A COURSE IN STATISTICS WITH R

A COURSE IN STATISTICS WITH R

Prabhanjan Narayanachar Tattar

Fractal Analytics Inc.

Suresh Ramaiah

Karnatak University, India

B.G. Manjunath

Dell International Services, India

This edition first published 2016

Registered office
John Wiley & Sons Ltd, The Atrium, Southern Gate, Chichester, West Sussex, PO19 8SQ, United Kingdom

For details of our global editorial offices, for customer services and for information about how to apply for permission to reuse the copyright material in this book, please see our website at www.wiley.com.

Library of Congress Cataloging-in-Publication Data applied for.

ISBN: 9781119152729

A catalogue record for this book is available from the British Library.

Cover Image: Tee_Photolive/Getty

Set in 10/12pt, TimesLTStd by SPi Global, Chennai, India.

1 2016

प्र(ण)ती

अण्णा हजारे
क्षितिज आकांक्षानां किनार्या पर्यंत खेचून आनन्याच्या प्रयत्यनासाठी...

Anna Hazare
For the efforts to bring them on the shore, the horizon hopes

Contents

List of Figures

List of Tables

Preface

The authors firmly believe that the biggest blasphemy a stat reader can commit is the non-reading of texts which are within her/his mathematical limits. The strength of this attitude is that since mathematical limits are really a perception and consequentially it would be in a decline with persistence, and the reader would then simply enjoy the subject like a dream. We made a humble beginning in our careers and proceeded with reading books within our mathematical limits. Thus, it is without any extra push or pressure that we began the writing of this book. It is also true that we were perfectly happy with the existing books and the purpose of this has not arisen as an attempt to improve on other books. The authors have taken the task of writing this book with a view which is believed to be an empirical way of learning computational statistics. This is also the reason why others write their books and we are not an exception.

The primary reason which motivated us to pick up the challenge of writing this book needs a mention. The Student's t-test has many beautiful theoretical properties. Apart from being a small sample test, it is known to be the Uniformly Most Powerful Unbiased, UMPU, test. A pedagogical way of arriving at this test is a preliminary discussion of hypothesis framework, Type I and II errors, power function, the Neyman-Pearson fundamental lemma which gives the Most Powerful test, and the generalization to the Uniformly Most Powerful test. It is after this flow that we appreciate the t-test as the UMPU test. For a variety of reasons, it is correct for software-driven stat books to skip over these details and illustrate the applications of the t-test. The purpose and intent are met and we have to respect such an approach.

We felt the intrinsic need of a computational illustration of the pedagogical approach and hence our coverage of statistical tests begins from a discussion of hypothesis framework through to the UMPU tests. Similarly, we have provided a demystification of the Iterative Reweighted Least Squares, IRLS, which will provide the reader with a clear view of how to estimate the parameters of the logistic regression. In fact, whenever we have an opportunity for further clarification of the computational aspects, we have taken it up. Thus, the main approach of this book has been to provide the R programs which fill the gap between formulas and output.

On a secondary note, the aim of this book is to provide the students in the Indian subcontinent with a single companion for their Masters Degree in Statistics. We have chosen the topics for the book in a way that the students will find useful in any Semester during their course. Thus, there is more flavor of the Indian subcontinent in this work. Furthermore, as scientific thinking is constant, it can be used by any person on this planet.

We have used R software for this book since it has emerged as one of the powerful statistical software, and each month at least one book appears which uses it as the primary software.

Preface

Acknowledgments

The R community has created a beautiful Open Source Software and the team deserves a special mention.

All the three authors completed their Masters Degrees at Bangalore University. We had a very purposeful course and take this opportunity to thank all our teachers at the Department of Statistics. This book is indeed a tribute to them.

Prof H.J. Vaman has been responsible, directly and indirectly, for each of us to pursue our doctoral degrees. His teaching has been a guidance for us and many of the pedagogical aesthetics adapted in this book bear his influence. The first author has collaborated with him on research papers and a lot of confidence has been derived from that work. We believe that he will particularly appreciate our chapter on "Parametric Inference".

At one point of time we were stuck when writing the chapter "Stochastic Processes". Prof S.M. Manjunath went through our rough draft and gave the necessary pointers and many other suggestions which helped us to complete the chapter. We appreciate his kind gesture. His teaching style has been a great motivation, and the influence will remain with us for all time.

We would like to take this opportunity to thank Dr G. Nanjundan of Bangalore University. His impact on this book goes beyond the Probability course and C++ training. Our association with him is over a decade and his countless anecdotes have brightened many of our evenings.

Professors A.P. Gore, S.A. Paranjape, and M.B. Kulkarni of the Department of Statistics, Poona University, have kindly allowed us to create an R package, titled gpk, from their book on the dataset. This has helped us to create a clear illustration of many statistical methods. Thank you, sirs.

The book began when the first author (PNT) was working as a Lead Statistician at CustomerXPs Software Private Limited. Thus, thanks are due to Rivi Varghese, Balaji Suryanarayana, and Aditya Lal Narayan, the founders of the company, who have always encouraged academic pursuits. PNT would also like to thank Aviral Suri and Pankaj Rai at Dell International Services, Bangalore. Currently, I am working as Senior Data Scientist at Fractal Analytics Inc.

Our friend Shakun Gupta kindly agreed to write "Open Source Software – An Epilogue" for us. In some way, the material may look out of place for a statistics text. However, it is our way of thanking the Open Source community. It is also appropriate to record that the book has used Open Source software to the maximum extent possible, Ubuntu Operating System, LaTeX, and R. In the context of the subcontinent, it is very relevant as the student should use the Open Source as much as possible.

The authors would like to express their sincere and profound thanks to the entire Wiley team for support and effort in bringing out the book in its present form. The authors also wish to place on record their appreciation for the criticisms and suggestions given by the anonymous referees.

PNT. The strong suggestion that this book should be written came from my father Narayanachar and a further boost of confidence promptly came from my mother Lakshmi. My wife Chandrika has always extended her support for this project, especially as the marriage had then been in its infant stage. This reminds me of the infant baby Pranathi, whose smiles and giggles would fill me with an unbounded joy. The family includes my brothers Arun Kumar and Anand, and their wives Bharthi and Madhavi. There are also three other naughties in our family, Vardhini, Yash, and Charvangi.

My friend Raghu always had a vested interest in this book. I also appreciate the encouragement given by my colleagues and friends Gyanendra Narayan, Ajay Sharma, and Abhinav Rai.

SR. It gives me immense pleasure to express my gratitude to my parents Ramaiah and Muna, and for giving me the wonderful quality of life and all my family members for their constant encouragement and support given to me while writing this book.

I thank my PhD supervisor Prof J.V. Janhavi for encouraging me to carry out this work. Lastly, it is my wife Sudha, who with great patience, understanding, support, and encouragement made the writing possible.

BGM. At the onset, I would like to express my deepest love and thankfulness to my father B.V. Govinda Raju and mother H. Vijaya Lakshmi and also to my friends Naveen, N.B. and N. Narayana Gowda, as their availability and encouragement was vital for the project. Moreover, I wish to express my heartfelt thanks to my beloved wife R. Shruthi Manjunath, for her unflinching understanding, strength, and support on this book was invaluable.

Besides, I would like to show my greatest gratitude to my PhD supervisor Prof Dr R.D. Reiss of the University of Siegen, for providing me with the opportunity to learn R at the University, which facilitated me to initiate this project.

Apart from all this, I would like to convey my thanks to Stefan Wilhelm, author and maintainer of the tmvtnorm: Truncated Multivariate Normal and Student t Distribution, R online package, for furnishing me with an opportunity to contribute to the package. Yet still, importantly, lively and productive discussion with him helped me to better understand the subject and also the successful realization of this book.

All queries, doubts, mistakes, and any communication related with the book may be addressed to the authors at the email acswithr@gmail.com. You can download all the R-codes used in the book from the website www.wiley.com/go/tattar/statistics

Prabhanjan Narayanachar Tattar
Fractal Analytics Inc.
acswithr@gmail.com

Suresh Ramaiah
Karnatak University, India

B.G. Manjunath
Dell International Services, India

Part I
The Preliminaries

1

Why R?

Package(s): `UsingR`
Dataset(s): `+AD1-9`

1.1 Why R?

Welcome to the world of Statistical Computing! During the first quartile of the previous century Statistics started growing at a great speed under the schools led by Sir R.A. Fisher and Karl Pearson. Statistical computing replicated similar growth during the last quartile of that century. The first part laid the foundations and the second part made the founders proud of their work. Interestingly, the beginning of this century is also witnessing a mini revolution of its own. The R Statistical Software, developed and maintained by the R Core Team, may be considered as a powerful tool for the statistical community. The software being a Free Open Source Software is simply icing on the cake.

R is evolving as the preferred companion of the Statistician. The reasons are aplenty. To begin with, this software has been developed by a team of Statisticians. Ross Ihaka and Robert Gentleman laid the basic framework for R, and later a group was formed who are responsible for the current growth and state of it. R is a command-line software and thus powerful with a lot of options for the user.

The legendary Prasanta Chandra Mahalanobis delivered one of the important essays in the annals of Statistics, namely, "Why Statistics?" It appears that Indian mathematicians were skeptical to the thought of including Statistics as a legitimate branch of science in general, and mathematics in particular. This essay addresses some of those concerns and establishes the scientific reasoning through the concepts of random samples, importance of random sampling, etc.

Naturally, we ask ourselves the question "Why R?" Of course, the magnitude of the question is oriented in a completely different and (probably) insignificant way, and we hope the reader will excuse us for this idiosyncrasy. The most important reason for the choice of R is that it is an open source software. This translates to the fact that the functioning of the software can be understood to the first line of code which steam rolls into powerful utilities. As an example, we can trace how exactly the important `mean` function works.

A Course in Statistics with R, First Edition. Prabhanjan Narayanachar Tattar, Suresh Ramaiah and B. G. Manjunath.

Companion Website: www.wiley.com/go/tattar/statistics

```
#  File src/library/base/R/mean.R
#  Part of the R package, http://www.R-project.org
#
#  A copy of the GNU General Public License is available at
#  http://www.r-project.org/Licenses/
mean <- function(x, ...) UseMethod("mean")
mean.default <- function(x, trim = 0, na.rm = FALSE, ...)
{
    if(!is.numeric(x) && !is.complex(x) && !is.logical(x)) {
        warning("argument is not numeric or logical: returning NA")
        return(NA_real_)
    }
    if (na.rm)
 x <- x[!is.na(x)]
    if(!is.numeric(trim) || length(trim) != 1)
        stop("'trim' must be numeric of length one")
    n <- length(x)
    if(trim > 0 && n > 0) {
 if(is.complex(x))
     stop("trimmed means are not defined for complex data")
 if(trim >= 0.5) return(stats::median(x, na.rm=FALSE))
 lo <- floor(n*trim)+1
 hi <- n+1-lo
 x <- sort.int(x, partial=unique(c(lo, hi)))[lo:hi]
    }
    .Internal(mean(x))
}
mean.data.frame <- function(x, ...) sapply(x, mean, ...)
```

Note that there is information about the address of the mean function, src/library/base/R/mean .R. The user can go to that address and open `mean.R` in any text editor. Now, if you find that the mean function does not work according to your requirement, modifications and new functions can be defined easily. For instance the default setting of the mean function is `na.rm=FALSE`, that is, if there are missing observations in a vector, see Section 2.3, the `mean` function will return `NA` as the answer. It is very simple to define a modified function whose default setting is `na.rm=TRUE`.

```
> x <- c(10,11,NA,13,14)
> mean(x)
[1] NA
> mean_new <- function(...,na.rm=TRUE) mean(...,na.rm=TRUE)
> mean_new(x)
[1] 12
> mean(x,na.rm=TRUE)
[1] 12
```

This is as simple as that. Thus, there are no restrictions imposed by the software on the user. The authors strongly believe that this freedom is priceless. If the decision to acquire the software is dictated by economic considerations, it is convenient that R comes freely.

Computation complexity is a reason for the need of software. As the modern statistical methods are embedded with complexity, it becomes a challenge for the developers of the methodology to complement the applications with appropriate computer programs. It has been our observation that many statisticians tend to address this dimension with relevant R packages. Venables and Ripley (2002) developed a very useful package `MASS`, an abbreviation for the title of their book *Modern Applied Statistics with S*. This package is shipped along with the software and is "recommended" as a priority package. In Section 1.8 we will see how many statisticians have adopted R as the language of their statistical computations.

1.2 R Installation

The website http://cran.r-project.org/ consists of all versions of R available for a variety of Operating Systems. CRAN is an abbreviation for Comprehensive R Archive Network. An incidental fact is that R had been developed on the Internet only.

The R software can be installed on a variety of platforms such as Linux, Windows, and Macintosh, among others. There is also an option of choosing 32- or 64-bit versions of the software. For a Linuxian, under appropriate privileges, R may be easily installed from the terminal using the command `sudo apt-get install r-base`. Ubuntu operating system users can find more help regarding R installation at the link http://ubuntuforums.org/showthread .php?t=639710.

After the installation is complete, the user can start the software by simply keying in R at the terminal. If the user is a beginner and not too familiar with the Linux environments, it is a possibility that she may be disappointed with its appearance as she cannot find much help there. Furthermore, the Linux expert may find this too trivial to explain/help a beginner. Some help for the beginner is available at http://freshmeat.net/articles/view/2237/.

A user of Windows first needs to download the recent versions executable file, currently R-3.0.2-win32.exe, and then merely double-click her way to completing the installation process. Similarly, Macintosh users can easily find the related files and methods for installation. The web links "R MacOS X FAQ" and "R Windows FAQ" should further be useful to the reader. The authors have developed the R codes used in this book and verified them for Linux and Windows versions. We are confident that they will compile without errors on Macintosh too.

1.3 There is Nothing such as PRACTICALS

The reader is absolutely free to differ from our point of view that "There is nothing such as PRACTICALS" and may skip this section altogether. There are two points of view from the authors which will be put forward here. First, with the decreasing cost of computers and availability of Open Source Software, OSS, see Appendix A, there is no need for calculator-based practicals. Also within the purview of a computer lab, a Statistics student/expertise needs to be more familiar with software such as R and SAS among others. Our second point of view is that the integration of theory with applications can be seamlessly achieved using the software modules.

It is apparently clear with the exponential growth of technology that the days of separate sessions for practicals of are a bygone era, and it's not an intelligent proposition to hang onto a weak rope, and blame it for our fall. It has been observed that in many of the developed Departments of the subject, calculator-based computations/practicals session have been done away with altogether. It is also noticed that many Statistical institutes do not teach C++/Fortran programming languages even at a graduate course, and a reason for this may be that statisticians need not necessarily be software programmers. There are many additional reasons for this reluctance. A practical reason is that computers have become very much cheaper, and if not within the financial reach of the students (especially in the developing countries), computing machines are easily available in most of their institutes. It is more often the case that the student has access to at least a couple of hours per week at her institute.

The availability of subject-specific interpretative software has also minimized the need of writing explicit programs for most of the standard practical methods in that subject. For example, in our Statistics subject, there are many software packages such as SAS, SYSTAT, STATISTICA, etc. Each of these contains inbuilt modules/menus which enable the user to perform most of these standard computations in a jiffy, and as such the user need not develop the programs for the statistical techniques in the applied area such as Linear Regression Analysis, Multivariate Statistics, among other topics of the subject.

It is true that one of the driving themes of this book is to convey as many ideas and concepts, both theoretical and practical, through a mixture of software programs and mathematical rigor. This aspect will become clear as the reader goes deeper into the book and especially through the asterisked sections or subsections. In short, this book provides a blend of theory and applications.

1.4 Datasets in R and Internet

The `R` software consists of many datasets and more often than not each package, see Section 2.6 for more details about an R package, contains many datasets. The command `try(data(package= "\,"))` enlists all the datasets contained in that package. For example, if we need to find the datasets in the package, say `rpart` and `methods`, execute the following:

```
> try(data(package="rpart"))
car.test.frame            Automobile Data from 'Consumer
+ Reports' 1990
car90                     Automobile Data from 'Consumer
+ Reports' 1990
cu.summary                Automobile Data from 'Consumer
+ Reports' 1990
kyphosis                  Data on Children who have had Corrective
+ Spinal Surgery
solder                    Soldering of Components on Printed-Circuit
+ Boards
stagec                    Stage C Prostate Cancer
> try(data(package="methods"))
no data sets found
```

The function for loading these datasets will be given in the next chapter. It has been observed that authors of many books have created packages containing all the datasets from their book and released them for the benefit of the programmers. For example, Faraway (2002) and Everitt and Hothorn (2006) have created packages titled `faraway` and `HSAUR2` respectively, which may be easily downloaded from http://cran.r-project.org/web/packages/, see Section 2.6.

Another major reason for a student to familiarize herself with a software is that practical settings rarely have small datasets ($n < 100$, to be precise). It is a good exposition to deal with industrial datasets. Thus, we feel that the beginners must try their hand at as many datasets as they can. With this purpose in mind, we enlist in the next subsection a bunch of websites which contain large numbers of datasets. This era really requires the statistician to shy away from ordinary calculators and embrace realistic problems.

1.4.1 List of Web-sites containing DATASETS

Practical datasets are available aplenty on the worldwide web. For example, Professors A.P. Gore, S.A. Paranjape, and M.B. Kulkarni of the Department of Statistics, Poona University, India, have painstakingly collected 103 datasets for their book titled "100 Datasets for Statistics Education", and have made it available on the web. Most of these datasets are in the realm of real-life problems in the Indian context. The datasets are available in the `gpk` package. We will place much emphasis on the datasets from this package and use them appropriately in the context of this current book, and also thank them on behalf of the readers too.

Similarly, the website http://lib.stat.cmu.edu/datasets/ contains a large host of datasets. Especially, datasets that appear in many popular books have been compiled and hosted for the benefit of the netizens.

It is impossible for anybody to give an exhaustive list of all the websites containing datasets, and such an effort may not be fruitful. We have listed in the following what may be useful to a statistician. The list is not in any particular order of priorities.

- http://ces.iisc.ernet.in/hpg/nvjoshi/statspunedatabook/databook.html
- http://lib.stat.cmu.edu/data sets/
- http://onlinelibrary.wiley.com/journal/10.1111/%28ISSN%291467-985X/homepage/datasets_all_series.htm
- http://www.commondata set.org/
- https://datamarket.com/data/list/?q=provider:tsdl
- http://inforumweb.umd.edu/econdata/econdata.html
- http://www.ucsd.edu/portal/site/Libraries/
- http://www.amstat.org/publications/jse/information.html
- http://www.statsci.org/data sets.html
- http://archive.ics.uci.edu/ml/data sets.html
- http://www.sigkdd.org/kddcup/index.php

We are positive that this list will benefit the user and encourage them to find more such sites according to their requirements.

1.4.2 Antique Datasets

Datasets available on the web are without any doubt very valuable and useful for a learner as well as the expert. Apart from the complexity and dimensionality, the sources are updated regularly and thus we are almost guaranteed great data sources. In the beginning of statistical development though, such a luxury was not available and the data collection mechanism was severely restricted by costs and storage restrictions. In spite of such limitations, the experimenters really compensated for them by their foresight and innovation. We describe in the rest of this section a set of very useful and antique datasets. We will abbreviate "Antique Datasets" as "AD". All the datasets discussed here are available in the books associated with the `ACSWR` package.

Example 1.4.1. AD1. Galileo's Experiments. The famous scientist Galileo Galilei conducted this experiment four centuries ago. An end of a ramp is elevated to a certain height with the other end touching the floor. A ball is released from a set height on the ramp and allowed to roll down a long narrow channel set within the ramp. The release height and the distance traveled before landing are measured. The goal of the experiment is to understand the word should be split like this: relationship between the release height and distance traveled. Dickey and Arnold's (1995) paper reignited interest in the Galileo dataset in the statistical community. This paper is available online at http://www.amstat.org/publications/jse/v3n1/datasets.dickey.html#drake. □

Example 1.4.2. AD2. Fisher's Iris Dataset. Fisher illustrated the multivariate statistical technique of the *linear discriminant analysis* method through this dataset. It is important to note here that though there are only three species with four measurements of each observation, and 150 observations, this dataset is very much relevant today. Rao (1973) used this dataset for the hypothesis testing problem of equality of two vector means. Despite the availability of large datasets, the `iris` dataset is a benchmark example for the *machine learning community*. This dataset is available in the `datasets` package. □

Example 1.4.3. AD3. The Militiamen's Chest Dataset. Militia means an army composed of ordinary citizens and not of professional soldiers. This dataset is available in an 1846 book published by the Belgian statistician Adolphe Quetelet, and the data is believed to have been collected some 30 years before that. It would be interesting to know the distribution of the chest measurements of a militia which had 5738 militia men. Velleman and Hoaglin (1984), page 259, has more information about this data. We record here that though the dataset is not available, the summaries of frequency count is available, which serves our purpose in this book. □

Example 1.4.4. AD4. The Sleep Dataset – 107 Years of Student's *t*-Distribution. The statistical analysis of this dataset first appeared in the 1908 remarkable paper of William Gosset. The paper titled *The Probable Error of Mean* had been published in the *Biometrika* journal under the pen name Student. The purpose of the investigation had been identification of an effective soporific drug among two groups for more sleep. The experiment had been conducted on ten patients from each group and since the large sample Z-test cannot be applied here, Gosset solved the problem and provided the small-sample t-test which also led to the well-known Student's t-distribution. The default R package `datasets` contains this dataset. □

Example 1.4.5. AD5. The Galton's Dataset. Francis Galton is credited with the invention of the linear regression model and it is his careful observation of the phenomenon of *regression toward the mean* which forms the crux of most of regression analysis. This dataset is available in the `UsingR` package of Verzani (2005) as the `galton` dataset. It is also available in the companion `RSADBE` package of Tattar (2013). The dataset contains 928 pairs of height of `parent` and `child`. The average height of the parent is 68.31 inches, while that of the child is 68.09 inches. Furthermore, the correlation coefficient between the height of parent and child is 0.46. We will use this dataset in the rest of this book. □

Example 1.4.6. AD6. The Michelson-Morley Experiment for Detection of Ether. In the nineteenth century, a conjectured theory for the propagation of light was the existence of an ether medium. Michelson conducted a beautiful experiment in the year of 1881 in which the drift caused by ether on light was expected to be at 4%. What followed later, in collaboration with Morley, was one of the most famous *failed experiments* in that the setup ended by proving the non-existence of ether. We will use this dataset on multiple occasions in this book. In the `datasets` package, this data is available under `morley`, whereas another copy is available in the `MASS` package as `michelson`. □

Example 1.4.7. AD7. Boeing 720 Jet Plane Air Conditioning Systems. The time between failures of air conditioning systems in Boeing jet planes have been recorded. Here, the event of failure is recurring for a single plane. Additional information is available regarding the air conditioning undergoing a major overhaul during certain failures. This data has been popularized by Frank Proschan. This dataset is available in the `boot` package by the data frame `aircondit`. □

Example 1.4.8. AD8. US Air Passengers Dataset. Box and Jenkins (1976) used this dataset in their classic book on time series. The monthly totals of international airline passengers has been recorded for the period 1949–1960. This data consists of interesting patterns such as seasonal variation, yearly increment, etc. The performance of various time series models is compared and contrasted with respect to this dataset. The `ts` object `AirPassengers` from the `datasets` package contains the US air passengers dataset. □

Example 1.4.9. AD9. Youden and Beale's Data on Lesions of Half-Leaves of the Tobacco Plant. A simple and innovative design is often priceless. Youden and Beale (1934) sought to find the effect of two preparations of virus on tobacco plants. One half of a tobacco leaf was rubbed with cheesecloth soaked in one preparation of the virus extract and the second half was rubbed with the other virus extract. This experiment was replicated on just eight leaves, and the number of lesions on each half leaf was recorded. We will illustrate later if the small sample size is enough to deduce some inference. □

1.5 http://cran.r-project.org

We mentioned CRAN in Section 2. The worldwide web link of CRAN is the title of this Section. A lot of information about R and many other related utilities of the software are available from this web source. The "R FAQ" web page contains a lot of common queries and helps the beginner to fix many of the initial problems.

"Manuals", "FAQs", and "Contributed" links on this website contains a wealth of information on documentation of the software. A journal called "The R Journal" is available at http://journal.r-project.org/, with the founders on the editorial board, who will help to keep track of developments in R.

1.5.1 *http://r-project.org*

This is the main website of the R software. The reader can keep track of the continuous stream of textbooks, monographs, etc., which use R as the computational vehicle and have been published in the recent past by checking on the link "Books". It needs to be mentioned here that this list is not comprehensive and there are many more books available in print.

1.5.2 *http://www.cran.r-project.org/web/views/*

The interest of a user may be in a particular area of Statistics. This web-link lists major areas of the subject and further directions to detailed available methods for such areas. Some of the major areas include Bayesian Inference, Probability Distributions, Design of Experiments, Machine Learning, Multivariate Statistics, Robust Statistical Methods, Spatial Analysis, Survival Analysis, and Time Series Analysis. Under each of the related links, we can find information about the problems which have been addressed in the R software. Information is also available on which additional package contains the related functions, etc.

As an example, we explain the link http://www.cran.r-project.org/web/views/Multivariate .html, which details the R package's availability for the broader area of multivariate statistics. This unit is maintained by Prof Paul Hewson. The main areas and methods in this page have been classified as (i) Visualizing Multivariate Data, (ii) Hypothesis Testing, (iii) Multivariate Distributions, (iv) Linear Models, (v) Projection Methods, (vi) Principal Coordinates/Scaling Methods, (vii) Unsupervised Classification, (viii) Supervised Classification and Discriminant Analysis, (ix) Correspondence Analysis, (x) Forward Search, (xi) Missing Data, (xii) Latent Variable Approaches, (xiii) Modeling Non-Gaussian Data, (xiv) Matrix Manipulations, and (xv) Miscellaneous utilities. Under each of the headings there will be a mention of the associated packages which will help in related computations and implementations.

In general, all the related web-pages end with a list of related "CRAN Packages" and "Related Links". Similarly, the url http://www.cran.r-project.org/web/packages/ lists all add-on packages available for download. As of April 10, 2015, the total number of packages was 6505.

1.5.3 *Is subscribing to R-Mailing List useful?*

Samuel Johnson long ago declared that "There are two types of knowledge. One is knowing a thing. The other is knowing where to find it." Subscribing to this list is the knowledge of the second type. We next explain how to join this club. As a first step, copy and paste the link www.r-project.org/mail.html into your web-browser. Next, find "web interface" and click on it, following which you will reach https://stat.ethz.ch/mailman/listinfo/r-announce. On this web-page, go to the section "Subscribing to R-announce". We believe that once you check the

URL http://www.r-project.org/contributors.html, you will not have any doubts regarding why we are pursuing you to join it.

1.6 R and its Interface with other Software

R has many strengths of its own, and is also true about many other software packages, statistics software or otherwise. However, it does happen that despite the best efforts and the intent to be as complete as possible, software packages have their limitations. The great Dennis Ritchie, for instance, had simply forgotten to include the power function when he developed one of the best languages in C. The reader should appreciate that if a software does not have some features, it is not necessarily a drawback. The missing features of a software may be available in some other package or it may not be as important as first perceived by the user. It then becomes useful if we have bridges across to the culturally different islands, with each of them rich in its own sense. Such bridges may be called *interfaces* in the software industry.

The interfaces also help the user in many other ways. A Bayesian who is well versed in the *Bayesian Inference Using Gibbs Samples* (BUGS) software may be interested in comparing some of the Bayesian models with their counterparts in the frequentist school. The BUGS software may not include many of the frequentist methods. However, if there is a mechanism to call, and frequentist methods of software such as R, SAS, SYSTAT, etc. are required, a great convenience is available for the user.

The bridge called interface is also useful in a different way. A statistician may have been working with BUGS software for many years, and now needs to use R. In such a scenario, if she requires some functions of BUGS, and if those codes can be called up from R and then fed into BUGS to get the desired result, it helps in a long way for the user. For example, a BUGS user can install the `R2WinBUGS` additional package in R and continue to enjoy the derived functions of BUGS. We will say more about such additional packages in the next chapter.

1.7 help and/or ?

Help is indispensable! Let us straightaway get started with the help in R. Suppose we need details of the `t.test` function. A simple way out is to enter `help(t.test)` at the R terminal. This will open up a new page in the R Windows version. The same command when executed in UNIX systems leads to a different screen. The Windows user can simply close the new screen using either "Alt+F4" or by using the mouse. If such a process is replicated in the UNIX system, the entire R session is closed without any saving of the current R session. This is because the screen is opened in the same window. The UNIX user can return to the terminal by pressing the letter `q` at any time. The R code `?t.test` is another way of obtaining the help on `t.test`.

Help on a topic, say `t.test,` can be obtained using `help(t.test)` or ?`t.test`

Programming skills and the ability to solve mathematical problems share a common feature. If it is not practiced for even a short period of time, as little as two months after years of experience, it undoes a lot of the razor sharpness and a lot of the program syntax is then forgotten. It may be likely that the expert in *Survival Analysis* has forgotten that the call function of the famous Cox Proportional Hazards model is `coxph` and not `coxprop`. A course of retrieval is certainly referred to in the related R books. Another way is using the help feature in a different manner `??cox`.

??, equivalently "help.search", helps you when ? fails

A search can also be made according to some keyword function, and we can also restrict it to a certain package in light of appropriate information.

help.search(keyword = "character", package = "base")

In the rest of this book, whenever help files give more information, we provide the related help at the right-hand end of the section in a box. For instance, the help page for the `beta` function is in the main help page `Special` and inquiring for `?beta` actually loads the `Special` help file.

1.8 R Books

Thanks to the user-friendliness of the software, many books are available with an "R-specific" focus. The purpose of this section is to indicate how R has been a useful software in various facets of the subject, although it will not be comprehensive. The first manual that deserves a mention is the notes of Venables and Smith (2014), the first version of which probably came out in 1997. Such is the importance of these notes that it comes with the R software and may be easily assessed. It is very readable and lucid in flow and covers many core R topics. Dalgaard (2002–9) is probably the first exclusive book on the software and it helps the reader to gain a firm footing and confidence in using the software. Crawley's (2007–13) book on R covers many topics and will be very useful on the deck of an R programmer. Purohit, et al. (2008) is a good introductory book and explains the preliminary applications quite well. Zuur, et al. (2009) is another nice book to start learning about the R software.

Dobrow (2013) and Horgan (2008) provide an exposition of probability with the software. Iacus (2008) deals with solving a certain class of "Stochastic Differential Equations" through the R software. Ugarte, et al. (2008) provides a comprehensive treatment of essential mathematical statistics and inference. Albert and Rizzo (2012) is another useful book to familiarize with R and Statistics. A useful reference for Bayesian analysis can be found in Albert (2007–9). It is important to note here that though Nolan and Speed (2000) have not written in the R-text book mold, they have developed very many R programs.

R produces some of the excellent graphics and the related development can be seen in Sarkar (2008), and Murrel (2006).

Freely circulated notes on Regression and ANOVA using R is due to Faraway (2002). Faraway has promptly followed these sets of notes with two books, Faraway (2006) and Faraway (2006). Nonlinear statistical model building in R is illustrated in Ritz and Streibig (2008). Maindonald and Braun (2010) is an early exposition to data analysis methods and graphics. Multivariate data analysis details can be found in Everitt and Hothorn (2011). Categorical data analysis in-depth treatment is found in Bilder and Loughin (2015).

The goal of this section is not to introduce all R books, but to give a glimpse into the various areas in which it can be aptly used. Appropriate references will be found in later chapters.

1.9 A Road Map

The preliminary R introduction is the content of Chapter 2. In this chapter we ensure that the user can do many of the basic and essential computations in R. Simple algebra, trigonometry, reading data in various formats, and other fundamentals are introduced in an incremental phase. Chapter 3 contains enhanced details on manipulation of data, as the data source may not be in a ready-to-use format. Its content will also be very useful to practitioners.

Chapter 4 on *Exploratory Data Analysis* will be the first statistical chapter. This chapter serves as an early level of analyses on the dataset and provides a rich insight. As the natural intent is to obtain an initial insight into the dataset, a lot of graphical techniques are introduced here. It may be noted that most of the graphical methods are suitable for continuous variables and we have introduced a slew of other graphical methods for discrete data in Chapter 16 on Categorical Data Analysis. The first four chapters forms Part I of this book.

The purpose of this book is to complement data analysis with a sound footing in the theoretical aspects of the subject. To proceed in this direction, we begin with *Probability Theory* in Chapter 5. A clear discussion of probability theory is attempted, which begins with set theory and concludes with the important *Central Limit Theorem*. We have enriched this chapter with a clear discussion of the challenging problems in probability, combinatorics, inequalities, and limit theorems. It may be noted that many of the problems and discussions have been demonstrated with figures and R programs.

Probability models and their corresponding distributions are discussed in Chapter 6. Sections 2 to 4 deal with univariate and multivariate probability distributions and also consider discrete and continuous variants. *Sampling Distributions* forms a bridge between probability and statistical inference. Bayesian sampling distributions are also dealt with in this chapter and we are now prepared for inference.

The Estimation, Testing Hypotheses, and Confidence Intervals trilogy is integrated with computations and programs in Chapter 7. The concept of families of distribution is important and the chapter begins with this and explores the role of loss functions as a measure which can be used to access the accuracy of the proposed estimators. The role of sufficient statistics and related topics are discussed, followed by the importance of the likelihood function and construction of the maximum likelihood estimators. The EM algorithm is developed in a step-by-step manner and we believe that our coverage of the EM algorithm is one of the pedagogical ones available in the books. Testing statistical hypotheses is comprehensively developed in Sections 7.9–7.15. The development begins with Type I and II errors of statistical tests and slowly builds up to multiple comparison tests.

Distribution-free statistical inference is carried out in Chapter 8 on *Nonparametric Inference*. The empirical distribution function plays a central role in non-parametrics and is also useful for estimation of statistical functions. Jackknife and bootstrap methods are essentially non-parametric techniques which have gained a lot of traction since the 1980s. Smoothing through the use of kernels is also dealt with, while popular and important non-parametric tests are used for hypotheses problems to conclude the chapter.

The problems of the frequentist school are parallelly conveyed in Chapter 9 titled *Bayesian Inference*. This chapter begins with the idea of Bayesian probabilities and demonstrates how the choice of an appropriate prior is critically important. The posterior distribution gives a unified answer in the Bayesian paradigm for all three problems of estimation, confidence intervals (known as credible intervals in the Bayesian domain), and hypotheses testing. Examples have been presented for each set of the problems.

Bayesian theory has seen enormous growth in its applications to various fields. A reason for this is that the (complex) posterior distributions were difficult to evaluate before the unprecedented growth in computational power of modern machines. With the advent of modern computational machines, a phenomenal growth has been witnessed in the Bayesian paradigm thanks to the Monte Carlo/Markov Chain methods inclusive of two powerful techniques known as the Metropolis-Hastings algorithm and Gibbs sampler. Part III starts by developing the required underlying theory of Markov Chains in Chapter 10. The Monte Carlo aspects are then treated, developed, and applied in Chapter 11.

Part IV titled "Linear Models" is the lengthiest part of the book. *Linear Regression Models* begins with a simple linear model. The multiple regression model, diagnostics, and model selection, among other topics, are detailed with examples, figures, and programs. *Experimental Designs* have found many applications in agricultural studies and industry too. Chapter 13 discusses the more popular designs, such as completely randomized design, blocked designs, and factorial designs.

Multivariate Statistical Analysis is split into two chapters, 14 and 15. The first of these two chapters forms the *core* aspects of multivariate analysis. Classification, Canonical Correlations, Principal Component Analysis, and Factor Analysis concludes Chapter 15.

If the regressand is a discrete variable, it requires special handling and we describe graphical methods and preliminary methods in Chapter 16 titled *Categorical Data Analysis*. The chapter begins with exploratory techniques useful for dealing with categorical data, and then takes the necessary route to chi-square goodness-of-fit tests. The regression problem for discrete data is handled in Chapter 17. The proceedings of statistical modeling in the final chapter parallels Chapter 12 and further considers probit and Poisson regression models.

2

The R Basics

Package(s): `gdata`, `foreign`, `MASS`, `e1071`

2.1 Introduction

A better way of becoming familiar with a software is to start with simple and useful programs. In this chapter, we aim to make the reader feel at home with the R software. The reader often struggles with the syntax of a software, and it is essentially this shortcoming that the reader will overcome after going through the later sections. It should always be remembered that it is not just the beginner, even the experts make mistakes when it comes to the structure of the syntax, and this is probably the reason why the "Backspace" key on the keyboard is always there, apart from many other keys round about for correcting previously submitted commands and/or programs.

Section 2.2 begins with the R preliminaries. The main topics considered here discuss and illustrate using R for finding absolute values, remainders, rounding numbers to specified number of digits, basic arithmetic, etc. Trigonometric functions and complex numbers are considered too, and the computations of factors and combinatorics is dealt with in this section. Useful R functions are then dealt with in Section 2.3. Summary of R objects, deliberating on the type of the R class, dealing with missing observations, and basic control options for writing detailed R programs have been addressed here. The importance of vectors and matrices are almost all prevalent in data analysis, and forms the major content of Section 2.4. Importing data from external files is vital for any statistical software. Section 2.5 helps the user import data from a variety of spreadsheets. As we delve into R programming, we will have to work with the R packages sooner or later. A brief discussion of installing the packages is revealed in Section 2.6. Running R codes will leave us with many objects which may be used again in a later session, and frequently we will stop a working session with the intent of returning to it at a later point in time. Thus, R session management is crucial and Section 2.7 helps in this aspect of programming.

A Course in Statistics with R, First Edition. Prabhanjan Narayanachar Tattar, Suresh Ramaiah and B. G. Manjunath.

Companion Website: www.wiley.com/go/tattar/statistics

2.2 Simple Arithmetics and a Little Beyond

Dalgaard (2008), Purohit, et al. (2008), and others, have often introduced R as a *out grown calculator*. In this section we will focus on the functionality of R as a calculator.

We will begin with simple addition, multiplication, and power computations. The codes/programs in R are read from left to right, and executed in that order.

```
> 57 + 89
[1] 146
> 45 - 87
[1] -42
> 60 * 3
[1] 180
> 7/18
[1] 0.3888889
> 4^4
[1] 256
```

It is implicitly assumed (and implemented too) that any reliable computing software must have included the *brackets, orders, division, multiplication, addition, and subtraction, BODMAS* rule. It means that if the user executes 4×3^3, the answer is 108, that is, order is first executed and then multiplication, and not 1728, multiplication followed by order. We verify the same next.

```
> 4*3^3
[1] 108
```

?Arith or ?S4groupGeneric, ?Syntax

2.2.1 *Absolute Values, Remainders, etc.*

The absolute value of elements or vectors can be found using the `abs` command. For example:

```
> abs(-4:3)
[1] 4 3 2 1 0 1 2 3
```

Here the argument `-4:3` creates a sequence of numerical integers $\{-4, -3, \cdots, 0, 1, 2, 3\}$ with the help of the colon : operator. Remainders can be computed using the R operator `%%`.

```
> (-4:3) %% 2
[1] 0 1 0 1 0 1 0 1
> (-4:3) %% 1
[1] 0 0 0 0 0 0 0 0
> (-4:3) %% 3
[1] 2 0 1 2 0 1 2 0
```

The *integer divisor* between two numbers may be calculated using the `%/%` operation.

```
> (-4:3) %/% 3
[1] -2 -1 -1 -1  0  0  0  1
```

Furthermore, we also verify the following:

```
> (-4:3) %% 3 + 3*((-4:3)%/%3) # Comment on what is being verified
+ here?
[1] -4 -3 -2 -1  0  1  2  3
```

A Word of Caution. We would like to bring to the reader's notice that though the operation `%/%` is integer division, `%*%` is not in any way related to it. In fact, this `%*%` operation is useful for obtaining the cross-products of two matrices, which will be introduced later in this chapter.

We conclude this small section with the `sign` operator, which tells whether an element is positive, negative, or neither.

```
> sign(-4:3)
[1] -1 -1 -1 -1  0  1  1  1
```

?base

2.2.2 *round, floor, etc.*

The number of digits to which R gives answers is set at seven digits by default. There are multiple ways to obtain our answers in the number of digits that we actually need. For instance, if we require only two digits accuracy for 7/18, we can use the following:

```
> round(7/18,2)
[1] 0.39
```

The function `round` works on a particular code under execution. If we require that each output to be fixed at two digits, say, consider this line of code.

```
> 7/118
[1] 0.059322
> options(digits=2)
> 7/118
[1] 0.059
```

It is often of interest to obtain the greatest integer less than the given number, or the least integer greater than the given number. Such tasks can be handled by the functions `floor` and `ceiling` respectively. For instance:

```
> floor(0.39)
[1] 0
> ceiling(0.39)
[1] 1
```

The reader is asked to explore more details about similar functions such as `signif` and `trunc`.

?round

2.2.3 *Summary Functions*

The `Summary` functions include `all, any, sum, prod, min, max,` and `range`. The last five of these is straightforward for the user to apply to their problems. This is illustrated by the following.

```
> sum(1:3)
[1] 6
> prod(c(3,5,7))
[1] 105
> min(c(1,6,-14,-154,0))
[1] -154
> max(c(1,6,-14,-154,0))
[1] 6
> range(c(1,6,-14,-154,0))
[1] -154    6
```

We are using the function `c` for the first time, so it needs an explanation. It is a *generic function* and almost omnipresent in any detailed R program. The reason being that it can combine various types of R objects, such as `vector` and `list`, into a single object. This function also helps us to create vectors more generic than the colon `:` operator.

Yes, `sum, prod, min, max,` and `range` functions when applied on an array respectively perform summation, product, minimum, maximum, and range on that array. Now we are left to understand the R functions `any` and `all`.

The `any` function checks if it is true that the array under consideration meets certain criteria. As an example, suppose we need to know if there are some elements of $(1, 6, -14, -154, 0)$ less than 0.

```
> any(c(1,6,-14,-154,0)<0)
[1] TRUE
> which(c(1,6,-14,-154,0)<0)
[1] 3 4
> all(c(1,6,-14,-154,0)<0) # all checks if criteria is met by
+ each element
[1] FALSE
```

In R, the function `summary` is all too prevalent and it is very distinct from the `Summary` that we are discussing here.

?Summary

2.2.4 *Trigonometric Functions*

Trigonometric functions are very useful tools in statistical analysis of data. It is worth mentioning the emerging areas where this is frequently used. Wavelet analysis, functional data analysis, and time series spectral analysis are a few examples. Such a discussion is however beyond the scope of this current book. We will contain ourself with a very elementary session. The value of π is stored as one of the *constants* in R.

```
> sin(pi/2)
[1] 1
> tan(pi/4)
[1] 1
> cos(pi)
[1] -1
```

Arc-cosine, arc-sine, and arc-tangent functions are respectively obtained using `acos`, `asin`, and `atan`. Also, the hyperbolic trigonometric functions are available in `cosh`, `sinh`, `tanh`, `acosh`, `asinh`, and `atanh`.

?Trig, ?Hyperbolic

2.2.5 Complex Numbers*[1]

Complex numbers can be handled easily in R. Its use is straightforward and the details are obtained by keying in `?complex` or `?Complex` at the terminal. As the arithmetic related to complex numbers is a simple task, we will look at an interesting case where the functions of complex numbers arise naturally.

The *characteristic function*, abbreviated as *cf*, of a random variable is defined as $\varphi_X(t) = E(e^{itX})$. For the sake of simplicity, let us begin with the *uniform random variable*, more details of which are available in Chapters 5 and 6, in the interval $[a, b]$. It can then be proved that the characteristic function of the uniform random variable is

$$\varphi_X(t) = \frac{e^{itb} - e^{ita}}{it(b-a)}. \tag{2.1}$$

To help the student to become familiarized with the characteristic function, Chung (2001), Chapter 6, provides a rigorous introduction to the theory of the characteristic function. Let us obtain a plot of the characteristic function of a uniform distribution over the interval [–1,1]. Here, $a = -1, b = 1$. An R program is provided in the following, which gives the required plot.

```
> # Plot of Characteristic Function of a U(-1,1) Random Variable
> a <- -1; b <- 1
> t <- seq(-20,20,.1)
> chu <- (exp(1i*t*b)-exp(1i*t*a))/(1i*t*(b-a))
> plot(t,chu,"l",ylab=(expression(varphi(t))),main="Characteristic
+ Function of Uniform Distribution [-1, 1]")
```

Any line which begins with # is a comment line, or the code following # in a line, and is ignored by R when the program is run. A good practice is to write comments in a program wherever clarity is required. It may refer to a comment, a problem specification, etc. Since the goal is to obtain the plot of the cf over the interval [–1,1], we have created two objects with `a <- -1`

[1]Asterisked sections/subsections may be omitted on first reading

and `b <- 1`. The semi-colon `;` ensures that the *a* and *b* are created on execution of two separate lines. Next, we create a sequence of points for *t* through `t <- seq(-20,20,0.1)`. That is, the `seq` function creates a vector which ranges from –20 to 20 with increments of 0.1, and hence `t` consists of the sequence $\{-20.0, -19.9, -19.8, \ldots, -0.2, -0.1, 0, 0.1, 0.2, \ldots, 19.9, 20.0\}$. Now, the format in the line `chu <- ()/()` mimics the expression 2.1 in the program. Note that `t` is a vector, whereas `a` and `b` have a single element. Since we have used `1i` in the expression for the `chu` object, `chu` is a *complex object*.

Next, we obtain the necessary plot by `plot(t,chu,"l",...)`, which plots the values of `chu` against the sequence `t` and then joins the consecutive pair of points with a straight line. The `plot` function will be dealt with in more detail in Chapter 4. The argument `main=` is used to specify the title for the graph. The code snippet `expression(varphi(t))` creates a mathematical expression for `ylab`. Part A of Figure 2.1 gives the plot of the characteristic function of the uniform distribution.

The characteristics function of a normal random variable $N(\mu, \sigma^2)$ and Poisson random variable $P(\lambda)$, see Bhat (2012), are respectively given by

$$\varphi_X(t) = e^{it\mu - \frac{1}{2}\sigma^2 t^2}, \text{ and} \tag{2.2}$$

$$\varphi_X(t) = e^{\lambda(e^{it}-1)}. \tag{2.3}$$

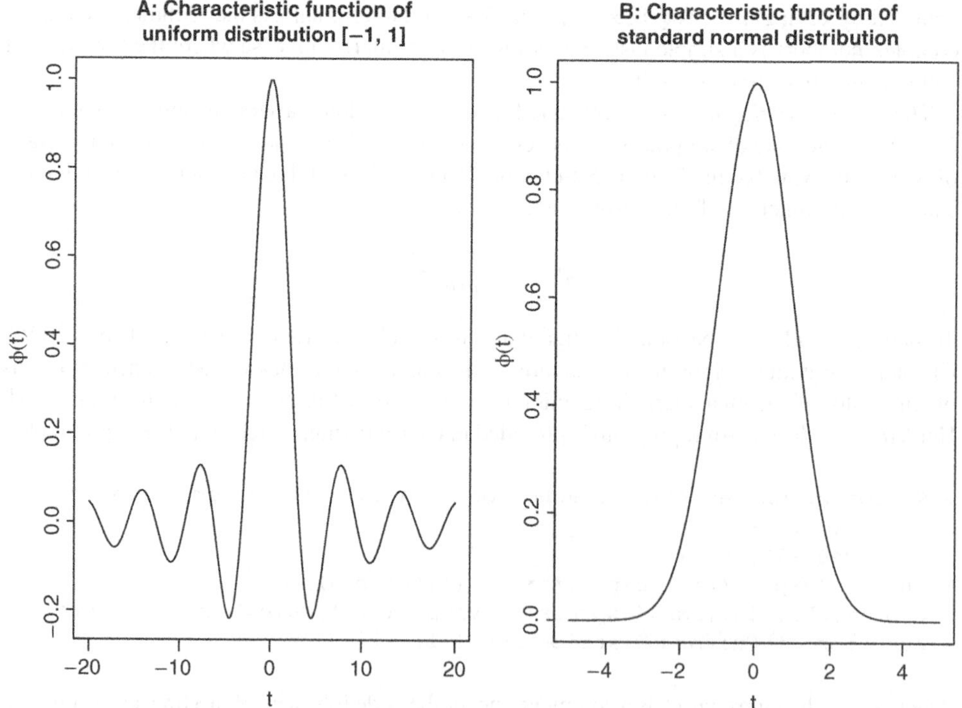

Figure 2.1 Characteristic Function of Uniform and Normal Distributions

We will obtain a plot for the cfs 2.2 and 2.3 in the next program.

```
> # Plot of Characteristic Function of a N(0,1) Variable
> mu <- 0; sigma <- 1
> t <- seq(-5,5,0.1)
> chsnv <- exp(1i*t*mu-.5*(sigma^2)*(t^2))
> plot(t,chsnv,"l",ylab=(expression(varphi(t))),main="Characteristic
+ Function of Standard Normal Distribution")
> # Plot of Characteristic Function of Poisson Random Variable
> lambda <- 6
> t <- seq(0,20,.1)
> chpois <- exp(lambda*(exp(1i*t)-1))
> plot(t,chpois,"l") # Warning omitted and left as exercise
+ # for the reader to interpret
```

The values of $\mu = 0$ and $\sigma^2 = 1$ are specified through `mu <- 0` and `sigma <- 1`. The t sequence is taken from –5 to 5 in `t <- seq(-5,5,0.1)`. The complex vector `chsnv` obtains the value of the cf for the `t` vector. The `plot` function works similarly to the cf for uniform distribution. The cf plot for Poisson distribution obviously has a problem and we leave it to the reader to figure it out. The plot of the cf of the standard normal distribution is given in the Part B of Figure 2.1.

?Complex or ?groupGeneric

2.2.6 *Special Mathematical Functions*

Here, by special functions, we mean certain mathematical entities that are difficult to calculate as the series/range increases. Factorials do have an in-built function in `factorial`. A few examples are in order.

```
> factorial(3)
[1] 6
> factorial(3000) # any guess?
[1] Inf
Warning message:
In factorial(3000) : value out of range in 'gammafn'
> lfactorial(3000) #lfactorial helps out
[1] 21024.02
```

The value of `21024.02` needs interpretation. Since the factorial is the product of positive integers to 1, `lfactorial` is the sum of log of the integers to 2. `log(1)` is zero. Thus, we check `lfactorial(3000)` as

```
> sum(log(3000:2))
[1] 21024.02
```

Let us verify the accuracy of the function `lfactorial` using the Stirling's approximation, see Feller (1968), page 52. The Stirling's approximation is useful to calculate the factorials of large numbers and is given by $n! \simeq \sqrt{2\pi} n^{n+1/2} e^{-n}$. We write a small `function` to obtain the Stirling's approximation. The `function` in R provides the base mechanism for defining new functions. It is a powerful technique and will be used freely throughout the course of this book.

```
> stirling <- function(n) {sqrt(2*pi)*n^{n+.5}*exp(-n)}
> stirling(100)
[1] 9.324848e+157
> factorial(100)/stirling(100)
[1] 1.000834
```

Consider the classical problem of selecting *r-out-of-n* objects. If we have to select k objects with replacement, that is the first drawn object is replaced in the pack before the second object is drawn, the number of ways of accomplishing the task is $\binom{n}{k}$. If $n = 10$ and $r = 4$, the `choose` function gives us the desired answer through the arguments `n` and `k`. That is, $\binom{n}{k}$ is calculated in R with `choose(n,k)`.

```
> choose(10,4)
[1] 210
> choose(10,10) # just verifying
[1] 1
> choose(100,10) # how about large n?
[1] 1.731031e+13
```

The selection problem without replacement does not have an explicit function though. We can help ourselves! We can select r out of n objects in ^nP_r number of distinct ways. It is known that $^nP_r = \frac{n!}{(n-r)!}$. A further simplification gives us $^nP_r = n \times (n-1) \cdots \times (n-r+1)$. Fortunately, we do not have to write extensive codes. It is fairly simple with the `prod` function, which multiplies all the elements specified in its argument `()`.

```
> prod(10:(10-4+1)) # permutations of 10 p 4
[1] 5040
> prod(100:(100-10+1)) #permutations of 100 p 10
[1] 6.281565e+19
```

?Special

2.3 Some Basic R Functions

In this section we introduce important classes of functions, which are essential from a statistical perspective.

2.3.1 Summary Statistics

Consider the Youden and Beale dataset, introduced earlier as AD-9. Here, we have two preparations of virus extracts and the data is available on the number of lesions produced by each extract on the eight leaves of tobacco plants. We read this data and assigned it to a new object yb. The summary statistics for the two extracts are as follows:

```
> data(yb)
> summary(yb)
 Preparation_1    Preparation_2
 Min.    : 7.00   Min.    : 5.00
 1st Qu.: 8.75    1st Qu.: 6.75
 Median :13.50    Median :10.50
 Mean    :15.00   Mean    :11.00
 3rd Qu.:18.50    3rd Qu.:14.75
 Max.    :31.00   Max.    :18.00
```

The summary considers each variable of the yb data frame and appropriately returns the summary for that type of variable. What does this mean? The two variables Preparation_1 and Preparation_2 are of the integer class. In fact, we need these two variables to be of the numeric class. For each class of objects, the summary function invokes particular methods, check methods from the utils package, as defined for an S3 generic function. We will not delve more into this technical aspect, except that we appreciate that R has one summary for a numeric object and another for a character object. For an integer object, the summary function returns the minimum, first quartile, median, mean, third quartile, and maximum. Minimum, mean, median, and maximum are fairly understood and recalled easily. Quartiles are a set of (three) numbers, which divide the range of the variables into four equal parts, in the sense that each part will have 25% of the observations. The range between minimum and first quartile will contain the smallest 25% of the observations for that variable, the first and second quartile (median) will have the next, and so on. The importance of these summaries will be realized in Chapter 4. For the yb data frame, it may be seen from the mean and median summaries that the Preparation_2 has a lesser number of lesions than Preparation_1. The first and third quantiles can also be obtained by using the codes quantile(x,.25) and quantile(x,.75) respectively. The percentiles, nine percentiles which divide the data into ten equal regions, can be obtained using the function quantile:

```
> quantile(yb$Preparation_1,seq(0,1,.1)) # here seq gives
+ 0, .1, .2, ...,1
  0%  10%  20%  30%  40%  50%  60%  70%  80%  90% 100%
 7.0  7.7  8.4  9.1  9.8 13.5 17.2 17.9 19.2 23.3 31.0
> quantile(yb$Preparation_2,seq(0,1,.1))
  0%  10%  20%  30%  40%  50%  60%  70%  80%  90% 100%
 5.0  5.7  6.4  7.3  9.4 10.5 11.6 13.7 15.8 17.3 18.0
```

The code `lapply(yb,summary)` also gives us the same values. The `lapply` will be considered in detail later in this chapter.

Tukey's `fivenum` gives another set of important summaries, which are detailed in Chapter 4. The `fivenum` summary, containing minimum, lower hinge, median, upper hinge, and maximum, see Chapter 4 for more details on *hinges*, for the two extracts of the virus preparation are as below:

```
> fivenum(yb$Preparation_1)
[1]  7.0  8.5 13.5 19.0 31.0
> fivenum(yb$Preparation_2)
[1]  5.0  6.5 10.5 15.5 18.0
```

We now consider some measures of dispersion. Standard deviation and variance of a sample are respectively obtained by the functions `sd` and `var`. Range is obtained using the `range` function.

```
> sd(yb$Preparation_1); sd(yb$Preparation_2)
[1] 8.176622
[1] 4.956958
> var(yb$Preparation_1); var(yb$Preparation_2)
[1] 66.85714
[1] 24.57143
> range(yb$Preparation_1); range(yb$Preparation_2)
[1]  7 31
[1]  5 18
```

In general, the median is more *robust* than the mean. A corresponding measure of dispersion is the *median absolute deviation*, abbreviated as MAD. The R function `mad` returns MAD. Another robust measure of dispersion is the *inter quartile range*, abbreviated as *IQR*, and the function available for obtaining it in R is `IQR`. These measures for the variables of the Youden and Beale data `yb` are thus computed in the next program.

```
> mad(yb$Preparation_1); mad(yb$Preparation_2)
[1] 7.413
[1] 5.9304
> IQR(yb$Preparation_1); IQR(yb$Preparation_2)
[1] 9.75
[1] 8
> #Too many functions. Want my own code!
> quantile(yb$Preparation_1,.75)-quantile(yb$Preparation_1,.25)
 75%
9.75
> quantile(yb$Preparation_2,.75)-quantile(yb$Preparation_2,.25)
75%
  8
```

The *skewness* and *kurtosis* are also very important summaries. Functions for these summaries are not available in the `base` package. The functions `skewcoeff` and `kurtcoeff` from the ACSWR package will be used to obtain these summaries. The functions skewness and kurtosis from the e1071 package are more generic functions, see Section 2.6, for installing and using an R package. We obtain the summaries for the Youden and Beale experiment data below.

```
> skewcoeff(yb$Preparation_1); kurtcoeff(yb$Preparation_1)
[1] 0.8548652
[1] 2.727591
> skewcoeff(yb$Preparation_2); kurtcoeff(yb$Preparation_2)
[1] 0.2256965
[1] 1.6106
```

2.3.2 *is, as, is.na, etc.*

The function is derives its nomenclature from the common usage of that word: Is it raining? We can use it to find if the class of a given object is numeric, logical, character, vector, matrix, function, etc., by respectively extending the is function to is.numeric, is.logical, is.character, is.vector, is.matrix, is.function, etc. The is function may be used for any kind of well-defined R class.

```
> is(5); is.numeric(5)
[1] "numeric" "vector"
[1] TRUE
> my_undefined_function <- function(n){}
> is.function(my_undefined_function)
[1] TRUE
> is.logical(T) # T or F can be used as abb of TRUE or FALSE
[1] TRUE
> is(pi)
[1] "numeric" "vector"
```

If we want to change the class of an R object, say from numeric to character, we can do that by using the function as. A vector object, say x <- c(1,4,2,6), is to be converted as a character vector.

```
> x <- c(1,4,2,6)
> xc <- as.character(x)
> xc; as.numeric(xc)
[1] "1" "4" "2" "6"
[1] 1 4 2 6
> x;xc
[1] 1 4 2 6
[1] "1" "4" "2" "6"
```

Missing data is very common in the real world. Analyses in which all the observations/ individuals having any missing elements are removed is called *complete case analysis* and known to be very inefficient. Of course, it is a far cry from getting involved with the scientific analysis of the missing data. We will focus on how it is indicated in R that an element of an object is missing.

A missing element in an object is denoted by NA as an abbreviation for "Not Available". Suppose that the fifth value of a vector of five elements is not available. We can include this information in an R object as follows:

```
> (x <- c(1,2,3,4,NA))
[1]  1  2  3  4 NA
> is.na(x) # Are elements of x missing?
[1] FALSE FALSE FALSE FALSE  TRUE
> xc <- na.omit(x) #xc for x complete
> xc
[1] 1 2 3 4
attr(,"na.action")
[1] 5
attr(,"class")
[1] "omit"
> which(is.na(x)) # Useful for advanced programming
[1] 5
```

We would like to know the summary of the x object sans its missing elements. We will see that there is some difference between operating on x and xc .

```
> summary(xc)
   Min. 1st Qu.  Median    Mean 3rd Qu.    Max.
   1.00    1.75    2.50    2.50    3.25    4.00
> summary(x,na.rm=TRUE)
   Min. 1st Qu.  Median    Mean 3rd Qu.    Max.    NA's
   1.00    1.75    2.50    2.50    3.25    4.00    1.00
```

?methods, ?as, ?NA, ?remove

2.3.3 *factors, levels, etc.*

The function gl generates factor levels, and this will be very useful for analysis of *Design of Experiments*. The arguments needed in this function include the number of observations n, and the number of replications, say k. A value-added flexibility of this function includes labeling the factors by certain names as desired by the user. The following examples show the usefulness of this function.

```
> (exp_levels <- gl(3,2)); is.factor(exp_levels)
[1] 1 1 2 2 3 3
Levels: 1 2 3
[1] TRUE
> exp_levels <- factor(exp_levels,labels=
+ c("fail","average","excellent"))
> exp_levels
[1] fail      fail      average   average   excellent excellent
```

```
Levels: fail average excellent
> levels(exp_levels)
> # Verifying and Learning about "levels" function
[1] "fail"      "average"   "excellent"
> levels(exp_levels) <- c("f","a","e") # Changing the labels
> exp_levels; nlevels(exp_levels)
[1] f f a a e e
Levels: f a e
[1] 3
```

The factors can be arranged as *ordinal* variables too. The approach to convert nominal factor variables to ordinal factor variables is given next.

```
> exp_levels.ord <- ordered(exp_levels,levels=c("f","a","e"))
> exp_levels; exp_levels.ord
[1] f f a a e e
Levels: f a e
[1] f f a a e e
Levels: f < a < e
> is.ordered(exp_levels); is.ordered(exp_levels.ord)
[1] FALSE
[1] TRUE
```

The ordered factors may sometimes need re-ordering or we may have certain levels which have no elements corresponding to them. In such cases we need to modify the levels of the variable which may be accomplished using the `relevel` and `droplevels` functions.

?factor, ?relevel,?droplevels

2.3.4 Control Programming

Loops form an integral part of many programming languages. `if`, `ifelse`, `for`, `while`, etc. are some of the basic control flow constructs of various languages. The control functions add a lot of value to the programs. However, and unfortunately, loops are a bane in R as they tend to be executed very slowly and thus need to be used very judiciously. We will start with a few examples of this family and later switch, not the control function `switch`, but to a powerful alternative of the `apply` family.

The syntax for the `if` and `if-else` control functions is as in the popular software languages. Here, the syntax for the two controls are respectively `if(cond) expr` and `if(cond) cons.expr else alt.expr`. That is, if the condition or the antecedent is met, which is a logical criteria, the expression is evaluated for the `if` control, and if the criteria is not met, the alternative expression is evaluated for the `if-else` control. We begin with simple examples.

```
> if(5 > 3) "I Win"
[1] "I Win"
> if(5 < 3) "I Win" else "You Lose"
[1] "You Lose"
```

Occasionally, we may need a program which needs to be executed in a manner until a certain criteria is met. Suppose that the value of the variables x and y are 100 and 10 respectively. Here, x/y = 10, and we are prepared to decrease x values and increase y values by one unit each time till the ration x/y is greater than 5. The following program helps us reach this goal with the help of the `while` control.

```
> x <- 100; y <- 10
> while(x/y>=5) {x<-x-1; y<-y+1}
> x;y
[1] 91
[1] 19
```

We can use the `while` control to find the number in the *Fibonacci series* which is less than 10 000:

```
> fs <- c() # The Fibonacci Series
> a <- 0; b <- 1
> while(b<10000){
+ fs <- c(fs,b)
+ temp <- b
+ b <- a+b
+ a <- temp}
> print(fs)
 [1]    1    1    2    3    5    8   13   21   34
[10]   55   89  144  233  377  610
[16]  987 1597 2584 4181 6765
```

Since the test criteria is verified at the top, we may like to put the test criteria at the end of the program, see Dalgaard (2008), page 45. This can be achieved by using a variation of the while loop, namely, `repeat`.

```
> x <- 100; y <- 10
> repeat{ x<-x-1; y<-y+1;
+ if(x/y<=5) break
+ }
> x;y
[1] 91
[1] 19
```

Oh! With the above program we have already introduced the important control parameter `break`. We will now introduce the useful `for` control function. We again undertake the simple task of computing the sum of the first 100 positive integers.

```
> x <- 1:100; sx <- 0
> for(i in 1:100) sx <- sx+x[i]
> sx
[1] 5050
```

At the start of this section, we commented that R is very slow in loops. Let us prove it with a very simple example.

```
> x <- 1:10000; sx <- 0
> system.time(for(i in 1:10000) sx <- sx+x[i])[3]
elapsed
  0.074
> system.time(sum(x))[3]
elapsed
      0
```

We have used the R function `system.time` to find the CPU time used for executing the program. This function may be used to find the CPU time of any R program and all that is required for finding it is to specify the entire program as an argument to the `system.time` function. This function returns an R object of class `proc_time`, whose third element `elapsed` is of interest to us and hence we have used `[3]` to find it.

Note that using a loop has (unnecessarily) increased the time of the program. We would advise the reader, as far as possible, to avoid using a loop and instead use other appropriate functions whenever they are available. Of course, it needs to be mentioned that the sum of the first 10 000 positive integers is 50 005 000.

?Control, ?apply

2.3.5 *Other Useful Functions*

In this subsection we introduce the reader to a selection of functions which we believe are important for statistical computing. This list is by no means exhaustive and as the reader transcends towards higher levels of computation, she may feel the contents here are unnecessary.

sort, rank, order. It happens frequently that we need to arrange a sequence in either increasing or decreasing order of magnitude. The `sort` function arranges a sequence of numeric or complex numbers in a monotone fashion. If the position of the numbers in a monotone sequence is required, we can use the `rank` function. Another useful function is `order`.

```
> sort(c(12,4,-8,54,23,-51))
[1] -51  -8   4  12  23  54
> sort(c(12,4,-8,54,23,-51),decreasing=TRUE)
[1]  54  23  12   4  -8 -51
> rank(c(12,4,-8,54,23,-51))
[1] 4 3 2 6 5 1
> order(c(12,4,-8,54,23,-51))
[1] 6 3 2 1 5 4
> order(c(12,4,-8,54,23,-51),decreasing=TRUE)
[1] 4 5 1 2 3 6
```

The function `order` returns the positions of the minimum to maximum in the original list of variables if arranged in increasing order (`decreasing=FALSE`, which is default).

Order can be used for arranging multivariate data in some monotone order. As a practical problem, consider the case of *censored data*. Here the lifetimes of certain experimental units are recorded and it is registered if the units failed or not. The following exhibit demonstrates the point.

```
> x <- c(12,8,5,89,23,64,37)
> x_ind <- c(1,1,1,0,1,0,1)
> o <- order(x)
> X <- cbind(x,x_ind)
> X[o,]
      x x_ind
[1,]  5     1
[2,]  8     1
[3,] 12     1
[4,] 23     1
[5,] 37     1
[6,] 64     0
[7,] 89     0
```

Run `example(order)` at the R terminal for more interesting and complex examples.
subset. Data preparation takes most of the time in industrial settings. For example, we may have a data file related to some clinical trial which contains all the observations. Suppose, there are many treatment groups and we are interested only in the set of individuals which received drug A. In such cases, we would like to prepare an R data frame containing information of related interested as follows:

```
> data(iris)
> iris_less <- subset(iris,Species %in% c("setosa","virginica"))
> iris_less[c(1:3,98:100),]
    Sepal.Length Sepal.Width Petal.Length Petal.Width   Species
1            5.1         3.5          1.4         0.2    setosa
2            4.9         3.0          1.4         0.2    setosa
3            4.7         3.2          1.3         0.2    setosa
148          6.5         3.0          5.2         2.0 virginica
149          6.2         3.4          5.4         2.3 virginica
150          5.9         3.0          5.1         1.8 virginica
```

Thus, we can use the command `subset` effectively and get the desired data frame. This function also applies to vectors and matrices. Equipped with control options in `select` and `drop`, it is a very powerful tool for purposes of data manipulation.
window. The `window` command applied to an R object extracts elements from the specified two times, `start` and `end`. Suppose we need the three-month moving averages of a time series of observations, **AD8** for instance. We consider the data for the first 24 months only. The next program achieves the goal.

```
> ad8_24 <- AirPassengers[1:24]
> ma3 <- c()
> for(i in 1:22) { ma3[i] <- mean(window(ad8_24,i,i+2))}
> ma3
```

```
 [1] 120.6667 ... 143.6667
 [7] 144.0000 ... 127.3333
[21] 134.0000 ... 129.0
```

The moving averages can be obtained using the `filter` function, try `filter (ad8_24,rep(1/3,3),sides=2)`. For more details, explore `filter`.

table. A simple use of this function is to obtain frequencies of a given factor. Agresti (2007), Chapter 2, considers the study of a survey of belief about the *Afterlife* among 1127 individuals. The respondents are asked if they believe in an afterlife or not.

```
> data(afterlife)
> table(afterlife$Males); table(afterlife$Females)
 NO YES
104 398
 NO YES
116 509
```

The table function can also be utilized to generate the *confusion matrix* in the *class prediction problems*. We consider a hypothetical example. If the true classes of ten observations are (A,A,A,A,B,B,B,C,C,C), and the best model has predicted the classes as (A,B,C,C,B,B,C,C,C,A), we can obtain the confusion matrix using the `table` function.

```
> true_classes <- c(rep("A",4),rep("B",3),rep("C",3))
> pred_classes <- c("A","B","C","C","B","B",
+ "C","C","C","A")
> conf_mat <- table(true_classes,pred_classes)
> conf_mat
            pred_classes
true_classes A B C
           A 1 1 2
           B 0 2 1
           C 1 0 2
```

Here the `rep` function finds more details with `?rep`, creates four replicates of "A", and three replicates for each of "B" and "C" for `true_classes`. The `table` function returns a *contingency table* for each combination of the vectors `true_classes` and `pred_classes`. This function will be very useful for analysis of *categorical data*.

?Comparison, ?xtfrm

*2.3.6 Calculus**

Differential and integral calculus are well incorporated in R, see Section 7.7 of Crawley (2013). The examples provided therein are a neat introduction to using the R functions `D` and `integrate`.

We undertake the task of proving that the *standard normal density* $f(x) = (2\pi)^{-1/2}e^{-x^2/2}$ is a probability density. Theorem 6.6 of Durrett (2009) or Section 7.4 of Chung and AitSahlia (2002), give the necessary proof. Our goal here is to understand the same proof through R as much as possible. At the outset, we assure that the R code `integrate(dnorm,-Inf,Inf)` is certainly not an acceptable proof.

To evaluate the integral $I = \int e^{-x^2/2}dx$ note that $I^2 = \int \int e^{-(x^2+y^2)}dxdy$. The proof is complete if we can prove that I^2 is equal to 2π. The trick here is to use the polar coordinates transformation: $x = r\ \cos(\theta)$ and $y = r\ \sin(\theta)$. We can rewrite θ and r in terms of x and y as $\theta = tan^{-1}(y/x)$ and $r = \sqrt{(x^2+y^2)}$.

Note that since r is the square root of two positive numbers, it is always positive. Furthermore, the range of θ is the interval $[0, 2\pi)$. We need to rewrite the expressions of I^2 in terms of r and θ. Towards this, we need to obtain $dxdy$ in terms of $drd\theta$. The following R codes give us the derivatives which are useful for computing the *Jacobian* of the transformation.

```
> expr1 <- expression(r*cos(theta))
> expr2 <- expression(r*sin(theta))
> D(expr1,"r");D(expr2,"r")
cos(theta)
sin(theta)
> D(expr1,"theta");D(expr2,"theta")
-(r * sin(theta))
r * cos(theta)
```

The mathematical quantities $r\cos(\theta)$ and $r\sin(\theta)$ are first created as the respective variables `expr1` and `expr2` using the `expression` function. The derivatives of these two quantities with respect to the variables r and θ are obtained in R using the `D` function. It will then be easier to obtain the Jacobian matrix. In terms of the symbols, it translates to the following:

$$\mathbf{J} = \det\begin{bmatrix} \frac{\delta x}{\delta r} & \frac{\delta x}{\delta \theta} \\ \frac{\delta y}{\delta r} & \frac{\delta y}{\delta \theta} \end{bmatrix} = \det\begin{bmatrix} \cos\theta & -r\sin\theta \\ \sin\theta & r\cos\theta \end{bmatrix}$$

$$= r\cos^2\theta - (-r\sin^2\theta) = r(\cos^2\theta + \sin^2\theta) = r$$

Thus, we can now rewrite I^2 in terms of r and θ as:

$$I^2 = \int_0^{2\pi} \int_0^{\infty} e^{-r^2/2} \mathrm{r} \mathrm{d}r \mathrm{d}\theta$$

We evaluate the second integral in the above equation using R. Thus:

```
> r_fun <- function(x) {x*exp(-x^2/2)}
> integrate(r_fun,0,Inf)
1 with absolute error < 2.8e-08
```

and hence, $I^2 = \int_0^{2\pi} \mathrm{d}\theta = 2\pi$. We have finally proved that I^2 is equal to 2π and thereby that the normal density is indeed a probability density function.

?integrate, ?deriv

2.4 Vectors and Matrices in R

The journey from a collection of random samples to summary statistics is a transformation of a vector to scalar-valued entities. Deriving the mean and standard deviation of a random sample instantly come to mind. We will learn more in this section about such vector functions. Gentle (2007) is a modern account of matrix computations using software with more emphasis on the theory. However in his book, for many of the matrix analyses, Gentle prefers R and Fortran. The most recent handbook on matrix analysis with more dedication towards statistics is Seber (2008).

2.4.1 Vectors

We begin with some elementary properties of vectors. Let $\mathbf{x} = (x_1, x_2, \cdots, x_p)$ and $\mathbf{y} = (y_1, y_2, \cdots, y_p)$ be two p-dimensional vectors. The basic operations of *scalar addition, multiplication*, etc., are defined in the following:

$$\mathbf{x} + c = (x_1 + c, x_2 + c, \cdots, x_p + c) \tag{2.4}$$

$$\mathbf{x} \times c = (x_1 \times c, x_2 \times c, \cdots, x_p \times c) \tag{2.5}$$

$$\mathbf{x} + \mathbf{y} = (x_1 + y_1, x_2 + y_2, \cdots, x_p + y_p) \tag{2.6}$$

Let us first understand the vector computations in R.

```
> x <- c(2,4,1,3)
> x+3 # scalar addition
[1] 5 7 4 6
> x*3 # scalar multiplication
[1]  6 12  3  9
> x+c(1,2,3,4) #adding two equal vectors
[1] 3 6 4 7
> x*c(1,2,3,4) #multiplying two equal vectors
[1]  2  8  3 12
> x+c(1,2) #adding two unequal vectors
[1] 3 6 2 5
> x*c(1,2) #multiplying two unequal vectors
[1] 2 8 1 6
> x+c(1,2,3); x*c(1,2,3) # what happens now?
[1] 3 6 4 4
Warning message:
In x + c(1, 2, 3) :
longer object length is not a multiple of shorter object length
[1] 2 8 3 3
Warning message:
In x * c(1, 2, 3) :
longer object length is not a multiple of shorter object length
```

In the example of scalar addition/multiplication, the number 3 is simply added/multiplied to each element of the vector x. Addition and multiplication of two equal vectors is also performed element wise. However, when we add or multiply unequal vectors, not allowed from a pure mathematical point of view, the computations are performed in a certain defined manner. First, the lengths of both the vectors are determined, and the minimum length vector is added element wise to the larger vector and the process is repeated for the remaining length of the larger vector. If the shorter vector length is an exact integer multiple of the lengthier one, R deems it appropriate. In cases where it is not true, a warning message is released. Let us now consider the working of the division operator.

```
> x/4; x/x
[1] 0.50 1.00 0.25 0.75
[1] 1 1 1 1
> x/c(1,2); x/c(1,2,3)
[1] 2.0 2.0 1.0 1.5
[1] 2.0000000 2.0000000 0.3333333 3.0000000
Warning message:
In x/c(1, 2, 3) :
  longer object length is not a multiple of shorter object length
```

Here, element-wise division is carried out and the rest of the operation is similar as in addition or multiplication. It should be remembered that the software vectors are treated as arrays and not necessarily as the vectors as in mathematics.

We will now relate vectors with Statistics. Section 2.3 of Gentle (2007) will be our core line of thinking and conceptual development.

Definition 2.4.1 *The* One Vector *is the vector with all elements equal to 1. It is also called the* summing vector, *as* $1^T\mathbf{x}$ *gives the sum of the elements of the vector* $\mathbf{x}$.

Definition 2.4.2 *The* inner product *of two vectors* $\mathbf{x}$ *and* $\mathbf{y}$ *is defined as*

$$\langle \mathbf{x}, y\rangle = \sum_i x_i y_i. \tag{2.7}$$

Let us consider two vectors $\mathbf{x} = [5, 4, 3, 8, 21]$ and $\mathbf{y} = [12, 2, 3, 16, 9]$. We can easily perform the inner product as

```
> x <- c(5,4,3,8,21); y <- c(12,2,3,16,9)
> sum(x*y) # gives us the inner product
[1] 394
```

Definition 2.4.3 *The* norm *of a vector* $\mathbf{x}$, *denoted by* $\| \,.\, \|$, *is a real-valued function, which satisfies the following three conditions:*

1. *if* $\mathbf{x} \neq 0, \| \mathbf{x} \| \geq 0$;
2. *for a scalar* a, $\| a\mathbf{x} \| = |a| \; \| \mathbf{x} \|$;
3. *and the triangle inequality,* $\| \mathbf{x} + y \| \leq \| \mathbf{x} \| + \| .\mathbf{y} \|$

For our purposes, we are interested in the norms induced by the inner product of vectors, which is given by

$$\| \mathbf{x} \| = \sqrt{\langle \mathbf{x}, \mathbf{x} \rangle} = \sqrt{\sum_i x_i^2}. \tag{2.8}$$

Furthermore, the normalized vector of a given vector $\mathbf{x}$ is defined as the vector divided by its *length**:

$$\tilde{\mathbf{x}} = \frac{1}{\| \mathbf{x} \|}\mathbf{x}. \tag{2.9}$$

* Here, length refers to the Euclidean distance of the vector from the origin, and in more technical language it is the Euclidean norm. This length of the vector can be confused with the `length` function, returning the number of elements of a vector, which is freely used as in R. However, it is often clear from the context and the fonts which is correct. We continue with the two vectors used earlier to become familiarized with the computations in R.

```
> normx <- sqrt(sum(x^2)); normy <- sqrt(sum(y^2))
+ # norms of vectors x and y
> normx;normy
[1] 23.55844
[1] 22.22611
> normalisedx <- x/normx; normalisedy <- y/normy
+ # vectors x and y normalised
> normalisedx; normalisedy
[1] 0.2122382 0.1697905 0.1273429 0.3395811 0.8914004
[1] 0.53990552 0.08998425 0.13497638 0.71987403 0.40492914
> sqrt(sum(normalisedx^2)); sqrt(sum(normalisedy^2)) # check
[1] 1
[1] 1
```

Definition 2.4.4 *Two vectors* $\mathbf{x}$ *and* $\mathbf{y}$ *are said to be* orthogonal vectors *if*

$$\langle \mathbf{x}, \mathbf{y} \rangle = 0, \tag{2.10}$$

and this is denoted as $\mathbf{x} \perp \mathbf{y}$.

Definition 2.4.5 *The* projection *of a vector* $\mathbf{y}$ *onto the vector* $\mathbf{x}$ *is defined by*

$$\hat{\mathbf{y}} = \frac{\langle \mathbf{x}, \mathbf{y} \rangle}{\| \mathbf{x} \|^2}\mathbf{x}. \tag{2.11}$$

A natural important property of the projection is that if the projection is subtracted from the vector that was projected, the *residual* is orthogonal to the projection. That is, the residual is defined as

$$\mathbf{r} = \mathbf{y} - \frac{\langle \mathbf{x}, \mathbf{y} \rangle}{\| \mathbf{x} \|^2}\mathbf{x} = \mathbf{y} - \hat{\mathbf{y}}, \tag{2.12}$$

and then the *angle* between two vectors is defined by

$$\text{angle}(\mathbf{x}, \mathbf{y}) = \cos^{-1}\left(\frac{\langle \mathbf{x}, \mathbf{y} \rangle}{\| \mathbf{x} \| \| \mathbf{y} \|}\right) \tag{2.13}$$

```
> angle_xy <- acos(sum(x*y)/(normx*normy))
> angle_xy
[1] 0.7189997
> cos(angle_xy)
[1] 0.7524649
```

Vectors and Basic Summary Statistics. The arithmetic mean of a vector **x** can be reformulated as a function of vectors, that is, $\bar{x} = 1_n{}^T\mathbf{x}/n$, where 1_n is the one vector of n elements. The mean can also be thought of as a vector whose elements are equal to $\bar{x}$, and such a vector is also denoted by $\bar{x}$ only. Since n is the (vector) length of the one vector, the mean vector can be considered as the projection of vector **x** onto that vector. The square of a norm of the vector $\| x\|^2$ is also useful in statistics, and particularly in the relation $\| \bar{x}\|^2 = n\bar{x}^2$, where the quantity $\bar{x}$ on the left-hand side is a vector and that on the right is a scalar.

```
> one <- rep(1,5)
> normone <- sqrt(sum(one^2))
> (sum(x*one)/(normone^2)); mean(x)
[1] 8.2
[1] 8.2
```

Definition 2.4.6 *The* centered counterpart *of a vector* **x**, *denoted* $\mathbf{x}_c$, *is defined as the vector*

$$\mathbf{x}_c = \mathbf{x} - \bar{x},$$

where $\bar{x}$ is the average of the elements of ***x***.

In general, any vector whose elements sum to 0 may be referred to as a centered vector. Since the mean of a vector is the vector projection of the vector onto one, the centered vector and the vector are orthogonal and the Pythagorean relationship holds, that is

$$\| \mathbf{x}\|^2 = \| \bar{\mathbf{x}}\|^2 + \| \mathbf{x}_c\|^2$$

The centered vector and Pythagorean relationship are now illustrated for the `x` vector.

```
> (xc <- x - mean(x))
[1] -3.2 -4.2 -5.2 -0.2 12.8
> normx^2; 5*mean(x)^2 + sum(xc^2)
[1] 555
[1] 555
```

?vector

2.4.2 *Matrices*

A matrix will be used here to represent an arrangement of real numbers in a two-dimensional array through row and column vectors. The dimension of a matrix is defined by the number of rows and columns, and thus if a matrix has n rows and m columns, the dimension of the matrix is $n \times m$. The dimension of a matrix is also known as the *order of the matrix*. The element of a matrix **A** in row i and column j will be denoted by $a_{ij}, i = 1, \cdots, n, j = 1, \cdots, m$, and the matrix is represented by

$$\mathbf{A} = \begin{bmatrix} a_{11} & a_{12} & \cdots & a_{1m} \\ a_{21} & a_{22} & \cdots & a_{2m} \\ \vdots & \vdots & & \vdots \\ a_{n1} & a_{n2} & \cdots & a_{nm} \end{bmatrix} = (a_{ij})_{n \times m}.$$

Matrices are easily created in R. First, we explain the beginning steps for clear understanding. The main syntax of the `matrix` function is `function(data = NA, nrow = 1, ncol = 1, byrow = FALSE, dimnames = NULL)`. The following simple examples clarify some ways of creating matrices.

```
> A <- matrix(nrow=5,ncol=6)
> A
     [,1] [,2] [,3] [,4] [,5] [,6]
[1,]   NA   NA   NA   NA   NA   NA
[2,]   NA   NA   NA   NA   NA   NA
[3,]   NA   NA   NA   NA   NA   NA
[4,]   NA   NA   NA   NA   NA   NA
[5,]   NA   NA   NA   NA   NA   NA
> B <- matrix(c(1:12),nrow=2)
> B
     [,1] [,2] [,3] [,4] [,5] [,6]
[1,]    1    3    5    7    9   11
[2,]    2    4    6    8   10   12
> C <- matrix(c(1:12),nrow=2,ncol=2)
> C
     [,1] [,2]
[1,]    1    3
[2,]    2    4
```

If `data` is not assigned/used while creating a matrix, the default values will be NA. The options of `nrow` and `ncol` can be used to fix the dimension of a matrix. It may be seen in the creation of the `C` matrix above that excess data is discarded. The reader should verify the result as a consequence of using the `byrow=TRUE` option while creating the `C` matrix.

It is sometimes to the user's advantage to assign names to the rows and columns of a matrix, which is accomplished by

```
> X <- matrix(20:11,nrow=2)
> rownames(X) <- rownames(X,do.NULL=FALSE,"Sl.No.")
> colnames(X) <- colnames(X,do.NULL=TRUE)
> colnames(X) <- c("john","mahesh","ganesh","ross","rupesh")
> X
        john mahesh ganesh ross rupesh
Sl.No.1   20     18     16   14     12
Sl.No.2   19     17     15   13     11
```

The reader may wish to explore more details about `case.names` and `variable.names`.

An important concept in the theory of matrices is the concept of *rank*. The rank of a matrix is defined as the maximum number of linearly independent vectors, row or column vectors. The rank of a matrix will be denoted by rank($\mathbf{A}$). It may be noted that for any scalar $a \neq 0$, rank($a\mathbf{A}$) = rank($\mathbf{A}$), and that rank($\mathbf{A}$) $\leq \min\{m, n\}$. A matrix is said to be of *full rank* if rank($\mathbf{A}$) $= \min\{m, n\}$.

A matrix is called a *square matrix* if the number of rows are equal to the number of columns, that is, $n = m$. The *diagonal elements* of a square matrix are $a_{ii}, i = 1, \cdots, n$. The sum of diagonal elements of square matrix is called the *trace of the matrix* and is denoted by tr($\mathbf{A}$). Mathematically, tr($\mathbf{A}$) $= \sum_i a_{ii}$. The *transpose of a matrix* is denoted by $\mathbf{A}'$ or $\mathbf{A}^T$, and is defined by $\mathbf{A}' = (a_{ji})_{m \times n}$, with $a_{ji} = a_{ij}, \forall i, j$.

If the off-diagonal elements are all 0, that is, $a_{ij} = 0, i \neq j$, and $a_{ii} = 1$, the matrix is called an *identity matrix* and it is generally denoted by $\mathbf{I}$. The (row-wise) array of a matrix $\mathbf{A}$ with elements $a_{ij}, i \geq j$, is said to form the *lower triangle* of the matrix, while the (column-wise) array of the matrix with elements $a_{ij}, i \leq j$, forms the *upper triangle*. Diagonal elements are included in the triangle matrices according to mathematical requirements. Also, if $a_{ij} = a_{ji}, \forall i, j$, the matrix is called a *symmetric matrix*. The concepts defined here are now illustrated in an R session.

```
> A <- matrix(1:9,nrow=3)
> diag(A)
[1] 1 5 9
> sum(diag(A)) # Trace of a matrix
[1] 15
> A[lower.tri(A,diag=TRUE)]
[1] 1 2 3 5 6 9
> A[upper.tri(A,diag=TRUE)]
[1] 1 4 5 7 8 9
```

The arithmetics of multiple matrices are now considered. Let $\mathbf{A} = (a_{ij})_{n \times m}$ and $\mathbf{B} = (b_{ij})_{n \times m}$ be two matrices of the same dimensions (order). Addition and subtraction is possible with matrices of the same order, and here $\mathbf{A} \pm \mathbf{B} = (a_{ij} \pm b_{ij})_{n \times m}$.

Matrix multiplication, also known as the *Cayley matrix multiplication* or *cross-product* of matrices, between two matrices $\mathbf{A} = (a_{ij})_{n \times m}$ and $\mathbf{B} = (b_{jk})_{m \times o}$ is defined if the number of columns of $\mathbf{A}$ is equal to the number of rows of $\mathbf{B}$ by the resultant matrix $\mathbf{C}$

$$\mathbf{C} = (c_{ik})_{n \times o}, c_{ik} = \sum_j a_{ij} b_{jk}.$$

Matrix computations are straightforward here. We first create two matrices A and B using the data.entry operator. Cross-products between two matrices, say A and B, may be performed using the %*% operator:

```
> A <- matrix(nrow=2,ncol=2)
> data.entry(A)
> A
     var1 var2
[1,]    4    5
[2,]    8   13
```

```
> B <- matrix(nrow=2,ncol=3)
> data.entry(B)
> B
     var1 var2 var3
[1,]   10   15    8
[2,]    4    6    9
> A%*%B
     var1 var2 var3
[1,]   60   90   77
[2,]  132  198  181
> B%*%A
Error in B %*% A : non-conformable arguments
```

Following the `data.entry` command, the reader should enter appropriate values on the popped-up window. Matrix operations must be carefully performed, as it can be seen above that `B%*%A` is not well defined.

The *determinant* of a square matrix $\mathbf{A} = (a_{ij})_{n \times n}$ is defined by

$$\det(\mathbf{A}) = |\mathbf{A}| = \sum \epsilon_{j_1 j_2 \cdots j_n} a_{1j_1} a_{2j_2} \cdots a_{nj_n},$$

where $\epsilon_{j_1 j_2 \cdots j_n}$ is ± 1 accordingly as $\{j_1 j_2 \cdots j_n\}$ is an even or odd number of permutations of the integer $\{1, 2, \cdots, n\}$, and the sum extends over all possible permutations. Fortunately, the simple R function `det` helps us to obtain the determinant of the matrix. If $|\mathbf{A}| = 0$, the matrix is said to be a *singular matrix*, and if $|\mathbf{A}| > 0$, it is called a *non-singular matrix*. The matrix $\mathbf{A}^{-1}$ is said to be inverse of a non-singular matrix $\mathbf{A}$ if $\mathbf{A}\mathbf{A}^{-1} = \mathbf{I}$. In the case of a singular matrix or a non-square matrix, *generalized inverse(s)* are defined. However, we will not go into its details here but merely note that the software can easily handle them.

The *determinant* of a matrix is computed using the `det` function: `det(A)` to give the answer as 12. The *inverse* and *generalized inverse* of a matrix are obtained using the `solve` and `ginv`, from the `MASS` package, functions:

```
> solve(A)
           [,1]       [,2]
var1  1.0833333 -0.4166667
var2 -0.6666667  0.3333333
> library(MASS)
> ginv(B)
            [,1]        [,2]
[1,]  0.04774536 -0.04244032
[2,]  0.07161804 -0.06366048
[3,] -0.06896552  0.17241379
```

Consider a square-matrix $\mathbf{A}$ of dimension $n \times n$. Consider the determinant $|\mathbf{A} - \lambda \mathbf{I}|$ as a function of the variable λ. The variable λ may be a complex-valued variable. The determinant $|\mathbf{A} - \lambda \mathbf{I}|$ would be a polynomial of degree n and is called the *characteristic polynomial* of $\mathbf{A}$, and the equation

$$|\mathbf{A} - \lambda \mathbf{I}| = 0, \tag{2.14}$$

is called the *characteristic equation* of **A**. The characteristic equation will have n roots, which are called the *eigenvalues* of **A**. The eigenvalues have important applications in statistical applications, as well as in stochastic processes, see Chapters 10 and 15.

The eigenvalues may be real, complex, or some combination of real and complex. The eigenvalues are ordered by the modulus values $|\lambda_1| \geq |\lambda_2| \geq |\lambda_n| \geq 0$. In the case where λ_1 is unique, it is called the *dominant eigenvalue*. Note that since any λ_i is a root of the equation $|\mathbf{A} - \lambda\mathbf{I}| = 0$, we have $|\mathbf{A} - \lambda_i\mathbf{I}| = 0$ and hence $\mathbf{A} - \lambda_i\mathbf{I}$ will be singular. Equivalently, it means that the null space of $\mathbf{A} - \lambda_i\mathbf{I}$ has a dimension of at least one, and this space is called the *eigenspace* of **A** corresponding to λ_i and any non-zero vector in this eigenspace is called the *eigenvector* of **A** corresponding to λ_i.

Now, let **A** be a matrix of dimension $n \times m$ with rank r. The matrix **A** can then be written as

$$\mathbf{A} = \mathbf{U}\boldsymbol{\Lambda}\mathbf{V}', \tag{2.15}$$

where $\boldsymbol{\Lambda}$ is a $r \times r$ diagonal matrix with positive diagonal elements, **U** is a $n \times r$ matrix such that $\mathbf{U}'\mathbf{U} = \mathbf{I}$, and **V** is an $m \times r$ matrix with $\mathbf{V}'\mathbf{V} = \mathbf{I}$. This representation of the matrix **A** is the well-known *singular value decomposition*.

Eigenvalues, eigenvectors, and singular value decomposition for appropriate matrices may be easily computed using the in-built R commands:

```
> eigen(A)
$values
[1] 16.2620873  0.7379127
$vectors
           [,1]       [,2]
[1,] -0.3775776 -0.8375173
[2,] -0.9259779  0.5464109
> eigen(B)
Error in eigen(B) : non-square matrix in 'eigen'
> svd(A)
$d
[1] 16.5370324  0.7256441
$u
           [,1]       [,2]
[1,] -0.3850756 -0.9228850
[2,] -0.9228850  0.3850756
$v
           [,1]       [,2]
[1,] -0.5396000 -0.8419215
[2,] -0.8419215  0.5396000
```

In this section, we have considered how the basic maths related to vectors and matrices are performed. Apart from the arithmetic, it is the methods related to the cross-product of the matrices, the determinants, inverses, eigen computations, and the Cholesky decomposition which are essential armor for a data analyst.

?matrix, ?matmult, ?solve, ?svd

2.5 Data Entering and Reading from Files

We undertake the task of storing the objects and also study how to read data from external files. The external data files may come in various formats and we will see how to read data of important file formats.

2.5.1 *Data Entering*

In the earlier sections, we used arrays, such as `1:5`, `c(1,6,-14,-154,0)`, etc. The second array mentioned above is one of the R commands. Specifically, the letter `c` stands for concatenation, or coercing, or combining various R objects in a single object. The following simple examples should help the reader:

```
> a <- c(1:7)
> a
[1] 1 2 3 4 5 6 7
> a2 <- c(1:6)
> a2
[1] 1 2 3 4 5 6
> c(4:-3) -> b
> b
[1]  4  3  2  1  0 -1 -2 -3
> D <- c(a,b)
> D
 [1]  1  2  3  4  5  6  7  4  3  2  1  0 -1 -2 -3
> (x <- c("Nominal", "Ordinal", "Others"))
[1] "Nominal" "Ordinal" "Others"
```

A few remarks are in order. We see that an array/object can be assigned to a new object as `->` or `<-`. The elements of an R object may be numeric or character. It should be noted here that the entire environment on the tail end of `<-` is assigned to the object on the side facing the arrow. Of course, there are more ways of creating new objects.

We can also use ≪- or -≫ for creating new objects.

```
> a «- c(1:7)
> a
[1] 1 2 3 4 5 6 7
```

There is a difference here though. The assignment operators ->,=, and -≫ work in a different manner to each other. The first two operators under consideration assign the environment when evaluated with = allowed at the top level, whereas the operator -≫ causes a search through the environment for an existing definition of the assignable variable. Of course, a detailed understanding of `environment` needs to be there in the first place, which can be obtained with `?environment`. We restrict ourselves here with an illustration, while introducing the new assignable operator `assign`.

```
> pi «- 23
Error: cannot change value of locked binding for 'pi'
> (pi <- 23)
[1] 23
> assign("b",c(1:3,192:195))
> b
[1]   1   2   3 192 193 194 195
```

We note that `pi` is a built-in constant of R, see `?Constants`.

Failing to remember the fact that R is *case sensitive* may lead to errors. For example, `C` is itself another R function which sets contrasts for a factor, and if care is not taken we may end up creating contrasts for an object when we intend to create a new object.

```
> a <- factor(1:3) #more about factors later
> c(a)
[1] 1 2 3
> C(a)
[1] 1 2 3
attr(,"contrasts")
      unordered
contr.treatment
Levels: 1 2 3
```

R makes a distinction between a row and a column vector, which can be seen by the example:

```
> letters # another sequence of constants, see also LETTERS
 [1] "a" "b" "c" "d" "e" ... "x" "y" "z"
> t(letters) # t for transpose
     [,1] [,2] [,3] [,4] [,5] ...[,24] [,25] [,26]
[1,] "a"  "b"  "c"  "d"  "e"  ...  "x"   "y"   "z"
```

The objects `letters`, along with `LETTERS`, `month.abb`, and `month.name` forms some of the important built-in constants of R.

We can easily find the number of elements in a vector using the `length` function; consider `x <- c(-3, 8)`:

```
> x <- c(-3:8)
> length(x)
[1] 12
```

We have created (used) some numeric vectors as well as character vectors. In some programs we may need to find the class of certain objects. We can find this by using either the mode function or the `class` function. The reader may verify the following:

```
> mode(c(0,.5,1)); class(c(0,.5,1))
[1] "numeric"
[1] "numeric"
> mode(a<-c(1:pi)); class(a<-c(1:pi))
```

```
[1] "numeric"
[1] "integer"
> mode(TRUE); class(FALSE); 1-TRUE; as.numeric(FALSE)
[1] "logical"
[1] "logical"
[1] 0
[1] 0
```

It had been stated previously that either of the mode or class functions can help us, but we have however ended up with two different answers. Let us understand what is happening. The function mode returns the type of stored object, whereas class returns a character vector of the names of the classes from which the object has inherited the class. In the above set of programs, we also have logical values TRUE and FALSE.

We will conclude this subsection with a presentation of the element-wise entry of a matrix. The matrix is considered in more detail in Section 2.4.

```
> X <- matrix(nrow=3,ncol=2)
> X[,1] <- scan()
1: 1
2: 2
3: 3
4:
Read 3 items
> X[,2] <- scan()
1: -3
2: -2
3: -1
4:
Read 3 items
> X
     [,1] [,2]
[1,]    1   -3
[2,]    2   -2
[3,]    3   -1
```

Here we have used an action of the scan function which allows the reader to specify the values through the console. In fact, this function can be used more elaborately to read data from external files, as will be seen next.

We next take up the task of reading data from external files.

?assign

2.5.2 Reading Data from External Files

In any R session we are working in a certain directory. The address of the current working directory may be known using the command getwd(). Suppose that we had a file named read_me_if_you_can.dat in the current directory. If the file is in a directory other than the working one, we can still access it. We use the function scan to read this file.

```
> scan("read_me_if_you_can.dat") # if file is in working directory
Read 5 items
[1] 10 20 30 40 50
> scan("/home/user/where_the_file_is/read_me_if_you_can.dat")
Read 5 items
[1] 10 20 30 40 50
```

The scanned data can be assigned to any new object, say `x <- scan()`. This example is a really simple one. It is very plausible that the external data file also contains variable names. Most often the variable names are indicated in the first line itself. Suppose we want to read the dataset of the Youden and Beale experiment introduced in Subsection 1.4.2. The first line of the file contains the names of the variable and each data point begins on a new line with the values of variables separated by a comma. We can read such a data file using the command read.table.

```
> yb <- read.table("/.../youden.csv",header=T,sep=",")
> yb
  Preparation_1 Preparation_2
1            31            18
2            20            17

7            10             5
8             7             6
```

Note: The option `header=T` is technically `header=TRUE`. The `TRUE` and `FALSE` are logical entities and may be abbreviated to the first letter itself. The option `sep=","` indicates that the values in the file are separated by a comma.

We could also have used `read.csv` instead of `read.table` for the above example.

?read.table

Reading data from other software formats will be treated in Section 3.3.

2.6 Working with Packages

We had introduced the reader to the web-link http://www.cran.r-project.org/web/packages. This page enlists all the packages that have been approved by the R team. Of course, there are many other developers who maintain their R package and which are available from them or their websites.

Let us first discuss the packages currently available with the installed R software. The Windows user can see `Packages` on the menu ribbon. The first option here is `Load Package`, which provides a list of all the packages which have already been installed in their current version. The code `library()` executed on the R console also does the same task and runs the same across all platforms. If you select the package `MASS`, it will be loaded for the session and you can start using all the functions and datasets from this package. Another alternative is to run `library(MASS)` or `require(MASS)` at the R console. All of them have the same results. Though a menu ribbon is not available for the UNIX user, she can use the latter two options. A nice option when loading an R packages is the `quietly` option, in that the general instructions or messages displayed when loading the package can be set off using this option. To understand this, first try `library(survival)` and note the message. Next, quit the R session and then start it again. Finally, try `library(survival,quietly=TRUE)` and mark your observation.

Now we consider the task of installing new packages. Suppose that you need to install the R package `gpk`. A good practice is to install the package within an R session. To install this package the user needs to simply run the code `install.packages("gpk")`. The message `Please select a CRAN mirror for use in this session` is first displayed and then you need to select a CRAN mirror. It is advisable that you select that mirror which is geographically closest to your place. We have assumed that you have a live Internet connection. In the case where you do not have a continuous connection, you may first download the package and then use the option, for Windows user, `Install package(s) from local zip files...`. The Windows package ends with an extension `zip`, that is, they are zipped files. For the Linux version, the extension is `tar.gz`, and such files may be installed using the command `R CMD INSTALL *.tar.gz` at the terminal. If the user has Internet connection, using the `install.packages` is advised since the command also downloads the related packages and installs them too.

A convention adopted in this book is the following. Software, programs, and packages evolve and mature over a time period. Furthermore, since the intent of this book is to provide effective coverage of several important domains of the subject, there is a need to refer to many important packages developed by many people across the globe. Thus, we have used many packages, and to ensure that the reader does not lose track of the package that will be used in a particular chapter, we describe the packages used at the beginning of that chapter. Thus, **Package(s):** will appear following the title of the chapter, giving a list of the packages used for that chapter. This book will also be using the companion package `ACSWR` and the `gpk` package too.

?install.packages

2.7 R Session Management

We have seen various essential techniques for use up to this point. Exporting data from foreign formats of data sources has also been explored. It is equally important to know how to manage and save your current R session, which may be useful for future use too. Let us discuss the functions which will help us to achieve this.

The authors preference at the beginning of most R sessions is to run the code `rm(list=ls())`. This is a useful trick in the initial stages of learning R, in the sense that it gives the user a clear session to begin! Here, the part code `ls()` lists all the variables in the current session and then is assigned to the `list` to be marked for deletion with the `rm` function.

In Section 2.5 we saw that `getwd()` accesses the current working directory. This directory may be changed to any other with, say, `setwd("/home/user/rlab")`. The reader should note that we use the forward slash / and not the backward slash \, which is a general practice for the Windows user. A small work around is to use the backward slash twice in succession to get the result for the Windows user, that is, `C:\\Users\\rlab`. To access the list of all the files in your current working directory, use `list.files()`.

Suppose that the following objects are present in the current R session: `gf`, `girder`, `girdernew`, `i`, `mf`, `ss`, `ssaov`. A specific object may be saved using the `save` function with `save(mf,file="mf.RData")`. Two or more objects may also be saved with `save(mf,gf,girder,file="my3objects.RData")`. All the objects of the session may be saved with `save.image(file="current_session.RData")`. The saved objects may be loaded in a later session with `load("current_session.RData")`.

To quit an R session, run the code `q()`.

2.8 Further Reading

Venables, et al. (2013), Version 3.0.2, is the most recent introductory course for a user to get the R basics correct. All the versions of this document are updated as and when a new R version is available. On the web, it is available at http://cran.r-project.org/doc/manuals/R-intro.pdf. According to the authors this document is a *must read* for any R beginner. A timeless classic introduction is Venables and Ripley (2002). Dalgaard (2008), Chapters 1 to 3, is a nice starting point too. The first seven chapters of Crawley (2007) provide a detailed background of R. Purohit, et al. (2008) which is a very concise and useful course at the beginning of R learning.

It is our view that any of the above sources give the user a good footing in R. Needless to say, even a first search on www will give various free introductions to R. A classic example of this fact is Wikipedia. Our observations have been that many complex statistical programs which follow a description of the theory are in R and also the codes generating the outputs are made available. The fact that such programs may have a few errors is not just attributable to them not being reviewed.

2.9 Complements, Problems, and Programs

Problem 2.1 Write a program to obtain the minimum between two corresponding elements of two vectors. As an example, for the two vectors `A=(1,2,3,4)` and `B=(4,3,2,1)`, your program should return the minimum as `(1,2,2,1)`. Repeat the exercise to obtain the maximum. After you are done with your program, use the `pmin` and `pmax` functions available in R.

Problem 2.2 Using the `options`, fix the number of digits of the output during a session to four digits.

Problem 2.3 Find the details about *complex numbers* and perform the basic arithmetic related to complex numbers. What do you expect when you perform `mean`, `median`, and `sd` on an array of complex numbers? Check the results in R console.

Problem 2.4 For a gamma integral, it is well known that $\Gamma(n) = (n-1)!$, where n is an integer. Verify the same for your choice of integers. Note that you are required to use `gamma` for the left-hand side and the `factorial` function for the right-hand side.

Problem 2.5 For the sequence `theta <- seq(0,pi,0.1)`, compute $\sin^2(\theta) + \cos^2(\theta)$ and comment. Furthermore, for $0 \leq \theta \leq \pi/2$, check whether you get $\sin(\theta) = \cos(\pi/2 - \theta)$.

Problem 2.6 For a number x, can you always say that `round(floor(x)) == floor (ro und(x))`. Also, test which of these relationships hold true: `floor (ceil ing(x)) == ceiling(floor(x))`, `floor(sign(x)) == sign(floor(x))`.

Problem 2.7 By using the `is.na` function to substitute the missing observations of a vector, you may select a numeric vector of your choice with missing values, with 0. Attempt to replace the missing values of a vector with the mean of the vector having valid elements.

Problem 2.8 Consider the factor vector `exp_levels <- gl(3,2)`, and now change the third and fourth elements to 1 with `exp_levels[3:4]<-1`. Now, 2 is an extra factor level which is not present as a factor for any of its elements. Drop it! Use `droplevels`.

Problem 2.9 For a numeric vector, do you expect `min(x) == -max(-x)`?

Problem 2.10 The Stirling function `stirling` is given as an approximation of $n!$. The R function `factorial` is also an approximation for the factorial operation. This means that `prod(1:n)` will not always be the same as $\prod_{j=1}^{n} j$. Find out the least n for which `factorial` does not agree with the result for `prod(1:n)`. Also, for `1:n`, plot the $n!$ values using the `prod`, `stirling` and `factorial` functions against `1:n` and make notes.

Problem 2.11 In Subsection 2.4.1, we computed the norm of a vector `x` as `sqrt (sum(x^2))`. With some *extra effort*, it is indeed possible to obtain the same using the R function `norm`. Explore the options `type` and complete the use of the `norm` function which gives the same answer as `sqrt(sum(x^2))`.

Problem 2.12 Create the matrix `A <- matrix(1:16,nrow=4)` in R. Using the functions `upper.tri`, `lower.tri`, and `diag`, obtain the identity matrix.

Problem 2.13 For the matrix `A<-matrix(c(1:12),nrow=2)`, find the determinant using the `det` function.

Problem 2.14 Check whether `ginv` and `solve` result in the same inverse matrix for a non-singular square matrix? In the case of a singular matrix, say `matrix(rep(1,4),nrow=2)`, what will be the generalized inverse?

3

Data Preparation and Other Tricks

Package(s): `gdata`, `chron`
Dataset(s): `100mrun.xls`, `Earthwormbiomass.xls`, `Bacteria.XLS`, `nerve.dat`, `atombombtest.xls`, `airquality`, `wine.dat`, `sat`, `faithful`, `2005-10.txt.gz`

3.1 Introduction

Data comes in various forms and complexities. It is a difficult task to even list the major/minor complexity levels of data preparation. The different forms of data, as well as complexity levels, may be known or unknown. Thus, it is difficult to have a standard set of guidelines for teaching data preparation methods.

Complexities arise on various counts, such as file types, files with missing data values, files with different kinds of attributes, etc. In some cases, it may be simply improbable for the user to read the data properly without repeated efforts of writing the codes over and over again. In Section 3.2, we use the options available in the R function `read.table` to import data of external files which pose some difficulties. The options may vary to accommodate data problems, avoiding certain number of lines of file, and so forth. A good practice during the learning curve is to validate the imported data into R and check if it is on the expected lines. Thus, it may help to see the imported data using the functions `head`, `tail`, `str`, `View`, etc., and such functions will be illustrated in Section 3.4. The R functions `aggregate`, `with`, and `assign` are effective in carrying out data manipulation without the need to create new R objects. The use of these functions will be seen in Section 3.5. Time and date vectors need special consideration and we will aid the reader with the math of it in Section 3.6. The complexity of dealing with text matter is one of the most detailed ones and the final technical Section 3.7 will consider the preliminary aspect of this new area. `Rscript` is a very important backend R tool and helps to run programs without the necessity of even opening the software. Furthermore, rich text editors are important too, and whenever it is possible to use them, the author would recommend that such editors be promptly deployed. This forms the topic of Section 3.8.

A Course in Statistics with R, First Edition. Prabhanjan Narayanachar Tattar, Suresh Ramaiah and B. G. Manjunath.

Companion Website: www.wiley.com/go/tattar/statistics

3.2 Manipulation with Complex Format Files

Section 2.5 introduced us to a method of reading data from external data files using the `scan` function. However, it is not the case that data is always well organized. The word *organized* here has a very vague meaning. After all, why would anybody write files which are *not* organized. It is nice to understand that "organized" is used in a rather internal sense here. The data that is "internally" stored and managed by R gives consistent results if we read the data according to the need of the hour. We will illustrate with some examples.

Example 3.2.1. The Hundred Meter Running Race. Consider the dataset `100mrun.xls` from Gore, et al. (2006). To obtain the file of interest, please visit http://ces.iisc.ernet.in/hpg/nvjoshi/statspunedatabook/databook.html and download `datafile sxls.zip` and unzip it and copy the file `100mrun.xls` to your working directory. The two columns give us the year of the Olympics and the winning recorded time. In spite of using the `read.xls` function from the package `gdata`, our problems are not over. The first row does not contain the variable names and is a descriptor of the file characteristic containing data about the 100 meters running race. The variable names appear on the second row, and we need to read the data from the second row onward. Hence, we ask R to skip the first line. We will first load the `gdata` package. The data is then properly read as below.

```
> library(gdata)
> newsome1 <- read.xls("100mrun.xls",sheet=1,skip=1)
> newsome1
   Year Time.sec.
1  1896     12.00
2  1900     11.00
3  1904     11.00

24 2000      9.87
```

The option `skip` ensures that the data is read from the second line of the `file`. Since the xls (xlsx) document may have multiple sheets, it is necessary for R to know from which sheet we are importing the data. This is met through the `sheet` option. The argument for the `sheet` option may either be the sheet number or the sheet name. □

Remark about `gdata`. This R package needs the `perl` software too. In general, Linux and McIntosh OS have this software by default and the `read.xls` function works fine. However, Windows OS does not contain the `perl` software and needs to be installed before using the `gdata` package. Thus, the user will need to first download and install the software from http://www.perl.org/get.html. Furthermore, the perl option needs to explicitly specified in the `read.xls` code. That is, we need a modification with `newsome1 <- read.xls("100mrun.xls",perl= "C:/Perl/bin/perl.exe",sheet=1,skip=1)` to ensure that the data is properly imported in R. If the sheets have names, and not numbers, the code changes slightly to `sheet='sheet name'`.

Example 3.2.2. The Earthworm Density. In this example, we have a few more added complexities. Here, we have to skip the first line of the xls file, which is a description of the data, where the option is `skip=1`. Columns I, II, and IV are numeric vectors, though Column IV contains years which may be considered both numeric as well as a factor. The variable names in the `xls` file will be changed with `col.names=c("Density","Biomass", "Crop","Year","Soil Layer")`. The data points are followed by a two-line citation of the research paper in which the data appears. We should not read this citation into R, and hence we specify that the number of rows which need to read should be 12 and this is done with the option `nrows=12`. The xls file containing this dataset is `Earthwormbiomass.xls`. The source of the dataset is the same as discussed in the previous example.

```
> some <- read.xls("Earthwormbiomass.xls",skip=1,nrows=12,
+ header=TRUE,sep=",", col.names=c("Density","Biomass","Crop",
+ "Year","Soil Layer"))
> some
  Density Biomass                 Crop Year Soil.Layer
1     210    15.1                Maize 1998       0-10
2     251    22.2                Maize 1999       0-10

12      3     0.6 Wheat and Mustard 1999      10-20
> sapply(some,class)
  Density    Biomass       Crop       Year Soil.Layer
"integer"  "numeric"   "factor"  "integer"   "factor"
```

The `sapply` function shows that we have properly read the data into R. □

Example 3.2.3. Removing Percentage Symbol from a Dataset. We consider the dataset `Bacteria.XLS` from the same source, as in the previous two examples. Here, the data in the second and third columns are percentage values, and accordingly end with a % symbol. We know from our experience that the value with the symbol is the percentage number. Unfortunately, R does not know this fact. The rest of the columns are numeric vectors.

We need to power our `read.xls` command with the `colClasses` option, which tells R to read all the columns as character vectors. The vectors can be straightaway made numeric using the `as.numeric` vector. For the second and third columns, we tell R that the decimals of the vector have to start by replacing % as a decimal start point. The program is given below which carries out the steps detailed here.

```
> bacteria <- read.xls("Bacteria.XLS",colClasses="character")
> sapply(bacteria,class)
   Response        salt       lipid          pH        Temp
"character" "character" "character" "character" "character"
> bacteria[,"Response"] <- as.numeric(bacteria[,"Response"])
> bacteria[,"salt"] <- type.convert(bacteria[,"salt"],dec="%")
> bacteria[,"lipid"] <- type.convert(bacteria[,"lipid"],dec="%")
> bacteria[,"pH"] <- as.numeric(bacteria[,"pH"])
> bacteria[,"Temp"] <- as.numeric(bacteria[,"Temp"])
> sapply(bacteria,class)
 Response      salt     lipid        pH      Temp
"numeric" "numeric" "numeric" "numeric" "numeric"
> bacteria
```

```
    Response salt lipid pH Temp
1      -5.55    0     0  3    0
2      -5.15    1     0  3    0
3      -5.05    0     5  3    0
             . . .
299     0.25    3    20  0    2
300     1.03    4    20  0    2
> sapply(bacteria,mean)
Response     salt     lipid        pH      Temp
  0.2693   2.0000   10.0000    1.5000    1.0000
```

Note that we are extracting the variables from a `data.frame` using their names for the first time. The `class` of the variables shows that all the variables have been imported as `character` variables, which is not the data that we really require. Thus, there is a need to change them. The `Response` is simply converted using the `as.numeric` function, that is, we are reinforcing that we need the `Response` as a numeric variable. Next, the variables `salt` and `lipid` are converted from character to numeric with the specification that the decimals for the numeric values are occurring at the `%` symbol, and we have to use the function `type.convert` to achieve the result. The rest of the program can be understood without any further explanation. Also note that we have used the `data.frame` names to index the columns instead of the column numbers, which is again a nice R feature. □

Example 3.2.4. Reading from the "nerve.dat" using the "scan" Function. We consider reading the `nerve` dataset, which was probably first used by Cox and Lewis (1966). This data is available on the web at http://www.stat.cmu.edu/larry/all-of-nonpar/=data/nerve.dat. The data consists of 799 observations of the waiting times between successive pulses along a nerve fiber. The dataset in the file is displayed as an arrangement of six observations per line, and we have 133 lines, and one more line containing the last observation. If we use the function `read.csv`, this dataset will be read as a `data.frame` consisting of six variables with 134 observations each. The first variable will contain 134 observations, whereas the 134-th observation for the remaining five variables will be a missing value `NA`. Using the `scan` function will properly read the dataset in the required format.

```
> nerve <- read.csv("nerve.dat",sep="\t") # Not the correct way
> dim(nerve)
[1] 133   6
> nerve <- scan("nerve.dat")
Read 799 items
```

Thus, we have been able to read data using the `read.csv` function. □

Example 3.2.5. Reading the "Wine and Raters" Frequency Dataset using the "ftable" Function. Example of judges and their ratings are of interest to consumers. Wine tasting is more of an art than a science. However, this cannot stop us from considering the data arising out of such experiments! Lindley does a wonderful analysis of such a scenario, see http://www.liquidasset.com/lindley.htm. The experiment involves two types of `Tastings`: `Chardonnay` and `Cabernet`. Each tasting has ten wines, labeled `A-J`. The 11 judges, labeled `1 to 11` across the file, unfolds as 1 Englishman in Steven Spurrier, 1 American in

Patricia Gallagher, and the remaining 9 are French. Each of these 11 tasters taste the 10 wines from both tastings. The rankings are made on a scale of 0 to 20. Thus, we have a total of 11 tasters times 10 wines times 2 tastings as 220 observations. The `Chardonnay` wines are also commonly known as white wines and the `Cabernet` as red wine. White wine is popular among Americans and red among the French. This is an example of ordinal data and we require a special function to handle it.

Frequency data, if properly entered in a file and saved as `.dat` or `.txt` file, may be conveniently read into R using the `read.ftable` function as follows:[1]

```
> wine <- read.ftable("wine.dat")
> wine
                    Tasters    1    2         10   11
Tastings   Wines
Chardonnay A                10.0 18.0       16.5 17.0
           B                15.0 15.0       16.0 14.5

           J                 0.0  8.0        5.0  7.0
Cabernet   A                14.0 15.0       16.5 14.0
           B                16.0 14.0       16.0 14.0

           J                 7.0  7.0        6.0  7.0
```

The function `read.ftable` is useful to read data from flat contingency tables. What is the advantage of reading the data as `table` objects? This framework allows easy handling of frequency in the sense that we can obtain the average ratings received by the ten wines across judges and tastings, or average `Chardonnay` and `Cabernet` ratings, and so forth. This needs the use of the `xtabs` function.

```
> xtabs(Freq~Wines,data=wine)/22
Wines
       A         B         C                J
14.272727 14.204545 13.636364     7.681818
> xtabs(Freq~Tastings,data=wine)/110
Tastings
Chardonnay   Cabernet
  11.35455   11.83636
> xtabs(Freq~Tasters,data=wine)/20
Tasters
     1      2        11
10.700 11.800    12.050
```

We have used two special features of R programming in ~ and `data`. In general ~ is used in R formulas, indicating a relationship that the variable on the left-hand side of the expression depends on the right-hand side. The variables on the right-hand side may be more than one. The evaluation of the formula depends on the function that is being deployed. The `data` option is used to specify that the variables used in the expression ~ are to be found in the data frame as declared.

[1]Output and R codes are edited and would differ from the actual one seen on running the R codes.

The table, ftable, xtabs, etc., are very useful functions for analysis of categorical data, see Chapter 16. □

We will check out one more example for the frequency table, which is predominantly useful for *categorical data analysis*.

Example 3.2.6. Preparing a Contingency Table. In this example we will read a dataset from an xls file, and then convert that data frame into a table or matrix form. Gore, et al. (2006) consider the frequencies of cancer deaths of Japanese atomic bomb survivors by extent of exposure, years after exposure, etc. This dataset has appeared in the journal "Statistical Sleuth". The data is first read from an Excel file which creates a data.frame object in R. This needs to be converted into a contingency table format, which is later achieved using the xtabs function in R. The next R program achieves exactly the same.

```
> library(gdata)
> atombomb <- read.xls("atombombtest.xls",header=TRUE)
> atombomb-
bxtabs <- xtabs(Frequency~Radians+Count.Type+Count.Age.Group,
+ data=atombomb)
> atombombxtabs
, , Count.Age.Group = '0-7'
       Count.Type
Radians At Risk Death Count
    0       262          10

    400      15           0
, , Count.Age.Group = '12-15'
       Count.Type
Radians At Risk Death Count
    0       240          19

    400      14           5
, , Count.Age.Group = '16-19'

       Count.Type
Radians At Risk Death Count
    0       243          12

    400      14           2
> class(atombombxtabs)
[1] "xtabs" "table"
```

This dataset will be used in Chapter 16. □

Example 3.2.7. Reading Data from the Clipboard. A common practice is "Copy and Paste". This practice is so prevalent that it is tempting to do that in R. Suppose that the data is to be copied from any external source, say SAS, Gedit, SPSS, EXL, etc., and then pasted into R. The common practice is merely to copy the matter which your computer then holds on the clipboard. For example, the matter, in the vertical display in a spreadsheet file, is the following:

```
NOP 10 28 ... 0 14 8
```

which we have copied to the clipboard. Next, do the following at the R console:

```
> read.table("clipboard",header=TRUE)
+ # Copy-paste methods die hard
   NOP
1   10
2   28
...
17   0
18  14
19   8
```

Thus, the copied matter in the clipboard may be easily imported in R. Note that you might prefer to copy certain columns/rows from the spreadsheet available in your machine to the clipboard. □

Example 3.2.8. Reading the Row Names. Thus far we have read external files with column names and we would like to find out if we can read the row names too. Consider an external file in a csv format. Here, we have taken the dataset from Everitt and Hothorn (2011) and saved the data in a csv file. This dataset is related to life expectancies for different countries and we have further information on the age and gender groups. In the csv file we have the first column which has the name of the countries and four different age groups for males and females. Particularly, we require the row names to be read by the country name and the column names to reflect the age group with gender. Using the code `life=read.csv("lifedata.csv",header=TRUE,row.names=1)`, we can read the data in the required format □

?read.table, ?read.ftable

3.3 Reading Datasets of Foreign Formats

Datasets may be available in formats other than csv or dat. It is also a frequent situation where we need to read data stored in xls (Microsoft Excel) format, sav (SPSS), ssd (SAS), dta (STATA), etc. For example, if the Youden-Beale data was saved in the first sheet of an xls file, we can use the command:

```
> yb <- read.xls("/.../youden.xls",header=TRUE,sheet=1)
Converting xls file to csv file... Done.
Reading csv file... Done.
```

Note that R first internally converts the xls file into a csv file, and then imports it into the session.

Similarly, we can read datasets of other software. Consider the `rootstock.dta` available from http://www.stata-press.com/data/r10/rootstock.dta. This is a popular dataset in the domain of *multivariate statistics*. The soft copy `rootstock.dta` has been generated from the Stata software. We assume that this dataset has been downloaded from the web and stored in the current working directory. We can read this dataset in R using the `foreign` packages `read.dta` function.

```
library(foreign)
rootstock <- read.dta("/.../rootstock.dta")
```

Section 1.4 listed many sources of data on the web. The laborious way of using them for analysis is to download them from the sources to the local hard disk and maybe to the current working directory. The technical way is to ask R to access and download the file and load the data into the working session. The next two small examples will clarify these ideas.

```
> rootstock.url <- "http://www.stata-press.com/data/r10/
+ rootstock.dta" # Example 1
> rootstock <- read.dta(rootstock.url)
> crime.url <- "http://www.jrsainfo.org/jabg/state_data2/
+ Tribal_Data00.xls" # Example 2
> crime <- read.xls(crime.url, pattern = "State")
```

Using the url link as a text string and appropriate importing functions such as `read.dta` and `read.xls`, we can import data in foreign formats to R.

3.4 Displaying R Objects

R objects are of varying nature and we may be interested in having a quick look at the dataset itself, and not through sophisticated tools such as graphics or statistical summaries. The `utils` package shipped along with R contains a host of functionalities for our purpose.

Suppose we want to see the first ten observations of the `100mrun.xls` dataset that we imported earlier. Or we may like to see the last five observations of the same dataset. In R, `head` and `tail` are the two functions which give us this facility:

```
> head(newsome1,10)
   Year Time.sec.
1  1896      12.0
2  1900      11.0

10 1936      10.3
> tail(newsome1,5)
   Year Time.sec.
20 1984      9.99

24 2000      9.87
```

Another compact way of visualizing an object is to horizontally display the dataset. This is provided by the `str` function.

```
> str(newsome1)
'data.frame': 23 obs. of  2 variables:
```

```
 $ X1896: int  1900 1904 1908 1912 1920 1924 1928 1932 1936 1948 ...
 $ X12  : num  11 11 10.8 10.8 10.8 10.6 10.8 10.3 10.3 10.3 ...
```

The `fix` function is used to display the dataset in a new window, whereas the `View` function is used to just view the dataset.

```
> fix(newsome1)
> View(newsome1)
> View(wine)
```

Check what exactly the `edit` function does to an R object.

Note that the window arising due to the `fix` function contains three tabs `Copy`, `Paste` and `Quit`, which may be used to change the dataset. The reader may find the `edit` function to be useful too. For more such interesting functions, run `library(help=utils)` at the R console and experiment.

library(help=utils)

3.5 Manipulation Using R Functions

Consider a dataset where we have one column for measurement values of different individuals and another column with group indicators for those individuals. Now, we need to obtain some summaries of these measurements by the group indicator. This task can be achieved with the `aggregate` function, and the next example illustrates this. The examples discussed in Section 2.4.5 are also useful for manipulation of data preparation.

Example 3.5.1. Use of the `aggregate` function. We have the `sat.csv` file which contains data on Student ID Number, Grade, Pass indicator, Sat score, and GPP grade. Now, we wish to obtain the sum of the Sat scores by the GPP grade. The `aggregate` function helps us to achieve the result.

```
> data(sat)
> aggregate(sat$Sat,by=list(sat$GPP),sum)
  Group.1    x
1       A 4055
2       B 5590
3       C 4393
4       D 2164
5       F  574
```

Here we have used the `by` option to specify the groups, and `sum` is the `FUN` option. Thus, we have obtained the group sum using the `aggregate` function. □

Consider a situation where you know what the name of the variables should be. However, for some technical reason you cannot declare them before they are actually assigned some value. The question is then how can we do such assignments in the flow of a program. As an artificial example, assume that you feed to R the current top ten Sensex companies of the day. Sensex refers to a number indicative of the relative prices of shares on the Mumbai Stock Exchange.

Now, you would like to create objects whose name is the company name and whose value is its Sensex closing value. We will use the `assign` function towards this end.

Example 3.5.2. Creating Variables in the Flow of a Program. Suppose that we have collected on our clipboard the top ten companies of Sensex for today. We then want to create ten new R objects which will have the end-of-day Sensex value. Check the one thing that has gone wrong with the below R program.

```
> Sensex <- read.table("clipboard",header=FALSE)
> Sensex
            V1       V2
1         Ram1 867.1884
2        Dyan3 866.1884
3    Kaps&Japs 865.1884
4  Rocks&Rolls 864.1884
5     JUSTBEST 863.1884
6     Sin_Gine 862.1884
7       Books1 861.1884
8  BikesMotors 860.1884
9          RCB 859.1884
10         JCF 858.1884
> for(i in 1:10) {
+ nam <- paste(as.character(Sensex[i,1]),"_",days(Sys.time()),sep="")
+ assign(nam,Sensex[i,2])
+ }
> ls()
 [1] "BikesMotors_14" "Books1_14"        "Dyan3_14"        "i"
 [5] "JCF_14"         "JUSTBEST_14"      "Kaps&Japs_14"    "nam"
 [9] "Ram1_14"        "RCB_14"           "Rocks&Rolls_14" "Sensex"
[13] "Sin_Gine_14"
> JUSTBEST_14
[1] 863.1884
> Books1_14
[1] 861.1884
> RCB_14
[1] 859.1884
```

In this program we have used the `paste` function to create distinct names of the R objects. The variable names construction uses elements from the first column of the `Sensex` object. As we need to create the variables along with the current date, we use the `Sys.time` function which returns the current date. Then, we use the `days` function from the `chron` package, which extracts the "day" from the date object. The variable names from the first column is concatenated with the day of the month using an underscore symbol "_" and the option `sep=""` which says that there should be no gap between the various arguments of the `paste` function. The `Sys.time` function will be dealt with in more detail in Section 3.6. □

With large data files it is memory-consuming to create new objects for some modifications of existing columns (or rows). Thus, there is this economic reason for modifying the objects without creating new ones. The R functions `with` and `within` meet the said requirement. For the `faithful` dataset, we will use the `within` function for carrying out necessary changes.

Example 3.5.3. Modifying `faithful` Dataset Using `within` R Function. In the `faithful` there are two variables in `eruptions` and `waiting` and both are measured in minutes. Suppose we seek to convert the eruption time into seconds and the waiting time is to be transferred on the logarithm scale. The `within` function can be used for this required manipulation.

```
> head(faithful)
  eruptions waiting
1     3.600      79
2     1.800      54
3     3.333      74
4     2.283      62
5     4.533      85
6     2.883      55
> faithful <- within(faithful,{
+ eruptions <- eruptions*60
+ waiting <- log(waiting)
+ })
> head(faithful)
  eruptions  waiting
1    216.00 4.369448
2    108.00 3.988984
3    199.98 4.304065
4    136.98 4.127134
5    271.98 4.442651
6    172.98 4.007333
```

The use of the `within` function helps in quick data preparation while avoiding creation of unnecessary new variables. □

?aggregate, ?with, ?assign

3.6 Working with Time and Date

Time and dates have always been a complex entity and it does not become any easier in programming languages either. A year has 7 months with 31 days, 4 months with 30 days, and 1 month with 28 days for 3 years and 29 days every fourth year. Even if we ignore a leap year, the number of weekdays, such as Monday, Tuesday, etc., in a year is different, and this is strangely distributed across the months. The number of days of a month, except for February in non-leap years, is not an integer multiple of 7, the number of days of a year is not an integer multiple of the number of months, or the number of weeks of a year. Similarly, time order is also a complex issue to deal with.

The number of ways in which we can write the date is in a further multiple ways. The complexity can be understood as the dates are written in different styles: "9-Sep-2010", "9-Sep-10","09-September-2010", "09-09-10","09/09/10", etc., all represent the same date. The month is written in numeric as well as text. The year may either be specified in full four digits or the last two digits of a century. We need to take into account all such complexities. Chapter 4 of Spector (2008) is a dedicated and rigorous treatment of handling dates, and we will deal with it in some detail.

As used in the previous section, the current time may be obtained using `Sys.time()`. Internally, for each time stamp, R stores a number. Similarly, `Sys.Date()` returns the current system date. This can be easily verified.

```
> Sys.time()
[1] "2011-06-14 23:28:34 IST"
> as.numeric(Sys.time())
[1] 1308074318
> as.numeric(Sys.time()+1)
[1] 1308074367
> as.numeric(Sys.time()+2)
[1] 1308074370
> Sys.Date()
[1] "2011-06-14"
```

We see that R is currently reading time up to seconds accuracy. Can the accuracy be increased? That is, we need to know the time in millisecond units. As is the practice, set the default number of digits at 3 using the `options` function.

```
> op <- options(digits.secs=3)
> Sys.time()
[1] "2011-06-14 23:33:43.964 IST"
```

Date objects belong to the classes `POSIXct` and `POSIXt`, where these two classes are of the date/times class. For more details, try `?POSIXct`. In Example 3.4.2 we had used a small function: `month.abb`. What is it really? Let us check it out.

```
> month.abb
 [1] "Jan" "Feb" "Mar" "Apr" "May" "Jun" "Jul" "Aug"
 [9] "Sep" "Oct" "Nov" "Dec"
> month.name
 [1] "January"  "February"          "June"
 [7] "July"     "August"            "December"
```

Let us store some date objects. To begin with we will consider the system date itself, and see the analysis (extraction actually) that may be performed with it.

```
> curr_date <- Sys.Date()
> curr_date
[1] "2015-04-13"
> years(curr_date); quarters(curr_date); months(curr_date)
[1] 2015
Levels: 2015
[1] "Q2"
[1] "April"
> days(curr_date); weekdays(curr_date); julian(curr_date)
```

```
[1] 13
31 Levels: 1 < 2 < 3 < 4 < 5 < 6 < 7 < 8  < ... < 31
[1] "Monday"
[1] 16538
attr(,"origin")
[1] "1970-01-01"
```

In the above display, some functions are from the `chron` package, whereas the rest are from the `base` package. Tables 4.1, 4.2, and 4.3 of Spector (2008) have details about various formats of dates and time. We will clarify a few of them here. As seen earlier, a single date may be written in distinct ways: `9-Sep-2010`, `9-Sep-10`, `09-September-2010`, `09-09-10`, `09/09/10`. The format can be specified through the `format` option as a string, and the conversion of text matter to date is achieved through the `Date` function. Let us now check how R understands these dates as one and the same.

```
> x1 <- as.Date('9-Sep-2010',format='%d-%b-%Y')
> x2 <- as.Date('9-Sep-10',format='%d-%b-%y')
> x3 <- as.Date('09-September-2010','%d-%B-%Y')
> x4 <- as.Date('09-09-10','%d-%m-%y')
> x5 <- as.Date('09/09/10','%d/%m/%y')
> x1;x2;x3;x4;x5
[1] "2010-09-09"
[1] "2010-09-09"
[1] "2010-09-09"
[1] "2010-09-09"
[1] "2010-09-09"
> x1==x2; x2==x3; x3==x4; x4==x5
[1] TRUE
[1] TRUE
[1] TRUE
[1] TRUE
```

Some algebra is possible with date objects, for example, `difftime`, `mean`, and `range`.

```
> x1+1
[1] "2010-09-10"
> difftime(x1,x2)
Time difference of 0 secs
> mean(c(x1,x2))
[1] "2010-09-09"
> range(c(x1,x2))
[1] "2010-09-09" "2010-09-09"
```

R is efficient in dealing with time and date variables and this section has given a brief exposition of it.

?Dates, ?DateTimeClasses

3.7 Text Manipulations

Data is not always in a ready-to-analyze format. We have seen that working with character or factor objects is not as convenient as working with numeric or integer objects. Working with text matter is a task with much higher complexity and inevitable inconvenience too. In fact, there is a specialized school working with such problems, known as *Text miners*. Here, we will illustrate the important text tools working our way through a complex text matter. The complexity of text functions is such that we feel that it is better to work with some examples instead of looking at their definitions. This approach forms the remainder of this section.

In Section 1.5, we indicated the importance and relevance of subscribing to the R mailing list. The mail exchanged among the subscribers is uploaded at the end of the day. Furthermore, all the mail in a month is consolidated in a tar compressed text file. As an example, the mail exchanged during the month of October in 2005 is available in the file `2005-10.txt.gz`, which can be downloaded from the R website. The first few lines of this text file are displayed below:

```
From lisawang at uhnres.utoronto.ca  Sat Oct  1 00:14:23 2005
From: lisawang at uhnres.utoronto.ca (Lisa Wang)
Date: Fri, 30 Sep 2005 17:14:23 -0500
Subject: [R] How to get to the varable in a list
Message-ID: <433DB8BF.3E0E22C7@uhnres.utoronto.ca>
Hello,
I have a list "lis" as the following:
```

We will first learn how to read such text files in R using the `readLines` function, which reads the different lines of a `txt` file as a `character` class.

```
> Imine <- readLines("2005-10.txt.gz")
> Imine[1:10]
 [1] "From lisawang at uhnres.utoronto.ca  Sat Oct  1 00:14:23 2005"
 [2] "From: lisawang at uhnres.utoronto.ca (Lisa Wang)"
 [3] "Date: Fri, 30 Sep 2005 17:14:23 -0500"
 [4] "Subject: [R] How to get to the varable in a list"
 [5] "Message-ID: <433DB8BF.3E0E22C7@uhnres.utoronto.ca>"
 [6] ""
 [7] "Hello,"
 [8] ""
 [9] "I have a list \"lis\" as the following:"
[10] ""
```

Verify for yourself the difference in actual text file `2005-10.txt.gz` and the R object `Imine`. The rest of the section will help you to extract information from such files. As an example, we will first extract `Date`, `Subject`, and `Message-ID` for the first mail of October 2005. We see that `Date` is in the third line of the object. We will ask R to return this line number with the use of functions `grep` and `grepl`.

```
> grep("Date",Imine[1:10])
[1] 3
```

```
> grepl("Date",Imine[1:10])
 [1] FALSE FALSE  TRUE FALSE FALSE FALSE FALSE FALSE FALSE FALSE
```

Thus, we see that the `grep` function finds in which line (row number) the text, commonly referred as a string, of interest occurs. The `grepl` is a logical function. The number of characters in a line can be found by the next line of codes through the R function `nchar`.

```
> unlist(lapply(Imine[1:10],nchar))
 [1] 61 48 37 48 50  0  6  0 37  0
```

The fourth line of the text file contains the subject of the mail. We want to obtain the subject sans the content header `Subject:  [R]`. Note that we have included the space after `[R]`. We will first find the position where the subject begins and next extract the exact matter using the R function.

```
> nchar("Subject:  [R] ")
[1] 13
> substring(Imine[4],14)
[1] "How to get to the varable in a list"
```

Thus, the function `substring` deletes the first `13` characters of the string and returns the rest of the string. Let us now extract the `Message Id` of this particular mail. As with the subject id, we have `Message-ID:` < as an indicator of the line of the object which contains the message ID. An added complexity is that we need to remove the sign > at the end of the message. We can see once more the utility of the `nchar` function.

```
> grep("Message-ID: <",Imine[1:10])
[1] 5
> nchar(Imine[5])
[1] 50
> nchar("Message-ID: <")
[1] 13
> substr(Imine[5],14,49)
[1] "433DB8BF.3E0E22C7@uhnres.utoronto.ca"
```

We will conclude this section with the extraction of the time and date of this message. The line containing the date and time is indicated by `Date:`. After doing extended manipulations we can obtain the date and time of the message. Recall from the previous section that the format of `30 Sep 2005 17:14:23` is `\%d %\B %\Y \%H:\%M:\%S`. Thus, we can extract the exact Date and Time of this email.

```
> grep("Date: ",Imine[1:10])
[1] 3
> temp <- strsplit(Imine[3],"Date: ")[[1]][2]
> temp
[1] "Fri, 30 Sep 2005 17:14:23 -0500"
> tempdate <- substring(temp,6,nchar(temp)-6)
> tempdate
```

```
[1] "30 Sep 2005 17:14:23"
> strptime(tempdate,"%d %B %Y %H:%M:%S")
[1] "2005-09-30 17:14:23"
```

Though this book does not deal with the emerging area of text mining, data also exists in rich and hidden forms in text format and files. The functions used here form the base and it will be useful for many text manipulations.

?grep, ?substring, ?substr, ?strptime

3.8 Scripts and Text Editors for R

In earlier sections we saw the need of using objects against just plain computing at the terminal. As the need and experience grows, the user finds it difficult to get the task accomplished, even within this framework. Consider the hypothetical scenario where the program runs into a few hundred lines. A mistake made at the 21st line is observed after 89 lines of code have been executed. There is thus this intrinsic need to write the R codes in a separate file and execute them. Consider the set of following codes:

```
yb <- read.table("/.../youden.csv",header=TRUE,sep=",")
quantile(yb$Preparation_1,seq(0,1,.1))
# here seq give 0, .1, .2, ...,1
quantile(yb$Preparation_2,seq(0,1,.1))
fivenum(yb$Preparation_1)
fivenum(yb$Preparation_2)
sd(yb$Preparation_1); sd(yb$Preparation_2)
var(yb$Preparation_1); var(yb$Preparation_2)
range(yb$Preparation_1); range(yb$Preparation_2)
```

Copy and paste these codes in any text editor, such as Notepad, vi, kate, gedit, etc., and save the file as `yb.R` or `yb.txt`. In the `File` option of the menu ribbon, a Windows user will find `New Script` and `Open Script` options. Using the `Open Script` option, load the `yb.R` file. Choose `Run line or selection` from the `Edit` option. We will then get the results the same as those obtained in Section 2.4.1. If there are any errors, we can modify the codes from the `yb.R` file, and thus the task of fixing the bugs is simplified. The Windows user may also explore the package `Rcmdr` explained in the next subsection.

3.8.1 *Text Editors for Linuxians*

Linuxians unfortunately do not have any Menu ribbon option available to them. Interestingly, we have a host of other options. As an example, just open the terminal and set the address to the working directory. At the terminal, run the following one-line code:

```
Rscript yb.R
```

We demonstrate two more options for Linuxians. Prof John Fox, McMaster University, and his team have developed a special package `Rcmdr`. Installing packages and loading libraries exercises will be explained in the next subsection. Enter the code below in the R session:

```
> library(Rcmdr)
```

and what you will see next is a user-friendly version of R. Yes, we have a new set of very useful tools. The options on the menu ribbon now includes File, Edit, Data, Statistics, Graphics, Models, Distributions, Tools, and Help. From the File menu, choose `Open script file` and open the file `yb.R` and then click on the `Submit` button. We get the same results as earlier.

The third option for a Linuxian is also better. You can go to the web http://rkward.sourceforge.net/ and download the RKWard 0.5.3 binaries. Of course knowing that Linuxians prefer the terminal, simply key in `sudo apt-get install rkward \verb`. Having installed RKWard, start it. This software is as user-friendly as many enterprise editions. The options on the ribbon are File, Edit, View, Workspace, Run, Analysis, Plots, Distributions, Windows, Settings, and Help options. If the reader is wondering why we are trivializing here, we justify it as we have seen a lot of users struggling in using R in the Linux environment. We will compromise here though by not repeating how to run `yb.R` in `RKWard`.

RStudio is quickly emerging as a popular variant and may be obtained from www.rstudio.com.

?Rscript

3.9 Further Reading

Spector (2008) is a comprehensive book dedicated to data preparation. Chapter 2 of Venables and Ripley (2002) contains data manipulation for R and S. We also recommend that the reader go through Chapter 9 of Zuur, et al. (2009) for common R mistakes.

3.10 Complements, Problems, and Programs

Problem 3.1 For the `data.frame some` in Example 3.2.2, what will be your expectation of the R code `summary(some)`? Validate the expectation by running the code too.

Problem 3.2 By considering the dataset `rootstock` imported in Section 3.3, export the data back to the working directory using the `write.dta` function from the `foreign` package.

Problem 3.3 Run `edit(newsome1)` as required in Section 3.4, and comment on how this function is different from the `View` function.

Problem 3.4 For any directory in your computer, use the function `list.files` to obtain the contents, inclusive of files and maybe other directories. Recollect that the default `list.files()` function returns the contents in the working directory, and hence you need to experiment with a directory other than `getwd()`.

Problem 3.5 The `attach` function, when applied on a `data.frame` object, loads the variables in the R session. How do you undo this operation? If the `attach` function is repeated more than once, what will be the result?

Problem 3.6 Suppose that the option `header=FALSE` is an error when an object is imported. Write appropriate codes which bring up the right variable names and deletes the wrong observations too. For example, suppose that the `chest` data is inappropriately imported with `chest <-read.csv("Chest_VH.csv",header=FALSE)`. A simple use of `names(chest) <- chest[1,]` and `chest <- chest[-1,]` will not fix the problem.

Problem 3.7 Using the `aggregate` function, as in Example 3.5.1, obtain the frequency instead of `sum`. Also, extend the `list` variables in the example to include both `GPP` and `Grade`, and hence obtain the sum of `Sat` for possible combinations of these two variables.

Problem 3.8 Using the `ifelse` conditional function, create a new `as.Date` type of function, which can read date objects available in a vector in two different forms.

Problem 3.9 Find the time difference between two time objects in units of `hours`, `days`, etc.

4

Exploratory Data Analysis

Package(s): `LearnEDA`, `e1071`, `sfsmisc`, `qcc`, `aplpack`, `RSADBE`
Dataset(s): `memory`, `morley`, `InsectSprays`, `yb`, `sample`, `galton`, `chest`, `sleep`, `cloud`, `octane`, `AirPassengers`, `insurance`, `somesamples`, `girder`

4.1 Introduction: The Tukey's School of Statistics

Exploratory Data Analysis, abbreviated and also simply referred to as EDA, combines very powerful and naturally intuitive graphical methods as well as insightful quantitative techniques for analysis of data arising from random experiments. The direction for EDA was probably laid down in the expository article of Tukey (1962), "*The Future of Data Analysis*". The dictionary meaning of the word "*explore*" means to search or travel with the intent of some kind of useful discovery, and in similar spirit EDA carries a search in the data to provide useful insights. EDA has been developed to a very large extent by the Tukey school of statisticians.

We can probably refer to EDA as a no-assumptions paradigm. To understand this we recall how the model-based statistical approaches work. We include both the classical and Bayesian schools in the model-based framework, see Chapters 7 to 9. Here, we assume that the data is plausibly generated by a certain probability distribution, and that a few parameters of such a distribution are unknown. In a different fashion, EDA places no assumptions on data-generating mechanism. This approach also gives an advantage to the analyst of making an appropriate guess of the underlying true hypothesis rather than speculating on it. The classical methods are referred by Tukey as "Confirmatory Data Analysis". EDA is more about attitude and not simply a bundle of techniques. No, these are not our words. More precisely, Tukey (1980) explains "Exploratory data analysis is an attitude, a flexibility, and a reliance on display, NOT a bundle of techniques, and should be so taught."

The major work of EDA has been compiled in the beautiful book of Tukey (1977). The enthusiastic reader must read the thought-provoking sections "How far have we come?" which is there in almost all the chapters. Mosteller and Tukey (1977) have further developed regression methods in this domain. Most of the concepts of EDA detailed in this chapter have been drawn from Velleman and Hoaglin (1984). Hoaglin, et al. (1991) extend further

A Course in Statistics with R, First Edition. Prabhanjan Narayanachar Tattar, Suresh Ramaiah and B. G. Manjunath.

Companion Website: www.wiley.com/go/tattar/statistics

the Analysis of Variance method in this school of thought. Albert's R package LearnEDA is useful for the beginner. Further details about this package can be found at http://bayes.bgsu .edu/EDA/R/Reda.html. From a regression modeling perspective, Part IV, Rousseeuw and Leroy (1987) offer very useful extensions.

In this chapter, we focus on two approaches of EDA. The preliminary aspects are covered in Section 4.2. The first approach is the graphical methods. We address several types of graphical methods here of visualizing the data. Those graphical methods omitted are primarily due to space restrictions and the author's limitations. These visualization techniques are addressed in Section 4.3. The quantitative methods of EDA are taken up in Section 4.4. Finally, exploratory regression models are considered in Section 4.5. Sections 4.3 and 4.4 form the second approach.

4.2 Essential Summaries of EDA

A reason for writing this section is that the summary statistics of EDA are often different from basic statistics. The emphasis is, more often than not, on summaries such as median, quartiles, percentiles, etc. Also, we define here a few summaries which we believe useful to gain insight into exploratory analyses. The concept of median, quartiles, and Tukey's five numbers, have already been illustrated in Section 2.3. A useful concept associated with each datum is *depth*, which is defined next.

Definition 4.2.1 Depth. *Suppose that the observations are arranged in ascending order. For each datum,* depth *is the minimum of the position from either end of the batch.*

Depth for a datum x is denoted by $d(x)$. We will denote the median by M. By definition, depth of median is $d(M) = (n + 1)/2$. We note that though in general the letter d stands for derivative, and we use the same for depth, there is not really any room for confusion. The ideas are illustrated using a simple program:

```
> x <- c(13,17,11,115,12,7,24)
> tab <- cbind(order(x),x[order(x)],c(1:7),c(7:1),pmin(c(1:7),
+ c(7:1)))
> colnames(tab) <- c("x_label","x_order","Position_from_min",
+ "Position_from_max","depth")
> tab
     x_label x_order Position_from_min Position_from_max depth
[1,]       6       7                 1                 7     1
[2,]       3      11                 2                 6     2
[3,]       5      12                 3                 5     3
[4,]       1      13                 4                 4     4
[5,]       2      17                 5                 3     3
[6,]       7      24                 6                 2     2
[7,]       4     115                 7                 1     1
```

In the above output, the second line of R code arranges the sample in increasing order, with the first column returning to their positions in the original sample using the order function. The third and fourth columns give their positions from minimum and maximum respectively. The fifth and last columns obtain the minimum of the positions from the minimum and maximum values using the `pmin` function, and thus return the depth of the sample values.

We begin with an explanation of *hinges*. The hinges are what everyone sees as the connectors between the door and its frame. In the past there would be three hinges to fix the door. The center one is at the middle of the length of the frame, and the other two hinges at the positions of one- and three-quarters of the height of the frame. Thus, if we assume the data as arranged in increasing (or decreasing) order along the height of the frame, the median is then the middle hinge, whereas 25% of the observations are below the lower hinge and 25% above the upper hinge. We naturally ask for the difference between the quartiles and hinges. Hinges are technically calculated from the depth of the median, whereas quartiles are not. Throughout this chapter, the lower-, middle-, and upper- hinges will be respectively denoted by LH, M, and UH. From the output of the previous table, it is clear that the lower and upper hinges are the averages of 11 and 12, equal to 11.5, and average of 17 and 24, equal to 20.5, respectively.

The Tukey's *five numbers* form one of the most important summaries in EDA. These five numbers are the minimum, lower hinge, median, upper hinge, and maximum. The five numbers are computed using the `fivenum` function, as seen earlier in Section 2.3.

Five number inter-difference, abbreviated as fnid, is defined as the consecutive differences of the five numbers, viz., {lower hinge – minimum}, {median – lower hinge}, {upper hinge – median}, and {maximum – upper hinge}. The five number inter-difference gives a fair insight into how the sample is spread out. It is easy to define a new function, which gives us the fnid using the `diff` operator: `fnid <- function(x) diff(fivenum(x))`.

As a quantitative measure of skewness, we introduce Bowley's relative measure of skewness based on Tukey's five numbers, to be called *Bowley-Tukey measure of skewness*, as follows:

$$\begin{aligned} S_{BT} &= \frac{(UH - M) - (M - LH)}{(UH - M) + (M - LH)}, \\ &= \frac{UH - 2M + LH}{UH - LH}. \end{aligned} \tag{4.1}$$

These concepts are illustrated in the next example of *Memory Recall Times*.

Example 4.2.1. Memory Recall Times. A test had been conducted with the purpose of investigating if people recollect pleasant memories associated with a word earlier than some unpleasant memory related with the same word. The word is flashed on the screen and the time an individual takes to respond via the keyboard is recorded for both types of the memories. This study was conducted by Dunn and Master (1982) and a useful URL is http://openlearn.open.ac.uk/mod/resource/view.php?id=165509. This dataset is available in the `ACSWR` package as the `memory` dataset.

We begin the exploratory analysis with the Tukey's five numbers `fivenum`, median absolute deviation `mad`, and inter-quartile range `IQR`.

```
> data(memory)
> lapply(memory,fivenum)
$Pleasant.memory
```

```
[1] 1.070 1.805 2.815 3.320 6.170
$Unpleasant.memory
[1]  1.450  2.335  3.600  6.690 10.930
> lapply(memory,mad)
$Pleasant.memory
[1] 1.134189
$Unpleasant.memory
[1] 2.557485
> lapply(memory,IQR)
$Pleasant.memory
[1] 1.3775
$Unpleasant.memory
[1] 4.2425
```

We can see from the above summaries that pleasant memories are recollected faster than unpleasant ones, since all the five number summaries for the time to recollect `Pleasant.memory` are less than the corresponding entries for `Unpleasant.memory`. The variation in the times to recollect `Pleasant.memory` is also less than those for `Unpleasant.memory`, as may be seen in the mad and `IQR` summaries.

The five-number inter-difference gives a fair insight into how the sample is spread out. For the memory dataset, we first define a new function in R named `fnid`, an abbreviation for five-number inter-difference.

```
> fnid <- function(x) diff(fivenum(x)) # difference of fivenum
> lapply(memory,fnid)
$Pleasant.memory
[1] 0.735 1.010 0.505 2.850
$Unpleasant.memory
[1] 0.885 1.265 3.090 4.240
```

It is interesting to note that each of the five number inter-differences for unpleasant memories is larger than the corresponding measure for pleasant memories.

For the memory data, we next compute the Bowley-Tukey measure of skewness.

```
> fnid_pleasant <- fnid(memory$Pleasant.memory)
> fnid_unpleasant <- fnid(memory$Unpleasant.memory)
> btskew_pleasant <- (fnid_pleasant[3]-fnid_pleasant[2])
+ /(fnid_pleasant[3]+fnid_pleasant[2])
> btskew_unpleasant <- (fnid_unpleasant[3]-fnid_unpleasant[2])/
+ (fnid_unpleasant[3]+fnid_unpleasant[2])
> btskew_pleasant; btskew_unpleasant
[1] -0.3333333
[1] 0.4190586
```

We have thus far seen how the data summaries are useful. □

?mad, IQR, fivenum

4.3 Graphical Techniques in EDA

4.3.1 Boxplot

The boxplot is essentially a one-dimensional plot, sometimes known as the *box-and-whisker* plot. The boxplot may be displayed vertically or horizontally, without any value changes in the information conveyed. Box and whiskers are two important parts here. The boxplot is always based on three quantities. The top and bottom of the box are determined by the upper and lower quartiles, and the band inside the box is the median. The whiskers are created according to the purpose of the analyses and defined according to the convenience of the experimenter and in line with the goals of the experiment. If complete representation of the data is required, then the whiskers are produced by connecting the end points of the box with the minimum and maximum value of the data. The rational of box and whiskers is that the quartiles divide the dataset into four parts, with each part containing one-quarter of the sample. The middle line of the box, the box, and the whiskers hence give an appropriate visual representation of the data.

If the goal is to find the *outliers*, also known as *extreme values*, below α_L and above α_U percentiles, the ends of the whiskers may be defined as data points which respectively gives us these percentile points. All observations below the lower whisker and those above the upper whisker may be treated as outliers. Some of the common choices of the cut-off percentiles are $\alpha_L = 0.02$ and 0.09, and $\alpha_U = 0.98$ and 0.91 respectively. Sometimes such percentiles may be based on the inter-quartile range *IQR*.

The role of NOTCHES. Inference for significant difference between medians can be made based on a boxplot which exhibit notches. The top and bottom notches for a dataset is defined by

$$Median \pm 1.57 \times \frac{IQR}{\sqrt{n}}. \tag{4.2}$$

A useful interpretation for notched boxplots is the following. If the notches of two boxplots do not overlap, we can interpret this as strong evidence that the medians of the two samples are significantly different. For more details about notches, we refer the reader to Section 3.4 of Chambers, et al. (1983).

Example 4.3.1. AD8. The Youden-Beale Experiment. We have used this dataset in Chapter 2, Section 4, and in a few other places too. We need to compare here if the two virus extracts have a varying effect on the tobacco leaf or not. We have already read this dataset into R on more than one occasion.

First, the boxplot is generated without the notches for `yb data.frame` using the `boxplot` function. The median for `Preparation_1` certainly appears higher than for `Preparation_2`, see Part A of Figure 4.1. Thus, we are tempted to check whether the medians for the two preparations are significantly different with the notched boxplot. Now, the boxplot is generated to produce the notches with the option `notch=TRUE`. Appropriate headers for a figure are specified with the `title` function. Most importantly, we have used a powerful graphical technique of R through `par`, which is useful in setting graphical parameters. Here, `mfrow` indicates that we need a multi-row figure with one row and two columns. For more details, check `?par`.

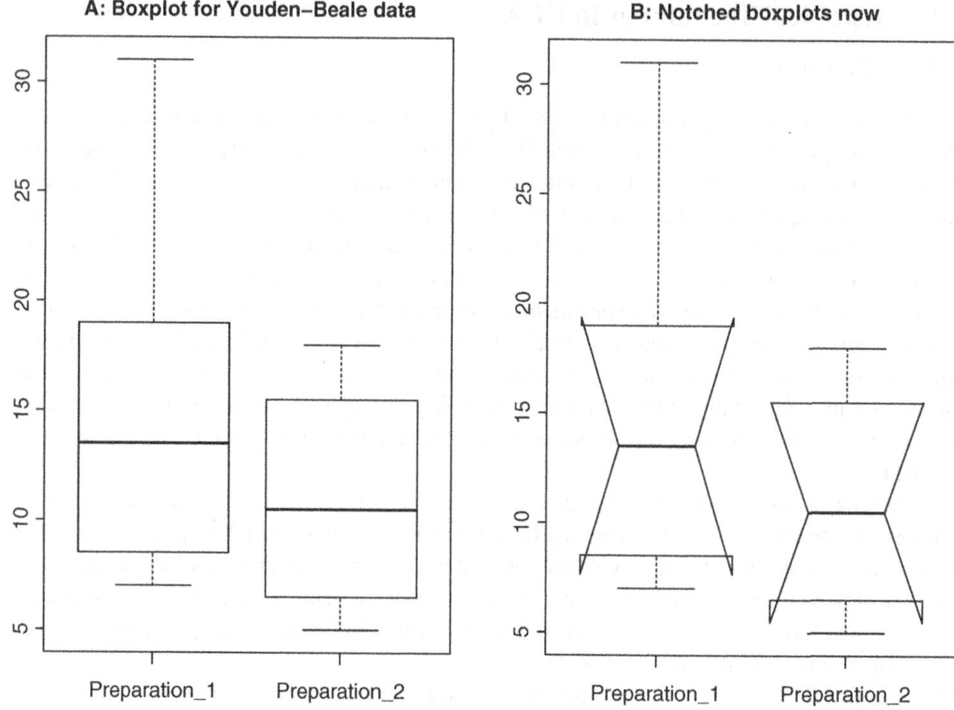

Figure 4.1 Boxplot for the Youden-Beale Experiment

```
> par(mfrow=c(1,2))
> boxplot(yb)
> title("A: Boxplot for Youden-Beale Data")
> boxplot(yb,notch=TRUE)
Warning message:
In bxp(list(stats = c(7, 8.5, 13.5, 19, 31, 5, 6.5, 10.5, 15.5,  :
  some notches went outside hinges ('box'): maybe set notch=FALSE
> title("B: Notched Boxplots Now")
```

We can see that the notches overlapping indicate that the medians are not significantly different, see Part B of Figure 4.1. This result may not be acceptable to Youden and Beale! However, the `Warning message` suggests that the notched boxplot may not be appropriate. Moreover, the data points are eight only and more data may be required for the notched boxplots. □

Example 4.3.2. The Michelson-Morley Experiment. In the late nineteenth century, a theory floated for the dispersion of light waves was that light also requires a medium of travel like any other waves, such as water waves or sound waves. The medium for light waves to propagate was conjectured to be *luminiferous ether*. Since it was well known at that time that light can travel through a vacuum too, it was believed that a vacuum must consist of luminiferous ether.

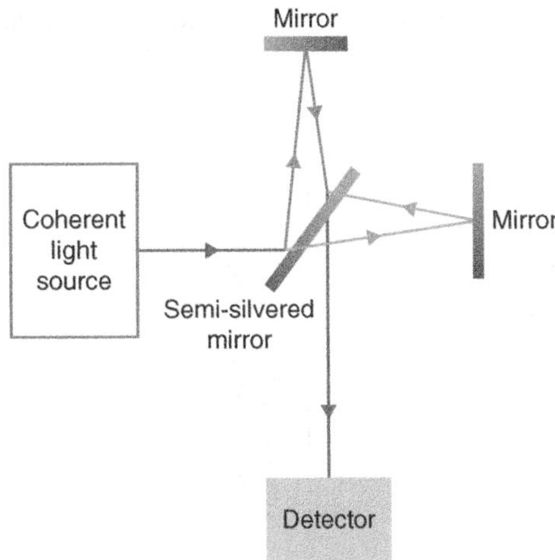

Figure 4.2 Michelson-Morley Experiment

Michelson devised an ingenious experiment for establishing the presence of ether. The device designed in this experiment is referred as an *interferometer*, in which a single source of light is sent through a half-silvered mirror, splitting the single light beam into two beams which travel at right angles to each other, see Figure 4.2. Each beam travels to the end of a long arm, and from this end they are reflected back to the middle of small mirrors. Both the beams are combined at this middle point of the small mirrors. If the ether medium exists, the beam which travels to and from parallel to the flow of ether should take more time than the beam which reflects perpendicularly, as the time gained from traveling downwards is less than the one traveling upwards. This phenomenon should result in a delay for one of the light beams. It is proved that such a shift would be approximately 4%. This is the famous *Michelson-Morley experiment*. Some related R programs for graphical plots of this experiment can be found at http://en.wikipedia.org/wiki/File:Michelsonmorley-boxplot.svg. In the dataset `morley`, the output `Speed` contains the kilometers per second information recorded as the speed of light minus the speed registered at the experimental unit. Twenty runs of the experiment is carried out at five different centers. If there is the presence of ether, we would expect this speed to be less than the speed of light in a free medium. The boxplot Figure 4.3 gives us a complete understanding of this data. We obtain it as follows.

```
> par(mfrow=c(1,2))
> boxplot(Speed ~ Expt, data=morley,xlab = "Experiment No.",
+ ylab="Speed of light (km/s minus 299,000)")
> abline(h=792.458, lty=3)
> boxplot(Speed ~ Expt, data=morley,xlab = "Experiment No.",
+ ylab="Speed of light (km/s minus 299,000)",notch=TRUE)
Warning message:
In bxp(list(stats = c(740, 850, 940, 980, 1070, 760, 800, 845, 890, :
  some notches went outside hinges ('box'): maybe set notch=FALSE
> abline(h=792.458, lty=3)
```

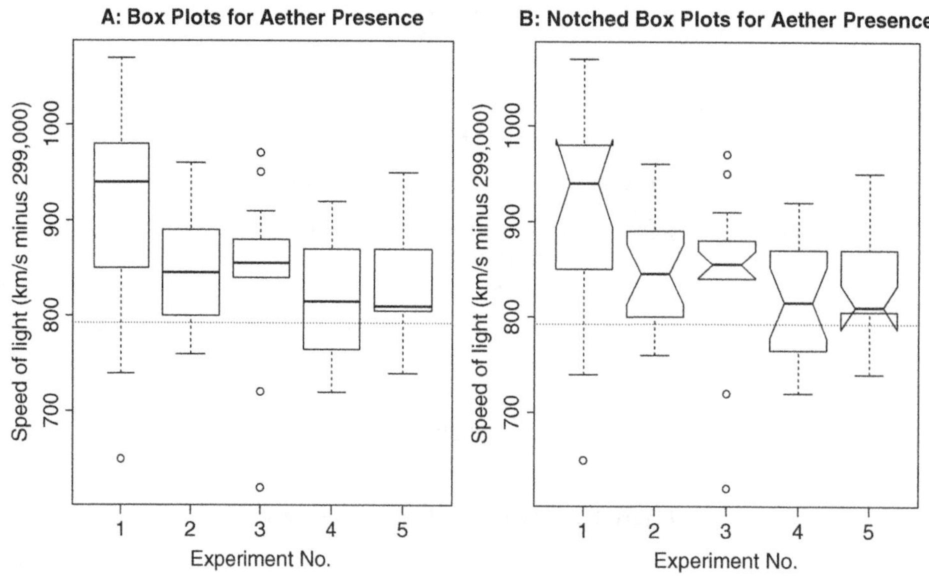

Figure 4.3 Boxplots for Michelson-Morley Experiment

Since the speed is almost in excess of the model value at 2.99×10^8 meters per second and we expected the speed to become less than this value in the presence of ether, we conclude that ether does not exist. Furthermore, most of the boxplots have overlapping notches, refer to Part B of Figure 4.3, and hence this indicates that medians of the observations across the different centers are identical. This experiment is one of the most important experiments in Physical Science. □

Example 4.3.3. Memory Recall Times. Contd. We now graphically examine the memory data using, of course, the R code `boxplot(memory)`.

```
> par(mfrow=c(1,2))
> boxplot(memory)
> title("A: Boxplot for Memory Recall")
```

Part A of Figure 4.4 clearly shows and confirms the results of the data summaries. □

Example 4.3.4. The Effect of Insecticides. McNeil (1977). Six insecticides, labeled `A to F`, were used in an agricultural experiment and the number of insects found dead after using them were counted. The dataset is available as `InsectSprays` in the package `datasets`. We first count the number of insect deaths due to each of the insecticides using the `aggregate` function with the `by=list` provided by the `spray` column. The notched boxplots are then obtained for each insect spray using the formula `boxplot(count~spray,data=InsectSprays, notch=TRUE)`.

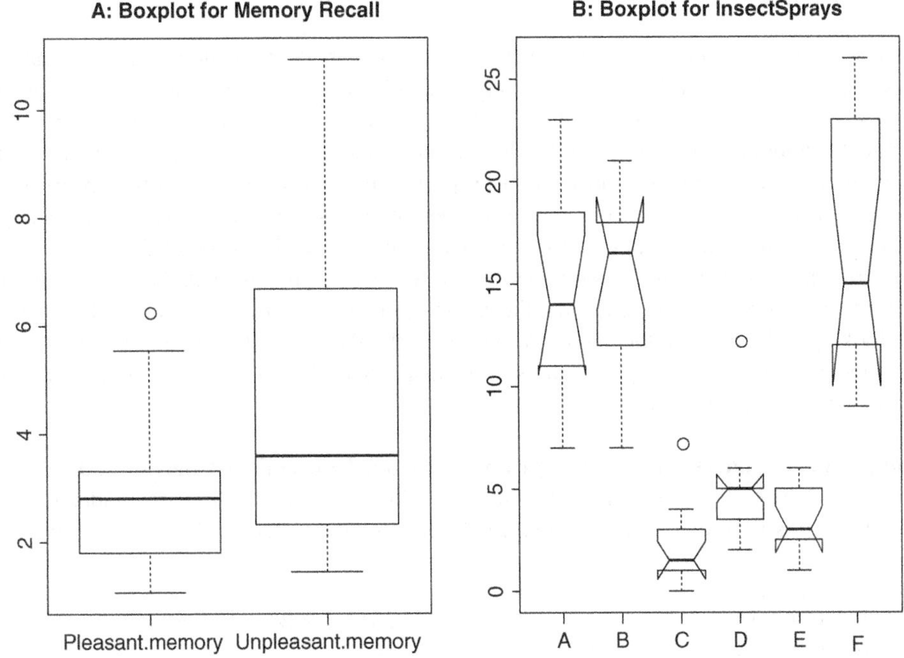

Figure 4.4 Boxplot for the Memory Data

```
> data(InsectSprays)
> aggregate(InsectSprays$count,by=list(InsectSprays$spray),sum)
  Group.1   x
1       A 174
2       B 184
3       C  25
4       D  59
5       E  42
6       F 200
> boxplot(count~spray,data=InsectSprays,notch=TRUE)
Warning message:
In bxp(list(stats = c(7, 11, 14, 18.5, 23, 7, 12, 16.5, 18, 21,  :
  some notches went outside hinges ('box'): maybe set notch=FALSE
```

The notches for sprays A, B, and F are overlapping, Part B of Figure 4.4, and thus indicate that their medians are not significantly different. Similar exploratory inference holds for sprays C to E. However, the notches for the latter group and the former group are non-overlapping with the medians less in magnitude. This leads us to conclude that if we were to select one of the insect sprays, we could choose any from A, B, and F (without looking any further?). We should be careful of two things here. First, some notches were outside the hinges of the box, and there was the presence of outliers for sprays C and D. □

?bxp

4.3.2 Histogram

The histogram was invented by the eminent statistician Karl Pearson and is one of the earliest types of graphical display. It goes without saying that its origin is earlier than EDA, at least the EDA envisioned by Tukey, and yet it is considered by many EDA experts to be a very useful graphical technique, and makes it to the list of one of the very useful practices of EDA. The basic idea is to plot a bar over an interval proportional to the frequency of the observations that lie in that interval. If the sample size is moderately good in some sense and the sample is a true representation of a population, the histogram reveals the shape of the true underlying uncertainty curve. Though histograms are plotted as two-dimensional, they are essentially one-dimensional plots in the sense that the shape of the uncertainty curve is revealed without even looking at the range of the x-axis. Furthermore, the Pareto chart, stem-and-leaf plot, and a few others may be shown as special cases of the histogram. We begin with a "cooked" dataset for understanding a range of uncertainty curves.

Example 4.3.5. Understanding Histogram of Various Uncertainty Curves. In the dataset `sample`, we have data from five different probability distributions. Towards understanding the plausible distribution of the samples, we plot the histogram and see how useful it is.

```
> data(sample)
> layout(matrix(c(1,1,2,2,3,3,0,4,4,5,5,0), nrow=2, ncol=6,
+ byrow=TRUE),respect=FALSE)
> matrix(c(1,1,2,2,3,3,0,4,4,5,5,0), nrow=2, ncol=6, byrow=TRUE)
     [,1] [,2] [,3] [,4] [,5] [,6]
[1,]    1    1    2    2    3    3
[2,]    0    4    4    5    5    0
> hist(sample[,1],main="Histogram of Sample 1",xlab="sample1",
+ ylab="frequency")
> hist(sample[,2],main="Histogram of Sample 2",xlab="sample2",
+ ylab="frequency")
> hist(sample[,3],main="Histogram of Sample 3",xlab="sample3",
+ ylab="frequency")
> hist(sample[,4],main="Histogram of Sample 4",xlab="sample4",
+ ylab="frequency")
> hist(sample[,5],main="Histogram of Sample 5",xlab="sample5",
+ ylab="frequency")
```

In the present case, we need five plots on a single graphical framework, and using `par` with either `mfrow=c(2,3)` or `mfrow=c(3,2)` leaves an empty plot. The `layout` graphics function helps to specify a complex plot. In the above R code, the graphical device is divided into 12 parts across 2 rows and 6 columns. The first plot of the device is plotted on first two parts of the first row, the second third and fourth part of first row, and so forth. The option of 0 says that such parts should not be used for plots.

The `hist` function works on a numeric vector. The option `main` helps in specifying a title for the histogram, and `xlab` and `ylab` can be used to specify labels for the axes.

Figure 4.5 is the output of the previous R program. The histogram of sample 1 is bell-shaped, and its peak (mode) is near 0. The mean and median are respectively `-0.1845` and `-0.1450`, again closer to 0. The standard deviation and variance are respectively `0.9714806` and

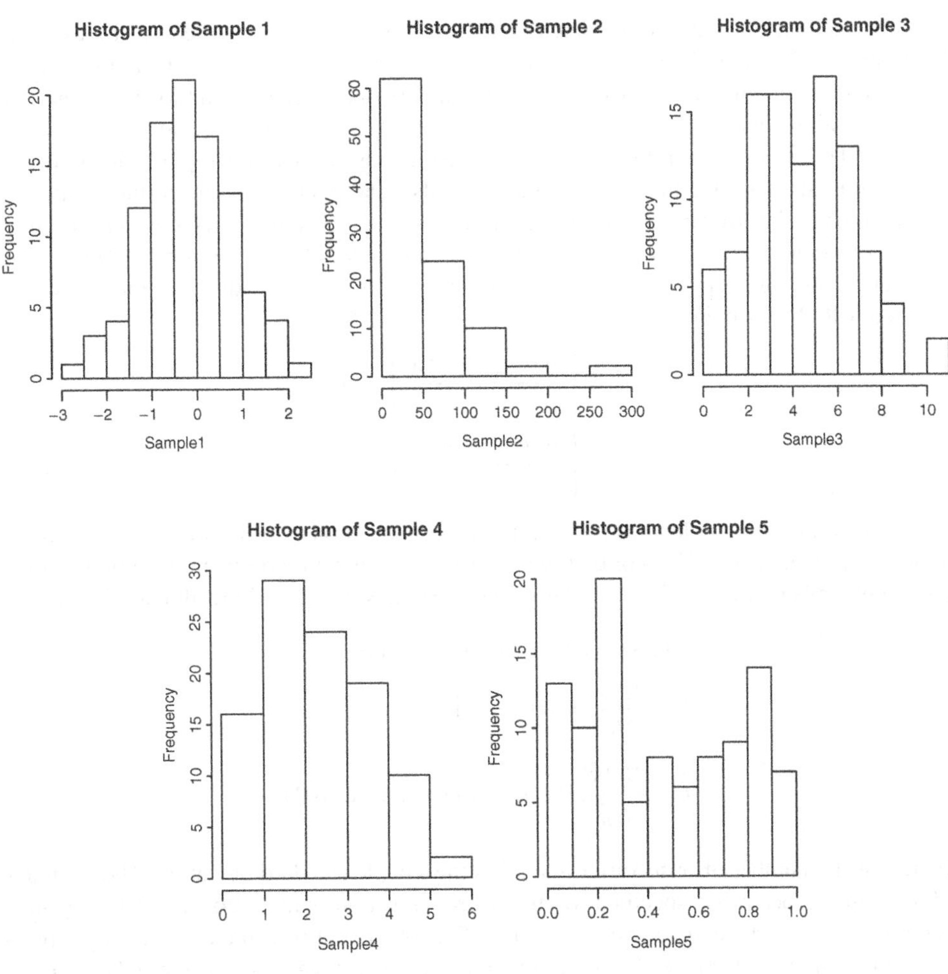

Figure 4.5 Different Types of Histograms

`0.9437745`. Verify these numbers! The shape indicated by the histogram and the summaries indicate that the distribution of the sample may be a normal distribution.

The histogram of Sample 2 is tailing off very fast after the value of 50. The distribution indicates positive skewness, and also the variance `2933.388` is approximately the square of the mean `53.27`. Furthermore, all the values are non-negative, which leads us to believe that the sampling distribution may be an exponential distribution. An important feature of Samples 3 and 4 is that all the values are non-negative integers. This makes us believe that the sampling distribution may be a discrete distribution. The mean and variance of Sample 3 is `4.98` and `5.2117`, whereas these numbers for Sample 4 are `2.83` and `1.7384`. The mean and variance of Sample 3 are almost equal, which is a characteristic of Poisson distribution and the variance being larger rules out the possibility of the sample being from a binomial distribution. Similarly, the variance of Sample 4 being less than its mean is a reflection that this sample may be from a binomial distribution. The interpretation of the fifth sample is left to the reader. □

A few fundamental questions related to the creation of histograms need to be asked at this moment. The central idea is to plot a bar over an interval. All the intervals together need to cover the range of the variables. For example, the number of intervals for the five histograms above are respectively 11, 6, 11, 6, and 10. How did R decide the number of intervals? The width of each interval for these histograms are respectively 0.5, 50, 1, 1, and 0.1. What is the basis for the width of the intervals? The reader may check them out with `length(hist$counts)` and `diff(hist$breaks)`. The intervals are also known as *bins*. Let us denote the number of intervals by k and the width of the bin by h. Now, if we know either the number of the interval or the bin width, the other quantity may be easily obtained with the formula:

$$k = \left\lceil \frac{\max_i x_i - \min_i x_i}{h} \right\rceil, \text{ or} \tag{4.3}$$

$$h = \left\lceil \frac{\max_i x_i - \min_i x_i}{k} \right\rceil, \tag{4.4}$$

where the argument $\lceil \ \ \rceil$ denotes the ceiling of the number. However, in practice we do not know either the number of bins or their width. The `hist` function offers three options for the bin width/number based on the formulas given by Sturges, Scott, and Freedman-Diaconis:

$$k = \lceil \log_2 n + 1 \rceil, \text{ Sturges formula,} \tag{4.5}$$

$$h = \frac{3.5\hat{\sigma}}{\sqrt[3]{n}}, \text{ Scott's formula,} \tag{4.6}$$

$$h = \frac{2IQR}{\sqrt[3]{n}}, \text{ Freedman-Diaconis formula,} \tag{4.7}$$

where n is the number of observations and $\hat{\sigma}$ is the sample standard deviation. The formulas 4.5–4.7 are respectively specified to the `hist` function with `breaks="Sturges"`, `breaks="Scott"`, and `breaks="FD"`. The other options include directly specifying the number of breaks with a numeric, say `breaks=10`, or through a vector `breaks=seq(-10,10,0.5)`.

Example 4.3.6. AD5. The Galton Data. The histogram gives a nice display of the variables. Here the goal would be to obtain a histogram for the height of parent and child on the same plot. However, we would clearly like to see all the frequency bars for parent as well as child. That is, if the frequency of the height for the parent is larger than for the child for a certain interval, it should be reflected the same as well as for the height of the variable of lesser frequency. The histograms should cover the range of both variables. With these technicalities in mind, the next program gives the required figure. The reader can first go through the program and follow it up with the description and the resulting figure.

```
> hist(galton$parent,freq=FALSE,col="green",density=10,xlim=c(60,75),
+ xlab="height",main="Histograms for AD5")
> hist(galton$child,freq=F,col="red",add=TRUE,density=10,angle=-45)
> legend(x=c(71,73),y=c(0.2,0.17),c("parent","child"),col=c("green",
+ "red"),pch="-")
```

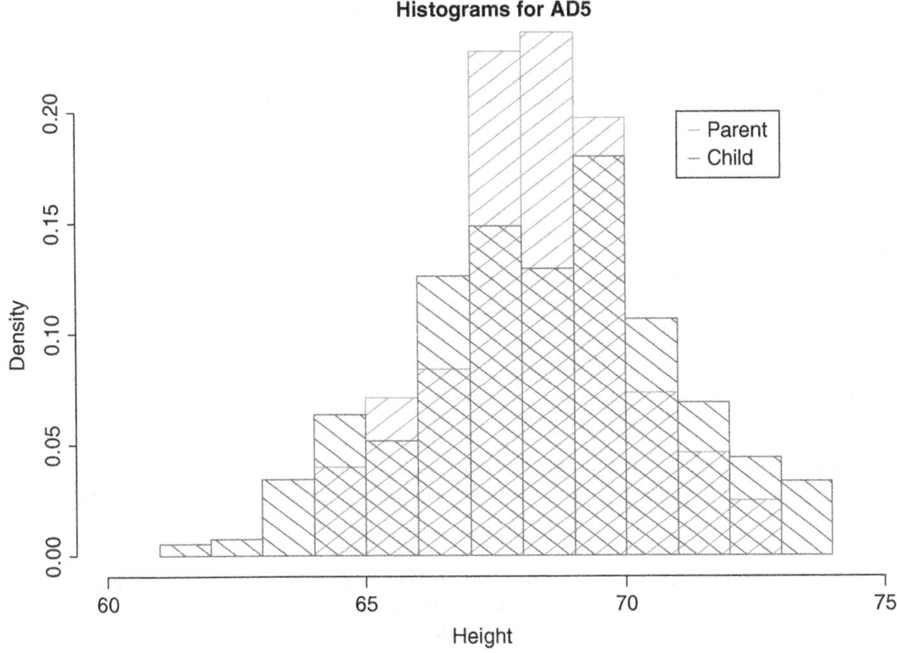

Figure 4.6 Histograms for the Galton Dataset

In the event of two variables having an unequal number of observations, the option `freq=FALSE` will ensure that the heights of two variables over an interval remain the same if their overall percentage of the bin remains equal. The limits for the height values is contained with `xlim=c(60,75)`. The histogram of the `parent`'s height is identified with `col="green",density=10`, and `add=TRUE,density=10,angle=-45` ensures that the embossed histogram is identifiable from that of the preceding one. The `legend` had been added to suitably complement the program. The reader should further interpret the results from Figure 4.6. □

4.3.3 Histogram Extensions and the Rootogram

The histogram displays the frequencies over the intervals and for moderately large number of observations, it reflects the underlying probability distribution. The boxplot shows how evenly the data is distributed across the five important measures, although it cannot reveal the probability distribution in a better way than a boxplot. The boxplot helps in identifying the outliers in a more apparent way than the histogram. Hence, it would be very useful if we could bring together both these ideas in a closer way than look at them differently for outliers and probability distributions. An effective way of obtaining such a display is to place the boxplot along the x-axis of the histogram. This helps in clearly identifying outliers and also the appropriate probability distribution.

The R package `sfsmisc` contains a function `histBxp`, which nicely places the boxplot along the x-axis of the histogram.

Example 4.3.7. Understanding Histogram of Various Uncertainty Curves. The short program for this problem is given below.

```
> par(mfrow=c(1,3))
> histBxp(sample$Sample_1,col="blue",boxcol="blue",xlab="x")
> histBxp(sample$Sample_2,col="grey",boxcol="grey",xlab="x")
> histBxp(sample$Sample_3,col="brown",boxcol="brown",xlab="x")
> title("Boxplot and Histogram Complementing",outer=TRUE,line=-1)
```

The combination of histogram and boxplot gives a very nice display of both the concepts, as seen in Figure 4.7. □

Generally, in histograms, bar height varies more in bins with long bars than in bins with short bars. In frequency terms, the variability of the counts increases as their typical size

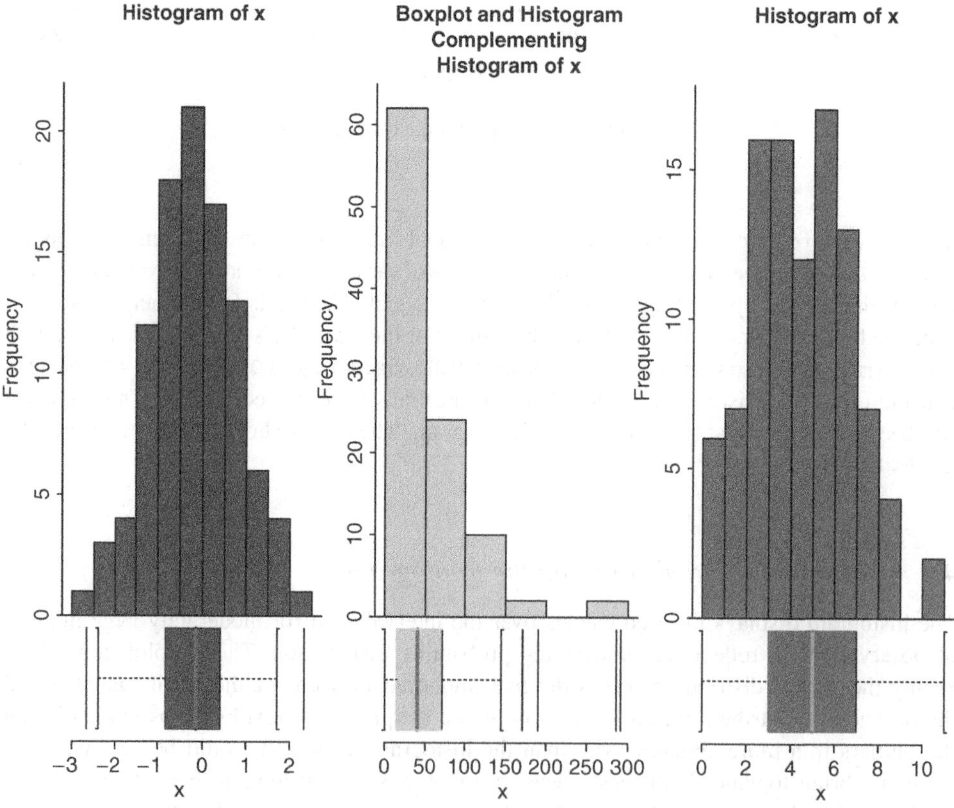

Figure 4.7 Histograms with Boxplot Illustration

increases. Hence, a re-expression can approximately remove the tendency for the variability of a count to increase with its typical size. The *rootogram* arises on taking the re-expression as the square root of the frequencies. This observation is important towards an understanding of the *transformations*.

Example 4.3.8. AD3. The "Militiamen Chests" Dataset. This dataset was introduced in AD3. In what follows, first the histogram is obtained, and then the rootogram.

```
> data(chest)
> attach(chest)
> names(chest)
[1] "Chest" "Count"
> militiamen <- rep(Chest,Count)
> length(militiamen)
[1] 5738
> bins <- seq(33,48)
> bins
 [1] 33 34 35 36 37 38 39 40 41 42 43 44 45 46 47 48
> bin.mids <- (bins[-1]+bins[-length(bins)])/2
> par(mfrow=c(1,2))
> h <- hist(militiamen, breaks = bins, xlab= "Chest Measurements
+ (Inches)", main= "A: Histogram for the Militiamen")
> h$counts <- sqrt(h$counts)
> plot(h,xlab= "Chest Measurements (Inches)",ylab= "ROOT FREQUENCY",
+ main= "B: Rootogram for the Militiamen")
```

Note that we do not have the real dataset for the chest width of the militiamen in terms of each datum. The data provides summary, actually frequencies, of the number of people having width 33 inches, 34 inches, and so forth. The program first recreates the data using the `rep` function, where each distinct chest width, `Chest`, is replicated the number of times as specified in `Count`. Next, the bin points are specified as integers varying from 33 to 48. A histogram for the militiamen's chest width data is first created and also assigned to a new object `h`, see Part A of Figure 4.8. Then, the frequency of the histogram is modified by taking the square-root transformation, that is, `h$counts <- sqrt(h$counts)` and the histogram is then regenerated, which is actually a rootogram. It may be seen from the plot that the rootogram *appears* smoother than the histogram, see Part B of Figure 4.8. □

4.3.4 Pareto Chart

The Pareto chart has been designed to address the implicit questions answered by the Pareto law. The common understanding of the Pareto law is that "majority resources" is consumed by a "minority user". The most common of the percentages is the 80–20 rule, implying that 80% of the effects come from 20% of the causes. The Pareto law is also known as the *law of vital few*, or the *80–20 rule*. The Pareto chart gives very smart answers by completely answering how much is owned by how many. Montgomery (2005), page 148, has listed the Pareto chart as one of the seven major tools of *Statistical Process Control*.

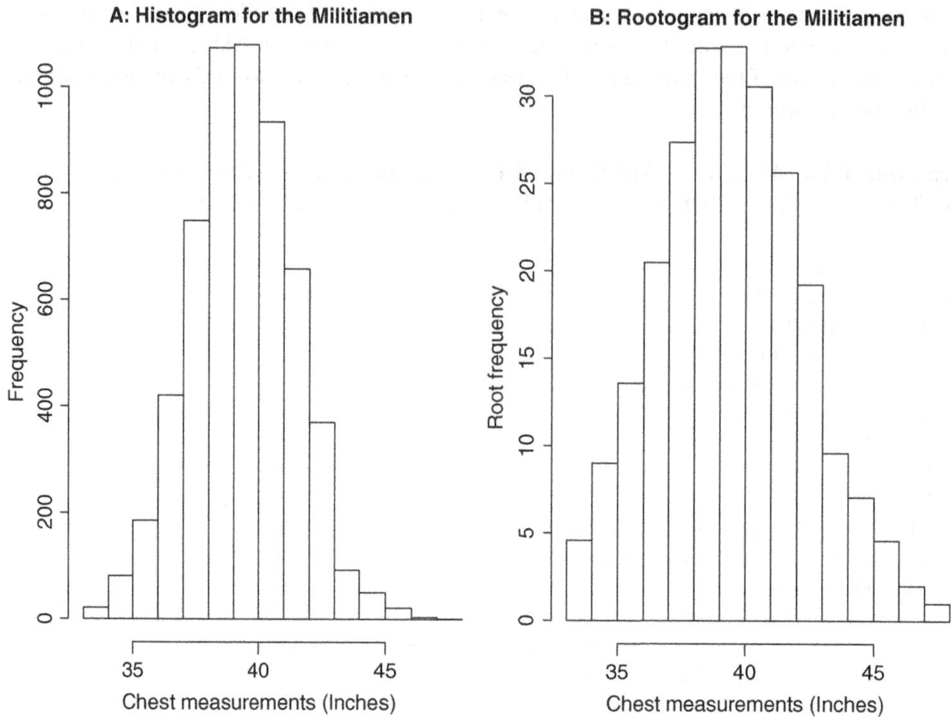

Figure 4.8 A Rootogram Transformation for Militiamen Data

R did not have any function for this plot and neither was there any add-on package which would have helped the user until 2004. However, one R user posed this question to the "list" in 2001 and an expert on the software promptly prepared exhaustive codes over a period of about two weeks. The codes are available at https://stat.ethz.ch/pipermail/r-help/2002-January/018406.html. The Pareto chart can be plotted using `pareto.chart` from the R package `qcc`. We will use Wingate's program and assume here that the reader has copied the codes from the web mentioned above and compiled it in the R session.

The Pareto chart contains three axes on a two-dimensional plot only. Generally, causes/users are arranged along the horizontal axis and the frequencies of such categories are conveyed through a bar for each of them. The bars are arranged in a decreasing order of the frequency. The left-hand side of the vertical axis denotes the frequencies. The cumulative frequency curve along the causes are then simultaneously plotted with the right-hand side of the vertical axis giving the cumulative counts. Thus, at each cause we know precisely its frequency and also the total issues up to that point of time.

Example 4.3.9. Cause and Frequencies. For a chart whose codes have been obtained from the Internet, we resort to the Internet again for a dataset. Click on the web-link http://www.otago.ac.nz/sas/qc/chap26/sect4.htm. From this page, copy and paste the Table 4.1.

Table 4.1 Frequency Table of Contamination and Oxide Effect

Obs	Cause	COUNT	PERCENT
1	Contamination	14	45.1613
2	Corrosion	2	6.4516
3	Doping	1	3.2258
4	Metalization	2	6.4516
5	Miscellaneous	3	9.6774
6	Oxide Defect	8	25.8065
7	Silicon Defect	1	3.2258

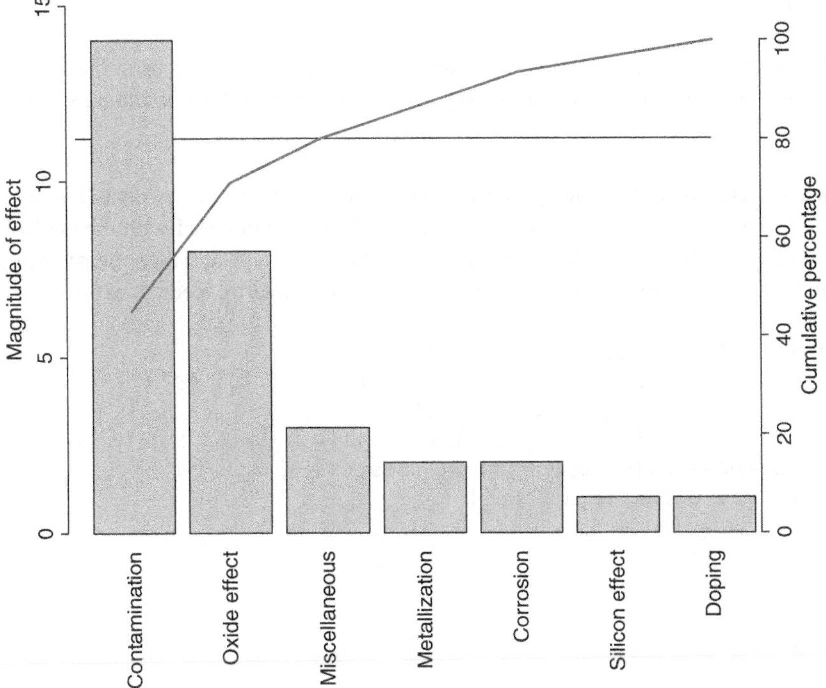

Figure 4.9 A Pareto Chart for Understanding The Cause-Effect Nature

```
> freq <- c(14,2,1,2,3,8,1)
> names(freq) <- c("Contamination","Corrosion","Doping",
+ "Metallization", "Miscellaneous", "Oxide Effect","Silicon Effect")
> pareto(freq)
```

It can be clearly seen from the Pareto chart in Figure 4.9 that `Contamination` and `Oxide Effect` account for more than 80% of the causes in this experiment. □

4.3.5 Stem-and-Leaf Plot

Velleman and Hoaglin (1984) describe the basic idea of stem-and-leaf display by allowing the digits of the data values to do the sorting into numerical order and then display the same. The steps for constructing stem-and-leaf are given in the following:

1. Select an appropriate pair of adjacent digits positioned in the data and split each observation between the adjacent digits. The digits selected on the left-hand side of the data are called *leading digits*.
2. Sort all possible leading digits in ascending order. All possible leading digits are called *stems*.
3. Write the first digit of each data value beside its stem value. The first digit is referred to as the *leaf*.

In Step 2, all possible stems are listed irrespective of whether they occur in the given dataset or not. The `stem` function from the `base` package will be useful for obtaining stem-and-leaf plots.

Example 4.3.10. AD4. The Sleep Data. The purpose of this famous dataset is to investigate if the drug `group==2` results in extra hours of sleep compared with the control group `group==1`. First, the extra sleep hours are sorted by the groups and then the `stem` function is applied over the groups to enable us to decide whether the drug leads to extra sleep hours.

```
> sort(sleep$extra[sleep$group==1])
 [1] -1.6 -1.2 -0.2 -0.1  0.0  0.7  0.8  2.0  3.4  3.7
> sort(sleep$extra[sleep$group==2])
 [1] -0.1  0.1  0.8  1.1  1.6  1.9  3.4  4.4  4.6  5.5
> stem(sleep$extra[sleep$group==1],scale=2)
  The decimal point is at the |
  -1 | 62
  -0 | 21
   0 | 078
   1 |
   2 | 0
   3 | 47
> stem(sleep$extra[sleep$group==2],scale=2)
  The decimal point is at the |
  -0 | 1
   0 | 18
   1 | 169
   2 |
   3 | 4
   4 | 46
   5 | 5
```

For the control group, the sleep hours vary from `-1.6` to `3.7`, whereas for the drug it varies from `-0.1` to `5.5` hours. In the former case, with `scale=2`, the leading digits would be `-1, -0, 0, 1, 2, 3`, and for the latter they are `-0, 0, 1, ...,5`. The `stem` plot for control group suggests the median value at about `0.35` and for the drug group at `1.75`, and thus the stem-and-leaf plot suggests an increase of about `1.4` sleep hours for the drug group.□

Example 4.3.11. The Cloud Seeding Data. Chambers, et al. (1983), page 381, contains the cloud seeding dataset. Rainfall in acre-feet for 52 clouds is measured, 50% of which have natural rain (control group), whereas the others are seeded. We need to visually compare whether seeding the clouds leads to an increase in rainfall in acre-feet. The stem-and-leaf plot will be used to analyze this cloud seed data. The `stem` function will again be used here.

The small code `summary(cloud)` shows that the rain in acre-feet for the `Control` group varies from `1.00` to `1202.60` and for the `Seeded` group from `4.10` to `2745.60`. The number of leading digits for this data will be too enormous and meaningless too. Hence, we resort to a logarithmic transformation of the data.

```
> data(cloud)
> summary(cloud)
    Control               Seeded
 Min.    :   1.00    Min.    :   4.10
 1st Qu.:  24.82    1st Qu.:  98.12
 Median :  44.20    Median : 221.60
 Mean   : 164.59    Mean   : 441.98
 3rd Qu.: 159.20    3rd Qu.: 406.02
 Max.   :1202.60    Max.   :2745.60
> stem(log(cloud$Seeded),scale=1)
  The decimal point is at the |
  1 | 4
  2 | 09
  3 | 457
  4 | 57889
  5 | 33556678
  6 | 1269
  7 | 449
> stem(log(cloud$Control),scale=1)
  The decimal point is at the |
  0 | 0
  1 | 66
  2 | 49
  3 | 123344679
  4 | 2456
  5 | 015889
  6 | 7
  7 | 1
```

From the stem-and-leaf plot, the median acre-feet rain for the seeded clouds appears around `5.4` and for the control clouds around `3.8`. The difference is certainly significant and the stem-and-leaf plot suggests that the rainfall is larger for the seeded clouds. □

Multiple histograms and boxplots were obtained on the same graphical device. Thus, to compare two stem-and-leaf plots, there is a need for a similar display arrangement. The infrastructure will now be discussed. Tukey has indeed enriched the EDA in ways beyond the discussion thus far. An important technique invented by Prof Tukey is the modification of the stem-and-leaf plot and this technique is available from the `aplpack` package in the `stem.leaf.backback` function. This technique will be illustrated through the two examples discussed previously.

If the trailing digits for stems are few, the interpretation of the stem-and-leaf plot becomes simpler. However, if there are a large number of trailing digits for a stem, it is inconvenient to interpret the display. Suppose that the stem is the integer 1 and there are nearly 15 observations among the trailing digits. This means that the stem part will have 15 numbers besides it, which will obscure the display. In an informal way, Prof Tukey suggests that such stems be further divided into sub-stems. The question is then how do we identify those sub-stems, which are part of neither the leading digits nor the trailing digits. Typically, the digits would be one of the ten integers 0 to 9. The notation for the sub-stems suggested by Prof Tukey is to identify the digits by the first letters of their spellings. Thus 2 (two) and 3 (three) will be denoted by **t**, 4 (four) and 5 (five) by **f**, 6 (six) and 7 (seven) by **s**. A convention for the digits 0, 1, 8, and 9 is the denote 0 (zero) and 1 (one) by the star symbol *, and 8 (eight) and 9 (nine) by the period "**.**".

Example 4.3.12. Tukey's Extension of the Stem-and-Leaf Plot. The `aplpack` package's `stem.leaf.backback` function will be used to arrange two stem-and-leaf plots in parallel, which help in direct comparisons. The cumulative frequencies from both the extremes are also provided for the stem-and-leaf plots and the point at which there is an overlap will help to identify the median. An awesome trick here!

We also consider one more dataset `octane` from the `RSADBE` package. In this problem, there are two methods of obtaining the octane rating of gasoline blends, and we need to check which method leads to higher ratings. The next batch of R codes gives the action on all the three datasets.

```
> stem.leaf.backback(sleep$extra[sleep$group==1],sleep$extra
+ [sleep$group==2], back.to.back=FALSE)
_______________________________
  1 | 2: represents 1.2, leaf unit: 0.1
sleep$extra[sleep$group == 1]
                    sleep$extra[sleep$group == 2]
_______________________________
   -2 |             |
   -1 |62     2     |
   -0 |21     4     |1       1
    0 |078   (3)    |18      3
    1 |             |169    (3)
    2 |0      3     |
    3 |47     2     |4       4
    4 |             |46      3
    5 |             |5       1
    6 |             |
_______________________________
n:     10          10
_______________________________
> stem.leaf.backback(log(cloud$Seeded),log(cloud$Control),
+ back.to.back=FALSE)
_______________________________
```

```
  1 | 2: represents 1.2, leaf unit: 0.1
log(cloud$Seeded)
                                log(cloud$Control)

______________________________________________________
   0* |              |0          1
   0. |              |
   1* |4         1   |
   1. |              |55         3
   2* |0         2   |4          4
   2. |8         3   |8          5
   3* |44        5   |012233    11
   3. |7         6   |678       (3)
   4* |              |234       12
   4. |57778    11   |59         9
   5* |234     (3)   |04         7
   5. |56678    12   |789        5
   6* |01        7   |
   6. |58        5   |7          2
   7* |44        3   |0          1
   7. |9         1   |
   8* |              |
______________________________________________________
n:      26                26
______________________________________________________
> library(RSADBE)
> data(octane)
> stem.leaf.backback(octane$Method_1,octane$Method_2,
+ back.to.back=TRUE)
_____________________________________________________________
  1 | 2: represents 12, leaf unit: 1
octane$Method_1
                                   octane$Method_2

_____________________________________________________________
    2            10|  8* |
    4            33|   t |3            1
    9         55544|   f |5            2
   16       7777666|   s |
  (2)            98|  8. |89           4
   14      11110000|  9* |
    6            32|   t |22333        9
    4             4|   f |4455        13
                   |   s |667777      (6)
    3             8|  9. |8899999     13
                   | 10* |011          6
                   |   t |3            3
    2            55|   f |
                   |   s |66           2
                   | 10. |
                   | 11* |
_____________________________________________________________
n:               32          32
_____________________________________________________________
```

The reader should verify if the medians as argued in the earlier examples are indeed correct. In light of the discussion in the paragraph preceding the example, interpret the symbols `*`, `t`, `f`, `s`, and "`.`". The number of bracket `(2)` for `Method_1` and `(6)` for `Method_2` indicates the median, that is, approximately 88 and 97. □

4.3.6 Run Chart

The run chart is also known as the *run-sequence* plot. In the run chart, the data value is simply plotted against its index number. For example, if $x_1, x_2, \dots, x_t$ is the data, plot $x_1, x_2, \dots, x_t$ against their index $1, 2, \dots, t$. The run charts can be plotted in R using the function `plot.ts`, which is very commonly used in time-series analysis.

Example 4.3.13. AD9. The Air Passengers Dataset. Consider the dataset of "Airline Passengers" in the US for the period 1949–1960. Plot the number of passengers against the month of the year label to obtain the run chart.

```
> par(mfrow=c(1,2))
> AirPassengers
     Jan Feb Mar Apr May Jun Jul Aug Sep Oct Nov Dec
1949 112 118 132 129 121 135 148 148 136 119 104 118
1950 115 126 141 135 125 149 170 170 158 133 114 140

1960 417 391 419 461 472 535 622 606 508 461 390 432
> plot.ts(AirPassengers)
> title("A: Run Chart for AD9")
```

The run chart in Part A of Figure 4.10 clearly shows that there is an increasing trend in the number of users. It may be seen that there is a seasonal variation whose size is roughly equal to the local mean. □

Example 4.3.14. Insurance Claims Data. Montgomery (2005), page 42, describes this dataset in which the number of days taken by the company to process and settle the claims of employee health insurance customers. The data is recorded for the number of days for settlement from the first to fortieth claim. Here, it is the claim number which plays the role of "time index" and not the number of days taken to settle the claim. Thus, to execute the run chart for this dataset, we have an insight into how the company has evolved from the first to the fortieth claim.

```
> data(insurance)
> plot(insurance$Claim,insurance$Days,"l",xlab="Claim Sequence",
+ ylab="Time to Settle the Claim")
> title("B: Run Chart for Insurance Claim Settlement")
```

We can see in Part B of Figure 4.10 that though there is a lot of upward and downward movements across the claims, it is gradually decreasing and thus shows that as the experience of the company increases in handling the claims, it is able to settle the claims in less time. □

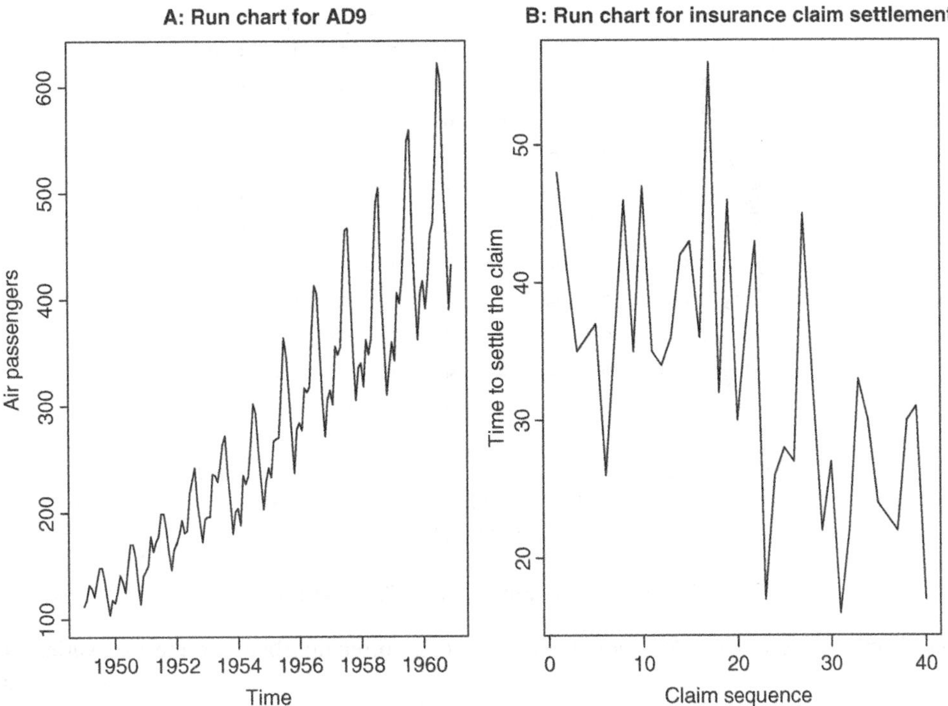

Figure 4.10 A Time Series Plot for Air Passengers Dataset

In certain ways, the graphical methods are useful for univariate data. The next technique is more useful for dealing with paired/multivariate data.

4.3.7 *Scatter Plot*

The reader is most certainly familiar with this very basic format of plots. Whenever we have paired data and there is a belief that the variables are related, its only natural to plot them against one other. Such a display is, of course, known as the *scatter plot* or the *x-y plot*. There is a subtle difference between them, see Velleman and Hoaglin (1984). We will straightaway start with examples.

Example 4.3.15. AD5. The Galton Data. As has been described in Section 4 of Chapter 1, we attempt an initial understanding of the relationship between the height of the child and the parent.

```
> library(UsingR)
> data(galton)
> plot(galton[,2],galton[,1],xlim=range(galton[,2]),ylim=
+ range(galton[,1]),xlab="Parent's Height",ylab="Child's Height")
```

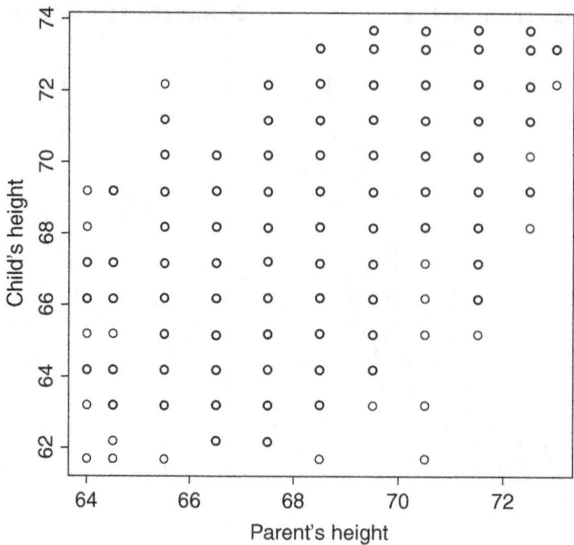

Figure 4.11 A Scatter Plot for Galton Dataset

The display, Figure 4.11, does not suggest a strong correlation between the two variables here. □

Example 4.3.16. Scatter Plots for Understanding Correlations. We consider a *cooked* data tailor-made for the use of scatter plots towards understanding correlations. This dataset is available in the file `some6samples.csv`.

```
> data(somesamples)
> attach(somesamples)
> par(mfrow=c(2,3))
> plot(x1,y1,main="Sample I",xlim=c(-4,4),ylim=c(-4,4))
> plot(x2,y2,main="Sample II",xlim=c(-4,4),ylim=c(-4,4))
> plot(x3,y3,main="Sample III",xlim=c(-4,4),ylim=c(-4,4))
> plot(x4,y4,main="Sample IV",xlim=c(-4,4),ylim=c(-4,4))
> plot(x5,y5,main="Sample V",xlim=c(-4,4),ylim=c(-4,4))
> plot(x6,y6,main="Sample VI",xlim=c(-4,4),ylim=c(-4,4))
```

The plots, Figure 4.12, titled `Sample I` and `Sample II`, resemble two clouds, and also appear to be mirror images of each other. If the first plot increases in the x value, this suggests an increase in y by a certain value, and the second plot suggests that increasing x should lead to a decrease in y by that certain value. That certain value is surely not 0 but does not look to be a high value either. The scenario in `Sample III` and `Sample IV` mirrors the relationship between the first two, except that we are sure that the "certain value" is high. The reader can further see that `Sample V` looks more or less like `Sample I`, with the cloud now denser than `Sample I` but sparser than `Sample III`. The exercise for the reader is to interpret `Sample VI`. □

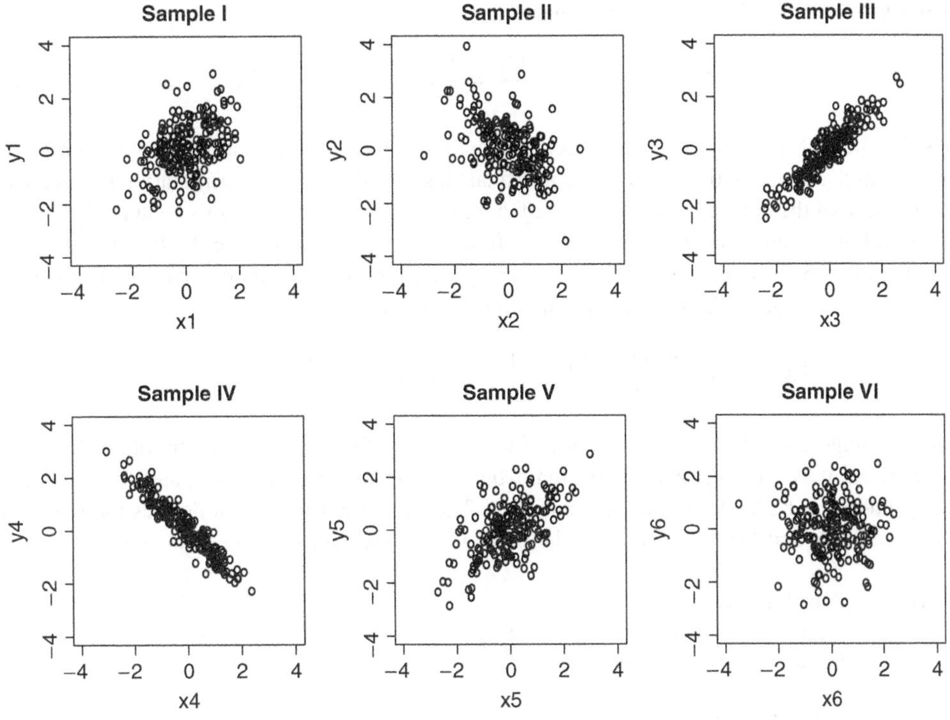

Figure 4.12 Understanding Correlations through Different Scatter Plots

The scatter plot will be later extended to multivariate data with more than two variables through an idea known as *matrix of scatter plots*. See Sections 12.4 and 14.2.

?plot

4.4 Quantitative Techniques in EDA

We discuss here two important methods of quantitative techniques in EDA. For advance concepts of quantitative techniques, refer to Hoaglin, et al. (1991). The methods described and demonstrated will lay a firm foundation towards the methods described in that book. The first method here is fairly simple, and the second one is more detailed.

4.4.1 Trimean

Trimean is a measure of location and is the weighted average of the median and two other quartiles. Since median is a measure of location, we may intuitively expect the trimean to be more robust than the median as well as the mean. If Q_1, Q_2, Q_3 are the lower, middle (median), and upper quartiles, the trimean is defined by

$$TM = \frac{Q_1 + 2Q_2 + Q_3}{4} = \frac{1}{2}\left(Q_2 + \frac{Q_1 + Q_3}{2}\right). \tag{4.8}$$

The last part of the above equation suggests that the trimean can be viewed as the average of median and average of the lower and upper quartiles. Weisberg (1992) summarized trimean as "a measure of the center (of a distribution) in that it combines the median's center values with the mid-hinge's attention to the extremes." In fact, we can even replace the lower and upper quartiles in the above expression by the corresponding hinges and then derive the trimean as a weighted average of the median and the hinges. That is,

$$TM^H = \frac{H_L + 2Q_2 + H_U}{4} = \frac{1}{2}\left(Q_2 + \frac{H_L + H_U}{2}\right).$$

As the hinges, the three of them, are obtained using the Tukeys' five numbers function `fivenum`, it is straightforward to obtain the trimean using either the quartiles (consider using the `quantile` function) or the hinges. The next small R session defines the required function in `TM` and `TMH`, and we also show that hinges and quartiles need not be equal.

```
> TM <- function(x) {
+   qs <- quantile(x,c(0.25,0.5,0.75))
+   return(as.numeric((qs[2]+(qs[1]+qs[3])/2)/2))
+                }
> TMH <- function(x) {
+   qh <- fivenum(x,c(0.25,0.5,0.75))
+   return((qh[2]+(qh[1]+qh[3])/2)/2)
+                  }
> TM(iris[,2]); TMH(iris[,2])
[1] 3.02
[1] 2.65
> ji4 <- jitter(iris[,4])
> quantile(ji4,c(0.25,0.75))
 25
0.29 1.80
> fivenum(ji4)[c(2,4)]
[1] 0.289 1.797
```

The functions are simple to follow and hence it is left to the reader to figure it out.

4.4.2 Letter Values

We have mentioned how EDA is about attitude, data driven stories, etc. Since the emphasis in EDA is on data, it makes a whole lot of sense to understand each "datum" as much as possible. Some natural examples of useful datum are minimum, maximum, etc. Median is also a useful datum when the size of data is odd. Recall that by definition, see Section 4.2, depth of a datum is the minimum of the position of the datum from either end of the batch. We can see from the outputs of Section 4.2 that the minimum and maximum values, also called extremes, have a depth of 1, the second largest and second smallest have a depth of 2, and so on. Thus, two observations, namely, the ith and $(n + 1 - i)^{th}$ ordered observations in ascending order have depth i.

The median splits the data into two equal halves. The upper and lower hinges do *that* to the upper and lower halves dataset what median does to the entire collection, that is, the hinges give us quarters of the dataset. We have seen earlier that the depth of the median, for a sample of size n is $(n + 1)/2$. It is fairly easy to see that the depth of the hinges is therefore

$$d(H) = \frac{[d(M)] + 1}{2}, \tag{4.9}$$

where $[d(M)]$ indicates the integer part of $d(M)$.

The next step is to define the half dividers of quarters, which results in eight equal divisions of the dataset. They are referred to as ***eights*** for simplicity, and we denote the eights by E. Furthermore, the depth of eights is given by

$$d(E) = \frac{[d(M)] + 1}{2}. \tag{4.10}$$

The concept will now be illustrated from Velleman and Hoaglin.

Example 4.4.1. Area of New Jersey Counties. Velleman and Hoaglin (1984). Data is available on the area of New Jersey counties and we want to find which cities fall in the halves, quarters, and eights of the dataset. See page 44 of Velleman and Hoaglin.

```
> areanj <- c(569, 234, 819, 221, 267, 500, 130, 329, 47, 423, 228,
+ 312, 476, 468, 642, 192, 365, 307, 527, 103, 362)
> counties <- c("Atlantic", "Bergen", "Burlington", "Camden",
+ "Cape", + "Cumberland", "Essex", "Gloucester", "Hudson",
+ "Hunterdon", "Mercer", + "Middlesex", "Monmouth", "Morris",
+ "Ocean", "Passaic", "Salem", "Somerset", "Sussex",
+ "Union", "Warren")
> njc <- data.frame(counties,areanj)
> njc <- njc[order(njc[,2]),]
> d_median <- (nrow(njc)+1)/2
> d_hinge <- (floor(d_median)+1)/2
> d_eights <- (floor(d_hinge)+1)/2
> d_median;d_hinge;d_eights
[1] 11
[1] 6
[1] 3.5
```

Though `floor` is not needed in this example, we have factored it into the program so that if this program is executed on other datasets, we get the right output. We modify the data frame `njc` for facilitating the computations of the hinges and the eights.

```
> indices <- c(1:d_median, (d_median-1):1)
> cbind(njc,indices)
    counties areanj indices
9     Hudson     47       1
```

```
20       Union    103      2

5         Cape    267      8
18    Somerset    307      9
12   Middlesex    312     10
8   Gloucester    329     11
21      Warren    362     10
17       Salem    365      9
10   Hunterdon    423      8

15       Ocean    642      2
3   Burlington    819      1
```

We can clearly see from the above display of R outputs that the median of area of New Jersey counties is 329 square miles, and that the lower and upper hinges are 228 and 476 square miles respectively. The depth of the eights is 3.5, and thus we need to take the average of the third and fourth observations from either end to calculate the eights. The lower and upper eights are thus (130+192)/2 = 161 and (527+569)/2 = 548 square miles respectively. □

Note that the measures such as hinges and eights are not the depth values, but are the values of the variable associated with the corresponding depth. Median, hinges, eights! Where to stop exactly will be a very legitimate question for any practitioner. Furthermore, depending on the size of the dataset, the eights may be 3.5 or even 3000. This question is what is precisely answered by **letter values**.

Letter values continue the division process further into sixteens, thirty-seconds, and so on until we reach the depth of a datum which will be equal to 1. Thus, we would have arrived at some of the most meaningful data division process. Velleman and Hoaglin (1984) suggest denoting the further letters, beyond eights, as D, C, B, A, Z, Y, X, W, and so on. Yes, we clarify here what to do with these eights, sixteens, etc. Recall that in Section 2 and in Subsection 4.3.1 we suggested extending measures of central tendency, dispersion, and skewness based on hinges. Similarly, we can generalize measures based on each of the letter values generated. Thus, we have further concepts such as *midhinges, mideights,* etc. These measures are referred to as *midsummaries*. Similarly, we can define measures of dispersion based on the ranges between the measures which lead to *H-spread*, *E-spread*, *D-spread*, etc.

We close this subsection with the use of function `lval` from the `LearnEDA` package developed by Prof Jim Albert.

Example 4.4.2. Area of New Jersey Counties. Contd. The `lval` function from Prof Jim Albert's R package `LearnEDA` will be used to obtain the letter values.

```
> library(LearnEDA)
> lval(areanj)
  depth  lo  hi  mids spreads
1  11.0 329 329 329.0       0
2   6.0 228 476 352.0     248
3   3.5 161 548 354.5     387
4   2.0 103 642 372.5     539
5   1.0  47 819 433.0     772
```

The letter values in this example end at thirty-two(th?), or equivalently at letter D. Note that there only 21 observations in the study. Thus, this should sound as a warning for the user that the letter values need not stop at the maximum number of observations, and that the process is terminated when the depth of one is reached. □

Now, we are prepared for exploratory regression models!

4.5 Exploratory Regression Models

The scatter plot helps to identify the relationship between two variables. If the scatter plot indicates a linear relationship between two variables, we would like to quantify the relationship between them. A rich class of the related confirmatory models will be taken in Part IV. In this section we will develop the exploratory approach for quantifying the relationship and hence we call these models *Exploratory Regression Models*. For the case of single input variables, also known as covariates, the output can be modeled through a *resistant line* and this development will be carried out in the next subsection 4.5.1, and the extension for two variables will be taken in subsection 4.5.2.

4.5.1 Resistant Line

We have so far seen EDA techniques handle reliable summaries in the form of median, mid-summaries, etc., and very powerful graphical displays such as histogram, Pareto chart, etc. We also saw how the x-y plots help in understanding the relationship between two variables. The reader would appreciate some EDA technique which models the relationship between two variables. Particularly, regression models of the form

$$y = \beta_0 + \beta_1 x + \epsilon, \tag{4.11}$$

are of great interest. Equation 4.11 is our first regression model. The answer to problems of this kind are provided by the ***resistant line***. Here, the term β_0 is referred to as the intercept term, β_1 as the slope term, while ϵ is the error or noise.

The motivation and development of the resistant line is very intuitive and extends in a natural way to employ the use of median, quartiles, hinges, etc. From a mathematical point of view, the slope term β_1 measures the changes in the output y for unit change in the input x, whereas β_0 is the intercept term. This rate of change is obtained by dividing the data into three regions.

We describe the resistant line mechanism by the following steps. The reader should follow the steps in Figure 4.13 too. A useful figure explaining the steps of resistant line modeling may be found in Figure 6 titled "Understanding the resistant line" of Tattar (2013). The initial estimate of the parameters are obtained through the following steps.

- The x-y plot is divided into three regions, containing an equal number of data points, according to the x-values only.
- In the right-hand region find the median of x values and also that of y, denote them as x_R and y_R, and obtain the pair (x_R, y_R).
- Repeat the exercises for the middle and left regions to obtain the points (x_M, y_M) and (x_L, y_L).

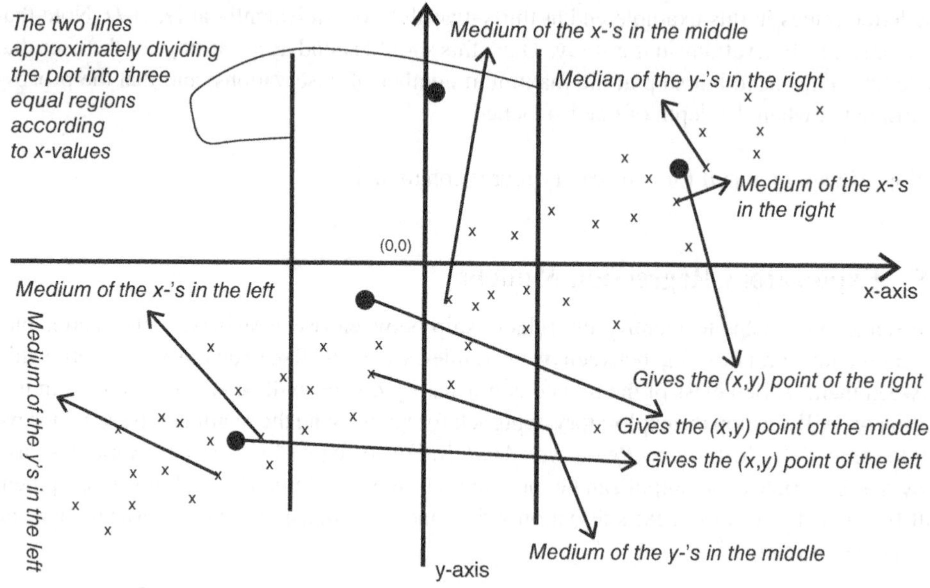

Figure 4.13 Understanding The Construction of Resistant Line

We note from the construction in Figure 4.13 that (x_R, y_R), (x_M, y_M) and (x_L, y_L) need not correspond to any of the paired data (x, y). Refer to Chapter 5 of Velleman and Hoaglin for more details.

The purpose of obtaining the triplets of the ordered pair $(x_L, y_L), (x_M, y_M), (x_R, y_R)$ is to put ourselves in the position where we can estimate the slope and intercept of the model given by Equation 4.11. We first estimate the slope, denoted by $\hat{\beta}_1^{RL}$, using the pair of points $(x_L, y_L), (x_R, y_R)$. Define

$$\hat{\beta}_1^{RL,0} = \frac{y_R - y_L}{x_R - x_L}. \tag{4.12}$$

We then use the *estimated* value of $\hat{\beta}_1^{RL}$ in the model and average over the three possible vital data points to obtain an estimate of the a value, denoted by $\hat{\beta}_0^{RL}$. Thus,

$$\hat{\beta}_0^{RL,0} = \frac{(y_L + y_M + y_R) - \hat{\beta}_1^{RL}(x_L + x_M + x_R)}{3}. \tag{4.13}$$

The initial estimate of $\hat{\beta}_0^{RL,0}$ and $\hat{\beta}_1^{RL,0}$ need improvization. Using the initial estimates, the residuals are obtained for the fitted model:

$$r_i^0 = y_i - \hat{\beta}_0^{RL,0} - \hat{\beta}_1^{RL,0} x_i, i = 1, \dots, n.$$

The slope and intercept terms are now obtained for the paired data $(x_i, r_i), i = 1, \dots, n$ and denoted by $\beta_0^{RL,1}, \beta_1^{RL,1}$. The residuals for the jth iteration of the slope and intercept will be denoted by $r_i^j, j = 1, 2, \ldots$, and for $j \geq 2$, the slope and intercept terms are updated with $\beta_0^{RL,j} = \beta_0^{RL,j} + \beta_0^{RL,j-1}$ and $\beta_1^{RL,j} = \beta_1^{RL,j} + \beta_1^{RL,j-1}$.

Let us put the theory of the resistant line behind us and see it in action during the following examples.

Example 4.5.1. AD4. The Galton Dataset. This dataset was used earlier as an example of an *x-y* plot. The scatter plot of the parents and the child reflected weak correlation in Figure 4.11, and now we examine and estimate the effect by using the resistant line model. The function `resistant_line` from the companion package will be used to build the model 4.11.

```
> library(UsingR)
> data(galton)
> rgalton <- resistant_line(galton$parent,galton$child,iterations=5)
> plot(galton$parent,galton$child,xlab="Parent's Height",
+ ylab="Child's Height")
> curve(rgalton$coeffs[1]+rgalton$coeffs[2]*(x-rgalton$xCenter),
+ add=TRUE)
> rgalton$coeffs
[1] 68.5  1.0
```

The fitted resistant line, see Figure 4.14, tells us that if the parents were taller by an inch, the child's height would be more than an inch taller too. □

For two *factors*, or covariates, an extension of the resistant line model 4.11, will be next considered.

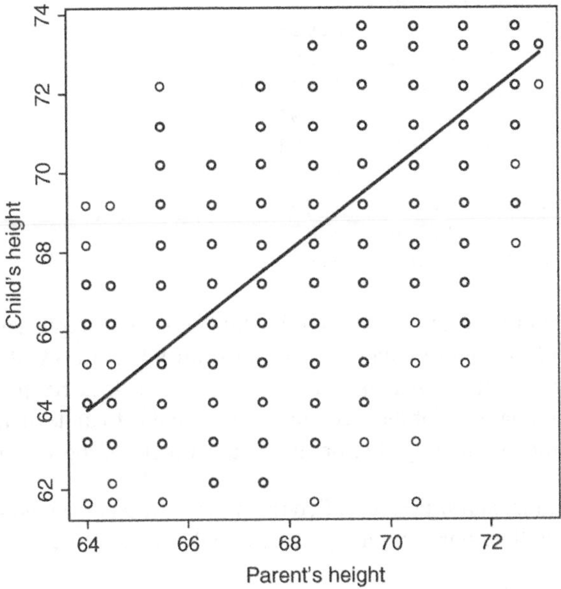

Figure 4.14 Fitting of Resistant Line for the Galton Dataset

4.5.2 Median Polish

For the AD5 dataset, we had height of the parent as an input variable and the height of the child as the output. Under the hypothetical case that we have *groups* for the height of father and mother as two different treatment variables, the resistant line model 4.11, in a very different technical sense, needs to be extended as follows:

$$y = \mu + \beta_i + \gamma_j + \epsilon, i = 1, \dots, m, j = 1, \dots, n, \tag{4.14}$$

where β_i and γ_j represent the two groups of height for the father and mother. The groups here may be something along the lines of Low, Medium, and High. In the study of *Experimental Designs*, Chapter 13, this model is occasionally known as the *two-way model*. In EDA, the solution for obtaining the parameters μ, β_i, $1, \dots, m$, and $\gamma_j, j = 1, \dots, n$ are given by the *Median Polish algorithm*. A slight technical difference needs to be pointed out for the use of median polish and resistant line models. Here, the input variables are categorical in nature and not continuous. This means that if we still need to understand the height of the child as a variable dependent on the height of the mother and of the father, the latter two variables need to be categorized into *bins*, say short (less than 5 feet), average (5–6 feet), and tall (greater than 6 feet).

To explain the median polish algorithm, we need to examine the dataset first.

Example 4.5.2. Strength Dataset of a Girder Experiment. In this experiment, the shear strength of steel plate girders needs to be modeled as a function of the four methods and nine girders, refer to Table 3.4 of Wu and Hamada (2000–9). The data will be displayed first and the analysis will be followed after the description of the median polish algorithm.

```
> data(girder)
> girder
     Aarau Karisruhe Lehigh Cardiff
S1.1 0.772     1.186  1.061   1.025
S2.1 0.744     1.151  0.992   0.905
S3.1 0.767     1.322  1.063   0.930
S4.1 0.745     1.339  1.062   0.899
S5.1 0.725     1.200  1.065   0.871
S1.2 0.844     1.402  1.178   1.004
S2.2 0.831     1.365  1.037   0.853
S3.2 0.867     1.537  1.086   0.858
S4.2 0.859     1.559  1.052   0.805
```

The array elements starting with `0.772` and finishing at `0.805` represent the shear strength of the steel plate girders. The row names, varying from `S1.1` to `S4.2`, represent the nine types of girders, and the column names, `Aarau`, `Karisruhe`, `Lehigh`, and `Cardiff` are the four methods of preparation of the steel plates. The goal is to understand the impact of the methods of preparation as well as girder on the shear strength of the steel plates. □

Now that we know the data structure, called the *two-way table*, the median polish algorithm is given next, which will help in estimating the row and column effects.

1. Compute the row medians of a two-way table and augment it to the right-hand side of the table. Subtract the row median in the respective rows of the table.

2. Take the median of the row medians as the initial total effect value of the row effect. Similar to the original elements of the table, subtract the initial total effect value from the row medians.
3. Compute the column medians of the original columns for the matrix in the previous step and append it to the bottom. Subtract from the data matrix the corresponding column medians.
4. Similar to Step 2, obtain the median of the column medians and add to the initial total effect value. Remove the current total effect median from each element of the column medians.
5. Repeat the four steps above until convergence of either the row or the column medians.

The `medpolish` function from the `MASS` package can be used to fit the median polish model. This will be illustrated in a continuation of the girder experiment.

Example 4.5.3. Strength Dataset of a Girder Experiment. Contd. The `medpolish` function can be readily applied over the `girder` data frame.

```
> medpolish(girder)
1: 1.96
2: 1.701
Final: 1.686

Median Polish Results (Dataset: "girder2")
Overall: 0.989
Row Effects:
      S1.1      S2.1               S3.2       S4.2
-0.005375 -0.053875          0.054625   0.033625
Column Effects:
    Aarau Karisruhe     Lehigh    Cardiff
  -0.2116    0.3330     0.0740    -0.0695
Residuals:
        Aarau Karisruhe   Lehigh Cardiff
S1.1   0.0000    -0.1306  0.0034  0.1109
S2.1   0.0205    -0.1171 -0.0171  0.0394
S3.1  -0.0104     0.0000  0.0000  0.0105
S4.1  -0.0239     0.0255  0.0075 -0.0120
S5.1  -0.0025    -0.0721  0.0519  0.0014
S1.2  -0.0179    -0.0045  0.0305  0.0000
S2.2   0.0451     0.0345 -0.0345 -0.0750
S3.2   0.0350     0.1604 -0.0316 -0.1161
S4.2   0.0480     0.2034 -0.0446 -0.1481
```

The median polish solution shows that the `Karisruhe` method of preparation helps in creating higher shear strength of the steel plates. □

4.6 Further Reading

We had mentioned Tukey's (1962) article "The Future of Data Analysis" as one of the starting points which may have led to the beginning of EDA. Tukey had the strong belief that data analysis must not be overwhelmed by model assumptions and they should have an effect on how you describe them. This belief and further work at the Bell Telephone Laboratories culminated in Tukey (1977). There is a lot of simplicity in Tukeys work, such that for small datasets we do not even need a calculator. A paper and pencil will help us to a great enough extent and depth. An advanced course to Tukey (1977) is available in Mosteller and Tukey (1977). In this book, EDA techniques for regression problems are discussed.

In the year 1991, Hoaglin, et al. produced a volume with EDA methods for Analysis of Variance (ANOVA). Hoaglin, et al. (1985) is another edited volume which is useful for exploring tables, shapes, and trends. In fact, many such ideas are described in Rousseeuw and Leroy (1987) for robust regression. We also make good use of Velleman and Hoaglin (1984), which has many Fortran programs for EDA techniques. The main reason for restating this is the fact that a user can import Fortran programs in R and use them easily again.

EDA is about any method which is exploratory in nature. Thus, many of the multivariate statistical analysis techniques are considered as EDA techniques. As an example, many experts consider Principal Component Analysis, Factor Analysis, etc. as EDA techniques. Martinez and Martinez (2005) and Myatt (2007) are two recent books which accept this point of view. We will see the multivariate techniques in Chapters 14 and 15.

We need to mention that Frieden and Gatenby (2007) have developed EDA methods using Fisher information. This is an important facet, as the Fisher information is very important and we introduce this concept in Chapter 7.

4.7 Complements, Problems, and Programs

Problem 4.1 Let `x` be a numeric vector. Create a new function, say `depth`, which will have a serial number as an argument, between `1:length(x)`, and its output should return the depth of the datum.

Problem 4.2 Obtain the EDA summaries as in `fivenum`, `IQR`, `fnid`, and `mad` for the datasets considered in Section 4.3. Note your observations based on the summaries and then investigate whether or not these notes are visible in the corresponding figures.

Problem 4.3 The part B of Figure 4.4, see Example 4.5, clearly shows the presence of outliers for the number of dead insects for insecticides `C` and `D`. Identify the outlying data points. Remove the outlying points, and then check if any more potential outliers are present.

Problem 4.4 Provide summary and descriptive statistics for the cooked dataset in Example 4.6, and interpret the results as provided by the histograms.

Problem 4.5 The number of intervals for the five histograms in Figure 4.5 can be seen as 11, 6, 11, 6, and 10. How do you obtain these numbers through R?

Problem 4.6 Create a function which generates a histogram with the intervals according to the percentiles of the data vector.

Problem 4.7 The histograms seen in Section 4.3 give a horizontal display. At times, a vertical display is preferable. Using the tips from the web http://stackoverflow.com/questions/11022675/rotate-histogram-in-r-or-overlay-a-density-in-a-barplot, obtain the vertical display of a histogram.

Problem 4.8 Imposing histograms on each other helps in comparison of similar datasets, as seen in Example 4.7. Repeating the technique for the Youden-Beale experiment, what will be the conclusion for the two virus extracts?

Problem 4.9 Explore the different choices of breaks given in Formulas 4.5 – 4.7 for the different histogram examples.

Problem 4.10 Using the R function `pareto.chart` from the `qcc` package, obtain the Pareto chart for the causes and frequencies, as in Example 4.10, and compare the results with Figure 4.9.

Problem 4.11 Using the `stem.leaf.backback` function, compare the averages of the two virus extracts for the Youden-Beale experiment, as discussed in Example 4.2. Similarly, compare the stem-and-leaf displays for the recall of pleasant and unpleasant memories of Example 4.4.

Problem 4.12 Create an R function, say `trimean`, for computing trimean, as given in Equation 4.8. Apply the new function for datasets of your choices considered in the chapter.

Problem 4.13 Obtain the letter values for three datasets in Example 4.13 using `lval` and check if the median comparisons can be extended through them.

Problem 4.14 Fit resistant line models for the six pairs of data discussed in Example 4.17. Validate the correlations as implied by the scatter plots in Figure 4.12.

Problem 4.15 For the datasets available in the files `rocket_propellant.csv` and `toluca_company.dat`, build the resistant line models. In the former file, the input variable is `Age_of_Propellant`, while in the latter file it is `Lot_Size`. The output variables in these respective files are `Shear_Strength` and `Labour_Hours`.

Part II

Probability and Inference

5

Probability Theory

Package(s): `prob`, `scatterplot3d`, `ConvergenceConcepts`

5.1 Introduction

Probability is that arm of science which deals with the understanding of uncertainty from a mathematical perspective. The foundations of probability are about three centuries old and can be traced back to the works of Laplace, Bernoulli, et al. However, the formal acceptance of probability as a legitimate science stream is just a century old. Kolmogorov (1933) firmly laid the foundations of probability in a pure mathematical framework.

An experiment, deterministic as well as random, results in some kind of outcome. The collection of all possible outcomes is generally called the *sample space* or the *universal space*. An example of the universal space of a deterministic experiment is the distance traveled as a consequence of the application of some force is $[0, \infty)$. On the other hand, for a random experiment of tossing a coin, the sample space consists of the set *{Head, Tail}*. The difference between these two types of experiments is the result of the final outcome. For a stationary object, if the application of a force results in an acceleration of $10m/s^2$, the distance traveled after 60 seconds is known by the formula $s = at^2/2 = 18000m$. That is, given the acceleration and time, the distance is uniquely determined. For a random experiment of coin tossing, the outcome is sometimes a *Head*, and at the other times it is *Tail*.

In this chapter, we will mainly focus on the essential topics of probability which will be required during rest of the book. We begin with the essential elements of probability and discuss the interesting problems using mathematical thinking embedded with in R programs. Thus, we begin with the sets and elementary counting methods and compute probabilities using the software in Section 5.2. Combinatorial aspects with useful examples will be treated in Section 5.3. The subject of *measure theory* is rightly required and we then discuss the core concepts required for the developments unfolding in Section 5.4. Conditional probability, independence, and Bayes formula are dealt with in Sections 5.5 and 5.6. Random variables and their important properties are detailed in Section 5.7. Convergence of random variables and other important sequences of functions of random variables are discussed through Sections 5.9–5.12.

A Course in Statistics with R, First Edition. Prabhanjan Narayanachar Tattar, Suresh Ramaiah and B. G. Manjunath.

Companion Website: www.wiley.com/go/tattar/statistics

We emphasize here that you may sometimes come across phrases such as "*graphical proof*", or "*it follows from the diagram that ...*". In most of these cases, the general statement holds true and admits an analytical proof, which actually means that it is the more mathematical proof that is admitting a cleaner *visual display*. The reader is cautioned here though that such visual displays do not necessarily imply that the mathematical proof is valid and hence we must resist the temptation to generalize statements based on the displays. The spirit adopted in this chapter in particular is to emphasize that probability concepts can be integrated well with a software and that programming may sometimes be viewed as the *e*-version of problem solving skills.

5.2 Sample Space, Set Algebra, and Elementary Probability

The *sample space*, denoted by Ω, is the collection of all possible outcomes associated with a specific experiment or phenomenon. A single coin tossing experiment results in either a head or a tail. The difference between the opening and closing prices of a company's share may be a negative number, zero, or a positive number. A (anti-)virus scan on your computer returns a non-negative integer, whereas a file may either be completely recovered or deleted on a corrupted disk of a file storage system such as hard-drive, pen-drive, etc. It is indeed possible for us to consider experiments with finite possible outcomes in R, and we will begin with a few familiar random experiments and the associated set algebra.

It is important to note that the sample space is uniquely determined, though in some cases we may not know it completely. For example, if the sequence *{Head, Tail, Head, Head}* is observed, the sample space is uniquely determined under binomial and negative binomial probability models. However, it may not be known whether the governing model is binomial or negative binomial. Prof G. Jay Kerns developed the `prob` package, which has many useful functions, including set operators, sample spaces, etc. We will deploy a few of them now.

Example 5.2.1. Tossing Coins: One, Two, ... If we toss a single coin, we have $\Omega = \{H, T\}$, where H denotes the head and T a tail. For the experiment of tossing a coin twice, the sample space is $\Omega = \{HH, HT, TH, TT\}$. The R function `tosscoin` with the option `times` gives us the required sample spaces when we toss one, two, or four coins simultaneously.

```
> tosscoin(times=1); tosscoin(times=2); tosscoin(times=4)
  toss1
1     H
2     T
  toss1 toss2
1     H     H
2     T     H
3     H     T
4     T     T
   toss1 toss2 toss3 toss4
1      H     H     H     H
2      T     H     H     H
3      H     T     H     H
  . . .
15     H     T     T     T
16     T     T     T     T
```

Thus, we can easily obtain the sample space for coin tossing experiments. A further option available in `makespace` for the `tosscoin` returns the probabilities of each element of the sample space which will be taken at a later stage. □

Example 5.2.2. Rolling Die: One, Two, ... Die rolling is a very popular experiment for the Probabilists. If the die has six sides, rolling one die has the sample space $\Omega = \{1, 2, \ldots, 6\}$, whereas rolling two die has the sample space of paired outcomes varying from one to six, that is, $\Omega = \{(i,j)|i,j = 1, 2, \ldots, 6\}$. In R, we can readily see the sample spaces of the die rolling experiments.

```
> rolldie(times=1); rolldie(times=2); rolldie(times=3)
  X1
1  1
2  2
3  3
4  4
5  5
6  6
   X1 X2
1   1  1
2   2  1
3   3  1
    . . .
35  5  6
36  6  6
    X1 X2 X3
1    1  1  1
2    2  1  1
     .   .   .
215  5  6  6
216  6  6  6
> rolldie(times=1,nsides=7) # My die has seven sides!
  X1
1  1
2  2
3  3
4  4
5  5
6  6
7  7
```

The function `rolldie` can roll dice as many times as is required with the option `times` and furthermore it may also deal with die of different numbers of sides, as seen in the option `nsides` in the last part of the previous program. We have of course curtailed the output in the above session. □

Mahmoud (2009) is a recent introduction to the importance of *urn models* in probability. Johnson and Kotz (1977) is a classic account of urn problems. These discrete experiments are of profound interest and are still an active area of research and applications.

Example 5.2.3. Urn Sample Space. Consider an urn which has five balls of red color, three balls of green color, and eight balls of blue color. Suppose we randomly pick one ball from the urn. Note that by definition of the sample space, which is a collection of all possible outcomes, the sample space associated with the experiment is $\Omega = \{\underbrace{Red, \dots, Red}_{5\ times}, \underbrace{Green, \dots, Green}_{3\ times}, \underbrace{Blue, \dots, Blue}_{8\ times}\}$.

Now consider further variants of the problem. First, we draw a ball, note its color, and place it back in the urn. Then we shake up the urn well enough to ensure that the next ball drawn is truly random. Yet another variant of the problem would be to not put the ball back in the draw and draw another one. What will the sample space be now?

The function `urnsamples` will help us to do these tasks. First, we need to carefully define the urn from which we wish to draw the samples. This is achieved using the `rep` function with the option `times`. Next, we use the `urnsamples` to find the sample space from the defined urn and required size, along with the information of whether or not we had placed the ball back in the urn.

```
> Urn <- rep(c("Red","Green","Blue"),times=c(5,3,8))
> urnsamples(x=Urn,size=1)
      out
1     Red

5     Red
6   Green

8   Green
9    Blue

16  Blue
>   urnsamples(x=Urn,size=2,replace=TRUE)
       X1    X2
1      Red   Red
2      Red   Red

135  Blue  Blue
136  Blue  Blue
> urnsamples(x=Urn,size=2,replace=FALSE)
       X1    X2
1      Red   Red
2      Red   Red

119  Blue  Blue
120  Blue  Blue
```

Thus, the function `urnsamples` helps us to obtain the sample space of drawing balls from the urns. □

Example 5.2.4. Card Experiments. A pack of cards contains a set of 13 cards of the 4 suites club, spade, heart, and diamond. Each suit contains cards labeled Ace, 2, 3, ..., 10, Jack, Queen, and King. Depending on the version of the card game being played, the pack may or may not contain two more cards labeled as Joker. Thus, the sample space Ω for the card game is specified as

```
> cbind(cards()[1:13,],cards()[14:26,],cards()[27:39,],
+ cards()[40:52,])
   rank suit rank    suit rank  suit rank  suit
1     2 Club    2 Diamond    2 Heart    2 Spade
2     3 Club    3 Diamond    3 Heart    3 Spade
3     4 Club    4 Diamond    4 Heart    4 Spade
4     5 Club    5 Diamond    5 Heart    5 Spade
5     6 Club    6 Diamond    6 Heart    6 Spade
6     7 Club    7 Diamond    7 Heart    7 Spade
7     8 Club    8 Diamond    8 Heart    8 Spade
8     9 Club    9 Diamond    9 Heart    9 Spade
9    10 Club   10 Diamond   10 Heart   10 Spade
10    J Club    J Diamond    J Heart    J Spade
11    Q Club    Q Diamond    Q Heart    Q Spade
12    K Club    K Diamond    K Heart    K Spade
13    A Club    A Diamond    A Heart    A Spade
> cards(jokers=T)[53:54,] # Jokers Rule, Sorry Mr.Super Man
    rank suit
53 Joker <NA>
54 Joker <NA>
```

The `cards` function along with the `cbind` function helped us to view the pack of 52 cards.□

Note that the sample space may be treated as a super set. It has to be exhaustive, covering all possible outcomes. Loosely speaking we may say that any subset of the sample space is an *event*. Thus, we next consider some set operations, which in the language of probability are events.

Let A, B be two subsets of the sample space Ω. The *union, intersection,* and *complement* operations for sets is defined as follows:

- The *union* of two sets A and B is defined as:

$$A \cup B = \{x | x \in A \ \text{ or } \ x \in B\}.$$

- The *intersection* of two sets A and B is defined as:

$$A \cap B = \{x | x \in A \ \text{ and } \ x \in B\}.$$

- The *complement* of a set A is defined as:

$$A^c = \{x | x \notin A\}.$$

- The *set difference*, or relative complement, of set B and A is defined by

$$B \backslash A = B - A = \{x | x \in B \, \text{and} \, x \notin A\}.$$

Software, and hence R, despite their strengths, will be used to illustrate the above using simple examples.

Example 5.2.5. Basic Set Operations For the Card Sample Space. The basic set operations are illustrated using the sample space for the card pack. The operations `union`, `intersect`, and `setdiff` of R gives us the relevant results. Some of these functions are available in both packages `base` and `prob`. The difference of their functioning across the packages, if any, may be found by the reader.

```
> S <- cards()
> A <- S[8:28,]; B <- S[22:35,]
> union(A,B)
   rank    suit
8     9    Club
9    10    Club

34    9   Heart
35   10   Heart
> intersect(A,B)
   rank    suit
22   10 Diamond
23    J Diamond
24    Q Diamond
25    K Diamond
26    A Diamond
27    2   Heart
28    3   Heart
> setdiff(S,A) # Result is complement of A
   rank  suit
1     2  Club
2     3  Club

51    K Spade
52    A Spade
```

The reader is advised to run the program and investigate the output, since the output has been curtailed here for brevity's sake. □

We will now consider a few introductory problems for computation of probabilities of events, which are also sometimes called *elementary events*. If an experiment has finite possible outcomes and each of the outcomes is as likely as the other, the natural and intuitive way of defining the probability for an event is as follows:

$$P(E) = \frac{\text{number of points in } E}{\text{number of points in } \Omega} = \frac{n(E)}{n(\Omega)},$$

where $n(.)$ denotes the number of elements in the set. The number of elements in a set is also called the *cardinality* of the set.

Example 5.2.6. Tossing Coins. Contd. By applying the above definition, we can compute the probabilities for the events in a coin tossing experiment. Notably, it is fairly straightforward that when we toss a fair coin, the probability of obtaining a head is 1/2, and that at least one head showing up when two coins are tossed is 3/4:

$$P(\{H\}) = \frac{1}{2} = 0.5,$$

$$P(\{HH, HT, TH\}) = \frac{3}{4} = 0.75.$$

However, we would like to use the function `tosscoin` and verify the same. First, the R program will be given followed by its logic.

```
> Omega <- tosscoin(times=1)
> sum(Omega=="H")/nrow(Omega)
[1] 0.5
> Omega2 <- tosscoin(times=2)
> sum(rowSums(Omega2=="H")>0)/nrow(Omega2)
[1] 0.75
```

For the object `Omega`, we first obtained the sample space using `tosscoin`. Now we checked how many of the events favor `H`, that is “Head”, using `sum`. Recollect, or verify if needed, that the function `tosscoin` returns a `data.frame` object, and hence `nrow` returns the total number of events of the sample space. Similarly, we need `rowSums`, and not the simple `sum`, to obtain our second answer. In the most likely case of the reader wondering if this tedious programmatic approach is feasible, let us ask the probability of obtaining heads in the range 4 to 7 when 10 coins are tossed. Now, using the arguments used so far, it would be really difficult. However, we can now write two lines of R code and get the answer.

```
> Omega10 <- tosscoin(times=10)
> sum((rowSums(Omega10=="H")>=4) & (rowSums(Omega10=="H")<=7))/
+ nrow(Omega10)
[1] 0.7734375
```

□

Example 5.2.7. Rolling Die. Contd. For the rolling of die experiment, the probability of obtaining an odd number is

$$P(\{1,3,5\}) = \frac{3}{6} = 0.5.$$

Now, how do we get the answer from the `rolldie` function? An integer x is odd if `x %% 2` returns 1, and this logic will be exploited to get the answer for the probability of a die to return an odd number. Thus, the next small R program returns the required answer.

```
> Omega_{R}oll1 <- rolldie(times=1)
> sum(Omega_Roll1%%2 ==1)/nrow(Omega_Roll1)
[1] 0.5
```

Frequently, we may be interested in some variations or transformations of the sample space. For example, consider the sample space arising as a consequence of rolling two dice. Here, the sample space is the collection of the couplets $\Omega = \{(i,j)|i,j = 1,2, \dots ,6\}$, and it has 36 points. Now, if we were to consider the sum of the numbers on both dice, the relevant sample space is $\Omega' = \{2,3, \dots ,11,12\}$. The number of elements in the modified sample space is now 11. How do we obtain such a sample space for the `rolldie` function? Let us work out how to answer the probability of the events in the modified sample space.

```
> S_Die <- rolldie(times=2)
> table(rowSums(S_Die))/nrow(S_Die)
      2       3              10      11
0.02778 0.05556         0.08333 0.05556
     12
0.02778
```

For a clearer understanding of the program here, note that the `table` function gives the frequency of the repeated values of a vector or a data.frame. Thus, if you first run `names(table(rowSums(S_Die)))` and `table(rowSums(S_Die))`, all doubts should be addressed. Now solve the problem related to `rolldie` in the exercise section to complete your understanding of the roll die experiment. □

It is also the case that even for elementary events, all the outcomes are not necessarily equally likely. The next example is a point in case.

Example 5.2.8. Thirteenth of a Month. We have been asked a question: What is the probability that the 13th of a month is a Friday? Assuming that the month is an arbitrary month, we would like to believe that there is no effect on the frequency of weekdays in a month. If simplicity is required, we will treat each month as February, which has exactly four frequencies of each weekday. A consequence of this simplicity is that our answer will be that the probability of the 13th of the month being a Friday is $1/7$. It turns out that a perfect cycle of the human calender is 400 years. Thus, for each month of these 400 years, we need to find the frequency of the weekdays on the 13th of that month. This is a daunting task! However, there is a calender in every laptop, and also in any good software such as R. Thus, the next module returns us the desired frequency of the weekdays for the 13th of the month.

```
> fullyears <- 1601:2000
> months <- 1:12
> testthirteenth <- NULL
> for(i in 1:length(fullyears)) {
+ for(j in 1:12){
+ testthirteenth <- c(testthirteenth,weekdays(as.Date(paste(
+ fullyears[i],"/", months[j],"/13",sep=""),"%Y/%m/%d")))
+ }
+ }
> table(testthirteenth)
testthirteenth
  Friday    Monday  Saturday    Sunday  Thursday   Tuesday Wednesday
     688       685       684       687       684       685       687
```

This detailed R program requires some discussion. The cycle of 400 years is declared in the variable `fullyears`, and the 12 months are entered in `months`. The two loops are coded in such a way that for each year the 12 months are checked for the weekday of the 13th. That is, for each month, we prepare the 13th day with the code `as.Date(paste(fullyears[i],"/",months[j],"/13",sep=""),"%Y/%m/%d")`. Next, its weekday is extracted with the function `weekdays` from the `base` package. This output is then stored in the character vector `testthirteenth`. Finally, for $400 \times 12 = 4800$ months, we obtain the frequency of the weekdays with `table(testthirteenth)`.

The above output shows that Friday has the maximum frequency, and hence it is safe to conclude that the probability of the 13th of a month being a Friday is more likely than any other weekday. More details of this problem may be obtained on Pages 26–27 of Parzen (1960), and we note that this problem was first solved in 1933! □

Example 5.2.9. Laplace Probability of Sunrise. Sometimes we find it useful to define the probability of events using empirical evidence. As an example, if we observed 568 heads out of 1014 throws of a coin, the empirical probability of a head is defined by $568/1014 = 0.5602$. Now, suppose that we have recorded the number of times the sun rises on N days, and we wish to predict the probability of sun rise for the day $(N + 1)$. The empirical definition of probability gives the answer as $N/N = 1$. Laplace suggested that for events which have occurred *M-out-of-N* times, the probability of that event occurring on the $(N + 1)$-th occasion is defined as $(M + 1)/(N + 2)$. Thus, if we have observed the sun to rise on 6 out of 6 days, the probability that the sun will rise on the 7th day will be $(6 + 1)/(6 + 2) = 7/8 = 0.875$.

At the outset, this answer may appear stupid! Nevertheless, this answer has far-reaching consequences, and we will arrive at it in at least one important context. Its importance is highlighted by the fact that this solution is sometimes known as *Laplace smoothing*. □

?match, library(help="prob")

5.3 Counting Methods

The events of interest may unfold in a number of different ways. We need mechanisms to find in how many different ways an event can occur. As an example, if we throw two die and count the sum of the numbers that appear on the two faces, the sum of 8 can occur in six different ways, viz., (6,2), (2,6), (5,3), (3,5), (4,4), (4,4). In this section, we will discuss some results which will be useful for a large class of problems and theorems.

The seasoned probabilist Kai Lai Chung has registered the importance of the role of permutations and combinations in a probability course. Over a period of years, he has obtained different answers for the number of ways a man can dress differently from a combination of three shirts and two ties. The answers vary from $3 + 2$ and 3×2 to 3^2 and 2^3. See page 46, Chung and AitSahlia (2003).

Theorem 5.3.1 *If an experiment consists of two parts, and if part I can occur in m ways, and part II in n ways, the experiment can be performed in $m \times n$ different ways.* □

Example 5.3.1. Basic Set Operations For the Card Sample Space. Contd. Consider a pack of 54 cards which contains the jokers. If two cards are picked, and we are interested in the event that there is one joker and one spade, the above theorem helps us to find the total number of ways we can have this arrangement. A joker can be picked in 2 ways and a spade in 13 different ways. Thus, $13 \times 2 = 26$ is the number of different ways of selecting a joker and a spade. We do not have to use R for every computation! □

A natural extension of the above experiment is shown by the next result.

Theorem 5.3.2 Fundamental Theorem of Counting. *Suppose that an experiment consists of k parts. Let the ith part occur in $m_i, i = 1, 2, \ldots, k$, number of ways. Then the experiment can be performed in $\prod_{i=1}^{k} m_i$ different ways.* □

Example 5.3.2. Basic Set Operations for the Card Sample Space. Contd. In a continuation of this example, suppose that now we are drawing four cards instead of two. We need to find the number of ways that the event consisting of exactly one spade, one joker, one diamond, and one heart occurs. In light of the above result, this event can occur in $2 \times 13 \times 13 \times 13 = 4394$ different ways. □

At the outset, the fundamental theorem of counting may appear very simple. Its strength will be used to derive the total number of ways a task can be done in the next subsection.

5.3.1 Sampling: The Diverse Ways

Sampling from a population can be carried out in many different ways. Suppose that we have m balls in an urn, and each ball carries a unique label along with it. Without loss of generality, we can label the balls 1 to m. In this case we say that the balls are ordered. If the label of the balls carry no meaning, or are not available, that is, indistinguishable, we are dealing with sampling problems with unordered units.

5.3.1.1 Sampling with Replacement and with Ordering

Consider the situation where we draw n units sequentially from m units. Before each draw, the balls in the urn are shaken well so that any ordered ball has the same chance of being selected. At each stage after the draw, the label of the drawn unit is noted and the order of labeled units is duly recorded before placing it back in the urn. Thus, if a_j denotes the label of the unit drawn on the jth occasion, we have an ordered n- tuple $(a_1, a_2, \ldots, a_n)$, with a_j taking a value between $1, 2, \ldots, m$, $\forall j = 1, 2, \ldots, n$. The fundamental counting theorem then gives the answer of doing this task in

$$m \times m \times \ldots \times m = m^n, \tag{5.1}$$

distinct ways.

5.3.1.2 Sampling without Replacement and with Ordering

Suppose that the experiment remains the same as above, with a variation being that the drawn ball is not put back in the urn. That is, at the first draw we have m units to choose from. At the second draw, we have $m - 1$ units to choose from, at the third draw $m - 2$ units, and so on. Thus, at the nth draw, we have $m - n + 1$ units for drawing the unit. Thus, sampling with replacement from ordered units can be performed in $m \times (m - 1) \times \ldots \times (m - n + 1)$ distinct ways. Since we cannot draw more than m units among m, we have the constraint of $n \leq m$. We have again applied the fundamental theorem of counting. Let us introduce a notation here of continued product: $(m)_n$ to denote $m \times (m - 1) \times \ldots \times (m - n + 1)$. That is

$$(m)_n = m \times (m - 1) \times \ldots \times (m - n + 1), 0 \leq n \leq m. \tag{5.2}$$

In popular terms, this is the *permutation* of n units sampled from a pool of m units. An interesting case is the permutation of obtaining all the m units. This experiment is about drawing all the units without replacement from the urn and is given by

$$m! = (m)_m = m \times (m - 1) \times \ldots \times 2 \times 1.$$

To see the behavior of the number of ways we can possibly draw, let us look at the permutation of drawing 1 to 12 units.

```
> sapply(1:12,factorial)
[1]   1 2 6 24 120 720 5040  40320 362880
[10] 3628800   39916800 479001600
```

The `sapply` function ensures that the `factorial` function is applied on each integer 1 to12.

5.3.1.3 Sampling without Replacement and without Ordering

We now consider a sampling variation of the previous experiment. In this experiment we do not record the order of the occurrence of the sampling unit. Alternatively, we can think of this experiment as seeing the final result of sampling the desired number of n units. We have seen that a sample of n units can be obtained in $n!$ different ways. Furthermore, the number of distinct ways of obtaining a sample of n units from m is given by the continued product $(m)_n$. Thus, the number of ways of obtaining an unordered sample of n units by sampling without replacement from m units is $(m)_n/n!$. By multiplying the numerator and denominator by $(m - n)!$, we get the desired result

$$\begin{aligned}\binom{m}{n} &= \frac{(m)_n(m-n)!}{n!(m-n)!} \\ &= \frac{m(m-1)\ldots(m-n+1)(m-n)\ldots 2.1}{n!(m-n)!} \\ &= \frac{m!}{n!(m-n)!}.\end{aligned} \tag{5.3}$$

Table 5.1 Diverse Sampling Techniques

	ordered = True	ordered = False
replace = True	m^n	$\frac{(m-1-n)!}{(m-1)!n!}$
replace = False	$\frac{m!}{(m-n)!}$	$\binom{m}{n}$

5.3.1.4 Sampling with Replacement and without Ordering

In this setup, we draw n balls one after another, replacing the drawn ball in the urn before the next draw. During this process, we register the frequencies of the labels drawn with possible repetitions without storing the order of occurrence. Note that in this case m may be less than n.

We summarize all the results in the table above.

Example 5.3.3. Random Sampling Numbers. Feller (1968), pages 31–2. Consider the population of 10 digits, $0, 1, \ldots, 9$. Suppose that we draw five digits, with replacement, randomly from it and wish to compute the probability of all the five digits being different. By earlier discussion, this probability is easily seen to be $p = (10)_5/10^5$, which on evaluation gives the answer, in R, as

```
> prod(10:6)/10^{5}
[1] 0.3024
```

Feller argues this probability through the use of *mathematical tables*. Let us begin with his discussion on the use of digits of the irrational number e. Consider the first 800 digits of e. The reader may obtain the first 2 million digits of e at http://apod.nasa.gov/htmltest/gifcity/e.2mil, and we too have obtained the values from it. The 800 digits can be grouped into 160 units, each unit consisting of a succession of 5 digits. Group the 160 units into 16 batches, with each batch containing 10 groups of 5 digits of the irrational number e. Finally, find the frequency of numbers in which the block has all distinct digits. We will first discuss the program for Fellers arguments.

```
> data(e800)
> dis_count <- NULL
> for(i in 1:16){
+       temp <- e800[(10*(i-1)+1):(10*i),]
+       dis_count[i] <- 0
+       for(j in 1:nrow(temp)){
+    if(length(unique(as.numeric(temp[j,])))==5) dis_count[i]
+ <- dis_count[i]+1
+ }
+ }
> dis_count # Matches exactly the numbers on Page 32 of
+ Feller (1968)
```

```
 [1] 3 1 3 4 4 1 4 4 4 2 3 1 5 4 6 3
> mean(dis_count)/10
[1] 0.325
```

Let us understand this program. The dataset `e800` consists of the first 800 digits of the irrational number e. The object `dis_count` represents the number of times we have unique digits among the five digits in a batch of ten such collections, and this is obtained through the loop `for(j in 1:nrow(temp))`. The search is carried out for all the 16 blocks in the loop `for(i in 1:16)`. Thus, the average of `dis_count` returns the probability of `0.325`, which is closer to the theoretical probability of `0.3024`. □

Example 5.3.4. Probability of *n* Balls Occupying *n* Cells. Consider an experiment where n balls are randomly placed among n cells and the problem is computation of the probability that each cell contains one ball. We can place n balls in n cells in $n!$ ways and the total number of ways in which the n balls can be placed among the n cells is n^n. Hence, the probability of the event of n randomly placed balls occupying the n cells is

$$P(n \text{ balls occupying } n \text{ cells}) = \frac{n!}{n^n}.$$

Consider $n = 10$. The small R program is then as follows.

```
> n <- 1:10
> prob_n_out_of_n <- factorial(n)/n^{n}
> plot(n,prob_n_out_of_n,type="h")
> title("Probability of All Cells Being Occupied")
```

The plot is given in Part A of Figure 5.1. □

Example 5.3.5. Probability of *n* Passengers Leaving at Different Floors. A building has $n = 10$ floors, excluding the ground floor, so let us suppose that the lift capacity is 10 people. We begin at the ground floor. The event of interest is that no two people leave at any given floor. Let us assume that we have 1 to 10 people at the beginning of the lift. The probability, starting with $r \leq n$ people, of the event is then given by

$$P(\text{all } r \text{ people leave at different floors}) = \frac{(n)_r}{n^r}$$

The R program below gives an interesting plot, Part B of Fiqure 5.1.

```
> n <- 10 # Floors
> r <- 1:10 # Number of Passengers
> prob_distinct_fn <- function(n,r) prod(n:(n-r+1))/n^{r}
> prob_all_distinct <- sapply(r,prob_distinct_fn,n=n)
> plot(r,prob_all_distinct,"h")
> title("B: Probability of Passengers Leaving at Distinct Floors")
```

Compare and contrast the two diagrams given in Figure 5.1. □

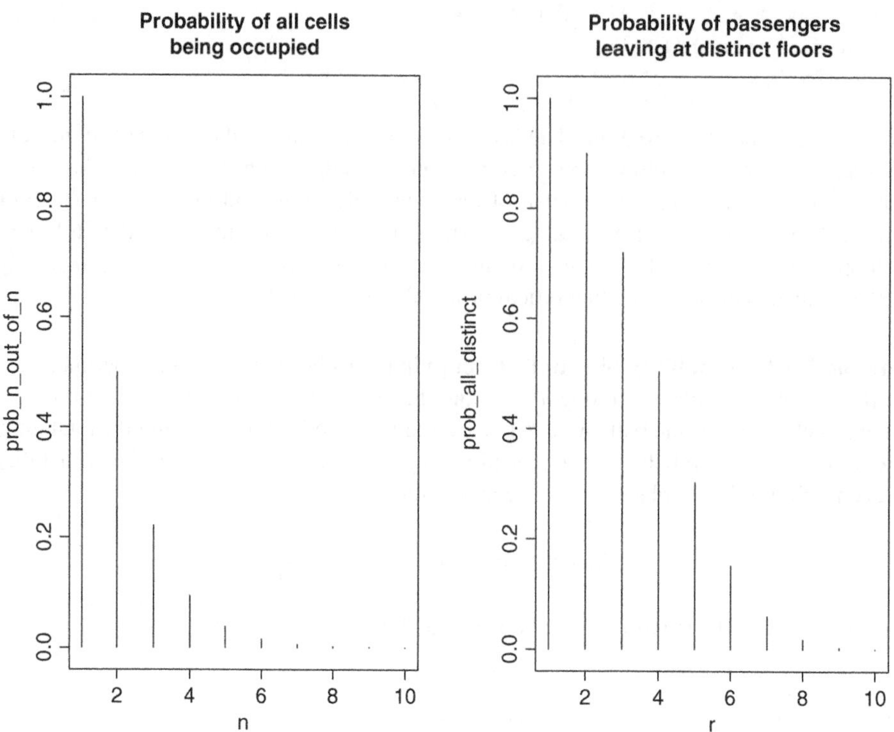

Figure 5.1 A Graph of Two Combinatorial Problems

5.3.2 The Binomial Coefficients and the Pascals Triangle

The *Pascal's triangle* is a simplistic and useful triangle for obtaining the *binomial coefficients*. To begin with, consider the following relationship:

$$\binom{m}{n} = \binom{m-1}{n-1} + \binom{m-1}{n}, 0 \leq n \leq m.$$

This relationship says that to obtain $\binom{m}{n}$, we can obtain it as the sum of ways of selecting n and $n-1$ objects from $m-1$. Thus, we can move to higher levels using the quantities at one level below it. This leads to the famous Pascal's triangle. A short program is given below to obtain the triangle.

```
> pascal <- function(n){
+ if(n<=1) pasc=1
+ if(n==2) pasc=c(1,1)
+ if(n>2){
+ pasc <- c(1,1)
+ j <- 2
+ while(j<n){
+       j <- j+1
+       pasc=c(1,as.numeric(na.omit(filter(pasc,rep(1,2)))),1)
+ }
```

```
+ }
+ return(pasc)
+ }
> sapply(1:7, pascal)
[[1]]
[1] 1
[[2]]
[1] 1 1
[[3]]
[1] 1 2 1
[[4]]
[1] 1 3 3 1
[[5]]
[1] 1 4 6 4 1
[[6]]
[1]  1  5 10 10  5  1
[[7]]
[1]  1  6 15 20 15  6  1
```

With the basics of combinatorics with us, we are now equipped to develop R solutions for some interesting problems in probability.

5.3.3 Some Problems Based on Combinatorics

Feller (1968) has a very deep influence on almost all the Probabilists. Diaconis and Holmes (2002) considered some problems from Feller's Volume 1 in the Bayesian paradigm. Particularly, we consider two of those three problems here: (i) The Birthday Problem, and (ii) The Banach Match Box Problem. The problems selected here serve the point that probability on some occasions can be very counter-intuitive. A survey of some of these problems may also be found in Mosteller (1962).

Example 5.3.6. The Birthday Problem. Suppose we have a group of k people. In the birthday problem, we have $n = 365$ cells. Thus, the total number of ways of arranging the k birthdays is 365^k different ways. The number of ways in which all the k birthdays are different is then the same as *k-out-of-n* permutations, that is, ${}^{365}P_k$. Hence, the probability of k different birthdays is ${}^{365}P_k/365^k$, the complement of which gives the probability of at least two birthdays being the same is $1-{}^{365}P_k/365^k$.

Williams (2001) has put forth his own experience of the *birthday problem* in the classroom:

> **True Story**. I learnt the value of statistics early. In a lecture to students, I had mentioned the result in Subsection 13O that if you have 23 people in a room then there is a probability of more than $\frac{1}{2}$ that two of them have the same birthday. One student came to see me that evening to argue that 23 wasn't anywhere near enough. We went through
>
> (*Continued*)

> the proof several times; but he kept insisting that there must be flaw in the basic theory. After some considerable time, I said. "Look, there must be 23 people still awake in College. Let's ask them their birthdays. To start with, when's yours?" "April 9th", he said. I replied (truthfully!) "So's mine".

The next R program gives us the birthday probabilities where we compute the probability of obtaining the same birthday if there are 2, 5, 10, 20, …, 50, people in a classroom.

```
> k <- c(2,5,10,20,30,40,50)
> probdiff <- c(); probat2same <- c()
> for(i in 1:length(k))  {
+    kk <- k[i]
+    probdiff[i] <- prod(365:(365-kk+1))/(365^{k}k)
+    probat2same[i] <- 1- prod(365:(365-kk+1))/(365^{k}k)
+                            }
> plot(k,probat2same,xlab="Number of Students in Classroom",
+       ylab="Birthday Probability",col="green","l")
> lines(k,probdiff,col="red","l")
> legend(10,1,"Birthdays are not same",box.lty=NULL)
> legend(30,.7,"Birthdays are same",,box.lty=NULL)
> title("A: The Birthday Problem")
```

The R numeric vectors `probdiff` and `probat2same` respectively compute ${}^{365}P_k$ and $1-{}^{365}P_k$. The code `prod(365:(365-kk + 1))/(365^kk)` gives ${}^{365}P_k$, and by using it we easily obtain `probat2same`. The `plot` functions, `lines`, `legend`, and `title` are simple to follow.

The birthday probabilities are summarized in Table 5.2. It can be seen from the table that we need to have just 50 people in a classroom to be almost sure of finding a pair of birthday mates. Part A of Figure 5.2 gives the visual display of the table probabilities. The meeting point of the complementary curves at 0.5 gives `k=23` as claimed in Williams (2001). □

Table 5.2 Birthday Match Probabilities

Size k	Probability of Different Birthdays	Probability of at least Two Same Birthdays
2	0.9973	0.0027
5	0.9729	0.0271
10	0.8831	0.1169
20	0.5886	0.4114
30	0.2937	0.7063
40	0.1088	0.8912
50	0.0296	0.9704

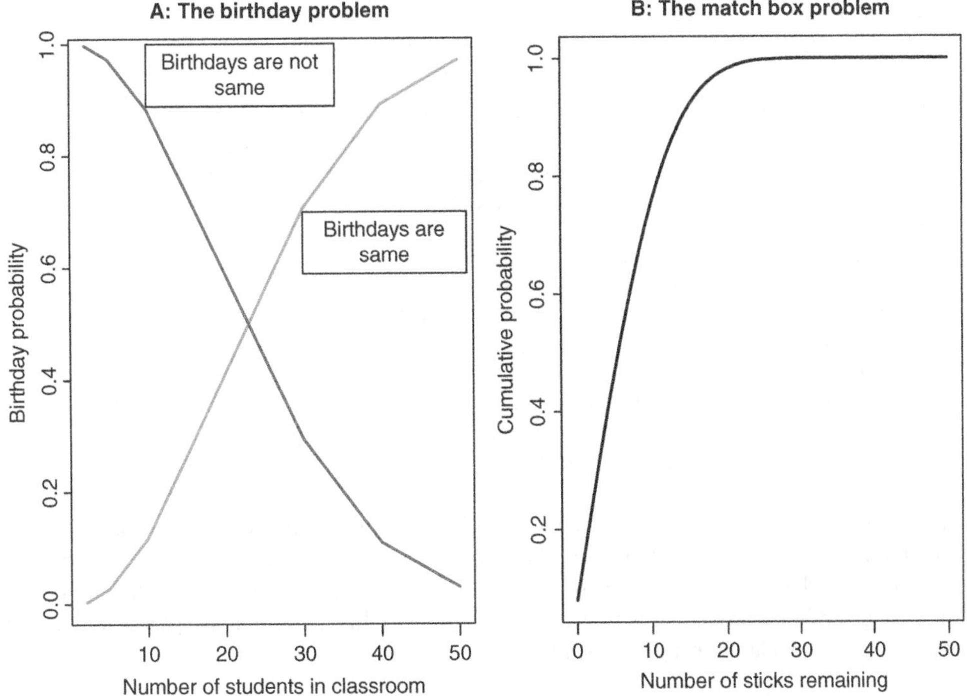

Figure 5.2 Birthday Match and Banach Match Box Probabilities

Example 5.3.7. The Banach Match Box Problem. This problem is credited to the famous mathematician Stephan Banach. Suppose that the mathematician keeps two match boxes, one each in the right and left pockets. For simplicity, we assume that both the match boxes have an equal number of sticks in the beginning. Whenever required, a match box is randomly selected from the pockets and used and then put back in its place. We are interested in finding the number of sticks remaining in the other box on the occasion of finding one of the boxes empty.

Suppose that each match box has 50 sticks at the beginning. Since each match box is selected with equal probability, we intuitively believe that when one of the match boxes is found empty, the other match box must also be nearly empty. The intuition further says that the probability of the other match box being nearly empty must be very high. If we are hard pressed to put our belief in numbers, we may say that the probability of the non-empty match box containing 5 or less sticks is very high, say 0.7, and that the probability of it having more than 5 sticks is less than 0.3.

Mathematically, the theory unfolds as follows. A probabilist has two match boxes in each of his two pockets, each containing N sticks. A stick is randomly selected from either the right or the left match box and is then used. We are interested in knowing the number of sticks left in the other match box when one of the two boxes is found to be empty. Let E denote the number of k sticks in a box when the other box is found empty. The well-known result about the probability of E is that

$$P(E) = \binom{2N-k}{N}\left(\frac{1}{2}\right)^{2N-k}. \tag{5.4}$$

The combinatorial probabilities can be obtained by the following R program:

```
> match_prob <- function(x) choose(2*N-x,N)*2^{-(2*N-x)}
> #Verifing Fellers Match Box Probabilities on Page 166
> N <- 50
> round(sapply(0:30,match_prob),6)
 [1] 0.079589 0.079589      0.067902 0.063568
 [9] 0.058783 0.053672      0.027677 0.023171
[17] 0.019082 0.015447      0.004041 0.002901
[25] 0.002034 0.001392
> plot(0:50,cumsum(sapply(0:50,match_prob)),xlab="Number of Sticks
+ Remaining", ylab="Cumulative Probability","l")
> title("The Match Box Problem")
```

The function `match_prob` computes the probability given by Equation 5.4. The `plot` function attempts to give the cumulative probability as discussed earlier, the code `cumsum` and its arguments. The cumulative probability plot of the number of sticks against the number of sticks is given in Figure 5.2. It is thus again a surprise to the reader that the plot is almost the exact reverse of what their intuition said. □

We will now digress a little here and have a close look at the failure of the definition of probability discussed thus far. It seems to our intuition that if $P(\Omega) = 1$, the probability for any subset $A \subset \Omega$ must exist. That is, any subset A must have a well defined *measure*. Ross and Pekoz (2007) consider a very elegant example of a subset A for which the measure cannot be defined in any rational way. Suppose that we begin at the top of a unit circle and take a step of one unit radian in a counter-clockwise direction. If required, we may perform more than one loop. The task is then computation of the probability of returning to the point from which we started our journey. Suppose that it takes a steps and b loops to return to the top of the circle. This implies that $a = 2b\pi$. As π is an irrational number, it cannot be expressed as the ratio of two integers $a/2b$. Thus, the probability of returning to the start point cannot be *measured*.

This and some other limitations of the definition of probability considered up to now are overcome using the Kolmogorov's definition of probability, which is based on Measure Theory. We will leave out the details of these *important discussions*!

?prod, ?choose, ?factorial, ?sample

5.4 Probability: A Definition

We will begin with a few definitions and lemmas.

5.4.1 *The Prerequisites*

Let us consider a class of sets of Ω, say $\{A_n\}_{n=0}^{\infty}$. The sequence $\{A_n\}_{n=0}^{\infty}$ is said to be *monotone increasing* if $A_n \subseteq A_{n+1}$ for each n. The sequence is said to be *monotone decreasing* if

$A_n \supseteq A_{n+1}$ for each n. We introduce two sequences *infimum* inf and *supremum* sup as below:

$$\inf_{k\geq n} A_k := \bigcap_{k=n}^{\infty} A_k,$$

$$\sup_{k\geq n} A_k := \bigcup_{k=n}^{\infty} A_k. \quad (5.5)$$

The symbol := is used to convey that the quantity on the left-hand side is by definition equal to that on the right-hand side. It is easier to see that the inf sequence is *monotone increasing sequence*, whereas the sup sequence is a *monotone decreasing sequence*. We further define sequences lim inf and lim sup as follows:

$$\lim \inf_{k\geq n} A_k := \bigcup_{n=1}^{\infty}\bigcap_{k=n}^{\infty} A_k,$$

$$\lim \sup_{k\geq n} A_k := \bigcap_{n=1}^{\infty}\bigcup_{k=n}^{\infty} A_k. \quad (5.6)$$

Definition 5.4.1 Limit of a Sequence. *Consider a sequence of sets $\{A_n\}_{n=1}^{\infty}$, with $A_n \in \Omega, \forall n$. We say that the* limit of the sequence $\{A_n\}_{n=1}^{\infty}$ *exists if*

$$\lim_{n\to\infty} \inf_{k\geq n} A_k = \lim_{n\to\infty} \sup_{k\geq n} A_k = A, \quad (say). \quad (5.7)$$

Example 5.4.1. Basic Set Operations. Let $A, B \in \Omega$ be any two arbitrary sets. Define

$$A_n = \begin{cases} A, & \text{if} \quad n = 1, 3, 5, \ldots, \\ B, & \text{if} \quad n = 2, 4, 6, \ldots. \end{cases}$$

By definition, it is easier to see that for $k \geq 1$, $\inf_{k\geq n} A_k = A \cap B$, whereas $\sup_{k\geq n} A_k = A \cup B$. Furthermore, the lim inf and lim sup are respectively $\lim \inf_{k\geq n} A_k = A \cap B$, and $\lim \sup_{k\geq n} A_k = A \cup B$. This implies for the sequence $\{A_n\}$ to have a limit, we must have $A \cap B = A \cup B$, which is possible if $A = B$. We attempt to write a small R program to illustrate the concepts here.

```
> # Illustrating limsup and liminf using R
> Omega <- letters
> A <- letters[1:5]; B <- letters[3:10]
> #n= 1, 2, ...
> n <- 1000 #We can't have infinity, so lets do with large n
> liminfsequence <- NULL; limsupsequence <- NULL
> An <- list() # Obtaining the An's
> for(i in 1:n){
+   if(i%%2 == 1) An[[i]] <- A else An[[i]] <- B
+ }
> # Obtaining the Bn's and Cn's
> Bn <- list()
> Cn <- list()
> for(i in 1:n){
+     Bn[[i]] <- An[[i]]
```

```
+      Cn[[i]] <- An[[i]]
+      for(j in (i+1):n){
+    Bn[[i]] <- intersect(Bn[[i]],An[[j]])
+    Cn[[i]] <- union(Cn[[i]],An[[j]])
+ }
+ }
Error in An[[j]] : subscript out of bounds
> #Purely from programming point of view ignore Bn[[n]] and Cn[[n]]
> for(i in 1:(n-1)){
+      liminfsequence <- Bn[[i]]
+      limsupsequence <- Cn[[i]]
+      for(j in (i+1):n){
+    liminfsequence <- union(liminfsequence,Bn[[i]])
+    limsupsequence <- intersect(limsupsequence,Cn[[j]])
+ }
+ }
> liminfsequence
[1] "c" "d" "e"
> limsupsequence
[1] "c" "d" "e" "f" "g" "h" "i" "j"
```

A purist may criticize the above program for incorrectly carrying out the first step of obtaining $\inf_{k\geq n} A_k$ in an erroneous way. The way we look at this criticism is that the steps carried out here are in the spirit of a *simulation study* for asymptotic results. In neither case, we never really reach ∞. On the other hand, this simple program (if the reader agrees!) illustrates some nice points, such as the fact that $\lim \inf_{k\geq n} A_k \subseteq \lim \sup_{k\geq n} A_k$. To see this point, experiment with different As and Bs. Of course, we have restricted ourselves to the case where the A_ks are a finite discrete set. □

Example 5.4.2. Limsum and Liminf for a Sequence of Sets. Consider a sequence of sets $\{A_n\}_{n=1}^{\infty}$ defined as follows:

$$A_n = \begin{cases} (-1/n, 1], & n = 1, 3, 5, \dots, \\ (-1, 1/n], & n = 2, 4, 6, \dots. \end{cases}$$

Here we need to consider two cases for computing the limsup and liminf. Consider first the case when n begins with an even number. Here $\cap_{k=n}^{\infty} A_k$

$$\cap_{k=n}^{\infty} A_k = \left(-1, \frac{1}{n}\right] \cap \left(\frac{-1}{n+1}, 1\right] \cap \left(-1, \frac{1}{n+2}\right] + \dots = \{0\},$$

whereas $\cup_{k=n}^{\infty} A_k$ is

$$\cup_{k=n}^{\infty} A_k = \left(-1, \frac{1}{n}\right] \cup \left(\frac{-1}{n+1}, 1\right] \cup \left(-1, \frac{1}{n+2}\right] + \dots = (-1, 1].$$

This leads to the liminf and limsup as $\cup_{n=1}^{\infty} \cap_{k=n}^{\infty} A_k = 0$, whereas $\cap_{n=1}^{\infty} \cup_{k=n}^{\infty} A_k = (-1, 1]$. If n begins with an odd number, the conclusion does not change, and this exercise is for the reader to verify. Hence, the limit does not exist for this sequence of sets. □

Definition 5.4.2 Field. *Let Ω be the sample space and consider a non-empty class of subsets of Ω, denoted by $\mathcal{F}$. We say that $\mathcal{F}$ is a* field *if it is closed under complementation and finite intersection, that is,*

1. $\Omega \in \mathcal{F}$.
2. $A \in \mathcal{F} \Rightarrow A^c \in \mathcal{F}$.
3. $A, B \in \mathcal{F} \Rightarrow A \cap B \in \mathcal{F}$.

It is also common to refer to the couplet $(\Omega, \mathcal{F})$ as a field. It may be easily proved that a field is also closed under finite union.

Example 5.4.3. A List of Fields. We need to verify that a class of sets $\mathcal{F}$ satisfies the three criteria of field in Definition 5.4.2 if it is to be a field. It is easy to see that the examples below are indeed fields.

1. Let Ω be any set. Then (ϕ, Ω) is a field which is also called the *trivial field*, where ϕ is the null set.
2. For an arbitrary set Ω, the collection of all subsets of Ω is a field. This field is referred to as the *power set*.
3. For the set Ω, the collection $\mathcal{F}_A := \{\phi, \Omega, A, A^c\}$, for any subset $A \subset \Omega$, is an example of a field.
4. Let $\mathcal{F}_1$ and $\mathcal{F}_2$ be any two fields of Ω. Then $\mathcal{F} = \mathcal{F}_1 \cap \mathcal{F}_2$, the intersection of two fields also results in a field. It is to be noted that an arbitrary intersections of field is also a field.
5. For a set Ω, the collections $\mathcal{F}_A := \{A, A^c, \phi, \Omega\}$ and $\mathcal{F}_B := \{B, B^c, \phi, \Omega\}$ are fields. However, the union $\mathcal{F}_A \cup \mathcal{F}_B = \{A, A^c, B, B^c, \phi, \Omega\}$ is not a field since $A \cup B$ is not in the class of unions.

A useful general class of field is developed next. □

Definition 5.4.3 Minimal Field. *Let $\mathcal{F}$ be any arbitrary collection of sets Ω. Let $\mathcal{F}_\alpha$ be a collection of fields, each of which contains $\mathcal{F}$. Then we define the* minimal field *by*

$$\mathcal{F}(\mathcal{A}) = \cap_\alpha \mathcal{F}_\alpha.$$

In plain words, the minimal field is the least collection of sets containing $\mathcal{F}$, which is a field.

Example 5.4.4. The Minimal Field of a Partition. A collection of sets is called a *partition* of Ω if the collection is mutually exclusive and exhaustive. That is, we say that the collection $\{A_i\}_{i=1}^n$ is a partition of Ω if $A_i \cap A_{i'} = \phi$ and $\sum_{i=1}^n A_i = \Omega$. A common practice in the case of mutually exclusive sets is to denote the union with a sum, that is, $\sum_{i=1}^n A_i = \cup_{i=1}^n A_i$. It is a straightforward exercise to verify that the collection $\{\phi, A_1, A_2, \ldots, A_n, A_1 + A_2, A_1 + A_3, \ldots, A_{n-1} + A_n, A_1 + A_2 + A_3, \ldots, A_{n-2} + A_{n-1} + A_n, \ldots, \Omega\}$ is a field. □

Fields need a generalization and especially in the case of countably infinite or continuous set Ω.

Definition 5.4.4 σ-field. *Let Ω be the sample space and consider a non-empty class of subsets of Ω, denoted by $\mathcal{F}$. We say that $\mathcal{F}$ is a σ-field if it is closed under complementation and countable union, that is,*

1. $\Omega \in \mathcal{F}$.
2. $A \in \mathcal{F} \Rightarrow A^c \in \mathcal{F}$.
3. $A_1, A_2, \ldots \in \mathcal{F} \Rightarrow \cup_{i=1}^{\infty} A_i \in \mathcal{F}$.

The couplet $(\Omega, \mathcal{F})$ is sometimes called the σ-field.

Example 5.4.5. A List of σ-fields. The reader may easily verify that each of the following collection of sets is an example of a σ-field.

1. If a collection $\mathcal{F}$ contains finite number of sets, and is also a field, then the collection is a σ-field too.
2. The intersection of an arbitrary number of σ-fields results in a σ-field.
3. If a collection $\mathcal{F}$ is a σ-field, it is possible to show that the lim sup and lim inf of any sequence is also contained in the σ-field.

A useful class of σ-fields will be taken up next. □

As earlier, we can define the minimal σ-field as an extension of the minimal field. There is an important class of σ-field, which will be defined now.

Definition 5.4.5 Borel σ-field. *Let $\Omega = \mathbb{R}$, $\mathbb{R}$ being the real line, and consider the class of sets $C = (-\infty, x], x \in \mathbb{R}$. Define $\sigma(C) \equiv \mathcal{B}(\mathbb{R})$ as the minimal σ-field of C. Then $\mathcal{B}(\mathbb{R})$ is called the* Borel *of subsets of* $\mathbb{R}$.

It may be verified that the Borel σ-field consists of the intervals, for all $a, b \in \mathbb{R}$, of the following types:

- $(-\infty, a]$
- (a, ∞)
- (a, b)
- $(a, b]$
- $[a, b)$
- $[a, \infty)$

The definition of $\mathcal{B}(\mathbb{R})$ may be extended to $\mathbb{R}^n$ and the reader may refer to Chung (2001). Starting with the sample space Ω, a general class of sets $\mathcal{F}$ has been defined. Next a formal definition of a *measure* is required.

Definition 5.4.6 Measure. *Let $(\Omega, \mathcal{F})$ be a σ-field. A function μ from $\mathcal{F}$ to the extended real line, including the positive and negative infinite numbers, is said to be a* measure *if it satisfies the following properties:*

1. *For any $A \in \mathcal{F}$, $\mu(A) \geq 0$.*
2. *For a collection of countable sets $\{A_n\}_{n=1}^{\infty}$ of pairwise disjoint sets in $\mathcal{F}$, the following is satisfied:*

$$\mu(\cup_{n=1}^{\infty} A_n) = \sum_{n=1}^{\infty} \mu(A_n).$$

3. *For an empty set $\phi \in \mathcal{F}$, $\mu(\phi) = 0$.*

Let us now look at two important types of *measures*.

Example 5.4.6. The Counting Measure. Consider a countable set Ω and let $\mathcal{F}$ be the collection of all possible subsets of Ω, and hence $\mathcal{F}$ is a σ-field. Define the *counting measure* μ as

$$\mu(A) = n(A), A \in \mathcal{F}.$$

The reader may verify that the counting measure satisfies the properties required of a measure. □

Example 5.4.7. The Lebesgue Measure. Consider the Borel σ-field over the real line $\mathbb{R}$, that is, $(\mathbb{R}, \mathcal{B}(\mathbb{R}))$. For a Borel set $A = [a, b) \in \mathcal{B}(\mathbb{R})$, A may be of any form, such as open interval, closed interval, etc., consider the measure defined by the length:

$$\mu(A) = b - a, a \leq b \in \mathbb{R}.$$

It may be verified that the length measure, called the *Lebesgue measure*, meets the requirement of a measure. Similarly, the Lebesgue measure may be defined as area, volume, etc., in higher dimensions. □

We are now equipped with the necessary tools for a proper construction of a probability measure.

5.4.2 The Kolmogorov Definition

Definition 5.4.7 The Finitely Additive Probability Measure. *Consider a field $(\Omega, \mathcal{F})$, where Ω is the sample space and $\mathcal{F}$ is a field. A function $P : \mathcal{F} \to [0, 1]$ is said to be a* finitely additive probability measure *if*

- $P(\Omega) = 1$.
- *If the events $A_1, A_2, \ldots, A_n \in \mathcal{F}$ are a sequence of disjoint sets, then*

$$P(\cup_{i=1}^{n} A_i) = \sum_{i=1}^{n} P(A_i).$$

The triplet $(\Omega, \mathcal{F}, P)$ is called the finitely additive probability space *or simply a* probability space.

Here, the finiteness refers to the collection of sets in $\mathcal{F}$ and additiveness refers to disjoint collection of events. Any set $A \in \mathcal{F}$ is called an event or (more precisely) a *measurable event*. Next, we list some properties of the finitely additive probability measure:

- $P(A^c) = 1 - P(A)$.
- $P(\phi) = 0$.
- If $A \subseteq B$, then $P(A) \leq P(B)$.
- $0 \leq P(A) \leq 1$.
- The *General Additive Rule*: $P(A \cup B) = P(A) + P(B) - P(A \cap B)$, and hence $P(A \cup B) \leq P(A) + P(B)$.

- For an arbitrary set A and a collection of mutually exclusive and exhaustive sets $B_1, B_2, \dots, B_n$:

$$P(A) = \sum_{i=1}^{n} P(A \cap B_i).$$

Example 5.4.8. Validation of a Measure to be a Finitely Additive Probability Measure. Consider $\Omega = \{1,2,3,4\}$ and let $\mathcal{F} = \{\phi, \Omega, \{1\}, \{4\}, \{2,3\}, \{1,4\}, \{1,2,3\}, \{2,3,4\}\}$. Define the probabilities with $P(\phi) = 0$, $P(\Omega) = 1$, $P(\{1\}) = 1/8, P(\{4\}) = 3/8$, $P(\{2,3\}) = 1/2, P(\{1,4\}) = 1/2$, $P(\{1,2,3\}) = 5/8$, $P(\{2,3,4\}) = 7/8$. First, we easily check that the class of sets $\mathcal{F}$ is indeed a field as it is closed under complementation and finite intersection (union).

Next, we see that all the defined probabilities are non-negative with $P(\Omega) = 1$. Consider an arbitrary collection of disjoint sets, say, $\{2,3\}, \{1\}, \{4\}$. Since$\{2,3\} \cup \{1\} \cup \{4\} = \Omega$, and $P(\{2,3\}) + P(\{1\}) + P(\{4\}) = 1/2 + 1/8 + 3/8 = (4+1+3)/8 = 1$, the second condition of probability measure is satisfied. Similarly, it can be verified with this example that for any arbitrary disjoint collection of events, the probability of union of the sets is equal to the sum of the probability of the events. Thus, the measure P is a finite additive probability measure. See Chapter 4 of Capiński and Zastawniak (2001). □

Example 5.4.9. Probability of a Symmetric Difference Event. The *symmetric difference* set operator for two events A and B is defined by

$$A \triangle B = \{A \cap B^c\} \cup \{B \cap A^c\}.$$

Note that by its definition, $A \triangle B = B \triangle A$. Further note that $\{A \cap B^c\}$ and $\{B \cap A^c\}$ are disjoint sets. We claim that for any sets $A, B, C \in \mathcal{F}$

$$P(A \triangle B) = P(A) + P(B) - 2P(A \cap B),$$

and the inequality $P(A \triangle C) \leq P(A \triangle B) + P(B \triangle C)$.

It is left to the reader as an exercise to prove that probability axioms are preserved under the symmetric difference. □

We now extend the finitely additive probability measure to the countably infinite case.

Definition 5.4.8 The Countably Additive Probability Measure. *Consider a σ-field $(\Omega, \mathcal{F})$, where Ω is the sample space and $\mathcal{F}$ is a σ-field. A function $P : \mathcal{F} \to [0,1]$ is said to be a* countably additive probability measure *if*

- $P(\Omega) = 1$.
- *If the events $A_1, A_2, \dots, \in \mathcal{F}$ are disjoint, then*

$$P(\cup_{i=1}^{\infty} A_i) = \sum_{i=1}^{\infty} P(A_i).$$

The triplet $(\Omega, \mathcal{F}, P)$ is called the countably additive probability space *or simply a* probability space.

Example 5.4.10. A Power Series Probability Measure. Let $\Omega = \mathbb{N}$, the set of natural integers, and let $\mathcal{F}$ be the power set of Ω. Define a measure as

$$P(\{i\}) = \frac{1}{2^i}, i = 1, 2, \ldots .$$

Then

$$P(\Omega) = \sum_{i=1}^{\infty} \frac{1}{2^i} = \sum_{i=0}^{\infty} (1/2)^i - 1 = \frac{1}{1 - 1/2} - 1 = 2 - 1 = 1.$$

It is further easy to see that the countably additiveness holds true for P. Thus, the measure P is a countably additive probability measure. □

Example 5.4.11. The Cantor Set. Consider the unit interval $\Omega = [0, 1]$. First, remove the open interval $(1/3, 2/3)$ from Ω so that we are now left with $\Omega' = [0, 1/3] \cup [2/3, 1]$. From each remaining interval remove the mid-thirds to obtain $\Omega'' = [0, 1/9] \cup [2/9, 1/3] \cup [2/3, 7/9] \cup [8/9, 1]$. This process is continued *ad infinitum*. The remaining Ω *ad infinitum* is well-known in *real analysis* as the *Cantor set*. It may be shown that the Cantor set is a Borel set, see Royden (1987). Define

$$E_n^c = \cup_{k=1}^{3^{n-1}} \left(\frac{3k-2}{3^n}, \frac{3k-1}{3^n} \right).$$

Note that for each n, E_n is the union of 2^n sets. The Cantor set is defined by

$$C = \cap_{n=1}^{\infty} E_n.$$

At each step we can see that E_n is an uncountable set. Since the intersection of uncountable sets is again an uncountable set, the Lebesgue measure of the Cantor set is expected to be a positive number. The Lebesgue measure of the Cantor set is obtained from those of E_n^c as

$$\mu(C) = \mu([0, 1]) - \mu \left(\cup_{n=1}^{\infty} \cup_{k=1}^{3^{n-1}} \left(\frac{3k-2}{3^n}, \frac{3k-1}{3^n} \right) \right).$$

For each n, the Lebesgue measure of E_n^c can be seen as $2^n/3^{n+1}$. Thus, we have

$$\mu(C) = 1 - \sum_{n=1}^{\infty} \frac{2^n}{3^{n+1}} = 1 - \frac{1}{3} \sum_{n=1}^{\infty} \frac{2^n}{3^n} = 1 - \frac{1}{3} \left(1 - \frac{1}{1 - \frac{2}{3}} \right) = 1 - 1 = 0.$$

Hence, it is a surprise that the Lebesgue measure of an uncountable set can be zero. A plot of the E_n's can be obtained from the following R program, see its output in Figure 5.3.

```
> n <- 0:6
> plot(c(0,1), c(0,6), type="n", xlab="The Unit Interval",ylab="n")
> title("The Cantor Set: A Visual Treat")
> points(c(0,1),c(0,0),"l",lwd=5)
> for(i in 2:7){
+       nn <- n[i]
+       points(c(0,1),c(nn,nn),"l",lwd=5)
+       for(j in 1:{3^{nn-1}}) points(c((3*j-2)/3^{nn},
+       (3*j-1)/3^{nn}),c(nn,nn),"l",lwd=5,col="white")
+       }
```

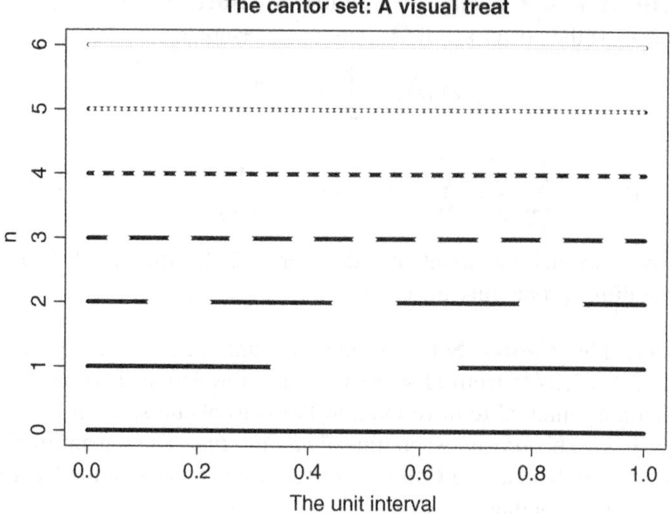

Figure 5.3 The Cantor Set

The code `points(c((3*j-2)/3^{nn},(3*j-1)/3^{nn}),c(nn,nn),...)` easily imitates the expression for E_n^c. Thus, R is useful to obtain a visual display of events leading to the Cantor set. □

5.5 Conditional Probability and Independence

An important difference *measure theory* and *probability theory* is in the notion of *independence of events*. The concept of independence is brought through conditional probability and its definition is first considered.

Definition 5.5.1 *Consider the probability space* $(\Omega, \mathcal{F}, P)$. *The* **conditional probability** *of an event B, given the event A, with* $P(A) > 0$*, denoted by* $P(B|A)$*,* $A, B \in \mathcal{F}$*, is defined by*

$$P(B|A) = \frac{P(B \cap A)}{P(A)}. \tag{5.8}$$

The next examples deal with the notion of conditional probability.

Example 5.5.1. The Dice Rolling Experiment. Suppose that we roll a die twice and note the sum of the outcomes as 9. The question of interest is then what is the probability of observing 1 to 6 on Die 1? Using the `rolldie` and `prob` functions from the `prob` package, we can obtain the answers.

```
> S <- rolldie(2,makespace=TRUE)
> prob(S,X1==1,given=(X1+X2==9))
[1] 0
```

```
> prob(S,X1==2,given=(X1+X2==9))
[1] 0
> prob(S,X1==3,given=(X1+X2==9))
[1] 0.25
> prob(S,X1==4,given=(X1+X2==9))
[1] 0.25
> prob(S,X1==5,given=(X1+X2==9))
[1] 0.25
> prob(S,X1==6,given=(X1+X2==9))
[1] 0.25
```

Conditional probabilities help in defining independence of events. □

Definition 5.5.2 *Consider the probability space* $(\Omega, \mathcal{F}, P)$ *and an event* $B \in \mathcal{F}$*, such that* $P(B) \neq 0$*. An event* $A \in \mathcal{F}$ *is said to be* independent *of* B *if*

$$P(A|B) = P(A). \tag{5.9}$$

Some properties of the independence, if events A and B are independent, are listed as:

- A and B^c are independent.
- A^c and B are independent.
- A^c and B^c are independent.

Example 5.5.2. The Intel Fiasco. This example is drawn from Horgan (2008). In the year 1994, Intel manufactured a chip which carried out 1 incorrect division in 9 billion opportunities. Intel transformed this story as an error occurring once in 27 000 years. A statistician will be typically performing millions of division every week. Let us see how this chip will be affecting him. By the data here:

$$P(\text{Error}) = \frac{1}{9000000000},$$

$$P(\text{No Error}) = \left(1 - \frac{1}{9000000000}\right),$$

$$P(\text{no errors in two divides}) = P(\text{no error in first divide}) \times P(\text{no error in second divide})$$

$$= \left(1 - \frac{1}{9000000000}\right)^2.$$

For a probabilist, if he performs a billion divisions, the probability of him making no error is then given by:

```
> proberror= 1 - 1/9000000000
> (noerrorbill=proberror^{1}000000000)
[1] 0.8948393
```

Suddenly, this probability looks very high. This is not a surprise for a Statistician, and naturally this fact forced Intel to withdraw the chip from the market. □

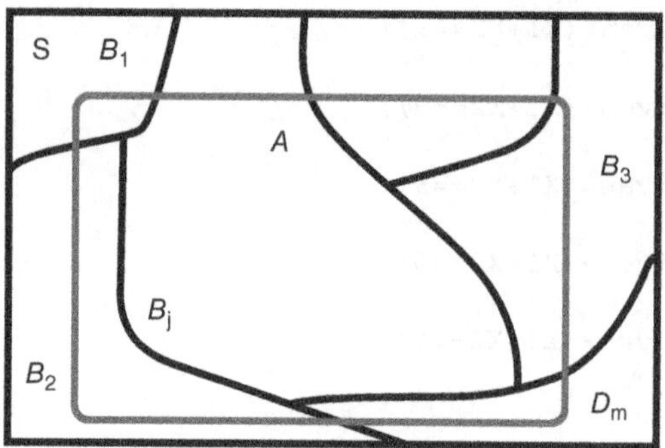

Figure 5.4 Venn Diagram to Understand Bayes Formula

5.6 Bayes Formula

An excellent exposition of the the Bayes formula is provided in Chapter 4 of Bolstad (2007). Consider a partition of the sample space Ω in a collection of m events $B_j, j = 1, 2, \dots, m$, also defined earlier in Section 5.4, from the probability space $(\Omega, \mathcal{F}, P)$. That is, $B_j \in \mathcal{F}, j = 1, \dots, m$. Consider an arbitrary event $A \in \mathcal{F}$. Then $A = \cup_{j=1}^m (A \cap B_j)$. Since B_j's form a partition of Ω, it can be visualized from the Venn diagram, Figure 5.4, that $A \cap B_j$'s are also a disjoint set of events. Hence,

$$P(A) = P(\cup_{j=1}^m (A \cap B_j)) = \sum_{j=1}^m P(A \cap B_j) = \sum_{j=1}^m P(A|B_j)P(B_j).$$

The last step of the above expression is obtained by the multiple rule of probability. The beauty of Bayes formula is that we can obtain *inverse probabilities*, that is, the probability of the cause given the effect. This famous Bayes formula is given by:

$$P(B_j|A) = \frac{P(A \cap B_j)}{P(A)} = \frac{P(A|B_j)P(B_j)}{\sum_{j=1}^m P(A|B_j)P(B_j)}.$$

Example 5.6.1. Classical Problem from Hoel, Port, and Stone (1971). Suppose there are three tables with two drawers each. The first table has a gold coin in each of the drawers, the second table has a gold coin in one drawer and a silver coin in the other drawer, while the third table has silver coins in both of the drawers. A table is selected at random and a drawer is opened which shows a gold coin. The problem is to compute the probability of the other drawer also showing a gold coin. The Bayes formula can be easily implemented in an R program.

```
> prob_GC <- c(1,1/2,0)
> prior <- c(1/3,1/3,1/3)
> post_GC <- prob_GC*prior
```

```
> post_GC/sum(post_GC)
[1] 0.6666667 0.3333333 0.0000000
```

Thus, the probability of the other drawer containing a gold coin is `0.6666667`. □

5.7 Random Variables, Expectations, and Moments

5.7.1 The Definition

Sample events on their own are not always of interest, as we may only be interested in general events. For instance, if 100 coins are thrown, we may not be interested in the probabilities of the event itself, but we may question the number of heads in the range of 10 to 40, or > 80. Thus, we need to consider functions of the events which help to answer generic questions. This will lead us to the concept of *random variable*.

Definition 5.7.1 *Consider a probability space* $(\Omega, \mathcal{F}, P)$. *A* random variable X *is any* $\mathcal{F}$*-measurable function from* Ω *to* $\mathbb{R}$*, that is,* $X : \Omega \to \mathbb{R}$.

In plain words, it is required that for any Borel set $A \in \mathbb{R}$, the inverse image $X^{-1}(A)$ must belong to $\mathcal{F}$:

$$X^{-1}(A) = \{\omega : X(\omega) \in A\} \in \mathcal{F}, \forall A \in \mathbb{R}.$$

A random variable will be simply abbreviated as *RV*. A commonly accepted convention is to denote the random variables by capital letters X, Y, Z, etc., and the *observed* values by small letters x, y, z, etc. respectively. Random variables are identified to be of three types: (i) *simple random variable*, (ii) *elementary random variable*, and (iii) *extended random variable*. A random variable X is said to be *simple* if there exists a finite partition of Ω in $A_1, \ldots, A_n$, n finite, implying $A_i \cap A_j = \phi, i \neq j, \cup_{i=1}^{n} A_i = \Omega$, such that

$$X = \sum_{i=1}^{n} x_i I\{A_i\}, \tag{5.10}$$

where $I\{A_i\} = 1$ if $x_i \in A_i, i = 1, \ldots, n$ and 0 otherwise. The random variable X is said to be *elementary* if for a countably infinite partition of Ω in $\{A_i\}_{i=1}^{\infty}$

$$X = \sum_{i=1}^{\infty} x_i I\{A_i\}. \tag{5.11}$$

Finally, the random variable X is said to be an *extended* random variable if $X : \Omega \to [-\infty, \infty]$. An extended RV is often split into a *positive part* and a *negative part* defined by

$$X^+ = \begin{cases} X, & \text{if } X \geq 0, \\ 0, & \text{if } X < 0, \end{cases}; X^- = \begin{cases} 0, & \text{if } X \geq 0, \\ -X, & \text{if } X < 0. \end{cases} \tag{5.12}$$

It can be easily seen that $X = X^+ - X^-$.

Example 5.7.1. Tossing Coins. Contd. Let X denote the number of heads in the experiment of tossing k coins. For example, if we throw three coins, then

$$X\{(HHH)\} = 3, \qquad X\{(HHT)\} = 2,$$
$$X\{(HTH)\} = 2, \qquad X\{(HTT)\} = 2,$$
$$X\{(THH)\} = 2, \qquad X\{(THT)\} = 2,$$
$$X\{(TTH)\} = 1, \qquad X\{(TTT)\} = 2.$$

Note that though the outcome of throwing three coins is one of the elements ω such as HHH, HHT, $\ldots$, TTT, we are more interested in knowing whether the number of heads is $1, 2, 3$. Is X an example of a simple random variable? □

Example 5.7.2. Rolling Dies. Contd. Suppose that we throw two die. Let X be the sum of outcomes of the two die. Then

$$X\{(i,j)\} = i + j, i, j = 1, 2, \ldots , 6.$$

Here, the sample events are $(\omega_1, \omega_2) = (i,j), i, j = 1, \ldots , n$, whereas we are interested in knowing whether the sum is $2, 3, \ldots , 12$. It is possible to define random variables in R for some random experiments. We will illustrate this in the example here. The necessary R codes are given next.

```
> S <- rolldie(2,makespace=TRUE)
> S <- addrv(S, U = X1+X2)
> for(i in 2:12) print(prob(S,U==i))
[1] 0.02777778
[1] 0.05555556
   ...
[1] 0.02777778
>  aggregate(S$probs,by=list(S$U),sum) # gives same result
```

Using the `rolldie` and `addrv` from the `prob` package, we can understand random variables for the die rolling experiments. It may be seen that X is a simple random variable. □

Example 5.7.3. Jiang's Example 2.2. Let $\Omega = [0, 1]$ and $\mathcal{F}$ be the Borel σ- field. The probability measure is the Lebesgue measure. Define a sequence of random variables $\{X_n\}_{n=1}^{\infty}$ as follows:

$$X_1(x) = \begin{cases} 1, & x \in [0, 1/2), \\ 0, & x \in [1/2, 1], \end{cases} \quad X_4(x) = \begin{cases} 1, & x \in [1/4, 1/2), \\ 0, & x \in \Omega \backslash [1/4, 1/2), \end{cases}$$

$$X_2(x) = \begin{cases} 0, & x \in [0, 1/2), \\ 1, & x \in [1/2, 1], \end{cases} \quad X_5(x) = \begin{cases} 1, & x \in [1/2, 3/4), \\ 0, & x \in \Omega \backslash [1/2, 3/4), \end{cases}$$

$$X_3(x) = \begin{cases} 1, & x \in [0, 1/4), \\ 0, & x \in \Omega \backslash [0, 1/4), \end{cases} \quad X_6(x) = \begin{cases} 1, & x \in [3/4, 1], \\ 0, & x \in \Omega \backslash [3/4, 1]. \end{cases}$$

$$\vdots \qquad\qquad \vdots$$

We need to first define the sequence properly. That is, we need an expression which will describe the probability distribution of X_n.

The first task towards this is to understand that the serial number list can be generated as a function of two series. The serial numbers $1, 2, 3, 4, \ldots$ can be obtained from the two series $m = 0, 1, 2, \ldots,$ and $i = 0, 1, 2, \ldots, 2^m - 1$. This can be seen below:

```
> m <- 0:4
> index <- 0
> serial_number <- c()
> for(k in 2:length(m)){
+     i <- 0:(2^{m[k]}-1)
+     for(j in 1:length(i)){
+ index <- index+1
+ serial_number <- c(serial_number,index)
+ }
+ }
> serial_number[1:10]
 [1]  1  2  3  4  5  6  7  8  9 10
```

We will use an R program to find the intervals over which X takes the value of 1.

```
> # myintervals[1,]=c(0,1)
> m <- 0:4
> myintervals <- matrix(nrow=1000,ncol=2)
> index <- 0
> for(k in 2:length(m)){
+     i=0:(2^{m[k]}-1)
+     for(j in 1:length(i)){
+ index=index+1
+ myintervals[index,1]=i[j]/{2^{m}[k]}
+ myintervals[index,2]=(i[j]+1)/{2^{m}[k]}
+ }
+ }
> myintervals[1:10,]
       [,1]  [,2]
 [1,] 0.000 0.500
 [2,] 0.500 1.000
 [3,] 0.000 0.250
 [4,] 0.250 0.500
 [5,] 0.500 0.750
 [6,] 0.750 1.000
 [7,] 0.000 0.125
 [8,] 0.125 0.250
 [9,] 0.250 0.375
[10,] 0.375 0.500
```

Is this all? The authors do not think so. Let us ask what will the plot of the random variables look like. Again, let us use a programming angle and plot the first eight random variables, see Figure 5.5.

```
> x <- seq(-0.1,1.1,0.01)
> rx <- function(x,a,b) ifelse({x>=a}&{x<=b},1,0)
> par(mfrow=c(2,4))
> for(i in 1:8){
+     plot(x,y=x*0+1,"n",xlab=expression(omega),
+     ylab=expression(X(omega)),ylim=c(0,1.1),
+     main=paste("Plot of X",i,sep=""))
+     lines(x,sapply(x,rx,a=myintervals[i,1],
+     b <- myintervals[i,2]),"l",cex=10)
+ }
```

Figure 5.5 displays the first eight random variables and should also further help the reader to visualize the random variables further in the sequence. This example will also be continued further. □

We next consider some important properties of random variables.

Properties of Random Variables

- Borel function f of a random variable X is also a random variable.
- If X is an RV, then $aX + b$ is also a RV for $a, b \in \mathbb{R}$.
- Let X_1 and X_2 be two RVs in a probability space $(\Omega, \mathcal{F}, P)$. Then $\min\{X_1, X_2\}$ and $\max\{X_1, X_2\}$ are also RVs.
- Consider an independent sequence of RVs $X_n, n \geq 1$. Define, for all $\omega \in \Omega$,

$$\sup_n X_n = \sup_n X_n(\omega), \qquad \inf_n X_n = \inf_n X_n(\omega),$$
$$\lim \sup_n X_n = \lim \sup_n X_n(\omega),\ \lim \inf_n X_n = \lim \inf_n X_n(\omega).$$

  Then $\sup_n X_n$, $\inf_n X_n$, $\lim \sup_n X_n$, and $\lim \inf_n X_n$ are all RVs.
- If $X_n(\omega)$ converges as $n \to \infty$ for every $\omega \in \Omega$, then $\lim_{n\to\infty} X_n$ is also an RV.

An RV is better understood through important summaries such as mean and variance. We next define *expectation* of RV, which further helps in obtaining these summaries.

5.7.2 Expectation of Random Variables

As an introductory, the expectation of a discrete RV is defined by $EX = \sum_x xp(x)$, and for a continuous RV, by $EX = \int_{R_X} xf(x)dx$. In light of the three types of RV discussed earlier, we need to now define the expectation of an RV for simple, elementary, and extended RVs defined in a probability space $(\Omega, \mathcal{F}, P)$. For the moment, we will assume that the extended RVs are non-negative RVs.

The *expectations* of simple RV and elementary RV as defined respectively in Equations 5.10 and 5.11 are given by

$$EX = \sum_{i=1}^{n} x_i P(A_i), \tag{5.13}$$

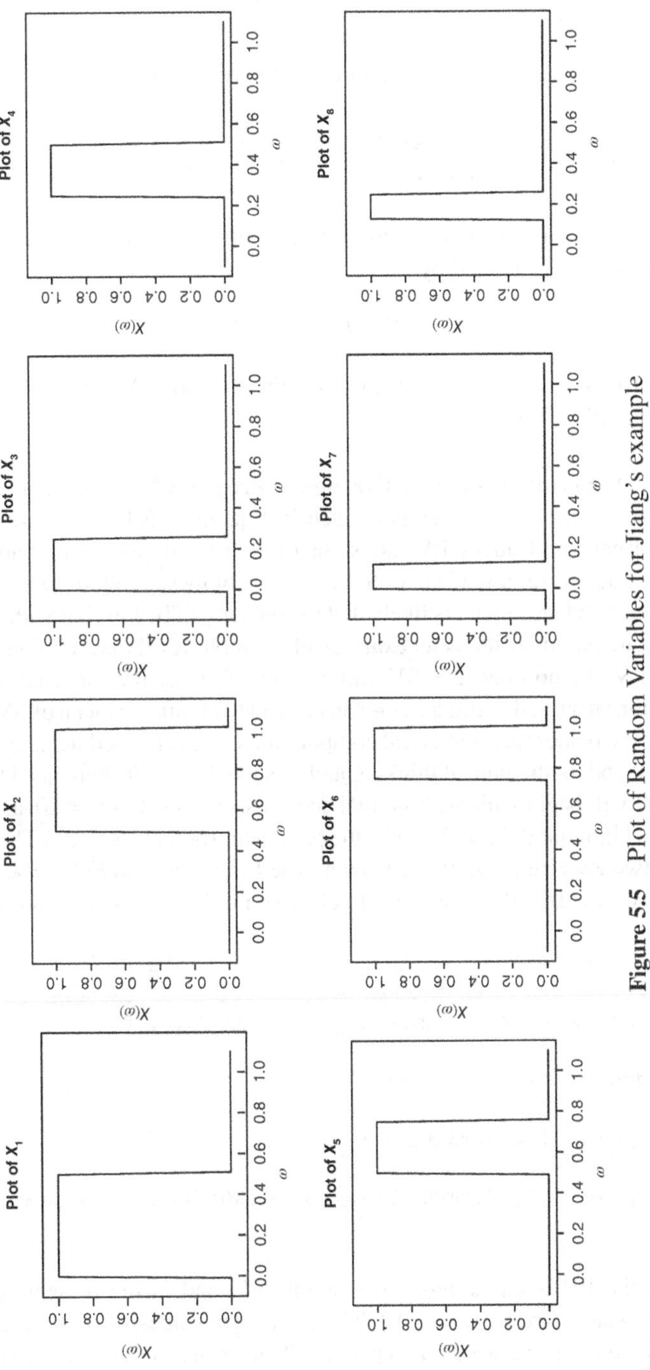

Figure 5.5 Plot of Random Variables for Jiang's example

$$EX = \sum_{i=1}^{\infty} x_i P(A_i). \tag{5.14}$$

The *expectation* of a non-negative random variable is defined by

$$EX = \lim_{n\to\infty} \sum_{i=1}^{n2^n} \frac{k-1}{2^n} P\left(\frac{k-1}{2^n} \le X < \frac{k}{2^n}\right). \tag{5.15}$$

It may be noted that the limit can be ∞ too. The expectation of an arbitrary (extended) RV, as given in Equation 5.12, is defined by

$$EX = EX^+ - EX^-, \tag{5.16}$$

provided that at least one of EX^+ and EX^- is finite. If both EX^+ and EX^- are infinite, the expectation of the RV is not defined.

Example 5.7.4. Expectation of RVs Through a Program.*[1] Mathematically, the expectations of the different types of RVs is defined in Equations 5.13–5.16. Binomial, Poisson, exponential, normal, and Cauchy RVs are some of the very important probability RVs in the subject, for more details refer to Chapter 6. The choice of these random variables is partly due to their importance and also that it is likely that the reader will be familiar with earlier exposure to the subject. The binomial RV is an example of a simple RV, Poisson of an elementary RV, or exponential RV of a non-negative RV, while normal Cauchy RVs are examples of arbitrary RVs. The functions `sum` and `integrate` can be used to obtain the mean of RVs. However, we need to caution the reader that numerical computations, as performed here, are not an alternative to analytical and mathematical thinking and as such the results here need to be taken with a lot of care. We will begin with the binomial and Poisson RVs. Let $n = 10$ and $p = 0.3$ be the parameters for a binomial RV and $\lambda = 5$ be the parameter for a Poisson RV. The expectation, or mean, of these two RVs are respectively known to be $E(X) = np$ and $E(X) = \lambda$. The probability mass function of these two RVs are respectively given in R by `dbinom` and `dpois`.

```
> sum(0:10*dbinom(0:10,size=10,p=0.3)) # Simple RV
[1] 3
> sum(0:1e7*dpois(0:1e7,lambda=5)) # Elementary RV
[1] 5
> sum(0:25*dpois(0:25,lambda=5))
[1] 5
> sum(0:30*dpois(0:30,lambda=5))
[1] 5
> sum(0:25*dpois(0:25,lambda=5))==sum(0:30*dpois(0:30,lambda=5))
[1] FALSE
```

Since the binomial RV is an example of a simple RV, and in the present case $n = 10$, the different integer values are 0, 1, …, 10. The parameter values of n and p are respectively declared with the options `size=10` and `p=0.3`. Thus, `sum(0:10*dbinom())` computes

[1]This example assumes familiarity with the probability models considered herein.

$\sum_{i=0}^{10} x_i p(x_i)$ as the required expectation $E(X)$ for the binomial RV. The R answer of `3` is acceptable, since it equals the theoretical value of np.

The non-negative integer values of the Poisson RV is the set 0, 1, 2, …, and as such we cannot create an R object consisting of infinite elements for any elementary RV. However, from a programming perspective, the values of X for which $p(x_i)$ will be close to zero will make an insignificant contribution towards this expectation and thus to begin with we will ignore values of X greater than `1e7` for $\lambda = 5$. Though the computed value of `5` for `sum(0:1e7*dpois(0:1e7,lambda=5))` meets the theoretical expected value, there is a small price to pay for ignoring the remaining range of the RV. This may be seen by restricting the `sum` over two sets `0:25` and `30`, which return the same value. However, they are not equal in the sense that the actual numbers differ in the decimal values which are not displayed on the screen.

Next, consider the computation of expectation of an extended RV. Basically, we will focus on continuous RVs and the use of the Formulas 5.15 and 5.16. To begin with, we will try to obtain the expectation of a uniform RV, see Section 6.3. The parameter θ determines the range of the uniform RV. The formula 5.15 requires us to partition the interval $[0, n]$ into $n2^n$—1 intervals. Thus, our computations of the expectations will not be accurate if $P(X > n)$ is significantly large, since the choice of n is limited accordingly as R can create large data objects depending on the available computer configurations. The computer configurations issue will not be discussed any further here. The intention of the program is to stress that as n increases, the computed expectation will be closer to the actual mean.

```
> partitions <- function(n) n*2^{n}
> Expectation_NNRV_Unif <- function(n,min,max){
+ k = 1:partitions(n)
+ EX = sum(((k-1)/(2^{n}))*(punif(k/2^{n},min,max)-
+ punif((k-1)/2^{n},min,max)))
+ return(EX)
+ }
> sapply(1:20,Expectation_NNRV_Unif,min=0,max=10)
 [1] 0.0250 0.1750 0.4312    5.0000 5.0000 5.0000
> sapply(1:20,Expectation_NNRV_Unif,min=0,max=0.5)
 [1] 0.0000 0.1250 0.1875   0.2500 0.2500 0.2500
> sapply(1:20,Expectation_NNRV_Unif,min=0,max=20)
 [1]  0.0125  0.0875  0.2156    8.1000  9.0250 10.0000
> sapply(1:20,Expectation_NNRV_Unif,min=0,max=30) # FAILS #
 [1] 0.008333 0.058333 0.143750   5.399999 6.016666 6.666666
> sapply(1:20,Expectation_NNRV_Unif,min=0,max=1.3467)
 [1] 0.1856 0.5539 0.6119   0.6733 0.6733 0.6733
```

The parameters of a uniform distribution can be specified through the `min` and `max` options of the function `punif`, which returns the cumulative probability. The number of partitions is created with the defined function `partitions`. The R function `Expectation_NNRV_Unif` is programmed in such a way as to mimic the expression on the right-hand side of Equation 5.15. The probability $P\left(\frac{k-1}{2^n} \leq X < \frac{k}{2^n}\right)$ is captured with `(punif(k/2^n,min,max)-punif((k-1)/2^n,min,max))`, while the term $\frac{k-1}{2^n}$ is obtained with `(k-1)/(2^n)`. Note that if the θ value is less than 20, the function

Expectation_NNRV_Unif works fine. Recall that the expected value of a uniform distribution is the average of min and max, and if the range is $[0, \theta]$, the expected value is $\theta/2$. The output given is curtailed and the running of the program at your own console clearly shows that as $n \to \infty$, the output becomes closer to EX, as given by the limit on the right-hand side of Equation 5.15. A similar exercise is repeated for the exponential distribution with the function Expectation_NNRV_Exp and will not be explained any further here.

```
> Expectation_NNRV_Exp <- function(n,rate){
+ k = 1:partitions(n)
+ EX = sum(((k-1)/(2^{n}))*(pexp(k/2^{n},rate)-
+ pexp((k-1)/2^{n},rate)))
+ return(EX)
+ }
> sapply(1:20,Expectation_NNRV_Exp,rate=10); 1/10
 [1] 0.0033 0.0224 0.0502   0.1000 0.1000 0.1000
[1] 0.1
> sapply(1:20,Expectation_NNRV_Exp,rate=0.9); 1/0.9
 [1] 0.12 0.50 0.78    1.11 1.11 1.11
[1] 1.1
> sapply(1:20,Expectation_NNRV_Exp,rate=0.5); 1/0.5
 [1] 0.086 0.451 0.836    1.998 1.998 1.999
[1] 2
> sapply(1:20,Expectation_NNRV_Exp,rate=0.1); 1/0.1
 [1] 0.023 0.153 0.353    5.372 5.663 5.940
[1] 10
```

Let us now look at an arbitrary RV, as defined in Equation 5.12. The focus will be on standard normal and Cauchy RVs, which are both extended RVs. For such RVs we define the positive and negative parts. The integrate(function,lower,upper) can be used to evaluate integrals of the form $\int_a^b f(x)dx$. It is important to note that R allows the options Inf and -Inf for ∞ and $-\infty$. Thus, using dnorm, dcauchy, and integrate with the appropriate options, we obtain EX^+ and EX^-, equivalently $\int_{R_X} |x| f(x)dx$. If both expectations are well defined, we can compute the expected value of the normal and Cauchy RVs.

```
> integrate(function(x) {x*dnorm(x)},lower=0,upper=Inf)
0.4 with absolute error < 1.1e-08
> integrate(function(x) {x*dnorm(x)},lower=-Inf,upper=0)
-0.4 with absolute error < 1.1e-08
> integrate(function(x) {abs(x)*dnorm(x)},lower=-Inf,upper=Inf)
0.8 with absolute error < 2.3e-08
> integrate(function(x) {x*dnorm(x)},lower=-Inf,upper=Inf)
0 with absolute error < 0
> integrate(function(x) {x*dcauchy(x)},lower=0,upper=Inf)
Error in integrate(function(x) { : maximum number of subdivisions
+ reached
> integrate(function(x) {x*dcauchy(x)},lower=-Inf,upper=0)
Error in integrate(function(x) { : maximum number of subdivisions
+ reached
> integrate(function(x) {abs(x)*dcauchy(x)},lower=-Inf,upper=Inf)
Error in integrate(function(x) { : maximum number of subdivisions
+ reached
```

```
> integrate(function(x) {x*dcauchy(x)},lower=-Inf,upper=Inf)
0 with absolute error < 0
```

It may be thus seen that the expectation exists for a normal RV, while it does not exist for the Cauchy RV. □

Let us now consider some properties of expectations of RVs.

Properties of Expectation of Random Variables

- If $\{A_i\}_{i=1}^n$ and $\{B_k\}_{k=1}^m$ are two partitions of a simple RV X such that

$$X = \sum_{i=1}^{n} x_i I(A_i) \text{ and } X = \sum_{k=1}^{m} x_k I(B_i),$$

  then

$$EX = \sum_{i=1}^{n} x_i p(A_i) = \sum_{k=1}^{m} x_k p(B_k).$$

- If X is a non-negative and simple RV, then $EX \geq 0$. This property continues to hold for non-negative RVs too.
- If X and Y are two non-negative (simple or otherwise) RVs, and $a, b \in \mathbb{R}$, then $E(aX + bY) = aEX + bEY$. This property is also known as the *linearity of expectations*.

The third counter-intuitive problem from Diaconis and Holmes (2002) will be discussed next.

Example 5.7.5. The Coupon Collectors Problem. Suppose that there are n coupons or stamps on the market, and the goal is to collect each of the coupons. The *coupon collectors problem* is to find the expected number of samples required to achieve that goal. At the outset, we may feel that a maximum of $2n$ or $3n$ is sufficient to meet the goal, as we believe that the probability of obtaining any coupon is the same as with any other coupon. Let us now look at the mathematical argument.

Let T denote the *random* time to collect all the n coupons, and let T_i be the time to collect the ith coupon after $i - 1$ coupons have already been collected. Viewing T and the T_i's as RVs, we can see that the probability of collecting a new coupon, given the previously collected ones, is $p_i = (n - i + 1)/n$, and that the RVs T_i has a *geometric distribution*[2] with expectation $1/p_i$. The *Linearity of Expectations* gives us

$$\begin{aligned}
E(T) &= E(T_1) + E(T_2) + \ldots + E(T_n) \\
&= \frac{1}{p_1} + \frac{1}{p_2} + \ldots + \frac{1}{p_n} \\
&= \frac{n}{n} + \frac{n}{n-1} + \ldots + \frac{n}{1} \\
&= n\left(\frac{1}{1} + \frac{1}{2} + \ldots + \frac{1}{n}\right) = nH_n
\end{aligned}$$

[2] See section 6.2 for more details on Geometric Distribution

In the last line of the above equation, H_n is the *harmonic mean*. It can be shown that as $n \to \infty$, $E(T)$ can be approximated by $n \ln(n) + 0.5772n + 1/2$. For different n values, we compute $E(T)$ in an R program.

```
> # The theoretical expectations for the coupon collectors problem
> # is given in this segment
> TEn <- function(n) n*log(n) # The Theoretical Expectations
> coupons_matrix <- matrix(nrow=100,ncol=3)
> colnames(coupons_matrix) <- c("Number_of_Coupons","TEn","BPEn")
> coupons_matrix[,1] <- 1:100
> coupons_matrix[,2] <- sapply(1:100,TEn)
> plot(1:1000,sapply(1:1000,TEn),"l",xlab="Number of Coupons",
+ ylab="Theoretical Expected Number",pch=10,col="orange")
> title("The Coupon Collectors Problem")
> abline(0,2,col="red",pch=1)
> abline(0,3,col="green",pch=2)
> abline(0,4,col="blue",pch=3)
> legend(0,6000, c("TEn","2n","3n","4n"),col=c("orange","red",
+ "green","blue"),pch=1:3)
```

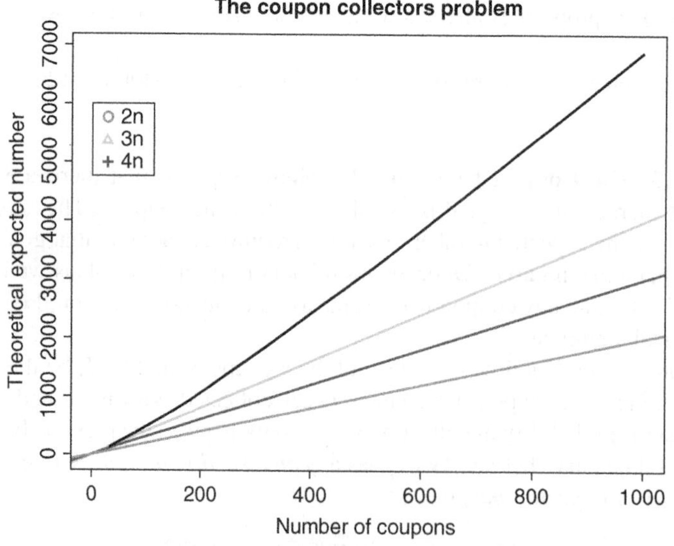

Figure 5.6 Expected Number of Coupons

Thus, we see from Figure 5.6 that there is a large difference between our perceived intuition and the theoretical values given by the mathematical solutions. □

Higher-order expectations are of interest for many RVs.

Definition 5.7.2 Moments of RV. *The n-th moment of an RV X is defined by* EX^n, $n = 1, 2, \ldots$. *The* central moments *of an RV X is given by* $E(X - EX)^n, n = 1, 2, \ldots$, *while the* absolute moments *are defined by* $E|X|^n$, *and finally the* absolute central moments *are* $E|X - EX|^n$.

The forthcoming section will consider three important functions related to an RV.

?addrv

5.8 Distribution Function, Characteristic Function, and Moment Generation Function

Let X be an $\mathcal{F}$-measurable random variable in the probability space $(\Omega, \mathcal{F}, P)$.

Definition 5.8.1 *For a random variable X, define*

$$F_X(x) = P(\{\omega : X(\omega) \leq x\}),$$

for $x \in R$. *Then* $F_X(x)$ *is called the* cumulative distribution function *of the random variable X, abbreviated as* cdf. *We now consider some properties of the cdf.*

Properties of the cdf

(a) The cdf F is a non-decreasing function, that is,

$$x < x' \to F(x) \leq F(x').$$

(b) The cdf F is right-continuous:

$$\lim_{h \downarrow 0} F(x + h) = F(x).$$

(c) $F(-\infty) = 0$ as we approach the null set.
(d) $F(\infty) = 1$ as we approach Ω.
(e) The set of discontinuity points of F is at most countable.

A related function is now defined.

Definition 5.8.2 *The* moment generating function, *abbreviated as* mgf, *of the random variable X is defined by*

$$M_X(t) = E(e^{tX}),$$

if the expectation on the right-hand side is finite for $|t| < a$ *with some* $a > 0$.

We list below some properties of the mgf, and the reader can refer to Gut (2007) for details.

Properties of the mgf

(a) If the mgf $M_X(t)$ is finite (in the above sense), the rth moment of X is the rth derivative (w.r.t. t) of the mgf $M_X(t)$ evaluated at $t = 0$.
(b) Define $Y = aX + b$, $a, b \in \mathbb{R}$, where the mgf of X is finite. Then

$$M_Y(t) = e^{tb} M_X(ta).$$

(c) A finite mgf determines the distribution of the RV uniquely.

The mgf does not exist for many important RVs, and thus we look at a function which will always exist.

Definition 5.8.3 *The* characteristic function, *abbreviated as* cf, *of the RV X is defined by*

$$\varphi_X(t) = E(e^{itX}).$$

The cf always exists for any random variable.

Properties of the cf

(a) $\varphi(0) = 1$, $|\varphi(t)| \leq 1$, $\varphi(-t) = \bar{\varphi(t)}$.
(b) $\varphi(t)$ is *uniformly continuous* on the real line.
(c) $\varphi(aX + b) = \varphi(at)e^{itb}$.

Example 5.8.1. Characteristic Function of a Power Series Distribution. Consider a discrete RV X with a probability function defined as

$$P(\{X = j\}) = \frac{1}{2^j}, j = 1, 2, \ldots .$$

By definition, the characteristic function is obtained in the following steps:

$$\varphi_X(t) = \sum_{k=1}^{\infty} \frac{e^{itk}}{2^k} = \sum_{k=0}^{\infty} \left(\frac{e^{it}}{2}\right)^k - 1$$
$$= \sum_{k=0}^{\infty} a^k - 1, \quad \text{where} \quad a = \frac{e^{it}}{2}.$$

The above expression can be easily evaluated if we can show that $|a| < 1$. Note that $|a| = |e^{it}|/2$, and since $|e^{it}| = \sqrt{\cos^2 t + \sin^2 t} = 1$, we have $|a| = 1/2 < 1$. Thus, using the result that for $|a| < 1$, the infinite series $\sum_{k=0}^{\infty} a^k = 1/(1-a)$, the characteristic function of the random variable X is

$$\varphi_X(t) = \frac{1}{1 - \frac{e^{it}}{2}} - 1 = \frac{e^{it}}{2 - e^{it}}.$$

A three-dimensional plot of the characteristic function is given by the following R codes.

```
> t <- seq(-10,10,0.1)
> cf_X <- function(t) {exp(1i*t)/(2-exp(1i*t))}
```

```
> scatterplot3d(t,Re(cf_X(t)),Im(cf_X(t)),
+ xlim=c(-11,11),ylim=c(-1,1),zlim=c(-1,1),
+ xlab="t",ylab="Real Part of CF", zlab="Complex Part of CF",
+ highlight.3d=TRUE, col.axis="blue",
+ col.grid="lightblue", pch=20,type="l")
> # Output Suppressed
```

In most cases, the cf plot does not have an interpretation! □

The concepts of cdf, mgf, and cf will be illustrated in more detail in Sections 6.2–6.4.

?scatterplot3d

5.9 Inequalities

The first inequality which comes to mind is the *triangle inequality*. It is claimed that this inequality has more than 200 different proofs! In probability theory, inequalities are useful when we do not have enough information about the distribution of the random variables. We will have practical scenarios where me may not know about the experiments any more than the fact that the random variables are independent, their mean, and probably standard deviation. We will now see the role of *probabilistic inequalities*.

5.9.1 The Markov Inequality

Theorem 5.9.1 *Let X be an $\mathcal{F}$- measurable non-negative RV defined in $(\Omega, \mathcal{F}, P)$ with $E(X) = \mu$. Then, for every $k > 0$, the Markov inequality says that*

$$P(X \geq k) \leq \frac{\mu}{k}.$$

□

Example 5.9.1. A Simple Illustration. Suppose that the average number of customers, denoted by X, arriving at a bank is 20 per hour. Then the probability of 50 or more customers arriving per hour is $P(X \geq 50) \leq 20/50 = 0.4$. □

Example 5.9.2. Horgan's Example 20.4. The mean diameter of a product is known to be 10, and the manufacturer wants an estimate of the proportion of products that will exceed 20. If X denotes the diameter of the product, the Markov's inequality helps the manufacturer to obtain the estimate as

$$P(X \geq 20) \leq \frac{10}{20} = 0.5.$$

□

5.9.2 The Jensen's Inequality

Definition 5.9.1 *Consider a finite mean RV X in a probability space $(\Omega, \mathcal{F}, P)$. Let $f : \mathbb{R} \to \mathcal{R}$ be a convex function. The Jensen's inequality states that*

$$E[f(x)] \geq f(E[X]). \tag{5.17}$$

Example 5.9.3. A Proof for Variance being Non-negative. Consider a probability space $(\Omega, \mathcal{F}, P)$ with a $\mathcal{F}$ measurable RV X. Clearly, $f(X) = X^2$ is a convex function and this implies that

$$E(X^2) \geq \{E(X)\}^2,$$

and thus further implies that $\text{Var}(X) = EX^2 - \{EX\}^2 \geq 0$. □

The Jensen's inequality is a very useful technique, especially when we deal with the theory of the subject.

5.9.3 The Chebyshev Inequality

Consider a random variable X with mean μ and variance σ^2. The Chebyshev's inequality states that

$$P(|X - \mu| \geq k\sigma) \leq \frac{1}{k^2}. \tag{5.18}$$

This inequality has a very useful interpretation: "Not more than $1/k^2$ of the distribution's values can be more than k standard deviations away from the mean." Note that the inequality does not make any assumptions about the probability distribution of X.

A *one-tailed* version of the Chebyshev's inequality is

$$P(X - \mu \geq k\sigma) \leq \frac{1}{1 + k^2}.$$

Example 5.9.4. Example 5.12.1. Contd. Suppose we also know that the variance of the customers arriving at the bank is 10. Then, the probability of 50 or more customers arriving per hour is obtained as below:

$$P(X > 50) = P(X - 20 > 30) = P(X - 20 > 3(10)) \leq \frac{1}{1 + 3^2} = 0.1.$$

□

The forthcoming section will deal with various convergence concepts of RVs.

5.10 Convergence of Random Variables

The concept of *convergence* is very strongly built in the $\epsilon - \delta$ argument. As Jiang (2010) emphasizes, the convergence concept embeds in itself the $\epsilon - \delta$ argument. Jiang refers to this tool as the A-B-C of *large sample theory*, and we will first discuss this in Example 1.1.

Example 5.10.1. Jiang's Example 1.1. Suppose that we have been asked to prove that as $n \to \infty$

$$\ln(n + 1) - \ln(n) \to 0.$$

Here, $\delta = \ln(n + 1) - \ln(n)$. By the $\epsilon - \delta$ argument, we need to show that there exists some n, however large, such that the δ will be less than ϵ, where ϵ is a very small non-negative number, that is,

$$\ln\left(1 + \frac{1}{n}\right) < \epsilon.$$

Of course, as a measurement of closeness, we need ϵ to be as close to 0 as possible. Let us consider a sequence of ϵ as $10^{-j}, j = 1, 2, \ldots, 8$. We will write a rudimentary R program for this task!

```
> # The jist of epsilon-delta argument
> epsilon <- 10^{-(1:8)}
> N <- NULL
> for(i in 1:length(epsilon)){
+     n <- 1
+     delta=10^{1}0
+     while(delta>epsilon[i]) {
+      n <- n+1
+   delta <- log(1+1/n)
+               }
+     N <- c(N,n)
+ }
> N
[1] 1e+01 1e+02 1e+03 1e+04 1e+05 1e+06 1e+07 1e+08
```

The sequence `epsilon <- 10^-(1:8)` examines the convergence for very small values of ϵ, which approach 0. The `while` loop increments the value of `N` by 1 until the `delta` becomes less than `epsilon`. The `for` loop runs the program for different `epsilon` values.

This program took approximately 30 minutes on a *modern laptop*. This shows that for a given ϵ, we can find an N which will ensure that after that number, $\delta = \ln(n+1) - \ln(n)$ will be smaller than the ϵ. Note that it is indeed possible to directly obtain the values of N, though such a program will not reflect the central idea of increasing n. The above program is, of course, not a proof! Now, $\ln\left(1 + \frac{1}{n}\right) < \epsilon$ implies $1 + 1/n < e^{\epsilon}$ and hence that $n > (1 + e^{\epsilon})^{-1}$. Thus, if we take $N = [(1 + e^{\epsilon})^{-1}] + 1$, where [.] denotes the integer part of a number, then for every $n \geq N$, we have satisfied the requirement $\ln\left(1 + \frac{1}{n}\right) < \epsilon$. □

In the rest of this section, we attempt to gain an insight into using R programs and to establish the results analytically.

5.10.1 Convergence in Distributions

Consider a sequence of probability spaces $\{(\Omega_n, \mathcal{F}_n, P_n)\}_{n=1}^{\infty}$, and let the random variable sequence $\{X_n\}_{n=1}^{\infty}$ be such that for each n, X_n is $\mathcal{F}_n$- measurable and $X_n \sim P_n$. Furthermore, let F_n be the cumulative distribution function associated with P_n. Also, let $(\Omega, \mathcal{F}, P)$ be another probability space and we consider an $\mathcal{F}$-measurable random variable X, whose P associated cumulative probability distribution function is F. Then we say that the sequence $\{X_n\}_{n=1}^{\infty}$ *converges in distribution* to X if as $n \to \infty$

$$F_n(x) \to F(x), \text{ for each continuity point } x \text{ of } F. \tag{5.19}$$

The standard notation for convergence in distribution is $F_n \underset{\rightarrow}{D} F$ or $F_n \underset{\rightarrow}{L} F$. Sometimes the convergence in the distribution is also denoted by $X_n \underset{\rightarrow}{L} X$.

Example 5.10.2. Convergence in Distribution for a Sequence of Uniform Random Variables. Let $\Omega_n = (0, 1/n)$, $\mathcal{F}_n$ a Borel σ-field on Ω_n, and let P_n be the uniform distribution over the interval $(0, 1/n)$, that is, we consider a sequence of (decreasing, in support) uniform distributions. We can then see that

$$\lim_{n\to\infty} F_n(x) = \lim_{n\to\infty} \begin{cases} 0, & \text{if } x < 0, \\ \frac{x}{n}, & \text{if } 0 < x < \frac{1}{n}, \\ 1, & \text{if } x \geq 1, \end{cases}$$

$$= \begin{cases} 0, & \text{if } x < 0, \\ 1, & \text{if } x \geq 0. \end{cases}$$

However, the cdf of a degenerate RV X is also given by

$$F_X(x) = \begin{cases} 0, & \text{if } x < 0, \\ 1, & \text{if } x \geq 0. \end{cases}$$

and hence we conclude that $X_n \underset{\rightarrow}{L} X$.

We illustrate this convergence in R.

```
> # Convergence of Uniform Random Variables
> supportud <- seq(-1,1,0.01)
> plot(supportud,punif(supportud,0,1),"l",xlab="x",
+ ylab=expression(paste("F","_","(n)",sep="")),col=1)
> n <- c(1,2,5,10,100,1000,10000)
> for(i in 2:length(n)) {
+       lines(supportud,punif(supportud,0,1/n[i]),col=i)
+         }
> pdegen <- c(rep(0,100),rep(1,101))
> lines(supportud,pdegen,"p")
```

How does the program work? The x values range is specified as `seq(-1,1,0.01)` and stored in the object `supportud`. Though X_n does not assume any negative value, the range is selected from –1, which gives a better plot. This aspect of generating elegant graphical plots is not a scientific matter, it is more of a personal preference. The uniform distribution function $F_n(x)$ is obtained with `punif(supportud,0,1)`, and it is then visualized with the `plot` graphical function. Since we need to examine the behavior of $F_n(x)$ for increasing n values, the n values are changed with `n <- c(1,2,5,10,100,1000,10 000)`. Using the `lines` option, the $F_n(x)$ are embossed on the existing plot. Thus, Part A of Figure 5.7 shows that as n increases, F_n approaches F. □

We next state an important result, see page 259 of Rohatgi and Saleh (2000).

Theorem 5.10.1 *Consider a sequence of probability spaces* $\{(\Omega_n, \mathcal{F}_n, P_n)\}_{n=1}^{\infty}$, *and the earlier setup of random variables with* $(\Omega, \mathcal{F}, P)$ *too. Let* f_n *and* f *be the probability density functions associated with the sequence of* F_n *and* F *respectively. If, as* $n \to \infty$

$$f_n(x) \to f(x), \text{ for almost all } x \text{ continuity points of } F, \tag{5.20}$$

then $X_n \underset{\rightarrow}{L} X$. □

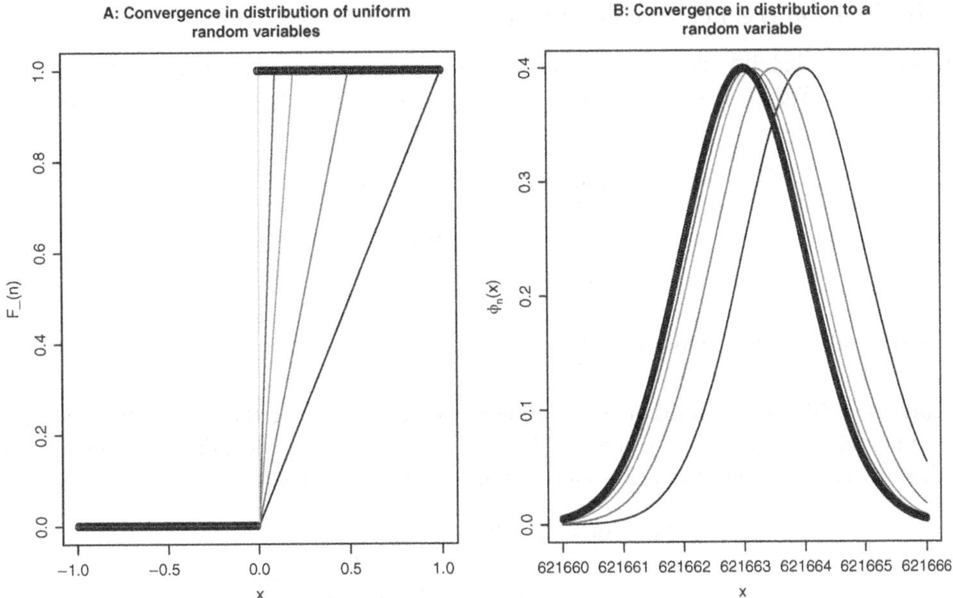

Figure 5.7 Illustration of Convergence in Distribution

The above theorem is now illustrated through an example.

Example 5.10.3. Convergence in Distribution to a Nondegenerate Random Variable. Consider a sequence of probability spaces $\{(\Omega_n, \mathcal{F}_n, P_n)\}_{n=1}^{\infty}$ with the probability measure P_n identified by normal probability measures $N(\mu + 1/n, 1)$. An R program next shows the convergence of the sequence X_n to a normal random variable with $N(\mu, 1)$.

```
> # Example of Convergence to a Continuous RV
> theta <- sample(1:10^{6},1)
> supportnor <- seq(theta-3,theta+3,0.01)
> n <- c(1,2,5,10,100,1000,10000)
> plot(supportnor,dnorm(supportnor,theta+1,1),xlab="x",
+ ylab=expression(paste(Phi,"n","(x)",sep="")),"l",col=1)
> for(i in 2:length(n)){
+      lines(supportnor,dnorm(supportnor,theta+1/n[i],1),col=i)
+ }
> lines(supportnor,dnorm(supportnor,theta,1),"p")
```

Since we require the probability density function of the normal RV, we are using the `dnorm` function. The purpose of the `sample` function is to generate a *random integer* in the range 1 to `10^6`. Details of this function are obtainable in Chapter 11. Note that different runs of the program will result in different outputs, since we are arbitrarily selecting the mean of the normal distribution from `1:10^6`. The rest of the program is easier to follow. What does Part B of Figure 5.7 say? □

5.10.2 Convergence in Probability

Consider a probability space $(\Omega, \mathcal{F}, P)$ and let $\{X_n\}$ be a sequence of random variables defined in this space. We say that the sequence $\{X_n\}$ *converges in probability* to a random variable X if for each $\epsilon > 0$

$$\lim_{n\to\infty} P(|X_n - X| \geq \epsilon) = 0, \tag{5.21}$$

or, equivalently

$$\lim_{n\to\infty} P(|X_n - X| < \epsilon) = 1. \tag{5.22}$$

Symbolically, we denote this as $X_n \underset{\rightarrow}{P} X$.

Example 5.10.4. Continuation of Example 5.7.3. Recall that the RVs X_i take the value 1 in the interval $[i/2^m, (i+1)/2^m]$, and 0 in the rest of Ω. Note that the length of the interval over which it takes the value 1 is $1/2^m$. Thus, for all $\epsilon \in (0, 1]$, we have

$$P(|X_n - 0| \geq \epsilon) = P(X_n = 1),$$
$$= \frac{1}{2^m} \rightarrow 0, \quad as \quad n \rightarrow \infty.$$

Thus the sequence of RVs converges to 0 in probability, that is, $X_n \underset{\rightarrow}{P} 0$. □

Convergence in probability implies convergence in distribution. However, the converse is not true.

5.10.3 Convergence in r^{th} Mean

We begin with a probability space $(\Omega, \mathcal{F}, P)$ and let $\{X_n\}$ be a sequence of random variables defined in it. We say that the sequence $\{X_n\}$ *converges in r^{th} mean* to an RV X if $E|X|^r < \infty$ and as $n \rightarrow \infty$

$$E|X_n - X|^r \rightarrow 0. \tag{5.23}$$

Example 5.10.5. A Sequence Converging in the Second Mean. Let $\{X_n\}_{n=1}^{\infty}$ be a sequence of random variables for whom the probability measure is defined by

$$P\{X_n = 1\} = 1 - \frac{1}{n}, P\{X_n = 0\} = \frac{1}{n}, n = 1, 2, \ldots .$$

Let us understand the behavior of X_n probabilities graphically.

```
> # Convergence in r-th Mean
> pr_xn_1 <- 1/{1:50}
> pr_xn_0 <- 1- 1/{1:50}
> par(mfrow=c(1,2))
> plot(1:50,pr_xn_1,xlab="X_n 's",
+ main="Probability of Xn Taking Value 1", type="h")
```

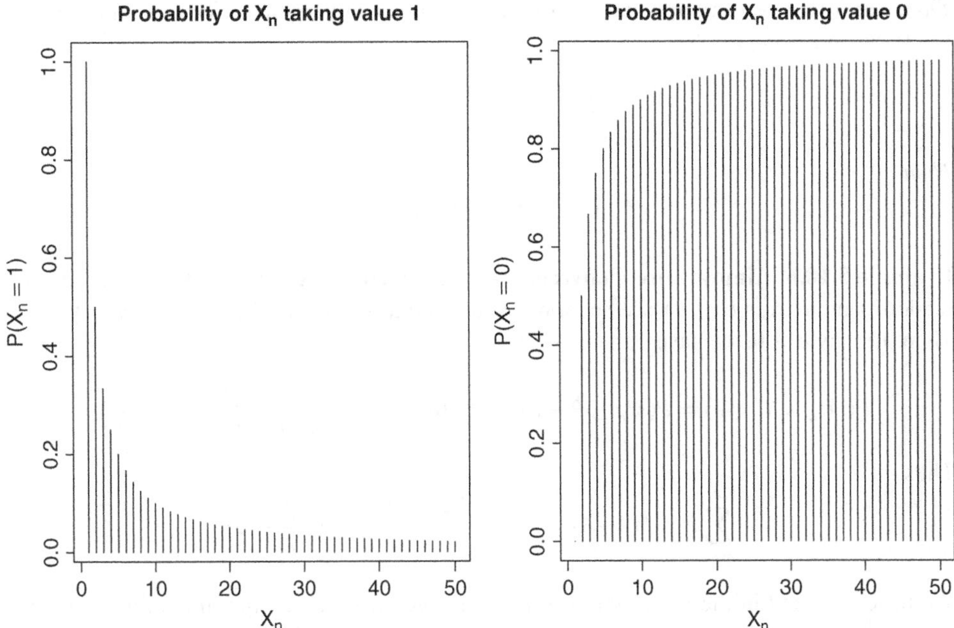

Figure 5.8 Graphical Aid for Understanding Convergence in r^{th} Mean

```
> plot(1:50,pr_xn_0,xlab="X_n 's",
+ main="Probability of Xn Taking Value 0", type="h")
```

Figure 5.8 shows that as n increases, the probability of X_n taking the value 0 is very close to 1. This is not the same as saying that the convergence in mean, for any r, is guaranteed. However, we can probably investigate if the sequence X_n converges in *some* order of mean to 0. Let us check for the convergence to 0 in the second mean.

$$E|X_n - 0|^2 = E|X_n|^2 = 0^2(1 - 1/n) + 1^2(1/n) = \frac{1}{n}.$$

Thus, as $n \to \infty$, $E|X_n - 0|^2 \to 0$ and we can say that X_n converges in the second mean to zero. □

5.10.4 Almost Sure Convergence

Let $\{X_n\}_{n=1}^{\infty}$ be a sequence of random variables on the probability space $(\Omega, \mathcal{F}, P)$. The sequence $\{X_n\}$ is said to *converge almost surely* to a RV X if

$$P\{\omega : X_n(\omega) \to X(\omega) \quad \text{as} \quad n \to \infty\} = 1.$$

The next result is very useful in establishing almost sure convergence. Almost sure convergence is denoted by $\xrightarrow{a.s.}$

Theorem 5.10.2 A Limsup Criteria for Almost Sure Convergence. *Suppose that for every $\epsilon > 0$, the following holds:*

$$\sum_{n=1}^{\infty} P(|X_n - X| \geq \epsilon) < \infty.$$

Then

$$X_n \underset{\longrightarrow}{a.s.} X, \quad \text{as} \quad n \to \infty.$$

□

Example 5.10.6. Almost Sure Convergence of Uniform Maxima. Let $X_1, X_2, \ldots, X_n$ be a random sample from $U(0, \theta)$, see Section 6.3, and define $M_n = \max(X_1, \ldots, X_n), n = 1, 2, \ldots$. Then, for any $\epsilon > 0$, we have

$$P(|M_n - \theta| \geq \epsilon) = P(M_n \leq \theta - \epsilon) = [F_U(\theta - \epsilon)]^n = \left(\frac{\theta - \epsilon}{\theta}\right)^n = \left(1 - \frac{\epsilon}{\theta}\right)^n.$$

Thus,

$$\sum_{n=1}^{\infty} P(\{|M_n - \theta| \geq \epsilon\}) = \sum_{n=1}^{\infty} \left(1 - \frac{\epsilon}{\theta}\right)^n = \frac{\theta}{\epsilon} < \infty.$$

We have assumed in the above that $\epsilon < \theta$. Thus, we have proved that the uniform maxima converges to θ. □

?expression, ?ifelse, library(help="ConvergenceConcepts")

5.11 The Law of Large Numbers

The "large" in the Law of Large Numbers, abbreviated as LLN, is a pointer that the number of observations are very large. This clarification is issued in interest of the student community, as we felt that quite a few of them have confused the "large" with the magnitude of X.

The LLN has two very important variants: (i) the Weak Law of Large Numbers, abbreviated as WLLN, and (ii) the Strong Law of Large Numbers, SLLN. The former is a convergence in probability criteria and the latter is almost sure convergence. Formal statements are given here. We discuss the concepts with a few analytical illustrations. For an understanding of these concepts through *simulation*, we refer the reader to Section 6 of Chapter 12.

5.11.1 The Weak Law of Large Numbers

Let $\{X_n\}_{n=1}^{\infty}$ be a sequence of random variables and define $S_n := \sum_{i=1}^{n} X_i, n = 1, 2, \ldots$. The sequence $\{X_n\}_{n=1}^{\infty}$ is said to obey the *weak law of large numbers*, WLLN, with respect to a sequence of constants $\{B_n\}, n = 1, 2, \ldots, B_n > 0, B_n \uparrow \infty$, if there exists a sequence of constants $\{A_n\}, n = 1, 2, \ldots$ which satisfies

$$\frac{S_n - A_n}{B_n} \underset{\rightarrow}{P} 0, \text{ as } n \to \infty$$

The sequence $\{A_n\}$ is called *centering sequence* and the sequence $\{B_n\}$ is called *norming sequence*. We state below a result which helps to determine whether the WLLN holds true for the sequence under consideration.

Theorem 5.11.1 A Criteria for WLLN to Hold True. *Let X_n be a sequence of pairwise uncorrelated RVs. Let $EX_i = \mu_i$ and $Var(X_i) = \sigma_i^2, i = 1, 2, \ldots$. Define $A_n = \sum_{i=1}^n \mu_i$ and $B_n = \sum_{i=1}^n \sigma_i^2, i = 1, 2, \ldots$. If $B_n \to \infty$ as $n \to \infty$, the WLLN holds true, that is,*

$$\sum_{i=1}^{n} \frac{X_i - \mu_i}{\sum_{i=1}^{n} \sigma_i^2} \to 0, \quad \text{as } n \to \infty.$$

□

Example 5.11.1. WLLN for Sum of Bernoulli Trials. Let $X_i \sim b(1, p), i = 1, 2, \ldots$. Here $A_n = np$ and $B_n = np(1—p)$. Thus, by application of the previous theorem, since $B_n \uparrow \infty$, we have

$$\frac{S_n}{n} \to p, \quad \text{as } n \to \infty,$$

which helps us to conclude that the WLLN holds for the sequence S_n. □

Theorem 5.11.2 A Necessary and Sufficient Condition for WLLN. *Let X_n be a sequence of iid RVs. Define $B_n = n$ and $S_n = \sum_{i=1}^n X_i$. Then $S_n/B_n \xrightarrow{P} 0$ if*

$$nP(|X_1| > n) \to 0, \quad \text{and}$$

$$E\{X_1 I_{|X_n| \le n}\} \to 0, \quad \text{as } n \to \infty.$$

□

Example 5.11.2. Non-universality of WLLNs: The Cauchy Sequence. Consider a random sample from a standard Cauchy distribution. That is, $X_i \sim Cauchy(0, 1)$. Then

$$nP(|X_n| > n) = n \int_{|x|>n} \frac{dx}{\pi(1 + x^2)} > \frac{n}{\pi} \int_n^{\infty} \frac{dx}{x_2} = \frac{1}{\pi}.$$

As the last term is independent of n, $nP(|X_n| > n)$ will not converge to 0. Hence, the WLLN does not hold for a Cauchy sequence. □

5.12 The Central Limit Theorem

5.12.1 The de Moivre-Laplace Central Limit Theorem

A complete de-mystification of the de Moivre-Laplace CLT appears in Ramasubramaniam (1997). Suppose that $X_i \sim Bernoulli(p), i = 1, 2, \ldots$. Let $S_n = \sum_{i=1}^n X_i, n = 1, 2, \ldots$. Define

$$Z_n = \frac{S_n - np}{\sqrt{np(1 - p)}}. \tag{5.24}$$

We will begin with a statement of this result.

Theorem 5.12.1 The de Moivre-Laplace CLT. *As* $n \to \infty$

$$P(a < Z_n \leq b) = \int_a^b \frac{1}{\sqrt{2\pi}} e^{-x^2/2} dx. \tag{5.25}$$

□

Typically, CLT is demonstrated using a simulation study. Though that approach is not wrong, we would like to make a few pointers here. In a simulation study we actually use the realized values of the RVs as in $x_1, x_2, \ldots, x_n$. However, the CLT is truly about the convergence of RVs as in $X_1, X_2, \ldots, X_n$. The principal point is that we cannot pretend that $\sqrt{n}(\bar{X}_n - \mu) \underset{\rightarrow}{D} N(0, \sigma^2)$ is the same as $\sqrt{n}\,(\bar{x}_n - \mu)\ \underset{\rightarrow}{D}\ N\,(0, \sigma^2)$. Thus, our illustration, at least in this section, will not resort to a simulation study.

We give an animated version of the convergence in the following program.

```
> n <- 10:1000
> p <- 0.4
> for(i in 1:length(n)){
+     plot(0:n[i],dbinom(0:n[i],p=0.4,n[i]),
+     "h",xaxt="n",yaxt="n",xlab="x",ylab="PDF")
+     title("The de Moivre's Laplace Central Limit Theorem")
+     curve(dnorm(x,mean=n[i]*0.4,sd=sqrt(n[i]*0.4*0.6)),
+     from=0,to=n[i],add=TRUE)
+ }
```

Change the values of p for different levels and enjoy the convergence. Consider the general iid case next.

5.12.2 CLT for iid Case

Let $X_1, X_2, \ldots$ be iid random variables with finite first and second moments, that is, $E(X_i^j) < \infty, j = 1, 2$. Define $S_n = \sum_{i=1}^n X_i, n = 1, 2, \ldots$. Let μ and σ^2 denote the mean and variance for X_i. The general CLT for the iid case is stated below.

Theorem 5.12.2 CLT for iid Random Sample. *As* $n \to \infty$

$$\frac{S_n - n\mu}{\sigma\sqrt{n}} \underset{\rightarrow}{D} N(0, 1). \tag{5.26}$$

□

Two equivalent forms of the CLT statement are that as $n \to \infty$

$$\sqrt{n}(\bar{X}_n - \mu)\ \underset{\rightarrow}{D}\ N(0, \sigma^2),$$

$$S_n = \sum_{i=1}^n X_i\ \underset{\rightarrow}{D}\ N(n\mu, n\sigma^2).$$

This statement appears very generic and we consider an illustration with varied distributions.

Example 5.12.1. CLT for Gamma Distribution. This illustration is an extension of a beautiful construct by Geyer, see http://www.stat.umn.edu/geyer/5101/examp/clt.html. Suppose $X \sim \text{Gamma}(\alpha, 1)$. We have an iid sample of size n. It is easier to see that $S_n = \sum_{i=1}^{n} X_i \sim \text{Gamma}(\alpha, n)$. For large n, the CLT says that S_n may be approximated by $N(n\alpha, n\alpha^2)$. We know that a Gamma distribution is skewed, and hence we first plot the density function of the gamma distribution and insert the approximate normal curve. In the long run, we expect the two curves to be identical. Thus, for different n values, we obtain Figure 5.9, which shows that the normal approximation indeed works fine.

```
> # 5.15.2 CLT for iid Case
> alpha <- 0.5
> n <- c(1,5,20,100,500,1000)
> cutoff <- 1e-3
> par(mfrow=c(2,3))
> for(i in 1:6){
+       from <- qgamma(cutoff/2, n[i]*alpha)
+       to <- qgamma(cutoff/2, n[i]*alpha,lower.tail=FALSE)
+       if(i==1) from <- 0
+       if(i==1) to <- 6
+       curve(dgamma(x,n[i]*alpha),from=from,to=to,ylab="f(x)",
+ xlab="x",main=paste("n = ",n[i],sep=""))
+       curve(dnorm(x,mean=n[i]*alpha,sd=sqrt(n[i]*alpha)),col="red",
+ add=TRUE)
+         }
> title("CLT for a Gamma Sum",outer=TRUE,line=-1)
```

Note that we are genuinely looking at the probability distribution function of S_n. □

Example 5.12.2. An iid Sample from Triangular Distribution. Let X be a random variable whose probability distribution is specified by a triangular distribution on the points a, b, c with $a \le c \le b \in \mathbb{R}$:

$$f(x,a,b,c) = \begin{cases} 0, & x < a, \\ \frac{2(x-a)}{(b-a)(c-a)}, & a \le x < c, \\ \frac{2}{b-a}, & x = c, \\ \frac{2(b-x)}{(b-a)(b-c)}, & c < x \le b, \\ 0, & x > b. \end{cases}$$

The parameters allow us to specify any three points on the real line. Let $X_1, X_2, \ldots,$ be replicates of X. The reader can verify this for a triangular distribution:

$$E(X) = \mu = \frac{a+b+c}{3},$$

$$Var(X) = \sigma^2 = \frac{a^2+b^2+c^2-ab-ac-bc}{18}.$$

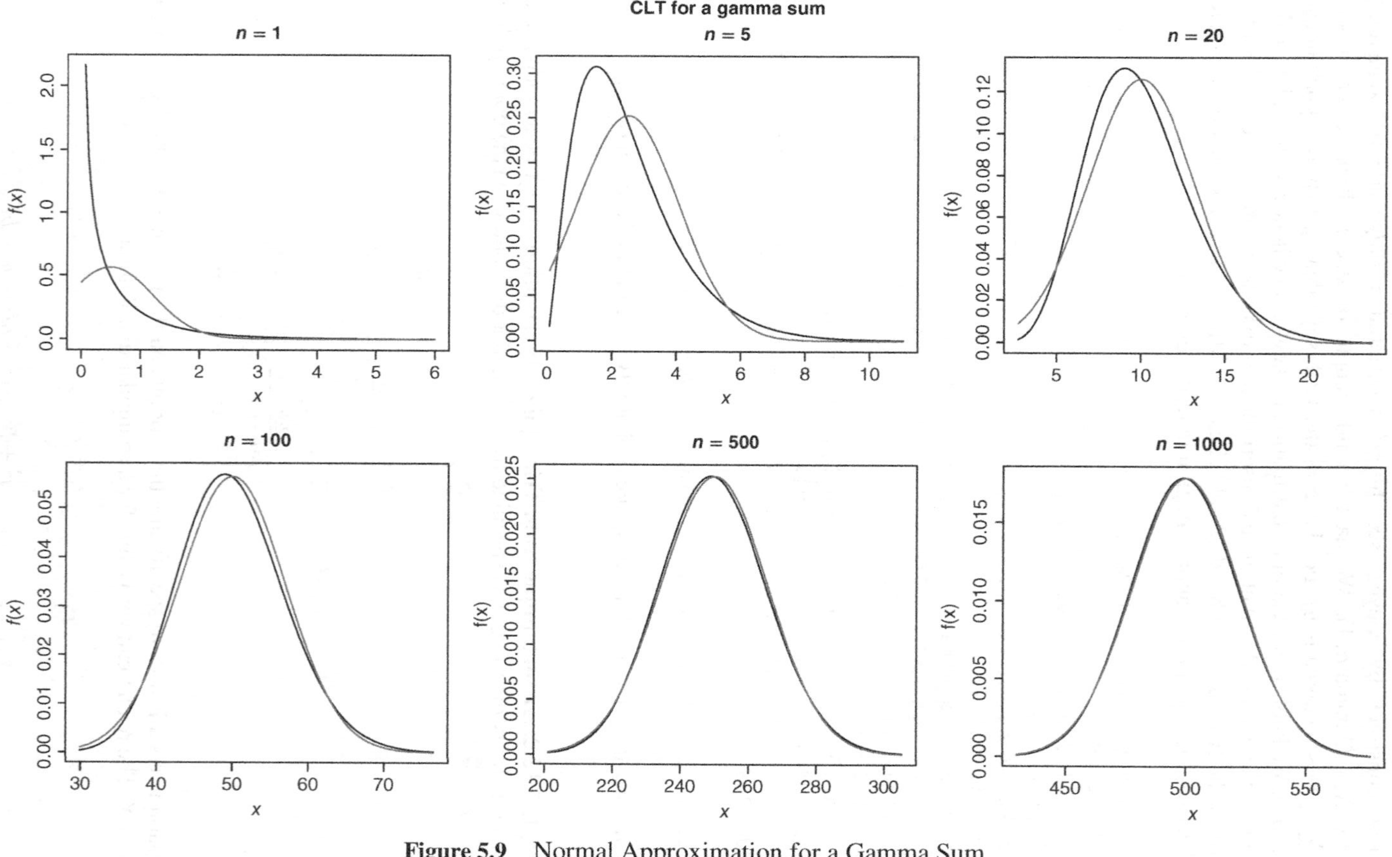

Figure 5.9 Normal Approximation for a Gamma Sum

Thus, the mean and variance are seen to be finite. Define $S_n = \sum_{i=1}^{n} X_i$. The iid CLT clearly says that in this case $(S_n - n\mu)/(\sigma\sqrt{n})$ converges to a standard normal distribution. A nice thing about the theory is that we now know how to approximate the average of the sample observations of a triangular distribution. It is important to note that the convolution sum of triangular random variables is not known for a general n. The CLT holding good for this example is shown through a simulation study in Chapter 11. □

The more general case of a sequence of independent RVs is considered next.

5.12.3 The Lindeberg-Feller CLT

The previous theorem along with Equation 5.26 handles a sequence of iid RVs. An extension of this result for the more generic case of a sequence of independent RVs is then required. The Lindeberg-Feller theorem gives a set of necessary and sufficient conditions which help establish CLT for a sequence of independent RVs. A few notations are in order towards this end.

Let $\{X_n\}_{n=1}^{\infty}$ be a sequence of RVs, and let their respective probability spaces be defined by the sequence $(\Omega_n, \mathcal{F}_n, P_n)$. In the case of the iid sequence, we have $P_n = P$. Assume that $EX_n = \mu_n$, and $VarX_n = \sigma_n^2 < \infty$. Define $S_n = \sum_{k=1}^{n}(X_k - \mu_k)$, $s_n^2 = \sum_{k=1}^{n} \sigma_k^2$, and $s_n = \sqrt{s_n^2}$. It may be noted by the reader here that s_n does not correspond to the realized value of the sum S_n. The next theorem is the famous result sought in this section.

Theorem 5.12.3 The Lindeberg-Feller CLT. *Consider a sequence of independent RVs $\{X_n\}_{n=1}^{\infty}$ defined on the respective probability spaces $(\Omega_n, \mathcal{F}_n, P_n)$. Suppose*

$$\frac{S_n}{s_n} \xrightarrow{D} N(0,1) \text{ and } \max_{1 \le k \le n} \frac{\sigma_k}{s_n} \to 0 \text{ as } n \to \infty. \tag{5.27}$$

A necessary and sufficient condition for 5.27 to hold is given by the Lindeberg *condition, if for every $\epsilon > 0$*

$$g_n(\epsilon) = \frac{1}{s_n^2} \sum_{k=1}^{n} \left(\int_{|x| > \epsilon s_n} x^2 dP_k(x) \right) \to 0, \text{ as } n \to \infty. \tag{5.28}$$

□

From a programming perspective, it is better to first consider the simpler case of a sequence of iid RVs for verifying the Feller condition 5.27 and also the Lindeberg condition 5.28. It will become more clear why the simpler case has been considered first.

Example 5.12.3. Sequence of Normal RVs. Let X_n's be iid RVs and each following the standard normal distribution. It is then known by the theorem in the previous subsection that the sum of these RVs follows a normal distribution. However, this example will be used here to give a clear understanding of the Lindeberg and Feller conditions. First, Feller conditions will be verified.

The R program unfolds as follows. The numeric vector `mean_k` declares all the means as 0, while `sigma_2_k` is used to define the sequence of σ_k's. Next, the important term of the sum of variances of the RVs s_n^2 is obtained using the `cumsum` function and stored as `sn_2`, and the small s_n is obtained with `sn <- sqrt(sn_2)`. The Feller condition requires us to obtain $\max_{1\le k\le n} \frac{\sigma_k}{s_n}$. This is easily obtained with the max function in a loop.

```
> mean_k <- rep(0,1000)
> sigma_2_k <- rep(1,1000)
> n <- length(sigma_2_k)
> sigma_k <- sqrt(sigma_2_k)
> sn_2 <- cumsum(sigma_2_k)
> sn <- sqrt(sn_2)
> Sn_by_sn <- sigma_k/sn
> Max_Sn_by_sn <- NULL
> for(i in 1:length(sigma_k)){
+ Max_Sn_by_sn[i] <- max(sigma_k[1:i]/sn[i])
+ }
> plot.ts(Max_Sn_by_sn,main=expression(paste("A: Feller
+ Condition for ", X[n],"~",N(0,1))),
+ xlab=expression(paste("as ",n %->% infinity)))
```

The resultant `Max_Sn_by_sn` is visualized to check if it really approaches 0 for large values of n. The numeric object `Max_Sn_by_sn` is simply plotted against the indices, and the `expression` and `paste` options are used meticulously to obtain the right labels for the x- and y- axes. It may be seen from Part A of Figure 5.11 that the Feller condition 5.27 is satisfied for the sequence of iid RVs from the standard normal distribution. Hence, a program is developed to verify if the Lindeberg conditions are also met.

```
> # Lindeberg Condition
> epsilon <- c(0.3,0.2,0.1,0.05)
> windows(height=20,width=20)
> par(mfrow=c(2,2))
> for(z in 1:4){
+ gn_epsilon <- NULL
+ curr_epsilon <- epsilon[z]
+ for(i in 1:n){
+ integral_term <- 0
+ sigma_2_temp <- sn_2[i]
+ sigma_temp <- sn[i]
+ for(j in 1:i){
+ integral_term <- integral_term + 2*integrate(function(x)
+ x^{2}*dnorm(x,mean=mean_k[j],
+ sd=sigma_k[j]),lower=curr_epsilon*sigma_temp,upper=Inf)$value
+ }
+ gn_epsilon[i] <- integral_term/sigma_2_temp
+ }
+ plot.ts(gn_epsilon,main=expression(paste("Lindberg Condition
+ for ", X[n],"~",N(0,1))),
+ xlab=expression(paste("as ",n %->% infinity)),
+ ylab=expression(g[n](epsilon)))
+ text(800,.8,bquote(epsilon == .(curr_epsilon)))
+ }
```

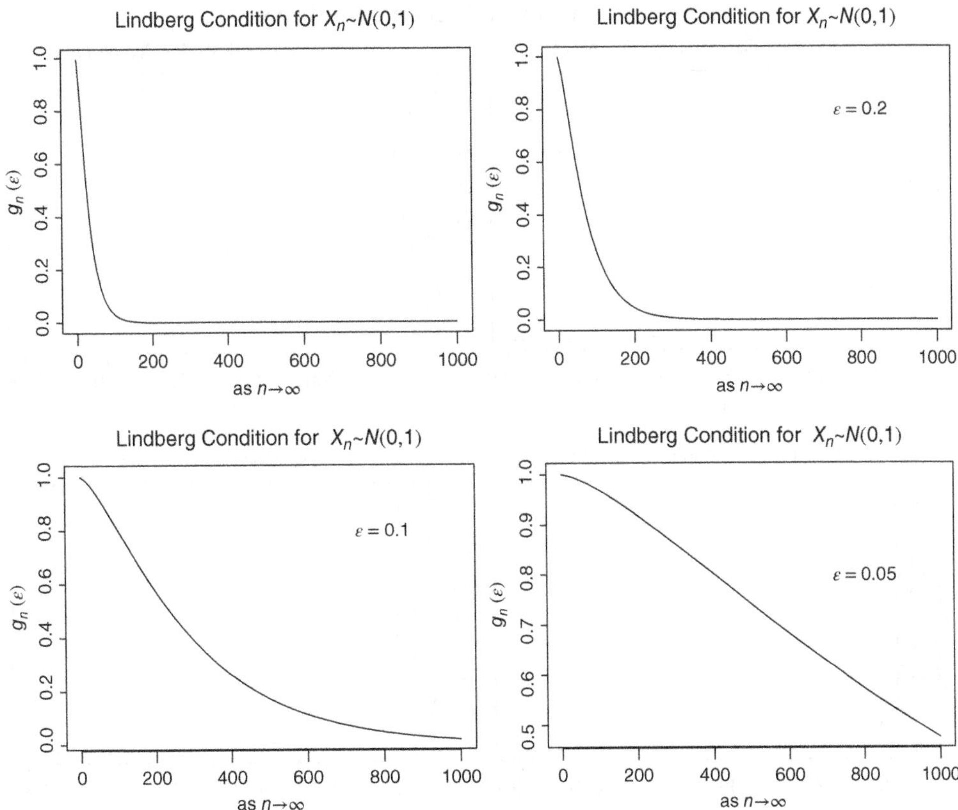

Figure 5.10 Lindeberg Conditions for Standard Normal Distribution

The Lindeberg condition 5.28 needs to be verified for every $\epsilon > 0$, but such a daunting task is not a necessity here and four values of `epsilon <- c(0.3,0.2,0.1,0.05)` are experimented with here. The Lindeberg expression needs to be handled carefully, and if it is not, the program may end up as a dampener. First, the integral needs to be evaluated over the range $|x| > \epsilon s_n$. Using the symmetric property of the normal distribution, the search is restricted over the range $x > \epsilon s_n$, and thus the options `lower=curr_epsilon*sigma_temp` and `upper=Inf` and the evaluated integral value is multiplied by 2. The integrand x^2 is handled with `function(x) x^2*dnorm`. The `for(j in 1:i)` obtains $g_n(\epsilon)$, and the higher loop `for(i in 1:n)` obtains $g_n(\epsilon)$ for different n's. The plot of $g_n(\epsilon)$ is obtained when the ϵ value is displayed using the `text` function with the `bquote` option to reflect the choice of ϵ. For each choice of ϵ, the $g_n(\epsilon)$ is seen to approach 0 in Figure 5.10. Thus, the CLT holds for this sequence of RVs. □

Example 5.12.4. Sequence of Normal RVs–$N(n,n^2)$. Now, consider the sequence of independent RVs $\{X_n\}_{n=1}^{\infty}$, where $X_n \sim N(n, n^2)$. This is an example of where the Lindeberg-Feller

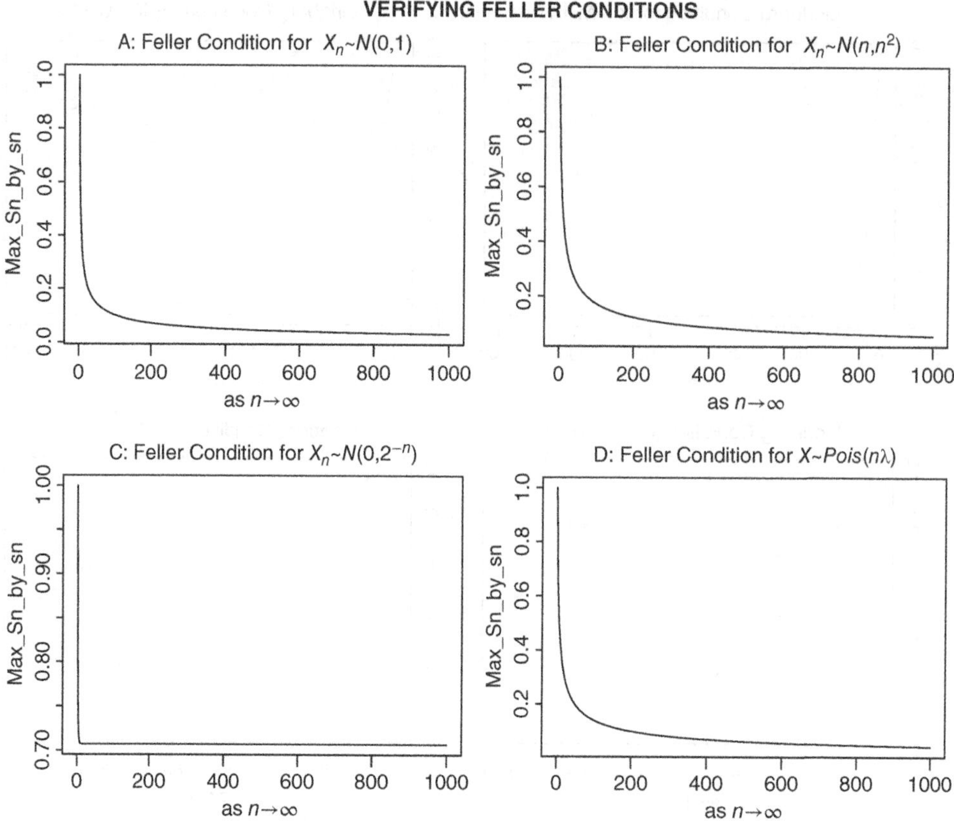

Figure 5.11 Verifying Feller Conditions for Four Problems

Theorem will be used to check if the CLT really holds or not. It is the Feller condition which will be first checked and if the condition 5.27 is satisfied, the Lindeberg condition will be detailed.

Clearly, the Feller part of the R program does not change much, except for the declaration of `mean_k` and `sigma_2_k`, and hence further description of the module is skipped. Part B of Figure 5.11 clearly shows that the Feller condition is satisfied for the sequence $\{X_n\}_{n=1}^{\infty}$. Similarly, the R program for the Lindeberg's condition does not require further explanation.

```
> ### Xn~N(n,n^{2}) ### CLT HOLDS GOOD
> # Feller Condition
> mean_k <- 1:1000
> sigma_2_k <- mea{n_k^{2}}
> n <- length(sigma_2_k)
> sigma_k <- sqrt(sigma_2_k)
> sn_2 <- cumsum(sigma_2_k)
> sn <- sqrt(sn_2)
```

```
> Sn_by_sn <- sigma_k/sn
> Max_Sn_by_sn <- NULL
> for(i in 1:length(sigma_k)){
+ Max_Sn_by_sn[i] <- max(sigma_k[1:i]/sn[i])
+ }
> plot.ts(Max_Sn_by_sn,main=expression(paste("B: Feller
+ Condition for ", X[n],"~","N(n,",n^{2},")")),
+ xlab=expression(paste("as ",n %->% infinity)))
> # Lindeberg Condition
> epsilon <- c(0.3,0.2,0.1,0.05)
> windows(height=20,width=20)
> par(mfrow=c(2,2))
> for(z in 1:length(epsilon)){
+ gn_epsilon <- 0
+ curr_epsilon <- epsilon[z]
+ for(i in 1:n){
+ integral_term <- 0
+ sigma_2_temp <- sn_2[i]
+ sigma_temp <- sn[i]
+ for(j in 1:i){
+ integral_term <- integral_term + 2*integrate(function(x)
+ x^{2}*dnorm(x,mean=mean_k[j],
+ sd=sigma_k[j]),lower=curr_epsilon*sigma_temp,upper=Inf)$value
+ }
+ gn_epsilon[i] <- integral_term/sigma_2_temp
+ }
+ plot.ts(gn_epsilon,main=expression(paste("Lindberg Condition
+ for ", X[n],"~",N(n,n^{2}))),
+ xlab=expression(paste("as ",n %->% infinity)),
+ ylab=expression(g[n](epsilon)))
+ text(800,3,bquote(epsilon == .(curr_epsilon)))
+ }
```

Note the change of $g_n(\epsilon)$ as ϵ decreases. This implies that for smaller ϵ, we need to draw large n to visualize the convergence of $g_n(\epsilon)$ to 0, see the right-hand bottom part of Figure 5.12. However, it is clearly seen that the Lindeberg condition is also satisfied for this sequence of RVs and hence the CLT will hold true. □

Example 5.12.5. Sequence of Normal RVs - $N(0, 2^{-n})$. Now, consider the sequence of independent RVs $\{X_n\}_{n=1}^{\infty}$ where $X_n \sim N(0, 2^{-n})$. The now familiar R program for the Feller condition results in part C of Figure 5.11. It is clearly seen that the Feller condition is not satisfied and that $\max_{1\le k\le n} \frac{\sigma_k}{s_n}$ stops at a value slightly above `0.7`. Hence, the CLT does not hold for this sequence of independent RVs.

```
> ### Xn~N(0,2^{-n}) ## CLT DOES NOT HOLD GOOD
> # Feller Condition
> mean_k <- rep(0,1000)
> sigma_2_k <- 2^{-c(1:1000)}
> n <- length(sigma_2_k)
```

```
> sigma_k <- sqrt(sigma_2_k)
> sn_2 <- cumsum(sigma_2_k)
> sn <- sqrt(sn_2)
> Sn_by_sn <- sigma_k/sn
> Max_Sn_by_sn <- NULL
> for(i in 1:length(sigma_k)){
+ Max_Sn_by_sn[i] <- max(sigma_k[1:i]/sn[i])
+ }
> plot(Max_Sn_by_sn)
> plot.ts(Max_Sn_by_sn,main=expression(paste("C: Feller Condition
+ for ", X[n],"~","N(0,",2^{-n},")")),xlab=expression(paste("as "
+ ,n %->%infinity)))
```

□

A stronger, but more restrictive, condition can be imposed, which can be used for examining the CLT for a sequence of independent RVs.

5.12.4 The Liapounov CLT

The Liapounov's CLT is given in the next theorem.

Theorem 5.12.4 The Liapounov CLT. *Consider a sequence of independent RVs* $\{X_n\}_{n=1}^{\infty}$ *defined in the respective probability spaces* $(\Omega_n, \mathcal{F}_n, P_n)$. *Let* $E(X_n) = \mu_n$, $Var(X_n) = \sigma_n^2 < \infty$, *and* $\nu_n = E|X_n - \mu_n|^{2+\delta}, 0 < \delta \leq 1$. *Define* $S_n = \sum_{k=1}^{n}(X_k - \mu_k)^2$, $s_n^2 = \sum_{k=1}^{n}\sigma_n^2$, $s_n = \sqrt{s_n^2}$, *and* $B_n = \sum_{k=1}^{n}\nu_k$. *If the* Liapounov*'s condition*

$$\frac{B_n}{s_n^{2+\delta}} \to 0 \, as \, n \to \infty, 0 < \delta \leq 1, \tag{5.29}$$

is satisfied for the sequence $\{X_n\}_{n=1}^{\infty}$, *then the CLT holds, that is,*

$$\frac{S_n}{s_n} \to N(0, 1) \, as \, n \to \infty.$$

□

Since the Liapounov's condition 5.29 requires a higher-order moment condition, it is more difficult in general to establish whether it holds for a given sequence of RVs. However, it is sometimes very useful for a sequence of discrete RVs.

Example 5.12.6. A Sequence of Poisson RVs with $X_n \sim$ Pois($n\lambda$). For a sequence of Poisson RVs $\{X_n\}_{n=1}^{\infty}$ with $X_n \sim$ Pois($n\lambda$), for $\delta = 1$, we have

$$E(X_n) = n\lambda = Var(X_n) = \nu_n,$$

$$s_n^2 = \sum_{k=1}^{n} k\lambda = \frac{n(n+1)}{2}\lambda, \text{ and}$$

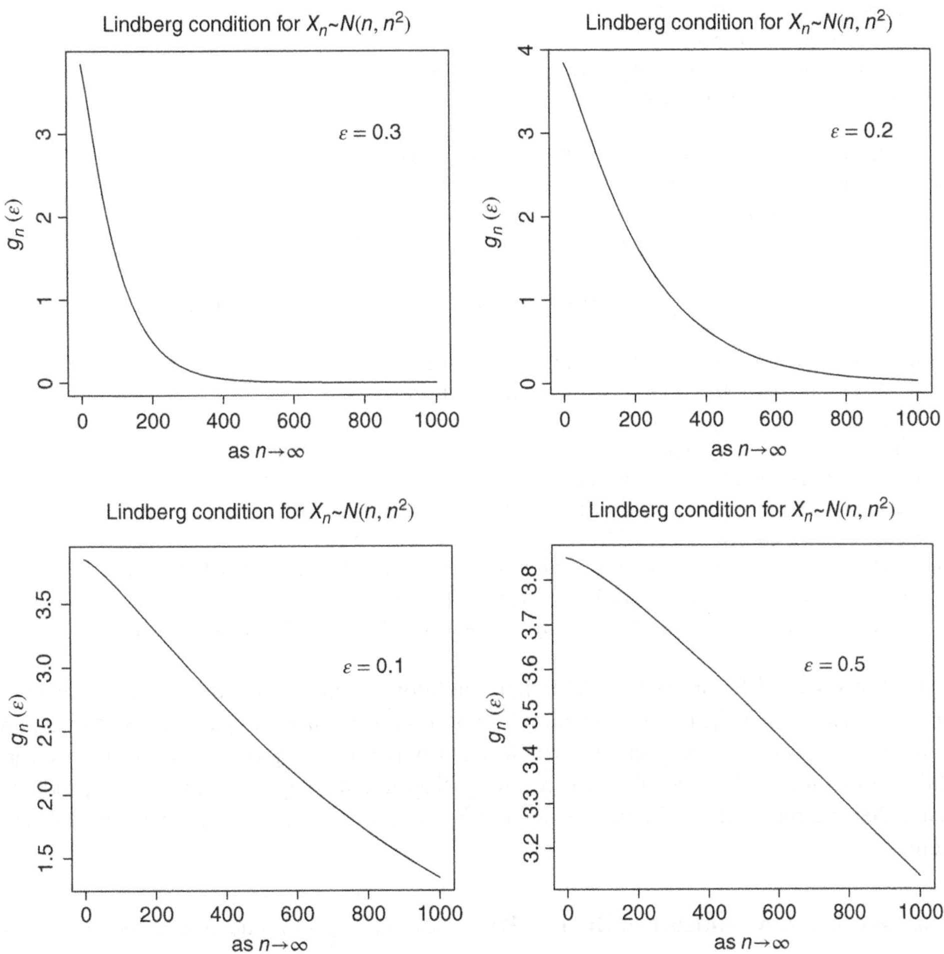

Figure 5.12 Lindeberg Conditions for Curved Normal Distribution

$$B_n = \sum_{k=1}^{n} k\lambda = \frac{n(n+1)}{2}\lambda.$$

It may be noted that the first three central moments for a Poisson RV are equal. Thus, we are checking whether the conditions required for the Liapounov's theorem is satisfied for $\delta = 1$. Since the Feller's condition is fairly easy to prove (at least in R), this aspect will be evaluated first.

```
> # # # Xn~Pois(n*lambda)
> # Feller Condition
> lambda <- 5 # A very arbitrary choice
> mean_k <- 1:100*lambda
```

```
> sigma_2_k <- mean_k
> n <- length(sigma_2_k)
> sigma_k <- sqrt(sigma_2_k)
> sn_2 <- cumsum(sigma_2_k)
> sn <- sqrt(sn_2)
> # Sn_by_sn <- sigma_k/sn # Not required
> Max_Sn_by_sn <- NULL
> for(i in 1:length(sigma_k)){
+ Max_Sn_by_sn[i] <- max(sigma_k[1:i]/sn[i])
+ }
> plot.ts(Max_Sn_by_sn,main=expression(paste("D: Feller Condition
+ for ", X, "~", "Pois(n", lambda,")")),
xlab=expression(paste("as ",n %->% infinity)))
> # Verify Liapounov's condition instead
> thirdCentral <- mean_k
> sn <- sqrt(cumsum(mean_k))
> Bn <- cumsum(thirdCentral)
> plot.ts(Bn/sn^{3},ylab="Liapounou's Condition",
+ xlab=expression(paste("as ", n %->% infinity)))
> text(80,0.4,expression(paste(frac(sum(E*"|"*X*"|"[k]^{2+delta},
+ k==1,n)),)) , col="purple", cex=0.8)
> text(80,0.365,expression(s[n]^{2+delta}),col="purple",cex=0.8)
```

Part D of Figure 5.11 shows that the Feller condition is satisfied for this sequence of Poisson RVs. Now, to evaluate the Liapounov's condition 5.29, first the quantities s_n and B_n are computed in sn and Bn respectively. The R quantity Bn/sn^3 gives us the Liapounov condition for various n. It is seen from the resulting diagram, the output of which is not produced here, that the required condition satisfies the X_n sequence, and hence the CLT holds good here. □

Example 5.12.7. A Sequence of Discrete RVs. Let $\{X_n\}_{n=2}^{\infty}$ be a sequence of RVs with PMF given by

$$P\left(X_n = \frac{n}{\ln(n)}\right) = P\left(X_n = -\frac{n}{\ln(n)}\right) = \frac{\ln(n)}{2n}, \text{ and}$$
$$P(X_n = 0) = 1 - \frac{\ln(n)}{n}. \tag{5.30}$$

It can be then seen that

$$\mu_n = E(X_n) = \frac{n}{\ln(n)}\frac{\ln(n)}{2n} + \frac{-n}{\ln(n)}\frac{\ln(n)}{2n} + 0 = 0,$$

$$\sigma_k^2 = Var(X_n) = \left(\frac{n}{\ln(n)}\right)^2\frac{\ln(n)}{2n} + \left(\frac{-n}{\ln(n)}\right)^2\frac{\ln(n)}{2n} + 0 = \frac{n}{\ln(n)}, \text{ and}$$

$$v_n = E|X - \mu_n|^3 = \left|\frac{n}{\ln(n)}\right|^3\frac{\ln(n)}{2n} + \left|\frac{-n}{\ln(n)}\right|^3\frac{\ln(n)}{2n} = \frac{n^2}{2(\ln(n))^2}.$$

The theoretical quantities μ_n, σ_k^2, and ν_n clearly help in setting up the R program. Using the same arguments as in the previous example, the R program is easily set up.

```
> # P(Xn=n/log(n))=log(n)/(2n) = P(Xn = -n/log(n));
# P(Xn=0) = 1-log(n)/n
> # E(Xn) = 0
> # Var(Xn) = n/log(n)
> # Feller Condition
> n <- 2:50
> sigma2 <- n/log(n)
> sigma <- sqrt(sigma2)
> sn2 <- cumsum(sigma2)
> sn <- sqrt(sn2)
> thirdCentral <- n^{2}/(2*(log(n)^{2}))
> Bn <- cumsum(thirdCentral)
> Max_Sn_by_sn <- sigma/sn
> par(mfrow=c(1,2))
> plot.ts(Max_Sn_by_sn,main=expression(paste("Feller Condition
+ for ", X[n])), xlab=expression(paste("as ",n %->% infinity)))
> # Verify Liapounov's condition instead
> plot.ts(Bn/sn^{3},ylab="Liapounov's Condition",
+ xlab=expression(paste("as ", n %->% infinity)),main=
+ expression(paste("Liapounov Condition for ", X[n])))
> text(40,0.8,expression(paste(frac(sum (E*"|"*X*"|"[k]^{2+delta},
+ k==1,n)),)), col="purple", cex=0.8)
> text(40,0.77,expression(s[n]^{2+delta}),col="purple",cex=0.8)
```

Figure 5.13 clearly shows that the Feller condition 5.27, as well as the Liapounov condition 5.29, are satisfied for the sequence of RVs considered here. Hence, the CLT holds for this sequence of RVs. □

?dgamma, ?qgamma

5.13 Further Reading

A futile exercise is being undertaken now as we promise the reader a complete bibliography on the sources of probability! With the possibility, that is positive probabilities, of some abuse, we have further classified the sources into different subsections.

5.13.1 Intuitive, Elementary, and First Course Source

Chung and AitSahlia (2004) is an appealing beginner's starting point. Chung and AitSahlia (2004) is a fourth edition enhancement of Chung (1979), which has been an excellent

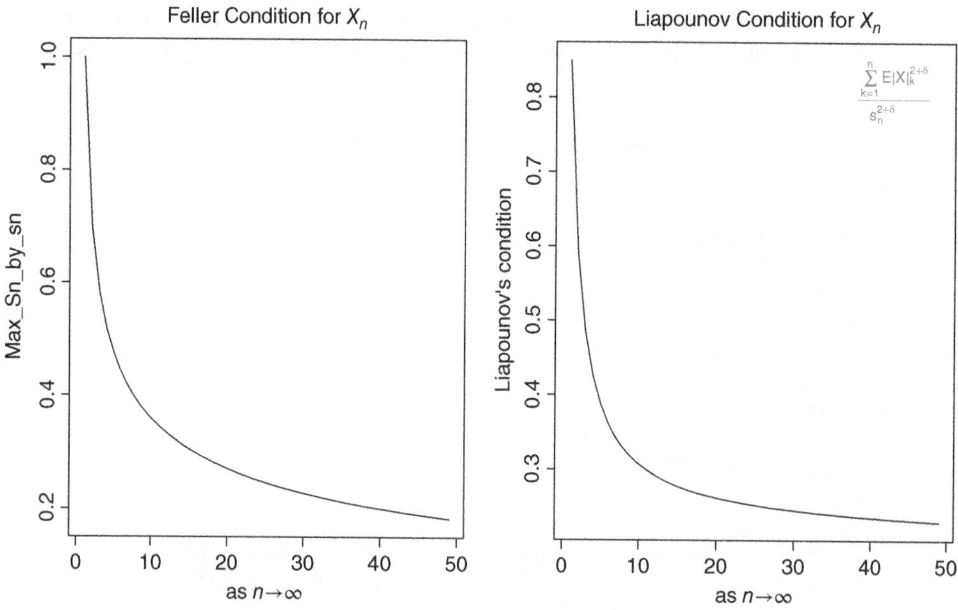

Figure 5.13 Liapounov Condition Verification

introduction since its first print. A higher secondary school introduction to probability has been written by two eminent Russian probabilists Gnedenko and Khinchin (1964). Ash (1969), Chandra and Chatterjee (2001), Gnedenko (1978), Durrett (2009), and Ross (2010) are some of the competitive first course texts on probability theory.

As far as intuition is concerned, one of the unrivalled works in the literature ever is the two volumes of Feller (1968 and 1971). A testimony and tribute to this fact is that almost any decent work on probability theory will cite Feller.

5.13.2 The Classics and Second Course Source

Feller's (1968 and 1971) two volumes are intuitive, classic, advanced courses, and also almost everything else too. The measure theoretic approach was first detailed in Kolmogorov (1933). This short book served as a cornerstone for the way probability would be written from that point onward. It is generally agreed that Loéve (1955) has been the first comprehensive take on the measure theoretic approach to probability and the last edition of his work appeared in two volumes, Loeve (1977). Chung (2000) has been another famous probabilitist researcher who has also written some of the best probability books.

Ash and Doléans-Dade (2000), Shiryaev (1995), Chow and Teicher (1995), Athreya and Lahiri (2005), Durrett (2010), and Breiman (1962, 1992), among others, are some of the excellent measure theoretic approaches to probability. Parthasarathy (1978) and Billingsley (1995) have also stood the test of time and are still a favorite of many probability readers. In most of the books mentioned in this paragraph, the first editions have appeared a couple of decades earlier than their most recent editions that we have listed here.

Rosenthall (2006) and Kallenberg (2002) are two of the modern texts on measure theoretic probability. In the Indian subcontinent, students and teachers have benefited from Bhat (2012) and Basu (1998) and both the books make a great read.

5.13.3 The Problem Books

If the intimidated people could have their way, we are sure that most of the authors mentioned in this subsection would be facing capital punishment! After all, the offense of these authors is not any less. Mosteller (1962), Grimmet and Stirzaker (2001), Cacoullus (1989), Schwarz (2007), Capiński and Zastawniak (2001), Nahin (2008), Sveshnikov (1968), and Chaumont and Yor (2003) all are guilty of the same offense. They batter the readers with a never-ending sequence of problems and thereby give a proof that is the way to understand infinity! To be fair to these authors, some of them have been really nice! They clearly mention that their book has only 40, 50, or 100 problems in contrast to some of them, who blatantly emphasize that the reader must solve 1000 problems!

5.13.4 Other Useful Sources

Johnson and Kotz (1969–73) have written a four-volume book on the distributions that arise in probability and statistics. An update to this work has appeared in the late 1990s by Johnson and Kotz and co-workers. DasGupta (2011) and DasGupta (2010) cover a lot of topics and modern advancements. Dworsky (2008) offers a different view and makes a smart read. Stoyanov (1997) is an entirely different type of book, with its focus mainly on counter examples.

5.13.5 R for Probability

Prof Jay Kerns' open source book, Kerns (2010), has been an influence on the first few sections of this chapter. Horgan (2008) and Baclawski (2008) are two introductory books who demonstrate a lot of probability aspect that can be understood through R.

5.14 Complements, Problems, and Programs

Problem 5.1 Consider the three sets from $\Omega =$ `LETTERS`: $A = \{``U", ``X", ``M", ``J", ``B", ``D"\}$, $B = \{``N", ``J", ``H", ``C", ``G", ``X"\}$, and $C = \{``H", ``V", ``N", ``K", ``D", ``F"\}$. Using the operators `intersect` and `union`, for the sets *A*, *B*, and *C*, verify the following:

1. $(A \cap B)' = A' \cup B'$ and $(A \cup B)' = A' \cap B'$.
2. $(A \cap B) \cup C = (A \cup C) \cap (B \cup C)$ and $(A \cup B) \cap C = (A \cap C) \cup (B \cap C)$.
3. Using the `sample` function, verify (i) and (ii) for arbitrary sets *A*, *B*, and *C*.

Problem 5.2 The R code `tosscoin(times=3)` returns an object of the `data.frame` class. However, a probabilist is familiar if the sample space is neatly written out as $\Omega = \{H, T\}$ or $\Omega = \{HH, HT, TH, TT\}$. Use the `paste` function to convert the `data.frame` object into ω elements such as H, HT, HHH, and so on, for any number of coin tosses.

Problem 5.3 The sample space of a die rolling becomes very large, depending on number of times we roll the die, and also on the number of sides of the die. Write a R program using the `rolldie` function from the `prob` package, *single line preferred*, which returns the total number of possible outcomes for (i) a die being rolled 1 to 6 times, (ii) the number of sides of the die vary from 3 to 10. An indicative syntax-based solution is along the lines `sapply(sapply(option2,rolldie,option1),nrow)`. Justify the use of `sapply` and the options.

Problem 5.4 Find out more details about the Roulette game and make a preliminary finding about it in the function `roulette`.

Problem 5.5 Run the codes `names(table(rowSums(S_Die)))` and `table (rowSums(S_Die))` from Example 5.2.7 and verify that you have completely understood the examples code. Now, roll four die and answer the probability of obtaining an odd number greater than ten.

Problem 5.6 For the thirteenth of a month problem, start with an arbitrary year, say 1857, and then run the program up to year 2256. Do you expect that the 13th will more likely be a Friday than any other day? Confirm your intuition with the R program.

Problem 5.7 In Example 5.3.3, the digits are drawn to solve a replacement problem. Obtain the probability of obtaining at least two even numbers in a draw of five using the leading digits of *e*.

Problem 5.8 What is the number of people whose birthday you need to ask so that the probability of finding a birthday mate is at least half? Write a brief R program to obtain the size as the probability varies from 0 to 1.

Problem 5.9 Construct a program which can conclude if the collection of sets over a finite probability space is a field.

Problem 5.10 Extend the program in the previous problem to verify if probabilities defined over an arbitrary collection of finite sets satisfies the requirement of being a probability measure.

Problem 5.11 Explore if the `addrv` function from the `prob` package can be used to handle more than two variables.

Problem 5.12 * For small σ values and μ around 0, write a program to obtain the expectation of a normal RV, which incorporates the expectation of an RV for an arbitrary RV, as given in Equation 5.16.

Problem 5.13 Extend the R function `Expectation_NNRV_Unif` for computing the expectation of a uniform RV over the interval $[-a, a], a \in \mathcal{R}$.

Problem 5.14 Evaluate the R program of de Moivre-Laplace CLT for different values of p.

Problem 5.15 Using the normal approximation, CLT result, for the triangular distribution for various values of a, b, and c, create an R program for evaluating $P(-c/2 < \bar{X} < c/2)$.

Problem 5.16 * Using the theoretical moments of the normal distribution, verify if the Liapounovs condition holds for the sequence of RVs developed in Example 5.12.4.

Problem 5.17 Let X_n follow a Poisson distribution $Pois(\lambda/n)$. Verify if the Feller condition holds for this sequence. If the Feller condition is satisfied, verify for the Liapounov's condition.

Problem 5.18 For an exponential RV with rate λ, the mean and variance are respectively known to be $1/\lambda$ and $1/\lambda^2$. Suppose X_n follows an exponential distribution with rate 2^n. Does the R program indicate that the Lindeberg condition will be satisfied for the defined sequence?

Problem 5.19 If the rate of exponential distribution for X_n is $n\lambda$, verify the Lindeberg and Feller condition for the sequence under consideration.

6

Probability and Sampling Distributions

Package(s): `scatterplot3d`, `mvtnorm`, `VGAM`

6.1 Introduction

In this chapter the focus will be two-fold. First, we will introduce and discuss common *probability models* in detail. This will cover probability models for univariate random variables, first including both discrete and continuous random variables. Apart from the associated probability measures, we will consider the cumulative probability distribution function, characteristics functions, and moment generating functions (when they exist). Sections 6.2 and 6.3 will cover some of the frequently arising probability models. Section 6.4 will deal with multivariate probability distributions of both discrete as well as continuous random vectors. A comprehensive listing source for probability distributions using R may be found at http://cran.r-project.org/web/views/Distributions.html.

The second purpose of this chapter is to show a different side of the probability models. The probability models which govern the uncertain phenomena discussed thus far implicitly assume that the parameters are known, or another way of their use is to obtain probabilities and not to be too concerned about the unknown parameters. In the real world, the parameters of probability models are not completely known and we infer their values which render the usefulness of these models. The statistical inference aspect of this problem is covered through Chapters 7 to 9. The bridge between probability models and statistical inference is provided by *sampling distributions*. The tool required towards this end is known as a *statistic*. The properties of the statistics are best understood using the law-of-large-numbers and the central limit theorem. Some results of these limit theorems were seen in the previous chapter. We will now begin with discrete random variables.

A Course in Statistics with R, First Edition. Prabhanjan Narayanachar Tattar, Suresh Ramaiah and B. G. Manjunath.

Companion Website: www.wiley.com/go/tattar/statistics

6.2 Discrete Univariate Distributions

We begin with discrete distributions. Many standard probability densities can be studied using built-in R commands. The three common and useful functions start with the letters `p`, `d`, and `q`, followed by a standard abbreviation of that distribution. Here, `p`, `d`, and `q` stand for the distribution function, density, and quantile function respectively. Of course, there is a fourth one too, which will be considered in Chapter 11.

6.2.1 *The Discrete Uniform Distribution*

Let X be an $\mathcal{F}$-measurable random variable oi the probability space $(\Omega, \mathcal{F}, P)$, where Ω is a finite set with N elements, say $\Omega = \{a, a+1, \dots, b-1, b\}$, where $b \geq a, a, b \in \mathcal{Z}$, $\mathcal{Z}$ is the set of integers, and let $\mathcal{F}$ be the power set of Ω. Here, $N = b - a + 1$. Define the probability measure P as follows. For any measurable set $A \in \mathcal{F}$, let

$$p(x) = P(X = x) = \begin{cases} \frac{1}{N}, & x \in \Omega, \\ 0, & \text{otherwise}. \end{cases} \tag{6.1}$$

The cdf, mgf, and cf, recall their definitions from Section 5.8, of discrete uniform distribution are respectively:

$$F_U(x) = \begin{cases} 0, & x < a, \\ \frac{x-a+1}{N}, & a \leq x \leq b, \\ 1, & \text{otherwise}, \end{cases} \tag{6.2}$$

$$M_U(t) = \frac{e^{at} - e^{(b+1)t}}{N(1 - e^t)}, \text{ and} \tag{6.3}$$

$$\varphi_U(t) = \frac{e^{iat} - e^{i(b+1)t}}{N(1 - e^{it})}. \tag{6.4}$$

The mean and variance of the discrete uniform distribution are given by

$$E(X) = \frac{a+b}{2}, \tag{6.5}$$

$$Var(X) = \frac{(b-a+1)^2 - 1}{12} = \frac{N^2 - 1}{12}. \tag{6.6}$$

On the surface the discrete uniform distribution may appear to be restricted and that it *may* not have practical applications. We next consider some real-life applications of the discrete uniform distribution.

Example 6.2.1. The Professor's Key Problem. Suppose a professor randomly selects a key from his key chain to open the door. If the key is not the correct one, the professor again randomly selects one of the other keys. The sampling continues until the lock is opened. The probability distribution of the right key being selected follows the discrete uniform distribution.

That is, if there are ten keys on the key chain, the average number of attempts it would take to open the door would be 5.5. □

Example 6.2.2. The German Tank Problem. A major task for the Western Allies during World War II was estimation of the number of tanks that Germany had manufactured. The scientists used data on the serial numbers on tanks (most significantly gearbox numbers), chassis and engine numbers, etc. The underlying distribution of the number of tanks was assumed to be discrete uniform. Check http://en.wikipedia.org/wiki/German_tank_problem for more details on this problem. □

6.2.2 *The Binomial Distribution*

Consider the probability space $(\Omega, \mathcal{F}, P)$, where $\Omega = \{0, 1, 2, \ldots, n\}$, and let $\mathcal{F}$ be the power set of Ω. Define the RV $X = j, j = 0, 1, 2, \ldots, n$. Clearly, the random variable X is $\mathcal{F}$- measurable. The *binomial probability measure* P is then defined by

$$p(x; n, p) = P(X = x) = \begin{cases} \binom{n}{x} \, p^x(1-p)^{n-x}, & x = 0, 1, \ldots, n, 0 \le p \le 1 \\ 0, & \text{otherwise.} \end{cases} \tag{6.7}$$

The cdf, mgf, and cf of the binomial distribution are:

$$F(x) = \begin{cases} 0, & x < 0 \\ \sum_{j=0}^{x} \binom{n}{j} \, p^j(1-p)^{n-j}, & x = 0, 1, \ldots, n, \\ 1, & x > 1, \end{cases} \tag{6.8}$$

$$M(t) = (1 - p + pe^t)^n, \tag{6.9}$$

$$\varphi(t) = (1 - p + pe^{it})^n. \tag{6.10}$$

The mean and variance of a binomial random variable are given by

$$E(X) = np, \tag{6.11}$$

$$Var(X) = np(1-p). \tag{6.12}$$

The binomial distribution arises in a lot of applications, especially when the outcome of the experiment can be labeled as Success/Failure, Yes/No, Present/Absent, etc. It is also useful in quality inspections in the industrial environment. We use `dbinom` to find the probabilities $P(X = x)$, `pbinom` for $P(X \le x)$, and `qbinom` for the quantiles.

Example 6.2.3. A Simple Illustration. Suppose that $n = 20$ and $p = 0.35$. The next program demonstrates the use of the R trio `d`, `p`, and `q`, which lead to a plot of the binomial density, cumulative probability function, and the quantiles of the distribution.

```
> n <- 20; p <- 0.35
> par(mfrow=c(1,3))
> plot(0:20,dbinom(0:n,n,p),xlab="x",ylab="P(X=x)",
+ main="A Binomial Distribution")
> plot(0:20,pbinom(0:n,n,p),xlab="x",ylab=expression(P(X<=x)),
+ main="Binomial Cumulative Distribution Function")
```

```
> plot(seq(0,1,.1),qbinom(seq(0,1,.1),n,p),xlab="Quantiles",ylab="X",
+ main="Quantiles of Binomial RV")
> # Output Suppressed
```

Note the use of `expression(P(X<=x))` and the resulting label on the y-axis. □

Example 6.2.4. Understanding Binomial Distributions. For $n = 10, p = 0.35$, we obtain the cdf, mgf, and cf plots, as given respectively in Equations 6.8–6.10. The necessary R program is given below:

```
> par(mfrow=c(1,3))
> n <- 10;p <- 0.35 # Plotting the CDF
> plot(0:10,pbinom(0:10,n,p),xlab="x-values",
+ ylab=expression(P(X<=x)),
+ main="Binomial Cumulative Distribution Function")
> t <- seq(-1,1,0.1) # The MGF
> mgf_binomial <- function(t,n,p) {(1-p+p*exp(t))^{n}}
> plot(t,mgf_binomial(t,n,p),xlab="t",ylab=expression(M(t)),
+ main="The Binomial MGF")
> t <- seq(-10,10,0.01) # The Characteristic Function
> cf_binomial <- function(t,n,p) {(1-p+p*exp(1i*t))^{n}}
> scatterplot3d(t,Re(cf_binomial(t,n,p)),Im(cf_binomial(t,n,p)),
+ xlim=c(-11,11),ylim=c(-1,1), zlim=c(-1,1), xlab="t",ylab=
+ expression(paste("Real Part of ",phi(t))), zlab=
+ expression(paste("Complex Part of ",phi(t))),highlight.3d=TRUE,
+ col.axis="blue",col.grid="lightblue", pch=20,type="l",
+ main=expression(phi(t)))
```

The resulting plot is given in Figure 6.1. Note the use of the `expression` option which has been exploited to ensure that we obtain the formulas for the labels. The CDF for binomial distribution is readily available in `pbinom` and the functions `mgf_binomial` and `cf_binomial` are defined respectively to obtain the formulas 6.9 and 6.10. The plot of mgfs' or cfs' do not offer much insight and will not be considered any further. □

Example 6.2.5. Understanding the Central Term of a Binomial Distribution. Let $b(n, p)$ denote the probability measure of a binomial RV with parameters n and p. The well-known *recursive formula* of binomial distribution is:

$$\frac{b(k, n, p)}{b(k-1, n, p)} = \frac{\binom{n}{k} p^k (1-p)^{n-k}}{\binom{n}{k-1} p^{k-1} (1-p)^{n-k+1}} = 1 + \frac{(n+1)p - k}{k(1-p)}. \tag{6.13}$$

Thus, we can see from Equation 6.13 that the binomial probabilities are increasing if $k < (n+1)p$ and decreasing if $k > (n+1)p$. If $(n+1)p = m$ is an integer, we have $b(m, n, p) = b(m-1, n, p)$. Finally, there exists only one integer m, such that

$$(n+1)p - 1 < m \leq (n+1)p.$$

This integer m is the *central term of a binomial distribution*. See Section 6.3 of Feller (1968) for more such interesting results. We will now write a small R program for understanding this

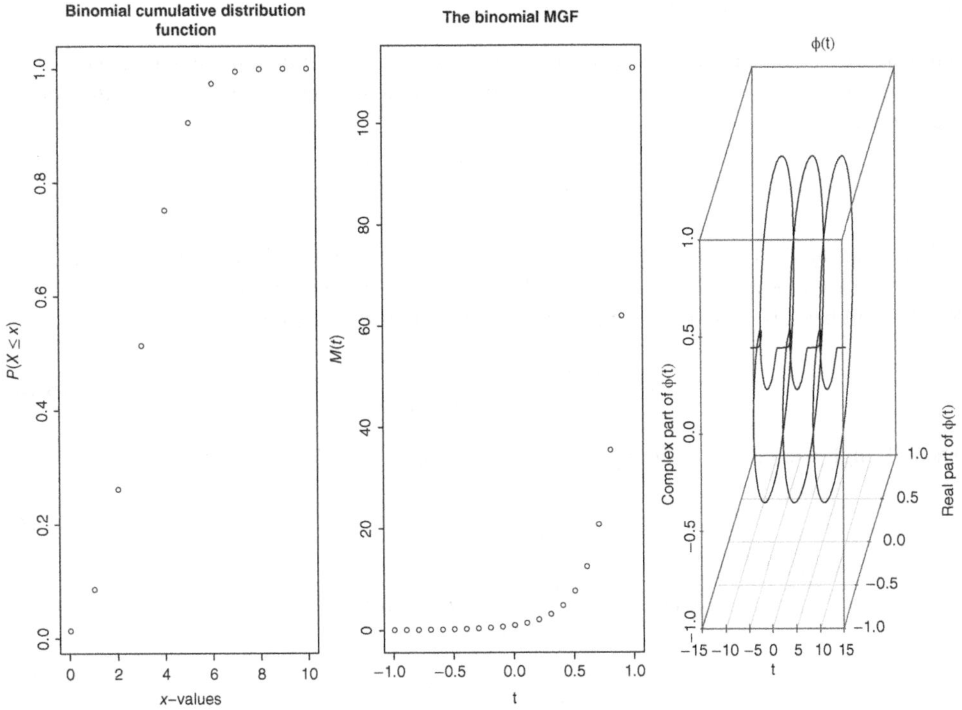

Figure 6.1 Understanding the Binomial Distribution

central term. Suppose that we vary n from 5 to 20 and set $p = 0.2$. For each of these binomial distributions, the program should return us the central term which makes use of the above stated inequality. Since our distributions are skewed to the left side, we expect the central term to occur in the beginning itself. The following R program reconfirms our belief.

```
> Understanding the Central Term of a Binomial Distribution
> n <- 20; p <- 0.2
> m <- NULL # Lets find the Central Terms
> for(k in 5:n){
+      mid_term <- 0
+      while((((k+1)*p-1)>mid_term) & ((k+1)*p>=mid_term) ) {
+   mid_term <- mid_term+1}
+      m[k-4] <- mid_term
+ }
> m
 [1] 1 1 1 1 1 2 2 2 2 2 3 3 3 3 3 4
```

The mid-term criteria $(n + 1)p - 1 < m \leq (n + 1)p$ is programmed with `while((((k+1)*p-1)>mid_term) & ((k+1)*p>=mid_term) )` and the `while` loop stops once the criteria is satisfied, then it returns to the mid-terms. □

6.2.3 The Geometric Distribution

Suppose we toss a coin until a head turns up. Let p denote the probability of a head on the toss of a coin. The probability of a head turning up for the first time on the nth toss of the coin is then given by

$$\underbrace{q\cdots q}_{n-1 \text{ times}}\, p, \quad q = 1 - p.$$

Let us define the related random variable in a more formal way. Define $\Omega = \{0, 1, 2, \dots\}$, and let $\mathcal{F}$ be the power set of Ω. We say that an $\mathcal{F}$- measurable RV is a *geometric or Pascal* RV if its probability mass function is given by the counting measure:

$$P(X = x) = p_x = \begin{cases} p(1-p)^x, & x = 0, 1, 2, \dots, 0 < p \leq 1, \\ 0, & \text{otherwise}. \end{cases} \tag{6.14}$$

The cdf, mgf, and cf of the geometric distribution are listed below:

$$F(x) = \begin{cases} 0, & x < 0 \\ 1 - (1-p)^{x+1}, & x = 0, 1, 2, \dots, \end{cases} \tag{6.15}$$

$$M(t) = \frac{pe^t}{[1 - (1-p)e^t]}, t < -\ln(1-p), \tag{6.16}$$

$$\varphi(t) = \frac{p}{1 - qe^{it}}. \tag{6.17}$$

The mean and variance of a geometric distribution are given by

$$E(X) = \frac{q}{p}, \tag{6.18}$$

$$Var(X) = \frac{q}{p^2}. \tag{6.19}$$

Note that the mean of a geometric RV is always less than its variance. This is because the mean is multiplied by $1/p$, which is always greater than 1. It is easier to verify by first declaring the p sequence as `p <- seq(0.01,1,.01)` and then by running `(1-p)/p <= (1-p)/p^2`. The geometric distribution has found applications in problems of estimating animal abundance, ticket control, vigilance systems, etc.

Example 6.2.6. Understanding the Mean and Variance. If the probability of arrival of a city bus at a station over a fixed time duration is high, we know from our experience of waiting for it that it will be less than in the cases where the probability of the bus arrival is less. This experience is captured by the above equations of mean and variance for a geometric distribution. The following R program and its result in Parts A and B of Figure 6.2 reflects the experience of these waiting times.

```
> p <- seq(0,1,0.02)
> mu <- (1-p)/p
> var <- (1-p)/p^(2)
> #par(mfrow=c(1,2))
> plot(p,mu,xlab="Probability of Success",ylab="Mean","l",
```

```
+ main="A: Mean of Geometric Distribution")
> plot(p,var,xlab="Probability of Success",ylab="Variance","l",
+ main="B: Variance of Geometric Distribution")
```

The program is straightforward to understand. □

Example 6.2.7. The Tail Probabilities of a Geometric Random Variables. For a geometric random variable, the tail probability $P(X \geq n)$ is

$$P(X \geq n) = \sum_{j=n}^{\infty} p(1-p)^j = p^n, n = 0, 1, 2, \ldots .$$

The following R program gives a plot of the tail probabilities for various values of p, check Part C of Figure 6.2.

```
> # The Tail Probabilities
> n <- 0:50
> p <- seq(0.05,1,0.05)
> plot(n,p[1]^{n},xlab="x",ylab="Tail Probabilities","l", col=1,
+ xlim=c(0,20),main="C: Tail Probabilities of Geometric RV")
> for(i in 2:20) lines(n,p[i]^{n},"l",col=i)
```

The tail probabilities simply involve computing p^n! □

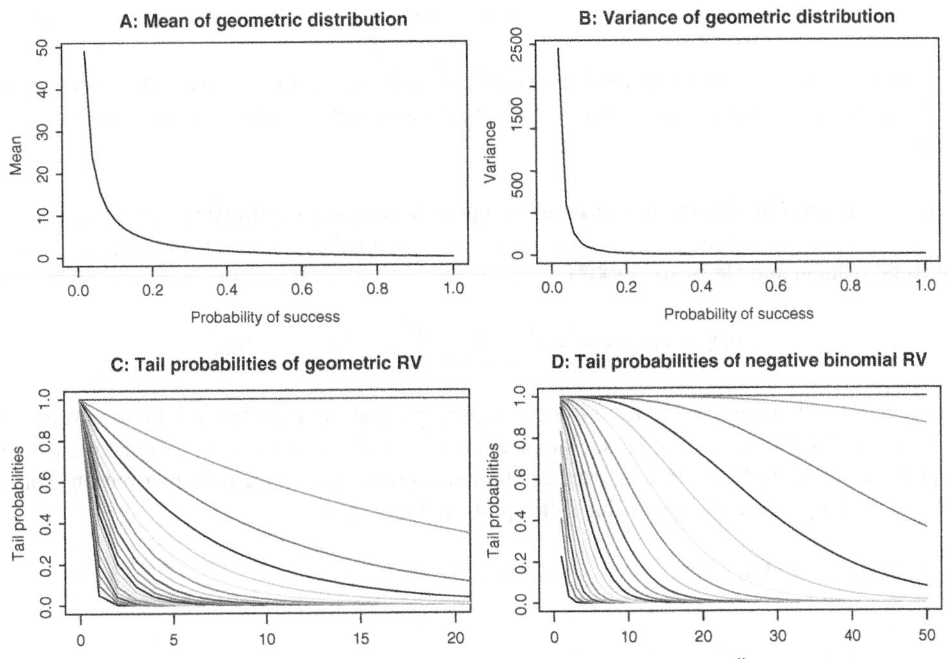

Figure 6.2 Understanding the Geometric Distribution

6.2.4 The Negative Binomial Distribution

Let $(\Omega, \mathcal{F}, P)$ be a probability space, with $\Omega = \{0, 1, \dots\}$, and $\mathcal{F}$ the power set of Ω. Let X be a random variable which counts the number of failures before observing exactly r successes. That is, we toss a coin repeatedly and wait until r heads turn up, and here X will be the number of tails observed before r heads. Such a random variable is called a *negative binomial RV* and the associated probability distribution is a *negative binomial distribution*. In this experiment, as $X = x$ failures are to be observed before r failures, the *negative binomial probability measure* is given by the counting measure:

$$P(X = x) = \begin{cases} \binom{x+r-1}{x} p^r(1-p)^x, & x = 0, 1, 2, \dots, \\ 0, & \text{otherwise.} \end{cases} \tag{6.20}$$

The mgf and cf of a negative binomial RV are given below:

$$M_X(t) = \left(\frac{p}{1-qe^t}\right)^r, \text{for } t < -\ln p, \tag{6.21}$$

$$\varphi_X(t) = \left(\frac{p}{1-qe^{it}}\right)^r, \text{for } t \in \mathcal{R}. \tag{6.22}$$

The mean and variance of a negative binomial RV are given below:

$$E(X) = r\frac{q}{p}, \tag{6.23}$$

$$Var(X) = r\frac{q}{p^2}. \tag{6.24}$$

The mean and variance relationship extends as with the geometric case. The distribution is found in many diverse areas such as birth-death-and-immigration process, queueing systems, etc.

Example 6.2.8. The Tail Probabilities of Negative Binomial Distribution. For the tail probabilities of a negative binomial distribution, we state the final expression from equation (7.23) of Balakrishnan and Nevzorov (2003):

$$P(X \geq m) = \frac{(m+r-1)!}{(m-1)!(r-1)!} \int_0^p x^{m-1}(1-x)^{r-1}dx.$$

We recognize that the integral term is a cumulative probability distribution of a *beta random variable* with parameters m and r, see sub-section 6.3.2. For the moment the reader can assume that the R function `pbeta` will return the cumulative probability of the beta distribution. Thus, using this the `pbeta`, the tail probabilities plot can be obtained.

```
> # Understanding the Tail Probabilities
> m <- 1:50
> r <- 5
> p <- seq(0.05,1,0.05)
> plot(m,pbeta(p[1],m,r),xlab="x",ylab="Tail Probabilities",
```

```
+ "l",col=1,xlim=c(0,50),ylim=c(0,1),main="D: Tail Probabilities
+ of Negative Binomial RV")
> for(i in 2:20) lines(m,pbeta(p[i],m,r),col=i)
```

The proportionality constant $(m + r - 1)!/((m - 1)!(r - 1)!)$ has been ignored without loss of generality. The plot for the tail probabilities of the negative binomial distribution is given in Part D of Figure 6.2. □

6.2.5 *Poisson Distribution*

Consider the probability space $(\Omega, \mathcal{F}, P)$, where $\Omega = \{0, 1, 2, \ldots\}$, and let $\mathcal{F}$ be the power set of Ω. Define a RV X with the *Poisson probability measure* given by

$$p(x; \lambda) = P(X = x) = \begin{cases} \frac{e^{-\lambda}\lambda^x}{x!}, & x = 0, 1, 2, \ldots, \lambda > 0, \\ 0, & \text{otherwise.} \end{cases} \tag{6.25}$$

Here, λ is the parameter of the RV X and is often known as *rate* of the RV. It may be shown that the mgf, cf, mean, and variance of a Poisson RV are given by

$$M_P(t) = e^{\lambda(e^t - 1)}, \tag{6.26}$$

$$\varphi_P(t) = e^{\lambda(e^{it} - 1)}, \tag{6.27}$$

$$E(X) = \lambda, \tag{6.28}$$

$$Var(X) = \lambda. \tag{6.29}$$

Note that the mean and variance of the Poisson distribution are equal. In fact, the first four central moments of the Poisson distribution are the same! The distribution is sometimes known as *the law of rare events*. It has found applications in problems such as the number of mistakes on a printed page, the number of accidents on a stretch of a highway, the number of arrivals at a queueing system, etc.

Example 6.2.9. The Percentiles and Quantiles of a Poisson Distribution. Suppose that X follows a Poisson distribution with $\lambda = 10$. Then, its percentiles are given by `qpois(seq(0,1,.1),10)`. Furthermore, the probability that X is greater than 15 is `1-ppois(15,10)`.

```
> qpois(seq(0,1,.1),10)
[1] 0 6 7 8 9 10 11 12 13 14 Inf
> 1-ppois(15,10)
[1] 0.0487404
```

As mentioned earlier in this section, `q` and `p` are used to obtain the quantiles and cumulative probability distribution for the Poisson RV. □

Example 6.2.10. Obtaining probabilities of a Poisson random variable when $P(X = 0)$ is known. Suppose that it is known that for a Poisson random variate $P(X = 0) = 0.2$. Then $P(X = 6)$ is obtained by first obtaining the rate λ and using it to calculate the required probability.

```
> lam <- -log(.2) # finds the parameter of the Poisson distribution
> dpois(6,lam)
[1] 0.004827729
```

Recall that $P(X = 0) = e^{-\lambda}$, and hence $-\ln(P(X = 0))$ gives the value of λ. □

Example 6.2.11. The probability distribution of Poisson random variables for different λ. In the previous example we saw the Poisson approximation for binomial distribution. We will simply look to see what happens to the Poisson distribution for large values of λ.

```
> par(mfrow=c(2,2))
> plot(0:20,dpois(0:20,lambda=2),xlab="x",
+ ylab="Probability",type="h")
> plot(0:50,dpois(0:50,lambda=5),xlab="x",
+ ylab="Probability",type="h")
> plot(0:100,dpois(0:100,lambda=20),xlab="x",
+ ylab="Probability",type="h")
> plot(0:150,dpois(0:150,lambda=110),xlab="x",
+ ylab="Probability",type="h")
```

For small values of λ, the discrete nature of Poisson RV is apparent. However, we note that for large values of λ, the pdf appears bell-shaped, see Figure 6.3. □

Example 6.2.12. The Poisson Approximation for Binomial Distribution. If the number of Bernoulli trials is more than 20, i.e. $n \geq 20$, and the probability of success is less than 0.05, the probability of x successes may be well approximated by a Poisson RV instead of the natural binomial distribution. The rule of thumb for this approximation is that $np \approx 1$. This is such a useful approximation that it is bound to be found in almost every book in the first course in statistics or probability. To see how this approximation works, we first look at the probability mass functions of both binomial distribution and the approximating Poisson distribution.

```
> n <- seq(20,41,3)
> p <- 1/n
> approxdiff <- n*0
> par(mfrow=c(2,4))
> for(i in 1:length(n)){
+       binomprob <- dbinom(c(0:n[i]),n[i],p[i])
+       poisprob <- dpois(c(0:n[i]),n[i]*p[i])
+       plot(c(0:n[i]),binomprob,xlab="x",
+ ylab = "Binomial and Poisson Probability",
+    ylim=c(0,.5),"l")
+       lines(c(0:n[i]),poisprob,ylim=c(0,.5),"l",col="red")
+       approxdiff[i] <- sum(binomprob-poisprob)
+ }
> title(main = "Poisson Approximation of Binomial RV",
+ outer=TRUE,line=-2)
> approxdiff
> # gives the cumulative sum of difference in approximation
[1] -7.765552e-18 -3.851576e-17    1.453942e-17
```

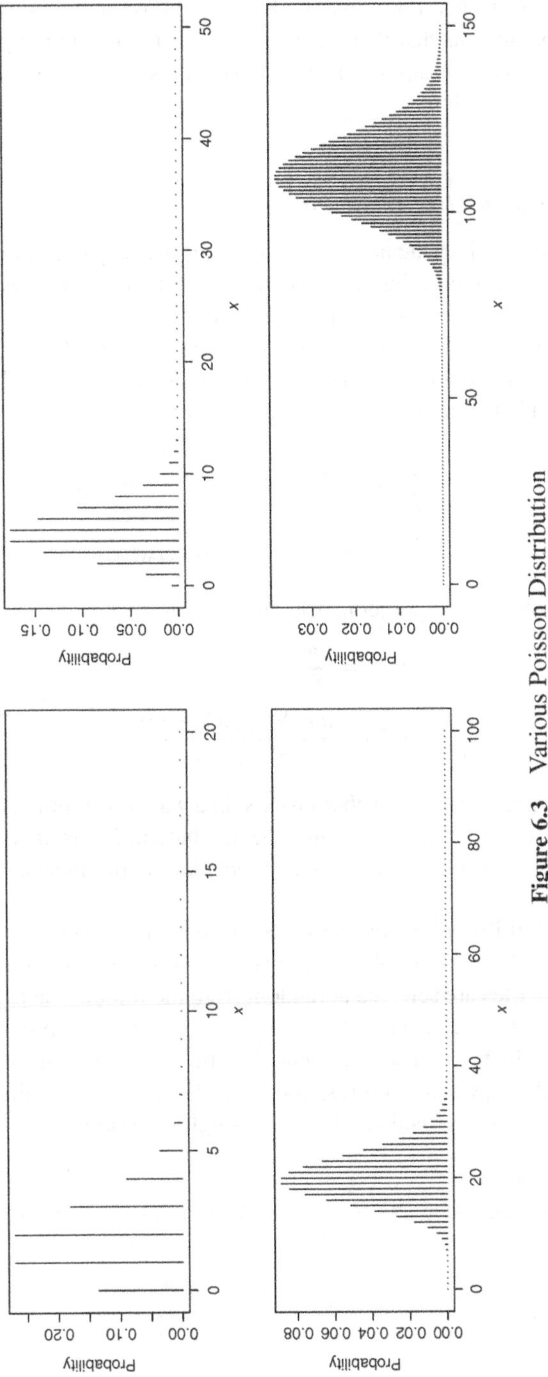

Figure 6.3 Various Poisson Distribution

The fact that the "red" curve of Poisson probabilities completely overshadows the black curve of binomial probabilities shows that the Poisson approximation is a very good approximation one. Figure 6.4 reveals that there is hardly any difference in the probability curves of the binomial distribution and its approximating Poisson distribution. The scenario when np is approximately equal to 1 is clear. □

6.2.6 *The Hypergeometric Distribution*

A hypergeometric RV describes the number of successes in a sequence of n draws from a finite population without replacement. Suppose that an urn contains N balls, m of which represent non-defective items (hence success!), and the remaining $N-m$ are defective items. We draw n items without replacement from the urn and note the number of non-defective items. Let X be the random variable denoting the number of non-defective items. Then the probability distribution of the number of non-defective items is given by

$$P(X=x)=\begin{cases}\dfrac{\binom{m}{x}\binom{N-m}{n-x}}{\binom{N}{n}}, & x=0,1,\ldots,\min\{n,m\},\\ 0, & \text{otherwise}.\end{cases} \tag{6.30}$$

The mean and variance of the hypergeometric distribution are

$$E(X)=\frac{nm}{N}, \tag{6.31}$$

$$Var(X)=\frac{nm(N-n)(N-m)}{N^2(N-1)}. \tag{6.32}$$

The mgf and cf of hypergeometric distribution exist in a way too complex in appearance for us to make good use of them. Further details may be obtained in Johnson and Kotz (1969). This distribution is found to be very useful in *capture-recapture* experiments.

Example 6.2.13. Probability of x successes!. Suppose that a folder on a drive of a hard disk contains $N=30$ files. Of the 30 books, 12 are statistical text and the remaining are science texts. Assume that five files are selected at random from the folder. The task is to compute the probability of obtaining 0, 1, …, and 5 statistical texts. To obtain the probabilities, we can use the inbuilt R function dhyper. The arguments for the parameters of the dhyper function are m, n, and k, which respectively correspond to N, $N-m$, and n in the above pmf for the hypergeometric RV. The answer is then given by a single-line program.

```
> dhyper(0:5,30,12,5)
[1] 0.000931 0.017457 0.112500 0.3145000 0.386590 0.167522
```

□

?Distributions

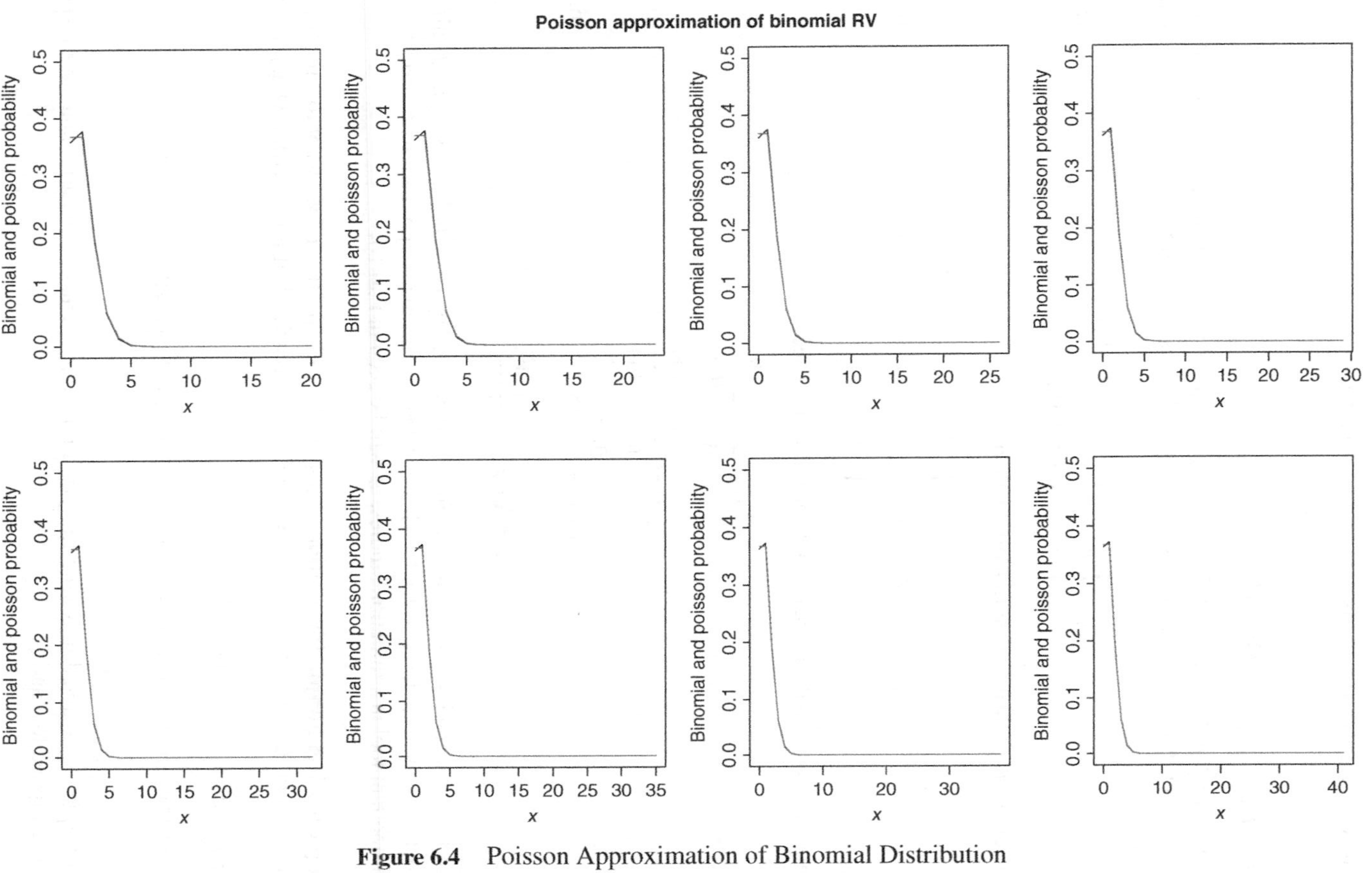

Figure 6.4 Poisson Approximation of Binomial Distribution

6.3 Continuous Univariate Distributions

Useful continuous distributions will be discussed here.

6.3.1 The Uniform Distribution

Consider a probability space $(\Omega, \mathcal{F}, P)$, where $\Omega = [\theta_1, \theta_2], \theta_2 > \theta_1, \theta_1, \theta_2 \in \mathbb{R}$, $\mathcal{F}$ is the Borel σ-field over Ω. An RV X is said to be a *uniform RV* if its probability density function (pdf) is given by

$$f(x) = \begin{cases} \frac{1}{\theta_2-\theta_1}, & \theta_1 < x < \theta_2, \theta_1, \theta_2 \in \mathbb{R}, \\ 0, & \text{otherwise}, \end{cases} \tag{6.33}$$

and its cumulative distribution function is then

$$F(x) = P(X \leq x) = \begin{cases} 0, & x \leq \theta_1 \\ \frac{x-\theta_1}{\theta_2-\theta_1}, & \text{if } \theta_1 < x \leq \theta_2, \\ 1, & x > \theta_2. \end{cases} \tag{6.34}$$

The mgf, cf, mean, and variance of uniform RV are listed in the following:

$$M_X(t) = \frac{e^{t\theta_2} - e^{t\theta_1}}{t(\theta_2 - \theta_1)}, \tag{6.35}$$

$$\varphi_X(t) = \frac{e^{it\theta_2} - e^{it\theta_1}}{it(\theta_2 - \theta_1)}, \tag{6.36}$$

$$E(X) = \frac{\theta_1 + \theta_2}{2}, \tag{6.37}$$

$$Var(X) = \frac{(\theta_2 - \theta_1)^2}{12}. \tag{6.38}$$

The uniform distribution over an interval $[\theta_1, \theta_2]$ is denoted by $U[\theta_1, \theta_2]$. The *standard* uniform distribution is over the interval [0, 1]. This distribution has many applications and serves as a very important tool in simulation studies, as will be seen in Part III.

Example 6.3.1. A Simple Illustration. Suppose $X \sim U(10, 20)$, and we want to compute the probabilities $P(10 < X < 15), P(12 < X < 18)$. We can easily do this in the following program:

```
> punif(15,min=10,max=20)
[1] 0.5
> punif(18,min=10,max=20)-punif(12,min=10,max=20)
[1] 0.6
```

The cdf $F_U(x)$ is obtained in R with the `punif` function. The options `min` and `max` respectively correspond to a and b. □

Example 6.3.2. Convolutions of Two Uniform Random Variables. Let X_1, X_2 be two independent standard uniform random variables. Define $Y = X_1 + X_2$. The pdf of Y is given by

$$p(y) = \begin{cases} y, & \text{if} \quad 0 \leq y \leq 1, \\ 2 - y, & \text{if} \quad 1 \leq y \leq 2, \\ 0, & \text{otherwise.} \end{cases}$$

We will obtain a plot of the pdf of Y.

```
> # Convolution of Two Standard Uniform Random Variables
> pdfy <- function(y){
+         pdfy=ifelse(y<=1,y, 2-y)
+         return(pdfy)
+ }
> y <- seq(0,2,0.05)
> pdf_y <- sapply(y,pdfy)
> plot(y,pdf_y,"l",ylab="Convolution Density")
```

The pdf of Y, as given in Equation 6.39, is captured in R with the function `pdfy`. It is clear from Part A of Figure 6.5 why the resulting distribution is popularly known as the *triangular distribution*. □

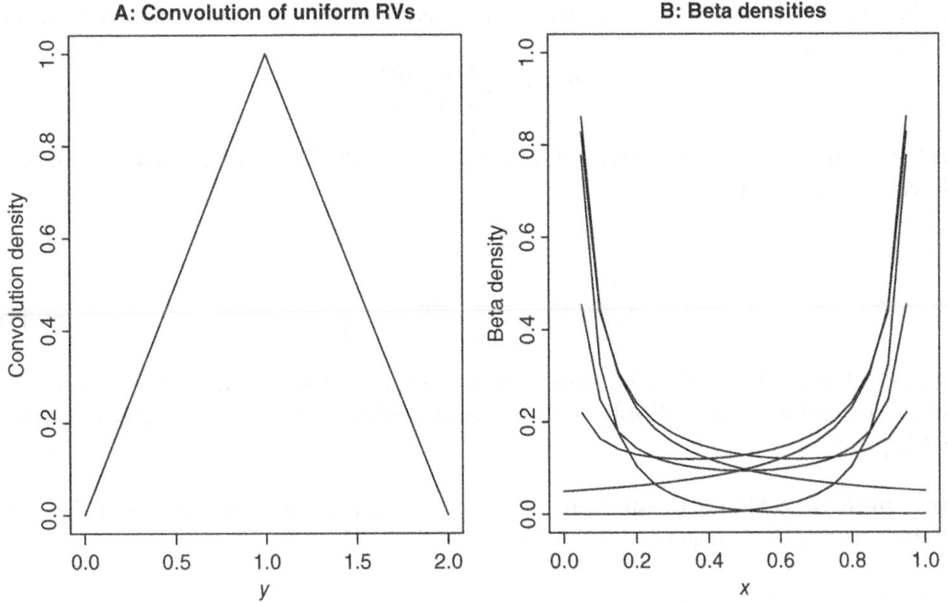

Figure 6.5 Convolution of Two Uniform Random Variables

Example 6.3.3. Mean and Variance of Uniform RV. Recall from Example 5.7.4 the definition of the R function `Expectation_NNRV_Unif`. This function made use of the definition of expectation function, as given in Equation 5.15. The `integrate` function can be used to quickly verify the mean and variance of a uniform RV over the interval $[\theta_1, \theta_2]$.

```
> EX <- integrate(function(x) {x*dunif(x,min=5,max=10)},
+ lower=5,upper=10)$value
> EX2 <-  integrate(function(x) {x^{2}*dunif(x,min=5,max=10)},
+ lower=5,upper=10)$value
> EX2-EX^{2}
[1] 2.083333
```

Note that in the above program `min` corresponds to θ_1 and `max` to θ_2. The program can be easily used for any values of the pair (θ_1, θ_2). □

6.3.2 *The Beta Distribution*

Consider the probability space $(\Omega, \mathcal{F}, P)$, with $\Omega = [0, 1]$, and $\mathcal{F}$ the Borel σ-field over Ω. We say that an RV is *beta RV* if its pdf is

$$f(x) = \begin{cases} \frac{1}{B(\alpha,\beta)} x^{\alpha-1}(1-x)^{\beta-1}, & 0 \leq x \leq 1, \alpha, \beta > 0, \\ 0, & \text{otherwise.} \end{cases} \tag{6.39}$$

In the above expression, the parameters α and β are non-negative values, and the function $B(\alpha, \beta)$ is given by

$$B(\alpha, \beta) = \frac{\Gamma(\alpha)\Gamma(\beta)}{\Gamma(\alpha+\beta)},$$

and $\Gamma(.)$ denotes the *gamma integral*, $\Gamma(t) = \int_0^I nfx^{t-1}e^{-x}dx$. The mean and variance of beta distribution is given by

$$E(X) = \frac{\alpha}{\alpha+\beta}, \tag{6.40}$$

$$Var(X) = \frac{\alpha\beta}{(\alpha+\beta)^2(\alpha+\beta+1)}. \tag{6.41}$$

The cf and mgf of beta RV is a bit more complex and hence it is not given here. The beta distribution is useful as a *prior* distribution in Bayesian analysis and this aspect will be illustrated in Chapter 9.

Example 6.3.4. A Simple Illustration. Suppose we want to compute probabilities $P(X < x_i)$, where $x_i = .1,.2,.3,.4,.5$, and $\alpha = \beta = 6$. Then

```
> p <- c(.1,.2,.3,.4,.5)
> pbeta(p,6,6)
[1] 0.0002957061 0.0116542054 0.0782247910 0.2465018675 0.5000000000
```

gives us the desired probabilities. □

Example 6.3.5. Different Density Shapes of Beta Distribution. In an attempt to understand the density, we give a small program for obtaining the density plots related to various beta densities using the dbeta function.

```
> # Various Beta Densities
> x <- seq(0,1,0.05)
> plot(x,dbeta(x,0.05,0.05),"l",
+ ylab="Beta Density Plot",xlab="x",ylim=c(0,1))
> lines(x,dbeta(x,0.05,0.5),"l"); lines(x,dbeta(x,0.05,1),"l")
> lines(x,dbeta(x,0.05,5),"l"); lines(x,dbeta(x,0.5,0.05),"l")
> lines(x,dbeta(x,1,0.05),"l"); lines(x,dbeta(x,5,0.05),"l")
```

The output is displayed in Part B of Figure 6.5. It may be seen that depending on the parameter values of α and β, the beta distribution can take a variety of shapes which in turn are useful for modeling a variety of practical scenarios. □

6.3.3 The Exponential Distribution

Consider the probability space $(\Omega, \mathcal{F}, P)$. Define $\Omega = \mathbb{R}^+$, and $\mathcal{F}$ as the the Borel σ-field over Ω. We say that the RV X follows an *exponential distribution* with mean θ if its pdf is

$$f(x;\theta) = \begin{cases} \frac{1}{\theta}e^{-\frac{x}{\theta}}, & x \geq 0, \theta > 0, \\ 0, & \text{otherwise}. \end{cases} \tag{6.42}$$

The mgf, cf, mean, and variance of exponential RV are given in the following set of equations:

$$M_X(t) = (1 - \theta t)^{-1}, \tag{6.43}$$

$$\varphi_X(t) = (1 - \theta it)^{-1}, \tag{6.44}$$

$$E(X) = \theta, \tag{6.45}$$

$$Var(X) = \theta^2. \tag{6.46}$$

The exponential RV is also usefully stated in a reparametrized form of the *rate* which is a reciprocal of the mean. This distribution has application in many areas of the subject such as reliability theory, survival analysis, queueing theory, etc.

Example 6.3.6. A Simple Illustration. If the mean of the exponential distribution is 30, and we desire to compute the percentiles at the points 13, 18, 27, and 45, we obtain the required percentiles using the pexp function. Suppose, we want to know the quantiles of an exponential distribution with mean time of 30 units. We can obtain them by the small code qexp(seq(0,1,.25),1/30). The next program gives us the results.

```
> t <- c(13,18,27,45)
> pexp(t,1/30)
[1] 0.3516557 0.4511884 0.5934303 0.7768698
> qexp(seq(0,1,.25),1/30)
[1] 0.000000 8.630462 20.794415 41.588831 Inf
```

The pexp and qexp R functions have been used to compute the cdf and quantiles of exponential distribution. □

Example 6.3.7. Conditional Probabilities in Exponential Distribution. Suppose that X is an exponential RV with mean 10. Assume that we have already noted that $X > 10$. In light of this information we would like to know the probability of X being greater than 16. That is, we wish to find $P(X \geq (6 + 10)|X \geq 10)$. Note that, for any $s, t > 0$

$$P(T \geq s + t|T > t) = \frac{P(\{t < T\} \cap \{T \geq s + t)\}}{P(T > t)}.$$

Hence, we will first calculate $P(10 < T \leq 16)/P(T > 10)$ and also $P(X \leq 6)$, that is $P(X \leq s)$.

```
> (pexp(16,1/10)-pexp(10,1/10))/(1-pexp(10,1/10))
[1] 0.4511884
> pexp(6,1/10)
[1] 0.4511884
```

Is this a coincidence for the case of $s = 6, t = 10$? Let us check this out for a range of s and t.

```
> theta <- 10
> s <- 1:5
> t <- 1:10
> checkequal <- function(a,b,theta){
+         temp <- round(((pexp(a+b,1/theta)-pexp(b,1/theta))/
+ (1-pexp(b,1/theta))),2)==round(pexp(a,1/theta),2)
+         return(temp)
+ }
> outer(s,t,checkequal,theta)
      [,1] [,2] [,3] [,4] [,5] [,6] [,7] [,8] [,9] [,10]
[1,] TRUE TRUE TRUE TRUE TRUE TRUE TRUE TRUE TRUE  TRUE
[2,] TRUE TRUE TRUE TRUE TRUE TRUE TRUE TRUE TRUE  TRUE
[3,] TRUE TRUE TRUE TRUE TRUE TRUE TRUE TRUE TRUE  TRUE
[4,] TRUE TRUE TRUE TRUE TRUE TRUE TRUE TRUE TRUE  TRUE
[5,] TRUE TRUE TRUE TRUE TRUE TRUE TRUE TRUE TRUE  TRUE
```

The checkequal function tests whether the probabilities $P(t < T \leq s + t)/P(T > t)$ and $P(X \leq s)$ are equal or not. The outer function carries out the checkequal function over a range of s and t values. In each case the probability has been found to be the same. This is not a surprise result and is in fact the most famous property of exponential distribution: *the memoryless property.* □

6.3.4 The Gamma Distribution

Consider the probability space $(\Omega, \mathcal{F}, P)$. Define $\Omega = \mathbb{R}^+$, and $\mathcal{F}$ as the the Borel σ-field over Ω. We say that an RV is a *gamma RV* with scale parameter θ and shape parameter k if its probability density function is

$$f(x, \theta, k) = \begin{cases} x^{k-1}\frac{e^{-x/\theta}}{\Gamma(k)\theta^k}, & x \geq 0, k, \theta > 0, \\ 0, & \text{otherwise.} \end{cases} \tag{6.47}$$

The mgf, cf, mean, and variance are contained in the list:

$$M_X(t) = (1 - \theta t)^{-k}, \tag{6.48}$$

$$\varphi_X(t) = (1 - \theta i t)^{-k}, \tag{6.49}$$

$$E(X) = k\theta, \tag{6.50}$$

$$Var(X) = k\theta^2. \tag{6.51}$$

It can be easily seen that the gamma distribution is an extension of the exponential distribution. It has also applications in Bayesian analysis as a natural *conjugate* prior for the standard deviation of a normal distribution, and also as a useful distribution for *frailty models* in survival analysis.

Example 6.3.8. The Gamma Density Plots. We will help the reader to reproduce the Gamma density plots, which appear on pages 213–4 of Rohatgi and Saleh (2000).

```
> # The Gamma Density Plots
> par(mfrow=c(2,2))
> x <- seq(0,2,0.1)
> plot(x,dgamma(x,shape=0.5,scale=0.5),
+ xlab="x",ylab="Gamma Density Plot","l")
> x <- seq(0,8,0.1)
> plot(x,dgamma(x,shape=2,scale=0.5),
+ xlab="x",ylab="Gamma Density Plot","l")
> lines(x,dgamma(x,shape=2,scale=1),"l")
> lines(x,dgamma(x,shape=2,scale=2),"l")
> x <- seq(0,20,0.1)
> plot(x,dgamma(x,shape=4,scale=2),xlab="x",
+ ylab="Gamma Density Plot","l")
> lines(x,dgamma(x,shape=4,scale=4),"l")
> x <- seq(0,35,0.1)
> plot(x,dgamma(x,shape=8,scale=2),
+ xlab="x",ylab="Gamma Density Plot","l")
```

The output of the this R program is Figure 6.6. □

6.3.5 The Normal Distribution

Consider the probability space $(\Omega, \mathcal{F}, P)$. Define $\Omega = \mathbb{R}$, and $\mathcal{F}$ as the Borel σ-field over Ω. An RV X is said to possess a normal distribution with mean μ and a variance σ^2 if its pdf is given by

$$f(x; \mu, \sigma^2) = \frac{1}{\sqrt{2\pi}\sigma} \exp\left(-\frac{(x-\mu)^2}{2\sigma^2}\right), x \in \mathbb{R}, \mu \in \mathbb{R}, \sigma > 0. \tag{6.52}$$

The mean and variance have already been defined. Thus, we will look at mgf and cf:

$$M_X(t) = e^{\mu t + \frac{1}{2}\sigma^2 t^2}, \tag{6.53}$$

$$\varphi_X(t) = e^{i\mu t - \frac{1}{2}\sigma^2 t^2}. \tag{6.54}$$

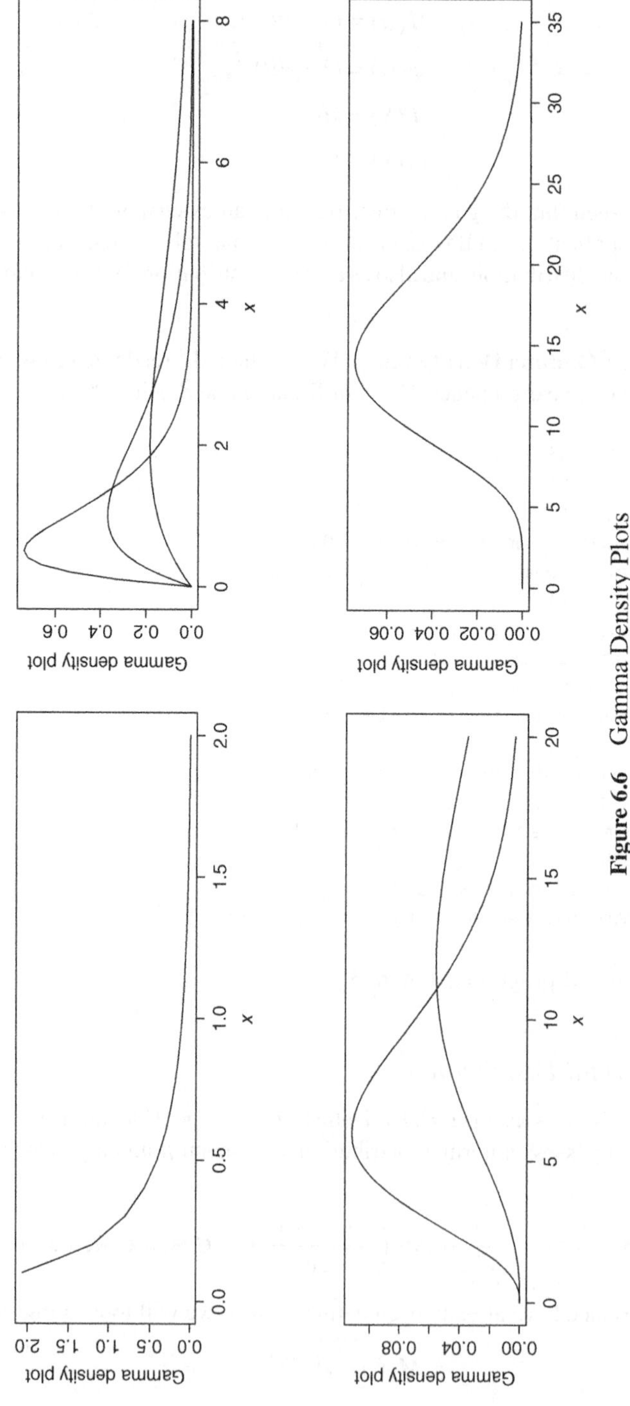

Figure 6.6 Gamma Density Plots

The normal distribution is almost omnipresent in the subject. It is very useful in error analysis, as will be seen in Chapters 12 and 13. Apart from direct applications, it also turns out to be the asymptotic distribution in many applications.

Example 6.3.9. A Simple Illustration. It is well-known that for a standard normal variable with $\mu = 0, \sigma^2 = 1$, $P(-1.68 < X < 1.68) = 0.90, P(-1.96 < X < 1.96) = 0.95$, and $P(-2.58 < X < 2.58) = 0.99$. Let us verify these statements using the dnorm function:

```
> integrate(dnorm,-1.68,1.68)$value
[1] 0.9070427
> integrate(dnorm,-1.96,1.96)$value
[1] 0.9500042
> integrate(dnorm,-2.58,2.58)$value
[1] 0.99012
```

Thus, the well-known results have been reaffirmed. □

Example 6.3.10. Some Shady Normal Curves. We will again consider a standard normal random variable, which is more popularly denoted in Statistics by Z. Some of the much needed probabilities are $P(Z > 0)$, $P(-1.96 < Z < 1.96)$, etc.

```
> par(mfrow=c(1,3))
> # Probability Z Greater than 0
> curve(dnorm(x,0,1),-4,4,xlab="z",ylab="f(z)")
> z <- seq(0,4,0.02)
> lines(z,dnorm(z),type="h",col="grey")
> # 95% Coverage
> curve(dnorm(x,0,1),-4,4,xlab="z",ylab="f(z)")
> z <- seq(-1.96,1.96,0.001)
> lines(z,dnorm(z),type="h",col="grey")
> # 95% Coverage
> curve(dnorm(x,0,1),-4,4,xlab="z",ylab="f(z)")
> z <- seq(-2.58,2.58,0.001)
> lines(z,dnorm(z),type="h",col="grey")
```

These probabilities are now shaded, see Figure 6.7. □

6.3.6 The Cauchy Distribution

Consider the probability space $(\Omega, \mathcal{F}, P)$. Define $\Omega = \mathbb{R}$, and $\mathcal{F}$ as the Borel σ-field over Ω. An RV X is said to a *Cauchy RV* if its pdf is of the form:

$$f(x; \mu, \sigma^2) = \frac{1}{\pi\sigma}\left[1 + \left(\frac{x-\mu}{\sigma}\right)^2\right]^{-1}, x \in \mathbb{R}, \mu \in \mathbb{R}, \sigma > 0. \tag{6.55}$$

The mean, variance, and mgf of the Cauchy RV do not exist. However, its cf is given by

$$\varphi_X(t) = e^{i\mu t - \sigma|t|}. \tag{6.56}$$

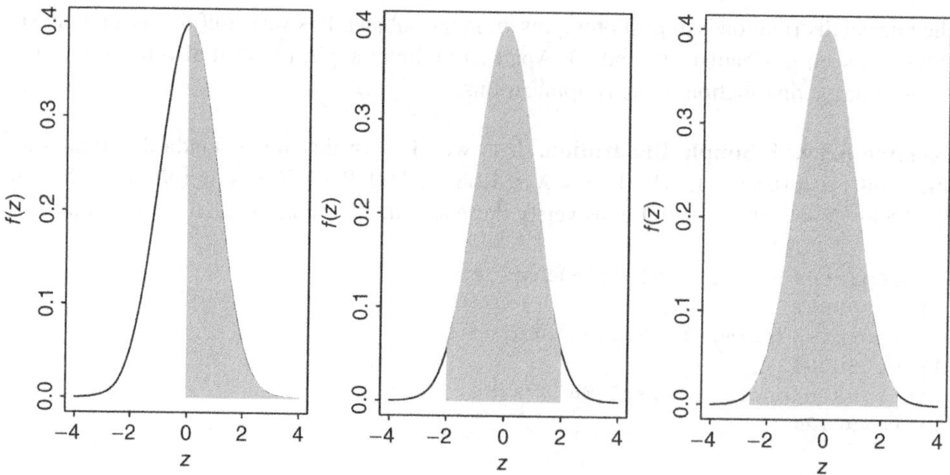

Figure 6.7 Shaded Normal Curves

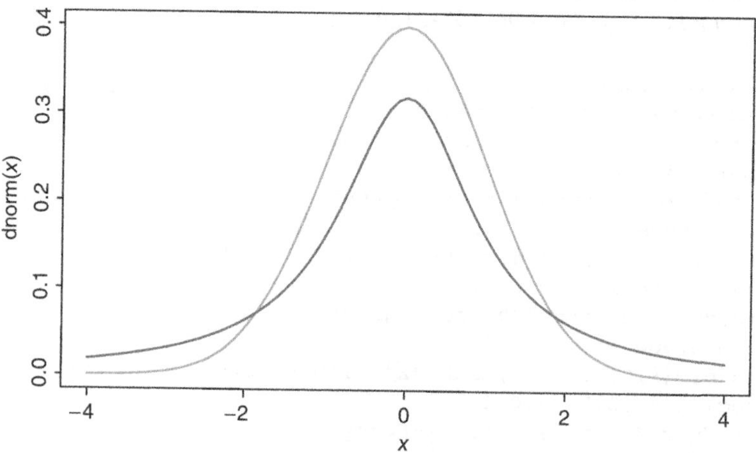

Figure 6.8 Whose Tails are Heavier?

Example 6.3.11. Whose tail is heavy? Normal or Cauchy? A plot of standard normal and Cauchy distribution is obtained to examine which of them is heavier.

```
> x <- seq(-4,4,0.1)
> plot(x,dnorm(x),"l",col="green")
> lines(x,dcauchy(x),"l",col="red")
```

The answer is obvious from the Figure 6.8. Can you prove it analytically? □

6.3.7 *The* t-*Distribution*

Consider the probability space $(\Omega, \mathcal{F}, P)$. Define $\Omega = \mathbb{R}$, and $\mathcal{F}$ as the the Borel σ-field over Ω. An RV X is said to follow a t-distribution if its pdf is given by

$$f(t,\nu) = \frac{\Gamma\left(\frac{\nu+1}{2}\right)}{\sqrt{\pi\nu}\Gamma\left(\frac{\nu}{2}\right)}\left(1+\frac{t^2}{2}\right)^{-(\nu+1)/2}, -\infty < t < \infty, \nu > 0. \tag{6.57}$$

The mean and variance of a t-RV are given below:

$$E(T) = \begin{cases} 0, & \text{if } \nu > 1, \\ \text{undefined}, & \text{otherwise.} \end{cases} \tag{6.58}$$

$$Var(T) = \begin{cases} \frac{\upsilon}{\nu-2}, & \text{for } \nu > 2, \\ \infty, & 1 < \nu \le 2, \\ \text{undefined}, & \text{otherwise.} \end{cases} \tag{6.59}$$

The cf exists in a complex form and it is not required for our purposes. This distribution is useful in construction of *statistical tests* and setting up *confidence intervals*.

Example 6.3.12. Cauchy Distribution as a Particular Case. In the above formula for expectation $E(T)$, we stated that the mean of a t-distribution exists only if $\nu > 1$. Let us consider the particular case of $\nu = 1$. In the density plot of the example "Whose tail is heavy? Normal or Cauchy?", if we add `lines(x,dt(x,df=1),"l",col="orange")`", we will see that the `red` color curve is overwritten by the orange color. Thus, we have a *graphical proof* that the Cauchy distribution is a particular case of the t-distribution. □

We close this section with statement of properties of the chi-square and F distributions.

6.3.8 *The Chi-square Distribution*

Consider the probability space $(\Omega, \mathcal{F}, P)$. Define $\Omega = \mathbb{R}^+$, and $\mathcal{F}$ as the the Borel σ-field over Ω. An RV is said to be a *chi-square* χ^2*- RV* if its pdf is given by

$$f(x,k) = \begin{cases} \frac{1}{2^{k/2}\Gamma(k/2)}x^{k/2-1}e^{-x/2}, & x \ge 0, k \in N^+, \\ 0, & \text{otherwise.} \end{cases} \tag{6.60}$$

The list of mean, variance, mgf, and cf for a chi-square RV are listed below:

$$E(X) = k, \tag{6.61}$$

$$Var(X) = 2k, \tag{6.62}$$

$$M_X(t) = (1-2t)^{-k/2}, \text{ if } t < 1/2, \tag{6.63}$$

$$\varphi_X(t) = (1-2it)^{-k/2}. \tag{6.64}$$

For the use and applications of χ^2 RV, see Section 6.6.

6.3.9 The F-Distribution

Consider the probability space $(\Omega, \mathcal{F}, P)$. Define $\Omega = \mathbb{R}^+$, and $\mathcal{F}$ as the the Borel σ-field over Ω. An RV is said to be a F- RV if its pdf is given by

$$f(x, m, n) = \begin{cases} \frac{1}{B\left(\frac{m}{2}, \frac{n}{2}\right)} \left(\frac{m}{n}\right)^{m/2} x^{\frac{m}{2}-1} \left(1 + \frac{m}{n}x\right)^{-\frac{m+n}{2}}, & x \geq 0, m, n \in N^+, \\ 0, & \text{otherwise.} \end{cases} \tag{6.65}$$

The mean and variance of an F- random variable are respectively given by

$$E(X) = \frac{n}{n-2}, \text{ if } n > 2, \tag{6.66}$$

$$Var(X) = \frac{2n^2(m+n-2)}{m(n-2)^2(n-4)}, \text{ if } n > 4. \tag{6.67}$$

Similar to the χ^2- RV, applications and R programs for F-RV will be developed in Section 6.6.

?Distributions, ?curve

6.4 Multivariate Probability Distributions

The previous two sections considered some important aspects of univariate (discrete and continuous) RVs. Random vectors are an extension of this concept, with each of its components itself being an RV. Of course, more often than not, the components of such random vectors are further correlated with each other. In this section we will consider four important random vectors. The purpose of this section is to emphasize the importance of these random vectors and towards this purpose the definitions are formally given. The role of software is not elaborated on here, except for giving pointers to the main functions. However, these distributions play a central role in inference of multivariate data.

6.4.1 The Multinomial Distribution

The binomial distribution encountered in the previous section is useful for binary sample outcomes. A natural extension is the probability distribution for the multi-cell distribution of a stochastic experiment. We say that a k-dimensional random vector $\mathbf{X} = (X_1, \ldots, X_k)$, $\sum_{i=1}^k X_i = n$, with probability vector $\boldsymbol{p} = (p_1, \ldots, p_k)$, $\sum_{i=1}^k p_i = 1$, is a *multinomial random vector* if its probability mass function is defined by

$$p(x_1, \ldots, x_k | n, \boldsymbol{p}) = \begin{cases} \frac{n!}{x_1! \cdots x_k!} p_1^{x_1} \cdots p_k^{x_k}, & \sum_{i=1}^k x_i = n, x_i = 0, 1, \ldots, n, \\ 0, & \text{otherwise.} \end{cases} \tag{6.68}$$

Some elementary properties of multinomial distribution are in order:

$$E(X_i) = np_i, i = 1, \ldots, k, \tag{6.69}$$

$$Var(X_i) = np_i(1 - p_i), i = 1, \dots, k, \tag{6.70}$$

$$\text{Cov}(X_i, X_j) = -np_ip_j, i \neq j = 1, \dots, k. \tag{6.71}$$

Marginal distribution of the multinomial distribution will follow a binomial distribution. In particular, when a *classification* problem involves more than two categories, the multinomial distribution will be very useful to study. The R function `dmultinom` will return the probabilities for a multinomial distribution. The multinomial probability model will be studied in more detail in Chapter 18.

The birthday problem may be handled using this distribution and we will see it in action in Chapter 9.

6.4.2 Dirichlet Distribution

The Dirichlet distribution arises from the *Dirichlet integral* and is found to be very useful in Bayesian statistics. In fact, it arises as a conjugate prior to the multinomial distribution discussed in the previous subsection, see Chapter 9.

A random vector $\mathbf{X} = (X_1, \dots, X_K)$ is said to have a *Dirichlet distribution* with parameters $(a_1, a_2, \dots, a_K)$ if the multivariate probability density function is given by

$$f(x_1, \dots, x_{K-1}|a_1, a_2, \dots, a_K) = \begin{cases} \frac{\Gamma(\sum_{i=1}^K a_i)}{\prod_{i=1}^K \Gamma(a_i)} \prod_{i=1}^K x_i^{a_i - 1}, & x_i > 0, a_i > 0, i = 1, \dots, K, \\ & \text{and } \sum_{i=1}^{K-1} x_i < 1, \\ 0, & \text{otherwise.} \end{cases} \tag{6.72}$$

The Dirichlet distribution is the multivariate extension of the beta distribution. It especially serves as a very important *prior distribution*, see Chapter 9, in the context of Bayesian analysis. Some R functions which are useful for computations may be found in the R packages `gtools`, `LearnBayes`, and `VGAM`.

6.4.3 The Multivariate Normal Distribution

We will begin with a well-defined probability space. Consider the probability space $(\Omega, \mathcal{F}, P)$. Let $\Omega = \mathbb{R}^p$ be a p-dimensional euclidean space, and $\mathcal{F}$ be the Borel σ-field over the p-dimensional sets of $\mathbb{R}^p$. A random vector $\mathbf{X}$ is said to have *multivariate normal distribution* with mean vector $\boldsymbol{\mu}$ and a positive definite variance-covariance matrix $\boldsymbol{\Sigma}$ if its density function is given by

$$f(\mathbf{x}) = \frac{1}{(2\pi)^{p/2}|\boldsymbol{\Sigma}|^{1/2}} e^{-\frac{1}{2}(\mathbf{x}-\boldsymbol{\mu})'\boldsymbol{\Sigma}^{-1}(\mathbf{x}-\boldsymbol{\mu})}, \quad \text{if } x_i \in \mathbb{R},$$

$$i = 1, 2, \dots, p, \boldsymbol{\mu} \in \mathbb{R}^p, |\boldsymbol{\Sigma}| > 0. \tag{6.73}$$

The mgf and cf of a multivariate normal random vector are given below:

$$M_{\mathbf{X}}(t) = \exp\left(\boldsymbol{\mu}'\mathbf{t} + \frac{1}{2}\mathbf{t}'\boldsymbol{\Sigma}\mathbf{t}\right), \tag{6.74}$$

$$\varphi_{\mathbf{X}}(t) = \exp\left(i\boldsymbol{\mu}'\mathbf{t} - \frac{1}{2}\mathbf{t}'\boldsymbol{\Sigma}\mathbf{t}\right). \tag{6.75}$$

Refer to Chapter 14 for a more elaborate use of the multivariate normal distribution. The R package mvtnorm consists of functions dmvnorm, pmvnorm, and qmvnorm, which respectively deal with the pdf, percentiles, and quantiles of multivariate normal distribution.

6.4.4 *The Multivariate* t *Distribution*

Consider a random vector **X**. We say that the random vector **X** is a p-variate t-distribution with degrees of freedom υ, mean vector $\boldsymbol{\mu}$, and correlation matrix **R**, if its probability density function is given by

$$f(\mathbf{x}, \nu, \boldsymbol{\mu}, \mathbf{R}) = \frac{\Gamma\left(\frac{\nu+1}{2}\right)}{(\pi\nu)^{p/2}\Gamma(\nu/2)|\mathbf{R}|^{1/2}}\left[1 + \frac{1}{\nu}(\mathbf{x} - \boldsymbol{\mu})'\mathbf{R}^{-1}(\mathbf{x} - \boldsymbol{\mu})\right]^{-(\nu+p)/2}. \qquad (6.76)$$

For a comprehensive treatment of the multivariate t distribution, see Kotz and Nadarajah (2004). Applications of this distribution may be found in Chapters 14 and 15. The pdf of this random vector for use in R is available in the mvtnorm package through the dmvt function. Similarly, pmvt and qmvt functions handle the percentile and quantile of the multivariate normal vector.

?ddirichlet, ?dmvnorm

6.5 Populations and Samples

The complete list of students in a classroom may be available in the attendance roll monitored by a class teacher. In the future, the denumeration of all Indians is expected to be available by the "Unique Identification" project initiated by the Government of India, see http://uidai.gov.in/. These two examples give us clarity on the population. Thus, we may say that the *population* is the collection of all possible existing units which have that trait under consideration.

Understandably, if observations of all the population units are available, the unknown values of the models can be perfectly known. However, this is generally not the case and we have to be content with a representative part of the population, which we refer to as the *sample*. The representative part here refers to the requirement that the units selected in the sample have as much information about the population as the units which have not been selected. For the purpose of this chapter, it would suffice to safely say that we have a *random sample* from the population. The random sample is mathematically defined as follows.

Definition 6.5.1 Random Sample *Let $X_1, X_2, \ldots, X_n$ be RVs having joint density function $f_{X_1,X_2,\ldots,X_n}(x_1, x_2, \ldots, x_n)$. Let us denote the density function by f. If the joint density function can be expressed as*

$$f_{X_1,X_2,\ldots,X_n}(x_1, x_2, \ldots, x_n) = \prod_{i=1}^{n} f_{X_i}(x_i), \qquad (6.77)$$

then $X_1, X_2, \ldots, X_n$ is said to be a random sample *of size n from a population with density $f(.)$.*

The information in the random sample needs to be summarized in as compact a manner as possible. This consolidation is elaborated through the next concept.

Definition 6.5.2 Statistic *Any function of the random variables, resulting in an observable random variable, which does not contain the parameter values, is called a* ***statistic****.*

Example 6.5.1. Statistics: Simple Examples. Let $X_1, X_2, \ldots, X_n$ be a random sample of size n from a population with density function $f(.|\theta)$. Define the following quantities:

$$T_1 \equiv \sum_{i=1}^{n} X_i, \quad T_2 \equiv \sum_{i=1}^{n} X_i^{3/2},$$

$$T_3 \equiv \prod_{i=1}^{n} X_i, \quad T_4 \equiv \frac{\theta}{\sum_{i=1}^{n} X_i}.$$

In the above bag, the first three qualify as statistics, whereas the last one does not. □

Example 6.5.2. Statistics: Sample Moments. As in the previous example, we let $X_1, X_2, \ldots, X_n$ be a random sample of size n from a population with density function $f(.|\theta)$. Define the rth *sample moment about 0*, denoted by M'_r, as

$$M'_r = \frac{1}{n} \sum_{i=1}^{n} X_i^r, r = 1, 2, \ldots .$$

Note that the sample moments do not involve any of the parameters of the density function f, and thus they are examples of a statistic. Similarly, the rth *sample moment about the mean* $\bar{X}_n$, denoted by M_r, are also examples of a statistic, and they are given by

$$M_r = \frac{1}{n} \sum_{i=1}^{n} (X_i - \bar{X}_n)^r, r = 1, 2, \ldots .$$

The sample moments about the mean are sometimes called the *central moments.* □

In the next section, we will focus on useful statistics when the random sample is drawn from a normal population.

6.6 Sampling from the Normal Distributions

Some of the important results regarding sampling from the normal distributions are listed in the forthcoming theorems.

Theorem 6.6.1 *Let $\bar{X}_n$ denote the sample mean for a random sample from a normal distribution $N(\mu, \sigma^2)$ of size n. Then the probability distribution of $\bar{X}_n$ is $N(\mu, \sigma^2/n)$, that is,*

$$\bar{X}_n \sim N(\mu, \sigma^2/n). \tag{6.78}$$

Note that the variance of the average reduces by a factor of order n. □

We can visualize this result for some sample sizes.

```
> # Understanding the behavior of Normal Sample Mean
> n <- c(2,5,10,20)
> sd_normal_mean <- sqrt(n)
> x <- seq(-3,3,0.1)
> plot(x,dnorm(x),"l",xlim=c(-3,3),ylim=c(0,2),
+ main="A: Understanding the Sample Normal Mean")
> for(i in 1:length(n)) {
+         points(x,dnorm(x,sd=1/sqrt(n[i])),"l")
+ }
```

We are plotting the density function based on the appropriate formula with standard deviation equal to the square-root of the sample size, see Part A of Figure 6.9. The `plot` function along with the `dnorm` function play the central role in obtaining the plot, while the options of `xlim`, `ylim`, and `main` present the output in an appropriate display.

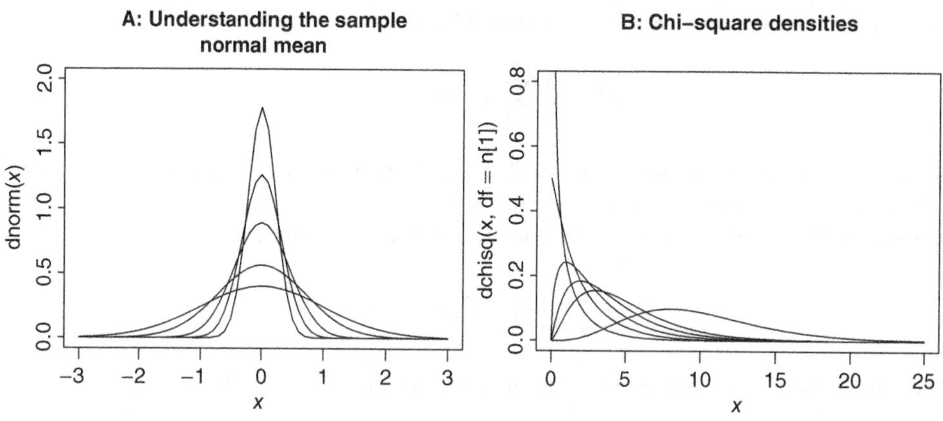

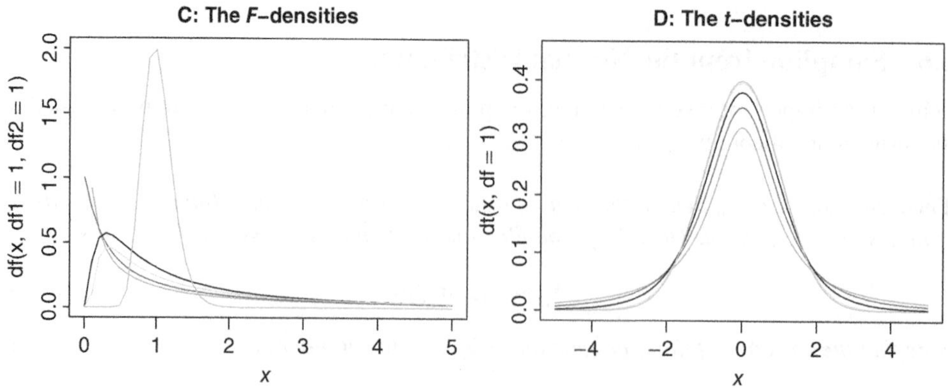

Figure 6.9 Some Important Sampling Densities

Theorem 6.6.2 *Suppose that $X_i \sim N(\mu_i, \sigma_i^2), i = 1, 2, \ldots, n$. Assume that the n random variables are independent. Define*

$$U \equiv \sum_{i=1}^{n} \left(\frac{X_i - \mu_i}{\sigma_i} \right)^2. \tag{6.79}$$

Then, U is distributed as a χ^2 RV with n degrees of freedom. □

The above theorem says that the sum of the squares of independent standard normal RVs has a χ^2-distribution with degrees of freedom equal to the number of terms in the sum. In the following, we will see the shape of chi-square densities for various degrees of freedom.

```
> # Understanding the shape of chi-square densities for various d.f.
> n <- c(1:5,10)
> x <- seq(0,25,0.1)
> plot(x,dchisq(x,df=n[1]),ylim=c(0,0.8),"l",
+ main="B: Chi-square Densities")
> for(i in 2:length(n)){
+         points(x,dchisq(x,df=n[i]),"l")
+ }
```

The `dchisq` function provides the density function of a χ^2 RV. See Part B of Figure 6.9. Some properties of a sample of standard normal RVs are collected in the next theorem.

Theorem 6.6.3 *Consider a random sample of size n from a standard normal population. Then the following results hold:*

1. *$\bar{X}$ is distributed as $N(0, 1/n)$.*
2. *$\bar{X}$ and $\sum_{i=1}^{n}(X_i - \bar{X})^2$ are independent.*
3. *$\sum_{i=1}^{n}(X_i - \bar{X})^2$ has a χ^2 distribution with $n - 1$ degrees of freedom.*

□

The F-distribution also arises as the ratio of two χ^2 RVs. A formal statement of this result is given next.

Theorem 6.6.4 *Let U be a χ^2 RV with m degrees of freedom, and let V be a χ^2 RV with n degrees of freedom. Assume that U and V are independent. Define*

$$X \equiv \frac{U/m}{V/n}. \tag{6.80}$$

Then the random variable X has an F distribution with m and n degrees of freedom. □

The R program for visualizing different F distributions appears in the following.

```
> # Understanding the F-Density Plots
> n <- c(1:5,10)
> x <- seq(0,5,0.1)
> plot(x,df(x,df1=1,df2=1),xlim=c(0,5),ylim=c(0,2),"l",
+ main="C: The F- Densities",col="green")
```

```
> points(x,df(x,df1=2,df2=1),"l",col="red")
> points(x,df(x,df1=5,df2=2),"l",col="blue")
> points(x,df(x,df1=100,df2=1),"l",col="yellow")
> points(x,df(x,df1=100,df2=100),"l",col="orange")
```

A plot related to different F-distributions is given in the "The F-Densities" Part C of Figure 6.9. The F-distribution plays an important role in comparing variances which will have important implications in analysis of *linear models*. The F-densities are obtained with the use of the `df` function. A related important sampling distribution for comparison of means is given by the t-distribution and we state this in the next theorem.

Theorem 6.6.5 *Let Z denote a standard normal variate. Consider an RV U which has a χ^2 distribution with k degrees of freedom. Assume that Z and U are independent random variables. Define*

$$t = \frac{Z}{\sqrt{U/k}}. \tag{6.81}$$

Then t has a Students t-distribution with k degrees of freedom. □

The t-distributions can also be easily visualized.

```
> # Understanding the t-densities
> n <- c(1:5,10)
> x <- seq(-5,5,0.1)
> plot(x,dt(x,df=1),xlim=c(-5,5),ylim=c(0,0.45),"l",
+ main="D: The t-Densities",col="green")
> points(x,dt(x,df=2),"l",col="red")
> points(x,dt(x,df=5),"l",col="blue")
> points(x,dt(x,df=30),"l",col="yellow")
> points(x,dt(x,df=Inf),"l",col="orange")
```

Different plots of the t-densities are displayed using the `dt` function in Part D of Figure 6.9.

We would now like to know what happens to the distribution of the sample mean and the sample sum in the general case. Especially if we are not sure if the underlying distribution is normal, we are curious about the sampling distribution properties. If the first two moments of the RVs are known to be finite and the observations are independent, the *central limit theorem* gives the answer, as also discussed earlier in Section 5.12.

Theorem 6.6.6 *Let $X_1, X_2, \ldots, X_n$ be a sequence of n iid RVs with mean μ and finite variance σ^2. The central limit theorem states that as the sample size n increases, the distribution of the sample average $\bar{X}_n$ approaches the normal distribution with mean μ and variance σ^2/n.* □

An illustration of the theorem has already been seen in Section 5.12.

?dnorm, ?curve, ?dchisq

6.7 Some Finer Aspects of Sampling Distributions

6.7.1 *Sampling Distribution of Median*

In this subsection, we will continue with the assumption of sampling from a normal distribution. In general, the focus is on the sampling distribution of the mean. We will now consider a few aspects of sampling distribution of a median.

Computation of a median is a fairly easy task. Let us state the requirements in a more formal way. Let $X_{(1)}, X_{(2)}, \ldots, X_{(n)}$ denote the ordered sample, that is, $X_{(1)} \leq X_{(2)} \leq \cdots \leq X_{(n)}$. If n is odd, the median is the middlemost $X_{((n+1)/2)}$ order statistic. We need to estimate the standard error of the median. Towards this, compute k as the integer part of the number obtained by

$$[k] = \frac{n+1}{2} - 2.58\sqrt{n/4}.$$

McKean-Schrader estimate of the variance of the median as given by

$$s_M^2 = \left(\frac{X_{(n-k+1)} - X_{(k)}}{5.1517}\right)^2. \tag{6.82}$$

A good coverage on these aspects appears in Section 5.4 of Wilcox (2009), which has been our source too. For other theoretical aspects of the sampling distribution of median, refer to Geyer (2001) . The concepts will be demonstrated using Student's sleep dataset.

```
> sleepgr1 <- sleep$extra[sleep$group==1]
> sleepgr1Median <- median(sleepgr1)
> n <- length(sleepgr1)
> sleepgr1Ascend <- sort(sleepgr1)
> k <- floor((n+1)/2 - 2.58*sqrt(n/4))
> sleepgr1MedianSE <- sqrt(((sleepgr1Ascend[n-k+1]-
+ sleepgr1Ascend[k])/5.1517)^{2})
> sleepgr1MedianSE
[1] 1.028787
```

6.7.2 *Sampling Distribution of Mean of Standard Distributions*

We will now consider three probability distributions, Poisson, Uniform, and Cauchy, and have a brief look at the sampling distribution of mean of a random sample from them.

Example 6.7.1. Poisson Distribution. Consider an random sample $X_1, \ldots, X_n$ from a Poisson distribution with parameter λ. We know that $\sum_{i=1}^{n} X_i$ follows a Poisson distribution with mean $n\lambda$. Using this fact we can obtain the sampling distribution of the mean of a Poisson random sample:

$$P\left(\bar{X} = \frac{k}{n}\right) = P\left(\sum_{i=1}^{n} X_i = k\right) = \frac{e^{-n\lambda}(n\lambda)^k}{k!}, k = 0, 1, 2, \ldots \tag{6.83}$$

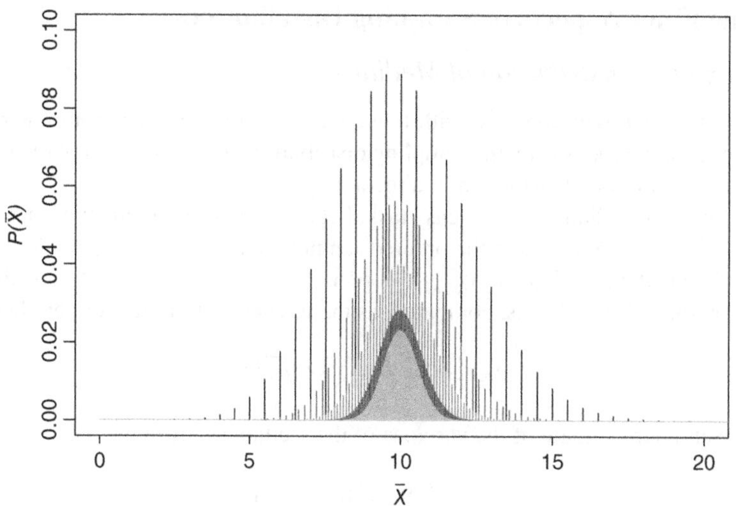

Figure 6.10 Poisson Sampling Distribution

The next R program helps to understand the distribution function of $\bar{X}$.

```
> n <- c(2,5,10,20,30,50)
> lambda <- 10
> i <- 6
> plot(seq(0,30*n[i],1)/n[i],dpois(seq(0,30*n[i],1),n[i]*lambda),
+ xlab=expression(bar(X)),ylab=expression(P(bar(X))),
+ type="h",col=i,xlim=c(0,20),ylim=c(0,0.1))
> for(i in 1:5) lines(seq(0,30*n[i],1)/n[i],dpois(seq(0,30*n[i],1),
+ n[i]*lambda),type="h",col=i)
```

Again, the R program is fairly easy to follow. Figure 6.10 shows that the sampling distribution may be approximated by a normal distribution. □

Example 6.7.2. Uniform Distributions. Consider a sample of size n from $U(0, 1)$. The exact density of $\bar{X}_n$, see page 238 of Mood, et al. (1974), is given by

$$f_{\bar{X}_n}(x) = \sum_{k=0}^{n-1}\left[(nx)^{n-1} - \binom{n}{1}(nx-1)^{n-1} + \binom{n}{2}(nx-2)^{n-1} - \cdots \right.$$
$$\left. +(-1)^k\binom{n}{k}(nx-k)^{n-1}\right] I_{(k/n,(k+1)/n)}(x). \tag{6.84}$$

We have not even considered the general case of θ. An exercise for the reader is to obtain the sample distributions of the mean for the first three n and sketch their densities. □

Example 6.7.3. Cauchy Distribution. Consider a random sample of size n from a Cauchy density:

$$f(x|\mu,\sigma^2) = \frac{1}{\pi\sigma\{1+[(x-\mu)/\sigma]^2\}}.$$

A remarkable fact about the Cauchy distribution is that the mean of the random sample has a Cauchy density with the same parameters μ and σ. Since this does not involve n, we cannot perform inference based on it! □

?dpois

6.8 Multivariate Sampling Distributions

We will now consider some aspects of multivariate sampling distributions. Chapter 6 of Giri (2004) gives a detailed account of multivariate sampling distributions.

6.8.1 *Noncentral Univariate Chi-square,* t, *and* F *Distributions*

Theorems 6.1 to 6.6 were related to the distribution of statistics, which were centered towards a guarantee that the mean would be zero. In varied applications we do not have the luxury of centering the statistics, and there will be the requirement of understanding such distributions. Thus, we are now looking at *noncentral distributions*.

Let $X_1, \ldots, X_n$ be independently distributed normal RVs with $X_i \sim N(\mu_i, \sigma_i^2), i = 1, \ldots, n$. Define

$$Z = \sum_{i=1}^{n} \frac{X_i^2}{\sigma_i^2}.$$

We also need to define a new quantity $\delta^2 = \sum_{i=1}^{n} \mu_i^2/\sigma_i^2$. The probability density function of Z is then given by

$$f(z|\delta^2) = \begin{cases} \frac{\exp\left\{-\frac{1}{2}(\delta^2+z)\right\} z^{\frac{n}{2}-1}}{\sqrt{\pi}2^{n/2}} \sum_{j=0}^{\infty} \frac{(\delta^2)^j z^j \Gamma(j+1/2)}{(2j!)\Gamma(n/2+j)}, & z \geq 0, \\ 0, & \text{otherwise.} \end{cases} \tag{6.85}$$

The parameter δ^2 is called the *non-centrality parameter*. The second parameter of a noncentral χ^2 distribution is the n degrees of freedom. For the χ^2 density plots, we will add curves with noncentrality parameters. The program is:

```
> n <- c(1:5,10)
> ncp <- n
> x <- seq(0,25,0.1)
> plot(x,dchisq(x,df=n[1]),ylim=c(0,0.3),
+ ylab="Non-central chi-square densities",
+ type="l",main="A: Chi-square Densities",col=1)
```

```
> points(x,dchisq(x,df=n[1],ncp=ncp[1]),"b",col=1)
> for(i in 2:length(n)){
+     points(x,dchisq(x,df=n[i]),"l",col=i)
+     points(x,dchisq(x,df=n[i],ncp=ncp[i]),"b",col=i)
+ }
```

All the density plots obtained here may be seen in Part A of Figure 6.11.

Consider a noncentral chi-square random variable $X \sim \chi^2_m(\delta^2)$, and another chi-square random variable $Y \sim \chi^2_n$. Assume that X and Y are independent random variables and define

$$F = \frac{\chi^2_m(\delta^2)/m}{\chi^2_n/n}.$$

The density function of F is given by a non-central F density function:

$$f_F(x) = \begin{cases} \dfrac{m}{n} \exp\left(-\dfrac{1}{2}\delta^2\right) \displaystyle\sum_{j=0}^{\infty} \dfrac{(\delta^2/2)\Gamma((m+n)/2+j)((m/n)x)^{m/2+j-1}}{\Gamma(m/2+j)\Gamma(n/2)(1+(m/n)x)^{(m+n)/2+j}}, & x \geq 0, \\ 0, & \text{otherwise}. \end{cases} \tag{6.86}$$

We will compare a few non-central F densities with their standard counterparts.

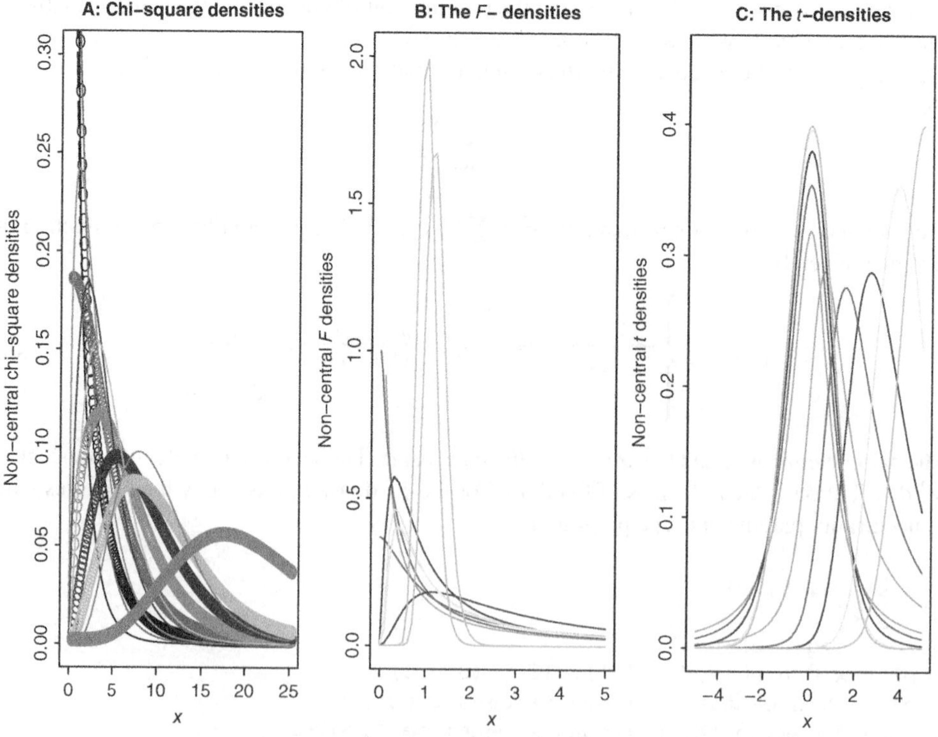

Figure 6.11 Non-central Densities

```
> x <- seq(0,5,0.1)
> plot(x,df(x,df1=1,df2=1),xlim=c(0,5),ylim=c(0,2),
+ ylab="Non-central F densities",
+ "l",main="B: The F- Densities",col="green")
> points(x,df(x,df1=2,df2=1),"l",col="red")
> points(x,df(x,df1=2,df2=1,ncp=2),"l",col="red")
> points(x,df(x,df1=5,df2=2),"l",col="blue")
> points(x,df(x,df1=5,df2=2,ncp=10),"l",col="blue")
> points(x,df(x,df1=100,df2=1),"l",col="yellow")
> points(x,df(x,df1=100,df2=1,ncp=15),"l",col="yellow")
> points(x,df(x,df1=100,df2=100),"l",col="orange")
> points(x,df(x,df1=100,df2=100,ncp=20),"l",col="orange")
```

The result of the above program is Part B of Figure 6.11. We will close this subsection with an introduction of the non-central t-distribution. Let $X \sim N(\mu, \sigma^2)$ and $Y/\sigma^2 \sim \chi^2_n$ be two independent random variables. Define

$$t = \frac{\sqrt{n}X}{\sqrt{Y}}.$$

Also define $\lambda = \mu/\sigma$. The probability density function of t is then given by

$$f(t) = \frac{n^{n/2} \exp\{-\lambda^2/2\}}{(n+t^2)^{(n+1)/2}} \sum_{j=0}^{\infty} \frac{\Gamma((n+j+1)/2)\lambda^j}{j!} \left(\frac{2t^2}{n+t^2}\right)^{j/2}, -\infty < t < \infty. \tag{6.87}$$

The non-centrality parameter is λ and the degrees of freedom is n. We will, as with the χ^2 and F distribution, sketch a few non-central t-densities and their standard counterparts.

```
> x <- seq(-5,5,0.1)
> plot(x,dt(x,df=1),xlim=c(-5,5),ylim=c(0,0.45),
+ ylab="Non-central t densities",
+ "l",main="C: The t-Densities",col="green")
> points(x,dt(x,df=1,ncp=1),"l",col="green")
> points(x,dt(x,df=2),"l",col="red")
> points(x,dt(x,df=2,ncp=2),"l",col="red")
> points(x,dt(x,df=5),"l",col="blue")
> points(x,dt(x,df=5,ncp=3),"l",col="blue")
> points(x,dt(x,df=30),"l",col="yellow")
> points(x,dt(x,df=30,ncp=4),"l",col="yellow")
> points(x,dt(x,df=Inf),"l",col="orange")
> points(x,dt(x,df=Inf,ncp=5),"l",col="orange")
```

6.8.2 *Wishart Distribution*

Let $\mathbf{X}_1, \ldots, \mathbf{X}_n$ be a k-dimensional random sample from $N(\boldsymbol{\mu}, \boldsymbol{\Sigma})$. Define

$$\mathbf{A} = \sum_{\alpha=1}^{n} (\mathbf{X}_\alpha - \bar{\mathbf{X}})(\mathbf{X}_\alpha - \bar{\mathbf{X}})^T. \tag{6.88}$$

The probability density function of **A**, provided **A** is a positive definite matrix, is then given by

$$f(\mathbf{A}) = \frac{|\mathbf{A}|^{\frac{n-p-1}{2}}}{2^{np/2}\pi^{p(p-1)/4}|\mathbf{\Sigma}|^{n/2}\prod_{i=1}^{p}\Gamma((n-i+1)/2)} \exp\left(\frac{-\text{tr}\mathbf{\Sigma}^{-1}\mathbf{A}}{2}\right). \tag{6.89}$$

The random variable **A** may be called the *Wishart RV* and its distribution as the *Wishart distribution*. The Wisharts distribution will be abbreviated symbolically as $W(n, \mathbf{\Sigma})$. We will require the Wishart distribution in Chapters 14 and 15, that is, in the context of *multivariate statistical analysis*. For more details about the Wishart distribution, refer to Chapter 7 of Anderson (2003) and Chapter 6 of Giri (2004).

6.8.3 Hotellings T^2 Distribution

We will give Timm's (2002) definition for Hotelling's T^2 distribution. Let $\mathbf{Y} \sim N(\boldsymbol{\mu}, \mathbf{\Sigma})$ and $\mathbf{Q} \sim W(n, \mathbf{\Sigma})$. Define *Hotelling's T^2 statistic* as

$$T^2 = n\mathbf{Y}^T\mathbf{Q}^{-1}\mathbf{Y} \tag{6.90}$$

Then, the sampling distribution of the Hotelling's T^2 statistic is proportional to a non-central F distribution

$$\frac{n-p+1}{p}\frac{T^2}{n} \sim F(p, n-p+1, \gamma) \tag{6.91}$$

where $\gamma = \boldsymbol{\mu}^T\mathbf{\Sigma}^{-1}\boldsymbol{\mu}$.

?dchisq, ?df, ?dt

6.9 Bayesian Sampling Distributions

In Section 5.6 we introduced the Bayes formula. That is, if $X \sim f_\theta$ and the prior information about θ is specified by $\pi(\theta)$, the posterior distribution is then given by

$$\pi(\theta|x) = \frac{f(x|\theta)\pi(\theta)}{\int_{R_\theta} f(x|\theta)\pi(\theta)d\theta}. \tag{6.92}$$

The expression in the denominator is referred to as the *marginal distribution* of X, and a standard notation for it is $m(x)$, that is, $m(x) = \int_{R_\theta} f(x|\theta)\pi(\theta)d\theta$.

Consider a random sample of size n from f_θ. The joint density function of $\mathbf{x}$ is then $f(\mathbf{x}|\theta) = \prod_{i=1}^{n} f(x_i|\theta)$. The posterior distribution of θ, given the data $\mathbf{x}$, will be referred as the ***Bayesian sampling distribution***. In this case, the Bayesian sampling distribution is obtained as

$$\pi(\theta|\mathbf{x}) = \frac{f(\mathbf{x}|\theta)\pi(\theta)}{\int_{R_\theta} f(\mathbf{x}|\theta)\pi(\theta)d\theta}. \tag{6.93}$$

Table 6.1 Bayesian Sampling Distributions

Probability Model	Parameters	Prior	Bayesian Sampling Distribution
Bernoulli	$b(1,p)$	$Be(a,b)$	$Be(a+\sum_{i=1}^n x_i, b+n-\sum_{i=1}^n x_i)$
Poisson	$P(\lambda)$	$Gamma(\alpha,\theta)$	$Gamma(\alpha+\sum_{i=1}^n x_i, \theta+n)$
Uniform	$U(0,\theta)$	$Pareto(a,b)$	
Normal	$N(\mu,\sigma^2)$, σ known	$N(\tau,\eta^2)$	$N\left(\frac{\sigma^2\tau+\eta^2\bar{x}}{\sigma^2+\eta^2}, \frac{\sigma^2\eta^2}{\sigma^2+\eta^2}\right)$
Exponential	$Exp\ (\theta)$	$Gamma(a,b)$	$Gamma(\alpha+\sum_{i=1}^n x_i, \theta+n)$

To the best of our knowledge, the term Bayesian sampling distribution is not used in the Bayesian literature. We make this distinction to reflect that the posterior distribution is now based on a random sample. The Bayesian sampling distributions are illustrated for one well-known probability model. For a reasoning of the choice of prior distributions, the reader may hop to Chapter 9 and return again. Alternatively, this section may be read in conjunction with that chapter. Table 6.1 spells out some of the very important Bayesian sampling distribution.

Example 6.9.1. The Poisson Model. Let $X_1, \dots, X_n$ be a random sample from a population where the uncertainty is explained by the Poisson distribution with rate λ. We will assume that λ follows a Gamma distribution with parameters (α, θ). Define $T = \sum_{i=1}^n X_i$. We will first obtain the marginal distribution of T. Here,

$$\begin{aligned}
\pi(t) &= \int_0^\infty f(\mathbf{x}|\lambda)\pi(\lambda)d\lambda \\
&= \int_0^\infty \frac{e^{-n\lambda}(n\lambda)^t}{t!}\frac{\lambda^{\alpha-1}e^{-\lambda/\theta}}{\theta^\alpha\Gamma(\alpha)}d\lambda \\
&= \frac{n^t}{t!\theta^\alpha\Gamma(\alpha)}\int_0^\infty e^{-n(\lambda\theta+1)/\theta}\lambda^{t+\alpha-1}d\lambda \\
&= \frac{n^t\theta^t\Gamma(\alpha+t)}{t!(n\theta+1)^{\alpha+t}\Gamma(\alpha)}.
\end{aligned}$$

Then, the posterior distribution of λ, after straightforward manipulation, is given by the $Gamma(\alpha+\sum_{i=1}^n x_i, \theta+n)$ distribution. □

6.10 Further Reading

As we noted that sampling distribution is a bridge between probability and statistical inference, most of the references related to them are to be found either in the probability texts or inference ones. The references mentioned in the flow of this chapter are useful connections for obtaining more details about sampling distribution.

6.11 Complements, Problems, and Programs

Problem 6.1 Classify the RVs in Section 6.2 as simple or elementary RVs. Obtain the expectation and variances of these RVs using Formula 5.13 or 5.11.

Problem 6.2 For the uniform and beta distribution, write R programs to obtain mean and variance using Equation 5.16.

Problem 6.3 Use `barplot`, if required get more details with `?barplot`, to understand the probability measure of discrete uniform distribution for various N values.

Problem 6.4 The central term of binomial RV had been discussed in Example 6.2.5. Suppose that the tail probabilities $P(X > x)$ are of interest. Fix the value of n and varying the p values from 0 to 1, obtain a plot of $P(X > x)$ against p.

Problem 6.5 Let X follow a geometric distribution. Set up an R program to evaluate $P(X > m + n|X > m)$ and $P(X \geq n)$, for non-negative integers m and n. Does the memoryless property of exponential RV, as seen in Example 6.3.5, hold for the geometric distribution? Test the condition for a Poisson RV too.

Problem 6.6 For a fixed p value in a negative binomial RV, see Equation 6.20, obtain a plot of the mean and variance for different r values and comment.

Problem 6.7 Using the `dpois` function, find the minimum value of λ, such that $P(X > 10) \geq 0.2$.

Problem 6.8 Using the `choose` function, create a new function for the pmf of hypergeometric distribution.

Problem 6.9 *Graphically* prove that $U(0, 1)$ and beta RV with $\alpha = \beta = 1$ have the same pdf.

Problem 6.10 Using the `integrate` and `dt` (for density of t-distribution), verify the mean and variance of the t RV.

Problem 6.11 Develop *cantour plots* for bivariate normal RV and comment. The reader may refer to the examples in Chapter 13, Section 4 for some help and hints on `cantour`, or Chapter 15.

Problem 6.12 Reconstruct Part A of Figure 6.9 using the `curve` function instead of the `plot` function. What are the apparent advantages of using the `curve` function, if any?

Problem 6.13 Under the assumption of normal distribution for some of the examples of Chapter 4, obtain an estimate of the standard error of the median.

7

Parametric Inference

Package(s): UsingR
Dataset(s): ns, ps, bs, cs, galton, sleep, airquality

7.1 Introduction

In Chapter 4 we came across one form of analyzing data, viz., the exploratory data analysis. That approach mainly made no assumptions about the probability mechanism for the data generation. In later chapters we witnessed certain models which plausibly explain the nature of the random phenomenon. In reality, we seldom have information about the parameters of the probability distributions. Historically, or intuitively, we may have enough information about the probability distributions, sparing a few parameters. In this chapter we consider various methods for inferring about such parameters, using the data generated under the assumptions of these probability models.

Parametric statistical inference arises when we have information for the model describing an uncertain experiment sans a few values, called parameters, of the model. If the parameter values are known, we have problems more of the probabilistic kind than statistical ones. The parameter values need to be obtained based on some data. The data may be a pure random sample in the sense of all the observations being drawn with the same probability. However, it is also the practical case that obtaining a random sample may not be possible in many stochastic experiments. For example, the temperature in the morning and afternoon are certainly not identical observations. We undertake statistical inference of uncertain experiments in this chapter.

In Chapter 6, we came across a pool of diverse experiments which have certain underlying probability models, say $P_\theta, \theta \in \Theta$. Under the assumption that P_θ is the truth, we now develop methods for inference about θ. We will begin with some important families of distribution in Section 7.2. This section and the next few sections rely heavily on Lehmann and Casella (1998). The form of *loss functions* plays a vital role on the usefulness of an estimator/statistic. For an observation from binomial distribution, we discuss some choice of loss functions in Section 7.3. Data reduction through the concepts of sufficiency and completeness are theoretically examined in Section 7.4. Section 7.5 empathizes the importance of the *likelihood*

A Course in Statistics with R, First Edition. Prabhanjan Narayanachar Tattar, Suresh Ramaiah and B. G. Manjunath.

Companion Website: www.wiley.com/go/tattar/statistics

principle through visualization and examples. The role of *information function* for obtaining the parameter values is also detailed in this section. The discussion thus far focuses on the preliminaries of point estimation.

Using the foundations from Sections 7.2–7.5, we next focus on the specific techniques of obtaining the estimates of parameters using *maximum likelihood estimator* and *moment estimator* in Section 7.6. Estimators are further compared for their unbiasedness and variance in Section 7.7. The techniques discussed up to this point of the chapter return us a single value of the parameter, which is seldom useful in appropriating inference for the parameters. Thus, we seek a range, actually interval, of plausible values of the parameters in Section 7.8. In the case of missing values, or a data structure which may be simplified through missing variables, the *EM algorithm* is becoming very popular and the reader will find it illustrated in Section 7.16.

Sections 7.9–7.15 offers a transparent approach to the problem of *Testing Statistical Hypotheses*. It is common for statistical software texts to focus on the testing framework using straightforward useful R functions available in `prop.test`, `t.test`, etc. However, here we take a pedagogical approach and begin with preliminary concepts of Type I and Type II errors. The celebrated Neyman-Pearson lemma is stated and then demonstrated for various examples with R programs in Section 7.10. The Neyman-Pearson lemma returns us to a unique powerful test which cannot be extended for testing problems of composite hypotheses, and thus we need slightly relaxed conditions leading to uniformly most powerful tests and also uniformly most powerful unbiased tests, as seen in Sections 7.11 and 7.12. A more generic class of useful tests is available in the family of *likelihood ratio tests*. Its examples are detailed with R programs in Section 7.13. A very interesting problem, which is still unsolved, arises in the comparison of normal means from two populations whose variances are completely unknown. This famous *Behrens-Fisher* problem is discussed with appropriate solutions in Section 7.14. The last technical section of the chapter deals with the problem of testing multiple hypotheses, Section 7.15.

7.2 Families of Distribution

We will begin with a definition of a group family, page 17 of Lehmann and Casella (1998).

Definition 7.2.1 Group. *A set G of elements is called a* group *if it satisfies the following four conditions:*

1. *The group multiplication operator on any two elements $a, b \in G$ results in an element $c \in G$. The element c is called the product of a and b and is denoted by $c = ab$.*
2. *The group multiplication operator satisfies the associative rule:*

$$(ab)c = a(bc).$$

3. *There exists an identity element $e \in G$, such that*

$$ea = ae = a, \forall a \in G.$$

4. *Each element $a \in G$ admits an inverse $a^{-1} \in G$, such that*

$$aa^{-1} = a^{-1}a = e.$$

The identity element of a group and the inverses of any element are unique. The two important properties of a group are (i) *closure under composition*, and (ii) *closure under inversion*.

Basically, for various reasons, we change the characteristics of random variables by either adding them, or addition or multiplication of some constants, etc. We need some assurance that such changes do not render the probability model from which we started useless. The changes which we subject the random variable to is loosely referred to as a transformation. Let us discuss these two properties in more detail.

Closure under composition. A 1:1 transformation may be addition or multiplication. We say that a class $\mathcal{T}$ of transformation is closed under composition if $g_1, g_2 \in \mathcal{T}$ implies $g_2 \cdot g_1 \in \mathcal{T}$.

Closure under inversion. For any 1:1 transformation g, the inverse of g, denoted by g^{-1}, undoes the transformation g, that is, $g^{-1}\{g(x)\} = x$. A class of transformations $\mathcal{T}$ is said to be closed under inversion if for any $g \in \mathcal{T}$, the inverse g^{-1} is also in $\mathcal{T}$.

Definition 7.2.2 Transformation Group. *A class G of transformations is called a* transformation group *if it is closed under composition and inversion.*

Definition 7.2.3 *A* group family *of distributions is a family of distributions obtained by subjecting a random variable with a fixed distribution to a suitable family of transformations.*

In plain words, if a random variable under a group family is subject to a transformation, the resulting distribution also belongs to the same class of distribution. The transformation may include addition, multiplication, sine, etc.

Example 7.2.1. The Location Family. Let $(\Omega, \mathcal{F}, P)$ be a probability space and consider an $\mathcal{F}$- measurable random variable X. Let F denote the fixed cumulative distribution function of X. Define $Y := X + a$, where $-\infty < a < \infty$ is a constant. Then the probability distribution of Y is given by

$$P(Y \leq y) = F_X(y - a). \tag{7.1}$$

The collection of distributions, for fixed F and $\{a : -\infty < a < \infty\}$, satisfying 7.1 is said to constitute a *location family*.

Suppose $X \sim N(0, \sigma_0^2)$, with known variance σ_0^2 and we define $Y = X + a$. It is then clear that

$$P(Y \leq y) = P(X + a \leq y) = F_X(y - a) = \Phi_X\left(\frac{y - a}{\sigma_0}\right).$$

Thus, the collection of normal distributions with known variance forms the class of location family. □

Example 7.2.2. The Scale Family. As in the setting of the previous example, we have a new transformation as $Y := bX$, where $b > 0$. Then the probability distribution of Y is given by

$$P(Y \leq y) = F_X(y/b). \tag{7.2}$$

The collection of distributions, satisfying 7.2, is said to constitute a *scale family*. If $X \sim N(\mu_0, \sigma^2)$, with known mean μ_0 and $Y := bX$, we have

$$P(Y \leq y) = P(bX \leq y) = F_X(y/b) = \Phi_X\left(\frac{y}{b}\right).$$

Thus, the collection of normal distributions with known mean forms the class of scale family. □

Example 7.2.3. The Location-Scale Family. We have the same setting as earlier, and now we consider the transformation $Y := a + bX$, where $-\infty < a < \infty, b > 0$. Then the probability distribution of Y is given by

$$P(Y \leq y) = F_X\left(\frac{y-a}{b}\right). \tag{7.3}$$

The collection of distributions, satisfying 7.3, is said to constitute a *location-scale family*. The family of normal distributions, for fixed but unknown mean and variance, is an example of a location-scale family. □

Table 4.1 of Lehmann and Casella (1998) gives an important list of location-scale families.

7.2.1 The Exponential Family

Definition 7.2.4 Exponential Family. *A family $\{P_\theta, \theta \in \Theta\}$ of distributions is said to form an s-dimensional exponential family if the density function associated with the distributions P_θ can be written in the form:*

$$p_\theta(x) = \exp\left[\sum_{i=1}^{s} \eta_i(\theta)T_i(x) - B(\theta)\right] h(x), \tag{7.4}$$

with respect to some measure function μ. Here, the functions of θ, $\eta_i, i = 1, \cdots, s$, and $B(.)$, are real valued function of the parameters, and $T_i, i = 1, \cdots, s$, are real-valued statistics. The density function of an exponential family may be written in the canonical form *as*

$$p(x|\eta) = \exp\left[\sum_{i=1}^{s} \eta_i T_i(x) - A(\eta)\right] h(x). \tag{7.5}$$

The canonical form is not necessarily unique.

Note that we speak of a family of probability distributions belonging to an exponential family, and as such we are not focusing on a single density, say $N(0, 1)$.

Example 7.2.4. The Binomial Exponential Family. Suppose $X \sim$ binomial(n, p), with $0 < p < 1$. The probability density function (with respect to the counting measure μ) of X is then given by

$$f(x|p) = \binom{n}{x} p^x (1-p)^{n-x} = \binom{n}{x} (1-p)^n \left(\frac{p}{1-p}\right)^x$$
$$= \binom{n}{x} \exp\left(\ln\left(\frac{p}{1-p}\right) x - \ln(1-p)n\right).$$

Define $h(x) = \binom{n}{x}$, $B(p) = \ln(1-p)n$, $T(x) = x$, and $\eta(p) = \ln\left(\frac{p}{1-p}\right)$. It is then clear that the binomial random variable belongs to the exponential family. □

Example 7.2.5. The Normal Family. Let $X \sim N(\mu, \sigma^2)$. We will now rewrite the pdf of X, which will show that it belongs to the exponential family.

$$f(x|\mu,\sigma^2) = \frac{1}{\sqrt{2\pi}\sigma}\exp\left\{-\frac{(x-\mu)^2}{2\sigma^2}\right\} = \frac{1}{\sqrt{2\pi}\sigma}\exp\left\{\frac{\mu}{\sigma^2}x - \frac{1}{2\sigma^2}x^2 - \frac{\mu^2}{2\sigma^2}\right\}.$$

Define $B(\sigma^2) = 1/(\sqrt{2\pi}\sigma)$, $\eta_1 = \mu/(\sigma^2)$, and $\eta_2 = 1/(2\sigma^2)$. Hence the family of normal distributions is seen as a two-dimensional exponential family. □

Example 7.2.6. The Curved Normal Family. Consider the particular case of $\mu = \sigma$ for a family of normal distributions. Then the density function of X is given by

$$f(x|\mu,\mu^2) = \frac{1}{\sqrt{2\pi}\mu}\exp\left\{\frac{x}{\mu} - \frac{x^2}{2\mu^2} - \frac{1}{2}\right\}, \mu > 0.$$

Note that though this is a two-parameter exponential family with natural parameters $\left(\frac{1}{\mu}, -\frac{1}{2\mu^2}\right)$, they are governed by a single parameter μ. Thus, the two-dimensional parameters $\left(\frac{1}{\mu}, -\frac{1}{2\mu^2}\right)$ lie on a curve in R^2, and hence attract the name of *curved exponential family*. □

7.2.2 Pitman Family

The exponential family meets the *regularity condition* since the range of random variable is not a function of the parameter θ. In many interesting cases, the range of the random variable depends on a function of its parameters. In such cases the regularity condition is not satisfied. A nice discussion about such non-regular random variables appears on Page 19 of Srivastava and Srivastava (2009).

The mathematical argument is as follows. Let $u(x)$ be a positive function of x and let $Q_1(\theta)$ and $Q_2(\theta)$, $Q_1(\theta) < Q_2(\theta)$ be the extended real-valued functions of parameter θ. We can then define a density by

$$f_X(x|\theta) = c(\theta)u(x), Q_1(\theta) < x < Q_2(\theta), \tag{7.6}$$

where

$$[c(\theta)]^{-1} = \int_{Q_1(\theta)}^{Q_2(\theta)} u(x)dx < \infty.$$

Thus, we can see that the range of X depends on θ, and hence the density is a *non-regular*. The family of such densities is referred to as the *Pitman family*. In Table 7.1, a list of some members of the Pitman family is provided, refer to Table 1.3 of Srivastava and Srivastava (2009).

We will next consider the role of loss functions.

Table 7.1 Pitman Family of Distributions

Name	Density	Parameter Space	Range
Uniform (continuous)	$f(x\|\theta) = 1/\theta$	$\theta > 0$	$0 < x < \theta$
Shifted Exponential	$f(x\|\theta) = e^{-(x-\theta)}$	$\theta > 0$	$x > \theta$
Shifted Geometric	$f(x\|\theta) = (1-p)p^{x-\theta}$	$0 < p < 1$	$x = \theta, \theta+1, \cdots, 0 < p < 1$

7.3 Loss Functions

A statistic, or an estimator, T is employed for estimation of a parameter, say $\theta, \theta \in \Theta$. The loss incurred as a consequence of using T is captured using a *loss function*. In convention with the standard notation, the loss function of a parameter inferred by using T will be denoted by $L(\theta, T)$. Some useful loss functions are now given.

$$\text{The Squared Error Loss Function}: L(\theta, T) = (\theta - T)^2,$$
$$\text{The Absolute Error Loss Function}: L(\theta, T) = |\theta - T|.$$

In this section we will consider the squared error loss function only. To evaluate the performance of an estimator T under a loss function $L(\theta, T)$, we require the notion of *risk function* defined as

$$R(\theta, T) = E_\theta L(\theta, T). \tag{7.7}$$

For a fixed θ, $R(\theta, T)$ calculates the risk of using the statistic T. The risk function is the average loss due to T. The risk function under the squared error loss functions is also popularly known as the *mean squared error* of the estimator. The next example illustrates the risk function for four different statistics T. Since T also leads more often to making some decisions, we sometimes also denote the statistic by d. In fact, the loss functions have a more prominent role in *decision theory*.

Example 7.3.1. Risk Functions for the Binomial Family. Suppose $X \sim b(100, p)$, and we have four statistics/estimators, see Table 7.2, for estimation of p. To verify that the risk functions are correctly given in the table, let us check them out:

$$\begin{aligned}
E(\delta_0 - p)^2 &= (p - 0.25)^2, \\
E(\delta_1 - p)^2 &= E\left(\frac{X}{n} - p\right)^2 = \frac{1}{n^2}E(X - np)^2 = \frac{p(1-p)}{n}, \\
E(\delta_2 - p)^2 &= E\left(\frac{X+3}{n} - p\right)^2 = \frac{1}{n^2}E((X - np)^2 + 2 \times 3 \times (X - np) + 3^2) \\
&= \frac{9 + np(1-p)}{n^2}.
\end{aligned}$$

Verify that the risk function for δ_4 is indeed as given by $R(p, \delta_4)$ in Table 7.2.

Table 7.2 Risk Functions for Four Statistics

Statistic T	Risk Function $R(L(p, T))$
$\delta_0 = 0.25$	$R(p, \delta_0) = E(\delta_0 - p)^2 = (p - 0.25)^2$
$\delta_1 = \frac{X}{n}$	$R(p, \delta_1) = E(\delta_1 - p)^2 = \frac{p(1-p)}{n}$
$\delta_2 = \frac{X+3}{n}$	$R(p, \delta_2) = E(\delta_2 - p)^2 = \frac{9+np(1-p)}{n^2}$
$\delta_3 = \frac{X+3}{(n+6)}$	$R(p, \delta_3) = E(\delta_3 - p)^2 = \frac{(9-8p)(1+8p)}{(n+6)^2}$

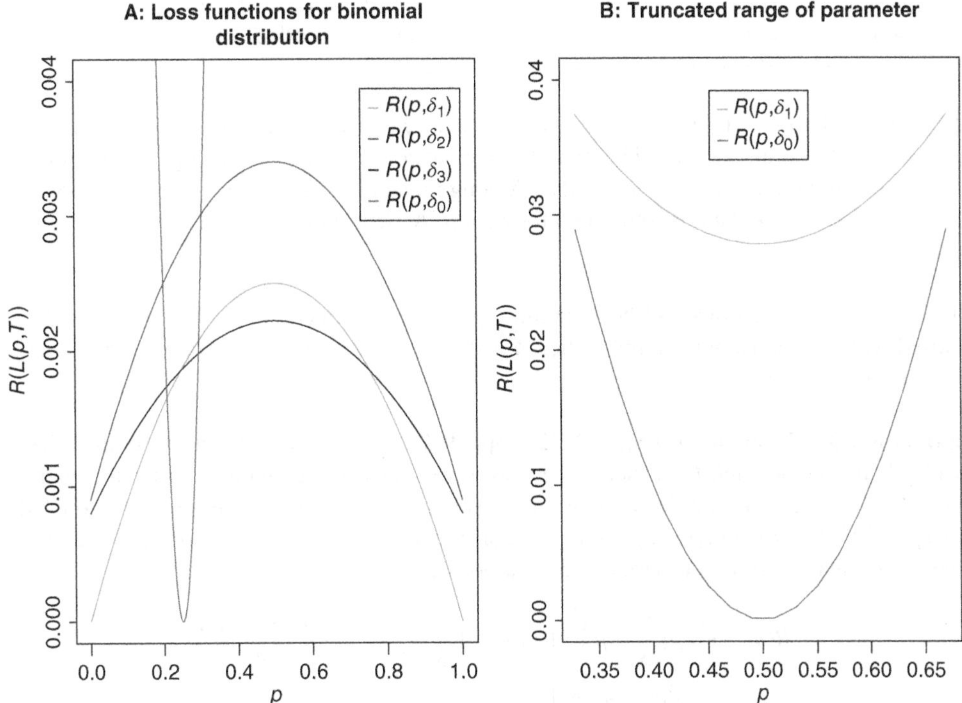

Figure 7.1 Loss Functions for Binomial Distribution

This example is adapted from Chapter 3 of Keener (2010). We now see how to plot the above tabled risk functions. First, we initialize the values of the parameter p in the R object `p <- seq(0,1,0.002)` and then calculate the risk functions for the four statistics in the respective R objects `Rdelta0, Rdelta1, Rdelta2, Rdelta3`. Next, the risk function for δ_1, that is $R(p, \delta_1)$, is plotted against the parameter values. Using the `lines` function, the remaining risk functions are obtained in the same plot. To obtain suitable legends for the risk functions, we first create an expression object in `exp_legends` and then use it in the `legend` function. The final output is given in Figure 7.1.

```
> # Risk Plots for 4 Loss Functions of Binomial Distribution
> p <- seq(0,1,0.002)
> Rdelta1 <- p*(1-p)/100
> Rdelta2 <- (9+100*p*(1-p))/100^{2}
> Rdelta3 <- (9-8*p)*(1+8*p)/106^{2}
> Rdelta0 <- (p-0.25)^{2}
> plot(p,Rdelta1,"l",xlim=c(0,1),ylim=c(0,0.004),xlab="p",
+ ylab=expression(R(L(p,T))),col="green")
> lines(p,Rdelta2,"l",col="blue")
> lines(p,Rdelta3,"l",col="black")
> lines(p,Rdelta0,"l",col="red")
> exp_legends <- expression(paste("R(p,",delta[1],")"),
+ paste("R(p,",delta[2],")"),
```

```
+ paste("R(p,",delta[3],")"),paste("R(p,",delta[0],")"))
> legend(x=c(0.8,1.0),y=c(0.004,0.003),exp_legends,
+ col=c("green","blue","black","red"),pch="-")
```

Referring to Part A of Figure 7.1, observe that the degenerate estimator, the red-colored curve, is a very bad example of an estimator and it may be considered as an analogy of the stopped watch showing the right time twice a day. Among the non-trivial estimators, δ_2, blue-colored curve, has more risk than the other two for each p. A clear winner cannot be picked from δ_1 and δ_3. □

The role of loss functions will become more prominent in Section 7.7. The section will be closed with an interesting example where the degenerate estimator is to be preferred over a reasonable estimator.

Example 7.3.2. Romano and Siegel's Example 9.21. Let X be a Bernoulli random variable with p being the probability of success. However, we now restrict the range of p to the interval $[1/3, 2/3]$. In light of a single observation, an estimator, say δ_1, is meaningful if we conclude that $p = 1/3$ if $X = 0$ and $p = 2/3$ if $X = 1$. Consider the degenerate estimator $\delta_0 = 1/2$. Now, the mean squared errors for these two estimators are

$$R(\delta_1, p) = p\left(\frac{2}{3} - p\right)^2 + (1-p)\left(\frac{1}{3} - p\right)^2 = \frac{3p^2 - 3p + 1}{9},$$

$$R(\delta_0, p) = \frac{4p^2 - 4p + 1}{4}.$$

The R program gives the plot of the risk functions.

```
> p <- seq(0.33,.67,0.02)
> Rdelta1 <- (3*p^2-3*p+1)/9
> Rdelta0 <- (4*p^2-4*p+1)/4
> plot(p,Rdelta1,"l",xlim=c(0.33,0.67),ylim=c(0,0.04),xlab="p",
+ ylab=expression(R(L(p,T))),col="green")
> lines(p,Rdelta0,"l",col="red")
> exp_legends <- expression(paste("R(p,",delta[1],")"),
+ paste("R(p,",delta[0],")"))
> legend(x=c(0.45,0.5),y=c(0.04,0.035),exp_legends,
+ col=c("green","red"),pch="-")
```

It appears from Part B of Figure 7.1 that the degenerate estimator is better than the reasonable estimator, which will be dealt with in Section 7.6. The important question here now is whether we can accept the degenerate estimator? □

7.4 Data Reduction

Statistical inference has two very important pillars: (i) The Sufficiency Principle, and (ii) The Likelihood Principle. Berger and Woolpert (1988) is a treatise for understanding these principles. In this section we will consider the sufficiency principle in depth.

7.4.1 Sufficiency

It is seen in Section 7.3 that many possible statistics exist for a given parameter. Some statistics have an advantage over others and a meaningful criteria needs to be arrived at to help in these type of decisions.

Definition 7.4.1 ***Sufficient Statistic.*** *A real valued statistic T is called* sufficient *for the parameter θ if and only if the conditional distribution of the random sample $X = (X_1, X_2, \cdots, X_n)$, given $T = t$ does not involve θ, for all $t \in S_T$, where S_T is the support (range) of the statistic T.*

Example 7.4.1. The Exponential Distribution. Let $X_1, X_2, \cdots, X_n$ be a random sample from an exponential distribution with mean θ, that is,

$$f(x) = \begin{cases} \frac{1}{\theta}\exp(-\frac{x}{\theta}), & x \geq 0, \theta > 0, \\ 0, & \text{otherwise}. \end{cases} \tag{7.8}$$

Consider the estimator $T = \sum_{i=1}^{n} X_i$. Then, it can be proved that

$$P(X_1 = x_1, \cdots, X_n = x_n | T = t) = \frac{\Gamma(n)}{t^{n-1}},$$

which is independent of θ. Hence, the information in T is sufficient for θ. □

Example 7.4.2. The Poisson Distribution. Let $X_1, X_2, \cdots, X_n$ be a random sample from a Poisson distribution with mean λ. Consider the statistic $T = \sum_{i=1}^{n} X_i$. It can be shown that

$$P(X_1 = x_1, \cdots, X_n = x_n | T = t) = \frac{t!}{\prod_{i=1}^{n} x_i!} n^{-t},$$

which is independent of λ, and hence we conclude that the statistic T is sufficient for the parameter λ. □

Example 7.4.3. Sufficient Statistics for Exponential Family. Corollary 6.16 of Lehmann and Casella (1998) gives a general result for obtaining sufficient statistics for the exponential family. Recollect the definition of an exponential family in its canonical form, equation 7.5:

$$p(x|\eta) = \exp\left[\sum_{i=1}^{s} \eta_i T_i(x) - A(\eta)\right] h(x).$$

Then $(T_1, \cdots, T_s)$ is sufficient if it is of full rank. In fact a more general result is true, which will be seen in the later part of this section. □

Thus far we began with statistics and verified whether it satisfied the sufficiency condition. It is not always possible to guess what may turn out to be sufficient statistics. The *Neyman Factorization theorem* gives a result which helps to obtain the sufficient statistics from the joint probability function of the random sample. A measure theoretic framework of this theorem is due to Halmos and Savage (1949), see page 289 of Mukhopadhyay (2000) for more details. The following theorem may be found in Casella and Berger (2002).

Theorem 7.4.1 Neyman Factorization Theorem. *Consider a random sample* $\mathbf{X} = (X_1, \cdots, X_n)$ *from* $f(x|\theta)$. *Let* $f(\mathbf{x}|\theta)$ *denote the joint pmf (pdf) of the random sample* $\mathbf{X}$. *A statistic* $T(\mathbf{X})$ *is sufficient for* θ *if there exist functions* $g(t|\theta)$ *and* $h(\mathbf{x})$, *such that for all possible* $\mathbf{x}$ *values and* $\theta \in \Theta$, *we can write the joint pmf (pdf) as*

$$f(\mathbf{x}|\theta) = g(T(\mathbf{X})|\theta)h(\mathbf{x}). \tag{7.9}$$

□

We will now use this result to obtain the sufficient statistics in some important cases.

Example 7.4.4. The Discrete Uniform Distribution. Let $(X_1, \cdots, X_n)$ be an iid sample from a discrete uniform distribution whose support is $1, \cdots, \theta$. The pmf is given by

$$f(x|\theta) = \begin{cases} \frac{1}{\theta}, & x = 1, 2, \cdots, \theta, \\ 0, & \text{otherwise.} \end{cases}$$

Define $T(\mathbf{x}) = \max_i \{x_i\}$ and consider the two functions:

$$g(t|\theta) = \begin{cases} \theta^{-n}, & t \leq \theta, \\ 0, & \text{otherwise,} \end{cases}$$

$$h(\mathbf{x}) = \begin{cases} 1, & x_i \in \{1, 2, \cdots, \theta\}, i = 1, 2, \cdots, n, \\ 0, & \text{otherwise.} \end{cases}$$

The joint pmf is then given by

$$f(\mathbf{x}|\theta) = \begin{cases} \frac{1}{\theta^n}, & x_i \in \{1, 2, \cdots, \theta\}, \\ 0, & \text{otherwise,} \end{cases}$$

$$= \begin{cases} g(t|\theta)h(\mathbf{x}), & t \leq \theta, \\ 0, & \text{otherwise.} \end{cases}$$

Thus, by the application of the Neyman factorization theorem, the maximum of the random sample is seen to be the sufficient statistic. □

Example 7.4.5. The Normal Distribution. Consider a random sample $(X_1, \cdots, X_n)$ from $N(\mu, \sigma^2)$. Here $\boldsymbol{\theta} = (\mu, \sigma^2)$. We have two parameters and both are assumed to be unknown. The joint pdf is then given by:

$$f_{\mu,\sigma^2}(\mathbf{x}) = \frac{1}{(\sigma\sqrt{2\pi})^n} \exp\left[-\frac{\sum_i (x_i - \mu)^2}{2\sigma^2}\right] = \frac{1}{(\sigma\sqrt{2\pi})^n} \exp\left[-\frac{\sum_i x_i^2}{2\sigma^2} + \frac{\mu \sum_i x_i}{\sigma^2} - \frac{n\mu^2}{2\sigma^2}\right].$$

Define $T(X_1, \cdots, X_n) = \left(\sum_i X_i, \sum_i X_i^2\right)$. Applying the Neyman factorization theorem, we can see that T is jointly sufficient for (μ, σ^2). □

If σ in the previous example is known, it can be seen that $T_1 = (X_1, \cdots, X_n)$, $T_2 = \sum_{i=1}^n X_i$, $T_3 = (X_1 + X_2, X_3 + X_4, \cdots, X_{n-1} + X_n)$, and other permutations are all sufficient for μ. Thus, we need a more general framework to identify the sufficient statistics. Furthermore, there may be more than one sufficient statistic and in such cases we need to pick one among them.

7.4.2 Minimal Sufficiency

Dynkin (1951) gave the criteria for a statistic to be *necessary*.

Definition 7.4.2 Necessary Statistics. *A statistic is said to be* necessary *if it is a function of every sufficient statistic.*

In the discussion before this subsection, it can be seen that the statistics T_2 can be mathematically written as a function of T_1 and T_3. Thus, if T_1, T_2, and T_3 are the only three sufficient statistics, though there are many more sufficient statistics in the scenario, then T_2 turns out to be a necessary statistic. This definition further guides towards the concept of *minimal sufficient* statistics.

Definition 7.4.3 Minimal Sufficient Statistics. *A statistic $T(X)$ is said to be a* minimal sufficient statistic *if it is a necessary and sufficient statistic.*

It is not practical to obtain a minimal sufficient statistic from its definition. Lehmann and Scheffé (1950) provide a result which is useful in obtaining a minimal sufficient statistic. We first describe this important result.

Theorem 7.4.2 *Let $f(\mathbf{x}|\theta)$ be the pmf (pdf) of a sample $\mathbf{X}$. A statistic $T(\mathbf{X})$ is said to be minimal sufficient for θ if for two data points $\mathbf{x}$ and $\mathbf{y}$ for the ratio $f(\mathbf{x}|\theta)/f(\mathbf{y}|\theta)$ is a constant.* □

Example 7.4.6. The Binomial Distribution. Suppose $X_i, i = 1, \cdots, n$, is a sequence of independent Bernoulli trials with probability of success being $p, 0 < p < 1$. For two data points $\mathbf{x}$ and $\mathbf{y}$, the ratio of joint pmf is given below:

$$\frac{f(\mathbf{x}|p)}{f(\mathbf{y}|p)} = \binom{n}{\sum_{i=1}^n x_i}\binom{n}{\sum_{i=1}^n y_i}^{-1} p^{\sum_{i=1}^n x_i - \sum_{i=1}^n y_i}(1-p)^{\sum_{i=1}^n y_i - \sum_{i=1}^n x_i}.$$

We can see that the ratio $f(\mathbf{x}|p)/f(\mathbf{y}|p)$ will be a constant function for p if $\sum_{i=1}^n x_i = \sum_{i=1}^n y_i$. Thus, $T(\mathbf{X}) = \sum_{i=1}^n X_i$ is a minimal sufficient statistic for p. □

Example 7.4.7. The Gamma Distribution. Consider a random sample $X_i, i = 1, \cdots, n$ from a gamma distribution. That is, the pdf of X is given by

$$f(x, \theta, k) = \begin{cases} x^{k-1}\frac{e^{-x/\theta}}{\Gamma(k)\theta^k}, & x \geq 0, k, \theta > 0, \\ 0, & \text{otherwise.} \end{cases}$$

The joint pdf of $\mathbf{X}$ is given by

$$f(\mathbf{x}|\theta, k) = \frac{\left(\prod_{i=1}^n x_i\right)^{k-1} e^{-\sum_{i=1}^n x_i/\theta}}{(\Gamma(k))^n \theta^{kn}}.$$

Then, for two different data points $\mathbf{x}$ and $\mathbf{y}$, consider the ratio

$$\frac{f(\mathbf{x}|\theta, k)}{f(\mathbf{y}|\theta, k)} = \left(\frac{\prod_{i=1}^n x_i}{\prod_{i=1}^n y_i}\right)^{k-1} e^{-(\sum_{i=1}^n x_i - \sum_{i=1}^n y_i)/\theta}.$$

Clearly, the ratio $f(\mathbf{x}|\theta, k)/f(\mathbf{y}|\theta, k)$ will be a constant function of (θ, k) if $\prod_{i=1}^n x_i = \prod_{i=1}^n y_i$ and $\sum_{i=1}^n x_i = \sum_{i=1}^n y_i$. Thus, it may be then seen that $T(\mathbf{X}) = (\sum_{i=1}^n x_i, \prod_{i=1}^n x_i)$ is minimal sufficient for (θ, k). □

Definition 7.4.4 Complete Statistics. *A statistic T is said to be* complete *for $P_\theta, \theta \in \Theta$ if, for any Borel function f, $E[f(T)] = 0, \forall \theta \in \Theta$ implies $f(T) = 0, a.s. P_\theta$. Furthermore, T is said to be* boundedly complete *if the condition holds for any bounded Borel function f.*

Example 7.4.8. Complete Statistic for Poisson Sample. Consider a sample $X_1, \cdots, X_n$ of size n from a Poisson distribution with rate λ. Define $T = \sum_{i=1}^n X_i$. It can be seen that if $E\{g(T)\} = 0$, then

$$E\{g(T)\} = \sum_{t=1}^{\infty} g(t) \frac{e^{-n\lambda}(n\lambda)^t}{t!} = 0, \forall \lambda > 0,$$

$$\updownarrow$$

$$\sum_{t=1}^{\infty} \frac{(n\lambda)^t}{t!} g(t) = 0, \forall \lambda > 0,$$

which can be seen to hold good if $g(t) = 0, \forall t$. Thus, T is seen to be a complete statistic. □

A useful result states that a complete sufficient statistic will be minimal and hence if the completeness of the sufficient statistic can be established, it will be minimal sufficient too. In the case of the exponential families of full rank, the statistic $(T_1, \cdots, T_s)$ will be a complete statistic. We had already seen that $(T_1, \cdots, T_s)$ is also sufficient, and hence for exponential families of full rank, it will be minimal sufficient. Since the examples of gamma, Poisson, etc., are members of an exponential family with full rank, the sufficient estimators/statistics seen earlier will be complete, and hence minimal sufficient too. The *likelihood principle* is developed in the next section.

7.5 Likelihood and Information

As mentioned at the beginning of the previous section, we will now consider the second important principle in the theory of statistical inference: the *likelihood principle*. The likelihood function is first defined.

7.5.1 The Likelihood Principle

Definition 7.5.1 *Let $f(\mathbf{x}|\theta)$ be the joint pmf (pdf) based on a random sample $X_1, \cdots, X_n$. For a observed value of the random vector $\mathbf{X} = \mathbf{x}$, the* likelihood function *is defined by*

$$L(\theta|\mathbf{x}) = f(\mathbf{x}|\theta). \tag{7.10}$$

A major difference between the likelihood function and (joint) pdf needs to be emphasized. In a pdf (or pmf), we know the parameters and try to make certain probability statements about the random variable. In the likelihood function the parameters are unknown and hence we use the data to infer certain aspects of the parameters. In simple and practical terms, we generally plot the pdf $f(x)$ against x values to understand it, whereas for the likelihood function plots, we plot $L(\theta|\mathbf{x})$ against the parameter θ. Obviously there is more to it than what we have simply said here, though what is detailed here suffices to understand the likelihood principle. Furthermore, it has been observed that many books lay far more emphasis on the *maximum likelihood estimator*, to be introduced in the Section 7.6, and the primary likelihood function is given a formal introduction. Barnard, et al. (1962) have been emphatic about the importance of the likelihood function. Pawitan (2001) is another excellent source for understanding the importance of likelihood. Moreover, Pawitan also provides R codes and functions towards understanding this principle. Naturally, this section is influenced by his book.

Example 7.5.1. The Binomial Distribution. Consider a sequence of Bernoulli trials, $X_1, \cdots, X_n$ where the probability of success is $p, 0 < p < 1$. Let $X = \sum_{i=1}^{n} X_i$ denote the number of success in the n trials. Then $X \sim b(n,p)$. The likelihood function for an observed value of $X = x$ is given by

$$L(p|x) = P_p(X = x) = \binom{n}{x} p^x (1-p)^{n-x}. \tag{7.11}$$

Before carrying out the inference, we can enrich our understanding by plotting the likelihood function as a function of p. At the end of $n = 10$ trials, suppose that X takes one of the values 0, 2, 5, 8, or 10. The next R program plots the likelihood for the various data.

```
> n <- 10; x <- 0
> likefn <- function(n,x,p){
+       choose(n,x)*p^{x}*(1-p)^{n-x}
+ }
> pseq <- seq(0,1,by=0.02)
> likefnbinom <- sapply(pseq,n=10,x=0,likefn)
> likefnbinom <- likefnbinom/max(likefnbinom)
> plot(pseq,likefnbinom,"l",xlab="p",ylab="Likelihood",col="red")
> legend(x=0,y=0.95,legend="L(p|x=0)",col="red",
+ box.col="white",box.lwd=0)
> likefnbinom <- sapply(pseq,n=10,x=2,likefn)
> likefnbinom <- likefnbinom/max(likefnbinom)
> lines(pseq,likefnbinom,col="green")
> legend(x=0.15,y=0.8,legend="L(p|x=2)",col="green",
+ box.col="white",box.lwd=0)
> likefnbinom <- sapply(pseq,n=10,x=5,likefn)
> likefnbinom <- likefnbinom/max(likefnbinom)
> lines(pseq,likefnbinom,col="brown")
> legend(x=0.42,y=0.8,legend="L(p|x=5)",col="brown",
+ box.col="white",box.lwd=0)
> likefnbinom <- sapply(pseq,n=10,x=8,likefn)
> likefnbinom <- likefnbinom/max(likefnbinom)
> lines(pseq,likefnbinom,col="grey")
> legend(x=0.6,y=0.95,legend="L(p|x=8)",col="grey",
+ box.col="white",box.lwd=0)
> likefnbinom <- sapply(pseq,n=10,x=10,likefn)
```

```
> likefnbinom <- likefnbinom/max(likefnbinom)
> lines(pseq,likefnbinom,col="blue")
> legend(x=0.8,y=0.95,legend="L(p|x=10)",col="blue",
+ box.col="white",box.lwd=0)
```

To define the function `likefn`, we first initialize the variables n and x with `n <- 10; x <- 0`. Though we use `choose(n,x)*p^{x}*(1-p)^{n-x}`, it is important to understand that the `choose` function may be omitted without loss of generality since it does not involve p. The `sapply` functionality helps obtain the likelihood values over the sequence `pseq`. The `plot`, `lines`, and `legend` functions do not need more explanation at this stage. Figure 7.2 shows that the likelihood functions attain the maximum values at 0, 0.2, 0.5, 0.8, and 1 respectively for the number of successes at 0, 2, 5, 8, and 10. □

Example 7.5.2. The Normal Likelihood Function. Suppose we have a single observation from the normal distribution $N(\mu, 1)$ and the value of the observation is noted as 2.45. The likelihood function is given by

$$L(\mu|x) = \frac{1}{\sqrt{2\pi}} e^{-(x-\mu)^2/2}. \tag{7.12}$$

The R codes return the desired likelihood plot. Here, we begin by declaring the x and σ values and then initialize a plausible range of the mean parameter in `museg`. The `likenorm` function computes the likelihood value over the specified range `museq` and we then normalize it to obtain values between 0 and 1. The `plot` function along with the options of `xlab` and `ylab` returns us a diagram as displayed in Part A of Figure 7.3. Since we had a single datum with value 2.45, the likelihood function plot reflects that the most likely value of μ is approximately 2.45 only, and this result is not too surprising!

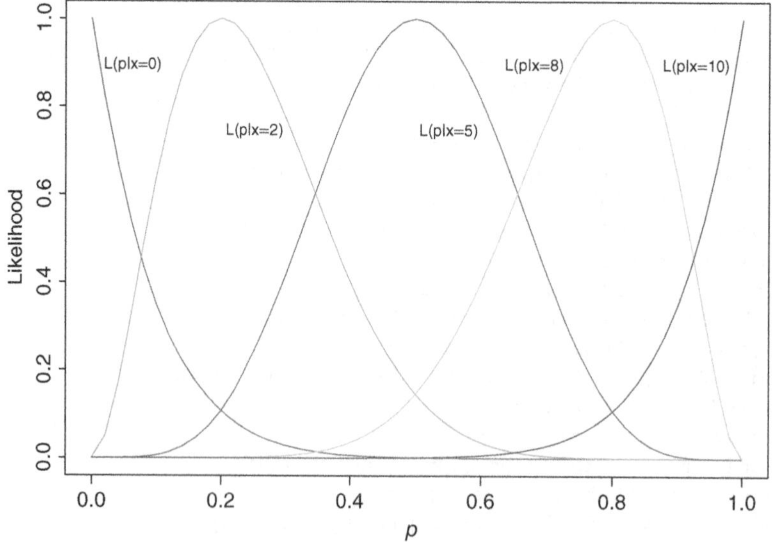

Figure 7.2 A Binomial Likelihood

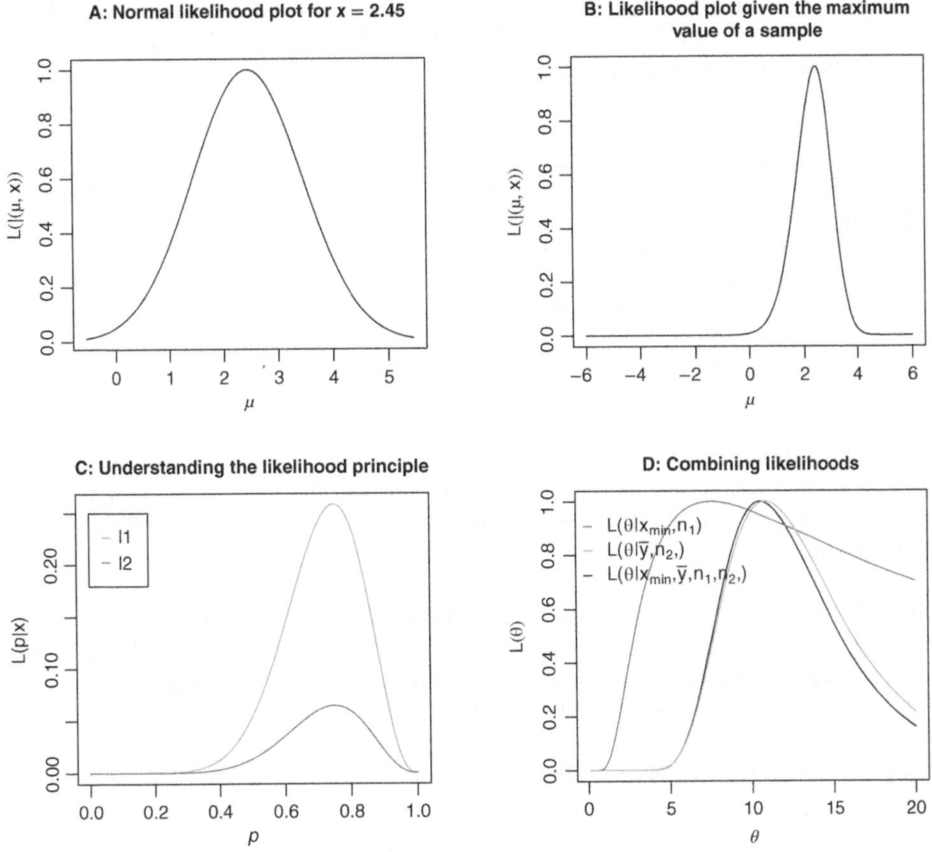

Figure 7.3 Various Likelihood Functions

```
> # Normalized Likelihood Function for a Datum
> # from Normal Distribution
> x <- 2.45; sigma <- 1
> museq <- seq(x-3*sigma,x+3*sigma,0.02)
> likenorm <- function(mu,x,sigma) dnorm(x,mu,sigma)
> likefnnorm <- sapply(museq,x=x,sigma=sigma,likenorm)
> likefnnorm <- likefnnorm/max(likefnnorm)
> plot(museq,likefnnorm,"l",xlab=expression(mu),
+ ylab=expression(L(mu|x)))
```

Consider the scenario when we have been told that there are $n = 5$ observations and the maximum of the observed sample is 3.5. The variance is assumed to be known at $\sigma = 1$. The likelihood function of the maximum of the sample is given by

$$L(\mu) = n\{\Phi(x_{(n)} - \mu)\}^{n-1}\phi(x_{(n)} - \mu), \tag{7.13}$$

where $x_{(n)}$ denotes the maximum value of the n data points $x_1, \cdots, x_n$, and $\Phi(.)$ is the cumulative distribution function of the standard normal RV. We next develop the necessary R codes for obtaining the likelihood plot as listed above. Note that the likelihood function `likenorm` needs to be defined carefully, as given in Equation 7.13. The rest of the R program is fairly easy to follow, so is not explained any further.

```
> # Normalized Likelihood Function for the
> # Maximum of the Random Sample
> n <- 5; xmax <- 3.5; sigma <- 1
> museq <- seq(-6,6,0.02)
> likenorm <- function(mu,x,sigma) (n*(pnorm(xmax-mu)^{n-1})
+ *dnorm(xmax-mu))
> likefnnorm <- sapply(museq,x=xmax,sigma=sigma,likenorm)
> likefnnorm <- likefnnorm/max(likefnnorm)
> plot(museq,likefnnorm,"l",xlab=expression(mu),
+ ylab=expression(L(mu|x)))
```

The result of the current R code is given in Part B of Figure 7.3. Note that the likelihood function is interpreted along the same lines as in Part A of the same figure, despite the data being specified in an entirely different way. This is a reason for us to emphasize the importance of likelihood plots. □

The likelihood function contains more information about the data and the parameters than some summary measures of the data. Plots of the likelihood, whenever possible, throw more light on random phenomenon and should be employed in as many cases as they permit. We will now formally state the likelihood principle.

Definition 7.5.2 The Likelihood Principle. *If the likelihood functions, say* $L(\theta|\mathbf{x})$ *and* $L(\theta|\mathbf{y})$*, corresponding to two sample points* **x** *and* **y** *are proportional to each other, that is,*

$$L(\theta|\mathbf{y}) = C(\mathbf{x},\mathbf{y})L(\theta|\mathbf{x}), \forall\theta \in \Theta, \tag{7.14}$$

then the conclusions drawn from **x** *and* **y** *should be identical.*

Example 7.5.3. Berger and Woolpert's Example 9. Let E_1 be an experiment where $X_1, \cdots, X_{12}$ are Bernoulli random variables with probability of success being p. Suppose we have observed that $\sum_{i=1}^{12} x_i = 9$. The likelihood function is then $L^1(p) = \binom{12}{9} p^9(1-p)^3$. In an experiment E_2 we proceed with Bernoulli trials until three failures are observed. The observed random variables here are Y_i's. Suppose that in the experiment E_2 we have observed $\sum Y_i = 9$. The likelihood function for E_2 is $L^2(p) = \binom{11}{9} p^9(1-p)^3$. We will obtain the likelihood plots. As with the earlier examples, we begin with initializing p values and define the the two likelihood functions in `l1` and `l2` and then plot them using `plot` and `lines` functions. The `legend` part is simple to follow.

```
> # Illustration of the Likelihood Principle
> p <- seq(0,1,0.01)
> l1 <- function(p) {choose(12,9)*p^{9}*(1-p)^{3} }
> l2 <- function(p) {choose(11,9)*p^{9}*(1-p)^{3} }
> plot(p,sapply(p,l1),"l",xlab="p",ylab="L(p|x)",col="green")
```

```
> lines(p,sapply(p,l2),"l",col="red")
> legend(x=0,y=0.25,legend=c("l1","l2"),col=c("green","red"),pch="-")
```

The graph, Part C of Figure 7.3, shows that the two likelihood functions are proportional to each other. It can also be seen that the maximum of the two likelihood functions occur at the same p value. Hence, any conclusions drawn from the two likelihood functions should result in the same answer. □

Example 7.5.4. Combining Likelihoods. Let $X_1, \cdots, X_n$ be a random sample from an exponential distribution with rate θ. From the definition, we know that the likelihood of X_i is

$$L(\theta|x_i) = \frac{1}{\theta}\exp\left\{-\frac{x_i}{\theta}\right\}, i = 1, \cdots, n.$$

The likelihood function for θ, given the complete random sample $x_1, \cdots, x_n$ is

$$L(\theta|\mathbf{x}) = \prod_{i=1}^{n} f(x_i|\theta) = \prod_{i=1}^{n} L(\theta|x_i).$$

Consequently, the log-likelihood for a sample will be the sum of the log-likelihoods. This is one method of combining likelihood functions for a random sample of size n.

Next, consider two samples from exponential distribution where the data for the first sample is $n_1 = 10$ and $x_{(1)} = 0.754$, and for the second sample $n_2 = 10$ and $\bar{y} = \frac{\sum_{i=1}^{n_2} y_i}{n_2} = 10.86$. The likelihoods for the two samples are then given by

$$L_1(\theta|x_{(1)}) = 10\left\{\exp\left(-\frac{x_{(1)}}{\theta}\right)\right\}^9 \frac{1}{\theta}\exp\left(-\frac{x_{(1)}}{\theta}\right),$$

$$L_2(\theta|y_1, \cdots, y_{10}) = \frac{1}{\theta^{10}}\exp\left\{-\frac{1}{\theta}\sum_{i=1}^{10} y_i\right\}.$$

The next R program is used to plot the combined likelihood, which gives us Part D of Figure 7.3. Note that the entire program is simply an extension of the earlier R codes, which have been explained in detail. Thus, Part D of Figure 7.3 shows that combining likelihood functions give a single curve to draw conclusions about the parameter.

```
> n1 <- 10; xmin <- 0.754
> thetaseq <- seq(0.1,20,0.1)
> likeexp1 <- function(theta,x)
+   (n1*(exp(-x/theta))^{n1-1}*exp(-x/theta)/theta)
> likefnexp1 <- sapply(thetaseq,x=xmin,likeexp1)
> n2 <- 10; ybar <- 10.86
> likeexp2 <- function(theta,x)
+   (exp(-10*ybar/theta)/theta^10)
> likefnexp2 <- sapply(thetaseq,x=ybar,likeexp2)
> likefnCombined <- likefnexp1*likefnexp2
> likefnexp1 <- likefnexp1/max(likefnexp1)
> likefnexp2 <- likefnexp2/max(likefnexp2)
```

```
> likefnCombined <- likefnCombined/max(likefnCombined)
> plot(thetaseq,likefnCombined,"l",
+       xlab=expression(theta),ylab=expression(L(theta)))
> lines(thetaseq,likefnexp1,"l",col="red")
> lines(thetaseq,likefnexp2,"l",col="green")
> exp_legends <- expression(paste("L(",theta,"|",x[min],",",
+ n[1],")"),paste("L(",theta,"|",bar(y),",",n[2],",)"),
+ paste("L(",theta,"|",x[min],",",bar(y),",",n[1],",",n[2],",)"))
> legend(x=c(-1,1),y=c(1,0.6),legend=exp_legends,col=c("red",
+ "green","black"), pch="-",box.col="white")
> title("D: Combining Likelihoods")
```

If you do not normalize the likelihood functions, do you expect similar curves? The reader is advised to actually do away with the normalization part and then verify if the final plots justify the intuitive answer. □

Remark. *For independent/random samples, it will be natural that the likelihood function will be a product of the likelihood function of each of the random variables. In general, it will be difficult to deal with products of functions and hence, without loss of generality, it is common practice to deal with the logarithm of likelihood function, that is, we will use more often* $\ln L(\theta|\mathbf{x})$ *than* $L(\theta|\mathbf{x})$.

More formal use of the likelihood function will be explained in the forthcoming subsection.

7.5.2 The Fisher Information

The likelihood function will now be more formally used towards the inference of the parameters. We will first define the *score function*.

Definition 7.5.3 Fisher Score Function. *Let* $L(\theta|\mathbf{x})$ *be the likelihood function based on a random sample* $\mathbf{x}$. *The Fisher score function for the parameter* θ *is defined by*

$$S(\theta) = \frac{\delta}{\delta\theta} \ln L(\theta|\mathbf{x}). \tag{7.15}$$

The natural question is how do we make use of the score function as given in Equation 7.15. We will first begin with an illustration of the sampling variance of score functions.

Example 7.5.5. Understanding the Sampling Variance of Score Function. This example illustrates the concepts detailed in chapter 8 of Pawitan (2001). We consider samples from normal, Poisson, binomial, and Cauchy distributions. For each of the distributions, we have 20 independent samples, each of size $n = 10$. The score function is plotted for each sample set and the behavior of the score function is then visualized. The scale parameter for a normal and a Cauchy distribution is known to be 1, whereas the mean, or location, for all the four distributions is approximately 4. The 20 sample datasets, for each distribution, is simulated.

The simulation technique is discussed in more detail in Chapter 11. However, for our purpose, we can treat them as real datasets.

To obtain the score function, we first need to obtain the log-likelihood functions. We state the log-likelihood functions as

$$\ln L(\mu) = -\frac{n}{2}\ln\sigma^2 - \frac{1}{2\sigma^2}\sum_{i=1}^{n}(x_i-\mu)^2, \text{ normal distribution,}$$

$$\ln L(\lambda) = -n\lambda + \sum_{i=1}^{n} x_i \ln(\lambda), \text{ Poisson distribution,}$$

$$\ln L(p) = \sum_{i=1}^{n}\{x_i\ln(p) + (n-x_i)\ln(1-p)\}, \text{ binomial distribution,}$$

$$\ln L(\mu) = -\sum_{i=1}^{n}\ln\{(1+(x_i-\mu)^2)\}, \text{ Cauchy distribution.}$$

Differentiating the log-likelihoods with respect to the parameters gives us the score function:

$$S(\mu) = \frac{\delta}{\delta\mu}\ln L(\mu) = \frac{n}{\sigma^2}(\bar{x}-\mu), \text{ normal distribution,} \tag{7.16}$$

$$S(\lambda) = \frac{\delta}{\delta\lambda}\ln L(\lambda) = \frac{n}{\lambda}(\bar{x}-\lambda), \text{ Poisson distribution,} \tag{7.17}$$

$$S(p) = \frac{\delta}{\delta p}\ln L(p) = \frac{n(\bar{x}-np)}{p(1-p)}, \text{ Binomial distribution,} \tag{7.18}$$

$$S(\mu) = \frac{\delta}{\delta\mu}\ln L(\mu) = \sum_{i=1}^{n}\frac{2(x_i-\mu)}{1+(x_i-\mu)^2}, \text{ Cauchy distribution.} \tag{7.19}$$

The R program for the score function of normal distribution is first explained. The simulated dataset is first loaded with the `data(ns)` file. We have 20 batches, each of size 10. The function `colMeans` returns the means for the 20 batches, while the function `normal_score_fn` defines the score function for the normal distribution. A sequence of plausible values for μ is specified through `seq(from=2,to=8,by=0.2)`. In practice, we may use the summary statistics to decide this range. The sub-code `sapply(mu,normal_score_fn,xbar=sample_means[1])`, and later with the index `i`, returns the score function values as required in Equation 7.16, and the `plot(...)` generates the plot of the score function for the first sample. The loop `for(i in 2:20)`, along with the `lines` function, completes the visualization for score function for the normal sample dataset. An important part of this code is given in `abline(v=4)` and `abline(h=0)`, which respectively produce a vertical line at the x-coordinate $\mu = 4$ and a horizontal line at the y-coordinate 0. What can you infer from Part A of Figure 7.4? In particular, the question is can you deduce the parameter value of μ for unknown scenarios using such a score function plot?

The detailed R program for Poisson, binomial, and Cauchy distributions are straightforward to follow through, and their outputs respectively form Parts C to D of Figure 7.4. The reader is especially advised to interpret the score function definitions in light of Equations 7.17–7.19.

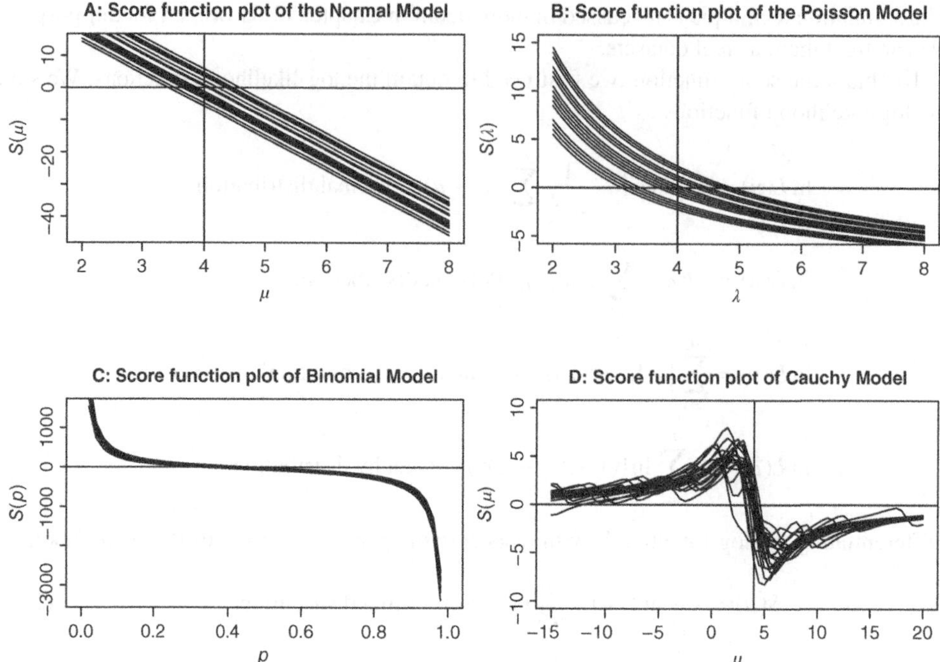

Figure 7.4 Understanding Sampling Variation of Score Function

```
> # Understanding the Sampling Variation of the Score Function
> # The Normal Model
> data(ns)
> n <- 10
> sample_means <- colMeans(ns)
> normal_score_fn <- function(mu,xbar) n*(xbar-mu)
> mu <- seq(from=2,to=8,by=0.2)
> plot(mu,sapply(mu,normal_score_fn,xbar=sample_means[1]),
+ "l",xlab=expression(mu),ylab=expression(S(mu)))
> title(main="A: Score Function Plot of the Normal Model")
> for(i in 2:20) lines(mu,sapply(mu,normal_score_fn,
+ xbar <- sample_means[i]),"l")
> abline(v=4)
> abline(h=0)
> # The Poisson Model
> data(ps)
> n <- 10
> sample_means <- colMeans(ps)
> poisson_score_fn <- function(theta,xbar) n*(xbar-theta)/theta
> theta <- seq(from=2,to=8,by=0.2)
> plot(theta,sapply(theta,poisson_score_fn,xbar=sample_means[1]),
+ "l",xlab=expression(lambda),ylab=expression(S(lambda)),
+ ylim=c(-5,15))
> title(main="B: Score Function Plot of the Poisson Model")
```

```
> for(i in 2:20)
+ lines(theta,sapply(theta,poisson_score_fn,xbar=
+ sample_means[i]),"l")
> abline(v=4)
> abline(h=0)
> # The Binomial Model
> data(bs)
> n <- 10
> sample_means <- colMeans(bs)
> binomial_score_fn <- function(p,xbar)
+        n*(xbar-10*p)/(p*(1-p))
> p <- seq(from=0,to=1,by=0.02)
> plot(p,sapply(p,binomial_score_fn,xbar=sample_means[1]),
+ "l",xlab=expression(p),ylab=expression(S(p)))
> title(main="C: Score Function Plot of Binomial Model")
> for(i in 2:20) lines(p,sapply(p,
+ binomial_score_fn,xbar=sample_means[i]),"l")
> abline(v=4)
> abline(h=0)
> # The Cauchy Model
> data(cs)
> n <- 10
> cauchy_score_fn  <-  function(mu,x)
+        sum(2*(x-mu)/(1+(x-mu)^{2}))
> mu <- seq(from=-15,to=20,by=0.5)
> plot(mu,sapply(mu,cauchy_score_fn,x=cs[,1]),
+ "l",xlab=expression(mu),ylab=expression(S(mu)),
+ ylim=c(-10,10))
> title(main="D: Score Function Plot of Cauchy Model")
> for(i in 2:20) lines(mu,sapply(mu,
+ cauchy_score_fn,x=cs[,i]),"l")
> abline(v=4)
> abline(h=0)
```

This current example thus provides a nice insight into the behavior of the sampling variance of the score functions. *It may thus also be noted that the expected value of a score function is 0.* □

An important exercise is to prove that the expectation of the score function equals zero, that is, $E_\theta S(\theta) = 0$, which we leave to the reader.

Definition 7.5.4 Fisher Information. *Let X be an RV with probability measure $p_\theta, \theta \in \Theta$. Assume that the following conditions hold:*

1. *Θ is an open set of R.*
2. *The partial derivative $\frac{\delta}{\delta\theta} f(x|\theta)$ is finite for all $x \in \Omega, \theta \in \Theta$.*
3. *The derivative with respect to θ can be interchanged with integral with respect to x.*

The Fisher Information *about θ contained in x is given by*

$$\mathcal{I}_X(\theta) = E_\theta\left[\left\{\frac{\delta}{\delta\theta}\ln f(X|\theta)\right\}^2\right]. \tag{7.20}$$

The expected Fisher information *is defined by*

$$\mathcal{I}(\theta) := E_\theta S(\theta). \tag{7.21}$$

In the above definition, the term *partial derivative* has been used in the sense that the parameter θ may be a vector and in which case we consider the derivative of the likelihood function with respect to each component of the vector.

A useful result regarding the expected Fisher information, under the assumptions of the regularity conditions of course, is

$$\texttt{var}_\theta S(\theta) = \mathcal{I}(\theta).$$

We will next find the Fisher information for a few well-known probability distributions.

Example 7.5.6. Poisson Distribution. Let X be a Poisson random variable with parameter λ. The log of the probability function is then given by

$$\ln f(x|\lambda) = -\lambda + x\ln(\lambda) - \ln(x!).$$

Differentiating the above wrt λ gives us

$$\frac{\delta}{\delta\lambda}\ln f(X|\lambda) = -1 + x\lambda^{-1}.$$

Note that $E(X^2) = \lambda(1+\lambda)$. Thus, we can obtain the Fisher information as follows:

$$E_\lambda\left[\left\{\frac{\delta}{\delta\lambda}\ln f(X|\lambda)\right\}^2\right] = E\left(\frac{x^2}{\lambda^2} - \frac{2x}{\lambda} + 1\right) = \frac{\lambda(1+\lambda)}{\lambda^2} - 2 + 1 = \frac{1+\lambda-\lambda}{\lambda} = \frac{1}{\lambda}.$$

□

The next result is an important one when we have to calculate the Fisher information for a random sample.

Theorem 7.5.1 Fisher Information for a Random Sample. *Consider a random sample $X_1, \cdots, X_n$ from p_θ. Let $\mathcal{I}_{X_1}(\theta)$ denote the information contained in a single observation. Then, the Fisher information contained in the random sample for θ is given by*

$$\mathcal{I}_{\mathbf{X}}(\theta) = n\mathcal{I}_X(\theta). \tag{7.22}$$

□

Example 7.5.7. Poisson Distribution. Contd. If we have a random sample of size n, the Fisher information about λ in the random sample is then given by

$$\mathcal{I}_{\mathbf{X}}(\lambda) = \frac{n}{\lambda}.$$

□

In the next section we will use the observed Fisher information in a random sample.

?choose, ?dnorm, ?pnorm, ?expression

7.6 Point Estimation

"Point Estimation" or "Estimation Theory" are some of the common names for dealing with the problem of estimation of parameters. Lehmann and Casella (1998) is one of the best sources for classical inference. Modern accounts of this domain are Casella and Berger (2002), Shao (2003), and Mukhopadhyay (2000). For details about the maximum likelihood technique implementation, refer to Millar (2011).

7.6.1 Maximum Likelihood Estimation

In the previous section we introduced the likelihood function. It will now be used to find estimators.

Let $X_1, \cdots, X_n$ be a random sample with common pdf or pmf $f(x, \theta)$, $x \in R, \theta \in \Theta$. The random variable X and/or θ may be scalar or vector. Recall the definition of likelihood function:

$$L(\theta, \mathbf{x}) = \prod_{i=1}^{n} f(x_i, \theta).$$

Definition 7.6.1 *The maximum likelihood estimate, abbreviated as MLE, of θ is the value $\hat{\theta} =: \hat{\theta}(\mathbf{x})$, for which $L(\theta, \mathbf{x})$ is a maximum, that is,*

$$L(\hat{\theta}) = \sup_{\theta \in \Theta} L(\theta|\mathbf{x}).$$

It is important to note that the MLE definition simply requires that the likelihood function be optimized. There is no specific method outlined on how to obtain the MLE. We will begin with a few graphical methods, which will be a continuation of some of our earlier examples.

Example 7.6.1. The Normal Likelihood Function. Example 7.5.1 Contd. Let us revisit the problem when we have a datum with value 2.45. The variance is known as 1 and we had obtained a plot of the likelihood function, over the grid of points `seq(x-3*sigma,x+3*sigma,0.02)`. We need to obtain the value of μ at which the likelihood function is a maximum value. Thus, using the `which` function we can obtain the maximum:

```
> thetaseq[which(likefnnorm==1)]
[1] 2.45
```

Note that we already know that the maximum of the likelihood function is 1 as we had normalized it. It may appear that what we have really done here is a trivial matter. After all, we started with 2.45 and closed the argument with 2.45. However, that is the best estimate of μ when we have only one observation.

Now, consider the next example where we have observed the maximum of five observations as 3.5. Here

```
> thetaseq[which(likefnnorm==1)]
[1] 2.44
```

Clearly, we have now done much better. Increasing the search of the grid area to `thetaseq<-seq(-6,6,0.001)` and `thetaseq<-seq(-6,6,0.001)` returns the MLE values as 2.438 and 2.4385 respectively. When performing such grid searches, it is recommended to vary the settings as much as it permits before accepting the final solution. □

Example 7.6.2. MLEs as Bird Eye of Examples of Section 7.5. For Example 7.5.1, we can easily deduce from the likelihood plots, Figure 7.3, that when we observe $x = 0, 2, 5, 8,$ or 10 out of $n = 10$ trials, the MLE for p, say $\hat{p}$, must be 0, 0.2, 0.5, 0.8, or 1 respectively.

Similarly, in the case of Example 7.5.3, irrespective of whether the sampling is from a binomial distribution or a negative binomial distribution, see Part C of Figure 7.3, the maximum value of p appears at 0.75.

The MLEs for μ based on the two samples, for Example 7.19, appear to be 2.5 (when $x_{(5)} = 3.5, n_1 = 5$) and 4 ($\bar{y} = 4, n_2 = 3$) respectively. However, for the combined likelihood, the MLE of μ is approximately 3.5, as seen in Part D of Figure 7.3. □

We will now attempt to obtain the MLEs when the parameters are continuous. A standard technique in calculus for obtaining the optimum value of a continuous function is by differentiating the function with respect to the continuous variable and setting the resultant expression to zero. In our case, such an expression turns out to be the score function which we saw in the previous Section 7.5. The MLE is then a root (solution) of the score function, that is, a solution of the equation:

$$S(\theta) = 0.$$

Note that in each of the four score function plots in Figure 7.4, the parameter values which correspond to the score function $S(\theta)$ at 0 is 4. This is not surprising since we had simulated the datasets to have the average (mean) of 4 only. Let us verify again with a plot of the score function for the normal sample and check if the plot helps to find the MLE in the spirit of Pawitan (2001).

Example 7.6.3. Example 7.19 Continued. Here, restating the facts, $n = 3, \bar{y} = 4$. In this case, the log-likelihood function is

$$\ln L(\mu) = -\frac{3}{2}\ln\sigma^2 - \frac{1}{2\sigma^2}\sum_{i=1} 3(x_i - \mu)^2,$$

and the score function is

$$S(\mu) = 3(4 - \mu).$$

A simple R program gives the score plot and suggests the MLE when the score function is equal to 0.

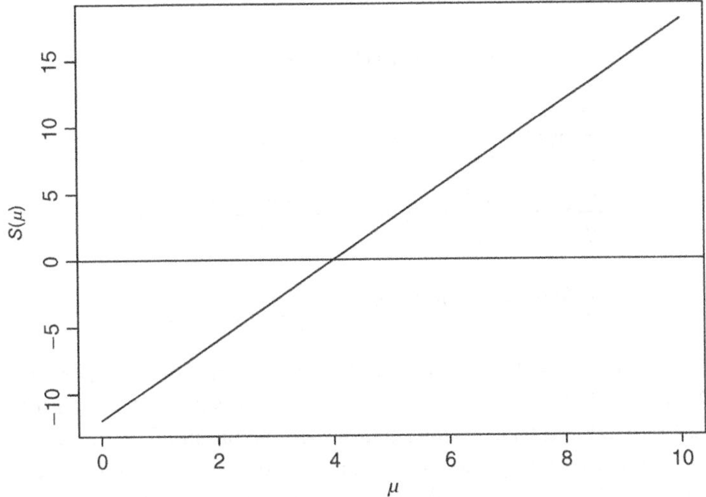

Figure 7.5 Score Function of Normal Distribution

```
> scorefunction <- function(mu) {3*(mu-4)}
> curve(scorefunction,from=0, to=10,xlab=expression(mu),
+ ylab=expression(S(mu)))
> abline(h=0)
```

In this case, the MLE is observed to be 4, as verified in Figure 7.5. □

In the case of an iid sample, R can be used efficiently to define the likelihood function and then solve the score function for obtaining the MLE. Two excellent introductions which illustrate this point may be found in Geyer (2003), see www.stat.umn.edu/geyer/5931/mle/mle.pdf, and Steenbergen (2006), see www.unc.edu/ monogan/computing/r/MLE_in_R.pdf. Also check Monahan (2011) for numerical methods in statistics, which also includes many interesting examples on MLE, see http://www4.stat.ncsu.edu/monahan/jul10/toc9r.html.

Setting the score functions equal to zero, and then obtaining an appropriate expression for the parameters, will give us estimators of the likelihood function, that is, the MLE. For the score-functions given in Equations 7.16–7.18, we obtain the MLEs by solving them as follows:

$$\hat{\mu}_{ML} = \bar{X} = \frac{\sum_{i=1}^{n} X_i}{n}, \text{ Normal distribution,} \tag{7.23}$$

$$\hat{\lambda}_{ML} = \bar{X} = \frac{\sum_{i=1}^{n} X_i}{n}, \text{ Poisson distribution,} \tag{7.24}$$

$$\hat{p}_{ML} = \bar{X} = \frac{\sum_{i=1}^{n} X_i}{n}, \text{ Binomial distribution.} \tag{7.25}$$

To be assured that $\hat{\mu}_{ML}$, $\hat{\lambda}_{ML}$, and $\hat{p}_{ML}$ as given above, are indeed the MLEs, we need to look at the derivatives of the score function and verify that they are negative. The derivatives of the score functions for the distributions are stated next:

$$\frac{d}{d\mu}S(\mu) = \frac{d^2}{d\mu^2}\ln L(\mu|x) = -\frac{n}{\sigma^2} \tag{7.26}$$

$$\frac{d}{d\lambda}S(\lambda) = \frac{d^2}{d\lambda^2}\ln L(\lambda|x) = -\frac{n}{\lambda^2}\bar{x}, \tag{7.27}$$

$$\frac{d}{dp}S(p) = \frac{d^2}{dp^2}\ln L(p|x) = -\frac{n(np^2 + \bar{x}(2p-1))}{(p(1-p))^2}, \tag{7.28}$$

$$\frac{d}{d\mu}S(\mu) = \frac{d^2}{d\mu^2}\ln L(\mu|x) = 2\sum_{i=1}^{n}\frac{1-(x_i-\mu)^2}{(1+(x_i-\mu)^2)^2}. \tag{7.29}$$

The derivatives of the log-likelihood function for normal and Poisson distribution, Equations 7.26 and 7.27, may easily be understood as negative, whereas it is not straightforward to obtain the answer for binomial and Cauchy distributions. In the binomial case, the reader may refer to a slightly different case at http://www.montana.edu/rotella/502/binom_like.pdf.

Note that the MLE for the Cauchy distribution has not been derived here and it requires a different way of solving the score function to obtain the MLE. We will be using three functions available in R, `optimize`, `mle` and `nlm` for obtaining the MLEs. Since we have emphasized the likelihood function, it is always good practice to report the values of the likelihood function, or its variants such as the log-likelihood function, or negative of the log-likelihood function.

Example 7.6.4. The Poisson Distribution. Death by Horse Kick. A classic example of the Poisson random variable is the death of army corps due to a kick by a horse. von Bortkiewicz reported this data of 122 deaths by horse kicks when a group of 10 Prussian army corps were under observation for a period of 20 years. Thus, we have $n = 200$ observations. Table 7.3 gives the data collected by von Bortkiewicz.

Let us try to find the MLE under the assumption that the number of deaths follows a Poisson random variable. Let λ be the average number of deaths due to horse kicks. The log-likelihood function is then specified by

$$\ln L(\lambda|\mathbf{x}) = \sum_{i=1}^{200} x_i \ln(\lambda) - n\lambda - \sum_{i=1}^{200}\ln(x_i!).$$

We will ignore the last term since it does not involve the parameter of interest. The R program which gives the MLE is given next.

Table 7.3 Death by Horse Kick Data

Number of Deaths in a Corp	Frequency
0	109
1	65
2	22
3	3
4	1

```
> n <- 200
> x <- rep(c(0,1,2,3,4),c(109,65,22,3,1))
> logl <- function(lambda){log(lambda)*sum(x) - n*lambda -
+ sum(log(factorial(x)))}
> optimize(logl,c(0,10),maximum=TRUE)
$maximum
[1] 0.6100066
$objective
[1] -206.1067
```

In this R program, the log-likelihood function is defined by `logl`. Using the `optimize` function, we optimize `logl` over the λ values. The components of the `optimize` function, `maximum` and `objective` respectively return the MLE and log-likelihood function value. Thus, the ML estimate is `0.6100066`. Note here that `logl(0.6100066)` returns exactly `-206.1067`. Now, to really test that you have obtained a maximum value of $\ln(\lambda|\mathbf{x})$, try the codes `logl(0.5)` and `logl(0.8)` and comment. A useful insight will also be to visualize `plot(seq(0.01,5,0.01),sapply(seq(0.01,5,0.01),logl),"l")`.

Another R technique to obtain the MLE is to use the `mle` function from the `stats4` package. To use this function, we need to first define the negative log-likelihood function and specify initial parameter values to the `mle` function.

```
> pois_nll <- function(lambda) -sum(dpois(x,lambda,log=TRUE))
> pois_mle <- mle(pois_nll,start=list(lambda=mean(x)),nobs=length(x))
> summary(pois_mle)
Maximum likelihood estimation
Call:
mle(minuslogl = pois_nll, start = list(lambda = mean(x)),
+ nobs = length(x))
Coefficients:
        Estimate Std. Error
lambda      0.61 0.05522666
-2 log L: 412.2134
```

The results of `mle` and `optimize` are equivalent, since `-2*logl(0.6100066)` gives `412.2134`. Thus, using both the `optimize` and `mle` functions, we are able to obtain the MLE. □

Example 7.6.5. Estimation of the Shape Parameter from a Gamma Sample. Consider a random sample of size $n = 20$, which is believed to arise from a Gamma distribution, that is,

$$f(x, \theta, k) = \begin{cases} x^{k-1} \frac{e^{-x/\theta}}{\Gamma(k)\theta^k}, & x \geq 0, k, \theta > 0, \\ 0, & \text{otherwise.} \end{cases} \tag{7.30}$$

From historical data, it is known that $\theta = 30$ and we have to obtain the MLE for k. The log-likelihood function is given by

$$\ln L(k|\mathbf{x}) = -\frac{\sum_{i=1}^{n} x_i}{\theta} + (k-1)\sum_{i=1}^{n} \ln(x_i) - nk\ln(\theta) - n\ln(\Gamma(k)).$$

It is found for the sample dataset that $\sum_{i=1}^{30} x_i = 221.59$ and $\sum_{i-1}^{20} \ln(x_i) = 9.03$. Substituting this information along with $\theta = 30$ and $n = 20$, we obtain the observed log-likelihood function as

$$\ln L(k|\mathbf{x}) = -7.39 + 9.03(k-1) - 60.02k - 20\ln(\Gamma(k)).$$

In R, we obtain the MLE with the next program:

```
> # MLE of Gamma shape parameter
> log_lik <- function(k) {-7.39 +9.03 * (k-1) -60.02*k
+ -20*(log(gamma(k))) }
> optimise(log_lik,c(0,10),maximum=TRUE)
$maximum
[1] 0.4016414
$objective
[1] -52.74936
```

Note here that `optimize` and `optimise` are the same functions only. The `log_lik` R function mimicks the expression in the previous equation. The MLE, given the data, is `0.3041274` and value of the log-likelihood function $\ln L(k|\mathbf{x})$ is `-40.9889`. □

The Cauchy distribution is slightly more complex and its MLE does not exist in a simple form. We resort to the numerical optimization technique, essentially the *Newton-Raphson* technique, through its score function as given in Equation 7.19.

Example 7.6.6. The Cauchy Distribution. In Example 7.5.5 we obtained the score function for the location parameter of a Cauchy distribution, which is recollected as follows:

$$S(\mu) = \sum_{i=1}^{n} \frac{2(x_i - \mu)}{1 + (x_i - \mu)^2}.$$

As noted in Example 5.21 of Knight (2000), the score function $S(\mu)$ is not monotone in μ, and hence it may have multiple solutions, technically roots of the equation. The Newton-Raphson technique can be used here to obtain $\hat{\mu}$. Starting with an initial estimate $\hat{\mu}^{(0)}$, the updated estimates are given by the equation

$$\hat{\mu}^{(k+1)} = \hat{\mu}^{(k)} + \frac{S(\hat{\mu}^{(k)})}{H(\hat{\mu}^{(k)})}, \tag{7.31}$$

where the *Hessian*, see Equation 7.29, is given by

$$H(\hat{\mu}) = 2\sum_{i=1}^{n} \frac{1 - (x_i - \mu)^2}{(1 + (x_i - \mu)^2)^2}. \tag{7.32}$$

In general, the *hessian* is a matrix of second-order partial derivatives. We will illustrate this estimation technique for the first sample of Example 7.5.5.

```
> data(cs)
> mysample <- cs[,1]
```

```
> n <- 10
> loglik <- muhat=NULL
> muhat[1] <- median(mysample)
> loglik[1] <- -sum(log(1+(mysample-muhat[1])^{2}))-n*log(pi)
> cauchy_score_fn <- function(mu,x){
+   sum(2*(x-mu)/(1+(x-mu)^{2}))
+ }
> cauchy_hessian_fn <- function(mu,x){
+   2*(sum((1-(x-mu)^{2})/(1+(x-mu)^{2})^{2}))
+ }
> mutest <- -10000000
> i <- 1
> while(abs(mutest-muhat[i])>0.0001){
+        mutest <- muhat[i]
+        i <- i+1
+        muhat[i] <- muhat[i-1]+cauchy_score_fn(muhat[i-1],mysample)
+  /cauchy_hessian_fn(muhat[i-1],mysample)
+        loglik[i] <- -sum(log(1+(mysample-muhat[i])^{2}))-n*log(pi)
+ }
> loglik
[1] -28.84483 -28.53130 -28.50123 -28.50120 -28.50120
> muhat
[1] 3.666913 4.081575 3.994956 3.992124 3.992121
```

The Cauchy score function in Equation 7.29 is computed with the function `cauchy_score_fn`. The initial estimate for μ is the sample median `median(mysample)`. The Hessian function given by Equation 7.32 is computed with the R function `cauchy_hessian_fn`. The improvements required by Equation 7.31 are updated with `muhat[i] <- muhat[i-1]+cauchy_score_fn(muhat[i-1],mysample)`, and the iterations are carried out until the difference between consecutive `muhat` values will be less than 0.0001, see the R code `while(abs(mutest-muhat[i])>0.0001)`. The numerical convergence is obtained at the 5th iteration and the MLE estimate $\hat{\mu}$ is `3.992121`.

The R function `mle` can also be used to obtain the answer and we leave it to the reader to complete this part. □

The MLE problems, and likelihood functions as well, thus far has been discussed in the context of a single unknown parameter only. In many applied contexts, it is a common theme that multiple parameters would be unknown. The approach remains the same, though the details will be obviously more. Let us consider a random sample from the normal distribution, where both the parameters μ and σ are unknown. Recollect that in Example 7.5.5 we had assumed $\sigma = 1$.

Example 7.6.7. MLE for a Normal Sample. Consider a random sample, of size n, from a normal distribution $N(\mu, \sigma^2)$, where both the parameters are unknown. The likelihood function is then given below by

$$L(\mu, \sigma^2|\mathbf{x}) = \frac{1}{\{\sqrt{2\pi}\sigma\}^n} \exp\left\{-\frac{1}{2\sigma^2}\sum_{i=1}^{n}(x_i - \mu)^2\right\}.$$

We will simply use the mle function to obtain MLEs of μ and σ.

```
> data(ns)
> x <- ns[,1]
> nlogl <- function(mean,sd) {-sum(dnorm(x,mean=mean,sd=sd,
+ log=TRUE)) }
> norm_mle <- mle(nlogl,start=list(mean=median(x),sd=IQR(x)),
+ nobs=length(x))
> summary(norm_mle)
Maximum likelihood estimation
Call:
mle(minuslogl = nlogl, start = list(mean = median(x), sd = IQR(x)),
    nobs = length(x))
Coefficients:
       Estimate Std. Error
mean 3.4290740  0.1908120
sd   0.6034005  0.1349205
-2 log L: 18.27551
```

Here, a simple option of the mle function in properly defining the log-likelihood function for two unknown parameters and a suitable value for the initial values help in obtaining the MLEs for μ and σ. □

We will close this sub-section with a very interesting example.

Example 7.6.8. Estimating the "Size" of Binomial Distribution. Assume that the number of trials for a binomial experiment, that is size, is unknown, and the probability of success p is known. In this example, the size will be denoted by k and probability of success by p. Examples 7.2.9 and 7.2.13 of Casella and Berger (2002) are the driving motivation behind the current example. Five data points are available (16, 18, 22, 25, 27), that is, $X_1 = 16, \ldots, X_5 = 27$. A quick temptation is to use the mle function. Let us do that and get the answer for $\hat{k}$ and $\hat{p}$.

```
> x <- c(16, 18, 22, 25, 27)
> nlog_binom <- function(size) {-sum(dbinom(x,size,
+ prob=0.5,log=TRUE)) }
> mle_x <- mle(nlog_binom,start=list(size=2*max(x)))
Error in optim(start, f, method = method, hessian = TRUE, ...) :
  non-finite finite-difference value [1]
In addition: Warning messages:
1: In dbinom(x, size, prob = 0.5, log = TRUE) : NaNs produced
2: In dbinom(x, size, prob = 0.5, log = TRUE) : NaNs produced
```

Unfortunately, on this occasion, R gave us errors and not answers. The reason being differentiating the likelihood function, or $\ln L(k, p|x)$ too, is not feasible. The MLE of k is not a straightforward routine and needs to be dealt with care. An important argument is that the likelihood function must be 0 for any k value less than $\max x_i$. We need to find k for which $L(k|x)/L(k-1|x) \geq 1$ and $L(k+1|x)/L(k|x) < 1$. We can use a while loop to find us the answer. □

We will close this discussion with some properties of the MLE.

1. If T is a sufficient statistic for the family of distributions P_θ and a unique MLE of θ exists, then the MLE is a function of the sufficient statistic T.
2. If T is an MLE for θ and $g(\theta)$ is a one-to-one function of θ, then $g(T)$ will be an MLE for $g(\theta)$.
3. Under certain *regularity conditions*, see Section 7.7, the MLE is a consistent estimator, and further

$$\sqrt{n}\left\{E_\theta\left(\frac{\delta \ln f_\theta(\mathbf{x})}{\delta\theta}\right)^2\right\}^{-1/2}(T-\theta)\rightarrow^D N(0,1). \tag{7.33}$$

7.6.2 *Method of Moments Estimator*

Karl Pearson invented the *method of moments* estimator. Suppose that $f(x;\boldsymbol{\theta})$ is the pmf (pdf), and that the parameters are k in number, $\boldsymbol{\theta} = (\theta_1, \cdots, \theta_k)$. The method of moments estimator means that we need to first find the k theoretical moments of $f(x;\boldsymbol{\theta})$ and assume that they are equal to the corresponding sample moments. We assume that we have a sample of size n. Thus, we have k equations for k unknown quantities. A solution for this set of equations leads to the method of moments estimator. Symbolically, we have the following setup:

$$\eta_1 = \int xf(x,\boldsymbol{\theta})dx \equiv \frac{\sum_{i=1}^n x_i}{n},$$

$$\eta_2 = \int x^2 f(x,\boldsymbol{\theta})dx \equiv \frac{\sum_{i=1}^n x_i^2}{n},$$

$$\vdots$$

$$\eta_k = \int x^k f(x,\boldsymbol{\theta})dx \equiv \frac{\sum_{i=1}^n x_i^k}{n}.$$

We will demonstrate the applications of the moment estimators through some examples of Mukhopadhyay (2000) and Casella and Berger (2002). An important point to note here is that the moment estimators can be computed. even if the complete density function is not known.

Example 7.6.9. Moment Estimator for Normal Distribution. Consider a sample $X_1, \cdots, X_n$ from $N(\mu, \sigma^2)$, where both the parameters are unknown. For a normal distribution it is known that $E(X) = \mu$ and $E(X^2) = \mu^2 + \sigma^2$. Thus, the moment estimators is a solution for the following set of two equations:

$$\mu = \frac{\sum_{i=1}^n X_i}{n},$$

$$\mu^2 + \sigma^2 = \frac{\sum_{i=1}^n X_i^2}{n}.$$

For a given sample, we first find the mean estimator and then insert it into the next equation to obtain an estimate of the variance. A little rearrangement gives the moment estimators as

$$\hat{\mu} = \bar{X},$$

$$\hat{\sigma}^2 = \frac{\sum_{i=1}^{2}(X_i - \bar{X})^2}{n}.$$

Suppose that we have observed the 10 values for an experiment as 7.96, 6.01, 9.30, 6.92, 7.70, 0.15, 5.24, 12.53, 8.69, and 6.94. We can then compute the moment estimators for mean and variance.

```
> x <- c(7.96, 6.01, 9.30, 6.92, 7.70, 0.15, 5.24, 12.53, 8.69, 6.94)
> mum <- mean(x)
> sigmam <- mean(x^{2})-mum^{2}
> mum;sigmam
[1] 7.144
[1] 9.094144
```

A simple program is all that is rquired in this example. □

Example 7.6.10. Moment Estimators for Binomial Distribution. Consider a random sample $X_1, \cdots, X_n$ from a binomial distribution (k, p), where both the parameters k and p are unknown. That is, the probability mass function of X is

$$p(X_i = x) = \binom{k}{p} p^x (1-p)^{k-x}, x = 0, 1, \cdots, k.$$

The first two sample moments equated to the population moments, see Example 7.2.2 of Casella and Berger (2002), leads to the system of two equations:

$$kp = \frac{\sum_{i=1}^{n} X_i}{n},$$

$$kp(1-p) + k^2p^2 = \frac{\sum_{i=1}^{n} X_i^2}{n},$$

which give the moment estimators:

$$\hat{k} = \frac{\bar{X}^2}{\bar{X} - \sum_{i=1}^{n}(X_i - \bar{X})^2/n},$$

$$\hat{p} = \frac{\bar{X}}{\hat{k}}.$$

Suppose that the number of crimes in 20 different localities is reported as 3, 0, 3, 2, 2, 2, 4, 1, 1, 4, 0, 2, 3, 1, 1, 2, 1, 2, 2, and 3. We need to find k and p, since the number of criminals across the localities is assumed to be unknown but equal. The next program is easier to follow and hence the explanation is omitted.

```
> x <- c(3, 0, 3, 2, 2, 2, 4, 1, 1, 4, 0, 2, 3, 1, 1, 2, 1, 2, 2, 3)
> khat <- (length(x)-1)*var(x)/length(x)
> khat <- mean(x)-khat
> khat <- mean(x)^{2}/khat
```

```
> phat <- mean(x)/khat
> khat;phat
[1] 5.412811
[1] 0.3602564
```

Notice the order of computation for $\hat{k}$! A small correction is in order here. The number of trials cannot be a fraction and hence $\hat{k} = 5.412811$ is not acceptable. The `floor` of this number is not acceptable, since the empirical evidence suggests that k is at least `5.412811`, and hence the `ceiling` should be accepted for the number of trials. Using this corrected k estimate, the reader should re-estimate $\hat{p}$. □

However, it is to be noted that the moment estimator is an ad hoc solution for obtaining estimators and it is severely restricted. Please refer to Mukhopadhyay (2000) and Casella and Berger (2002) for more pointers in this regard.

?which, ?optim, ?nlm, ?constrOptim

7.7 Comparison of Estimators

In the previous sections we considered two main methods of estimation. It is possible to propose several estimators for the same parameter and we would have to then justify the use of one estimator over other. That is, we need criteria for comparison of estimators. We will begin with *unbiased estimator* as a criterion for comparison purposes.

7.7.1 Unbiased Estimators

Definition 7.7.1 Unbiased Estimator. *A real valued statistic $T(\mathbf{X}) \equiv T(X_1, \cdots, X_n)$ is said to be an* unbiased estimator *for $g(\theta)$ if*

$$E_\theta(T) = g(\theta), \forall \theta \in \Theta. \tag{7.34}$$

Furthermore, a statistic $T(\mathbf{X})$ is said to be a biased estimator *of $g(\theta)$ if it is not an unbiased estimator. The bias of an estimator is defined by*

$$b_\theta(T) = E_\theta(T) - g(\theta), \theta \in \Theta. \tag{7.35}$$

It needs to be recorded that the lack of bias is a property of an estimator and not of a sample. An unbiased estimator reaches the target $g(\theta)$ on average and its bias will be 0 for all values of θ. An important measure of the performance of a statistic is provided by its Mean Squared Error.

Definition 7.7.2 Mean Squared Error. *Consider an estimator $T(\mathbf{X})$ for $g(\theta)$. Then, the mean squared error, abbreviated as* MSE, *of T is given by*

$$MSE_T = E(T - g(\theta))^2, \forall \theta \in \Theta. \tag{7.36}$$

If T is unbiased, its MSE is just its variance.

A result which connects variance, bias, and MSE is given next.

Theorem 7.7.1 Bias, Variance, and MSE Relationship. *Let $T(\mathbf{X})$ be an estimator of $g(\theta)$. The bias, variance, and MSE are related by*

$$MSE_T = E_\theta(T - g(\theta))^2 = V_\theta(T) + b_\theta^2(T). \tag{7.37}$$

Thus, for an unbiased estimator, the MSE will coincide with the variance of the estimator. □

Example 7.7.1. MSE's for Estimators from Poisson Distribution. Consider a random sample of size $n = 5$ from a Poisson distribution with unknown parameter λ. Following estimators are proposed for λ:

$$T_1 = X_1 + X_2 + X_3, \quad T_2 = \frac{X_1 + X_2 + X_3}{3},$$
$$T_3 = \bar{X}, \quad T_4 = \frac{\sum_{i=1}^5 iX_i}{15}.$$

Using the linearity of expectations and independence, we can easily see that

$$E(T_1) = 3\lambda, E(T_2) = \lambda,$$
$$E(T_3) = \lambda, E(T_4) = \lambda.$$

Thus, we can see that $T_2, T_3,$ and T_4 are unbiased estimators, whereas T_1 is a biased estimator. For the unbiased estimators, the MSEs are the variance of the estimators. Again, using the linearity property, we can obtain the variances of these unbiased estimators as below:

$$MSE_{T_2} = V_\lambda(T_2) = \frac{\lambda + \lambda + \lambda}{3^2} = \frac{\lambda}{3},$$
$$MSE_{T_3} = V_\lambda(T_3) = \frac{5\lambda}{5^2} = \frac{\lambda}{5},$$
$$MSE_{T_4} = V_\lambda(T_4) = \frac{\lambda \sum_{i=1}^5 i^2}{15^2} = \frac{55}{225}\lambda.$$

From the above expressions, it is seen that the MSE is minimum for T_3.

We will now obtain the MSEs of the biased estimator T_1. Here

$$MSE_{T_1} = V_\mu(T_1) + b_\mu(T_1) = 3\lambda + (3\lambda - \lambda)^2 = 3\lambda + 4\lambda^2.$$

□

Example 7.7.2. Non-existence of Unbiased Estimator. Suppose that $X \sim b(n, p)$ and we are investigating if an unbiased estimator exists for $g(p) = 1/p$. Here $T = X$ is sufficient for p. Suppose that there is a function $k(t)$ which is an unbiased estimator of $g(p)$, that is,

$$\sum_{j=0}^{n} k(j) \binom{n}{j} p^j (1-p)^{n-j} = 1/p, 0 < p < 1.$$

We can rewrite this expression as

$$\sum_{j=0}^{n} k(j) \binom{n}{j} p^{j+1} (1-p)^{n-j} - 1 = 0.$$

Note that the first term on the life-hand side above is a polynomial of degree $n+1$ and the sum must equal 0 if an unbiased estimator exists for $g(p)$. This leaves us with $-1 = 0$, which is a contradiction. Thus, an unbiased estimator cannot exist for $g(p)$. This example has been adapted from Example 1.2 of Lehmann and Casella (1998). □

In the previous Example 7.7.1, we had four unbiased estimators $T_2, T_3,$ and T_4. Among these we will prefer the estimator with the least variance. This leads to the following definition.

Definition 7.7.3 Uniformly Minimum Variance Unbiased Estimator. *Let C denote the class of all unbiased estimators for $g(\theta)$. Assume that C is non-empty. We say that an estimator $T \in C$ is* uniformly minimum variance unbiased estimator, UMVUE, *if for any member $T' \in C$, we have*

$$V_\theta(T) \leq V_\theta(T'), \forall \theta \in \Theta. \tag{7.38}$$

In the following, we will first consider improving the unbiased estimators using sufficient statistics via the Rao-Blackwellization process. Next we will state what will be the lower bound for variance of unbiased estimators using Cramér-Rao inequality. Finally, we will briefly discuss how to obtain UMVU estimators.

7.7.2 Improving Unbiased Estimators

If we have an unbiased estimator, and we seek an improvement of it in terms of reduction in variance, we have an affirmative answer in the *Rao-Blackwell* theorem.

Theorem 7.7.2 Rao-Blackwell Theorem. *Let T be an unbiased estimator of real-valued parametric function $g(\theta), \theta \in \Theta$. Suppose that $\boldsymbol{U}$ is a jointly sufficient statistic for θ. Define $W = E_\theta(T|\boldsymbol{U} = u)$. Then the following results hold:*

1. *W is an unbiased estimator for $g(\theta)$.*
2. *$V_\theta(W) \leq V_\theta(T), \forall \theta \in \Theta$.* □

An illustration of how the Rao-Blackwell theorem works is required here.

Example 7.7.3. Improving an Unbiased Estimator of Bernoulli Sample. Consider n trials from a Bernoulli experiment and let $X_i \sim b(1, p), 0 < p < 1$. Consider $T = X_1$ as an estimator of p. Clearly $E_p(T) = E_p(X_1) = p$ and we can see that it is an unbiased estimator. However, as X_1 takes values 0 or 1, it is not a meaningful estimator of p. We have seen earlier that $U = \sum_{i=1}^n X_i$ is a sufficient statistic. Define $W = E_p(T|U = u)$. The Rao-Blackwellization can be now seen in action:

$$\begin{aligned} W = E_p(T|U = u) &= 1 \times P(X_1 = 1|U = u) + 0 \times P(X_1 = 0|U = 0) \\ &= \frac{P(X_1 = 1 \cap U = u)}{P(U = u)} \\ &= \frac{P(X_1 = 1 \cap \sum_{i=2}^n X_i = u - 1)}{P(U = u)} \end{aligned}$$

$$
\begin{aligned}
&= \frac{P(X_1 = 1)P(\sum_{i=2}^{n} X_i = u-1)}{P(U=u)}, X_1 \text{ and } \sum_{i=2}^{n} X_i \text{ are independent} \\
&= \frac{p\binom{n-1}{u-1}p^{u-1}(1-p)^{n-u}}{\binom{n}{u}p^u(1-p)^{n-u}} \\
&= \frac{\binom{n-1}{u-1}}{\binom{n}{u}} \\
&= \frac{u}{n} = \bar{x}.
\end{aligned}
$$

Let us compare the variances of W and T. By the definitions, we see that the variance of T is $p(1-p)$, whereas the variance of W is $p(1-p)/n$, which is a *reduction* unless $n = 1$. □

The reader may consult Mukhopadhyay (2000) for more interesting examples of Rao-Blackwellization. We have taken one important step towards reducing the variance via sufficiency and we should now ask what is the best we can do further. Under some mild regularity conditions, the answer is provided by Cramér-Rao's lower bound. We need the following assumptions.

(a) The support of X is independent of θ.
(b) $\frac{\partial}{\partial\theta}L(\theta, x)$ exists $\forall\theta, x$.
(c) $\frac{\partial}{\partial\theta}\int L(\theta, x)dx = \int \frac{\partial}{\partial\theta}L(\theta, x)dx$.
(d) $\frac{\partial}{\partial\theta}\int t(x)L(\theta, x)dx = \int t(x)\frac{\partial}{\partial\theta}L(\theta, x)dx$.
(e) $\mathcal{I}_X(\theta) < \infty, \forall\theta \in \Theta$.

Theorem 7.7.3 Cramér-Rao Inequality. *Suppose that $T(X)$ is an unbiased estimator of a real-valued parametric function $g(\theta)$. Under the assumption $\frac{d}{d\theta}g(\theta)$ exists, and together with the assumptions listed above, we have*

$$
V_\theta(T) \geq \frac{g'(\theta)^2}{n\mathcal{I}_X(\theta)}. \tag{7.39}
$$

□

As the above inequality involves the Fisher information, Lehmann and Casella (1998) refer to the Cramér-Rao inequality as the *information inequality*. The Cramér-Rao inequality can be derived using the characteristic function, see Kay and Xu (2008).

Example 7.7.4. The Poisson Distribution. Consider a random sample of size n from $Pois(\lambda)$, and let the parameter of interest be $g(\lambda) = \lambda$. Then $g' = 1$ and $\mathcal{I}_X(\lambda) = n/\lambda$. Thus, the Cramér-Rao lower bound for an unbiased estimator is λ/n. Recall that $V_\lambda(\bar{X}) = \lambda/n$. As the sample mean attains the Cramér-Rao lower bound for variance of unbiased estimator, we can claim the $\bar{X}$ is the UMVUE. □

We will close this section with an important result which leads towards deriving UMVUE for some special family of probability distributions.

Theorem 7.7.4 Lehmann-Scheffé Theorem. *Suppose that T is an unbiased estimator for a real-valued parametric function $g(\theta)$. Suppose that $\mathbf{U}$ is a complete sufficient statistic for θ. Define $W = E_\theta(T|\mathbf{U}=\mathbf{u})$. Then, the statistic W is the unique UMVUE of $g(\theta)$.* □

Example 7.7.5. UMVU Estimator for $e^{-\lambda}$ of Poisson Distribution. For a Poisson random sample, suppose we are interested in finding the UMVUE of probability of zero, that is $g(\lambda) = e^{-\lambda}$. An initial estimator of $g(\lambda)$ based on a single observation is $T = I(X_1 = 0)$ as $E_\lambda(T) = P(X_1 = 0) = e^{-\lambda}$. Rao-Blackwellization of this unbiased estimator, of the sufficient statistic $\sum_{i=1}^n X_i$ gives us the following:

$$\begin{aligned}
E(T|U = u) &= P(X_1 = 0|U = u)\\
&= \frac{P\left(X_1 = 0 \cap \sum_{i=2}^n X_i = u\right)}{P(\sum_{i=1}^n X_i = u)}\\
&= \frac{e^{-\lambda}\frac{e^{-(n-1)\lambda}((n-1)\lambda)^u}{u!}}{\frac{e^{-n\lambda}(n\lambda)^u}{u!}}, \text{ by independence}\\
&= \left(\frac{n-1}{n}\right)^u.
\end{aligned}$$

Rao-Blackwellization suggests the estimator as $W = ((n-1)/n)^{\sum_{i=1}^n X_i}$. By the expression (7.5.14) of Mukhopadhyay (2000), we have $V_\lambda(W) = e^{-2\lambda}(e^{\lambda/n} - 1)$.

The Cramér-Rao lower bound for $g(\lambda)$ turns out to be $\lambda e^{-2\lambda}/n$. Thus, the variance of the Rao-Blackwellized estimator turns out to be greater than the Cramér-Rao lower bound. However, as W is a function of the complete sufficient statistic $\sum_{i=1}^n X_i$, the Lehmann-Scheffé theorem guarantees that W is the UMVUE. □

7.8 Confidence Intervals

Point estimates of the parameters are useful as already seen. However, there is often a need to complement them with other techniques, and a very brief discussion on the technique of *confidence intervals* will be discussed here. It is admitted that this topic requires more depth, and is restricted only in part by the important problem of *hypotheses testing*, which is covered in a more rigorous and R way. Another reason for skipping over the details on confidence intervals in part is that most of the R statistical functions, the confidence intervals, are also provided as part of the output when we use the well-known tests. In fact, the R function `confint` is also available, which extracts the confidence intervals with desired confidence widths for the regression models.

Definition 7.8.1 Confidence Interval. *A confidence interval for a parameter $\theta \in \Theta$ is a random set $A \in \Theta$, which is predicted to contain the parameter with a defined probability, that is, a $100(1-\alpha)$, $\alpha \in [0, 1]$, confidence interval is such that*

$$P(\theta \in A) = 1 - \alpha. \tag{7.40}$$

The reader may refer Chapter 5 of Tattar (2013) for confidence interval functions `binom_CI`, `normal_CI_ksd`, and `normal_CI_uksd`. Chapter 8 of Ugarte, et al. (2008) is a comprehensive account of the confidence intervals construction in R. A reason for not developing this section in more detail is that most of the statistical tests in R such as `t.test`, `var.test`, `binom.test` give the confidence intervals as side products in the output. Furthermore, the function `confint` is applicable to many statistical models fitted in R.

7.9 Testing Statistical Hypotheses–The Preliminaries

In earlier sections we explored various techniques of estimating the unknown parameters. The next task is validation of these parameters. Especially, we would like to deduce if the estimated parameters are in agreement with certain conjectures. We will now introduce some important terminology.

Consider a random sample whose underlying probability law is a pmf or a pdf $f(x, \theta), \theta \in \Theta$.

Definition 7.9.1 Hypothesis. *A hypothesis is an assertion about the unknown parameter θ. If the assertion specifies that the parameter takes a single value over Θ, we refer to the hypothesis as* simple, *or else we say that it is* composite.

Example 7.9.1. Various types of hypothesis. Let us consider the standard distributions and see what may form the hypothesis:

1. The Poisson Distribution: $H : \lambda = 1$.
2. The Binomial Distribution: $H : p = 0.7$.
3. The Normal Distribution $N(\mu, \sigma^2)$, σ known: $H : \mu = 0$.
4. The Exponential Distribution: $H : \lambda > 50$.
5. The Uniform Distribution: $H : \theta \leq 10$.
6. The Normal Distribution $N(\mu, \sigma^2)$: $H : (\mu, \sigma) = (0, 1)$.

The first three hypotheses are simple, whereas the remaining are composite. □

Testing the hypotheses problem is the statistical criteria of choosing between two plausible hypotheses, that is, we find a mechanism to choose between hypotheses H and K. Formally, the testing hypotheses problem is

$$H : \theta \in \Theta_0 \text{versus } K : \theta \in \Theta_1, \tag{7.41}$$

where Θ_0 and θ_1 are two subsets of Θ and mutually exclusive, that is, $\Theta_0 \subset \Theta, \Theta_1 \subset \Theta$ and $\Theta_0 \cap \Theta_1$ is empty. The choice among Θ_0 and Θ_1 is to be based on a random sample $X_1, \cdots, X_n$ of size n. The values in the sample space which lead to rejection of the hypothesis H has a special name.

Definition 7.9.2 *The subset of Ω which lead to rejection of H is referred as the* critical region *or the* rejection region. *The critical region will be denoted by $\mathcal{R}$.*

We need an instrument which will decide between H or K. A formal definition is as follows.

Table 7.4 Type I and II Error

Hypothesis Test	H True	K True
Accept H	No Error	Type II Error
Accept K	Type I Error	No Error

Definition 7.9.3 *A* hypothesis test *is a rule which specifies the following:*

- *The sample values for which the decision is to accept H.*
- *The sample values for which we accept K and reject H.*

A standard notation for a hypothesis test is ϕ. In terms of the rejection region, we can define the test as

$$\phi = \begin{cases} 1, & \text{if } \mathbf{x} \in \mathcal{R}, \\ 0, & \text{otherwise.} \end{cases}$$

The tests can also be defined in terms of decision rules. Let d_0 and d_1 denote the decisions of accepting or rejecting the hypothesis H. Note that if $d_0 = 1$, then $d_1 = 0$.

The hypothesis test may lead to two types of error, which is brought out in Table 7.4.

It is customary to denote the probabilities of Type I and II errors by α and β respectively, that is,

$$\alpha = P(\text{Type I Error}) = P\{\mathbf{X} \in \mathcal{R} \text{ when } H \text{ is true}\}, \tag{7.42}$$

$$\beta = P(\text{Type II Error}) = P\{\mathbf{X} \in \mathcal{R}^c \text{ when } K \text{ is true}\}. \tag{7.43}$$

Ideally, we would like to construct a hypothesis test that will keep both types of errors to a minimum. Unfortunately, it is not possible to do this, and hence we seek hypothesis tests which assign an upper bound on the probability of Type I errors and attempt to minimize Type II errors subject to this bound. A formal definition captures the requirement.

Definition 7.9.4 Level of Significance. *A test ϕ for the testing problem of $H : \theta \in \Theta_0$ against $K : \theta \in \Theta_1$ is said to have a* level of significance $\alpha, 0 \leq \alpha \leq 1$, *if*

$$E_\theta \phi(\mathbf{X}) \leq \alpha. \tag{7.44}$$

The concept of Type I and Type II errors will be demonstrated in the next example with a small R program.

Example 7.9.2. Computing Probabilities of Type I and Type II Errors. Consider a random sample of size $n = 25$, that is $X_1, \cdots, X_{25}$, from an exponential distribution with parameter θ, and denote the sample mean by $\bar{X} = \sum_{i=1}^{25} X_i/n$. We are interested in testing $H : \theta = 10$ against the hypothesis $K : \theta = 20$. Consider four tests defined below:

$$\phi_1 = \text{Reject } H \text{ iff } \frac{\sum_{i=1}^{5} X_i}{5} > 15,$$

$$\phi_2 = \text{Reject } H \text{ iff } \frac{\sum_{i=1}^{15} X_i}{15} > 15,$$

$$\phi_3 = \text{Reject } H \text{ iff } \frac{\sum_{i=1}^{25} X_i}{25} > 13,$$

$$\phi_4 = \text{Reject } H \text{ iff } \frac{\sum_{i=1}^{25} X_i}{25} > 18.$$

We wish to compute the probability of Type I and Type II errors for the above four tests. Towards this, we need to re-formalize the tests in terms of the gamma distribution with the important result that for a sample of size n from an exponential distribution with parameter θ, the sample mean distribution is a gamma distribution with parameters $(n, n/\theta)$. A simple tweak will give us the necessary probabilities.

```
> theta_h <- 10; theta_k <- 20;
> x <- 15; n <- 5
> 1-pgamma(x,n,n/theta_h) # Type I Error of Test 1
[1] 0.1321
> pgamma(x,n,n/theta_k) # Type II Error of Test 1
[1] 0.3225
> x <- 15; n <- 15
> 1-pgamma(x,n,n/theta_h) # Type I Error of Test 2
[1] 0.0386
> pgamma(x,n,n/theta_k) # Type II Error of Test 2
[1] 0.1648
> x <- 13; n <- 25
> 1-pgamma(x,n,n/theta_h) # Type I Error of Test 3
[1] 0.07536
> pgamma(x,n,n/theta_k) # Type II Error of Test 3
[1] 0.02614
> x <- 18; n <- 25
> 1-pgamma(x,n,n/theta_h) # Type I Error of Test 4
[1] 0.0004492
> pgamma(x,n,n/theta_k) # Type II Error of Test 4
[1] 0.3262
```

The R program shows that the test ϕ_1 has large Type I and II error probabilities. Though the test ϕ_4 has a very less Type I probability, its Type II error probability is very high. The choice between tests ϕ_2 and ϕ_3 depends on which error needs to be given more emphasis. □

Example 7.9.3. Uniform Distribution. Consider a random sample of size n from $U(0, \theta)$. We wish to test the hypothesis $H : \theta \leq 1/2$ against $K : \theta = 1$. A test function is given by

$$\phi(\mathbf{X}) = I(\max(\mathbf{X}) > 1/2).$$

The density function of $M = \max(\mathbf{X})$ is given by

$$f(m) = \begin{cases} \frac{nm^{n-1}}{\theta^n}, & 0 < m < \theta, \\ 0, & \text{otherwise.} \end{cases}$$

Suppose $n = 8$ and we want to compute the size of the test and its power. Under the null hypothesis

$$E_H\phi(\mathbf{x}) = \int_0^{1/2} \frac{8m^7}{\theta^8} dm = 0.444,$$

as seen from the minor program:

```
> myfun <- function(n,theta,x) n*x^{n}/theta^{n}
> integrate(myfun, lower=0, upper=1/2,theta=1/2,n=8)
0.4444444 with absolute error < 4.9e-15
```

The function `myfun` is an R replica of $E_H\phi(\mathbf{x})$ and with the `integrate` function and the options `theta=1/2` and `n=8`, computes the Type I error. The Type II error value is left to the reader as an exercise. □

The level of significance places an upper bound on the probability of Type I error. However, sometimes we need to find from the data the probability of rejecting the hypothesis H.

Definition 7.9.5 p-value. *The p-value is the smallest level α_0, such that we would reject the hypothesis H at level α_0 with the observed data.*

The concept of the p-value will be especially useful in a lot of the hypotheses testing problems to be seen in Part IV. We will need one more concept here.

Definition 7.9.6 *The* power of a test *is the probability of rejecting the hypotheses H when $\theta \in \Theta$ is the true parameter value.*

The power of a test, also called the *power function*, will be denoted by $Q(\theta)$. If H and K are simple hypotheses, we have $Q(\theta_H) = \alpha$ and $Q(\theta_K) = 1 - \beta$, where θ_H and θ_K are the hypothesized values of the parameter. This notation of the power function should not be confused with the similarly used notation in Section 7.16 of the EM algorithm.

Example 7.9.4. Continuation of Example 7.9.2. The power function for the four tests are given by:

$$Q_{\phi_1}(\theta) = 1 - \frac{1}{\Gamma(5)\theta^5} \int_0^{15} x^{5-1} e^{-x/\theta} dx,$$

$$Q_{\phi_2}(\theta) = 1 - \frac{1}{\Gamma(15)\theta^{15}} \int_0^{15} x^{15-1} e^{-x/\theta} dx,$$

$$Q_{\phi_3}(\theta) = 1 - \frac{1}{\Gamma(25)\theta^{25}} \int_0^{13} x^{25-1} e^{-x/\theta} dx,$$

$$Q_{\phi_4}(\theta) = 1 - \frac{1}{\Gamma(25)\theta^{25}} \int_0^{18} x^{25-1} e^{-x/\theta} dx.$$

Plotting of the power function of tests gives an indication of the behavior of the test functions.

```
> Q1 <- function(x)  {1-pgamma(15,shape=5,rate=5/x)}
> Q2 <- function(x)  {1-pgamma(15,shape=15,rate=15/x)}
> Q3 <- function(x)  {1-pgamma(13,shape=25,rate=25/x)}
> Q4 <- function(x)  {1-pgamma(18,shape=25,rate=25/x)}
> curve(Q1,from=0.1,to=40,n=400,xlab=expression(theta),
+ ylab=expression(Q(theta)),
+ "l",col='red',add=FALSE,ylim=c(0,1))
> curve(Q2,from=0.1,to=40,n=400,"l",col='green',add=TRUE)
> curve(Q3,from=0.1,to=40,n=400,"l",col='blue',add=TRUE)
> curve(Q4,from=0.1,to=40,n=400,"l",col='yellow',add=TRUE)
> title(main="Various Power Functions")
> exp_legends <- expression(paste(Q[phi[1]],"(",theta,")"),
+ paste(Q[phi[2]], "(",theta,")"),paste(Q[phi[3]],
+ "(",theta,")"),paste(Q[phi[4]],"(",theta,")"))
> legend(x=c(30,40),y=c(0.7,0.5),exp_legends,col=
+ c("red","green","blue", "yellow"),lwd=rep(1.5,4))
> abline(v=c(10,20))
```

The R functions Q1, Q2, Q3, and Q4 are the corresponding implementation of the power functions stated before them. The `curve` function plots the power function curves. Discuss which test you will prefer, based on the power function plots in Figure 7.6. □

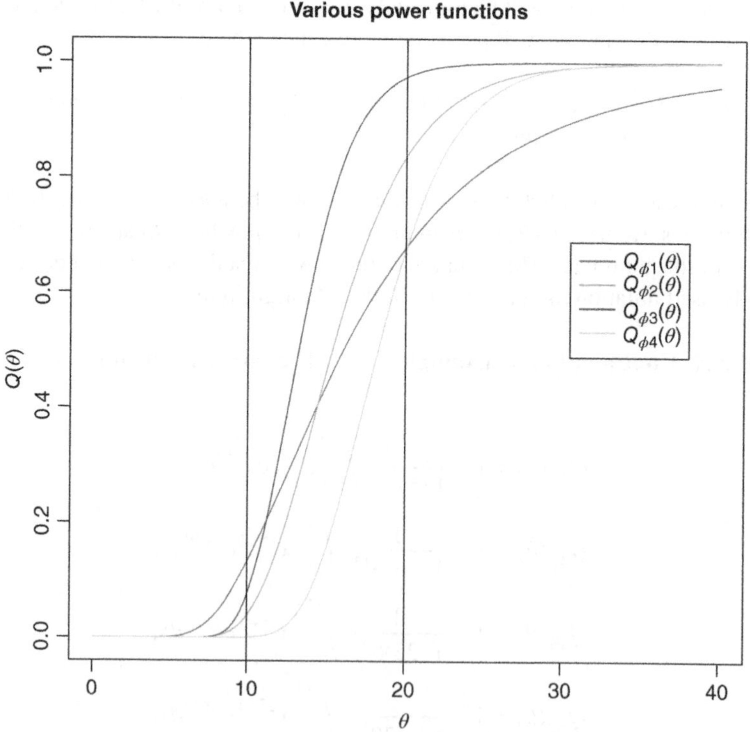

Figure 7.6 Power Function Plot for Normal Distribution

The next section will present a nice technique to obtain meaningful tests.

?pnorm, ?integrate

7.10 The Neyman-Pearson Lemma

The Neyman-Pearson lemma is one of the ground-breaking results in statistics. It begins with the problem of testing a simple hypothesis $H : \theta = \theta_0$ against the simple hypothesis $K : \theta = \theta_1$. The requirement of a size α test with maximum power leads to the definition of a most powerful test.

Definition 7.10.1 Most Powerful Test. *A test ϕ is said to be the most powerful test of H against K if*

$$E_H(\phi(\mathbf{x})) = \alpha, \ \ and \ , \tag{7.45}$$

$$Q_\phi(\theta_1) \geq Q_{\phi'}(\theta_1). \tag{7.46}$$

for any other level α test ϕ'.

The most powerful test is abbreviated as the MP test. We now state the lemma.

Theorem 7.10.1 The Neyman-Pearson Lemma. *Let P_0 and P_1 be probability distributions with respective densities p_{θ_0} and p_{θ_1} with respect to a measure μ. The Neyman-Pearson lemma for testing $H : p_{\theta_0}$ versus $K : p_{\theta_1}$ then states the following:*

- Existence. *There exists a test ϕ and constants k and γ such that*

$$E_{\theta_0}(\phi(\mathbf{x})) = \alpha, \tag{7.47}$$

$$\phi(\mathbf{x}) = \begin{cases} 1, \ if \ p_{\theta_1} > kp_{\theta_0}, \\ \gamma, \ if \ p_{\theta_1} = kp_{\theta_0}, \\ 0, \ if \ p_{\theta_1} < kp_{\theta_0}. \end{cases} \tag{7.48}$$

- Sufficient Condition for MP Test. *If a test satisfies (7.47) and (7.48) for some k, then it is MP for H against K.*
- Necessary Condition for MP Test. *If ϕ is an MP test at level α for H against K, then for some k it satisfies (7.48) almost everywhere μ. Furthermore, it satisfies (7.47) unless there exists a test of size less that α with power 1.* □

The test $\phi(\mathbf{x})$ may be rewritten in the form of likelihood functions as

$$\phi(\mathbf{x}) = \begin{cases} 1, \ \text{if} \ L(\theta_1, \mathbf{x}) > kL(\theta_0, \mathbf{x}), \\ \gamma, \ \text{if} \ L(\theta_1, \mathbf{x}) = kL(\theta_0, \mathbf{x}), \\ 0, \ \text{if} \ L(\theta_1, \mathbf{x}) < kL(\theta_0, \mathbf{x}), \end{cases}$$

$$= \begin{cases} 1, \ \text{if} \ \frac{L(\theta_1, \mathbf{x})}{L(\theta_0, \mathbf{x})} > k, \\ \gamma, \ \text{if} \ \frac{L(\theta_1, \mathbf{x})}{L(\theta_0, \mathbf{x})} = k, \\ 0, \ \text{if} \ \frac{L(\theta_1, \mathbf{x})}{L(\theta_0, \mathbf{x})} < k. \end{cases} \tag{7.49}$$

We will discuss some aspects of the Neyman-Pearson lemma before its applications. Some key points in this lemma are emphasized in the following:

(a) Points are increased in the critical region until the size of the test reaches α. To understand this, note that we consider the likelihood ratio $L(\theta_1|\mathbf{x})/L(\theta_0|\mathbf{x})$ and then rate the points of $\mathbf{X}$ on the basis of the ratio of the explanation of $\mathbf{x}$ under K to the explanation under H. Thus, the points with higher values of the likelihood ratio enjoy a better explanation under K in comparison with H.
(b) The power of MP tests increases for corresponding increases in the test sizes.
(c) The *risk set* for H against K is defined by

$$R = \{(\alpha, Q) : \alpha = E_{\theta_0}\phi(\mathbf{X}), Q = E_{\theta_1}(1 - \phi(\mathbf{X}))\}. \tag{7.50}$$

(d) The risk set R defined in Equation 7.50 is a *convex* and *compact* set.

The Neyman-Pearson lemma will be illustrated through various examples now.

Example 7.10.1. MP Test for Normal Distribution. We consider a random sample of size n from $N(\mu, \sigma^2)$, σ^2 known in $X_1, \cdots, X_n$. The problem is to test the hypothesis $H : \mu = \mu_0$ against the alternative $K : \mu = \mu_1, \mu_1 > \mu_0$. As the comparison problem involves two simple hypotheses, we can use the Neyman-Pearson lemma. In terms of the likelihood function, the MP test function takes the form

$$\phi(\mathbf{x}) = \begin{cases} 1, \text{ if } \frac{L(\mu_1|\mathbf{x})}{L(\mu_0|\mathbf{x})} > k, \\ 0, \quad \text{otherwise.} \end{cases}$$

Since the likelihood function is of the form $L(\mu|\mathbf{x}) \propto \exp\left\{(-2\sigma^2)^{-1}\sum_{i=1}^n (x_i - \mu)^2\right\}$, the MP test is to reject the hypothesis H if

$$\exp\left\{\sigma^{-2}(\mu_1 - \mu_0)\sum_{i=1}^n x_i\right\} > k.$$

Alternatively, we can state that the test procedure is to reject H if $\bar{x} > k$. We need the size of the test to be α, and to achieve this, standardize the test procedure and thus it is required that

$$\phi(\mathbf{x}) = \begin{cases} 1, \text{ if } \sqrt{n}\left(\frac{\bar{x}-\mu_0}{\sigma}\right) > z_\alpha, \\ 0, \qquad \text{otherwise,} \end{cases}$$
$$= \begin{cases} 1, \text{ if } \bar{x} > \frac{\sigma z_\alpha}{\sqrt{n}} + \mu_0, \\ 0, \quad \text{otherwise,} \end{cases}$$

where z_α is the upper $100\alpha\%$ of the standard normal distribution. It is easy to verify that $E(\phi(\mathbf{x})) = \alpha$. Some examples are demonstrated in R.

```
> MPNormal <- function(mu0, mu1, sigma, n,alpha) {
+    if(mu0<mu1) k <- qnorm(alpha,lower.tail = FALSE)*
+ sigma/sqrt(n) + mu0
```

```
+    if(mu0>mu1) k <- mu0 - qnorm(alpha,lower.tail = FALSE)*
+ sigma/sqrt(n)
+    return(k)
+ }
> MPNormal(mu0=0, mu1=0.5,sigma=1,n=10,alpha=0.05)
[1] 0.5201
> MPNormal(mu0=0, mu1=-0.5,sigma=1,n=10,alpha=0.05)
[1] -0.5201
> MPNormal(mu0=0, mu1=0.5,sigma=1,n=10,alpha=0.1)
[1] 0.4053
> MPNormal(mu0=0, mu1=-0.5,sigma=1,n=10,alpha=0.1)
[1] -0.4053
> MPNormal(mu0=10, mu1=15,sigma=2,n=10,alpha=0.05)
[1] 11.04
> MPNormal(mu0=10, mu1=5,sigma=2,n=10,alpha=0.05)
[1] 8.96
> MPNormal(mu0=10, mu1=15,sigma=2,n=10,alpha=0.1)
[1] 10.81
> MPNormal(mu0=10, mu1=5,sigma=2,n=10,alpha=0.1)
[1] 9.189
```

The R function `MPNormal` is created to take care of both scenarios (i) $\mu_1 > \mu_0$, and (ii) $\mu_1 < \mu_0$. Basically, the function returns the value of k, which leads to rejecting the hypothesis H if $\bar{x} > k$. The function `MPNormal` is available in the `ACSWR` package. □

Example 7.10.2. MP Test for Binomial Distribution. Consider a binomial distribution $b(n,p)$, where $n = 3$. We want to test $H : p = 0.95$ against $K : p = 0.10$. The target is construction of the MP test of size $\alpha = 0.001$. Since the value of the parameter p is greater under H than K, the MP test criteria will reject H for some k, such that $X < k$. Next, by the significance value, we require

$$P_{0.95}\{X < k\} + \gamma P_{0.95}\{X = k\} = 0.001.$$

Since the second term in the above equation $\gamma P_{0.95}\{X = k\}$ is a positive number, it is clear that we need to find k, such that $P_{0.95}\{X < k\} < 0.001$. Let us use the `pbinom` function to identify k:

```
> pbinom(0:3,prob=0.95,size=3)
[1] 0.000125 0.007250 0.142625 1.000000
```

It is clear from the above that the value of k should be 1. Plugging in this value of k, we can easily find γ as

```
> dbinom(1,prob=0.95,size=3)
[1] 0.007125
> (0.001-0.0001)/0.0071
[1] 0.1267606
```

Thus the MP level $\alpha(=0.001)$ for H against K is given by

$$\phi(x) = \begin{cases} 1, & \text{if } x < 1, \\ 0.1267, & \text{if } x = 1, \\ 0, & \text{otherwise.} \end{cases}$$

□

In the previous example, the value of p under K was less than under H. Let us consider the same problem with roles reversed.

Example 7.10.3. MP Test for Binomial Distribution. Contd. Consider a random sample of size n from Bernoulli, where the probability of success is $p, 0 < p < 1$. We are now interested in testing $H : p = p_0$ against $K : p = p_1$, where $p_1 > p_0$. The α- level MP test, after sacrificing a few vital steps, is defined by

$$\text{Reject } H \text{ if } \sum_{i=1}^{n} X_i \text{ is large.}$$

The form of the MP test is then

$$\phi(\mathbf{X}) = \begin{cases} 1, \text{ if } & \sum_{i=1}^{n} X_i > k, \\ \gamma, \text{ if } & \sum_{i=1}^{n} X_i = k, \\ 0, & \text{otherwise.} \end{cases}$$

We need to obtain the values of γ and k to complete the hypothesis frame. First we find the smallest integer k such that $P_{p_0}(\sum_{i=1}^{n} X_i > k) < \alpha$. Then, we find γ by

$$\gamma = \frac{\alpha - P_{p_0}(\sum_{i=1}^{n} X_i > k)}{P_{p_0}(\sum_{i=1}^{n} X_i = k)}.$$

An interesting program `MPbinomial` has been developed, which will readily return us the values of γ and k. For different values of $p_0, p_1, n,$ and α, the values of γ and k are returned, which will be the α-level MP test. The function `MPbinomial` will be applied for different p values under the hypotheses H and K. It is available in the companion `ACSWR` package.

```
> MPbinomial <- function(Hp, Kp, alpha,n){
+         k <- min(which((1-pbinom(0:n,size=n,prob=Hp))<alpha))-1
+         gamma <- (alpha-1+pbinom(k,size=n,prob=Hp))/dbinom
+ (k,size=n,prob=Hp)
+         return(list=c(k,gamma))
+ }
> MPbinomial(Hp=0.25,Kp=0.9,alpha=0.1,n=10)
[1] 4.0000 0.1498
> MPbinomial(Hp=0.5,Kp=0.9,alpha=0.1,n=10)
[1] 7.0000 0.3867
> MPbinomial(Hp=0.5,Kp=0.9,alpha=0.2,n=10)
[1] 6.0000 0.1371
> MPbinomial(Hp=0.75,Kp=0.9,alpha=0.2,n=10)
```

```
[1] 9.0000 0.7655
> MPbinomial(Hp=0.3,Kp=0.9,alpha=0.1,n=50)
[1] 19.0000  0.2726
> MPbinomial(Hp=0.3,Kp=0.9,alpha=0.2,n=50)
[1] 18.0000  0.7695
> MPbinomial(Hp=0.6,Kp=0.9,alpha=0.1,n=100)
[1] 66.0000  0.2238
> MPbinomial(Hp=0.6,Kp=0.9,alpha=0.2,n=100)
[1] 64.0000  0.3471
```

The Neyman-Pearson test for the hypotheses testing problem `MPbinomial` has not been explained in detail, although it should not be difficult to follow. Note that unlike the `MPNormal` function, we need two values of k and γ to be returned here. □

The reader may not be too comfortable with writing different programs, for the reason that p_0 may be lesser or greater than p_1. Recall that the `MPNormal` function takes care of both scenarios. The next function takes care of this.

```
MPbinomial <- function(Hp, Kp, alpha,n) {
  if(Hp<Kp){
    k <- min(which((1-pbinom(0:n,size=n,prob=Hp))<alpha))-1
    gamma <- (alpha-1+pbinom(k,size=n,prob=Hp))/dbinom(k,size=n,
+ prob=Hp)
    return(list=c(k,gamma))
  }
  else {
    k <- max(which((pbinom(0:n,size=n,prob=Hp))<alpha))
    gamma <- (alpha-pbinom(k-1,size=n,prob=Hp))/dbinom(k,size=n,
+ prob=Hp)
    return(list=c(k,gamma))
  }
}
```

Example 7.10.4. MP Test for Poisson Distribution. Let $X \sim Pois(\lambda)$ and assume that n replicates of it are available. The testing problem is hypothesis $H : \lambda = \lambda_0$ against the hypothesis $K : \lambda = \lambda_1$. We now allow λ_0 to be either greater or less than λ_1. The `MPPoisson` function returns the desired values of γ and k at a specified level α.

```
> MPPoisson <- function(Hlambda, Klambda, alpha,n) {
+   Hlambda <- n*Hlambda
+   Klambda <- n*Klambda
+   nn <- n*Hlambda
+   if(Hlambda<Klambda) }
+     k <- min(which((1-ppois(0:nn,lambda=Hlambda))<alpha))-1
+     gamma <- (alpha-1+ppois(k,lambda=Hlambda))/dpois
+  (k,lambda=Hlambda)
+     return(list=c(k,gamma))
+   {
+   else {
```

```
+       k <- max(which((ppois(0:nn,lambda=Hlambda))<alpha))
+       gamma <- (alpha-ppois(k-1,lambda=Hlambda))/dpois
+ (k,lambda=Hlambda)
+       return(list=c(k,gamma))
+     }
+ }
> MPPoisson(Hlambda=5,Klambda=10,alpha=0.2,n=10)
[1] 56.0000  0.5875
> MPPoisson(Hlambda=5,Klambda=10,alpha=0.15,n=10)
[1] 57.0000  0.1557
> MPPoisson(Hlambda=5,Klambda=10,alpha=0.1,n=10)
[1] 59.0000  0.3206
> MPPoisson(Hlambda=5,Klambda=10,alpha=0.05,n=10)
[1] 62.0000  0.5725
> MPPoisson(Hlambda=15,Klambda=10,alpha=0.2,n=50)
[1] 727.0000   0.4001
> MPPoisson(Hlambda=15,Klambda=10,alpha=0.15,n=50)
[1] 722.000   0.128
> MPPoisson(Hlambda=15,Klambda=10,alpha=0.1,n=50)
[1] 715.0000   0.5068
> MPPoisson(Hlambda=15,Klambda=10,alpha=0.05,n=50)
[1] 705.0000   0.7362
```

The `MPPoisson` is tailored to Poisson distribution on the same lines as `MPNormal` and `MPbinomial` functions. □

We will now move to the next type of hypotheses testing problem.

?qnorm, ?pbinom, ?ppois,

7.11 Uniformly Most Powerful Tests

The general *one-sided* hypothesis testing problem for a single real valued parameter $\theta \in \Theta$ is stated as:

$$H : \theta \leq \theta_0 \text{ against } K : \theta > \theta_0, \theta_0 \in \Theta.$$

Note that the hypotheses H and K are composite hypotheses. A definition of the *size* of a test for composite hypothesis is required.

Definition 7.11.1 Size of a Test. *A test ϕ for testing $H : \theta \in \Theta_0$ against $K : \theta \in \Theta_1$ is said to be of size α if*

$$\sup_{\theta \in \Theta_0} E_\theta \phi(X) = \alpha. \tag{7.51}$$

Definition 7.11.2 Class of Size α Tests. *The collection of all size α tests forms the* class of level α *tests:*

$$C_\alpha = \left\{ \phi | \sup_{\theta \in \Theta_0} E_\theta \phi(X) \leq \alpha \right\}. \tag{7.52}$$

We can now define the *Uniformly Most Powerful Tests.*

Definition 7.11.3 Uniformly Most Powerful Tests. *A test $\phi \in C_\alpha$ for testing $H : \theta \in \Theta_0$ against $K : \theta \in \Theta_1$ is said to be the Uniformly Most Powerful, UMP, test of size α if it satisfies the following conditions:*

$$\sup_{\theta \in \Theta_0} E_\theta \phi(X) = \alpha, \tag{7.53}$$

$$E_\theta \phi_0(X) \geq E_\theta \phi(X), \quad \forall\ \theta \in \Theta_1, \ \textit{and}\ \forall\ \phi_0 \in C_\alpha. \tag{7.54}$$

Let us first consider the problem of testing $H : \theta = \theta_0$ against $K : \theta > \theta_0$. In this case the UMP test may be easily obtained. Towards this, fix a value $\theta_1 > \theta_0$ and set up the Neyman-Pearson MP test for $H : \theta = \theta_0$ against $K : \theta = \theta_1$. Then the MP test continues to be a UMP test if the test remains unaffected by the specific choice of θ_1.

Example 7.11.1. UMP Test for Binomial Distribution. In continuation of Example 7.10.3, suppose the interest is in testing the hypothesis $H : p = p_0$ against $K : p > p_0$. Then the values of k and γ continue to be the same as returned by the `MPbinomial` function, since the function does not use the p_1 argument in the rest of the program. Thus we can claim that the MP tests obtained in Example 7.10.3 are the UMP test against the appropriate hypothesis that $K : p > p_0$. □

We note that the UMP tests do not exist in general for one-sided testing problems. However, the UMP tests exist for a family of distribution satisfying a particular property. The mathematical property which is necessary for the existence of UMP tests is defined next.

Definition 7.11.4 Monotone Likelihood Ratio. *Areal parameter family of distributions is said to have a* monotone likelihood ratio, *MLR, in a statistic $T(\mathbf{x})$ if the ratio of density functions*

$$\frac{f(\mathbf{x}|\theta_2)}{f(\mathbf{x}|\theta_1)},$$

is a non-decreasing function of $T(\mathbf{x})$ for $\theta_1 < \theta_2$.

A result due to Karlin and Rubin states that whenever there exists a statistic $T(\mathbf{x})$ for which $f(\mathbf{x}|\theta)$ admits the MLR property, a UMP test can be constructed for the one-sided hypothesis.

Theorem 7.11.1 Karlin and Rubin Theorem for UMP Tests. *Assume that the family of distributions $\{f_\theta, \theta \in \Theta\}$ of $\mathbf{X}$ admits the MLR property in a statistic $T(\mathbf{x})$. Consider the testing problem $H : \theta \leq \theta_0$ against $K : \theta > \theta_0$. Then the UMP size α test exists and its form is given by*

$$\phi(\mathbf{x}) = \begin{cases} 1, & \textit{if } T(\mathbf{x}) > t_0, \\ \gamma, & \textit{if } T(\mathbf{x}) = t_0, \\ 0, & \textit{otherwise}. \end{cases} \tag{7.55}$$

□

Example 7.11.2. UMP Test for Exponential Distribution. In an experiment involving electronic tubes, an experimenter collects data on the failure times from a random sample of 20 units. Assume that the failure time follows an exponential distribution with mean time θ. The aim of the experiment is to test $H : \theta \leq 350$ against $K : \theta > 350$. The observed data contains the 20 failure times as 9.9, 35.6, 57.9, 94.6, 141.4, 154.4, 163.3, 226.7, 244.3, 337.2, 391.8, 417.2, 444.6, 461.2, 497.1, 582.6, 606.8, 616.0, 784.7, and 794.7.

Define $T(\mathbf{X}) = \sum_{i=1}^{n} X_i$. Clearly, $T(\mathbf{X})$ is sufficient for θ and the density function of exponential distribution is monotone in $T(\mathbf{X})$. Thus, the size θ UMP test is given by

$$\phi(\mathbf{X}) = \begin{cases} 1, & \text{if } T(\mathbf{x}) > k, \\ 0, & \text{otherwise.} \end{cases}$$

Note that $T \sim Gamma(n, \theta)$ and hence we can determine k in the following steps. To obtain a size α UMP test we require

$$E_\theta \phi(T) = \alpha,$$

which translates to

$$\int_t^\infty Gamma(n, \theta) dy = \alpha, \text{ or}$$

$$\int_0^t Gamma(n, \theta) dy = 1 - \alpha.$$

This integral can be easily evaluated to obtain t using the `qgamma` function. The R program below gives us the required results.

```
> UMPExponential <- function(theta0, n, alpha){
+ t <- qgamma(1-alpha, shape=n,scale=theta0)
+ return(t)
+ }
> UMPExponential(theta0=350,n=20,alpha=0.05)
[1] 9757.734
> x <- c(9.9, 35.6, 57.9, 94.6, 141.4, 154.4, 163.3, 226.7,
+ 244.3, 337.2, 391.8, 417.2, 444.6, 461.2, 497.1, 582.6,
+ 606.8, 616.0, 784.7, 794.7)
> (t <- sum(x))
[1] 7062
```

Since the observed t value `7062` is less than `9757.734`, we fail to reject the hypothesis $H : \theta \leq 350$. □

Example 7.11.3. UMP Test for Uniform Distribution. Consider a random sample $X_1, \cdots, X_n$ from $U(0, \theta)$. The problem of interest is $H : \theta \leq \theta_0$ against $K : \theta > \theta_0$. It is then known that $M = \max\{X_i\}$ is a sufficient statistic for θ. Recall the distribution of M:

$$f(m|\theta) = \begin{cases} \frac{nm^{n-1}}{\theta^n}, & 0 < m < \theta, \\ 0, & \text{otherwise.} \end{cases}$$

Clearly, $f(m|\theta)$ is monotone decreasing in θ. Thus, by the application of the Karlin-Rubin theorem, the UMP test is given by

$$\phi_(\mathbf{X}) = \begin{cases} 1, & \text{if } M(\mathbf{x}) > k, \\ 0, & \text{otherwise.} \end{cases}$$

To obtain a size α test, we need to evaluate

$$\alpha = P_{\theta_0}\{M > k\} = 1 - \left\{\frac{k}{\theta_0}\right\}^n.$$

For a dummy dataset, we have

```
> UMPUniform <- function(theta0,n,alpha)
+ return(theta0*(1-alpha)^{1/n})
> UMPUniform(0.6,10,0.05)
[1] 0.5969303
```

Thus, if the M value is greater than `0.5969303`, we reject the hypothesis H. □

Example 7.11.4. UMP Test for Normal Distribution. The one-sided hypothesis testing problem is $H : \mu \le \mu_0$ against $K : \mu > \mu_0$ for a random sample of n observations from $N(\mu, \sigma^2)$. Here, we assume that the variance σ^2 is known. It can be easily proved that the UMP test function is of the form:

$$\phi(\mathbf{X}) = \begin{cases} 1, & \text{if } \sqrt{n}(\bar{X} - \mu_0)/\sigma > z_\alpha, \\ 0, & \text{if } \sqrt{n}(\bar{X} - \mu_0)/\sigma \le z_\alpha. \end{cases}$$

Note that if the problem is of testing $H : \mu > \mu_0$ against $K : \mu \le \mu_0$, the above test function with the inequalities sign reversed on the right-hand side of the equation will continue to be an UMP test. The power function for the previous hypotheses is given by

$$P(\text{Rejecting } H|\mu) = P(\bar{X} \ge \mu_0 + z_\alpha\sigma/\sqrt{n}|\mu).$$

In the next program, we create R functions which will enable us to test the hypotheses and also obtain the power function.

```
> # UMP Test for Normal Distribution
> # H:mu <= mu_0 vs K: mu > mu_0
> UMPNormal <- function(mu0, sigma, n,alpha){
+         qnorm(alpha)*sigma/sqrt(n)+mu0
+  }
> UMPNormal(mu0=0, sigma=1,n=1,alpha=0.5)
[1] 0
> powertestplot <- function(mu0,sigma,n,alpha){
+         mu0seq <- seq(mu0-3*sigma, mu0+3*sigma,(6*sigma/100))
+         betamu <- pnorm(sqrt(n)*(mu0seq-mu0)/sigma-qnorm(1-alpha))
+         plot(mu0seq,betamu,"l",xlab=expression(mu),ylab="Power of
+ UMP Test",
```

```
+         main = expression(paste("H:",mu <= mu[0]," vs K:",
+ mu>mu[0])))
+         abline(h=alpha)
+         abline(v=mu0)
+   }
> powertestplot(mu0=0,sigma=1,n=10,alpha=0.05)
> # H:mu > mu_0 vs K: mu <= mu_0
> UMPNormal <- function(mu0, sigma, n,alpha){
+         mu0-qnorm(alpha)*sigma/sqrt(n)
+ }
> UMPNormal(mu0=0, sigma=1,n=1,alpha=0.5)
[1] 0
> powertestplot <- function(mu0,sigma,n,alpha){
+         mu0seq=seq(mu0-3*sigma, mu0+3*sigma,(6*sigma/100))
+         betamu = pnorm(sqrt(n)*(mu0-mu0seq)/sigma-qnorm(1-alpha))
+         plot(mu0seq,betamu,"l",xlab=expression(mu),ylab="Power of
+  UMP Test",
+         main = expression(paste("H:",mu >= mu[0]," vs K:",
+ mu<mu[0])))
+         abline(h=alpha)
+         abline(v=mu0)
+ }
> powertestplot(mu0=0,sigma=1,n=10,alpha=0.05)
```

It may be noted from Figure 7.7 that the power function reaches value α exactly at μ_0. We conclude this example with a small discussion of the sample size determination so that the UMP test attains a specified power. Thankfully, in R, we have an inbuilt function for determining the sample size for normal samples in `power.t.test`.

```
> power.t.test(delta=0.5,sd=1,sig.level=0.025,type="one.sample",
+ alternative="one.sided",power=0.9)
     One-sample t test power calculation
              n = 43.99552
          delta = 0.5
             sd = 1
      sig.level = 0.025
          power = 0.9
    alternative = one.sided
```

Since the sample size cannot be a fraction, we need to have a minimum sample of size $n = 44$, so that the power of the test is 0.9. □

?power.t.test

7.12 Uniformly Most Powerful Unbiased Tests

The general hypotheses of interest is of the form: $H : \theta = \theta_0$ against $K : \theta \neq \theta_0$. We will begin with an example.

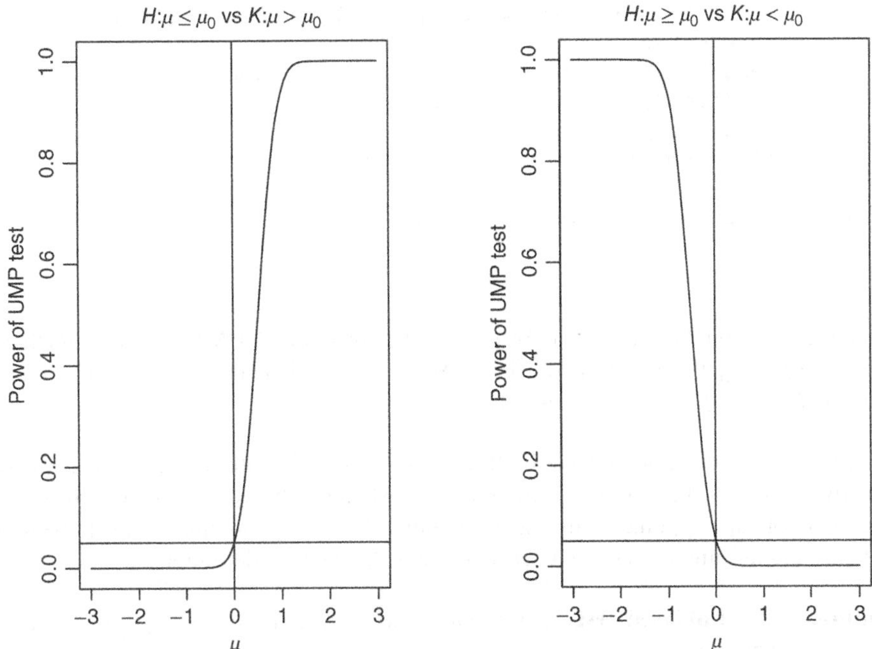

Figure 7.7 UMP Tests for One-Sided Hypotheses

Example 7.12.1. Non-existence of UMP Test for Testing Simple Hypothesis Against Two-sided Hypothesis for Normal Distribution. For the problem of testing $H : \mu = \mu_0$ against $K : \mu \neq \mu_0$ based on a sample of size n from $N(\mu, \sigma^2)$, where σ is known, let us first consider two UMP size α tests for two testing problems: (a) $H_1 : \mu = \mu_0$ against $K_1 : \mu > \mu_0$, and (b) $H_2 : \mu = \mu_0$ against $K_2 : \mu < \mu_0$. Consider the following two tests:

$$\phi_1(\mathbf{X}) = \begin{cases} 1, \text{ if } \sqrt{n}(\bar{X} - \mu_0)/\sigma > z_\alpha, \\ 0, \text{ if } \sqrt{n}(\bar{X} - \mu_0)/\sigma \leq z_\alpha, \end{cases}$$

$$\phi_2(\mathbf{X}) = \begin{cases} 1, \text{ if } \sqrt{n}(\bar{X} - \mu_0)/\sigma \leq z_\alpha, \\ 0, \text{ if } \sqrt{n}(\bar{X} - \mu_0)/\sigma > z_\alpha. \end{cases}$$

From the examples in previous sections, it is clear that the tests ϕ_1 and ϕ_2 are two UMP tests of size α for testing problems (a) and (b) respectively. Let us obtain a plot of the power functions for these two tests.

```
> pdf("Non_Existence_UMP_Normal.pdf")
> powertestplot <- function(mu0,sigma,n,alpha){
+        mu0seq <- seq(mu0-3*sigma, mu0+3*sigma,(6*sigma/100))
+        betamu <- pnorm(sqrt(n)*(mu0-mu0seq)/sigma-qnorm(1-alpha))
+        betamu2 <- pnorm(sqrt(n)*(mu0seq-mu0)/sigma-qnorm(1-alpha))
+        plot(mu0seq,betamu,"l",xlab=expression(mu[0]),
+        ylab="Power of UMP Test",main = expression(paste("H:",mu
```

```
+         = mu[0]," vs K:",mu != mu[0])),col="red",xaxt="n")
+         points(mu0seq,betamu2,"l",col="blue")
+         legend(2,0.6,c(expression(phi[1]),expression(phi[2])),
+         col=c("red","blue"),lty=c(1,1))
+         abline(h=alpha)
+         abline(v=mu0)
+ }
> powertestplot(mu0=0,sigma=1,n=10,alpha=0.05)
> dev.off()
1
```

We can then see from Figure 7.8 that for $\mu > \mu_0$, the power of the UMP test ϕ_1 is less than ϕ_2, whereas for $\mu < \mu_0$, the power of ϕ_2 is less than ϕ_1. Hence, there does not exist a UMP size α for testing $H : \mu = \mu_0$ against $K : \mu \neq \mu_0$. □

It needs to be noted though that a UMP test for a simple hypothesis against the two-sided alternative exists for the uniform distribution, see Mukhopadhyay (2000). We will return to the problem of such hypotheses for the normal distribution. A condition needs to be relaxed for identifying meaningful tests and hence we consider the next definition.

Definition 7.12.1 Unbiased Tests. *A size α test ϕ for testing $H : \theta \in \Theta_0$ against $K : \theta \in \Theta_1$ is said to be* unbiased *if*

$$E_\theta\phi(\mathbf{X}) \geq \alpha, \forall\theta \in \Theta_1. \tag{7.56}$$

Let $\mathcal{U}_\alpha$ denote the collection of all size α unbiased tests. The next definition follows naturally.

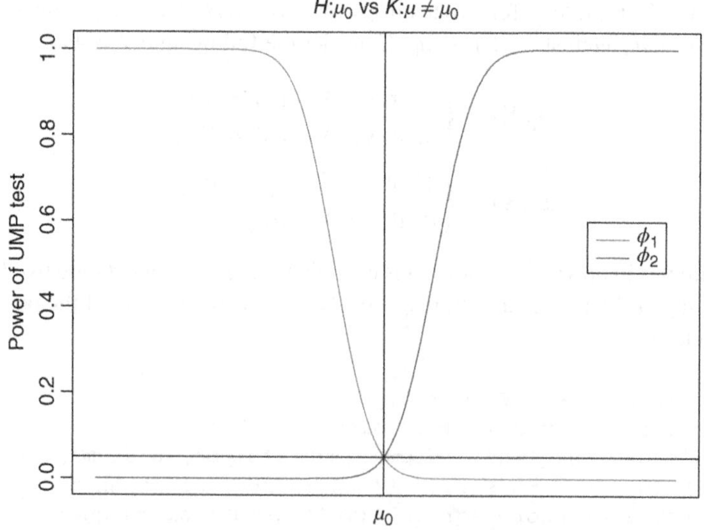

Figure 7.8 Non-Existence of UMP Test for Normal Distribution

Definition 7.12.2 Uniformly Most Powerful Unbiased, UMPU, size α Test. *An unbiased size α test $\phi_0 \in \mathcal{U}_\alpha$ is said to be a UMPU test if it has maximum power at each $\theta \in \Theta_1$, that is:*

$$E_\theta \phi_0(\mathbf{X}) \leq \alpha, \forall \theta \in \Theta_0, \tag{7.57}$$

$$E_\theta \phi_0(\mathbf{X}) \geq E_\theta \phi_1(\mathbf{X}), \ \textit{for any} \ \phi_1 \in \mathcal{U}_\alpha. \tag{7.58}$$

The main reason for discussing the results in this fashion thus far is the integration of statistical concepts with R. It is believed that the reader is now convinced that the details of statistical theory can be understood using a software package. We now skip rest of the details, though illustrations are given, and simply leave it as an exercise for the reader to verify that the Student's t-test is indeed a UMPU test. In fact, we need a host of other related and interesting concepts, such as *similarity*, to prove that the Student's t-test is indeed a UMPU test. The details may be found in Lehmann and Romano (2005) and Srivastava and Srivastava (2009).

7.12.1 *Tests for the Means: One- and Two-Sample* t-*Test*

Assume that $x_1, x_2, \cdots, x_n$ is a random sample from $N(\mu, \sigma^2)$ with both the parameters being unknown. Suppose we are interested in testing $H : \mu = \mu_0$. The parameters μ and σ^2 are respectively estimated using the sample mean and the sample standard deviation. The t-test is then given by

$$t = \frac{\bar{x} - \mu_0}{s/\sqrt{n}}, \tag{7.59}$$

which has a t-distribution with $n - 1$ degrees of freedom. The t-test in R software may be found in the `stats` package whose constitution is given as

```
t.test(x, y = NULL,
       alternative = c("two.sided", "less", "greater"),
       mu = 0, paired = FALSE, var.equal = FALSE,
       conf.level = 0.95, ...)
```

The following is clear from the above display:

1. The default function is a one-sample test with a two-sided alternative being tested for $\mu = 0$ and 95% confidence interval as an output.
2. The user has the options of specifying the nature of alternatives, μ, and the confidence interval level.

Example 7.12.2. A t-test for the Galton Data. For the famous Galton dataset, suppose that we want to test if the height of the child equals the height of the parent. Using the t-test, we get the following answer.

```
> library(UsingR)
> summary(galton)
     child             parent
```

```
  Min.   :61.70   Min.   :64.00
  1st Qu.:66.20   1st Qu.:67.50
  Median :68.20   Median :68.50
  Mean   :68.09   Mean   :68.31
  3rd Qu.:70.20   3rd Qu.:69.50
  Max.   :73.70   Max.   :73.00
> t.test(galton$child,mu=mean(galton$parent))
  One Sample t-test
data:  galton$child
t = -2.6583, df = 927, p-value = 0.00799
alternative hypothesis: true mean is not equal to 68.30819
95 percent confidence interval:
 67.92626 68.25068
sample estimates:
mean of x
 68.08847
```

Thus, we can see from the p-value, and the confidence interval too, that we need to reject the hypotheses that the height of the child is equal to the height of the parent. □

In the above example we specified that μ_0 is the mean of the parent height. However, a more appropriate test will be a direct comparison as to whether the height of the child is the same as the height of the parent.

Let $X_1, X_2, \cdots, X_{n_1}$ be a random sample from $N(\mu_x, \sigma_x^2)$, and $Y_1, Y_2, \cdots, Y_{n_2}$ a random sample from $N(\mu_y, \sigma_y^2)$, with σ unknown. Here, we assume that the variances are equal, though unknown. Suppose that we are interested to test the hypothesis $H : \mu_x = \mu_y$ against the hypothesis $K : \mu_x \neq \mu_y$. The two-sample t-test is then given by

$$t = \frac{\bar{X} - \bar{Y}}{s_{xy}}, \tag{7.60}$$

which has a t-distribution with $n_1 + n_2 - 1$ degrees of freedom, with s_{xy} being the pooled standard deviation.

Example 7.12.3. Illustration through `sleep` dataset in R, or the AD4. The dataset is not large and this is compensated for by its antiquity. The `t.test` can be applied on the `sleep` data site straightaway.

```
> plot(extra ~ group, data = sleep) # output suppressed
> t.test(extra ~ group, data = sleep)
 Welch Two Sample t-test
data:  extra by group
t = -1.8608, df = 17.776, p-value = 0.07939
alternative hypothesis: true difference in means is not equal to 0
95 percent confidence interval:
 -3.3654832  0.2054832
sample estimates:
mean in group 1 mean in group 2
           0.75            2.33
```

At size $\alpha = 0.1$, the hypothesis that the heights are equal needs to be rejected, whereas at $\alpha = 0.05$ level, it may be seen from the p-value and 95% confidence interval that there is not enough evidence in the dataset to reject the hypothesis of equal heights of parent and child. □

?qgamma, ?qnorm, ?expression, ?pnorm, ?power.t.test

7.13 Likelihood Ratio Tests

Consider the generic testing problem $H: \theta \in \Theta_0$ vs $K: \theta \in \Theta_1$. As earlier, it is assumed that a random sample $X_1, \cdots, X_n$ of size n is available.

Definition 7.13.1 The Likelihood Ratio Test. *For the problem of testing $H: \theta \in \Theta_0$ vs $K: \theta \in \Theta_1$, the likelihood ratio test is to reject H iff $\lambda(\mathbf{x}) < c$, for some constant c, where*

$$\lambda(\mathbf{x}) = \frac{\sup_{\theta \in \Theta_0} L(\theta|\mathbf{x})}{\sup_{\theta \in \Theta} L(\theta|\mathbf{x})}. \tag{7.61}$$

The constant c is to be determined from the size restriction:

$$\sup_{\theta \in \Theta_0} P(L(\theta|\mathbf{x}) < c) = \alpha.$$

The following examples deal with the construction of likelihood ratio tests.

Example 7.13.1. The Binomial Distribution. Suppose that $X \sim b(n,p)$ and the problem of testing involves $H: p \leq p_0$ against $K: p > p_0$. The likelihood ratio test requires the determination of $\lambda(x)$ such that

$$\lambda(x) = \frac{\sup_{p \leq p_0} \binom{n}{x} p^x (1-p)^{n-x}}{\sup_{0 \leq p \leq 1} \binom{n}{x} p^x (1-p)^{n-x}}.$$

In Example 5.9.6. we saw that the pmf of random variable X initially increases, and then reaches the maximum at $p = x/n$, and then decreases. Thus

$$\sup_{p \leq p_0} p^x (1-p)^{n-x} = \begin{cases} p_0^x (1-p_0)^{n-x}, & \text{if } p_0 < x/n, \\ \left(\frac{x}{n}\right)^x \left(1 - \frac{x}{n}\right)^{n-x}, & \text{if } x/n < p_0. \end{cases}$$

Thus, the likelihood ratio test becomes

$$\lambda(x) = \begin{cases} \frac{p_0^x (1-p_0)^{n-x}}{(x/n)^x (1-(x/n)^{n-x})}, & \text{if } p_0 < x/n, \\ 1, & \text{if } x/n < p_0. \end{cases}$$

The completion of the R program to obtain the likelihood ratio test is left as an exercise for the reader. □

The likelihood ratio tests are obtained for the normal distribution in the following subsections.

7.13.1 Normal Distribution: One-Sample Problems

In Section 7.11 we saw that UMP tests do not exist for many crucial types of hypothesis problems. As an example, for a random sample of size n from $N(\mu, \sigma^2)$, σ known, the UMP test does not exist for testing $H : \mu = \mu_0$ against $K : \mu \neq \mu_0$. We will consider these types of problems in this subsection.

Example 7.13.2. Testing $H : \mu = \mu_0$ against $K : \mu \neq \mu_0$ when σ is known. In this problem, $\Theta_0 = \mu_0$, and $\Theta_1 = \mathbb{R}$. The likelihood function is given by

$$L(\mu|\mathbf{x}, \sigma^2) = \{\sigma\sqrt{2\pi}\}^{-n} \exp\left\{-\frac{1}{2\sigma^2}\sum_{i=1}^{n}(x_i - \mu)^2\right\}.$$

It is straightforward to see that the maximum of $L(\mu|\mathbf{x}, \sigma^2)$ over Θ_0 is simply given by the likelihood function at $\mu = \mu_0$, that is,

$$\sup_{\Theta_0} L(\mu|\mathbf{x}, \sigma^2) = \{\sigma\sqrt{2\pi}\}^{-n} \exp\left\{-\frac{1}{2\sigma^2}\sum_{i=1}^{n}(x_i - \mu_0)^2\right\}.$$

For the denominator term of $\lambda(\mathbf{x})$, note that maximum over Θ occurs at the MLE $\bar{x}$, that is:

$$\sup_{\Theta} L(\mu|\mathbf{x}, \sigma^2) = \{\sigma\sqrt{2\pi}\}^{-n} \exp\left\{-\frac{1}{2\sigma^2}\sum_{i=1}^{n}(x_i - \bar{x})^2\right\}.$$

Thus, the likelihood ratio becomes

$$\lambda(x) = \exp\left\{-\frac{1}{2\sigma^2}\left(\sum_{i=1}^{n}(x_i - \mu_0)^2 - \sum_{i=1}^{n}(x_i - \bar{x})^2\right)\right\},$$
$$= \exp\left\{-\frac{1}{2\sigma^2}\left(n(\bar{x} - \mu_0)^2\right)\right\}.$$

The LR test procedure will be to reject H if $n(\bar{X} - \mu_0)^2/\sigma^2 > k$, that is, if the value of $|\bar{X} - \mu_0|$ is too large or too small. The value of k is determined by the size of the required test. The final form of the LR test is given by

$$\phi_{LR}(\mathbf{X}) = \begin{cases} 1, & \text{if } |\sqrt{n}(\bar{X} - \mu_0)/\sigma| > z_{\alpha/2}, \\ 0, & \text{otherwise.} \end{cases}$$

A small R function `LRNormalMean_KV` is given below:

```
> LRNormalMean_KV = function(x,mu0,alpha,sigma){
+ ifelse(abs(sqrt(length(x))*(mean(x)-mu0)/sigma)>qnorm(1-alpha/2),
+ "Reject Hypothesis H","Fail to Reject Hypothesis H")
+ }
```

The user may use this function to test for sample datasets of his choice. □

Example 7.13.3. Testing $H : \mu = \mu_0$ against $K : \mu \neq \mu_0$ when σ is unknown. Unlike the previous problem, here the the hypothesis H is composite, as σ is unknown. We will first begin with two quantities:

$$\hat{\sigma}^2 = \frac{\sum_{i=1}^n (x_i - \mu_0)^2}{n}, \tag{7.62}$$

$$\hat{\sigma}^{*2} = \frac{\sum_{i=1}^n (x_i - \bar{x})^2}{n}. \tag{7.63}$$

It can then be shown that

$$\sup_{\Theta_0} L(\mu|\mathbf{x}, \sigma) = \frac{1}{(\hat{\sigma}\sqrt{2\pi})^n} \exp(-n/2), \tag{7.64}$$

$$\sup_{\Theta} L(\mu|\mathbf{x}, \sigma) = \frac{1}{(\hat{\sigma}^*\sqrt{2\pi})^n} \exp(-n/2). \tag{7.65}$$

The likelihood ratio then becomes

$$\lambda(\mathbf{x}) = \left\{ \frac{\hat{\sigma}^{*2}}{\hat{\sigma}^2} \right\}^{n/2} = \left[1 + \frac{n(\bar{x} - \mu_0)^2}{\sum_{i=1}^{n} (x_i - \bar{x})^2} \right]^{-n/2}.$$

The test procedure is given by

$$\phi_{LR}(\mathbf{x}) = \begin{cases} 1, \text{ if } \frac{n(\bar{X}-\mu_0)^2}{\sum_{i=1}^n (X_i-\bar{X})^2} > k, \\ 0, \quad \text{otherwise,} \end{cases}$$

$$= \begin{cases} 1, \text{ if } |\sqrt{n}(\bar{X} - \mu_0)/S| > t_{n-1,\alpha/2}, \\ 0, \quad \text{otherwise,} \end{cases}$$

where S is the sampling variance. We close this example with the R function `LRNormalMean_UV`.

```
> LRNormalMean_UV <- function(x,mu0,alpha){
+ S <- sd(x); n <- length(x)
+ ifelse(abs(sqrt(length(x))*(mean(x)-mu0)/S)>qt(n-1,1-alpha/2),
+ "Reject Hypothesis H","Fail to Reject Hypothesis H")
+ }
```

Test the working of the likelihood ratio function `LRNormalMean_UV` on any dataset of your choice. □

Example 7.13.4. Testing $H : \sigma = \sigma_0$ against $K : \sigma \neq \sigma_0$ when both μ and σ are unknown. As in the previous example, the hypothesis H is composite here. Define the sample mean and variance by

$$\bar{X} = \frac{\sum_{i=1}^{n} X_i}{n},$$

$$S^2 = \frac{\sum_{i=1}^{n} (X_i - \bar{X})^2}{n-1}, n \geq 2.$$

Since the MLE of μ is $\bar{X}$, we have

$$\sup_{\Theta_0} L(\mu, \sigma^2) = \frac{1}{(\sigma_0 \sqrt{2\pi})^n} \exp\left\{ -\frac{\sum_{i=1}^{n} (x_i - \bar{x})^2}{2\sigma_0^2} \right\}.$$

Define $\hat{\sigma}^{*2}$, as in Equation 7.63. However, for Θ, we have

$$\sup_{\Theta} L(\mu, \sigma^2) = \frac{1}{(\hat{\sigma}^* \sqrt{2\pi})^n} \exp(-n/2).$$

Thus, the likelihood ratio is given by

$$\lambda(\mathbf{x}) = \left[\frac{\hat{\sigma}^{*2}}{\sigma_0^2} \exp\left\{ -\frac{\hat{\sigma}^{*2}}{\sigma_0^2} + 1 \right\} \right]^{n/2}.$$

The likelihood ratio test is finally given by

$$\phi_{LR}(\mathbf{x}) = \begin{cases} 1, \text{ if } \frac{\hat{\sigma}^{*2}}{\sigma_0^2} \exp\left\{ 1 - \frac{\hat{\sigma}^{*2}}{\sigma_0^2} \right\} > k, \\ 0, \qquad \text{otherwise}, \end{cases}$$

$$= \begin{cases} 1, \quad \text{if } \frac{(n-1)S^2}{\sigma_0^2} < \chi^2_{n-1,\alpha/2}, \\ \qquad \text{or } \frac{(n-1)S^2}{\sigma_0^2} > \chi^2_{n-1,1-\alpha/2}, \\ 0, \qquad \text{otherwise}. \end{cases} \tag{7.66}$$

The R function `LRNormalVariance_UM` closes the example.

```
> LRNormalVariance_UM <- function(x,sigma0,alpha){
+     S <- var(x); n <- length(x)
+     chidata <- ((n-1)*S)/(sigma0^2)
+     ifelse((chidata<qchisq(df=n-1,p=alpha/2)||
+     (chidata>qchisq(df=n-1,p=1-alpha/2))),
+     "Reject Hypothesis H","Fail to Reject Hypothesis H")
+ }
```

Thus, using the `LRNormalVariance_UM` function, the likelihood ratio test in the case of the unknown variance can be carried out. □

7.13.2 Normal Distribution: Two-Sample Problem for the Mean

As in the previous subsection, we will only consider the testing problem related to means. A very brief summary is given here.

The general problem is described as follows. Let $X_{11}, \cdots, X_{1n_1}$ be a random sample from $N(\mu_1, \sigma^2)$, and $X_{21}, \cdots, X_{2n_2}$ a random sample from $N(\mu_2, \sigma^2)$. Assume that all the three parameters μ_1, μ_2, and σ^2 are unknown. For a specified level α, the aim is to obtain the likelihood ratio test for testing $H : \mu_1 = \mu_2$ against $K : \mu_1 \neq \mu_2$. Define the following quantities:

$$\bar{X}_i = \frac{\sum_{j=1}^{n_i} X_{ij}}{n_i}, i = 1, 2, \tag{7.67}$$

$$S_i^2 = \frac{\sum_{j=1}^{n_i} (X_{ij} - \bar{X}_i)^2}{n_i - 1}, i = 1, 2, \tag{7.68}$$

$$S_p^2 = \frac{(n_1 - 1)S_1^2 + (n_2 - 1)S_2^2}{n_1 + n_2 - 2}. \tag{7.69}$$

The size α likelihood ratio test for H against K is given by

$$\phi_{LR}(\mathbf{x}) = \begin{cases} 1, \text{ if } \frac{|\bar{X}_1 - \bar{X}_2|}{\sqrt{1/n_1 + 1/n_2 S_p}} > t_{n_1+n_2-2, \alpha/2}, \\ 0, \quad \text{otherwise.} \end{cases} \tag{7.70}$$

The next R function, `LRNormal2Mean`, with an illustration, gives the likelihood ratio test.

```
> LRNormal2Mean <- function(x,y,alpha){
+      xbar <- mean(x); ybar <- mean(y)
+      nx <- length(x); ny <- length(y)
+      Sx <- var(x); Sy <- var(y)
+      Sp <- ((nx-1)*Sx+(ny-1)*Sy)/(nx+ny-2)
+      tcalc <- abs(xbar-ybar)/sqrt(Sp*(1/nx+1/ny))
+      conclusion=ifelse(tcalc>qt(df=nx+ny-2,p=alpha/2),
+ "Reject Hypothesis H","Fail to Reject Hypothesis H")
+      return(c(tcalc,conclusion,Sp))
+ }
> lisa <- c(234.26, 237.18, 238.16, 259.53, 242.76, 237.81,
+ 250.95, 277.83)
> mike <- c(187.73, 206.08, 176.71, 213.69, 224.34, 235.24)
> LRNormal2Mean(mike,lisa,0.05)
[1] "4.06112227911276"        "Reject Hypothesis H"
+ "332.808456944444"
```

To the best of our knowledge, R does not have an implementation for the likelihood ratio test.

?qnorm, ?qchisq, ?ifelse

7.14 Behrens-Fisher Problem

In the two-sample problems for normal distributions considered earlier, the problem of testing $H : \mu_1 = \mu_2$ against $K : \mu_1 \neq \mu_2$, when σ_1 and σ_2 are unknown and distinct, has not been considered. There has been a special reason for this. It has been proved by Linnik (1968) in this case that the UMPU test does not exist and there has been a lot of controversy surrounding the solutions proposed to date and it is even today an *open problem*.

The problem was first attempted by Behrens in 1929 and by Fisher in 1935. Kim and Cohen (1995) provide an excellent review of the solutions proposed by various statisticians. Schéffe (1943), Aspin (1948), Lindley (1965), Robinson (1976), and Welch (1938, 1947) are some of the important works in this direction.

Suppose that we have n_1 observations from $N(\mu_1, \sigma_1^2)$ and n_2 observations from $N(\mu_2, \sigma_2^2)$. As earlier, let $\bar{X}_1, \bar{X}_2, S_1^2, S_2^2, S_p^2$ denote the sample means, variances, and pooled variance. The Student's t-test pivotal statistic with $n_1 + n_2 - 2$ degrees of freedom is given by

$$t = \frac{\bar{X}_1 - \bar{X}_2}{\sqrt{1/n_1 + 1/n_2 S_p}}.$$

However, the Student's t-test procedure makes the assumption of the variances being equal. Thus, the use of the t-test is inappropriate here. An *ad-hoc* solution is the following. Compute t^* by

$$t^* = \frac{\bar{X}_1 - \bar{X}_2}{\sqrt{S_1^2/n_1 + S_2^2/n_2}},$$

and compare it with the critical value obtained from a t variable with $\min(n_1 - 1, n_2 - 1)$ degrees of freedom. For a dataset from Kim and Cohen's review paper, an R program is given next.

```
> adhocBF <- function(x,y,delta,alpha){
+   tstar <- (delta-mean(y)+mean(x))/sqrt(var(x)/length(x)+var(y)/
+ length(y))
+   v <- min(length(x)-1,length(y)-1)
+   pval <- 2*(1-pt(tstar,v))
+   confint <- c(mean(y)-mean(x)-qt(1-alpha/2,v)
+ *sqrt(var(x)/length(x)+
+   var(y)/length(y)),mean(y)-mean(x)+qt(1-alpha/2,v)*
+   sqrt(var(x)/length(x)+var(y)/length(y)))
+   return(list=c(tstar,pval,confint))
+ }
> x <- c(8,10,12,15)
> y <- c(1,7,11)
> adhocBF(x,y,delta=0,alpha=0.05)
[1]   1.5049258   0.2712717 -18.9736452   9.1403119
```

A more satisfactory solution for the Behrens-Fisher problem is given by Welch and we will discuss his solution with an R program.

Compute the value of test statistic t as the same given by t^*. Define $g_i = S_i^2/n_i, i = 1, 2$. Define

$$\hat{\upsilon} = \frac{(g_1 + g_2)^2}{g_1^2/(n_1 - 1) + g_2^2/(n_2 - 1)} \tag{7.71}$$

The Welch solution is to carry out the test by using the value t^* and comparing it with a t random variate with $\hat{\upsilon}$ degrees of freedom. As may be expected, in general $\hat{\upsilon}$ is not an integer. In such a case we round off the value to the nearest integer.

```
> WelchBF <- function(x,y,alpha){
+      gx <- var(x); gy <- var(y)
+      t <- (mean(x)-mean(y))/sqrt(gx/length(x)+gy/length(y))
+      vhat <- (gx+gy)^2/(gx^2/(length(x)-1) + gy^2/(length(y)-1))
+      pval <- 2*(1-pt(t,round(vhat)))
+      ci <- qt(c(alpha/2,1-alpha/2),round(vhat))
+      return(list=c(t,pval,ci))
+ }
> WelchBF(x,y,alpha=0.05)
[1]  1.5049258  0.2294048 -3.1824463  3.1824463
```

For more details related to the Behrens-Fisher problem, refer to the review article of Kim and Cohen.

?qt

7.15 Multiple Comparison Tests

Consider the following hypothesis:

$$H : \theta_1 = \theta_2 = \cdots = \theta_s = 0. \tag{7.72}$$

Here, we have a set of hypotheses to be tested and this framework is popularly known as the *multiple comparision test*. Such hypotheses are very common in Experimental Designs, see Chapter 15. Suppose that $\theta_i, i = 1, 2, \cdots, s$, denotes the mean yield due to the i-th treatment. In its general setup, the hypothesis says that none of the treatment means are significant. In case we fail to reject H, the conclusion is indeed that none of the treatment means are significant and the analysis stops. However, if we reject the hypothesis H, a host of questions then arise. In this case, the conclusion says that at least one treatment is significant and the interest is then to identify such a treatment. A slight variant of the problem is testing to some pre-specified level, which is generally known as the mean of the *control* treatment.

Let us begin with a naive approach. That is, we consider s hypotheses instead of a single hypothesis and consider the problem of testing $H_i : \theta_i = 0, i = 1, \cdots, s$. Suppose each hypothesis is tested at level α. A simple exploration shows the dire consequence of this naive approach. The forthcoming program will show that the probability of one or more false rejections increases drastically with s.

```
> n <- c(1,2,5,10,50)
> alpha <- 0.05
```

```
> prob_rejection <- function(n,alpha) (1-(1-alpha)^{n})
> round(sapply(n,prob_rejection,alpha),2)
[1] 0.05 0.10 0.23 0.40 0.92
```

That is, the Type I error grows very fast and with $s = 50$, we are almost certain of having committed the error. This motivates the next definition.

Definition 7.15.1 Family-wise Error Rate. *Consider a family of hypotheses $H_i : \theta_i \in \Theta_i$. Then, the Family-wise Error Rate, abbreviated as* FWER, *is defined as the probability of one or more false rejections of the hypotheses. In symbols, if V is the number of false rejections among the s hypotheses, then*

$$FWER = P(V \geq 1). \tag{7.73}$$

The goal of the multiple testing problem is to restrict the *FWER* to a pre-specified level α:

$$FWER \leq \alpha. \tag{7.74}$$

In the next section we will focus on two simple, yet useful, procedures for the multiple testing problem.

7.15.1 Bonferroni's Method

The Bonferroni's method is a simple consequence of using the *Bonferroni inequality*. Let $\hat{p}_i$ be the *p*-value associated with hypothesis $H_i, i = 1, \cdots, s$. Then reject the family of hypotheses $H_i, i = 1, \cdots, s$ if $\hat{p}_i \leq \alpha/s$, for any $i = 1, \cdots, s$. It may be easily verified is this case that

$$FWER \leq \alpha.$$

An illustration will be provided for the example provided in R.

Example 7.15.1. Bonferroni's Method for Testing if Ozone depends on the Month. Consider the `airquality` dataset from the `datasets` package. The data is available on the ozone levels measured in parts per billion from 1300 to 1500 hours at Roosevelt Island, and Month variable denotes the month number. The problem is to test if the ozone level depends on the month number.

```
> data(airquality)
> boxplot(airquality$Ozone ~ airquality$Month) # Output suppressed
> airquality$Month <- factor(airquality$Month)
> pairwise.t.test(airquality$Ozone,airquality$Month, p.adj = "bonf")
 Pairwise comparisons using t tests with pooled SD
data:  airquality$Ozone and airquality$Month
  5       6       7       8
6 1.00000 -       -       -
7 0.00029 0.10225 -       -
8 0.00019 0.08312 1.00000 -
9 1.00000 1.00000 0.00697 0.00485
> pairwise.t.test(airquality$Ozone, airquality$Month,
+ p.adj = "bonf")$p. value<=0.05/10
```

```
        5     6     7    8
6 FALSE    NA    NA   NA
7  TRUE FALSE    NA   NA
8  TRUE FALSE FALSE   NA
9 FALSE FALSE FALSE TRUE
```

Using the `pairwise.t.test` function with the option `p.adj="bonf"`, the multiple hypotheses can be tested using the Bonferroni solution in R. Since some p-values are less than α/s, we reject the family of hypotheses. □

7.15.2 Holm's Method

Consider the ordered p-values $\hat{p}_{(1)} \leq \cdots \leq \hat{p}_{(s)}$ and let the associated hypotheses be $H_{(1)}, \cdots, H_{(s)}$. The *Holm* procedure is a *stepdown* procedure and is described below, adapted from page 351 of Lehmann and Romano (2005).

Step 1. If $\hat{p}_{(1)} \geq \alpha/s$, accept $H_1, \cdots, H_s$ and stop. If $\hat{p}_{(1)} < \alpha/s$, reject $H_{(1)}$ and test the remaining $s-1$ hypotheses at level $\alpha/(s-1)$.
Step 2. If $\hat{p}_{(2)} \geq \alpha/(s-1)$ with $\hat{p}_{(1)} < \alpha/s$, accept $H_{(2)}, \cdots, H_{(s)}$ and stop. If $\hat{p}_{(1)} < \alpha/s$ and $\hat{p}_{(2)} < \alpha/(s-1)$, reject $H_{(1)}$ and $H_{(2)}$ and test the remaining $s-2$ hypotheses at level $\alpha/(s-2)$.
Step 3. Continue the steps until $H_{(s)}$.

For proof that the Holm's method meets the requirement $FWER \leq \alpha$, see Theorem 9.1.2 of Lehmann and Romano (2005). We will close the discussion with an example.

Example 7.15.2. Bonferroni's Method for Testing if Ozone depends on the Month. Contd. In continuation of the previous example, we now investigate similar hypotheses for the Holm's method. The reader should pay more attention to the R program.

```
> pairwise.t.test(airquality$Ozone, airquality$Month, p.adj = "holm")
+ $p. value
             5          6           7           8
6 1.0000000000         NA          NA          NA
7 0.0002638036 0.05112741          NA          NA
8 0.0001949061 0.04987333 1.000000000          NA
9 1.0000000000 1.00000000 0.004878798 0.003878108
> holmmat <- pairwise.t.test(airquality$Ozone,
+ airquality$Month, p.adj = "holm")$p. value
> holmmat[lower.tri(holmmat,diag=TRUE)]<(0.05/(1:10))
 [1] FALSE  TRUE  TRUE FALSE FALSE FALSE FALSE FALSE  TRUE  TRUE
```

Using the `pairwise.t.test` function with the option `p.adj="bonf"`, the multiple hypotheses is tested with the Holm solution in R. The same conclusion is reached as in the previous example. □

?pairwise.t.test

7.16 The EM Algorithm*

7.16.1 Introduction

The Expectation-Maximization Algorithm, more popularly known as the EM algorithm, is a very popular tool, not only among the statisticians, but also among the data miners. Wu and Kumar (2009) have selected the EM algorithm as one among the top ten useful algorithms for data miners. McLachlan and Krishnan (1998, 2008) give a rigorous mathematical introduction with a large number of illustrations of the EM algorithm. Little and Rubin (1987, 2002) is also one of the earliest books to give a detailed account of the algorithm. Dempster, Laird, and Rubin (1977) introduced the breakthrough EM algorithm and enhanced statistical methods which can accommodate missing data. This paper is also popularly referred to as the **DLR** paper. The introductory literature has so far been in reversed chronological order.

It is important to understand that the EM algorithm is not really an algorithm in the traditional usage of the technical word "algorithm". It is a generic tool which gives rise to different statistical methods depending on the context of the application. Ripley in a reply to an R user has rightly explained this de facto as "The EM algorithm is not an algorithm for solving problems, rather an algorithm for creating statistical methods."

In the context of handling missing data, Schafer (2000) has rightly said that "The key ideas behind EM and data augmentation are the same: to solve a difficult incomplete-data problem by repeatedly solving tractable complete-data problems." Terry Speed (2008) has also said this about the EM algorithm: "I know many statisticians are deeply in love with the EM algorithm."

"EMMIX" is probably one of the few softwares which implements the EM algorithm for the mixture of multivariate normal or t- distribution.

7.16.2 The Algorithm

In general, the EM algorithm is stated in two steps: the E-step and the M-step. We will begin with a description as given in McLachlan and Krishnan (2008). Let $\mathbf{Y}$ be a random vector and $\mathbf{y}$ be its observed value. The sample space of $\mathbf{Y}$ is denoted by $\Omega_{\mathbf{Y}}$. We will denote the pdf of $\mathbf{Y}$ by $g(\mathbf{y}, \theta)$, where $\theta = (\theta_1, \cdots, \theta_d)^T \in \Theta_Y$ is the vector of unknown parameters.

To make use of the EM algorithm, we will always pretend that $\mathbf{y}$ is *incomplete* in the sense that the experiment consists of some values which we treat as *missing data*. That is, we will assume that we have missing data in $\mathbf{z}$, and if this is augmented with $\mathbf{y}$, we will have the complete data in $\mathbf{x} = \{\mathbf{y}, \mathbf{z}\}$. Let $\Omega_{\mathbf{X}}$ denote the sample space of $\mathbf{X}$.

The pdf of the complete observation $\mathbf{x}$ will be denoted by $g_c(\mathbf{x}, \theta)$. Thus, under the assumption that $\mathbf{x}$ is completely observed, the log-likelihood of $\mathbf{x}$ is given by

$$\ln L_c(\theta|\mathbf{x}) = \ln g_c(x, \theta). \tag{7.75}$$

Clearly, as the sample space of the $\mathbf{x}$'s is larger than the $\mathbf{y}$'s, we have a many-to-one mapping from $\mathcal{X}$ to $\mathcal{Y}$. Thus, the observed data can be written as the function $\mathbf{y} = \mathbf{y}(\mathbf{x})$. Hence, we have the relationship

$$g(\mathbf{y}, \theta) = \int_{\Omega_X(y)} g_c(\mathbf{x}, \theta).d\mathbf{x}$$

Assume that we have an initial value as an estimate of θ in $\theta^{(0)}$. Using the observed data $\mathbf{y}$ and $\theta^{(0)}$, we next specify the conditional probability distribution of $g_c(\mathbf{x}|\mathbf{y}, \theta^{(0)})$. Since the complete data log-likelihood $\ln g_c(\mathbf{x}, \theta)$ is not observable, we will replace it by its conditional expectation given $\mathbf{y}$ and $\theta^{(0)}$. This conditional expectation is the famous *Q-function* defined by

$$Q(\theta|\theta^{(0)}) = \int_{\mathcal{X}(\mathbf{y})} \ln L_c(\theta|\mathbf{x}) g_c(\mathbf{x}|\mathbf{y}, \theta^{(0)}) d\mathbf{x}. \tag{7.76}$$

This is the famous *E-step* of the EM algorithm. In the M-step, we maximize $Q(\theta|\theta^{(0)})$ to obtain $\theta^{(1)}$ such that

$$Q(\theta^{(1)}|\theta^{(0)}) \geq Q(\theta|\theta^{(0)}). \tag{7.77}$$

Thus, the EM algorithm can be summarized as below:

- **E-Stem:** Calculate $Q(\theta|\theta^{(k)})$, where

$$Q(\theta|\theta^{(k)}) = E_{\theta^{(k)}}\{\ln g_c(\theta)|\mathbf{y}\}. \tag{7.78}$$

- **M-Step:** Select any value $\theta^{(k+1)}$ of $\theta \in \Theta_Y$, such that

$$Q(\theta^{(k+1)}|\theta^{(k)}) \geq Q(\theta|\theta^{(k)}), \forall \theta \in \Theta_Y. \tag{7.79}$$

The convergence criteria for the EM algorithm is that the difference $L(\theta^{(k+1)} - \theta^{(k)})$ should be approximately 0. This explanation of the EM algorithm in two steps can be found almost everywhere. However, we have found the five steps detail of the EM algorithm by Gupta and Chen (2011) to be more friendly and despite a repetition of the above content, we will state it here.

1. Set $k = 0$ and obtain an initial estimate for θ as $\theta^{(0)}$.
2. Assume that $\theta^{(k)}$ as the truth and using the observed data $\mathbf{y}$, completely specify the conditional probability distribution $g_c(\mathbf{x}|\mathbf{y}, \theta^{(k)})$ for the complete data $\mathbf{x}$.
3. Obtain the conditional expected log-likelihood Q-function:

$$Q(\theta|\theta^{(k)}) = E_{\theta^{(k)}}\{\ln g_c(\theta)|\mathbf{y}\}.$$

4. Find $\theta^{(k+1)}$, which maximizes $Q(\theta|\theta^{(k)})$.
5. Set $k := k + 1$ and go to the first step.

We understand that the EM algorithm is best illustrated through applications.

7.16.3 Introductory Applications

We will consider problems which have been widely used illustrating the EM algorithm.

Example 7.16.1. The Multinomial Distribution. Consider an observation from a multinomial distribution, say $\mathbf{y}$, that is, we have

$$\mathbf{y} = (y_1, y_2, y_3, y_4).$$

Suppose that the probability vector associated with the multinomial distribution is specified by

$$\mathbf{p} = \left(\frac{1}{2} + \frac{p}{4}, \frac{1}{4}(1-p), \frac{1}{4}(1-p), \frac{p}{4}\right), 0 \leq p \leq 1.$$

A popular dataset in the context of a multinomial distribution is $\mathbf{y} = (125, 18, 20, 34)$. This example has been used in Rao (1973), DLR, and McLachlan and Krishnan (1998, 2008), among many other researchers. The goal of the problem is estimation of p based on the observed data $\mathbf{y}$. The probability mass function, $g(y, p)$, is then given by

$$g(y,p) = \frac{n!}{y_1!y_2!y_3!y_4!}\left(\frac{1}{2}+\frac{p}{4}\right)^{y_1}\left(\frac{1}{4}(1-p)\right)^{y_2}\left(\frac{1}{4}(1-p)\right)^{y_3}\left(\frac{p}{4}\right)^{y_4}.$$

Thus, the log-likelihood function, sans the constant terms, may be written as

$$\ln L(p) = y_1 \ln(2+p) + (y_2+y_3)\ln(1-p) + y_4 \ln(p).$$

It is important to note that the score function for the above log-likelihood function can be solved explicitly for obtaining the MLE $\hat{\theta}$. Let us use the MLE technique seen in the Section 7.6.

```
> y <- c(125, 18, 20, 34)
> logl <- function(p)  {
+   y[1]*log(2+p)+(y[2]+y[3])*log(1-p)+y[4]*log(p)
+   }
> optimize(logl,c(0,1),maximum=TRUE)
$maximum
[1] 0.6268298
$objective
[1] 67.3841
```

However, we will treat this problem as a missing data problem. In the original formulation we have four cells. The first cell with probability $\frac{1}{2}+\frac{p}{4}$ can be split into two sub-cells with probabilities $\frac{1}{2}$ and $\frac{p}{4}$, and we will denote the frequencies of these two cells by y_{11} and y_{12}, which will meet the requirement $y_1 = y_{11} + y_{12}$. Define the complete data vector as

$$\mathbf{x} = (y_{11}, y_{12}, y_2, y_3, y_4).$$

The multinomial cell probabilities for $\mathbf{x}$ are then specified by

$$\mathbf{p}' = \left(\frac{1}{2}, \frac{p}{4}, \frac{1}{4}(1-p), \frac{1}{4}(1-p), \frac{\theta}{4}\right), 0 \le p \le 1.$$

and the log-likelihood function for the complete data vector is

$$\ln L_c(p) \propto (y_{12}+y_4)\ln p + (y_2+y_3)\ln(1-p).$$

Using the score function of the above log-likelihood, we can obtain the MLE as

$$\hat{p}_c = \frac{y_{12}+y_4}{y_{12}+y_2+y_3+y_4}.$$

We have used $\hat{p}_c$ to represent the ML estimator based on the complete data. However, we cannot straightaway compute it, as y_{12} is not observed. This sets up room for the EM algorithm. The E-step will help in obtaining an estimate of the missing data (y_{11}, y_{12}), and the M-step will update the estimate of the parameters.

In the E-step, we recognize that as the probability distribution of the complete data vector **X** is a multinomial distribution, conditional on **y**, y_{12} has a binomial distribution with probability

$$\frac{1/2}{\left(\frac{1}{2}+\frac{p^{(k)}}{4}\right)},$$

where $p^{(k)}$ is the estimate at the iteration k. Thus, the k-th iteration estimate of y_{12} is given by

$$y_{12}^{(k)} = \frac{y_1/2}{\left(\frac{1}{2}+\frac{p^{(k)}}{4}\right)} = \frac{2y_1}{2+p^{(k)}}, \tag{7.80}$$

and for y_{11} it is simply

$$y_{11}^{(k)} = y_1 - y_{12}^{(k)}.$$

It is further easier to see that an estimate of p, for the M-step, is given by

$$p^{(k+1)} = \frac{y_{12}^{(k)} + y_4}{n - y_{11}^{(k)}} = \frac{\frac{2y_1}{2+p^{(k)}} + y_4}{\frac{2y_1}{2+p^{(k)}} + y_2 + y_3 + y_4}. \tag{7.81}$$

An R program which implements the E- and M-step detailed above is given next.

```
> p0 <- 0.5
> estep <- function(y,p0){
+         temp <- c(2*y[1]/(2+p0),p0*y[1]/(2+p0),y[2],y[3],y[4])
+         return(temp)
+ }
> emconvergence <- function(y,p0){
+         pold <- p0
+         pnew <- p0+0.5
+         while(abs(pnew-pold)>0.0000000001){
+         pold <- p0
+         x <- estep(y,p0) # E-Step
+         pnew <- (p0*y[1]/(2+p0)+y[4])/(p0*y[1]/(2+p0)+y[2]+y[3]+y[4])
+         # M-Step
+         p0 <- pnew
+    }
+         return(pnew)
+ }
> pmle <- emconvergence(y,p0)
> pmle
[1] 0.6268215
```

Note that in the `estep` function, the small piece of code `2*y[1]/(2+p0)` implements the E-step as required in Equation 7.80. Similarly, the code on the right-hand side of the line `pnew` clearly captures the M-step given in Equation 7.81. The `while` loop ensures convergence up to the required accuracy. The ML estimate `0.6268215` in the EM algorithm is closer to the one obtained using the `optimize` function, as seen earlier. □

Example 7.16.2. Application of Multinomial Distribution in Genetics. A very interesting application of the multinomial distribution occurs in *genetics*. Rao (1973), DLR, and McLachlan and Krishnan (1998, 2008), Monahan (2011), and many other texts discuss this application at great length. The problem is estimation of gene frequencies of blood antigens A and B by observing four main blood groups AB, A, B, O. Let p and q respectively denote gene frequencies A and B. Let $\boldsymbol{\pi} = (\pi_1, \pi_2, \pi_3, \pi_4)$ be the probabilities of the group AB, A, B, O. As the sampling mechanism here is with replacement, the cell probabilities are obtained in the following way:

$$\pi_1 = P(AB) = (pq) + (qp) = 2pq,$$
$$\pi_2 = P(A) = p(2 - p - 2q),$$
$$\pi_3 = P(B) = q(2 - q - 2p),$$
$$\pi_4 = P(O) = (1 - p - q)(1 - q - p) = (1 - p - q)^2.$$

Symbolically, we have conveyed how we get π_1 and π_4. It is an exercise for the reader to similarly derive the other two probabilities. Of course, if you get π_3, π_2 follows by symmetry. The parameters of interest in this problem is of course $\boldsymbol{\theta} = (p, q)$. Also, define $r = 1 - p - q$. The observed data is $\mathbf{y} = (n_{AB}, n_A, n_B, n_O) = (17, 182, 60, 176)$. The log-likelihood function is then given by

$$\ln L(\boldsymbol{\theta}) = 2n_O \ln(1 - p - q) + n_A \ln p(2 - p - 2q) + n_B \ln q(2 - q - 2p) + n_{AB} \ln 2pq.$$

Equivalently, the log-likelihood can be written in terms of $\boldsymbol{\pi}$ as

$$\ln L(\boldsymbol{\theta}) = n_O \ln \pi_4 + n_A \ln \pi_2 + n_B \ln \pi_3 + n_{AB} \ln \pi_1.$$

In terms of $\boldsymbol{\theta}$, the log-likelihood does not admit closed-form expression and we will introduce a new framework which will help in deployment of the EM algorithm. Define the *complete-data* vector by

$$\mathbf{x} = (n_O, \mathbf{z}')'$$

where $\mathbf{z} = (n_{AA}, n_{AO}, n_{BB}, n_{BO})'$ represents the missing data corresponding to the frequencies $n_{AA}, n_{AO}, n_{BB},$ and n_{BO}. In Table 7.5, we present cells and their corresponding frequencies.

Table 7.5 Multinomial Distribution in Genetics

Original Problem			Modified for EM Algorithm		
Category	Cell Probability	Observed Frequency	Category	Cell Probability	Observed Frequency
O	r^2	n_O	O	r^2	n_O
A	$p^2 + 2pr$	n_A	AA	p^2	n_{AA}
B	$q^2 + 2qr$	n_B	AO	$2pr$	n_{AO}
AB	$2pq$	n_{AB}	B	q^2	n_{BB}
			BO	$2qr$	n_{BO}
			AB	$2pq$	n_{AB}

The complete data log-likelihood function is then given by

$$\begin{aligned}
\ln L_c(p,q) &= 2n_O \ln r + 2n_{AA} \ln p + n_{AO} \ln p + n_{AO} \ln r \\
&+ 2n_{BB} \ln q + n_{BO} \ln q + n_{BO} \ln r + n_{AB} \ln p + n_{AB} \ln q \\
&= 2\left(n_{AA} + \frac{n_{AO}}{2} + \frac{n_{AB}}{2}\right) \ln p + 2\left(n_{BB} + \frac{n_{BO}}{2} + \frac{n_{AB}}{2}\right) \ln q \\
&+ 2\left(n_O + \frac{n_{AO}}{2} + \frac{n_{BO}}{2}\right) \ln r \\
&= 2n_A^+ \ln p + 2n_B^+ \ln q + 2n_O^+ \ln r,
\end{aligned}$$

where $n_A^+ = n_{AA} + \frac{n_{AO}}{2} + \frac{n_{AB}}{2}$, $n_B^+ = n_{BB} + \frac{n_{BO}}{2} + \frac{n_{AB}}{2}$, and $n_O^+ = n_O + \frac{n_{AO}}{2} + \frac{n_{BO}}{2}$.

The E- and M-step unfold as follows. In the E step, we find the missing data by using the current conditional expectation of the sufficient statistic of $\boldsymbol{\theta}$, which is essentially n_A^+ and n_B^+. To obtain them, assume that the current estimate of $\boldsymbol{\theta} = (p, q)$ is available in the form of $\boldsymbol{\theta}^k = (p^k, q^k)$. Note that the computation of n_A^+ and n_B^+ requires values on the unobserved data $n_{AA}, n_{AO}, n_{BB},$ and, n_{BO}. Consider the first element n_{AA}. Now, conditional on the observed data $\mathbf{y}$, n_{AA} has a binomial distribution with sample size n_A and probability given by

$$\frac{p^{(k)2}}{p^{(k)2} + 2p^{(k)}r^{(k)}},$$

where (k) denotes the current iteration. That is, current conditional expectation of n_{AA} given $\mathbf{y}$ is

$$E_{\boldsymbol{\theta}^{(k)}}\{n_{AA}\} = n_{AA}^k = n_A \frac{p^{(k)2}}{p^{(k)2} + 2p^{(k)}r^{(k)}}. \tag{7.82}$$

Similarly, the following may be verified:

$$E_{\boldsymbol{\theta}^{(k)}}\{n_{AO}\} = n_{AO}^k = \frac{2n_A p^{(k)} r^{(k)}}{p^{(k)2} + 2p^{(k)}r^{(k)}}, \tag{7.83}$$

$$E_{\boldsymbol{\theta}^{(k)}}\{n_{BB}\} = n_{BB}^k = n_B \frac{q^{(k)2}}{q^{(k)2} + 2q^{(k)}r^{(k)}}, \tag{7.84}$$

$$E_{\boldsymbol{\theta}^{(k)}}\{n_{BO}\} = n_{BO}^k = \frac{2n_B q^{(k)} r^{(k)}}{q^{(k)2} + 2q^{(k)}r^{(k)}}. \tag{7.85}$$

Then, the M step consists of the following:

$$p^{(k+1)} = \frac{n_{AA}^{(k)} + n_{AO}^{(k)}/2 + n_{AB}/2}{n}, \tag{7.86}$$

$$q^{(k+1)} = \frac{n_{BB}^{(k)} + n_{BO}^{(k)}/2 + n_{AB}/2}{n}, \tag{7.87}$$

$$r^{(k+1)} = 1 - p^{(k+1)} - q^{(k+1)}. \tag{7.88}$$

The following R program for the first five iterations of the EM algorithm gives the solution for the problem on hand.

```
> y <- c(176,182,60,17)
> n <- sum(y)
> p0 <- 0.26399
> q0 <- 0.09299
> r0 <- 1-p0-q0
> log_lik=n_aa=n_ao=n_bb=n_bo=p_new=q_new=r_new=NULL
> for(i in 1:5){
+      log_lik[i] <- 2*y[1]*log(r0)+y[2]*log(p0^{2}+2*p0*r0)+y[3]
+         *log(q0^{2}+2*q0*r0)+y[4]*log(2*p0*q0)
+      n_aa[i] <- y[2]*p0^{2}/(p0^{2}+2*p0*r0)
+      n_ao[i] <- (2*y[2]*p0*r0)/(p0^{2}+2*p0*r0)
+      n_bb[i] <- y[3]*q0^{2}/(q0^{2}+2*q0*r0)
+      n_bo[i] <- (2*y[3]*q0*r0)/(q0^{2}+2*q0*r0)
+      p_new[i] <- (n_aa[i]+n_ao[i]/2+y[4]/2)/n
+      q_new[i] <- (n_bb[i]+n_bo[i]/2+y[4]/2)/n
+      r_new[i] <- 1-p_new[i]-q_new[i]
+      p0 <- p_new[i];q0 <- q_new[i];r0 <- 1-p0-q0
+ }
> p_new;q_new;r_new;log_lik
[1] 0.2643643 0.2644311 0.2644422 0.2644440 0.2644443
[1] 0.09315619 0.09316760 0.09316866 0.09316879 0.09316881
[1] 0.6424795 0.6424013 0.6423892 0.6423872 0.6423869
[1] -492.5360 -492.5353 -492.5353 -492.5353 -492.5353
```

The vector objects n_aa, n_ao, n_bb, and n_bo are related with the computations for the E-step, as given in the system of Equations 7.82–7.85, while p_new, q_new, and r_new deal with the M-steps given in Equations 7.86–7.88. The rest of the program is simpler to follow. The results may be verified with Table 2.8 of McLachlan and Krishnan (1998, 2008). □

?optimize

7.17 Further Reading

7.17.1 Early Classics

Fisher! In the 1920s, Sir R.A. Fisher wrote a series of ground-breaking papers on inference. Fisher (1925-1954) has given a first account on what should form the fundamentals of inference. Kendall and Stuart (1945–79) is one of the earliest and rigorous development of inference. Cramér's (1946) book is one of the landmarks for inference. Lehmann (1958) gave a detailed account related to testing of hypotheses. Rao (1965–73) is one of the all-time classics and goes beyond the "linear" indicated in its title. Wilks (1962), Zacks (1971), and Cox and Hinkley (1973) are some of the other rigorous books on statistical inference.

Let us now look at some of the earlier books which introduce the subject at an elementary level. Snedecor and Cochran (1937–89) may have been the first book on "Statistical Methods". Mood, et al. (1950–74) is one of the earliest, elegant and elementary introduction to statistics. Hoel, et al. (1971), Hogg and Craig (1978), Hogg and Tanis (1977), and DeGroot and Schervish (2012), are also some of the best books written at their level.

In the Indian subcontinent, Das (1996) and Goon, et al. (1963) have written very useful texts.

7.17.2 *Texts from the Last 30 Years*

We do not intend to retain the chronological year of publication and jot down the texts which readily come to mind. As seen, chapter, Mukhopadhyay (2000), Rohatgi and Saleh (2000), and Casella and Berger (2000) have influenced this chapter a lot. Pawitan (2001) has been freely used for illustration of many concepts. Geisser and Johnson (2006) is a very compact work and will be useful to brush up on the details for an expert. Sen, et al. (2009) is a very concise course on the recent topics in inference. Wasserman (2004) is an advanced text which the reader will find useful for the modern development of the subject. Keener (2010), Dekking, et al. (2005), Liese and Miescke (2008), Knight (2000), Schervish (1995), and Shao (2003) are some of the finest written texts.

McLachlan and Krishnan (2008) is the first book to detail the EM algorithm. Huber and Ronchetti (2009) deals with the *robustness* of inference tools. As with the bibliography section of Chapter 5, we have again repeated a futile exercise.

7.18 Complements, Problems, and Programs

Problem 7.1 For different values of μ, obtain a plot of the curved normal family.

Problem 7.2 Italicize the y-axis label in the `expression` part in Example 7.3.1.

Problem 7.3 Find a sufficient statistic for λ when $X \sim Pois(\lambda)$.

Problem 7.4 Suppose X follows a negative binomial distribution with parameters as defined in Equation 6.20. Assume that for obtaining $r = 6$ failures, x is noted as 10. Obtain the likelihood function plot and then graphically infer about the ML estimate of p.

Problem 7.5 In a directory on a particular folder of a hard disk drive, there are $N = 50$ files. Suppose that in a random selection of $n = 12$ files, 9 are observed to be e-books. Under the assumption of a hypergeometric distribution, and by using the likelihood function approach, give the ML estimate of m. Check Equation 6.30 if required to complete the R program.

Problem 7.6 For the two likelihood functions of the multinomial distribution in Examples 7.9.1 and 7.9.2, plot the likelihood function for obtaining the ML estimates.

Problem 7.7 Section 7.6 makes use of the function `optimize` and `mle` to obtain the ML estimate. Will these techniques, return the ML estimate for the parameters in the previous two examples? If the technique fails, test across values of the parameters and data, what may be the reason behind it?

Problem 7.8 Using the Fishers score function technique, obtain the ML estimate in the previous three examples.

Problem 7.9 For the `galton` dataset from `UsingR` package, what will be the conclusion of the MP test that the height of the child is $H : \mu = 68$ against $K : \mu = 75$, given that variance is known to be 1.7873.

Problem 7.10 If the variance is unknown in the previous example, carry out the likelihood-ratio test, see `LRNormalMean_UV`, and draw the conclusion at the $\alpha = 0.05$ level of significance.

Problem 7.11 In Section 7.12, it was mentioned that for a sample from a uniform distribution an UMP test exists for the hypothesis test problem of $H : \theta = \theta_0$ against $K : \theta \neq \theta_0$. Obtain the UMP test and, if possible, an appropriate R program.

Problem 7.12 Assume that the variances for the two treatments of the Youden-Beale problem are unknown and there is no reasonable way they can be assumed to be equal. Use the two tests (R programs) developed in Section 7.14 in `adhocBF` and `WelchBF` to draw the right conclusions.

Problem 7.13 Carry out the multiple hypothesis testing problem, see `glht` function from the `multcomp` package, for the median polish regression model fitted in Section 4.5.2.

Problem 7.14 Interpret the R program in Example 7.10.2.

Problem 7.15 The *t*-test used on the `galton` dataset is `t.test(galton$child,mu=mean(galton$parent))`. However, there is a "pairing" between the height of the child and the parent. Is the test `t.test(galton$child, galton$parent,paired=TRUE)` more appropriate?

8

Nonparametric Inference

Package(s): `boot`, `UsingR`, `ISwR`
Dataset(s): `nerve`, `swiss`, `depression`, `galton`, `Mucociliary`, `x_bimodal`

8.1 Introduction

The statistical methods discussed in the previous chapter are restricted by many assumptions. As an example, the inference is valid only if the assumed distribution is also the underlying truth distribution. Non-parametric methods are versatile and not restricted by many assumptions.

In this chapter we first consider estimation problems and then the testing problems. We will begin with the importance of the empirical distribution function (edf) and state the *fundamental theorem of statistics* in Section 8.2. The edf is further explored for estimation of statistical functionals. The jackknife and bootstrap methods are considered in the next Section 8.3. Smoothing techniques for estimation problems are covered in Section 8.4. Finally, we conclude the chapter with some of the very important non-parametric tests in Section 8.5.

8.2 Empirical Distribution Function and Its Applications

Let $X_1, X_2, \ldots, X_n$ be a random sample from an unknown distribution function F on the real line. The *empirical distribution function*, abbreviated as edf, is then defined by

$$\hat{F}_n(x) = \frac{1}{n}\sum_{i=1}^{n} I(X_i \leq x), \tag{8.1}$$

where $I\{\}$ is an indicator function. The edf is very intuitive and plays a highly useful tool in non-parametric inference. The asymptotic properties of edf are best explained by the Glivenko-Cantelli theorem, sometimes called the *fundamental theorem of statistics*. The asymptotic and other useful properties of edf are stated next, see Chapter 2 of Wasserman (2006).

A Course in Statistics with R, First Edition. Prabhanjan Narayanachar Tattar, Suresh Ramaiah and B. G. Manjunath.

Companion Website: www.wiley.com/go/tattar/statistics

Theorem 8.2.1 *Let $\hat{F}_n(x)$ be the empirical distribution function of F. Then*

- *For any fixed x*

$$E\hat{F}_n(x) = F(x), \quad and \quad Var(\hat{F}_n(x)) = \frac{F(x)(1-F(x))}{n}. \tag{8.2}$$

- The Glivenko-Cantelli Fundamental Theorem of Statistics *states that*

$$\sup_x |\hat{F}_n(x) - F(x)| \underset{\longrightarrow}{a.s.} 0. \tag{8.3}$$

□

We will require the help of the Dvoretzky-Kiefer-Wolfowitz (DKW) inequality for construction of confidence sets.

Theorem 8.2.2 *The Dvoretzky-Kiefer-Wolfowitz (DKW) inequality says that for any $\epsilon > 0$*

$$P\left(\sup_x |\hat{F}_n(x) - F(x)|\right) \le 2e^{-2n\epsilon^2}.$$

Now, define the lower and upper confidence limit for $\hat{F}_n$ by

$$L(x) = \max\{\hat{F}_n(x) - \epsilon_n, 0\},$$
$$U(x) = \min\{\hat{F}_n(x) + \epsilon_n, 1\},$$

where $\epsilon_n = \sqrt{\ln(2/\alpha)/(2n)}$. Then, for all F and all n

$$P(L(x) \le F(x) \le U(x), \forall x) \ge 1 - \alpha. \tag{8.4}$$

□

These ideas will be followed up with an application to the `nerve.dat` dataset using the useful `ecdf`.

Example 8.2.1. The Nerve Data. We consider the Nerve dataset popularized by Cox and Lewis (1946). In this experiment, 799 waiting times are recorded for successive pulses along a nerve fiber. This problem was introduced in Section 2 of Chapter 3. Let X be a random variable denoting the time between successive pulses. The empirical (cumulative) distribution functions, with the help of the `ecdf` function, and the 95% confidence intervals are obtained for this dataset by the following R program.

```
> date(nerve)
> nerve_ecdf <- ecdf(nerve)
> knots(nerve_ecdf) # Returns the jump points of the edf
 [1] 0.01 0.02 ... 0.29 0.30
[31] 0.31 0.32 ... 0.61 0.62
[61] 0.63 0.64 ... 1.35 1.38
> summary(nerve_ecdf) # the usual R summaries
Empirical CDF:     88 unique values with summary
```

```
   Min. 1st Qu.  Median    Mean 3rd Qu.    Max.
 0.0100  0.2275  0.4450  0.4789  0.6825  1.3800
> nerve_ecdf(nerve) # returns the percentiles at the data points
  [1] 0.63204005 0.11389237 ... 0.59449312 0.08260325
 [14] 0.48310388 0.34292866 ... 0.51939925 0.34292866

[781] 0.96745932 0.34292866 ... 0.11389237 0.31163955
[794] 0.51939925 0.20025031 ... 0.38297872 0.91239049
> plot(nerve_ecdf,verticals=TRUE,do.points=FALSE,main="95%
+ CI for Empirical DF of Nerve Waiting Times", xlab="
+ Waiting Times in Seconds",ylab="Empirical DF",col="green")
> alpha <- 0.05 # the level of significance
> en <- sqrt(log(2/alpha)/(2*length(nerve)))
+ #en stands for the epsilon n term
> L_DKW <- pmax(nerve_ecdf(nerve)-en,0) #The lower DKW limit
> U_DKW <- pmin(nerve_ecdf(nerve)+en,1) #The lower DKW limit
> points(sort(nerve),L_DKW[order(nerve)],"l",col="red")
> points(sort(nerve),U_DKW[order(nerve)],"l",col="red")
> legend(x=c(1,1.5),y=c(0.8,0.6),legend=c("Empirical CDF",
+ "Lower Limit","Upper Limit"),col=c("green", "red","red"),pch="-")
```

The non-parametric empirical distribution function is fitted with the `ecdf` function and for the `nerve` dataset, the fitted edf is created in `nerve_ecdf`. There are 88 unique values of the `nerve` object, verified with `length(unique(nerve))`, which is not included in the program, and it is at these unique points that the edf $\hat{F}(x)$ will have the jump points. The corresponding jump point values in the `nerve` variable are obtained with `knots(nerve_ecdf)`, and as a confirmation of the program, the reader may try `knots(nerve_ecdf)==sort(unique(nerve))`. Invoking the fitted empirical distribution function on the dataset returns the percentiles at the data values, `nerve_ecdf(nerve)`. The `plot` function on the `nerve_ecdf` object invokes the settings of `plot.ecdf` and thus we obtain the curve colored green in Figure 8.1. The upper and lower values for $F(x)$ are derived with `L_DKW` and `U_DKW`, and are then added to the figure with the `points` function with suitable labels as given in `legend`. □

The empirical cdf is useful in estimating many other parameters and the technique to do the same is dealt with in the next subsection.

8.2.1 Statistical Functionals

The empirical cdf $\hat{F}$ as an estimator of F is seen to have useful statistical properties. Though the cdf F may be completely unknown, we are also interested in estimation of the mean, variance, etc. Similar to the "plug-in" estimator in Section 7.6, we can use the empirical cdf to obtain the quantities of interest. Let us begin with an important definition.

Definition 8.2.1 *A* statistical functional *is any function of the probability distribution function F.*

A list of the examples of statistical functionals, including mean and variance, are given in Table 8.1.

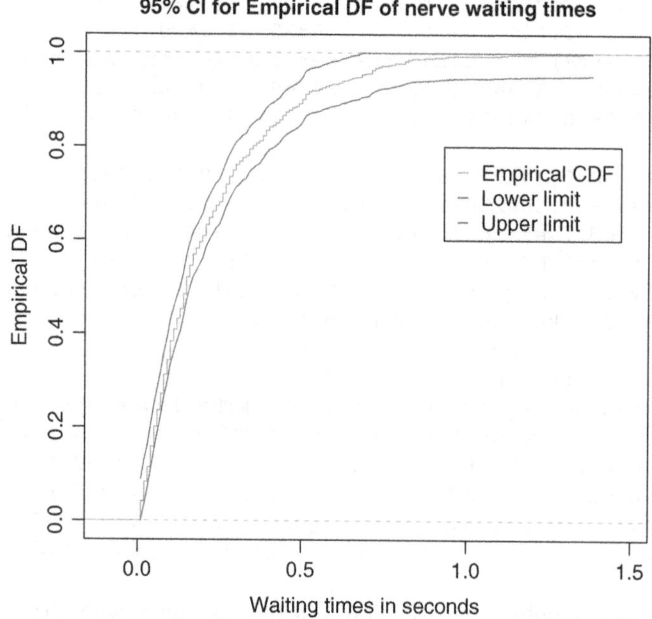

Figure 8.1 A Plot of Empirical Distribution Function for the Nerve Dataset

Table 8.1 Statistical Functionals

Statistical Functionals (Parameters)	Mathematical Expression for the Functionals
Mean (μ)	$\int xdF(x)$
Variance (σ^2)	$\int (x-\mu)^2 dF(x)$
Median (m)	$F^{-1}(1/2)$
Correlation (ρ)	$\dfrac{E(X-\mu_X)(Y-\mu_Y)}{\sigma_X\sigma_Y}$
Skewness (κ)	$\dfrac{E(X-\mu)^3}{\sigma^3}$

Statistical functionals of complex forms pose difficulties when there is the requirement of statistical inference about them. The "plug-in" estimators may be used for inference of complex statistical functions. A formal statement about this is the next definition.

Definition 8.2.2 *The* plug-in estimator *of* $\theta = T(F)$ *is defined as*

$$\hat{\theta}_n = T(\hat{F}_n). \tag{8.5}$$

□

Note that empirical distribution function $\hat{F}$ is discrete, which puts a mass of $1/n$ on each variable X_i. This translates into a useful relationship that if the integral $T(F) = \int g(x)dF(x)$ is a linear functional, the plug-in estimator $T(\hat{F}_n)$ can be estimated as

$$T(\hat{F}_n) = \frac{1}{n}\sum_{i=1}^{n} g(X_i). \tag{8.6}$$

Assume that an estimate of the standard error of the functional $T(\hat{F}_n)$ is available, which we will denote by $\hat{se}_{T(\hat{F}_n)}$. In such a case, we have the result that the asymptotic distribution of the plug-in estimator is the normal distribution $N(T(\hat{F}_n), \hat{se}_{T(\hat{F}_n)})$. Then, a $100(1-\alpha)$ % confidence interval for $T(F)$ can be constructed with

$$T(\hat{F}_n) \pm z_{\alpha/2}\hat{se}_{T(\hat{F})}. \tag{8.7}$$

Example 8.2.2. Estimating some Functionals and Illustration Using the Nerve Dataset. We can see from the previous table that the mean $\mu = \int xdF(x)$ is a linear functional, and thus its estimator can be derived as

$$\hat{\mu} = \int xd\hat{F}(x) = \frac{1}{n}\sum_{i=1}^{n} X_i = \bar{X}_n.$$

The second equivalence in the above equation follows here as $g(x) = X_i$. There is not a computational issue here and using the simple R function `mean` does the required work. Furthermore, the standard error of $\bar{X}_n$ is equal to $\sqrt{V(\bar{X})} = \sigma/\sqrt{n}$. Let $\hat{\sigma}$ be an estimator of σ. The confidence interval for μ is then given by $\bar{X}_n \pm z_{\alpha/2}\hat{\sigma}/\sqrt{n}$, where $z_{\alpha/2}$ is the $\alpha/2$ quantile of the standard normal distribution.

By definition, we have

$$\sigma^2 = \int x^2 dF(x) - \left(\int xdF(x)\right)^2.$$

The plug-in estimator for the variance is then given by

$$\hat{\sigma}^2 = \int x^2 d\hat{F}(x) - \left(\int xd\hat{F}(x)\right)^2 = \frac{1}{n}\sum_{i=1}^{n} X_i^2 - \left(\frac{1}{n}\sum_{i=1}^{n} X_i\right)^2 = \frac{1}{n}\sum_{i=1}^{n}(X_i - \bar{X}_n)^2.$$

As earlier, we have used here the fact that $g(x) = X_i$. This above expression for the estimate of the variance may be used in the formulas for the confidence intervals of the mean parameter.

Next, we look at the task of a non-parametric estimation of the skewness parameter using the plug-in estimator of the parameter. By definition and further plug-in, we can estimate the skewness as below:

$$\begin{aligned}\hat{\kappa} &= \frac{\int (x-\mu)^3 d\hat{F}_n(x)}{\left(\int (x-\mu)^2 d\hat{F}_n(x)\right)^{3/2}} = \frac{\int \left(x - \int xdF(x)\right)^3 d\hat{F}_n(x)}{\left(\int (x - \int xdF(x))^2 d\hat{F}_n(x)\right)^{3/2}}\\ &= \frac{\int \left(x - \int xd\hat{F}(x)\right)^3 d\hat{F}_n(x)}{\left(\int (x - \int xd\hat{F}(x))^2 d\hat{F}_n(x)\right)^{3/2}} = \frac{\int (x-\hat{\mu})^3 d\hat{F}_n(x)}{\left(\int (x-\hat{\mu})^2 d\hat{F}_n(x)\right)^{3/2}} = \frac{\frac{1}{n}\sum_{i=1}^{n}(X_i - \hat{\mu})^3}{\hat{\sigma}^3}\end{aligned}$$

```
> # Mean, Variance, and Skewness in Statistical Functionals
> mean_nerve <- mean(nerve)
> mean_nerve
[1] 0.2185732
> var_nerve <- sum((nerve-mean_nerve)^2)/length(nerve)
+ # the "var" R function has scaling by (n-1)
> var_nerve
[1] 0.0437051
> skew_nerve <- mean((nerve-mean_nerve)^3)/(var_nerve^(3/2))
> skew_nerve
[1] 1.761249
```

Computations were not really difficult for the problem on hand here. An alternative way of obtaining the variance will be through the R function `var` and we leave it to the reader to carry out that minor, yet subtle, change. □

?ecdf, ?knots, ?stepfun

8.3 The Jackknife and Bootstrap Methods

In a breakthrough paper, Quenouille (1949) invented a technique for bias reduction of statistics and this technique has been later renamed by the eminent scientist J.W. Tukey as the *jackknife method*. Tukey observed that the jackknife technique can be extended to obtain the variance of complex statistics. The jackknife method has probably laid the foundation work for the *leave-one-out* resampling statistical technique. Efron (1979) invented the bootstrap method, which gives a general solution for the computation of standard errors and confidence intervals. A detailed discussion of these two powerful techniques is beyond the scope of this book and the enthusiastic reader may consult Shao and Tu (1995) for more in-depth details. We will be content with a couple of important topics and illustrate them through the software.

8.3.1 *The Jackknife*

Consider a random sample $X_1, X_2, \ldots, X_n$ from a probability distribution function F. Let $T = T(X_1, X_2, \ldots, X_n)$ be an estimator for a parameter θ, and let the bias be represented by $bias(T_n) = E(T_n) - \theta$. Define $T_{(-i)}$ as the statistic, which does not consider the ith observation. The *jackknife bias estimate* is then defined by

$$b_{jack} = (n-1)(\bar{T}_n - T_n),$$

where $\bar{T}_n = \sum_{i=1}^{n} T_{(-i)}/n$. The *bias-corrected jackknife estimator* is

$$T_{jack} = T_n - b_{jack}. \tag{8.8}$$

The jackknife estimator can be equivalently written as

$$T_{jack} = \frac{1}{n}\sum_{i=1}^{n} \tilde{T}_i, \tag{8.9}$$

with $\tilde{T}_i = nT_n - (n-1)T_{(-i)}$. The elements $\tilde{T}_i$ can be viewed as the contribution of the ith observation towards T_n. These elements are called *pseudo-values*. The *variance of the jackknife estimator* is then given by

$$v_{jack} = \frac{\tilde{s}^2}{n}, \tag{8.10}$$

where

$$\tilde{s}^2 = \frac{\sum_{i=1}^{n}\left(\tilde{T}_i - \frac{1}{n}\sum_{i=1}^{n}\tilde{T}_i\right)^2}{n-1}.$$

This idea will be illustrated for the estimation of the skewness parameter.

Example 8.3.1. Confidence Intervals for the Skewness Estimator. Recall that the nonparametric estimator of the skewness is given by

$$\hat{\kappa} = \frac{\frac{1}{n}\sum_{i=1}^{n}(X_i - \hat{\mu})^3}{\hat{\sigma}^3}.$$

We want to construct a 95% confidence interval for $\hat{\kappa}$. The estimated value of $\hat{\kappa}$ is 1.76. The forthcoming program gives us the required confidence interval.

```
> # Jackknife Estimator for Skewness of the Nerve Data set
> delete_mean_nerve=delete_var_nerve=delete_skew_nerve=nerve*0
> for(i in 1:length(nerve)){
+ delete_mean_nerve[i] <- mean(nerve[-i])
+ delete_var_nerve[i] <- sum((nerve[-i]-delete_mean_nerve[i])^2)
+ /(length(nerve)-1)
+ delete_skew_nerve[i] <- mean((nerve[-i]-delete_mean_nerve[i])^3)
+ /(delete_var_nerve[i]^(3/2))
+ }
> se_skew_nerve <- sqrt(((length(nerve)-1)/length(nerve))*
+ (sum((delete_skew_nerve-skew_nerve)^2)))
> se_skew_nerve
[1] 0.1719727
```

The first line `delete_mean_nerve= =nerve*0` sets up the task of initialization of the required vectors. To compute $\tilde{T}_i = nT_n - (n-1)T_{(-i)}$ for each i, the `for` loop at each stage removes the i-th datum and obtains the skewness value for the remaining data. That is, the `for` loop is the step towards the *leave-one-out* computations. The remaining program completes other steps of the jackknife technique for the skewness parameter. The 95% confidence interval is then given by $1.76 \pm 2(0.17) = (1.42, 2.10)$. □

An alternative to the jackknife, which in some cases is also a generalization, is the bootstrap technique, which will be discussed in the next sub-section.

8.3.2 The Bootstrap

Efron (1979) proposed the *bootstrap methods* and it is now one of the very important and widely used techniques. With this method the observations are redrawn among themselves towards arriving at some statistical inference of related parameters. In fact, a motivation for doing this is a strong inspiration from the well-known *urn problems* of the combinatorial probability theory. The basic idea is to consider the data as balls in an urn, and obtain a first lot of k balls with replacement and do the inference about the unknown population parameters. We then repeat this process a large number of times for obtaining reliable statistical inference. This forms the basis of the bootstrap method proposed by Efron.

The bootstrap method is useful for estimating the variance of a statistic T_n. As earlier, let $X_1, X_2, \ldots, X_n$ be a random sample of size n with a probability distribution F. If the sampling distribution of T_n is a complex one, we can approximate its variance using the bootstrap method. The steps involved are listed in the following.

1. Draw a random sample of size n with replacement among $X_1, X_2, \ldots, X_n$. Denote this random sample by $X_1^*, X_2^*, \ldots, X_n^*$.
2. Compute T_n from $X_1^*, X_2^*, \ldots, X_n^*$. Denote this by T_n^*.
3. Repeat the above two steps a large number of times, say B. Denote these quantities by $T_{n,1}^*, T_{n,2}^*, \ldots, T_{n,B}^*$.
4. The bootstrap approximation of the variance of T_n is then given by

$$v_{boot}(T_n) = \frac{1}{B}\sum_{j=1}^{B}\left(T_{n,j}^* - \frac{1}{B}\sum_{r=1}^{B} T_{n,r}^*\right)^2. \tag{8.11}$$

The General Bootstrap Principle. We obtain a random sample of size n, with replacement, from the n observations. Let the observations be denoted by $\mathbf{X} = (X_1, X_2, \ldots, X_n)$. We now treat this random sample as a *population*. Next, draw a random sample of size n from $\mathbf{X}$ with replacement. The ideas can be clearly absorbed by this hypothetical example. Let there be four observations in a sample, say (5, 14, 17, 12). One possible realization of the redrawn sample by treating (5, 14, 17, 12) as a population can be (5, 17, 5, 12). The redrawn sample is referred as the *bootstrap sample*. We denote the bootstrap sample by $\mathbf{X}^{*1}$. The estimator $T(\mathbf{X})$ is computed for the bootstrap sample $\mathbf{X}^{*1}$. We repeat this process of redrawing and obtaining the bootstrap sample a large number of times, say B. For each of the bootstrap samples, we compute the estimator, denoted by $\mathbf{X}^{*1}, \mathbf{X}^{*2}, \ldots, \mathbf{X}^{*B}$. The sampling distribution of bootstrap estimators helps us to carry out the related inference about the parameter θ. In the next example, we understand the working of the bootstrap through the famous aspirin example.

Example 8.3.2. The Aspirin Study. The *New York Times* conducted a *double-blind* experiment to investigate if consuming small doses of aspirin reduced the risk of heart attack among healthy middle-aged men. The data is given in Table 8.2.

The *odds ratio*, abbreviated as OR, of heart attack rate for the aspirin/placebo group is computed as $OR = (104/11037)/(189/11034) = 0.55$. The same study also has information on the people who had heart attack strokes and the odds ratio here is $OR = (119/11037)/(98/11034) = 1.21$. This translates to an unusual situation. The study reports that taking small doses of aspirin reduces heart attack by about 50% in comparison with the placebo group, whereas the same treatment increases the risk of a heart attack stroke by about 20% more. We would like to construct bootstrap confidence intervals based on the data reported in the above two tables. The program below achieves this goal.

Table 8.2 The Aspirin Data: Heart Attacks and Strokes

Treatment Group	Attacks		Strokes	
	Heart Attacks	Subjects	Strokes	Subjects
Aspirin	104	11037	119	11037
Placebo	189	11034	98	11034

```
> aspirin_overall <- c(rep(1,104),rep(0,11037-104))
> placebo_overall <- c(rep(1,189),rep(0,11034-189))
> aspirin_strokes <- c(rep(1,119),rep(0,11037-119))
> placebo_strokes <- c(rep(1,98),rep(0,11034-98))
> or_overall=or_strokes=c()
> for(i in 1:1000){
+ bao <- sample(aspirin_overall,11037,replace=TRUE)
+ bpo <- sample(placebo_overall,11034,replace=TRUE)
+ bas <- sample(aspirin_strokes,11037,replace=TRUE)
+ bps <- sample(placebo_strokes,11034,replace=TRUE)
+ or_overall[i] <- (sum(bao)/11037)/(sum(bpo)/11034)
+ or_strokes[i] <- (sum(bas)/11037)/(sum(bps)/11034)
+ }
> quantile(or_overall,c(0.025,0.975))
     2.5%     97.5%
0.4319186 0.6852233
> quantile(or_strokes,c(0.025,0.975))
     2.5%     97.5%
0.9330137 1.6018372
```

Using the `rep` function, we are attempting to recreate the aspirin data in Table 8.2 with the variables `aspirin_overall`, `placebo_overall`, `aspirin_strokes`, and `placebo_strokes`. The number of bootstrap replicates is chosen as $B = 1000$, see the `for` loop. Using the `sample` function with the option of `replace=TRUE`, we are generating the bootstrap samples, and for each such bootstrap sample, the odds ratio for heart attacks and strokes is calculated. The `quantile` function gives us the 95% confidence intervals for the odds ratio of heart attacks and strokes. The bootstrap confidence intervals confirm the result obtained earlier. □

The R core package `boot` contains the `boot` function, which can be readily used for the bootstrap technique.

Example 8.3.3. Bootstrapping Non-parametric Skewness for Nerve Dataset. Contd. The `boot` function needs to be given a function as an argument and the data on which the function needs to be operated upon for the related statistic. Thus, first define the `skew_nonparametric` function which computes the skewness for a vector object. The `boot` function also needs to be told the number of required bootstrap samples through the option `R = 1000`, say,

```
> # Bootstrap Estimator for Skewness of the Nerve Data Set
> library(boot)
> skew_nonparametric=function(x,i){
+    mx <- mean(x[i])
+    vx <- sum((x[i]-mx)^2)/length(x[i])
+    sx <- mean((x[i]-mx)^3)/(vx^(3/2))
+    return(sx)
+    }
> boot(nerve,skew_nonparametric,1000)
ORDINARY NONPARAMETRIC BOOTSTRAP
Call:
boot(data = nerve, statistic = skew_nonparametric, R = 1000)
Bootstrap Statistics :
    original       bias    std. error
t1* 1.761249 -0.01118149   0.1621611
```

Now the reader can contrast the results here with the jackknife technique for the `nerve` data. □

8.3.3 Bootstrapping Simple Linear Model*

Consider the simple linear regression model, to be dealt with in more detail in Chapter 12, for n pairs of data $(X_i, Y_i), i = 1, \ldots, n$:

$$Y_i = \beta_0 + \beta_1 X_i + \epsilon_i, i = 1, \ldots, n.$$

Suppose, using the least squares method, we obtain the fitted model as

$$\hat{Y}_i = \hat{\beta}_0 + \hat{\beta}_1 X_i.$$

We have two methods for bootstrapping the simple linear regression model. First, we can bootstrap the residuals and then predict the regressands for such resampled residuals, and based on the estimated regression coefficients for each bootstrap sample, we obtain a large number of such bootstrap regression coefficients. Inference can be carried out from the sampling distribution of the bootstrap regression coefficients. The second method is of course to resample the values of paired regressand and regressor variables, and obtain bootstrap regression coefficients from the resampled design matrix. Details for both the methods may be found in Chapter 26 of Draper and Smith (1998).

Bootstrapping the Residuals. We will denote the estimated residual, for the above fitted model, by $\hat{\boldsymbol{\epsilon}}$. As earlier, we will denote the design matrix by $\mathbf{X}$, and the first column will be 1's for the intercept term. The bootstrap method can be described in three steps:

1. Draw a sample of size n with replacement from $\hat{\boldsymbol{\epsilon}}$ and denote it by $\boldsymbol{\epsilon}^*$.
2. For the resampled $\boldsymbol{\epsilon}^*$, obtain the new regressands using $\mathbf{Y} = \mathbf{X}'\hat{\boldsymbol{\beta}} + \hat{\boldsymbol{\epsilon}}$.
3. Finally, calculate $\boldsymbol{\epsilon}^*$ for the model $\mathbf{Y}^* = \mathbf{X}'\boldsymbol{\beta} + \hat{\boldsymbol{\epsilon}}^*$.

We repeat this process a large number of times, B. Inference about the vector of regression coefficients can be carried out on the basis of the sampling distribution of B estimates of bootstrapped regression coefficients $\boldsymbol{\epsilon}^*$. This bootstrap method is demonstrated for the simple linear regression model.

Example 8.3.4. The Galton Dataset. We fit a model for the height of the child as a linear function of the the height of the parent.

```
> library(UsingR)
> cplm <- lm(child~parent,galton)
> # Boostrapping the Residuals
> resid <- lm(child~parent,galton)$residuals
> bcoef <- matrix(nrow=100,ncol=2)
> for(i in 1:100){
+ newy <- cbind(rep(1,nrow(galton)),galton$parent)
+ %*%cplm$coefficients
+ +sample(resid,nrow(galton),replace=TRUE)
+ bcoef[i,] <- lm(newy~galton$parent)$coefficients
+ }
> quantile(bcoef[,2],c(0.025,0.975))
     2.5%     97.5%
0.5726571 0.7123394
```

Since 0 is not in the above bootstrap confidence interval, we conclude that the height of the parent has significant effect on the height of the child. □

Bootstrapping the Observations. This method is a straightforward application of the general bootstrap method explained earlier. For the paired data $(X_i, Y_i), i = 1, \ldots, n$, we list the procedure in the following steps:

1. Obtain a sample of size n with replacement from the above n points $(X_i^*, Y_i^*), i = 1, \ldots, n$.
2. Obtain the regression coefficients of the above bootstrap sample.
3. Repeat the above two steps a large number of times, say B.

Example 8.3.5. The Galton Dataset. Contd. Example 8.3.4 will be continued for bootstrapping the observations.

```
> # Bootstrapping the Observations
> bcoef <- matrix(nrow=100,ncol=2)
> for(i in 1:100) {
+ tempgalton <- galton[sample(1:nrow(galton),nrow(galton),
+ replace=TRUE),]
+ bcoef[i,] <- lm(child~parent,tempgalton)$coefficients
+ }
> quantile(bcoef[,2],c(0.025,0.975))
     2.5%     97.5%
0.5688382 0.7232253
> lm(child~parent)$coefficients
(Intercept)      parent
 23.9415302   0.6462906
```

Since the value 0 does not lie in the 95% bootstrap confidence interval, we conclude that the height of the parent has significant effect on the height of the child. □

?boot, library(help=boot)

8.4 Non-parametric Smoothing

In Section 8.2, we saw the applications of the empirical distribution function (edf). It is seen then that the edf is an estimator of the cumulative distribution function F with useful statistical properties. Consider a random sample $X_1, \dots, X_n$ with pdf f. The density function is defined as

$$f(x) = \lim_{h \downarrow 0} \frac{F(x+h) - F(x)}{h}. \tag{8.12}$$

The estimation of f is a complex problem and we will use *kernels* to deal with it. We will use Silverman (1985) and Simonoff (1996) as the main references for developments in this section. An intuitive approach of *histogram smoothing* is first considered.

8.4.1 Histogram Smoothing

Consider a random sample $X_1, \dots, X_n$ of size n from f. Divide the line into a set of K bins of equal width h. Let us denote points of the division of the line by $b_0 < b_1 < \cdots < b_K$. An intuitive estimator of the distribution function $F(x)$ is

$$\hat{F}(x) = \frac{\#\{x_i \le x\}}{n}.$$

Thus, for a bin $(b_j, b_{j+1}], j = 0, 1, \dots, K-1$, an estimator of the density is given by

$$\hat{f}(x) = \frac{\#\{x_i \le b_{j+1}\} - \#\{x_i \le b_j\}}{nh}, x \in (b_j, b_{j+1}]. \tag{8.13}$$

We will consider a simple illustration of this technique using an R program.

Example 8.4.1. Histogram Smoothing for Forged Swiss Bank Notes. The `swiss` dataset from the `ACSWR` package consists of measurements on the width of bottom margin and image diagonal length for forged and real notes. The histogram smoothing method is applied to understand the width of bottom margins for the forged notes. In the next program, histogram smoothing is put into action with $K = 6, 14,$ and 28 number of bins.

```
> par(mfrow=c(1,3))
> data(swiss)
> hist(swiss$Bottforg,breaks=28,probability=TRUE,col=0,
+ ylim=c(0,.5),xlab="Margin width (mm)",ylab="Density")
> hist(swiss$Bottforg,breaks=12,probability=TRUE,col=0,
+ ylim=c(0,.5),xlab="Margin width (mm)",ylab="Density")
> hist(swiss$Bottforg,breaks=6,probability=TRUE,col=0,
+ ylim=c(0,.5),xlab="Margin width (mm)",ylab="Density")
```

Now, to obtain the histogram smoothing for estimating the density function with $K = 6, 14$ and 28 number of bins, the histogram is obtained with the `hist` function and option of `breaks=6`, `14` and `28` respectively.

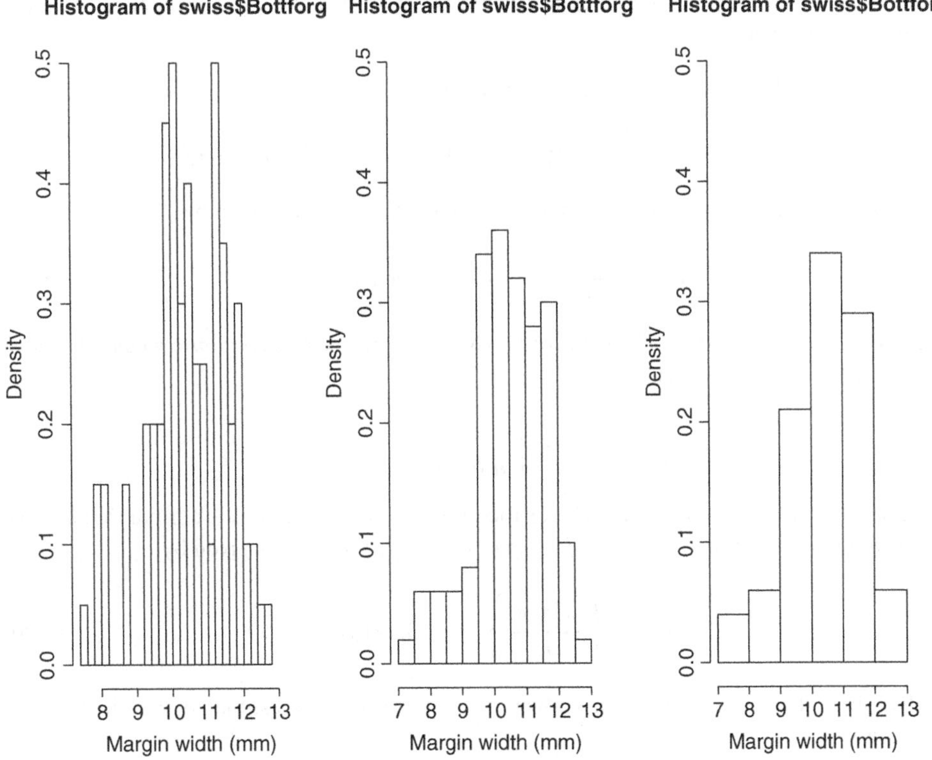

Figure 8.2 Histogram Smoothing for Forged Swiss Notes

It may be seen from Figure 8.2 that for $K = 28$ bins there are 3 modes at approximately 8 mm, 10 mm, and 11.5 mm. Similarly, for $K = 12$ bins there are 2 modes at 10 mm and 11.5 mm, whereas for $K = 6$ bins there is just 1 mode at 10.5 mm, roughly. Thus, we see that the choice of the number of bins is critical. □

Statistical techniques are then required to evaluate the estimator $\hat{f}(x)$ for $f(x)$. At a given point x the *squared error* is $SE(x) = \{\hat{f}(x) - f(x)\}^2$, and the *expected squared error* $MSE(x) = E_f\{\hat{f}(x) - f(x)\}^2$. However, for estimation of f, the performance needs to be evaluated for the range of x values. Thus, the user should be looking at the *integrated square error*:

$$ISE = \int_{-\infty}^{\infty} \{\hat{f}(x) - f(x)\}^2 dx. \tag{8.14}$$

The bias and variance, see Chapter 4 of Simonoff (1996), of the estimator $\hat{f}(x)$ are given by

$$\text{Bias}\{\hat{f}(x)\} = \frac{f'(x)}{2}\{h - 2(x - b_j)\} + O(h^2), x \in (b_j, b_{j+1}], \tag{8.15}$$

$$\text{Var}\{\hat{f}(x)\} = \frac{f(x)}{nh} + O(1/n), \tag{8.16}$$

where $O(u) \to 0$ as $u \to 0$, and $f'(x)$ is the derivative of $f(x)$. At a given point x, the mean squared error is then given by

$$\begin{aligned} \text{MSE}\{\hat{f}(x)\} &= \text{Var}\{\hat{f}(x)\} + \text{Bias}^2\{\hat{f}(x)\} \\ &= \frac{f(x)}{nh} + \frac{f'(x)^2}{4}\{h - 2(x - b_j)\}^2 + O(h^3) + O(1/n). \end{aligned} \tag{8.17}$$

The *mean integrated square error*, abbreviated as *MISE*, is then given by

$$MISE = \frac{1}{nh} + \frac{h^2 R(f')}{12} + O(h^3) + O(1/n), \tag{8.18}$$

where $R(f') = \int \{f'(x)\}^2 dx$. The value of h, which minimizes the *asymptotic mean integrated square error*, *AMISE*, is given by

$$h^* = \left\{\frac{6}{nR(f')}\right\}^{1/3}. \tag{8.19}$$

However, the true f is not known. Under the assumption that the f is a normal density, the rule-of-thumb for optimum h^*, since $\int \{f'(x)\}^2 dx = 1/\{4\sqrt{\pi}\sigma^3\}$, is given by

$$h^* \approx \sigma\left\{\frac{24\sqrt{\pi}}{n}\right\}^{1/3} \approx 3.491\sigma n^{-1/3}. \tag{8.20}$$

Finally, since the value of σ is not known, we replace it by its estimated sample standard deviation s:

$$h^* \approx 3.491 s n^{-1/3}. \tag{8.21}$$

In practice, the sample standard deviance is not robust, and highly sensitive to outliers, and a sensible estimate is obtained by replacing s by the *inter-quantile range*, *IQR*. The concept is illustrated through the continued example of Swiss bank notes.

Example 8.4.2. Histogram Smoothing for Forged Swiss Bank Notes. Contd. The optimum bin width is obtained and histogram smoothing is then applied.

```
> n <- length(swiss$Bottforg)
> s <- sd(swiss$Bottforg)
> iqr <- IQR(swiss$Bottforg)
> hstars <- 3.491*s*n^{-1/3}
> nobreaks <- (max(swiss$Bottforg)-min(swiss$Bottforg))/hstars
> hstariqr <- 2.6*iqr*n^{-1/3}
> nobreaks2 <- (max(swiss$Bottforg)-min(swiss$Bottforg))/hstariqr
> hist(swiss$Bottforg,breaks=round(nobreaks),probability=TRUE,col=0,
+ ylim=c(0,.5),xlab="Margin width (mm)",ylab="Density")
```

To compute the optimum number of bins h^*, as required in Equation 8.20, an estimate of the standard deviation s is given by *IQR* and obtained in the program with the `IQR` function. It may now be seen from Figure 8.3 that we have a negatively skewed distribution with the mode occurring at 10.5 mm approximately. □

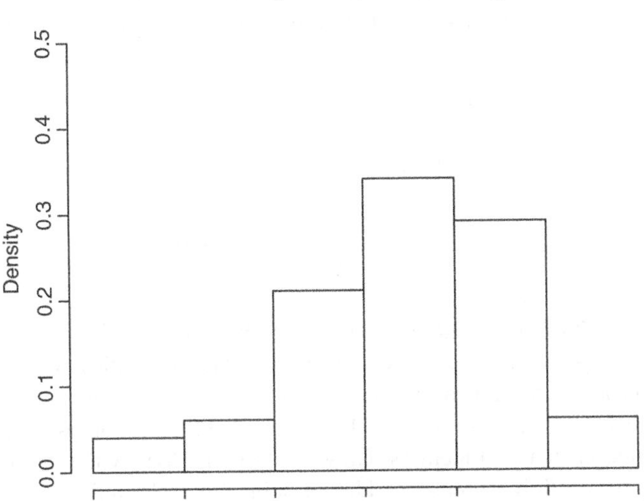

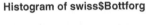

Figure 8.3 Histogram Smoothing using Optimum Bin Width

The histogram smoothing technique has vital drawbacks. First, it is a discontinuous approximation of the density function f. Furthermore, it is affected by the choice of origin, bin width, besides not being convenient to generalize for higher dimensional problems. These drawbacks are overcome by using *kernels*, which will be considered in subsection 8.4.2 below.

8.4.2 Kernel Smoothing

Rewrite the expression for the pdf $f(x)$ in a slightly different (and equivalent) form:

$$f(x) = \lim_{h \to 0} \frac{F(x+h) - F(x-h)}{2h}. \tag{8.22}$$

Now, as the estimator $\hat{f}$ in Equation 8.13 is for the $f(x)$ given in Equation 8.12, an intuitive estimator of $f(x)$ based on the above expression is

$$\hat{f}(x) = \frac{\#\{x_i \in [x-h, x+h)\}}{2nh}, x \in (x-h, x+h]. \tag{8.23}$$

The discontinuity in the histogram smoothing technique arises on account of the formula given in expression 8.13. Thus, the alternative is then to replace the expression on the right-hand side by a continuous function, here *kernels*, which ensures continuity. This motivates the next definition.

Definition 8.4.1 Kernel Function *A real, integrable, non-negative function K on $\mathcal{R}$, which is symmetrical about 0, is said to be a* kernel. *That is, a kernel satisfies the following properties:*

$$\int_{\mathcal{R}} K(x)dx = 1,$$

$$\int_{\mathcal{R}} xK(x)dx = 0,$$

$$\sigma_K^2 = \int_{\mathcal{R}} x^2 K(x)dx < \infty. \tag{8.24}$$

A list of kernels, see http://robjhyndman.com/etc5410/density.pdf, is given in Table 8.3. For all the kernels, $u = \frac{x-x_i}{n}, i = 1, \ldots, n$. The uniform kernel is the simplest of the kernels. It takes the value 1/2 if the absolute value of u is less than 1. A drawback of the uniform kernel is that the estimated density function is not smooth and may have some jumps. The Epanechnikov kernel provides smooth density functions. These two kernels along with triangle, biweight, and triweight kernels have a finite support, and hence points beyond u units will not add any contribution to the density at such points. The Gaussian kernel does not have support restrictions and hence it takes into consideration all the data values.

To understand the nature of these kernels, let us use R to obtain the plot of these functions, see Part A of Figure 8.4. The `density` function from R gives a tool for the kernel technique and we simply use it to understand the shape of the various kernels. The `kernel` option in the `density` function helps to specify the choice of required kernels. The graphical functions `plot`, `main`, `lines`, etc., have often been seen earlier.

```
> plot(density(0,bw=1,kernel="rectangular"),main="Kernel Shapes",
+ ylim=c(0,0.4),xlab="x")
> lines(density(0,bw=1,kernel="triangular"),col="red")
> lines(density(0,bw=1,kernel="epanechnikov"),col="green")
> lines(density(0,bw=1,kernel="biweight"),col="blue")
> lines(density(0,bw=1,kernel="gaussian"),col="orange")
> legend(-3,.4,legend=c("rectangular","triangular","epanechnikov",
+ "biweight","gaussian"),col=c("black","red","green",
+ "blue","orange"),lty=1,cex=0.7)
```

Table 8.3 Kernel Functions

Kernel Name	Kernel Form
Uniform	$\frac{1}{2}, \lvert u\rvert \leq 1$
Triangle	$(1-\lvert u\rvert), \lvert u\rvert \leq 1$
Epanechnikov	$\frac{3}{4}(1-u^2), \lvert u\rvert \leq 1$
Biweight	$\frac{15}{16}(1-u^2)^2, \lvert u\rvert \leq 1$
Triweight	$\frac{35}{32}(1-u^2)^3, \lvert u\rvert \leq 1$
Gaussian	$\frac{e^{-u^2/2}}{\sqrt{2\pi}}, \lvert u\rvert < \infty$

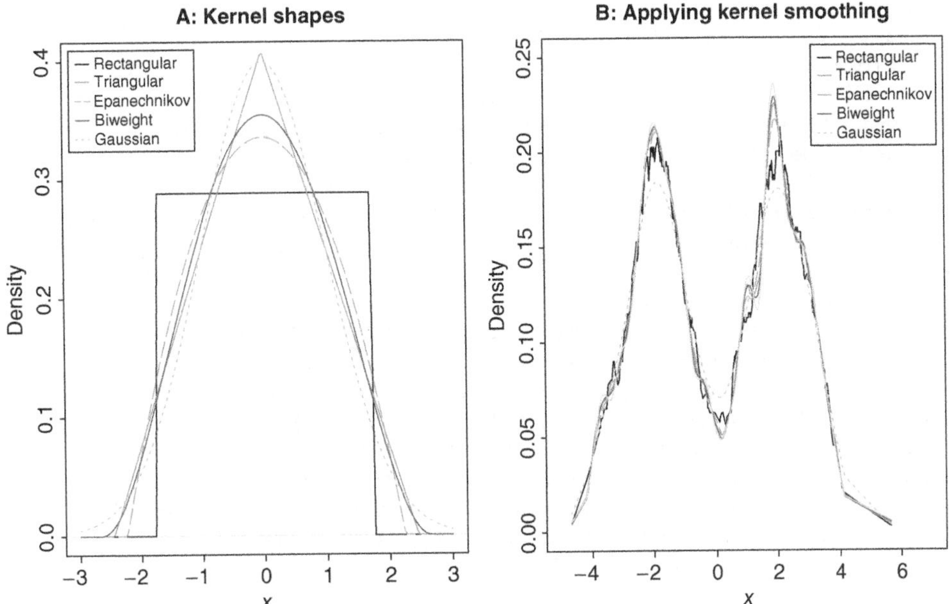

Figure 8.4 A Plot of Various Kernels

Now, using an *appropriate* kernel, an estimator of the pdf $\hat{f}(x)$ is given by

$$\hat{f}(x) = \frac{1}{nh}\sum_{i=1}^{n} K\left(\frac{x - x_i}{h}\right). \tag{8.25}$$

The use of `density` function is obviously an efficient way of deploying kernel smoothing. However, the formulas of the various kernels is explained in the next example through a program building from raw codes.

Example 8.4.3. Understanding the Use of Kernel Smoothing. A simulated dataset is available in the `x_bimodal` data frame of the companion package. As the name of the data frame indicates, there are two modes at –2, and 2 and we have 400 observations. A bin of width `h <- 0.5` is considered for the kernel smoothing. The computations related to all the kernels given in Table 8.3 are initiated in the objects `dens_kernel_name`, that is, `dens_unif` is initiated for the uniform kernel. The kernel values are computed at all the values of the data points of `x_bimodal`. The first important step is to calculate the value of the argument u through `u <- (x_bimodal[i]-x_bimodal)/h`. The object `xlogical` ensures that the support restrictions for all the kernels, except the Gaussian kernel, are obtained while the final values are stored in the object `dens_kernel_name`.

```
> data(x_bimodal)
> h <- 0.5; n <- length(x_bimodal)
> dens_unif <- NULL; dens_triangle <- NULL; dens_epanechnikov <- NULL
> dens_biweight <- NULL; dens_triweight <- NULL
> dens_gaussian <- NULL
```

```
> for(i in 1:n)  {
+   u <- (x_bimodal[i]-x_bimodal)/h
+   xlogical <- (u>-1 & u <= 1)
+   dens_unif[i] <- (1/(n*h))*(sum(xlogical)/2)
+   dens_triangle[i] <- (1/(n*h))*(sum(xlogical*(1-abs(u))))
+   dens_epanechnikov[i] <- (1/(n*h))*(sum(3*xlogical*(1-u^2)/4))
+   dens_biweight[i] <- (1/(n*h))*(15*sum(xlogical*(1-u^2)^2/16))
+   dens_triweight[i] <- (1/(n*h))*(35*sum(xlogical*(1-u^2)^3/32))
+   dens_gaussian[i] <- (1/(n*h))*(sum(exp(-u^2/2)/sqrt(2*pi)))
+ }
> plot(x_bimodal,dens_unif,"l",ylim=c(0,.25),xlim=c(-5,7),xlab="x",
+      ylab="Density",main="B: Applying Kernel Smoothing")
> points(x_bimodal,dens_triangle,"l",col="red")
> points(x_bimodal,dens_epanechnikov,"l",col="green")
> points(x_bimodal,dens_biweight,"l",col="blue")
> points(x_bimodal,dens_triweight,"l",col="yellow")
> points(x_bimodal,dens_gaussian,"l",col="orange")
> legend(4,.23,legend=c("rectangular","triangular","epanechnikov",
+ "biweight","gaussian"),col=c("black","red","green",
+ "blue","orange"),lty=1)
```

Using the `plot` function along with `points`, the fitted densities are plotted in Part B of Figure 8.4. The Gaussian kernel appears the most smooth of all the kernels, and there is a lot closeness between the remaining densities. □

Example 8.4.4. Kernel Smoothing for Forged Swiss Bank Notes. Example 8.4.2 Contd. A rectangular/uniform kernel is first applied on the bottom margin variable with a bandwidth of 0.08 with `bw=0.08`. The `bw` is a smoothing bandwidth value, and the kernel is accordingly scaled such that it is the standard deviation of the smoothing kernel. The `plot` function can be directly applied on an object of class `density`.

```
> par(mfrow=c(1,3))
> plot(density(swiss$Bottforg,kernel="rectangular",bw=0.08),
+ main="A: Uniform Kernel with h=0.08")
> plot(density(swiss$Bottforg,kernel="gaussian",bw=0.04),
+ main="B: Gaussian Kernel with h=0.04")
> plot(density(swiss$Bottforg,kernel="gaussian",bw=0.16),
+ main="C: Gaussian Kernel with h=0.12")
```

It may be seen from Part A of Figure 8.5 that the density fitted by the rectangular kernel is very poor, while Part C shows that fitting a Gaussian kernel with `bw=0.16` is a much better fit, as the three modes can be clearly seen. □

*8.4.3 Nonparametric Regression Models**

The simple linear regression model was introduced earlier in Section 4.5; recall Equation 4.11 for the linear form as $Y = \beta_0 + \beta_1 X + \epsilon$. Suppose that we have n independent pairs of

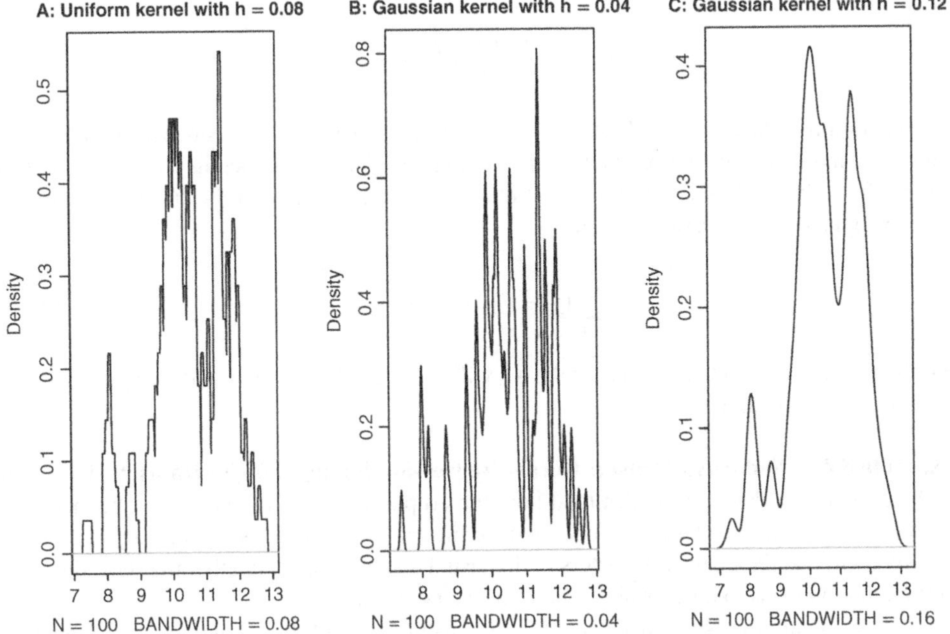

Figure 8.5 Understanding "Kernel" Choice for Swiss Notes

observations $(X_i, Y_i), i = 1, 2, \ldots, n$. The *non-parametric regression model* is given by

$$Y_i = m(X_i) + \epsilon_i, \tag{8.26}$$

where the term $m(x)$ is the *regression curve*, and is defined as the conditional expectation $m(x) = E(Y|x)$. The assumption about the error term is that it has mean zero $E(\epsilon) = 0$ and variance $\texttt{Var}(\epsilon|x) = \sigma^2(x)$, that is, the variance term is not necessarily constant.

The Nadaraya-Watson Regression Technique

The *Nadaraya-Watson kernel estimator* of the regression curve $m(x)$ is given by

$$\hat{m}_{NW}(x) = \frac{\sum_{i=1}^{n} K\left(\frac{x-x_i}{h}\right) y_i}{\sum_{i=1}^{n} K\left(\frac{x-x_i}{h}\right)}. \tag{8.27}$$

The Nadaraya-Watson kernel estimator can be rewritten as a function of y_i's $\hat{m}_{NW}(x) = \sum_{i=1}^{n} w_i y_i$ with

$$w_i = \frac{1}{nh} \frac{K\left(\frac{x-x_i}{h}\right)}{\hat{f}(x)}, \tag{8.28}$$

where

$$\hat{f}(x) = \frac{1}{nh}\sum_{i=1}^{n} K\left(\frac{x - x_i}{h}\right).$$

The derivation of the Nadaraya-Watson estimator is not considered here, since it would require definition and details of the product kernel estimate of $f(x, y)$. The details may be sought in Simonoff (1996) or Wasserman (2006). It may be noted however that $\hat{m}_{NW}(x)$ is the solution of the weighted least squares problem:

$$\sum_{i=1}^{n} (y_i - \beta_0)^2 K\left(\frac{x - x_i}{h}\right). \tag{8.29}$$

For the rectangular and Gaussian kernels, we will illustrate this concept with an application of the `faithful` dataset.

Example 8.4.5. Nadaraya-Watson Kernel Regression for the *faithful* Dataset. The main problem with this data is to understand how the eruption time of the volcano influences the waiting time. First, a scatter plot is obtained for the `waiting` variable against `eruptions`. It is apparent that there are two clusters in the visual display, conveying that the short duration of the eruption leads to a less waiting time for the eruption.

First, we obtain the Nadaraya-Watson kernel estimator with the choice of kernel being a rectangular one, the option is `kernel="box"`, and bandwidth of `0.25`. The bandwidth is then increased to `0.5` and `0.75`. The exercise is then repeated with the Gaussian kernel and the option is accordingly changed to `kernel="normal"`.

```
> plot(faithful$eruptions,faithful$waiting,xlab="Duration of the
+ Eruptions",ylab="Waiting Time for the Eruption")
> lines(ksmooth(faithful$eruptions,faithful$waiting,kernel="box",
+ bandwidth=0.25),col="green",lwd=1)
> lines(ksmooth(faithful$eruptions,faithful$waiting,kernel="box",
+ bandwidth=0.5),col="green",lwd=2)
> lines(ksmooth(faithful$eruptions,faithful$waiting,kernel="box",
+ bandwidth=0.75),col="green",lwd=3)
> legend(x=c(1.5,3.15),y=c(90,75),c("Box, Width=0.25","Box,
+ Width=0.50","Box, Width=0.75"),col="green",lwd=1:3)
> lines(ksmooth(faithful$eruptions,faithful$waiting,kernel="normal",
+ bandwidth=0.25),col="red",lwd=1)
> lines(ksmooth(faithful$eruptions,faithful$waiting,kernel="normal",
+ bandwidth=0.5),col="red",lwd=2)
> lines(ksmooth(faithful$eruptions,faithful$waiting,kernel="normal",
+ bandwidth=0.75),col="red",lwd=3)
> legend(x=c(3.25,5.2),y=c(48,60),c("Normal, Width=0.25","Normal,
+ Width=0.50","Normal, Width=0.75"),col="red",lwd=1:3)
```

It may be seen from Figure 8.6 that the rectangular kernel does not provide a smooth curve for the regression model. The Gaussian kernel leads to smooth curve fitting. However, with bandwidths `0.5` and `0.75`, the curve overfits the data and hence the choice of `0.25` seems more apt as it captures the local variation quite well. □

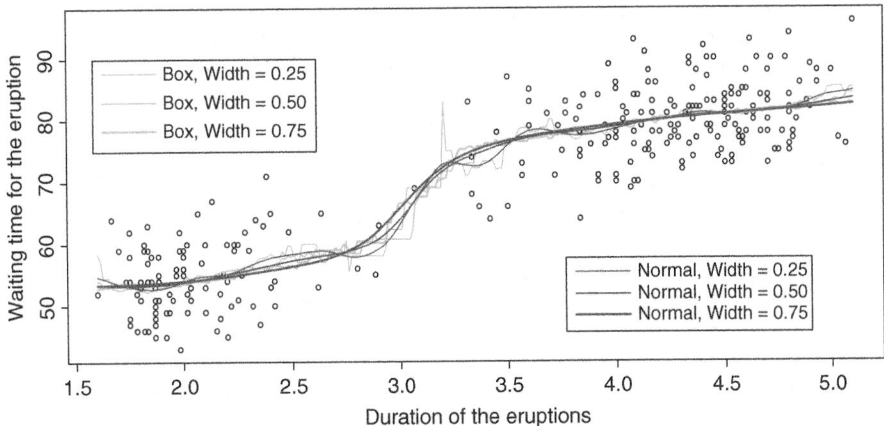

Figure 8.6 Nadaraya-Watson Kernel Regression for Faithful Dataset

The LOESS Technique

The *local polynomial regression* generalizes the weighted least squares criteria given in Equation 8.29 to a pth order polynomial:

$$\sum_{i=1}^{n} (y_i - \beta_0 - \beta_1(x - x_i) - \beta_2(x - x_i)^2 - \cdots - \beta_p(x - x_i)^p)^2 K\left(\frac{x - x_i}{h}\right). \tag{8.30}$$

The *loess* technique is a particular (and modified) case of the local polynomial regression model with the degree of the polynomial up to 2. The bandwidth of loess is specified by the nearest neighbors and such an option is provided in the R `loess` function in `span`. We will quickly run through the previous Example 8.4.5 with different scan coverage and the `family` option of `gaussian` and `symmetric`.

Example 8.4.6. The *faithful* Dataset. Contd. The `loess` function will be first used with the options of `scan` at `0.25, 0.5, 0.75` for the `gaussian` family and the exercise will be repeated for the `symmetric` family.

```
> par(mfrow=c(1,2))
> plot(faithful$eruptions,faithful$waiting,xlab="Duration of the
+       Eruptions", ylab="Waiting Time for the Eruption")
> tt1 <- loess(waiting~eruptions,data=faithful,span=0.25,
+ family="gaussian")
> points(tt1$x,fitted(tt1),col="red")
> tt2 <- loess(waiting~eruptions,data=faithful,span=0.5,
+ family="gaussian")
> points(tt2$x,fitted(tt2),col="green")
> tt3 <- loess(waiting~eruptions,data=faithful,span=0.75,
+ family="gaussian")
> points(tt3$x,fitted(tt3),col="blue")
> title("Gaussian Kernel")
```

```
> legend(x=c(1.75,3),y=c(90,78),c("span=0.25","span=0.50",
+         "span=0.75"),col=c("red","green","blue"),pch="o")
> plot(faithful$eruptions,faithful$waiting,xlab="Duration of the
+         Eruptions",ylab="Waiting Time for the Eruption")
> tt4 <- loess(waiting~eruptions,data=faithful,span=0.25,
+ family="symmetric")
> points(tt4$x,fitted(tt4),col="red")
> tt5 <- loess(waiting~eruptions,data=faithful,span=0.5,
+ family="symmetric")
> points(tt5$x,fitted(tt5),col="green")
> tt6 <- loess(waiting~eruptions,data=faithful,span=0.75,
+ family="symmetric")
> points(tt6$x,fitted(tt6),col="blue")
> legend(x=c(1.75,3),y=c(90,78),c("span=0.25","span=0.50",
+         "span=0.75"),col=c("red","green","blue"),pch="o")
> title("Symmetric Kernel")
```

It may be seen from Figure 8.7 that there is not much to choose between the family being Gaussian or symmetric. On the other hand, the span of `span=0.75`, which means 75% of the neighborhood points are taken into consideration for smoothing purposes, is too smooth and misses out on the local variation. Though `span=0.25` captures a lot of local variation, the average `0.5` seems to be smoother. □

?hist, ?IQR, ?eval, ?density

8.5 Non-parametric Tests

The above sections so far have focused on the problem of non-parametric estimation. The goal of this section is to consider non-parametric tests for hypotheses relating to the parameters of

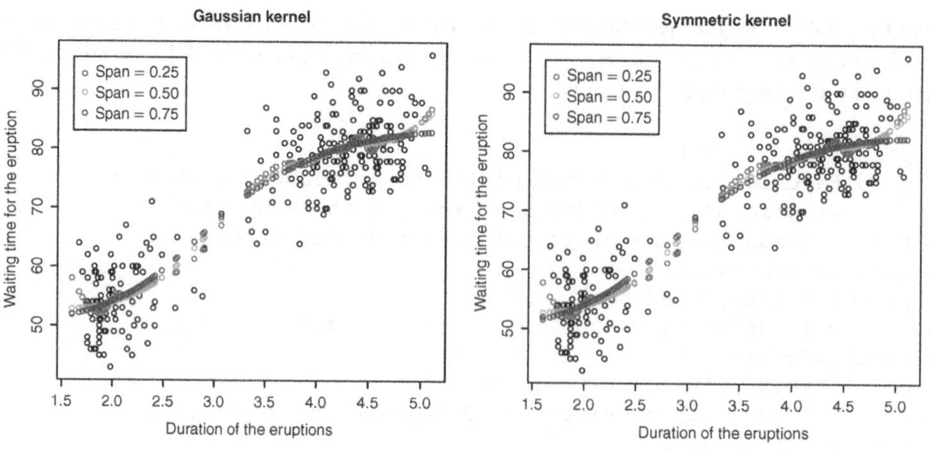

Figure 8.7 Loess Smoothing for the Faithful

location and scale, as well as the distribution function among the one- and k-sample problems. In this section we consider some of the most popular non-parametric tests:

- The Wilcoxon Signed-Ranks Test
- Mann-Whitney test
- Wald-Wolfowitz run test
- Kolmogorov-Smirnov test
- Kruskal test
- Siegel-Tukey test

Non-parametric tests are also known as *distribution-free tests*. These are not to be confused with *assumption free* tests.

8.5.1 The Wilcoxon Signed-Ranks Test

The *Wilcoxon signed-rank test* was first proposed in Wilcoxon (1945). As the name indicates, the test procedures consider the ranks of the observations and their signs, which will be elaborated on in more detail in the following subsections. The Wilcoxon signed-rank test can be used in both one- and two-sample cases. We will begin with the one-sample problem.

The One-Sample Case

Let $X_1, X_2, \dots, X_n$ be iid RVs with the common absolutely continuous distribution function F, which is assumed to be symmetric about its median θ. Suppose that we are interested in testing $H : \theta = 0$ against the hypothesis that $H : \theta \neq 0$, where $\theta = E_F(X)$. This test can also be extended to one-sided tests. The two main and very important assumptions for this test are that the n observations are independent and that the underlying probability distribution F is absolutely continuous. The Wilcoxon signed-rank test is constructed in the following steps. First, obtain $|X_i|, i = 1, \dots, n$ and note the ranking of $|X_i|$ as $R_i, i = 1, \dots, n$. Note that if we are interested in testing the hypothesis $H : \theta = \theta_0$, we need the ranking of $|X_i - \theta_0|, i = 1, \dots, n$. Define the indicator variables:

$$\psi_i = \begin{cases} 1, & \text{if } X_i > 0, \\ 0, & \text{if } X_i \leq 0. \end{cases}$$

The Wilcoxon signed-rank test is then given by the sum of *positive signed ranks*:

$$T^+ = \sum_{i=1}^{n} \psi_i R_i. \tag{8.31}$$

The statistic T^+ is known as the *Wilcoxon statistic*. The one-sided upper-tail test of $H : \theta = 0$ against the alternative $K : \theta > 0$ is to reject the hypothesis H if $T^+ > t_\alpha$, where t_α is the upper-tail probability of the distribution of the Wilcoxon signed-rank T^+ statistic under H. Here, α is the level of significance. Similarly, the one-sided lower-tail test of $H : \theta = 0$ against the alternative $K : \theta < 0$ is to reject the hypothesis H if $T^+ \leq \frac{n(n+1)}{2} - t_\alpha$, whereas the two-sided test against the alternative $K : \theta \neq 0$ is to reject the hypothesis H if $T^+ \geq t_{\alpha/2}$ or if $T^+ \leq \frac{n(n+1)}{2} - t_{\alpha/2}$.

Hollander and Wolfe (1999) also suggest the use of a large-sample approximation for the Wilcoxon statistic by noting that under the hypothesis H, the mean and variance of the

Wilcoxon statistic T^+ are respectively given by:

$$E_H(T^+) = \frac{n(n+1)}{4},$$
$$Var_H(T^+) = \frac{n(n+1)(2n+1)}{24}.$$

The standardized version of T^+ is thus

$$T^* = \frac{T^+ - E_H(T^+)}{\sqrt{Var_H(T^+)}} = \frac{T^+ - \frac{n(n+1)}{4}}{\sqrt{\frac{n(n+1)(2n+1)}{24}}}.$$

Under the hypothesis H, as $n \to \infty$, $T^* \underset{\rightarrow}{D} N(0, 1)$. The inference is carried out in the usual way. In the next example, both the techniques will be illustrated.

Example 8.5.1. Freund and Wilson (2003). Suppose that the mean weight of peanuts put in jars is required to be 8 oz. The observed weights for 16 jars are 8.08, 7.71, 7.89, 7.72, 8.00, 7.90, 7.77, 7.81, 8.33, 7.67, 7.79, 7.79, 7.94, 7.84, 8.17, and 7.87. Here, we are interested in testing $H : \mu = 8.0$. This hypothesis can be testing with the aid of `wilcox.test`.

```
> peanuts <- c(8.08,7.71,7.89,7.72,8.00,7.90,7.77,7.81,8.33,7.67,
+ 7.79,7.79,7.94,7.84,8.17,7.87)
> wilcox.test(peanuts,mu=8)
 Wilcoxon signed rank test with continuity correction
data:  peanuts
V = 23.5, p-value = 0.04081
alternative hypothesis: true location is not equal to 8
Warning messages:
1: In wilcox.test.default(peanuts, mu = 8) :
  cannot compute exact p-value with ties
2: In wilcox.test.default(peanuts, mu = 8) :
  cannot compute exact p-value with zeroes
> wilcox.test(peanuts,mu=8,exact=FALSE,correct=FALSE)
 Wilcoxon signed rank test
data:  peanuts
V = 23.5, p-value = 0.03809
alternative hypothesis: true location is not equal to 8
```

Since the p-value is very small, for the exact Wilcoxon test as well as for the large-sample approximation non-parametric test, we reject the hypothesis H. □

The Two-Sample Case

If we have bivariate random samples $(X_1, Y_1), (X_2, Y_2), \ldots, (X_n, Y_n)$, we can proceed as in the one-sample case by ranking the differences $Z_1 = Y_1 - X_1, Z_2 = Y_2 - X_2, \ldots, Z_n = Y_n - X_n$. Here, the X_i's form one group and the Y_i's the other one. We assume that the $2n$ observations are independent of each other. In general, the (paired) two-sample Wilcoxon test is based on replacing the data pair (X_i, Y_i) with their differences Z_i, ignoring their group, and then calculating the sum of ranks in one group. The computation process is elaborated on as:

- Remove the observations if $Z_i = 0$, and let m denote the reduced number of pairs.
- Arrange the absolute values $|Z_i|$ in ascending order and let R_i denote the rank of $|Z_i|$.
- Define the indicator variables:

$$\psi_i = \begin{cases} 1, & \text{if } Z_i > 0, \\ 0, & \text{if } Z_i \leq 0. \end{cases}$$

- Finally, compute the Wilcoxon rank-sign tests T^+ and T^-, as earlier, by

$$T^+ = \sum_{i=1}^{n} \psi_i R_i, \tag{8.32}$$

$$T^- = \sum_{i=1}^{n} (1 - \psi_i) R_i. \tag{8.33}$$

- Define $S = \min(T^+, T^-)$, and compare S with critical values.

Test 6 of Sheshkin (2004) gives a comprehensive coverage of the Wilcoxon signed-rank test.

Example 8.5.2. The Hamilton Depression Scale Factor. The Hamilton depression scale factor IV is a measurement of mixed anxiety and depression and is named after its inventor. In a double-blind experiment, this scale factor is obtained for nine patients on their entry in a study, denoted by X. Post a tranquilizer T, the scale factor IV is again obtained for the same set of patients, which is denoted by Y. Here, an improvement due to tranquilizer T corresponds to a reduction in factor IV values. We use `wilcox.test` from R for testing if the tranquilizer T has been effective or not.

```
> data(depression)
> attach(depression)
> names(depression)
[1] "Patient_No" "X"          "Y"
> wilcox.test(Y-X, alternative = "less")
Wilcoxon signed rank test
data:  Y - X
V = 5, p-value = 0.01953
alternative hypothesis: true location is less than 0
> wilcox.test(Y-X, alternative = "less",exact=FALSE,correct=FALSE)
> #Hollander-Wolfe Large Sample Approximation Test
Wilcoxon signed rank test
data:  Y - X
V = 5, p-value = 0.01908
alternative hypothesis: true location is less than 0
```

The hypothesis $H : \theta = 0$ is rejected in favor of the alternative $K : \theta < 0$, since the p-values for the two-sample Wilcoxon test and its large sample approximation test, respectively at `0.01953` and `0.01908`, are small, and hence it is concluded that there has been an improvement due to the tranquilizer. □

Example 8.5.3. Energy Spend of Lean and Obese Men. The objective of this study is to examine if the energy spent by obese men and lean men is the same. The related data `energy` is available in the `ISwR` package. The Wilcoxon test for the energy spent by `lean` and `obese` persons in R is given below:

```
> wilcox.test(expend~stature,data=energy)
Wilcoxon rank sum test with continuity correction
data: expend by stature
W = 12, p-value = 0.002122
alternative hypothesis: true location shift is not equal to 0
Warning message:
In wilcox.test.default(x = c(7.53, 7.48, 8.08, 8.09, 10.15, 8.4, :
cannot compute exact p-value with ties
```

With the p-value being very close to zero, the hypothesis H that the energy spent by obese and lean men is the same will be rejected. □

8.5.2 *The Mann-Whitney test*

The Wilcoxon sign-rank test is useful for *paired data*. However, in the general two-sample problems, we may not have the paired data setup. The Mann-Whitney test is an extension of the Wilcoxon test, and is also known as the *Wilcoxon-Mann-Whitney* test or the *Wilcoxon rank-sum* test.

Let $X_1, \ldots, X_m$ be m observations from a population with distribution F, and $Y_1, \ldots, Y_n$ be n observations from a second population with distribution G. To set up the Wilcoxon rank-sum test, we assume that (a) the m observations are independent under F and the n under G, (b) the two populations are independent of each other, and (c) both the distributions F and G are absolutely continuous distributions.

Let $\Delta = E(Y) - E(X)$, and the hypothesis of interest be $H : \Delta = 0$. The Mann-Whitney test is set up as follows. Combine the X's and Y's and arrange them in ascending order. Let S_j denote the rank of $Y_j, j = 1, \ldots, n$. The Mann-Whitney statistic is then defined as

$$W = \sum_{j=1}^{n} S_j. \tag{8.34}$$

The one-sided upper-tail test of the hypothesis $H : \Delta = 0$ against the hypothesis $K : \Delta > 0$ is to reject the hypothesis H if $W \geq w_\alpha$, where w_α is the quantile corresponding to the upper-tail probability of the Wilcoxon rank-sum W statistic. As earlier with the one-sample case, the one-sided lower-tail test of the hypothesis $H : \Delta = 0$ against the hypothesis $K : \Delta < 0$ is to reject the null hypothesis if $W \leq n(n + m + 1) - w_\alpha$, whereas the two-sided test against the hypothesis $K : \Delta \neq 0$ is to reject the hypothesis H if $W \geq w_{\alpha/2}$ or if $W \leq n(n + m + 1) - w_{\alpha/2}$.

The large-sample approximation test statistic of Hollander and Wolfe (1999) also proceeds in the following way. The mean and variance of W, under the hypothesis H, are given by

$$E_H(W) = \frac{n(n+m+1)}{2},$$

$$Var_H(W) = \frac{nm(n+m+1)}{12}.$$

Thus, the standardized version of W is given by

$$W = \frac{W - E_H(W)}{\sqrt{Var_H(W)}} = \frac{W - \frac{n(n+m+1)}{2}}{\sqrt{\frac{nm(n+m+1)}{12}}}, \tag{8.35}$$

which for a large sample size converges to the standard normal distribution. Refer to Test 12 of Sheskin (2004) for more details.

Example 8.5.4. Some Urban-Rural Comparisons. Problem 6.9 of Gibbons and Chakraborti (2004) consider a random sample of 9 rural counties and 7 urban non-counties among a group of 67 Alabama counties for the population percent change. The data has been obtained from the 2000 census statistics. We need to compare if the population percent change among the rural and non-rural counties are the same or not. The R program is executed below.

```
> # The Mann-Whitney Test
> x <- c(1.1,-21.7,-16.3,-11.3,-10.4,-7,-2,1.9,6.2)
> # Percent Change in the Rural Counties
> y <- c(-2.4,9.9,14.2,18.4,20.1,23.1,70.4)
> # Percent Change in the Nonrural Counties
> wilcox.test(y,x)
 Wilcoxon rank sum test
data:  y and x
W = 59, p-value = 0.002098
alternative hypothesis: true location shift is not equal to 0
> wilcox.test(y,x,exact=FALSE)
 Wilcoxon rank sum test with continuity correction
data:  y and x
W = 59, p-value = 0.004263
alternative hypothesis: true location shift is not equal to 0
```

The p-value being closer to zero leads to rejection of the hypothesis H that the population percent change in the rural and non-rural counties are equal. □

The `wilcox.test` is very useful in setting up non-parametric tests, as seen in the different examples here. The option of `exact` is also seen to give useful large sample approximation when required.

8.5.3 The Siegel-Tukey Test

Siegel and Tukey (1960) proposed a non-parametric test for comparison of the spread among two populations. The Siegel-Tukey test is a non-parametric test for testing the equality of spread among two populations. This test can handle an unequal number of observations in the two populations. Consider, as earlier, a population A with m units and another population B with n units. The total number of observations is $N = m + n$. The observations are pooled together and arranged in ascending order. The hypothesis testing problem is $H : \sigma_A^2 = \sigma_B^2, \mu_{med,A} = \mu_{med,B}$ against is $K : \sigma_A^2 > \sigma_B^2$. Here $\mu_{med,A}, \mu_{med,B}$ denote the median of group A and B respectively.

Under the hypothesis H, it is expected that the ranks of the units from the two populations will be well mixed. That is, under the pooled sample, the sum of ranks for each sample will be approximately $N(N+1)/4$. If this is indeed the case, we believe the hypothesis H to be true, or else it is not so. Under the hypothesis K, we expect one of the group's rank sums to be far more than in the other sample.

The main assumptions of the Siegel-Tukey test are that (a) the units are random samples from their respective populations, (b) the two samples are respectively drawn from their populations independent of each other, (c) the data from each population is ordinal data, and (d) the medians of both the population are assumed to be equal.

Let $X_1, \ldots, X_m$ denote a random sample from the first population and $Y_1, \ldots, Y_n$ a sample from the second population. Let the pooled ordered sample be denoted by $W_1 \leq W_2 \leq \cdots \leq W_N$ and define the variables:

$$Zi = \begin{cases} 1, & \text{W is a x value,} \\ 0, & \text{W is a y value.} \end{cases}$$

The *Siegel-Tukey test* is given by the expression:

$$S_N = \sum_{i=1}^{N} a_i Z_i, \tag{8.36}$$

where the a_i's are some weights decided as follows. Assume that N is even. Then on the left-hand side we assign $a_1 = 1$, and move to the right-hand side with $a_N = 2, a_{N-1} = 3$. Next, we return to the left-hand side and assign $a_2 = 4, a_3 = 5$, and continue moving in either direction until N. We will illustrate these a_is in a dummy dataset, see Table 8.4.

If N is odd, the middle observation is thrown out and the weights for reduced N are used. Hence, a general formula for obtaining a_i's is given by:

$$a_i = \begin{cases} 2i, & i \text{ even, } 1 \leq i \leq N/2, \\ 2i-1, & i \text{ odd, } 1 \leq i \leq N/2, \\ 2(N-i)+2, & i \text{ even, } N/2 < i \leq N, \\ 2(N-i)+1, & i \text{ odd, } N/2 < i \leq N. \end{cases}$$

The probability distribution of S_N is the same as that for the Wilcoxon test statistic. Hence, the same tables may be used. For a comprehensive coverage of the Siegel-Tukey test, the reader

Table 8.4 Determining Weights of the Siegel-Tukey Test

i	1	2	3	4	5	6
x	1	2	3			
y				4	5	6
W	1	2	3	4	5	6
Z	1	1	1	0	0	0
a	1	4	5	6	3	2

may refer to Test 14 in Sheskin (2004). Here, we will use a large-sample approximation using the following facts:

$$E(S_N) = \frac{m(N+1)}{2},$$
$$Var(S_N) = \frac{mn(N+1)}{12}.$$

The next program illustrates the Siegel-Tukey procedure for a dataset from Gibbons and Chakraborti (2003).

```
> x <- c(0.028, 0.029, 0.011, -0.030, 0.017, -0.012, -0.027,-0.018,
+ 0.022, -0.023)
> y <- c(-0.002, 0.016, 0.005, -0.001, 0.000, 0.008, -0.005,-0.009,
+ 0.001, -0.019)
> siegel.tukey(x,y)
[1] -3.4016802571  0.0003348647
```

The reader should note that the function `siegel.tukey` from the `ACSWR` package follows the formulas detailed earlier. For the dataset under consideration, the conclusion is to reject the hypothesis that the spread of the two distributions is equal.

8.5.4 The Wald-Wolfowitz Run Test

The Wald-Wolfowitz run test is yet another non-parametric test of the hypothesis $H : F = G$, where F and G are the probability distribution functions of two samples. The distributions F and G are assumed to be absolutely continuous. As earlier, let $X_1, \dots, X_m$ be a random sample of size m from F, and let $Y_1, \dots, Y_n$ be a random sample of size n from G.

A *run* is defined as a succession of one or more identical symbols, which are preceded and followed by a different symbol, or no symbol. The *length* of a run is the number of identical symbols in that run. Finally, we define an RV R as the total number of runs in the pooled sample of X's and Y's, arranged in ascending order. If the hypothesis H holds true, we expect the X's and Y's to be well mixed, and thus a large value for R.

It may be shown that for a large value of $N(= m + n)$, an approximation for the mean and variance of R are respectively given by

$$\mu_R = 1 + \frac{2mn}{m+n},$$
$$\sigma_R^2 = \frac{2mn(2mn - m - n)}{(m+n-1)(m+n)^2}.$$

Thus, it can be seen that as $n \to \infty$

$$R \sim N\left(1 + \frac{2mn}{m+n}, \frac{2mn(2mn - m - n)}{(m+n-1)(m+n)^2}\right). \tag{8.37}$$

Using the above result, it is possible to carry out appropriate inference for the related hypotheses.

Example 8.5.5. Incidence and Degree of Aggression Scores for Boys and Girls. Rohatgi and Saleh (2000), Problem 7 of Section 13.6, lists a dataset for incidence and degree of aggression scores for 15 3-year-old boys and 15 3-year-old girls. We need to investigate if there is gender differences for these scores. R base does not have a function for carrying out the Wald-Wolfowitz run test, and the authors are not aware of any package to help us out in this context. It may be possible that some user may have developed it. However, we will write an explicit program for this as the code development is also a bit of fun here. The next R program solves this problem.

```
> # The Wald-Wolfowitz Run Test
> boys <- c(96,65,74,78,82,121,68,79,111,48,53,92,81,31,40)
> girls <- c(12,47,32,59,83,14,32,15,17,82,21,34,9,15,51)
> ww.test(boys,girls)
[1] 0.002950069
```

The function `ww.test` in the `ACSWR` package is set up as follows. First, the indices for X and Y are generated in `xind` and `yind`. The vector data of `x` and `y` are then combined in `xy`, using the concatenate and generic function `c`, and this is then repeated for `xind` and `yind` in `xyind`. Then a matrix is set up using `cbind` for the combined data in the `grand` object. This new object is then ranked using the values in `xy`. The function `run-function` within the `ww.test` function obtains the number of runs in the two samples. The number of runs is determined in a logical way, and the reader needs to figure this out, in the line `num_of_runs <- sum(diff(grand[,2])!=0)+1`. The computation of `mu0` and `var0` does not require further explanation, and neither do the rest of the arguments. Now, using the function `ww.test`, we obtain the p-value for comparison of the gender difference.

Since the p-value is very small, we reject the hypothesis H that the gender difference is insignificant. □

8.5.5 *The Kolmogorov-Smirnov Test*

The One-Sample Problem

Let $X_1, X_2, \ldots, X_n$ be a random sample from a probability distribution F. The empirical distribution function, as given in Section 8.2 of this chapter, is $\hat{F}_n(x) = \sum_{i=1}^{n} I(X_i \leq x)/n$. Suppose we wish to test the hypothesis $H: F(x) = F_0(x), \forall x$ against the alternative $K: F(x) \neq F_0(x),\ for\ some\ x$. The *Kolmogorov-Smirnov* test for the hypothesis H is given by

$$D_n = \sup_x |F_n(x) - F_0(x)|, \tag{8.38}$$

$$= \max_{1 \leq i \leq n} \left\{ \max \left[F_0(X_{i:n}) - \left(\frac{i-1}{n} \right), \frac{1}{n} - F_0(X_{i:n}) \right] \right\}, \tag{8.39}$$

where $X_{1:n} \leq \cdots \leq X_{n:n}$ are the ordered RVs. For more details, see Section 8.3 of Govindarajulu (2007).

Example 8.5.6. Distribution of the Height of Children in the Galton Dataset. Suppose that historically it is known that the distribution of height of parents follows a normal distribution with a mean of 68 and a standard deviation of 1.78. For the Galton dataset, we wish to investigate if the height of children is also the same. The Kolmogorov-Smirnov test is then performed in R as detailed here.

```
> # The One-Sample Kolmogorov-Smirnov Test
> library(UsingR)
> data(galton)
> ks.test(galton$child,"pnorm",mean=68,sd=1.78)
 One-sample Kolmogorov-Smirnov test
data:  galton$child
D = 0.1831, p-value < 2.2e-16
alternative hypothesis: two-sided
Warning message:
In ks.test(galton$child, "pnorm", mean = 68, sd = 1.78) :
  cannot compute correct p-values with ties
```

The function `ks.test` is fairly straightforward to use in the case of a two-sample problem. In the case of a one-sample problem, the hypothesized distribution F_0 needs to be specified in a careful way. In this example, we wanted to test if $F_0 \sim N(68, 1.78^2)$. Now, this distribution needs to be specified in the `ks.test` function with the options `pnorm`, and `mean=68` and `sd=1.78`.

Typically, the results from a software program needs to be interpreted properly. Here, the R program is saying that it has not handled the ties properly. Thus, we need to adjust for the ties in an adequate way. Having said this, it is not within the scope of the current chapter to address this issue, and we conservatively conclude that the distribution of the height of the children is not distributed as normal with mean 68 and standard deviation 1.78. □

The Two-Sample Problem

Suppose that $X_1, X_2, \ldots, X_m$ is a random sample from a probability distribution F, and $Y_1, Y_2, \ldots, Y_n$ is a random sample from a probability distribution G. Assume that we are interested in determining if the two samples originate from the same population, that is, we would like to verify our intuition by testing the hypothesis $H : F = G = F'$, say. Notice that we are not making any assumptions for the distribution of F and G, or F'. In this case we need to resort to non-parametric methods. Let $F_m(x)$ and $G_n(x)$ be the empirical distribution functions related to F and G respectively. The *two-sample Kolmogorov-Smirnov test* is then given by

$$D_{m,n} = \sup_x |F_m(x) - G_n(x)|. \tag{8.40}$$

The test procedure is to reject H if $D_{m,n} \geq c_\alpha$, where c_α is determined such that

$$P(D_{m,n} \geq c_\alpha | H_0) \leq \alpha.$$

Exact computation of the probabilities for small m and n values may be seen in Table I of Gibbons and Chakraborti (2004). Refer to Test 7 of Sheskin (2004) for more details related to the KS-test. We will next illustrate the two-sample test for the Galton dataset.

Example 8.5.7. Are the Distributions of Height of Children and Parents Equal? In continuation of the previous example, we now do not specify the distribution of the height of parents. The R implementation is straightforward:

```
> ks.test(galton$child,galton$parent)
Two-sample Kolmogorov-Smirnov test
data:  galton$child and galton$parent
D = 0.2425, p-value < 2.2e-16
alternative hypothesis: two-sided
Warning message:
In ks.test(galton$child, galton$parent) :
  cannot compute correct p-values with ties
```

The conclusion of the above program is left to the reader! □

*8.5.6 Kruskal-Wallis Test**

We have earlier used the Wilcoxon test for testing the hypothesis of equality of two location parameters (median). A generalization of the testing for equality of k location parameters is provided by the Kruskal-Wallis test statistic. In the general setting we have k treatments and we are interested in testing if their effects are equal or otherwise. The Kruskal-Wallis test a non-parametric ANOVA technique. The parametric ANOVA methods are detailed in Chapters 13 to 15.

Let n_j denote the number of observations under treatment $j, j = 1, 2, \ldots, k$. The total number of observations in the study is $N = \sum_{j=1}^{k} n_j$. For a *one-way* layout we can display the data, as in Table 8.5.

The assumptions for the use of the test method are the following: (a) all the N observations are independent, (b) the cumulative distribution function $F_j, j = 1, \ldots, k$ is assumed to be continuous, and (c) the distribution functions F_j are characterized by $\tau_j, j = 1, \ldots, k$, where τ_j is the unknown treatment effect.

The hypothesis of interest is $H : \tau_1 = \cdots = \tau_k$, which is tested against the hypothesis that $K : \tau_i \neq \tau_j$, for some $i \neq j$. The test procedure includes the following steps.

- Arrange all the N observations from smallest to largest value.
- Let r_{ij} denote the rank of X_{ij} in the above pooled data.

Table 8.5 Data Arrangement for the Kruskal-Wallis Test

Treatment 1	Treatment 2	…	Treatment k
X_{11}	X_{12}	…	X_{1k}
X_{21}	X_{22}	…	X_{2k}
⋮	⋮		⋮
$X_{n_1 1}$	$X_{n_2 2}$	…	$X_{n_k k}$

- Obtain the rank sum and rank average for each of the k samples:

$$R_j = \sum_{i=1}^{n_j} r_{ij}, j = 1, \dots, k,$$

$$R_j = \frac{R_j}{n_j}, j = 1, \dots, k.$$

The Kruskal-Wallis test statistic, denoted by H, is given by

$$T_{KW} = \left(\frac{12}{N(N+1)} \sum_{j=1}^{k} \frac{R_j^2}{n_j} \right) - 3(N+1) \tag{8.41}$$

The test procedure is to reject H if $T_{KW} \geq h_\alpha$, where h_α is found by a special statistical table.

Example 8.5.8. Mucociliary Clearance. Table 6.1 of Hollander and Wolfe (1999) lists the data for Half-Time of Mucociliary Clearance. We need to test if the time across various treatments is equal or not.

```
> data(Mucociliary)
> Mucociliary$Rank <- rank(Mucociliary$Time)
> aggregate(Mucociliary$Rank,by=list(Mucociliary$Treatment),sum)
                    Group.1  x
1                Asbestosis 33
2           Normal Subjects 36
3 Obstructive Airways Disease 36
> kruskal.test(Time~Treatment,data=Mucociliary)
 Kruskal-Wallis rank sum test
data:  Time by Treatment
Kruskal-Wallis chi-squared = 0.7714, df = 2, p-value = 0.68
```

The `kruskal.test` readily gives the required answer. The large p-value indicates that there is no evidence to reject the hypothesis H for equality of the location parameters. □

?wilcox.test, ?rank, ?ks.test, ?kruskal.test

8.6 Further Reading

An interesting remark about non-parametrics is that due to computational limitations, the early history of the subject was more dedicated to testing problems and less on estimation. The computational advantage during the last three decades is changing this facet and we can increasingly see more estimation methods developed in the domain of non-parametrics. Thus, we can see many early non-parametric texts focusing more on testing problems.

Siegel (1956) appears to us as the first non-parametrics text and it was also especially written for the *behavioral sciences*. Conover (1999), Gibbons and Chakraborti (2003), Desu and Raghavarao (2004), Govindarajulu (2007), and Sprent and Smeeton (2001) deal with many non-parametric testing procedures. Lehmann (1975) is a rigorous treatment of this subject. The previous section has been influenced by Hollander and Wolfe (1999). The authorative handbook on testing by Sheshkin (2004) will be very handy for practitioners. Though we do not consider an approach, Hajék, et al. (1999) is essential reading for any person who wants to study the subject in a detailed framework.

Efron and Tibshirani (1993) is a detailed monograph on bootstrap methods. Further details about the bootstrap can be obtained in Shao and Tu (1996) and Chernick (2008).

Smoothing techniques have been detailed in Silverman (1985) and Simonoff (1996). Wasserman (2006) is yet another comprehensive treatise on the modern aspects of non-parametrics.

8.7 Complements, Problems, and Programs

Problem 8.1 For the `swiss$Bottforg` data vector, obtain the empirical cdf and estimate the statistical functionals of skewness and kurtosis.

Problem 8.2 Find the 90% bootstrap confidence intervals for skewness and kurtosis estimates of the previous problem.

Problem 8.3 For the `parent` height in the `galton` set, obtain the histogram smoothing and the kernel smoothing estimates and draw the right inference.

Problem 8.4 Compare the Behrens-Fisher test results with the Mann-Whitney non-parametric test for the Youden-Beale data.

Problem 8.5 The `nerve` dataset, as discussed in Section 8.2, deals with the cumulative distribution function. Estimate the density function of the `nerve` data using histogram smoothing, and uniform, Epanechnikov, biweight, and Gaussian kernels.

Problem 8.6 For the parameters estimated in Section 7.6 under the assumption of certain distributions, use the Kolmogorov-Smirnov tests for one-sample to test the hypothesis that the fitted models are the true model.

Problem 8.7 The `t.test` is used to compare the `sleep` data, Youden-Beale data, etc. In each case, test the Kolmogorov-Smirnov two-sample test and conclude whether or not both the tests agree.

9

Bayesian Inference

Package(s): `LearnBayes`, `VGAM`

9.1 Introduction

We encountered the Bayes formula in Section 5.6 and some important Bayesian sampling distributions in Section 6.9. Bayesian probabilities are of interest in themselves and such probabilities also highlight the requirement for appropriate choice of prior distributions for unknown parameters. The Bayesian probabilities will be discussed in depth in Section 9.2. Useful theoretical aspects of the Bayesian paradigm are then discussed in Section 9.3. Bayesian inference for standard probability distributions will be taken up in Sections 9.4.1–9.4.5. An advantage of the Bayes paradigm is that a single approach helps to answer the three inferential problems of estimation, intervals, and testing hypotheses, and we will consider *credible intervals* in Section 9.5. Finally, hypotheses testing problem will be dealt with in Section 9.6 using *Bayes factors*.

9.2 Bayesian Probabilities

In general, almost all Bayesian texts assume that the reader learned probability theory in a separate course and so there is almost no discussion of *Bayesian probabilities*. As a matter of factual non-coincidence, an observation has been that either the word "Bayes" does not appear in many classical probability texts, or merely gets a simple honorable mention. This is not a surprise as most Bayesian texts define "posterior distribution" only in the context of data and not as a probability model. There are a lot of surprises when we consider Bayesian probabilities themselves and so there is no strong requirement to have data as a starting point when learning Bayesian statistics. A simple example of Bayesian probability has already been seen in Example 5.6.1 of Section 5.6. This section will follow the paper of Diaconis and Holmes (2002). The philosophy of Bayesian approach can be found in the classic book of Jeffreys (1961).

A Course in Statistics with R, First Edition. Prabhanjan Narayanachar Tattar, Suresh Ramaiah and B. G. Manjunath.

Companion Website: www.wiley.com/go/tattar/statistics

Example 9.2.1. Bayesian Probability of Success and Revisiting Example 5.2.9 of Laplace Probability of Sunrise. Consider an observation X which follows binomial distribution $b(n,p)$. Here, X can take any integer value between 0 and n. An *indifferent* approach for specifying a prior distribution is that p can assume any value equally between 0 and 1, that is, we use a uniform prior for p:

$$\pi(p) = 1, 0 \le p \le 1. \tag{9.1}$$

The posterior distribution is given by

$$\begin{aligned}
\pi(p|x) &= \frac{\binom{n}{x} p^x (1-p)^{n-x}}{\int_0^1 \binom{n}{x} p^x (1-p)^{n-x} dp} \\
&= \frac{p^x (1-p)^{n-x}}{\int_0^1 p^{(x+1)-1} (1-p)^{(n-x+1)-1} dp} \\
&= \frac{1}{\text{Beta}\,(x+1, n-x+1)} p^{(x+1)-1} (1-p)^{(n-x+1)-1}.
\end{aligned}$$

Application to an interesting problem is in order. Recollect that we had defined the probability that the sun will rise on the 7th day, if we have observed the sun to rise on 6 out of 6 days, will be (6 + 1)/(6 + 2) = 7/8 = 0.875. The posterior mean of p is then

$$\hat{p} = \frac{x+1}{x+1+n-x+1} = \frac{x+1}{n+2}.$$

Thus, if we had observed the sun to rise on 6 out of 6 days, the Bayesian estimate for the probability of sunrise on the next day, under a non-informative prior, is (6 + 1)/(6 + 2) = 7/8 = 0.875. □

Thus, all the inference for p may be based only on the posterior distribution.

Example 9.2.2. Uniform Prior for the Birthday Problem. The birthday problem will be considered under different setups for different priors. As a beginning, a multinomial distribution with $n = 365$ cells may be used, where each cell has the same probability of getting a new ball. Under a uniform prior, equivalently non-informative prior, the probability of a match when k balls are dropped into the n cells is given by

$$P(\text{match}) = 1 - \prod_{i=1}^{k-1} \frac{1-i/n}{1+i/n}. \tag{9.2}$$

The next R program gives the Bayesian probabilities of a match when k balls are dropped into the n cells.

```
> # Prob(a match) = 1- prod_{i=1}^{k-1} {(1-i/n)/(1+i/n)}
> n <- 365
> k <- c(2,5,10,20,30,40,50)
> prob_match_fun <- function(n,k) 1-prod((1-1:k/n)/(1+1:k/n))
> prob_match <- sapply(k,prob_match_fun,n=n)
```

```
> prob_no_match <- 1-prob_match
> cbind(k,prob_match,prob_no_match)
      k prob_match prob_no_match
[1,]  2 0.01630411  0.9836958949
[2,]  5 0.07890755  0.9210924518
[3,] 10 0.26022659  0.7397734053
[4,] 20 0.68377152  0.3162284780
[5,] 30 0.92198997  0.0780100274
[6,] 40 0.98891780  0.0110822028
[7,] 50 0.99909607  0.0009039281
```

The R code `1-prod((1-1:k/n)/(1+1:k/n))` calculates the probability on the right-hand side of Equation 9.2 . Of course, it is of interest to contrast these probabilities with classical ones, refer to Table 9.1. We can thus see that even the use of the uniform prior changes the probabilities significantly. □

Table 9.1 Birthday Probabilities: Bayesian and Classical

Size k	Classical Birthday Probabilities	Bayesian Birthday Probabilities
2	0.00273973	0.01630411
5	0.02713557	0.07890755
10	0.11694818	0.26022659
20	0.41143838	0.68377152
30	0.70631624	0.92198997
40	0.89123181	0.98891780
50	0.97037358	0.99909607

Example 9.2.3. The Coupon Collector's Problem Under the Bayesian Paradigm. In Example 5.7.5, the coupon collectors were discussed in detail and the answer was obtained for the expected number of coupons to be purchased to complete the collection. The problem will be looked at in a different framework now. As earlier, let T continue to denote the number of coupons n to be purchased for the complete collection. It helps to imagine a coupon as an urn and that if the ith coupon is chosen, the ith urn is non-empty. Equivalently, all the coupons are collected if all the urns are non-empty. Then, the probability $P(T \leq t)$, see Section 2.2 of Mahmoud (2008) for details, is given by

$$P(T \leq t) = \sum_{j=0}^{n} (-1)^j \binom{n}{j} \left(1 - \frac{j}{n}\right)^t, t = n, n+1, \ldots . \tag{9.3}$$

It may be noted here that though some components of the sum in Equation 9.3 may be negative, the overall probability is always positive. A small program will illustrate this next for the number of urns at $n = 5$ and $t = 5, 6, \ldots, 10$.

```
> n <- 5; t <- 5:10
> ProbAllUrns <- NULL
```

```
> for(i in 1:length(t)) {
+   tt <- 0:n*0
+   for(j in 0:n) {
+     tt[j+1] <- ((-1)^{j})*choose(n,j)*((1-j/n)^{t}[i])
+                 }
+   ProbAllUrns[i] <- sum(tt)
+                       }
> ProbAllUrns
[1] 0.0384 0.1152 0.2150 0.3226 0.4271 0.5225
> tt
[1]  1.000e+00 -5.369e-01  6.047e-02 -1.049e-03  5.120e-07  0.000e+00
```

The terms `tt` show that the terms of the sum for $P(T \leq 10)$ are negative, though the probability itself is not. If a village celebrates the birthday of its occupants, we can then answer how many people are required in its population so that the probability of every day being celebrated as a birthday is at least 1/2 by computing $n = 365$ and allowing $t \geq 365$. It may be verified for $t = 2287$, the probability will be `0.5004`.

The *Bayesian probability* $P_{Bayes}(T \leq t)$, under a uniform prior that any coupon is as likely to be picked as any other coupon, see Equation 3.3 of Diaconis and Holmes (2002), is given by

$$P_{Bayes}(T \leq t) = \frac{\binom{t-1}{n-1}}{\binom{t+k-1}{n-1}}, t = n, n+1, \ldots . \tag{9.4}$$

The expression $P_{Bayes}(T \leq t)$ is very computationally demanding. For example, if we try to obtain the numerator term with $t = 2287$, which in the expression 9.3 refers to the probability 1/2, with `choose(2286,364)`, we run into the `Inf` problem. Thus, we customize a function `logChoose` and then compute the probabilities $P_{Bayes}(T \leq t)$. The function `logChoose` simply executes the combinations on a logarithmic scale.

```
> logChoose <- function(n,r) {
+   lcr <- sum(log(1:n)) - sum(log(1:(n-r))) - sum(log(1:r))
+   return(lcr)
+                            }
> n <- 365
> t <- 2287
> exp(logChoose(t-1,n-1)-logChoose(t+n-1,n-1))
[1] 4.595884e-26
> exp(logChoose(2*t-1,n-1)-logChoose(2*t+n-1,n-1))
[1] 2.353723e-13
> exp(logChoose(5*t-1,n-1)-logChoose(5*t+n-1,n-1))
[1] 8.978454e-06
> exp(logChoose(10*t-1,n-1)-logChoose(10*t+n-1,n-1))
[1] 0.00299862
> exp(logChoose(100*t-1,n-1)-logChoose(100*t+n-1,n-1))
[1] 0.5593746
> exp(logChoose(191844-1,n-1)-logChoose(191844+n-1,n-1))
[1] 0.5003025
```

For the classical counterpart sample size of $n = 2287$, the Bayesian probability is `4.596e-26`, to almost zero. In fact, even if the size is increased by 10 times to $n = 22870$, the Bayesian answer is `0.002999`, again close to zero. To match the probability of 1/2, the Bayesian answer of the sample size is as high as `191844`. Thus, the answer becomes here even more intriguing. However, it is not too much of a surprise, and the enthusiastic reader should refer to the Diaconis and Holmes paper. □

Diaconis and Holmes also deal with these problems using the Dirichlet prior. Jeffreys (1939–61) is a treatise on the philosophy of Bayes paradigm.

9.3 The Bayesian Paradigm for Statistical Inference

In the classical approach, we have seen that estimation and testing problems have different approaches. In the Bayesian school, we have a unified framework for addressing all of the inferential aspects. The posterior distribution of the parameters suffice for estimation, testing, and confidence interval problems. In Sections 7.4 and 7.5 of Chapter 7, we noted the importance of the sufficiency and likelihood principles. The Bayesian paradigm serves as a *duality principle* which considers both of these perspectives, see Section 1.2 of Robert (2007). To understand the Bayesian paradigm, consider a probability function $f(x|\theta)$, and let the prior distribution about θ be specified as $\pi(\theta)$. The Bayesian paradigm then bases the inference about θ on the *posterior distribution*, denoted by $\pi(\theta|x)$, given by:

$$\pi(\theta|x) = \frac{f(x|\theta)\pi(\theta)}{\int f(x|\theta)\pi(\theta)d\theta}. \tag{9.5}$$

Recall by the definition of sufficient statistic and the Neyman factorization theorem that a statistic $T(x)$ is sufficient if

$$f(x|\theta) = g(T(x)|\theta)h(x).$$

Since the Bayesian inference depends on $f(x|\theta)$, it will always take into consideration the sufficient statistic, and hence it can be said that the Bayesian paradigm will satisfy the sufficiency principle. In the next subsection, we will briefly state Bayesian sufficiency and later check for the likelihood principle.

9.3.1 *Bayesian Sufficiency and the Principle*

Ghosh, et al. (2006) discuss the Bayesian sufficiency in their Appendix E. The concept of sufficiency here remains the same as seen in Section 7.4.

Definition 9.3.1 Bayesian Sufficiency. *A statistic T is said to be sufficient in a Bayesian sense if for all priors $\pi(\theta)$ the posterior distribution can be written as*

$$\pi(\theta|x) = \pi(\theta|T(x)) \tag{9.6}$$

By their definitions, a sufficient statistic is always Bayesian sufficient. However, Blackwell and Ramamoorthi (1982) give a counter example that the Bayesian sufficient statistic need not be a sufficient statistic in the context of a hypothesis testing problem. See also Section 7.9 of Geisser and Johnson (2006). The *sufficiency principle* is given next.

Definition 9.3.2 Sufficiency Principle. *Let x and y be two observations factorizing through the same value of a sufficient statistic T, implying $T(x) = T(y)$. Then the inference based on the two observations x and y must be the same for the parameter θ.*

The Examples 7.4.1 to 7.4.7 all provide sufficient statistics and the inference for the parameters to be carried out using them. For instance, in Example 7.4.1, $T = \sum_{i=1}^n X_i$ is sufficient for θ in the case of exponential distribution, while $T = (\sum_{i=1}^n X_i, \sum_{i=1}^n X_i^2)$ is jointly sufficient for (θ, σ^2) for a sample from a normal distribution when both parameters are unknown.

9.3.2 *Bayesian Analysis and Likelihood Principle*

The likelihood principle was introduced in Section 7.5. Recollect from Example 7.5.3 where the inference for p had to be based on $p^9(1-p)^3$. However, we had two proportionality constants which would lead to different conclusions in the classical inference. The Likelihood principle though requires that the inference should be the same as long as the two sample points are proportional to each other. Since the Bayesian inference about p would depend completely on the posterior distribution, the Likelihood principle is automatically satisfied. This point will be clearly demonstrated in examples that follow in the remainder of this chapter.

The choice of prior distributions will be discussed in the following.

9.3.3 *Informative and Conjugate Prior*

Consider a prior distribution $\pi(\theta)$ for a random sample from $f(x|\theta)$.

Definition 9.3.3 *Suppose that υ is a parameter of interest. Let $\mathcal{P}$ be the family of distribution of $\pi(\theta)$. We say that the prior $\pi(\theta)$ is a* conjugate prior *for θ if the posterior density function $\pi(\theta|x)$ also belongs to $\mathcal{P}$.*

Table 6.1 gives some examples of the conjugate prior and the related posterior distribution in what has been referred to as the Bayesian sampling distribution. Specifically recall that if the prior distribution for p in the binomial distribution is a beta distribution, the posterior distribution is also a beta distribution, see also the discussion following Example 9.2.1. In the case of multinomial distribution, which is an extension of binomial, the Dirichlet prior is an example of a conjugate prior, since the posterior distribution is also a Dirichlet distribution.

It should be noted that the parameters of the prior distribution need to be completely specified. The important question is how are the parameters specified? A very partial answer is provided here and precise answers can be obtained in the literature given in the Further Reading section at the end of this chapter. Suppose that it is intended to estimate the average life of an electronic device at a certain facility, and exponential distribution is assumed to govern the age of the device. It may be possible that the expert engineering team has a good scientific reason for specifying the range of the average age device with certain probabilities, say they expect the average life of the device to be between 10 months to 36 months, with a probability 0.95. It is also possible that data may be available for a sample of 20 units each over the past 24 months and the sampling distribution of the averages of the months may be used to specify the prior parameters of a gamma distribution.

9.3.4 *Non-informative Prior*

The prior information may not always be strong or reliable enough to form a prior distribution $\pi(\theta)$. It is also possible that expert information is not available or that the experiment is being performed for the first time and hence there would be no data to form a prior distribution. In such scenarios, the role of the *non-informative priors* comes into prominence. The non-informative prior has already been used in Section 9.2. For instance, in the coupon collector's problem, any coupon is as likely to be selected as any other coupon.

We will briefly discuss two types of non-informative priors: (i) Laplace prior, and (ii) Jeffrey's prior. Recall the uniform prior for probability of success p in Example 9.2.1, that is, $\pi(p) = 1, 0 \leq p \leq 1$. It means, of course, that any value of p is as likely as any other, that is, there is no information about p being really conveyed. Similarly, the Laplace prior in other examples are also non-informative.

The Jeffrey's prior is related to the Fisher information given in Equation 7.20. The Jeffrey's prior distribution is defined as proportional to the square-root Fisher information, that is,

$$\pi(\theta) \propto I^{1/2}(\theta). \tag{9.7}$$

Recall that in Example 7.5.6, it was proved that $\mathcal{I}_\lambda = 1/\lambda$, and thus the Jeffreys non-informative prior is $1/\sqrt{\lambda}$.

9.4 Bayesian Estimation

In many cases, the posterior distribution does not admit a closed form expression. In general, it may be a difficult expression to evaluate. For the moment assume that we do not have the time (and the skills) for learning advanced techniques. That is, the probability model and the posterior distribution which have closed form expressions are considered.

9.4.1 *Inference for Binomial Distribution*

Consider a random sample of size n from Bernoulli trials. Let the probability of success be denoted by p. As seen earlier, for a specified prior distribution $\pi(p)$, and the data $\mathbf{x} = (x_1, \ldots, x_n)$, the posterior distribution is obtained by

$$\pi(p|\mathbf{x}) = \frac{\pi(p)\binom{n}{x}p^x(1-p)^{n-x}}{\int \pi(p)\binom{n}{x}p^x(1-p)^{n-x}dp}.$$

So far we have not specified the form of the prior distributions. The prior distribution may be discrete or continuous. First consider the discrete prior and then follow it up with a continuous prior. As in the general scenario, the marginal distribution $\int \pi(p)f(\mathbf{x}|p)dp$ is not of interest and is ignored and we continue to focus on $\pi(p)\binom{n}{x}p^x(1-p)^{n-x}$.

9.4.1.1 Inference Using a Discrete Prior

For a discrete prior $\pi(p) = (p_1, \ldots, p_k)$, the integral in the denominator of the posterior distribution reduces to a sum over the k points and the Bayes formula can be used to obtain the posterior probabilities. The Bayesian inference for the Bernoulli distribution with a discrete prior is considered next.

Example 9.4.1. A Discrete Prior for the Proportion of Heavy Sleepers. Consider an example from Albert (2009). A small survey has been conducted to find out if the students receive the recommended sleep of eight hours. Let p denote the proportion of students who have at least eight hours of sleep. Suppose that the experimenter believes the proportion p belongs to the intervals (0,0.1),(0.1,0.2), ..., (0.9,1) with the weights 1, 5.2, 8, 7.2, 4.6, 2.1, 0.7, 0.1, 0, and 0. That is, the probability p of belonging in the interval is now specified by a histogram. Bayesian inference using the *histogram prior* will be taken in Section 11.6. Thus, the prior over intervals is tweaked to specific points, namely the center of the intervals. That is, suppose that the experimenter believes that the weights of p taking the values 0.05, 0.15, ..., 0.95 are respectively 1, 5.2, 8, 7.2, 4.6, 2.1, 0.7, 0.1, 0, and 0. A normalization can be used to translate the weights into prior probabilities. In terms of symbols, $\pi_i, i = 1, \ldots, 10$ takes the values 0.05, ..., 0.95 with respective probabilities 0.03, …, 0. Given that 11 out of 27 students had a minimum sleep of eight hours the previous night, here $n = 27$ and $x = 11$, the posterior probabilities can be obtained with the use of Bayes formula 5.10:

$$p(\pi_i|x = 11) = \frac{\pi_i \times p^{11}(1-p)^{16}}{\sum_{i=1}^{10} \pi_i \times p^{11}(1-p)^{16}}.$$

The posterior probabilities are easily obtained by first multiplying the prior probabilities with the likelihood function and then following it with a normalization.

```
> p <- seq(0.05, 0.95, by = 0.1) # plausible values of the parameter
> prior <- c(1, 5.2, 8, 7.2, 4.6, 2.1, 0.7, 0.1, 0, 0)
> # belief in plausible values
> prior <- prior/sum(prior)
> # translating the belief into probability
> x <- 11; n <- 27
> lik_prior <- prior*p^{11}*(1-p)^{16}
> posterior_prob <- lik_prior/sum(lik_prior)
> round(posterior_prob,2)
[1] 0.00 0.00 0.13 0.48 0.33 0.06 0.00 0.00 0.00 0.00
```

Thus, the prior probabilities are transformed into posterior ones using a simple expression. □

Example 9.4.2. Bolstad's Example 6.9. Bolstad (2007) constructs Bayesian inference for binomial distribution given a discrete prior. Suppose that it is known a priori that the probability of success is one of the three values 0.4, 0.5, or 0.6, and each is as likely to occur as the others. The coin is tossed $n = 4$ times and $x = 3$ successes are observed. The problem is then to obtain the posterior probabilities. The lucid manner in which Bolstad transcends from the

Bayes formula to inference is remarkable and in Chapter 6 of his book, all the steps are cleanly outlined through the use of neat tables, Tables I to IV, which are as follows:

- In Table I, specify the discrete prior values, say $p_1, \dots, p_k$, in column 1 and the discrete prior probabilities, $\pi_1, \dots, \pi_k$, in column 2. The rest of the columns are labeled as 0, 1, $\dots, n$.
- For the ith row, obtain the probabilities $P(X = i|p = p_j), i = 0, 1, \dots, n, j = 1, \dots, k$. This will complete Table I.
- For Table II, retain the number of columns. The first three rows are unchanged and we need to append the table with one more row. From the third column onwards, obtain the column sums and enter the result as the fourth row. This will be given as the *marginal distribution* of X.
- We need to obtain the posterior probabilities $P(\pi_j|X = 3)$! This can be obtained by dividing the column corresponding to $X = 3$ by its column sum, as obtained in the previous step. This is Table III.
- Refer to page 110 of Bolstad (2007) and interpret Table IV.

However, we will simply use the Bayes formula and R codes as in the previous example to obtain the posterior probabilities.

```
> n <- 4; x <- 3
> prior <- rep(1/3,3)
> p <- c(0.4,0.5,0.6)
> likelihood <- p^{x}*(1-p)^(n-x)*choose(n,x)
> posterior <- prior*likelihood
> posterior <- posterior/(sum(posterior))
> round(posterior,2)
[1] 0.21 0.33 0.46
```

We have now seen a systematic translation from prior to posterior probabilities through a pedagogical program. □

9.4.1.2 Inference using a Continuous Prior

If the prior distribution for probability of success p follows the standard uniform distribution $U(0, 1)$, we saw in Example 9.2.1 the technique of obtaining the posterior distribution. However, a uniform prior is a non-informative prior, or a flat prior. If the user has information about the skewness of the parameter, such information may be conveyed through a prior which follows a beta distribution. This may be easily seen by reverting to the diagram in Part B of Figure 6.5. The beta distribution will be a natural conjugate prior for p, in that the posterior distribution will also be a beta distribution. Thus, if the prior distribution for p is taken to be Beta (α, β), it may show mathematically, refer to Table 6.1, that the posterior distribution for p follows the beta distribution Beta $(\alpha + x, \beta + n - x)$:

$$\pi(p|x) = \frac{1}{\text{Beta}\,(x + \alpha, n - x + \beta)} p^{x+\alpha-1}(1 - p)^{n-x+\beta-1}.$$

Based on the data, the estimate of p will be the mean of the posterior beta distribution $(\alpha + x)/(\alpha + x + \beta + n - x) = (\alpha + x)/(\alpha + \beta + n)$.

Example 9.4.3. Again Revisiting Laplace Probability of Sunrise. For near certain events, it is natural to specify that the probability curve be very high at 1 and very low at 0, say for example, plot `plot(x,dbeta(x,5,0.05))` for `x <- seq(0,1,0.05)`. It is obvious that for n days, we would observe $x = n$ number of sunrises. In the present case, the estimate of p will be $(\alpha + n)/(\alpha + \beta + n)$. Now, suppose we have a friend who plays the devils advocate and says the prior should be `dbeta(x,0.05,5)`. The next small program will give the Bayes estimate of p.

```
> alpha <- 5; beta <- 0.05
> n <- seq(1e2,1e3,1e2)
> (alpha+n)/(alpha+n+beta)
 [1] 1 1 1 1 1 1 1 1 1 1
> alpha <- 0.05; beta <- 5
> (alpha+n)/(alpha+n+beta)
 [1] 0.952 0.976 0.984 0.988 0.990 0.992 0.993 0.994 0.994 0.995
```

It may be that when we have a large number of observations, the prior influence has little impact on the concluding estimate. This observation is known as *data washing away the prior*. □

9.4.2 *Inference for the Poisson Distribution*

9.4.2.1 Inference using a Discrete Prior

Let us begin with a discrete prior and obtain the posterior probabilities using the Bayes formula. As with the binomial distribution, we will demonstrate the details with an example.

Example 9.4.4. A Discrete Prior for Poisson Distribution. Let $X \sim \text{Pois}(\lambda)$, and assume that the mean λ can take values 1, 2, 3, or 4 with respective probabilities 1/8, 1/4, 1/2, and 1/8. Suppose that we have observed $X = 3$ and then have been asked to return the posterior probabilities. A simple application of the Bayes theorem will then return us the required probabilities. As the method of application follows the binomial distribution, we will skip the details and ask the reader to furnish them. The R program below gives the posterior probabilities.

```
> lambda <- c(1,2,3,4)
> prior <- c(1/8,1/4,1/2,1/8)
> x <- 3
> likeli <- dpois(x=3,lambda=lambda)
> priorlikeli <- likeli*prior
> posterior <- priorlikeli/sum(priorlikeli)
> posterior
[1] 0.0405 0.2384 0.5920 0.1291
```

The computations are fairly easy to understand. □

9.4.2.2 Inference using a Continuous Prior

It has been seen in Section 6.9 that if we have a random sample of size n from *Pois*(λ), and the conjugate prior is specified by *Gamma*(α, θ), then the Bayesian sampling distribution is given by

$$p(\lambda|x_1, \dots, x_n, \alpha, \theta) = \begin{cases} \lambda^{\theta+n-1} \frac{e^{-\lambda / \left(\alpha+\sum_{i=1}^{n} x\right)}}{\Gamma(\theta+n)(\theta+n)^{\alpha+\sum_{i=1}^{n} x_i}}, & \lambda > 0, \alpha, \theta > 0, \\ 0, & \text{otherwise.} \end{cases}$$

Let us consider the birth rates example of Hoff (2010).

Example 9.4.5. Birth Rates Example. Hoff (2010) considers the birth rates for two populations: (i) women with less than a Bachelors degree, and (ii) women educated at Bachelors degree level or higher. Here $X_{1,1}, \dots, X_{1,n_1}$ denotes the number of children for $n_1 = 111$ women who did not have a Bachelors degree, and $X_{2,1}, \dots, X_{2,n_2}$ denotes $n_2 = 44$ women in the other group. The sufficient statistics resulted in the data $\sum_{i=1}^{n_1} x_{1,i} = 217$ and $\sum_{i=1}^{n_2} x_{2,i} = 66$. Assuming the same gamma prior for the two groups with parameters $\alpha = 2, \theta = 1$, the posterior distribution for the two groups, each group has parameter $\lambda_i, i = 1, 2$, can be summarized as

$$\lambda_1 \sim \text{Gamma}(2 + 217, 1 + 111)$$
$$\lambda_2 \sim \text{Gamma}(2 + 66, 1 + 44)$$

Let us obtain the posterior means for λ_1 and λ_2.

```
> (2+217)/(1+111) # Posterior mean of group 1
[1] 1.955357
> (2+66)/(1+44) # Posterior mean of group 2
[1] 1.511111
```

This shows that women without the Bachelors degree on average have 2 children, whereas the other group has about 1.5. □

9.4.3 Inference for Uniform Distribution

Consider a random sample $X_1, \dots, X_n$ of size n from a uniform distribution $U(0, \theta)$, that is,

$$p(x) = \begin{cases} \frac{1}{\theta}, & 0 \leq x \leq \theta, \theta > 0, \\ 0, & \text{otherwise.} \end{cases}$$

Minka (2001) considers the Bayesian inference for uniform distribution. The conjugate prior for uniform distribution is the *Pareto distribution*:

$$p(\theta) = \begin{cases} \frac{Kb^K}{\theta^{K+1}}, & \text{if } \theta \geq b, \\ 0, & \text{otherwise.} \end{cases} \tag{9.8}$$

Minka represents the Pareto distribution by $Pa(b, K)$. The Pareto density asserts that θ must be greater than b, though not much greater. It may be observed that as $K \to 0$ and $b \to 0$, the Pareto prior reduces to a non-informative prior. An exercise for the reader is to plot a few Pareto densities. Let $\mathbf{x} = \{x_1, \ldots, x_n\}$ denote the dataset. The joint distribution of $\mathbf{x}$ and θ is given by

$$p(\mathbf{x}, \theta) = \frac{Kb^K}{\theta^{K+n+1}}, \max\{\mathbf{x}\} \leq \theta.$$

The posterior density for θ is given by

$$p(\theta|\mathbf{x}) = \frac{p(\mathbf{x}, \theta)}{p(\mathbf{x})} \sim Pa(c, n + K), \tag{9.9}$$

where $c = \max(m, b)$ and $m = \max\{\mathbf{x}\}$. We will clarify the concepts with a dummy example.

Example 9.4.6. The Taxicab Problem. Minka had mainly developed the methods here for estimation of the number of taxis in a city. We are illustrating with a dummy data example and refer the reader to Minka's paper for more details and depth. Suppose that the maximum number observed in 103 (distinct) taxis is 9184 and our prior parameters are specified by $b = 10000$ and $K = 10$. We need to estimate θ from this information. The posterior distribution of θ given $m = 9184, b = 10000, K = 10$ is

$$p(\theta|m, b, K) = \frac{10 \times 10000^{10}}{\theta^{11}}, \theta \geq 10000$$

The next R program gives a plot of the posterior distribution of θ, see Figure 9.1.

```
> m <- 9184
> n <- 103
> b <- 10000
> K <- 10
> theta <- seq(1000,20000,500)
> plot(theta,as.numeric(sapply(theta,pareto_density,scale=b, shape=
+ K)),"l",xlab=expression(theta),ylab="The Posterior Density")
> (n+1)*m/n
[1] 9273
```

The function `pareto_density` from the companion package is used to obtain values of the Pareto density. A more complete function for the Pareto density is the `dpareto` function from the `VGAM` package. An estimator of θ is provided by the posterior mean, which is $\frac{n+1}{n}m$ and thus our estimate of the number of taxis in the town is `9273.165`. Recollect that the estimate from a classical inference perspective is the sample maximum for θ, which will be 9184. □

9.4.4 *Inference for Exponential Distribution*

Consider the exponential distribution with rate λ:

$$f(x|\lambda) = \begin{cases} \lambda e^{-\lambda x}, & x \geq 0, \lambda > 0, \\ 0, & \text{otherwise.} \end{cases}$$

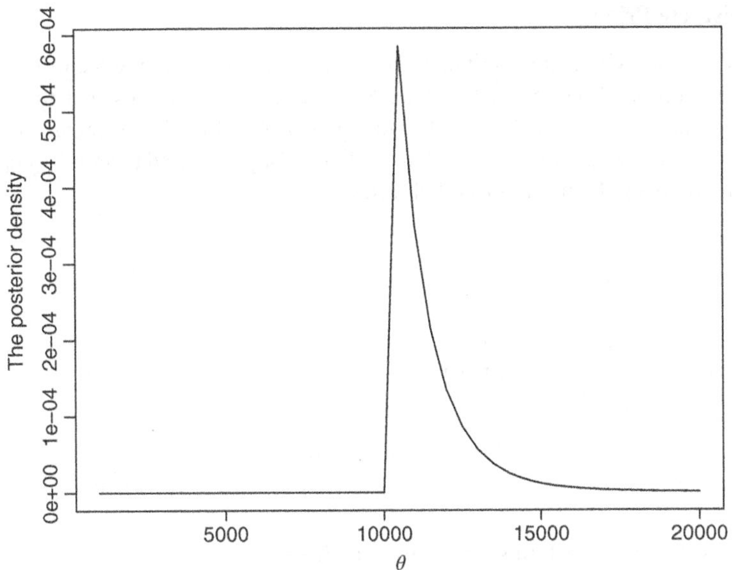

Figure 9.1 Bayesian Inference for Uniform Distribution

From Section 6.9, the conjugate prior for λ is given by the gamma distribution:

$$\pi(\lambda|\alpha,\beta) = \begin{cases} \frac{\beta^\alpha}{\Gamma(\alpha)}\lambda^{\alpha-1}\exp(-\lambda\beta), & \alpha,\beta,\lambda > 0, \\ 0, & \text{otherwise.} \end{cases}$$

Suppose we have an iid sample of size n in $X_1, \ldots, X_n$. Define $\bar{X} = \sum_{i=1}^n X_i/n$. The posterior distribution is then given by

$$\pi(\lambda|\bar{x},\alpha,\beta) = \frac{(\beta + n\bar{x})^{\alpha+n}}{\Gamma(\alpha+n)}\lambda^{\alpha+n-1}\exp(-\lambda\{\beta + n\bar{x}\}). \tag{9.10}$$

Example 9.4.7. Proschan's Air Conditioner Failure Times. We will begin with the assumption that the time between failures of the air-conditioning equipment in ten Boeing 720 aircraft follows an exponential distribution. Assume that the prior distribution for the failure rate is specified by Gamma(0.1,0.05). The posterior distribution is then given by Gamma(12.1,1297.05). The Bayes estimator for λ is given by the mode of the posterior distribution, which is 1297.05/12.1 = 107 hours. □

9.4.5 Inference for Normal Distributions

In Section 6.9 we had stated the Bayesian sampling distributions for a normal model. In this section, it will be put into action.

Using a Discrete Prior

The Bayes formula will again continue to be a useful tool for updating the prior probabilities into posterior probabilities given the data. Suppose the prior values that the mean μ can possibly take are –3, –2, –1, 0, 1, 2, 3 with equal probability. The standard deviation σ is known as 1 and an observation is noted at 1.13. The Bayes formula can be computed in the routine way to obtain the posterior probabilities.

```
> mu <- -3:3
> prior <- rep(1/7,7)
> x <- 1.13
> lik_norm <- dnorm(x,mu,1)
> posterior <- lik_norm*prior
> posterior <- posterior/sum(posterior)
> posterior
[1] 0.000 0.003 0.042 0.212 0.398 0.275 0.070
```

Inference for μ when σ is known, Continuous Prior

A non-informative prior for μ is specified by

$$\pi(\mu|\mathbf{x}) = 1, -\infty < \mu < \infty. \tag{9.11}$$

That is, this prior assumes that all the possible values of μ are equally possible. Of course, this is an example of improper prior since $\int \pi(\mu)d\mu = \infty$. However, the Jeffrey's prior is this flat prior only. It can be easily seen that the posterior distribution is the normal distribution $N(\bar{x}, \sigma^2)$. This distribution can then be used for inference on μ.

Example 9.4.8. Estimation of Average Height of Child in the Galton Dataset. We will assume that the height of the child follows a normal distribution. Here $n = 928$, and we assume that the variance of the height is known as $\sigma^2 = 6$. Using the non-informative prior, the posterior distribution of μ follows the normal distribution $N(\overline{x}, 6)$. Thus, the Bayes estimate for the average height of the child, the posterior mode, is given by $\hat{\mu} = 68.08847$. □

Now consider the case of *informative prior*. Assume that the prior for μ is specified by $N(\tau, \eta^2)$, where both τ and η^2 are known. The posterior distribution is then specified by $N\left(\frac{\sigma^2\tau+\eta^2\bar{x}}{\sigma^2+\eta^2}, \frac{\sigma^2\eta^2}{\sigma^2+\eta^2}\right)$.

Example 9.4.9. Estimation of Average Height of Child in the Galton Dataset. Contd. Let us continue with the assumption that the variance of the height of children is known as $\sigma^2 = 6$. Assume that the prior for μ is specified by $N(68, 3.2)$. The simpler computations are given next.

```
> data(galton)
> xmean <- mean(galton$child)
> variance <- 6
> priormean <- 68
> priorvar <- 3.2
```

```
> postmean <- (variance*priormean + priorvar*xmean)/
+ (variance+priorvar)
> postvariance <- (variance*priorvar)/(variance+priorvar)
> postmean
[1] 68.03077
```

The `galton` dataset is used from the `UsingR` package. The Bayes estimate for the average height of the child, the posterior mode, is given by $\hat{\mu} = 68.03077$. □

For an enriched example of inference from a normal distribution when μ is known, but σ is not known, see Section 3.2 of Albert (2009).

Inference when μ and σ are both Unknown

As earlier, and so many times over, consider a sample $X_1, \ldots, X_n$ of size n for $N(\mu, \sigma^2)$. We will begin with the case of **non-informative priors**. That is, $\pi(\mu, \sigma^2) \propto 1/\sigma^2$. The posterior density is then given by

$$\begin{aligned}\pi(\mu, \sigma^2|\mathbf{x}) &\propto \frac{1}{(\sigma^2)^{n/2+1}} \exp\left(-\frac{1}{2\sigma^2}\left\{\sum_{i=1}^{n}(x_i-\bar{x})^2 + n(\mu-\bar{x})^2\right\}\right)\\ &= \pi(\mu|\sigma^2, \mathbf{x})\pi(\sigma^2|\mathbf{x}) \qquad (9.12)\end{aligned}$$

where

$$\pi(\mu|\sigma^2, \mathbf{x}) \propto \exp\left\{-\frac{1}{2\sigma^2}n(\bar{x}-\mu)^2\right\} \qquad (9.13)$$

is a normal distribution $N(\bar{x}, \sigma^2/n)$, and

$$\pi(\sigma^2|\mathbf{x}) \propto (\sigma^2)^{n/2+1} \exp -\left\{\frac{(n-1)s^2}{2\sigma^2}\right\} \qquad (9.14)$$

where $s^2 = \sum_{i=1}^{n}(x_i - \bar{x})^2$. Thus, we see that $\pi(\mu|\sigma^2, \mathbf{x})$ is a normal distribution with mean $\bar{x}$ and variance σ^2/n, and $\pi(\sigma^2|\mathbf{x})$ is a *scaled inverse chi-square* distribution with $n-1$ degrees of freedom.

Informative Priors. When both the parameters are not known, the use of the conjugate prior simplifies the analysis. For the normal distribution, the conjugate prior is specified by *normal-inverse gamma distribution NIG*(μ_0, c, a, b), where $-\infty < \mu_0, c < \infty$ and $a, b > 0$. See Ntzoufras (2009) for details. The posterior distribution is specified by *NIG*$(\tilde{\mu}, \tilde{c}, \cap, \tilde{b})$, where

$$\begin{aligned}\tilde{\mu} &= \frac{nc}{1+nc}\bar{x} + \frac{1}{1+nc}\mu_0\\ \tilde{c} &= \frac{nc}{n(1+nc)}\\ \tilde{a} &= a + \frac{n}{2}\\ \tilde{b} &= b + \frac{SS}{2}\end{aligned}$$

where

$$SS = \sum_{i=1}^{n} x_i^2 + \frac{\mu_0^2}{c} - \frac{(nc\bar{x} + \mu_0)^2}{c(nc+1)}$$

Illustration of Bayesian inference for normal distribution, for many reasons, is better done in Chapter 11.

9.5 The Credible Intervals

For many technical reasons, Bayesians typically do not use the term "confidence interval" and prefer to call such an interval in their domain as *credible intervals*.

Definition 9.5.1 Credible Sets. *Given the dataset* $\mathbf{x}$ *and the prior distribution* π*, let* $\pi(\theta|\mathbf{x})$ *be the posterior distribution. Then, for any given set* $A \subset \Theta$*, the* credible probability *of A is given by*

$$P(\theta \in A|\mathbf{x}) = \int_A \pi(\theta|\mathbf{x})d\theta. \tag{9.15}$$

The set A is called a credible set (interval) *for* θ*.*

Furthermore, if $P(\theta \in A|\mathbf{x}) \geq 1 - \alpha$*, the set A is called* α*-credible set for* θ*.*

It is clear from the definition of a credible set that we may have many sets which may meet the requirement. However, we need that credible set which has minimum length. This motivates the next definition.

Definition 9.5.2 Highest Posterior Density Credible Set. *Let* A_x *denote a credible set and let* k_α *be the largest bound such that*

$$P^\pi(\theta \in A_x^\alpha|\mathbf{x}) \geq 1 - \alpha.$$

We say that A_x *is the* highest posterior density, HPD, α*-credible set if*

$$\{\theta : \pi(\theta|\mathbf{x}) > k_\alpha\} \subset A_x^\pi \subset \{\theta : \pi(\theta|\mathbf{x}) \geq k_\alpha\}. \tag{9.16}$$

In the rest of this section we will reconsider some of the examples developed earlier in this chapter and obtain the credible intervals for them.

Example 9.5.1. ***Example 9.4.5*** Contd. For the birth rates example, we obtained the posterior distribution, under the assumption of gamma prior, for the two groups of women less than Bachelors degree and above Bachelors degree as $\lambda_1 \sim \text{Gamma}(2+217, 1+111)$ and $\lambda_2 \sim \text{Gamma}(2+66, 1+44)$ respectively. Then, credible intervals for λ_1 and λ_2 can be simply obtained as shown below.

```
> qgamma(c(0.025,0.975),(2+217),(1+111)) # posterior 95% CI
[1] 1.704943 2.222679
> qgamma(c(0.025,0.975),(2+66),(1+44)) # posterior 95% CI
[1] 1.173437 1.890836
```

The qgamma function is easily used to obtain the credible intervals. Since the credible intervals for the two groups overlap, it cannot be concluded that the birth rates are significantly different for the two groups. □

Example 9.5.2. ***Example 9.4.6.*** **The Taxicab Problem.** Contd. For the hypothetical example of the taxicab problem, we obtained the posterior distribution of θ as a Pareto distribution with parameters $b = 10000, K = 10$. Using the pareto_quantile function from the companion library, we can obtain the credible intervals as below.

```
> pareto_quantile(c(0.05,0.95),scale=10000,shape=10)
[1] 10051 13493
```

Thus, the 95% credible interval for the number of taxis in the city is (10051,13493). □

9.6 Bayes Factors for Testing Problems

Consider the problem of testing hypotheses $H : \theta \in \Theta_0$ versus $K : \theta \in \Theta_1$, where $\Theta_0 \cap \Theta_1 = \phi$ and $\Theta_i \subset \Theta, i = 1, 2$. We dealt with such problems in the classical framework in Sections 7.10–7.14. A few problems will now be handled in the Bayesian framework.

We begin with a proper prior specified by $g(\theta)$. Let $\mathbf{X} = (X_1, \ldots, X_n)$ be a random sample from f_θ. The likelihood function is then given by $L(\theta|\mathbf{x})$. Under the hypotheses, define the prior probabilities by $\pi_i = \int_{\Theta_i} g(\theta)d\theta, i = 0, 1$, and the posterior probabilities by $p_i = \int_{\Theta_i} g(\theta|\mathbf{x})d\theta = \int_{\Theta_i} L(\theta|\mathbf{x})g(\theta)d\theta, i = 0, 1$.

The a priori odds ratio and posterior odds ratio of two hypotheses are respectively given by:

$$\frac{\pi_0}{\pi_0} = \frac{\int_{\Theta_0} g(\theta)d\theta}{\int_{\Theta_1} g(\theta)d\theta}, \tag{9.17}$$

$$\frac{p_0}{p_i} = \frac{\int_{\Theta_0} L(\theta|\mathbf{x})g(\theta)d\theta}{\int_{\Theta_1} L(\theta|\mathbf{x})g(\theta)d\theta}. \tag{9.18}$$

The *Bayes factor* for testing H against K is then given by

$$BF = \frac{p_0/p_1}{\pi_0/\pi_1}. \tag{9.19}$$

Though there are no hard and fast rules for using the BF, we list below some rules of thumb:

- If $BF \geq 1$, then the hypothesis H is supported.
- If $0.316 \leq BF < 1$, we have minimal evidence against H.
- If $0.1 \leq BF < 0.316$, we have substantial evidence against H.
- If $0.01 \leq BF < 0.1$, we have strong evidence against H.
- If $BF < 0.1$, we have decisive evidence against H.

Example 9.6.1. Normal Distribution. Consider a random sample of $n = 10$ from $N(\mu, 3^2)$. The prior for μ is specified by the conjugate prior $N(5, 1)$. The value of sufficient statistic

$T = \sum_{i=1}^{10} X_i$ is $t = 25$. We are interested in testing $H : \theta < 5$ against the alternative hypothesis given in $K : \theta > 5$. The posterior distribution is then given by $N\left(\frac{\sigma^2\tau+\eta^2\bar{x}}{\sigma^2+\eta^2}, \frac{\sigma^2\eta^2}{\sigma^2+\eta^2}\right) = N\left(\frac{3^2 \times 5+1^2 \times 2.5}{3^2+1^2}, \frac{3^2 \times 1^2}{3^2+1^2}\right) = N(4.75, 0.9)$. Let us compute the Bayes factor.

```
> pi_H <- pnorm(5,mean=5,sd=1) # prior prob under H
> pi_K <- 1-pnorm(5,mean=5,sd=1) # prior prob under K
> p_H <- pnorm(5,mean=4.75,sd=sqrt(0.9)) # posterior prob under H
> p_K <- 1-pnorm(5,mean=4.75,sd=sqrt(0.9)) # posterior prob under K
> BF <- p_H*pi_K/(p_K*pi_H)
> BF
[1] 1.52
```

The computations are again not too complicated and hence the explanation is left to the reader. Thus, the BF test supports the hypothesis H. □

Example 9.6.2. Binomial Distribution. Suppose we observe n Bernoulli trials with probability of success being p. The prior distribution for p is specified through the beta distribution with parameters (α, β), say (2,2), and hence the posterior distribution is given by the beta distribution $(\alpha + x, \beta + n - x)$. Consider the hypothesis testing problem of $H : p = 0.2$ against hypothesis $K : p = 0.9$. Assume that out of $n = 10$ trials, we have observed $x = 6$.

```
> pi_H <- dbeta(0.2,2,2) # prior prob under H
> pi_K <- dbeta(0.9,2,2) # prior prob under K
> p_H <- dbeta(0.2,6+2,4+2) # posterior prob under H
> p_K <-  dbeta(0.9,6+2,4+2)# posterior prob under K
> BF <- p_H*pi_K/(p_K*pi_H)
> BF
[1] 0.493
```

Thus, the BF test says that there is mild evidence against the hypothesis H. □

9.7 Further Reading

Jeffreys (1939–61) may have been the first treatise on Bayesian statistics. de Finetti's (1974–5) two volumes made a nice prediction that every Statistician will be a Bayesian by 2020. Savage (1954) has firmly laid the foundation for Bayesian analysis. Box and Tiao (1973) is an early book which has complete focus on Bayesian inference. It also discusses Bayesian methods for regression analysis. Berger (1985) develops the Bayesian methodology from a decision perspective. Bernardo and Smith (1994), Robert (2007), Press (2003), Ghosh, et al. (2006), and Carlin and Louis (2000) are some of the best books for Bayesian analysis.

Berger and Woolpert's (1985) monograph gives a distinct clarity on how the Bayesian school meets the sufficiency and likelihood principle. Samaniego (2010) offers a course which does a lot of comparison between the frequentist and Bayesian school.

For this chapter, we have relied on Bolstad (2007), Albert (2009), and Hoff (2010).

9.8 Complements, Problems, and Programs

Problem 9.1 Verify that the probability of sunrise is a proper probability measure. Extend the result in Example 9.2.1 to more than two possible events of an experiment.

Problem 9.2 For a beta prior $Be(a, b)$ on the probability of success in a Bernoulli trial, find the probability of sunrise. For a large n, obtain the plot of the probability for various a and b values.

Problem 9.3 Under a symmetric Dirichlet prior, with symmetric parameter c, the probability of a birthday match, see Diaconis and Holmes (2002) is given by

$$P_c(\text{match}) = 1 - \prod_{i=1}^{k-1} \frac{(n-i)c}{nc+i}.$$

Write an R program to compute the probability of a match when c is 0.5, 1, 2, 5, 20, 200.

Problem 9.4 Varying the value of m in the taxicab problem, explore the difference between the classical estimator and the Bayes estimate for N.

Problem 9.5 Find 95% credible intervals for the examples discussed in Section 9.4.

Part III

Stochastic Processes and Monte Carlo

10

Stochastic Processes

Package(s): `sna`
Dataset(s): `testtpm`, `testtpm2`, `testtpm3`

10.1 Introduction

Stochastic processes commonly refer to a collection of random variables. Such a collection may vary over time, sample number, geographical location, etc. It is to be noted that a stochastic process may consist of finite, countably infinite, or uncountably infinite collections of random variables. An important characteristic of the stochastic process is that it allows us to relax the assumption of independence for a sequence of random variables.

Definition 10.1.1 A Stochastic Process *is a collection of random variables*

$$\mathbb{X} = \{X_t, t \in A\}, \tag{10.1}$$

where A may be a finite set, or countable set, or an interval.

A few examples are in order.

Example 10.1.1. Examples of Stochastic Processes. We will consider situations where a stochastic process may be discrete or continuous.

- **The maximum temperature of the day**. Let X_n denote the maximum temperature recorded on the nth day. Then, the collection $\{X_n : n = 1, 2, \dots\}$ forms an example of a stochastic process.

  Since a very hot day is unlikely to be immediately followed by a chilly day, it may be easily seen that the X_n does not form an independent sequence of random variables.
- **The Closure Points of the SENSEX**. Consider the points of closure at the end of the day of BSE-SENSEX. This collection is also an example of a stochastic process.

A Course in Statistics with R, First Edition. Prabhanjan Narayanachar Tattar, Suresh Ramaiah and B. G. Manjunath.

Companion Website: www.wiley.com/go/tattar/statistics

- **Sum of Heads in n successive throws of a coin**. Define

$$X_i = \begin{cases} 1, & \text{head appears on the i-th toss of the coin,} \\ 0, & \text{tail appears.} \end{cases}$$

For $i = 1, 2, \ldots, n, \ldots$, define the sum of heads as

$$S_n = \sum_{i=1}^{n} X_i, n = 1, 2, \ldots . \tag{10.2}$$

Then, $S_n, n = 1, 2, \ldots$, is a collection of random variables which forms a stochastic process. Again, it may be easily seen that $P(S_{n+1} \leq S_n) = 0$, and hence S_n forms a sequence of dependent RVs.

- **Number of Customers arriving at a Ticket Counter**. Let $\{N(t), t \in [0, \infty)\}$ denote the number of customers arriving at a ticket counter up to time t. Then $\{N(t), t \in [0, \infty)\}$ is again a stochastic process. □

Section 10.2 will ensure that the probability space for the stochastic process is properly defined. A very important class of stochastic process is the *Markov Chains*, and this will be detailed in Section 10.3. The chapter will close with a brief discussion of how Markov Chains are useful in the practical area of *computational statistics* in Section 10.4.

10.2 Kolmogorov's Consistency Theorem

As seen in the introductory section, a stochastic process is a collection of infinite random variables. It needs to be ensured that the probability measures are well defined for such a collection of RVs. An affirmative answer in this direction is provided by Prof Kolmogorov. The related definitions and theorems (without proof) have been adapted from Adke and Manjunath (1984) and Athreya and Lahiri (2005). We consider the probability space $(\Omega, \mathcal{F}, P)$ and follow it up with a sequence of RVs $\{X_\alpha, \alpha \in A\}$. Here A is any non-empty set. Then for any $(\alpha_1, \alpha_2, \ldots, \alpha_k) \in A$, the random vector $(X_{\alpha_1}, X_{\alpha_2}, \ldots, X_{\alpha_k})$ has a joint probability distribution $\mu_{(\alpha_1, \alpha_2, \ldots, \alpha_k)}$ over $(R^k, \mathcal{B}(R^k))$, and here $\mathcal{B}(R^k)$ is the Borel σ-field over R^k.

Definition 10.2.1 Finite Dimensional Distributions. *The family* $\{\mu_{(\alpha_1, \alpha_2, \ldots, \alpha_k)}(.) \equiv P((X_{\alpha_1}, X_{\alpha_2}, \ldots, X_{\alpha_k}) \in \cdot) : (\alpha_1, \alpha_2, \ldots, \alpha_k) \in A^k, 1 \leq k < \infty\}$ *of probability distributions is called the* family of finite dimensional distributions, *abbreviated as* fdd, *associated with the stochastic process* $\{X_\alpha : \alpha \in A\}$.

For any $(\alpha_1, \alpha_2, \ldots, \alpha_k) \in A^k, 2 \leq k < \infty$, and any $B_1, B_2, \ldots, B_k \in \mathcal{B}(R)$, the family of fdds satisfies the following two conditions:

[C1].

$$\mu_{(\alpha_1, \alpha_2, \ldots, \alpha_k)}(B_1 \times \ldots \times B_{k-1} \times R) = \mu_{(\alpha_1, \alpha_2, \ldots, \alpha_{k-1})}(B_1 \times \ldots \times B_{k-1}). \tag{10.3}$$

[C2]. For any permutation $i_1, i_2, \ldots, i_k$ of $1, 2, \ldots, k$:

$$\mu_{(\alpha_{i_1}, \alpha_{i_2}, \ldots, \alpha_{i_k})}(B_{i_1} \times B_{i_2} \times \ldots \times B_{i_k}) = \mu_{(\alpha_1, \alpha_2, \ldots, \alpha_k)}(B_1 \times B_2 \times \ldots \times B_k). \tag{10.4}$$

Kolmogorov's consistency theorem addresses the issue that if there exists a family of distributions $Q_A \equiv \{\upsilon_{\alpha_1,\ldots,\alpha_k} : (\alpha_1, \ldots, \alpha_k) \in A^k, 1 \leq k < \infty\}$ in finite dimensional Euclidean spaces, then there exists a real valued stochastic process $\{X_\alpha, \alpha \in A\}$ whose fdds coincides with Q_α.

Theorem 10.2.1 [Kolmogorov's Consistency Theorem] *Let A be a non-empty set, and let* $Q_A \equiv \{\upsilon_{(\alpha_1,\ldots,\alpha_k)} : (\alpha_1, \ldots, \alpha_k) \in A^k, 1 \leq k < \infty\}$ *be a family of probability distributions such that for each* $(\alpha_1, \ldots, \alpha_k) \in A^k, 1 \leq k < \infty\}$*:*

- $\upsilon_{(\alpha_1,\ldots,\alpha_k)}$ *is a probability measure on* $R^k, \mathcal{B}(R^k)$.
- *The conditions C1 and C2 hold, that is,* $\forall B_1, \ldots, B_k \in \mathcal{B}(\mathcal{R}), 2 \leq k < \infty$, *we have*

$$\upsilon_{(\alpha_1,\alpha_2,\ldots,\alpha_k)}(B_1 \times B_2 \times \ldots \times B_{k-1} \times \mathcal{R}) = \upsilon_{(\alpha_1,\alpha_2,\ldots,\alpha_{k-1})}(B_1 \times B_2 \times \ldots \times B_{k-1}),$$

and for any permutation $i_1, i_2, \ldots, i_k$ *of* $1, 2, \ldots, k$ *we have*

$$\mu_{(\alpha_{i_1},\alpha_{i_2},\ldots,\alpha_{i_k})}(B_{i_1} \times B_{i_2} \times \ldots \times B_{i_k}) = \mu_{(\alpha_1,\alpha_2,\ldots,\alpha_k)}(B_1 \times B_2 \times \ldots \times B_k).$$

Then there exists a probability space $(\Omega, \mathcal{F}, P)$ *and a stochastic process* $X_A \equiv \{X_\alpha : \alpha \in A\}$ *in* $(\Omega, \mathcal{F}, P)$ *such that* Q_A *is the family of finite dimensional distributions associated with* X_A. □

Having being assured of the existence of probability measures for the stochastic processes, let us now look at the important family of stochastic processes: Markov Chains.

10.3 Markov Chains

In earlier chapters, we assumed the observations were independent. In many random phenomenon, the observations are not independent. As seen in the examples in Section 10.1, the maximum temperature of the current day may depend on the maximum temperature of the previous day. The sum of heads in n trials depends on the corresponding sum in the first $n-1$ trials. *Markov Chains* are useful for tackling such dependent observations. In this section, we will be considering only discrete phenomenon.

To begin with, we need to define the *state space* associated with the sequence of random variables. The state space is the set of possible values taken by the stochastic process. In Example 10.1.1 of Section 10.1, the state space for the sum of heads in n throws of a coin is $\mathbf{S} = \{0, 1, 2, \ldots\}$. The state space considered in this section is at most countably infinite. At time n, the stochastic process $\mathbf{X}$ will take one of the values in S, that is, $X_n = j, j \in S, n = 1, 2, \ldots$.

Definition 10.3.1 Markov Chain. *The stochastic process* $\mathbf{X} = \{X_n, n = 0, 1, \ldots\}$ *with state space* $\mathbf{S}$ *is said to be a Markov Chain if for each* $j \in \mathbf{S}$ *and* $n = 0, 1, \ldots$*, the following statement holds good:*

$$P\{X_{n+1} = j | X_n = i, X_{n-1} = i_{n-1}, \ldots, X_1 = i_1, X_0 = i_0\} = P\{X_{n+1} = j | X_n = i\} = p_{ij}, \quad (10.5)$$

for any set of states $i_0, i_1, \ldots, i_{n-1}, i$.

This definition says that the probability of X_{n+1} being observed in a state j, given the entire history $X_n = i, X_{n-1} = i_{n-1}, \dots, X_1 = i_1, X_0 = i_0$, depends only on the recent past state of X_n, and not on the history. The matrix array $\mathbf{P} = \{p_{ij}\}$ is called the *Transition Probability Matrix*, abbreviated as TPM, of the Markov Chain.

Example 10.3.1. The Ehrenfest Model Consider a system of two urns. Among the two urns, we have $2n$ balls. At each instance, a ball is selected from one of the urns and placed in the other. Assume that there are i balls in Urn I, and the remaining $2n - i$ balls in Urn II. Then at any instance, the probability of selecting a ball from Urn I and placing it in Urn II is $i/2n$, and the other way of placing a ball from Urn II to Urn I is $(2n - i)/2n$. At each instant we let the number i of balls in the Urn I to be the state of the system. Thus, the state space is $\mathbf{S} = \{0, 1, 2, \dots, 2n\}$. Then we can pass from state i only to either of the states $i - 1$ or $i + 1$, and the transition probabilities are given by

$$p_{ij} = \begin{cases} \frac{i}{2n}, & \text{if } j = i - 1, \\ 1 - \frac{i}{2n}, & \text{if } j = i + 1, \\ 0, & \text{otherwise.} \end{cases} \tag{10.6}$$

Here, $\mathbf{S} = \{0, 1, \dots, 2n\}$. Suppose that $n = 2$. Then the TPM of such an Ehrenfest model is given by

$$\mathbf{P} = \left(\begin{array}{c|ccccc} & 0 & 1 & 2 & 3 & 4 \\ \hline 0 & 0 & 1 & 0 & 0 & 0 \\ 1 & 1/4 & 0 & 3/4 & 0 & 0 \\ 2 & 0 & 1/2 & 0 & 1/2 & 0 \\ 3 & 0 & 0 & 3/4 & 0 & 1/4 \\ 4 & 0 & 0 & 0 & 1 & 0 \end{array}\right)$$

It can be shown that the above TPM $\mathbf{P} = \{p_{ij}\}$ forms a Markov Chain, that is, the definition 10.5 is satisfied for all i. The `Ehrenfest` function is first defined here and obtained for the cases of $n = 2, 3$. The program will be described following the brief R session.

```
> Ehrenfest <- function(n) {
+ States <- c(0, seq(1,2*n))
+ TPM <- matrix(0,nrow=length(States),ncol=length(States),dimnames=
+ list(seq(0,2*n),seq(0,2*n)))
+ tran_prob <- function(i,n) {
+ tranRow <- rep(0,2*n+1)
+ if(i==0) tranRow[2] <- 1
+ if(i==2*n) tranRow[(2*n+1)-1] <- 1
+ if(i!=0 & i!=2*n) {
+ j=i+1
+ tranRow[j-1] <- i/(2*n)
+ tranRow[j+1] <- 1-i/(2*n)
+ }
+ return(tranRow)
+ }
+ for(j in 0:(2*n))TPM[j+1,] <- tran_prob(j,n)
```

```
+ return(TPM)
+ }
> Ehrenfest(2)
     0   1    2   3    4
0 0.00 1.0 0.00 0.0 0.00
1 0.25 0.0 0.75 0.0 0.00
2 0.00 0.5 0.00 0.5 0.00
3 0.00 0.0 0.75 0.0 0.25
4 0.00 0.0 0.00 1.0 0.00
> Ehrenfest(3)
       0      1      2      3      4      5      6
0 0.0000 1.0000 0.0000 0.0000 0.0000 0.0000 0.0000
1 0.1667 0.0000 0.8333 0.0000 0.0000 0.0000 0.0000
2 0.0000 0.3333 0.0000 0.6667 0.0000 0.0000 0.0000
3 0.0000 0.0000 0.5000 0.0000 0.5000 0.0000 0.0000
4 0.0000 0.0000 0.0000 0.6667 0.0000 0.3333 0.0000
5 0.0000 0.0000 0.0000 0.0000 0.8333 0.0000 0.1667
6 0.0000 0.0000 0.0000 0.0000 0.0000 1.0000 0.0000
```

The `Ehrenfest` function accepts n as an input and returns the TPM for the Ehrenfest model associated with $2n$. The two objects are defined in this function; `States` and `TPM`. The object `States` generates the related state space **S**. Essentially, the number of balls in Urn I varies from $0, 1, \dots, 2*n-1, 2n$, and for each of the possible states, we need to obtain the transition probabilities to the other states according to Equation 10.6 . The R function `tran_prob` within the `Ehrenfest` function gives us this row probabilities. The transition probability row for the cases $i = 0$ and $i = 2n$ is obtained in a routine manner. The `if` condition `i!=0 & i!=2*n` is coded to ensure that the computations on the right-hand side of Equation 10.6 are completely met. The indexing is defined in a slightly vague way with `j=i+1`. However, it should not be intriguing to reason out why it is required in this way, and especially a similar trick is used in the loop `for(j in 0:(2*n)) TPM[j+1,]`. The function `Ehrenfest` is defined in a way which will return the TPM for the Ehrenfest model, and `Ehrenfest(2)` and `Ehrenfest(3)` give us the required TPMs. □

Example 10.3.2. The Gambler's Walk. Suppose that a gambler starts at 0 and throws a coin. If heads turn up, he takes a step to the right and moves to 1. Otherwise, he moves to the left at −1. Assume that the probability of getting a head is $p, 0 < p < 1$. The state space **S** is the set of natural integers, that is, $\mathbf{S} = \{0, \pm1, \pm2, \pm3, \dots\}$. The transition probability matrix TPM of the Gamblers walk is then defined by

$$\mathbf{P} = \left(\begin{array}{c|cccccc} & \dots & -2 & -1 & 0 & 1 & 2 \dots \\ \hline -2 & \dots & 0 & p & 0 & 0 & 0 \dots \\ -1 & \dots & (1-p) & 0 & p & 0 & 0 \dots \\ 0 & \dots & 0 & (1-p) & 0 & p & 0 \dots \\ 1 & \dots & 0 & 0 & (1-p) & 0 & p \dots \\ 2 & \dots & 0 & 0 & 0 & (1-p) & 0 \dots \end{array}\right)$$

How do you verify that **P** satisfies Equation 10.5 ?

In the next subsection, we will consider how the states of a Markov Chain can be classified into a meaningful set of various characteristics.

10.3.1 *The* m*-Step TPM*

The TPM $\mathbf{P} = \{p_{ij}\}$ is a one-step transition probability array, namely, its elements give the probability of moving from state i to state j in the next step. The m-step transition probability of a movement from state i to state j is defined by

$$P\{X_{m+n} = j | X_n = i\} = p_{ij}^{(m)}, i, j \in \mathbf{S}. \tag{10.7}$$

Let $\mathbf{P}^{(m)} = \{p_{ij}^{(m)}\}$ denote the m-step transition probability matrix. It can be shown that

$$\mathbf{P}^{(m)} = \underbrace{\mathbf{P} \;\; \mathbf{P} \ldots \mathbf{P}}_{m \text{ times}}. \tag{10.8}$$

Equation 10.8 is based on the well-known *Chapman-Kolmogorov equation*. The Chapman-Kolmogorov lemma says that for any $n \geq 0, m \geq 0, i, j \in S$

$$p_{ij}^{n+m} = \sum_{k \in S} p_{ik}^{n} p_{kj}^{m}.$$

We can easily use the Chapman-Kolmogorov relationship to obtain the m-step TPM of a Markov Chain. The R program for obtaining the m-step TPM through `msteptpm` is given in the next illustration.

Example 10.3.3. The Ehrenfest Model. Consider the Ehrenfest model for $2n = 4$ balls. The 4-step TPM for the Ehrenfest Markov model can be easily obtained using R. This is done as follows:

```
> msteptpm <- function(TPM,m){
+ if(m==1) return(TPM) else {
+ temp <- TPM
+ for(i in 1:(m-1)) temp=temp
+ return(temp)
+ }
+ }
> EF2 <- Ehrenfest(2)
> msteptpm(as.matrix(EF2),4)
        0      1    2      3       4
0 0.15625 0.0000 0.75 0.0000 0.09375
1 0.00000 0.5312 0.00 0.4688 0.00000
2 0.12500 0.0000 0.75 0.0000 0.12500
3 0.00000 0.4688 0.00 0.5312 0.00000
4 0.09375 0.0000 0.75 0.0000 0.15625
> EF2
```

The `for` loop in the `msteptmp` function simply carries out the required computation required in Equation 10.8. The interpretations are as follows. If we begin in Urn I with 0 balls, the probability of Urn I containing 1 to 4 balls after four steps is `0.0000`, `0.75`, `0.0000`, and `0.09375` respectively. Similarly, the probabilities in the rest of the matrix $\mathbf{P}^4$ may be interpreted. □

10.3.2 Classification of States

In the Ehrenfest example we see that it is possible to move from a particlar state to one of its adjacent states only. However, it is possible for us to move from state 1 to states 3 and 4 in 2 and 3 steps. The question that then arises is how to identify the accessible states? Towards this discussion, a few definitions are required.

Definition 10.3.2 Accessible State. *A state $j \in \mathbf{S}$ is said to be accessible from state $i \in \mathbf{S}$ if for some $n \geq 0$, we have $p^n_{ij} > 0$.*

Accessibility is denoted by $i \to j$.

Definition 10.3.3 Communicative States. *If state j is accessible from state i, and vice versa, we say that the states* communicate *with each other.*

Communication between two states is denoted by $i \leftrightarrow j$. The collection of the states where each communicates with the other is said to belong to the same *class*. Some properties of communication, without proof, are listed below:

- $i \leftrightarrow i, i \in \mathbf{S}$.
- If $i \leftrightarrow j$, then $j \leftrightarrow i, i, j \in \mathbf{S}$.
- If $i \leftrightarrow j$ and $j \leftrightarrow k$, then $i \leftrightarrow k, i, j, k \in \mathbf{S}$.

Definition 10.3.4 Absorbing State. *A state $i \in \mathbf{S}$ is said to be an* absorbing state *if $p^n_{ij} = 0$, $\forall n, \forall j \neq i$.*

Definition 10.3.5 Recurrent/Transient State. *A state $i \in \mathbf{S}$ is said to be a* recurrent (transient) state *if*

$$P(X_n = i \text{ for infinitely many } n \geq 1) = 1(0).$$

Definition 10.3.6 Irreducible Markov Chains. *A Markov Chain is said to be* irreducible *if there is only one class of states. Alternatively, if each of the states of the Markov Chain communicates with every other state, we have an irreducible Markov Chain.*

Irreducible Markov Chains are also called *ergodic* Markov Chains. A stronger requirement than irreducibility is given next.

Definition 10.3.7 Regular Markov Chain. *A Markov Chain is said to be a* regular Markov Chain *if there exists some n such that $p^n_{ij} > 0, \forall i, j \in \mathbf{S}$.*

It can be easily seen that the presence of an absorbing state implies that the Markov Chain is neither regular nor irreducible.

A state i is said to have *period d* if $p_{ii}^n = 0$ whenever n is not divisible by d and d is the greatest integer with this property. The period of a state is denoted by $d(i)$. If it is not possible to return to state i and be retained in i (starting from state i of course), the period of the state i is infinite. On the other hand, if a state has period 1, we call that state *aperiodic*.

Digraph is a powerful visualizing tool for understanding the accessible and communicating states of a Markov Chain. Here, we use the package sna for achieving this. Note that this package is developed for the purpose of an emerging field *Social Network Analysis*. The gplot function from this package is useful for our purpose though.

Example 10.3.4. Digraph Plots for Markov Chains. Contd. The TPM of Markov Chains may be visualized using digraphs. In R, we use the gplot graph function of the sna package to achieve this. We plot the digraphs of the Ehrenfest Markov model, and some three artificial TPMs. The R program next gives the necessary codes.

```
> library(sna,quietly=TRUE)
> ehrenfest <- Ehrenfest(2)
> rownames(ehrenfest) <- colnames(ehrenfest)=0:4
> ehrenfest
     0   1    2   3    4
0 0.00 1.0 0.00 0.0 0.00
1 0.25 0.0 0.75 0.0 0.00
2 0.00 0.5 0.00 0.5 0.00
3 0.00 0.0 0.75 0.0 0.25
4 0.00 0.0 0.00 1.0 0.00
> data(testtpm)
> rownames(testtpm) <- colnames(testtpm)
> testtpm
       A    B     C    D    E      F
A 1.0000 0.00 0.000 0.00 0.00 0.0000
B 0.2500 0.50 0.000 0.25 0.00 0.0000
C 0.0000 0.00 0.000 1.00 0.00 0.0000
D 0.0625 0.25 0.125 0.25 0.25 0.0625
E 0.0000 0.00 0.000 0.25 0.50 0.2500
F 0.0000 0.00 0.000 0.00 0.00 1.0000
> data(testtpm2)
> rownames(testtpm2) <- colnames(testtpm2)
> testtpm2
  A B    C    D   E    F
A 0 1 0.00 0.00 0.0 0.00
B 1 0 0.00 0.00 0.0 0.00
C 0 0 0.25 0.45 0.0 0.30
D 0 0 0.00 0.50 0.5 0.00
E 0 0 0.25 0.00 0.5 0.25
F 0 0 0.00 0.00 0.3 0.70
> data(testtpm3)
> rownames(testtpm3) <- colnames(testtpm3)
> testtpm3
    A   B   C   D   E   F   G
A 0.3 0.1 0.2 0.2 0.1 0.1 0.0
B 0.0 0.5 0.0 0.0 0.0 0.0 0.5
```

```
C 0.0 0.0 0.4 0.6 0.0 0.0 0.0
D 0.0 0.0 0.3 0.2 0.0 0.5 0.0
E 0.0 0.0 0.2 0.3 0.4 0.1 0.0
F 0.0 0.0 1.0 0.0 0.0 0.0 0.0
G 0.0 0.8 0.0 0.0 0.0 0.0 0.2
> par(mfrow=c(2,2))
> gplot(ehrenfest,diag=TRUE,vertex.cex=6,vertex.sides=4,
+ vertex.col=1:5,vertex.border=2:6,vertex.rot=(0:4)*100,
+ displaylabels=TRUE, main="A: Digraph for Ehrenfest Model")
> gplot(testtpm,diag=TRUE,vertex.cex=6,vertex.sides=4,vertex.col=1:6,
+ vertex.border=2:7,vertex.rot=(0:5)* 100,displaylabels=TRUE,
+ main="B: Digraph for testtpm")
> gplot(testtpm2,diag=TRUE,vertex.cex=6,vertex.sides=4,
+ vertex.col=1:6,vertex.border=2:7,vertex.rot=(0:5)*100,
+ displaylabels=TRUE, main="C: Digraph for testtpm2")
> gplot(testtpm3,diag=TRUE,vertex.cex=6,vertex.sides=4,
+ vertex.col=1:7, vertex.border=2:8,vertex.rot=(0:6)*100,
+ displaylabels=TRUE, main="D: Digraph for testtpm3")
```

The digraphs helps us to understand the nature of states, Figure 10.1. We can classify the states into transition states and recurrent states. Let us discuss the digraph in detail.

In the Ehrenfest model we see that $0 \leftrightarrow 1$, $1 \leftrightarrow 2$, $2 \leftrightarrow 3$, and $3 \leftrightarrow 4$. Hence, we can see by the *commutative* property of accessible states that all the states communicate with each other. Thus, we have an irreducible Markov Chain. In an irreducible Markov Chain, all the states are recurrent states (a proof is not in the scope of this text).

For the example where the TPM is given by `testtpm`, we make the following observations. The pair of communicative states are the following: $B \leftrightarrow D, D \leftrightarrow E, D \leftrightarrow C$, and consequently these states are accessible from each other. However, it is clear from the diagraph that states A and F are absorbing states as no other state is accessible from them. Thus `testtpm` is not a regular or irreducible Markov Chain.

In the case of `testtpm2`, it is easily seen to be decomposible into two Markov Chains. One Markov Chain consists of states A and B, and the other C, D, E, F. In light of the fact that $p_{AB} = p_{BA} = 1$, we can easily conclude the periodicity of the two states is 2. Interpretation for `testtpm3` is left as an exercise. □

10.3.3 Canonical Decomposition of an Absorbing Markov Chain

In the previous discussion we have seen different types of TPM characteristics for the Markov Chains. In an irreducibile Markov Chain, all the states are recurrent states. However, if there is an absorbing state, as in `testtpm`, we may be interested in the following issues:

1. The probability of the process ending up in an absorbing state.
2. The average time for the Markov Chain to get absorbed.
3. The average time spent in each of the transient states.

The *canonical decomposition* helps with the answer to the above questions.

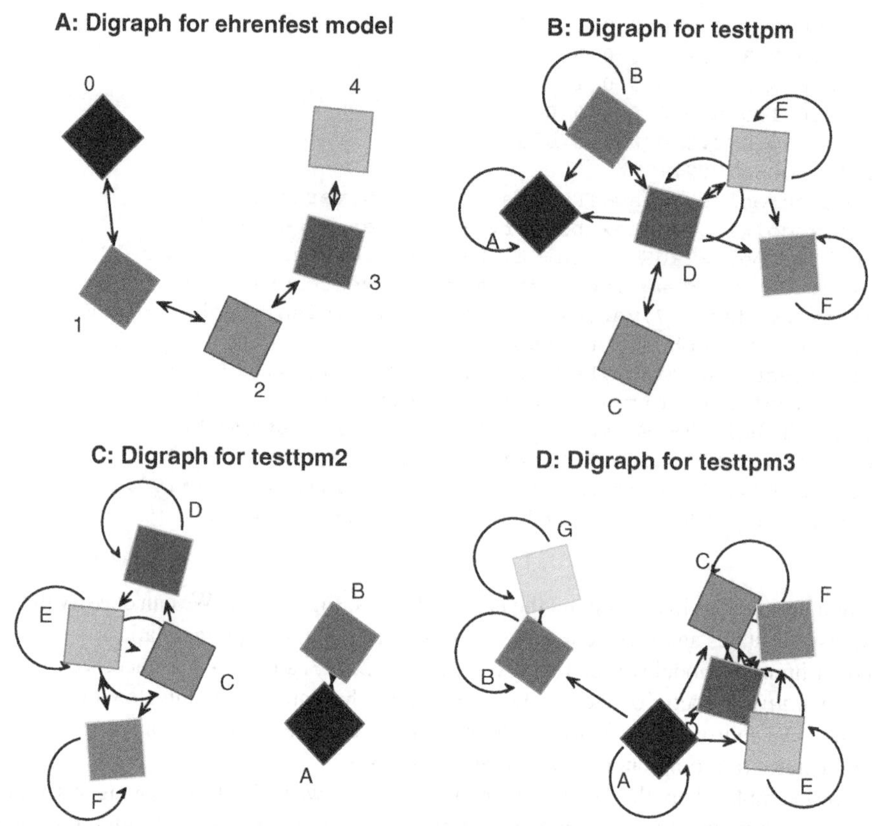

Figure 10.1 Digraphs for Classification of States of a Markov Chain

Arrange the states of an absorbing Markov Chain in the form of (TRANSIENT, ABSORBING). For example, reorder the states of `testtpm2` as $S = (\underbrace{B, C, D, E,}_{\text{TRANSIENT}} \underbrace{A, F}_{\text{ABSORBING}})$. Let r be the number of absorbing states and t the number of transient states. The total number of states is $p = r + t$. Arrange the TPM as below:

$$P = \left(\begin{array}{l|c|c} & \text{TRANSIENT} & \text{ABSORBING} \\ \hline \text{TRANSIENT} & \mathbf{Q} & \mathbf{R} \\ \text{ABSORBING} & \mathbf{0} & \mathbf{I} \end{array}\right) \tag{10.9}$$

Here $\mathbf{I}$ is an $r \times r$ identity matrix, $\mathbf{0}$ an $r \times t$ zero matrix, $\mathbf{Q}$ a $t \times t$ matrix, and $\mathbf{R}$ a non-zero $t \times r$ matrix. Let us closely look at the matrix $\mathbf{Q}$ and calculate $\mathbf{Q}^n$ for some large n. Note that it is very easy to rearrange the matrix in the required form in R.

```
> testtpm <- as.matrix(testtpm)
> testtpm <- testtpm[c(2,3,4,5,1,6),c(2,3,4,5,1,6)]
> Q <- testtpm[c(1:4),c(1:4)]
```

```
> R <- testtpm[c(1:4),c(5,6)]
> Q
     B     C    D    E
B 0.50 0.000 0.25 0.00
C 0.00 0.000 1.00 0.00
D 0.25 0.125 0.25 0.25
E 0.00 0.000 0.25 0.50
> R
       A      F
B 0.2500 0.0000
C 0.0000 0.0000
D 0.0625 0.0625
E 0.0000 0.2500
> testtpm
     B     C    D    E      A      F
B 0.50 0.000 0.25 0.00 0.2500 0.0000
C 0.00 0.000 1.00 0.00 0.0000 0.0000
D 0.25 0.125 0.25 0.25 0.0625 0.0625
E 0.00 0.000 0.25 0.50 0.0000 0.2500
A 0.00 0.000 0.00 0.00 1.0000 0.0000
F 0.00 0.000 0.00 0.00 0.0000 1.0000
> msteptpm(testtpm,n=100)[c(1:4),c(1:4)]
             B            C            D            E
B 1.635836e-10 3.124169e-11 2.022004e-10 1.635836e-10
C 2.499335e-10 4.773305e-11 3.089348e-10 2.499335e-10
D 2.022004e-10 3.861685e-11 2.499335e-10 2.022004e-10
E 1.635836e-10 3.124169e-11 2.022004e-10 1.635836e-10
```

We can easily then see that

$$\text{As } n \to \infty \Rightarrow \mathbf{Q}^n \to \mathbf{0}. \tag{10.10}$$

The *Fundamental Matrix* for an absorbing Markov chain is given by

$$\mathbf{N} = (\mathbf{I} - \mathbf{Q})^{-1}. \tag{10.11}$$

The elements n_{ij} of $\mathbf{N}$ gives the expected number of times the process will be in transient state j if the process started in state j. For the `testtpm` example, we have the answers in the output given below:

```
> N <- solve(diag(rep(1,nrow(Q)))-Q)
> N
          B         C        D         E
B 2.6666667 0.1666667 1.333333 0.6666667
C 1.3333333 1.3333333 2.666667 1.3333333
D 1.3333333 0.3333333 2.666667 1.3333333
E 0.6666667 0.1666667 1.333333 2.6666667
```

Starting from a transient state i, the expected number of steps before the Markov Chain is absorbed and the probabilities of it being absorbed into one of the absorbing states are respectively given by

$$\mathbf{t} = \mathbf{Nc} \tag{10.12}$$

$$\mathbf{B} = \mathbf{NR} \tag{10.13}$$

where c is an t column of 1 and **t** and **B** are respectively the expected number of steps and probabilities of the absorption matrix. For our dummy example, the computation concludes with the program below.

```
> t <- N
> t
      [,1]
B 4.833333
C 6.666667
D 5.666667
E 4.833333
> B <- N %*% R
> B
     A    F
B 0.75 0.25
C 0.50 0.50
D 0.50 0.50
E 0.25 0.75
```

The three questions asked about an absorbing Markov Chain are also applicable to an Ergodic Markov Chain in a slightly different sense. This topic will be taken up next.

10.3.4 Stationary Distribution and Mean First Passage Time of an Ergodic Markov Chain

If we have an ergodic Markov Chain, we know that each state will be visited infinitely often. However, this implies that over the long run, the number of times it will be in a given state may be obtained.

Definition 10.3.8 Stationary Distribution. *A vector* $\boldsymbol{\pi}$ *is called the* stationary distribution *of an ergodic Markov Chain if*

$$\pi_j \geq 0, \sum_{j=1}^{p} \pi_j = 1, \tag{10.14}$$

$$\boldsymbol{\pi}\mathbf{P} = \boldsymbol{\pi}. \tag{10.15}$$

A stationary distribution $\boldsymbol{\pi}$ is a (left) eigenvector of the TPM whose associated eigenvalue is equal to one. For an ergodic Markov Chain, the next program gives us the stationary distribution.

```
> stationdistTPM <- function(M){
+       eigenprob <- eigen(t(M))
```

```
+         temp <- which(round(eigenprob$values,1)==1)
+         stationdist <- eigenprob$vectors[,temp]
+         stationdist <- stationdist/sum(stationdist)
+         return(stationdist)
+ }
> P <- matrix(nrow=3,ncol=3) # An example
> P[1,] <- c(1/3,1/3,1/3)
> P[2,] <- c(1/4,1/2,1/4)
> P[3,] <- c(1/6,1/3,1/2)
> stationdistTPM(P)
[1] 0.24 0.40 0.36
```

The function uses the `eigen` function to obtain the eigenvalues and eigenvectors.

The *mean recurrence time* of an ergodic Markov Chain is given by

$$\tau = 1/\pi. \tag{10.16}$$

For the previous example:

```
> 1/stationdistTPM(P)
[1] 4.166667 2.500000 2.777778
```

We will next consider the concept of passage time.

Definition 10.3.9 First Passage Time *The* first passage time *from state i to state j is the number of transitions made by the stochastic process to move from state i to state j.*

Definition 10.3.10 Mean First Passage Time *For an ergodic Markov Chain in state i, the expected number of steps to reach state j for the first time is called the* mean first passage time *from i to j.*

The matrix of mean first passage time is denoted by $\mathbf{M} = \{m_{ij}\}$. We will next briefly state the formulas to obtain **M**. Let **W** be a matrix where each row consists of the stationary probability vector. Define $\mathbf{Z} = (\mathbf{I} - \mathbf{P} + \mathbf{W})^{-1}$, where **I** is an identity matrix, and **W** is a matrix where each row is the stationary probability vector $\boldsymbol{\pi}$. The elements of **M** are then given by

$$m_{ij} = \frac{z_{jj} - z_{ij}}{\pi_j}.$$

For the Ehrenfest model, the mean recurrence times are given below:

```
> ehrenfest <- as.matrix(ehrenfest)
> w <- stationdistTPM(ehrenfest)
> W <- matrix(rep(w,each=nrow(ehrenfest)),nrow=nrow(ehrenfest))
> Z <- solve(diag(rep(1,nrow(ehrenfest)))-ehrenfest+W)
> M <- ehrenfest*0
> for(i in 1:nrow(ehrenfest)){
+       for(j in 1:nrow(ehrenfest)){
+ M[i,j] <- (Z[j,j]-Z[i,j])/W[j,j]
```

```
+ }
+ }
> M
         0        1        2        3        4
0  0.00000 1.000000 2.666667 6.333333 21.33333
1 15.00000 0.000000 1.666667 5.333333 20.33333
2 18.66667 3.666667 0.000000 3.666667 18.66667
3 20.33333 5.333333 1.666667 0.000000 15.00000
4 21.33333 6.333333 2.666667 1.000000  0.00000
```

For details, refer to Chapter 11 of Grinstead and Snell (2002).

10.3.5 Time Reversible Markov Chain

Consider a stationary and ergodic Markov Chain with stationary distribution $\boldsymbol{\pi}$.

Definition 10.3.11 *An ergodic Markov Chain with a stationary distribution π_j is said to be a* time reversible Markov Chain *if the conditional distribution of X_{n+1} given $X_{n+2} = x$ is the same as the conditional distribution of X_{n+1} given $X_n = x$.*

In simple words, for a stationary ergodic Markov Chain with $\ldots, X_{n-2}, X_{n-1}, X_n, X_{n+1}, X_{n+2}, \ldots$, the backward chain $\ldots, X_{n+2}, X_{n+1}, X_n, X_{n-1}, X_{n-2}, \ldots$ is also a Markov Chain. An intuitive explanation of the phenomenon is that given the present state, the past and future states are independent events. The TPM of the reversed Markov Chain is given by $\mathbf{Q} = \{Q_{ji}\}$:

$$
\begin{aligned}
Q_{ji} = P(X_n = j | X_{n+1} = i) &= \frac{P(X_n = j, X_{n+1} = i)}{P(X_{n+1} = i} \\
&= \frac{P(X_n = j)P(X_{n+1} = i | X_n = j)}{P(X_{n+1} = i)} \\
&= \frac{\pi_j P_{ij}}{\pi_i}. \qquad (10.17)
\end{aligned}
$$

The Gamblers random walk in a finite state space is an example of time reversible Markov Chain.

?'%*%', ?gplot, ?solve, ?diag, ?eigen

10.4 Application of Markov Chains in Computational Statistics

Modern computations are driven by hi-speed computers and without the latter some of the algorithms cannot be put to good use. In this section two of the famous *Monte Carlo* techniques will be discussed whose premise is in the usage of Markov Chains, viz., the *Metropolis-Hastings* algorithm and the *Gibbs sampler*. The current section relies on Chapter 10 of Ross (2006).[1] Robert and Casella (1999–2004) is also an excellent exposition for the two algorithms to be discussed here.

[1]This section may be read in conjunction with Chapter 11

10.4.1 The Metropolis-Hastings Algorithm

Consider a finite sequence of positive numbers $\{b_j\}_{j=1}^k$, for some large integer k. The positive numbers may be interpreted as the weights of an RV W taking the values $j, j = 1, \ldots, k$. Define $B = \sum_{j=1}^k b_j$, and suppose that B is a difficult number to compute. The PMF of X is then given by

$$P(X = j) = \pi_j = \frac{b_j}{\sum_{i=1}^k b_i}. \tag{10.18}$$

It will be seen in Chapter 11 that for large k values, simulation from the probability distribution π_j becomes a daunting task. The Metropolis-Hastings algorithm builds a *time-reversible* Markov Chain argument for simulation from π_j. The requirement is then to find a Markov Chain with TPM $\mathbf{P} = \{p_{ij}\}_{i,j=1}^k$, which is easier to simulate and its stationary distribution must be the same as π_j. Let $\mathbf{Q} = \{q_{ij}\}_{i,j=1}^k$ represent the TPM of an irreducible time-reversible Markov Chain. A Markov Chain $\{X_n\}_{n=1}^\infty$, useful for simulation from π_j, is set up as follows. Suppose that the current state is i, that is, $X_n = i, i = 1, \ldots, k$. Generate an RV X with PMF $q_{ij}, j = 1, \ldots, k$, $P(X_{n+1} = j) = q_{ij}, j = 1, \ldots, k$. Then X_{n+1} is assigned the state j with probability α_{ij}, or the state i with probability $1 - \alpha_{ij}$. The simulation problem is solved if we can determine these $\{\alpha_{ij}\}$ probabilities. The TPM $\mathbf{P}$ of the Markov Chain should thus satisfy the following condition:

$$p_{ij} = q_{ij}\alpha_{ij}, \quad \text{when } i \neq j, \tag{10.19}$$

$$p_{ii} = q_{ii} + \sum_{j \neq i} q_{ij}(1 - \alpha_{ij}). \tag{10.20}$$

The Markov Chain with TPM $\mathbf{P}$ is a time reversible Markov Chain if

$$\pi_i q_{ij} \alpha_{ij} = \pi_j q_{ji} \alpha_{ji}.$$

This relationship is satisfied for the choice of α_{ij} given by

$$\alpha_{ij} = \min\left(\frac{\pi_j q_{ji}}{\pi_i q_{ij}}, 1\right) = \min\left(\frac{b_j q_{ji}}{b_i q_{ij}}, 1\right). \tag{10.21}$$

The reader should verify the need of 1 in Equation 10.21! The *Metropolis-Hastings* algorithm for generation of a Markov Chain $\{X_n\}_{n=1}^\infty$ can be summarized as follows:

1. Select a time-reversible irreducible Markov Chain $\mathbb{Q} = \{q_{ij}\}_{i,j=1}^k$.
2. Choose an integer j, $1 \leq j \leq k$.
3. Set $n := 0, X_0 = j$, and generate an RV X such that $P(X = j) = q_{X_n j}$.
4. Generate a random number U between 0 and 1, see Section 11.2, and set $X_{n+1} = X$ if

$$U < \alpha_{XX_n} = \min\left(\frac{b_X \; q_{X,X_n}}{b_{X_n} \; q_{X_n,X}}, 1\right), \tag{10.22}$$

   else, $X_{n+1} = X_n$.
5. Set $n := n + 1$ and return to Step 2.

The quantity α is called the *Metropolis-Hastings acceptance probability*.

Alternately, the Metropolis-Hastings algorithm can be stated for the continuous RVs case too, see Chapter 7 of Robert and Casella (1999–2004) for more details. Assume that f represents the pdf of interest and that a conditional density $q(y|x)$ is available, which is a dominating measure with respect to f. The Metropolis-Hastings algorithm can be implemented in practice if the two conditions hold: (i) the density f is known to the extent that the ratio $f(y)/q(y|x)$ is known up to a constant which is independent of x, and (ii) the density $q(y|x)$ is either explicitly available or symmetric in the sense of $q(y|x) = q(x|y)$. The density f is known as the *target density*, while q is called the *instrumental* or *proposal density*. The Metropolis-Hastings algorithm starting with x_t is then given by

1. Simulate $Y_t \sim q(y|x_t)$.
2. Simulate X_{t+1} as follows:

$$X_{t+1} = \begin{cases} Y_t, & \text{with probability } \alpha_{x_t Y_t}, \\ x_t, & \text{with probability } 1 - \alpha_{x_t Y_t}, \end{cases} \tag{10.23}$$

where

$$\alpha_{x_t Y_t} = \min\left\{ \frac{f(Y_t)}{f(x_t)} \frac{q(x_t|Y_t)}{q(Y_t|x_t)}, 1 \right\}.$$

The Metropolis-Hastings algorithm will be illustrated following a discussion of the *Gibbs sampler*.

10.4.2 Gibbs Sampler

The Gibbs sampler is a particular case of the Metropolis-Hastings algorithm. However, its intuitive and appealing steps have made it more popular and thus wide applications are carried using it. The algorithm description is as follows.

Suppose $\mathbf{X} = (X_1, \dots, X_p)$ is a (discrete) random vector with probability measure $p(\mathbf{x})$. Assume that the measure $p(\mathbf{x})$ is specified up to a constant, that is, $p(\mathbf{x}) = cg(\mathbf{x})$, where c is a multiplicative constant. The Gibbs sampler deals with the problem of generating an observation from $p(\mathbf{x})$. The Gibbs sampler essentially uses the Metropolis-Hastings algorithm with the state space $\mathbf{S}$ as $\mathbf{x} = (x_1, \dots, x_p)$. The transition probabilities in this state space are set up as follows. Assume that the present state is $\mathbf{x}$. A coordinate of the state space $\mathbf{x}$ is selected at random, that is, an observation from the index $1, 2, \dots, p$, is selected as a sample from a discrete uniform distribution with p number of points. The main assumption of the Gibbs sampler is that for any state i and values $x_j, j \neq i$, a random variable X can be simulated with pmf

$$P(X = x) = P\{X_i = x | X_j = x_j, j \neq i\}. \tag{10.24}$$

Now, the coordinate i is selected at random and using the elements of $\mathbf{x}$ an observation with value x is simulated which will replace the previous x_i value. Thus, the new state is $\mathbf{y} = \{x_1, \dots, x_{i-1}, x, x_{i+1}, \dots, x_p\}$. In other words, the Gibbs sampler uses the Metropolis-Hastings algorithm where

$$q(\mathbf{x}, \mathbf{y}) = \frac{1}{p} P\{X_i = x | X_j = x_j, j \neq i\} = \frac{p(\mathbf{y})}{pP\{X_j = x_j, j \neq i\}}. \tag{10.25}$$

The necessity of the stationary distribution to be $p()$ requires that the new vector $\mathbf{y}$ be accepted as the new state with probability

$$\alpha(\mathbf{x},\mathbf{y}) = \min\left(\frac{p(\mathbf{y})q(\mathbf{y},\mathbf{x})}{p(\mathbf{x})q(\mathbf{x},\mathbf{y})}, 1\right). \tag{10.26}$$

Applications of the Metropolis-Hastings algorithm and Gibbs sampler will be described in the next subsection.

10.4.3 Illustrative Examples

Three examples for each of the algorithms will be discussed briefly. As a fitting tribute to the inventor of the algorithm, the next example of a random walk generation will be discussed, which was originally illustrated by Hastings (1970) in his breakthrough paper. The first two examples are from Robert and Casella (2004).

Example 10.4.1. Random Walk Generation. Random walk/Gamblers walk is seen in Section 10.3 as an important example of a Markov Chain. Consider the continuous version of random walk where the sequence of RVs $\{X_t\}_{t=1}^{\infty}$ is given by

$$X_{t+1} = X_t + \epsilon_t, t = 1, 2, \ldots .$$

Here, ϵ's are generated independently of the X's and $\epsilon_t \sim N(0, 1)$. In the original work, Hastings considers a uniform distribution on $[-\delta, \delta]$ as the proposal density, see Robert and Casella (2004). Then, the probability of acceptance is

$$\alpha_{x_t Y_t} = \min\left\{\exp\left(\frac{x_t^2 - y_t^2}{2}\right), 1\right\}.$$

The R program is thus set up in the following.

```
> yMH <- 0
> Trials <- 15000
> delta <- .1
> for(i in 2:Trials){
+ z <- runif(1,-delta,delta)
+ alpha <- min(1,exp((yMH[i-1]^2-z^2)/2))
+ wp <- runif(1)
+ ifelse(wp<alpha,yMH[i]<-z,yMH[i]<-yMH[i-1])
+ }
> plot.ts(yMH,main="A: Gamblers Walk")
```

The random walk begins at 0, `yMH <- 0`, and the proposal density is initiated as the uniform distribution with $[-0.1, 0.1]$, `runif(1,-delta,delta)`.[2] Now, at each (next) iteration of

[2]Simulation from discrete and continuous distributions are formally introduced in the next chapter. At this stage, *runif* may be assumed to generate observations from uniform distribution.

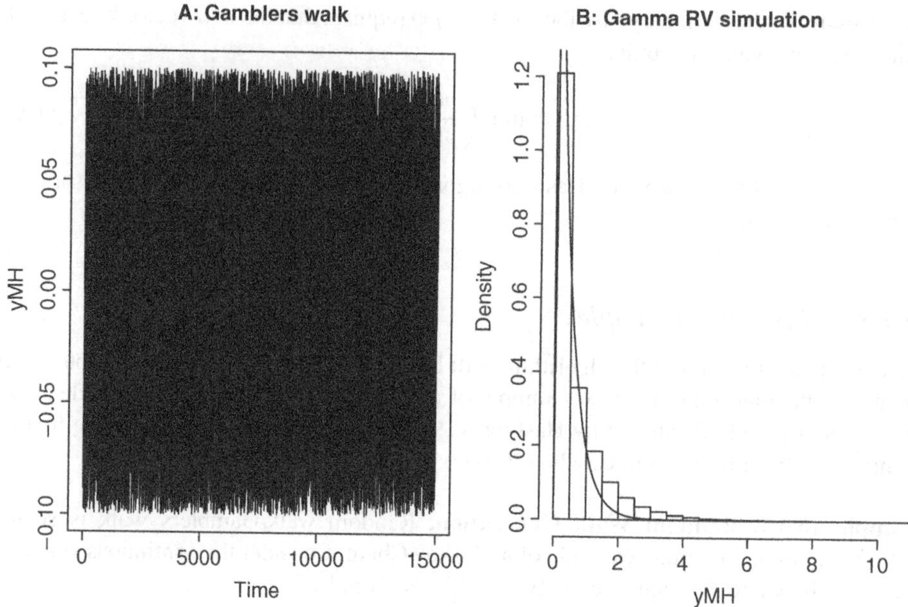

Figure 10.2 Metropolis-Hastings Algorithm in Action

the random walk, a point `z` is generated in this interval and the Metropolis-Hastings acceptance probability `alpha` is calculated. A random observation is then generated in the unit interval and if the acceptance probability is higher than this number `wp<alpha`, the random walk is updated to that of `yMH[i]<-z`, or else the previous iteration `yMH[i-1]` is retained. The result of the program is given in Part A of Figure 10.2.

Example 10.4.2. Simulation from Gamma Distribution. Simulation from gamma distribution is always a complex task, that is, until we resort to built-in modules. To simulate observations from Gamma(θ, k), the Metropolis-Hastings algorithm is set up as follows. Assume that $k = \lfloor\theta\rfloor/\theta$, where $\lfloor.\rfloor$ denotes the integer part of the argument. Next, generate $Y \sim$ Gamma$(\lfloor\theta\rfloor, \lfloor\theta\rfloor/\theta)$. The Metropolis-Hastings algorithm for simulation from gamma distribution is given by the following:

1. Simulate an observation $Y_t \sim$ Gamma$(\lfloor\theta\rfloor, \lfloor\theta\rfloor/\theta)$.
2. Set the next value of observation as follows:

$$X_{t+1} = \begin{cases} Y_t, & \text{with probability } \alpha, \\ x_t, & \text{with probability } 1-\alpha, \end{cases}$$

where

$$\alpha = \min\left[\left(\frac{Y_t}{x_t}\exp\left\{\frac{x_t - Y_t}{\theta}\right\}\right)^{\theta-\lfloor\theta\rfloor}, 1\right].$$

The R program which implements this Metropolis-Hastings algorithm is given next.

```
> theta <- 2.3; k <- 1
> b <- floor(theta)/theta
> yMH <- 1/theta
> Trials <- 1e5
> for(i in 2:Trials){
+ z <- rgamma(1,shape=b,rate=k)
+ alpha <- min(1,((yMH[i-1]/z)*exp((z-yMH[i-1])/theta))^(theta-floor
+(theta)))
+ wp <- runif(1)
+ ifelse(wp<alpha,yMH[i]<-z,yMH[i]<-yMH[i-1])
+ }
> hist(yMH,prob=TRUE,main="B: Gamma RV Simulation")
> curve(dgamma(x,shape=b,rate=theta),add=TRUE)
```

The algorithm is implemented as follows. First, the values of θ and k are arbitrarily chosen as `theta <- 2.3` and `k <- 1`. An initial value of `yMH` is selected as $1/\theta$. The values of `z` and `yMH[i]` are easily seen to follow the steps of the Metropolis-Hastings algorithm. The actual gamma curve is imposed to check if the simulated values of the y in the Metropolis-Hastings algorithm is a good sample or not. The final result is shown in Part B of Figure 10.2. □

Next, the use of Gibbs sampler will be illustrated.

Example 10.4.3. Generating n Random Points at d Distance in a Circle. Some of the probability problems are indeed interesting! Suppose that we are asked to find the probability that if a sample of n points are randomly selected from a circle with unit radius, what is the probability that each of the points is at least at a d distance from the other points? Though this problem can be completely solved using the Gibbs sampler, the problem of obtaining such a sample is discussed here. The answer may be obtained easily though and it is an exercise for the reader.

Now, without loss of generality, the circle may be assumed to have 0 as its origin. The Gibbs sample for obtaining the required sample distribution is implemented in the following algorithm:

1. Initialize n points such that no two points are within a distance of d.
2. Select one of the points from 1–n at random, say I.
3. Simulate a point at random in the circle.
4. If the simulated point is within a distance of d with respect to any of the $n-1$ points except the Ith one, reject the simulated observation.
5. If the simulated point is not within d distance of any of the $n-1$ points, replace the Ith point with the simulated point.
6. Repeat the above process a large number of times, say N.

The final collection of n points has the desired probability. The next program codes the above algorithm. First, a circle is drawn with the n initial points and all the points are given at the end of the algorithm.

```
> radius <- 1
> ddist <- 0.1
```

```
> n <- floor(2*pi/ddist)
> GetRandomPoint <- function(radius){
+ rr <- runif(1,0,radius)
+ theta <- runif(1,0,2*pi)
+ return(c(rr*sin(theta),rr*cos(theta)))
+ }
> # Testing the working of GetRandomPoint
> windows(width=10,height=10)
> theta <- seq(0,2*pi,length.out=200)
> plot(radius*sin(theta),radius*cos(theta),"l",xlab="x",ylab="y")
> abline(h=c(-1,1),v=c(-1,1))
> InitialPoints <- cbind(radius*sin(seq(1:n)*(1/(2*pi))),radius*
+cos(seq(1:n)
+ *(1/(2*pi))))
> points(InitialPoints,col="red")
> # Gibbs sampling
> Trials <- 1000
> testCounter <- 0
> for(i in 1:Trials){
+ CurrPoints <- InitialPoints
+ testPoint <- GetRandomPoint(radius)
+ testIndex <- sample(1:n,1)
+ CurrPoints <- CurrPoints[-testIndex,]
+ CurrPoints <- rbind(testPoint,CurrPoints)
+ if(min(as.matrix(dist(CurrPoints,upper=TRUE))[1,-1])>=ddist){
+ InitialPoints[testIndex,] <- testPoint
+ testCounter <- testCounter+1
+ }
+ }
> points(InitialPoints,col="green")
> min(dist(CurrPoints))
[1] 0.1002729
```

If the distance d is given, we can generate at most `n <- floor(2*pi/ddist)` points on the circumference of the circle. The function `GetRandomPoint` generates a random point within the unit circle around the origin. This is easily seen since `rr <- runif(1,0,radius)` has a random distance of less than or equal to the radius, while a random angle is generated with `theta <- runif(1,0,2*pi)`. It is easy to see that the polar transformation leads to a random point in the unit circle. A circle is first generated on the graphics window, and its explanation may be followed by the reader. The `InitialPoints` are then plotted on the circumference of the circle and each point is colored as red.

The Gibbs sampler implementation is now explained. It is a difficult proposition to simulate the n initial points and hence a deterministic choice is made here. Thus, the points are initialized with `InitialPoints`, where `radius*sin(seq(1:n)*(1/(2*pi)))` gives the x-coordinate and `radius*cos(seq(1:n)*(1/(2*pi)))` returns the y-coordinate. The Gibbs sampler implementation is indeed easier to follow here. The result is shown in Figure 10.3.

□

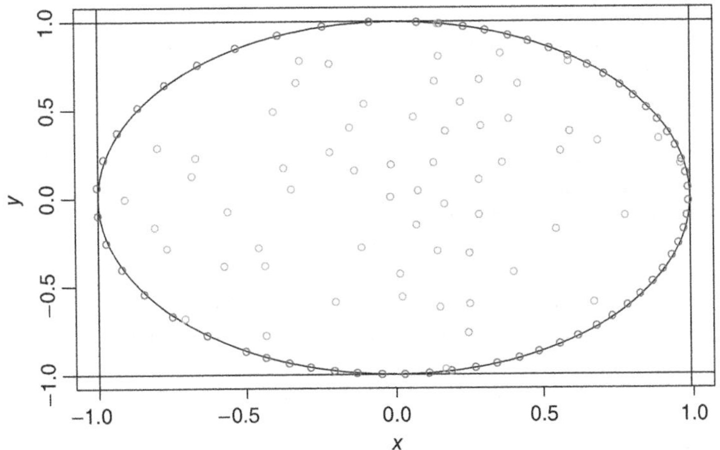

Figure 10.3 Gibbs Sampler in Action

Example 10.4.4. Exponential RVs with Sum Greater than some *c*. Suppose $X_i \sim Exp(1/\lambda_i)$. Define $S \equiv \sum_{i=1}^{n} X_i$. The problem is to generate the random vector $\mathbf{X} = (X_1, \ldots, X_n)$ given that the event $S > c$ has been observed, where c is a large positive number. The Gibbs sampling algorithm to solve this problem is given in the following:

1. Initialize a vector $\mathbf{x} = (x_1, \ldots, x_n)$ such that each $x_i \geq 0$ and $\sum_{i=1}^{n} x_i > c$.
2. Select an observation at random, that is, choose an integer from $1, 2, \ldots, n$. Suppose that the integer chosen is $I(= i)$.
3. Simulate an observation from exponential distribution with rate λ_i, say Y, and set, see page 254 of Ross (2006), the value of x_i as
$$X = Y + \left(c - \sum_{j \neq i} x_j\right)^+,$$
where $(a)^+$ takes the value a if $a > 0$ and 0 otherwise.
4. Repeat the previous steps a large number of times.

The expression for X needs an explanation. When $I = i$, we need to simulate an exponential observation X with rate $1/\lambda_i$ conditional on the event $X + \sum_{j \neq i} x_j > c$. Equivalently, we need to simulate an observation of X which is conditional on the event $c - \sum_{j \neq i} x_j$. A useful result here is that if an exponential RV is greater than a positive constant, then it is distributed as an exponential distribution (with rate λ_i) plus that constant. Hence, the value of X is chosen as that given in the above equation.

The implementation of the program is given in the following:

```
> # Exponential Sum S = sum_i=^n X_i > c
> n <- 15
> constant <- 200
```

```
> rate <- 1/(1:n)
> x0 <- sort((constant*rate)/sum(rate))
> Trials <- 1e5
> xGS <- x0
> for(i in 1:Trials){
+ currIndex <- sample(1:n,1)
+ Sum <- sum(xGS[-currIndex])
+ xGS[currIndex] <- max(constant-Sum,0)-log(runif(1))/rate[currIndex]
+ }
> xGS
 [1]    1.33068757   0.07708722     13.07502344    9.00714096
[12]    1.50248658  21.37157461   21.83680094 104.26333132
> 1/rate
 [1]  1  2  3  4  5  6  7  8  9 10 11 12 13 14 15
```

In the above program the average of the i-th exponential RV is i. The program is again simple to follow and hence it is left to the reader to interpret it. □

The next problem is a continuation of the exponential RVs sum.

Example 10.4.5. Probability of Product of Exponential RVs. Suppose that $n = 5$, and that $\lambda_i = 1/i$. Assume that the sum is observed to be 15 and the problem is to find the probability that the product exceeds 120, that is, we need to compute

$$P\left\{\prod_{i=1}^{5} X_i > 120 \mid \sum_{i=1}^{5} = 15\right\}.$$

This example is again adapted from Ross (2006), page 260. To obtain this probability, the Gibbs sampler will randomly select two observations from $n = 5$. Let us denote the two selected observations as U and V, which are independent with rates $1/\lambda_U$ and $1/\lambda_V$. Without loss of generality, assume that $\lambda_U < \lambda_V$. Then, the conditional distribution of U given $U + V = a$ is

$$f_{U|U+V=a} \propto \exp\{-(\lambda_V - \lambda_U)u\}, 0 < u < a.$$

Thus, the conditional distribution of U is again an exponential distribution with rate $\lambda_V - \lambda_U$, which is conditioned to be less than a. Hence, the conditional distribution of U and V, given the other values is the conditional distribution of two exponential distributions with rate λ_V and λ_V given that their sum is $15 - \sum(\mathbf{X}_{-U,-V})$, where $\sum(\mathbf{X}_{-U,-V})$ indicates that the elements U and V are removed from $\mathbf{X}$. Now, the values of U and V can be simulated by first simulating an observation from $f_{U|U+V=a}$, which is conditional on $15 - \sum(\mathbf{X}_{-U,-V})$ and setting the value of V to meet the constraint $\sum_{i=1}^{5} x_i = 15$. This process is then repeated a large number of times, so that the proportion of times the product exceeds 120 is accepted as the required probability. The next R program implements this Gibbs sampling technique.

```
> itexp <- function(u, m, t) { -log(1-u*(1-exp(-t*m)))/m }
> rtexp <- function(n, m, t) { itexp(runif(n), m, t) }
> # http://www.r-bloggers.com/r-help-follow-up-truncated-exponential/
> rate <- 1/(1:5)
```

```
> x0 <- c(1.08,2.38,2.84,3.84,4.86)
> Sx0 <- sum(x0); Px0 <- 120
> Trials <- 1000; prodYes <- 0
> for(i in 1:Trials){
+ twoIndex <- sort(sample(1:5,2))
+ a <- sum(x0)-sum(x0[-twoIndex])
+ x0[twoIndex[1]] <- rtexp(1,rate[twoIndex[2]-rate[twoIndex[1]]],a)
+ x0[twoIndex[1]] <- Sx0-x0[twoIndex[1]]-sum(x0[-twoIndex])
+ if(prod(x0)>Px0) prodYes <- prodYes+1
+ }
> prob_beta <- prodYes/Trials
> prob_beta
[1] 0.317
```

Two functions are required to simulate observations from the truncated exponential distribution and these programs have been adapted from the link given in the program. The initial vector `x0` is quite arbitrary. The `twoIndex` randomly draws two observations, and a performs the computation as described earlier. The reader can now complete the remainder of the description, and based on the 1000 trials, the estimated probability is `0.317`.

The purpose of this section has been to introduce the two algorithms discussed here. However, it must be said that there is much more detail to the use and applications of these algorithms than even indicated here. However, it is the stochastic process part of these algorithms which is of interest here. The applications of these techniques to Bayesian inference will be considered in the next chapter.

?qpois

10.5 Further Reading

Feller's two volumes are again useful for a host of theories and applications of stochastic processes. Doob (1953) is the first book on stochastic processes. Karlin and Taylor's (1975, 1981) two volumes have been a treatise on this subject. Taylor and Karlin (1998) is another variant of the two volumes by Karlin and Taylor. Bhattacharya and Waymire (1990–2009) has been found to be very useful by the students. Ross (1996) and Medhi (1992) are nice introductory texts.

Feldman and Valdez-Flores (2010) considers the modern applications of stochastic processes. Adke and Manjunath (1984) consider statistical inference related to the finite Markov process.

10.6 Complements, Problems, and Programs

Problem 10.1 The TPM of a gamblers walk consists of infinite states. Restricting the matrix over $[-n,n]$ states, that is considering only the corresponding rows and columns and not the *restricted* gamblers walk, obtain the digraph using the `sna` package.

Problem 10.2 Using the `msteptpm` function, obtain $\mathbf{P}^{10}$ for `testtpm`, `testtpm2`, and `testtpm3` TPM's.

Problem 10.3 Carry out the canonical decomposition for `testtpm3`.

Problem 10.4 Find the stationary distribution for the Ehrenfest Markov Chain.

11

Monte Carlo Computations

Package(s): `plotrix`, `LearnBayes`, `ConvergenceConcepts`

11.1 Introduction

Simulation of observations from random experiments has always been of profound interest. Generation of random numbers has always been crucial for statisticians, both for theory and applications. The emergence of the computer and its speed has greatly benefited from the endurance of random numbers. The truth is that machines cannot really produce random numbers in the sense that the generated sequence will eventually repeat itself identically, which is more formally called the *cycle of the generator*. However, this does not restrict their usage for most practical situations if the required random numbers are less than the cycle of the generator. See also the important page: http://www.cran.r-project.org/web/views/Distributions.html

The current chapter unfolds along the following lines. Section 11.2 discusses how random numbers may be simulated using *random generators*. Three different techniques are developed here and a pressing case is made for the use of the *linear congruential generator*. A different way of dealing with these random numbers will be that such numbers may be treated to follow the uniform distribution $U(0, 1)$. The standard uniform distribution forms the base of most simulation techniques. Using the techniques described here, some very interesting probability problems are dealt with in Sub-section 11.2.2. Simulation from discrete and continuous distributions are dealt with in Section 11.3. Also, the role of simulation towards understanding, along with a relook, towards limit theorems and CLT as seen in Chapter 5, is dealt with in the same section. The core concept of this chapter on the *Monte Carlo* technique is developed in Section 11.4. Direct sampling from a distribution is not feasible in all cases and we need to resort to sampling from other distributions. This approach is called the *accept-reject* technique and will be developed in Section 11.5. The Gibbs sampler and Metropolis-Hastings algorithm have already been investigated in Section 10.4. Their application to Bayesian inference is developed in Section 11.6.

A Course in Statistics with R, First Edition. Prabhanjan Narayanachar Tattar, Suresh Ramaiah and B. G. Manjunath.

Companion Website: www.wiley.com/go/tattar/statistics

11.2 Generating the (Pseudo-) Random Numbers

Generation of random numbers has a lot of applications in real life. The 14-digit number that is written on your mobile recharge voucher, numbers on be-lucky-to-win scratch cards, match your mobile numbers on those given in a series of draws of newspapers, etc., are all some scenarios which require generation of random numbers. Thus, there is that need of a random number generator (RNG,) which ensures that the numbers in the draw look random. This is purely in the sense that there is no systematic pattern in the sequence of generated numbers.

It used to be a difficult task to generate random numbers three decades ago. Computers have eased this job for us, just as they have aided with solving a billion other problems.

11.2.1 Useful Random Generators

The eminent mathematician von Neumann proposed one of the earliest techniques for generating random numbers with the *middle-square method*. In this simple setup, a number is squared and its head and tail are chopped off to obtain the middlemost number. This is better understood through a simple illustration. Consider the four-digit number 4253 as the *initial seed*. The square of this number is `18088009`, a eight-digit number. Now, remove the first two leading digits `1` and `8`, and then the trailing digits `0` and `9`. We are then left with `0880`. Set the middle-square number for generating the next random number, and continue the process until you get the desired numbers. An R program created in the `vonNeumann` function implementing this task is given for seeds `11`, `675248`, and `8653`.

```
> vonNeumann <- function(x,n){
+ rx <- NULL
+ d <- max(2,length(unlist(strsplit(as.character(x),""))));
+ getNext <- function(x,d){
+ temp <- x^2
+ tbs <- as.numeric(unlist(strsplit(as.character(temp),"")))
+ # to be split
+ tbs_n <- length(tbs);
+ diff_n <- 2*d - tbs_n;
+ dn <- ceiling(d/2)
+ ifelse(diff_n == 0, tbs <- tbs, tbs <- c(rep(0,diff_n),tbs))
+ tbs_n <- length(tbs)
+ NEXT <- tbs[-c(1:dn,((tbs_n-dn+1):tbs_n))]
+ return(as.numeric(paste(NEXT,collapse="")))
+ }
+ rx[1] <- x
+ for(i in 2:(n+1)) rx[i] <- getNext(rx[i-1],d)
+ return(rx)
+ }
> vonNeumann(x=11,n=10)
 [1] 11 12 14 19 36 29 84  5  2  0  0
> vonNeumann(x=675248,n=10)
```

```
[1] 675248 959861 333139          341914
> vonNeumann(x=8653,n=100)
  [1] 8653 8744 4575    1354 8333 4388
 [30] 2545 4770 7529    8100 6100 2100
 [59] 4100 8100 6100    6100 2100 4100
 [88] 8100 6100 2100    4100 8100 6100
```

The two arguments of the `vonNeumann` function are the initial seed `x` and the required number of observations `n`. Then `length(unlist(strsplit(as.character(x),"")))` first characterizes the numeric, splits it, and obtains the number of digits in it. The `getNext` function obtains the next random number in the sequence. Though this function is slightly complex, the reader must attempt to demystify it. The `getNext` function is then repeated n times to obtain the random sequence of required numbers.

The limitations of this approach are easily seen as follows. In the first example (of `x=11`), we end up with a sequence of 0's, and in the third case, we have a recurring pattern of the numbers of `6100 2100 4100 8100`. Thus, the middle-squared method is not really useful for generating a large sequence of random numbers.

Let us consider generation of random numbers in the unit interval [0, 1]. If we begin with two random seeds, say x_{i-1} and x_{i-2} for some i, and generate further (pseudo) random numbers using $x_i = (x_{i-1} + x_{i-2})\text{mod}1$, an apparent random sequence may seem appropriate, see page 15 of Ripley (1987). Let us write a small program through the function `Ripley2.2` for this method and understand its mathematical logic and generate observations for the seeds `0.563` and `0.624`.

```
> Ripley2.2 <- function(x,n){
+ rx <- NULL
+ rx <- x
+ for(i in (length(x)+1):(length(x)+n)) {
+ rx[i] <- (rx[i-1]+rx[i-2]) %% 1 }
+ return(rx)
+ }
> Ripley2.2(c(0.563,0.624),50)
[1] 0.56300000 0.62400000 0.18700000 0.81100000 0.99800000

[49] 0.12299945 0.06399912 0.18699857 0.25099769
```

An obvious drawback of this method is that x_i can never be a random number between x_{i-1} and x_{i-2}.

A powerful algorithm for generating pseudo-random numbers is the *linear congruential generator*, abbreviated to LCG. In this algorithm, we start with an initial number x_0 , a multiplier a, an incremental value c, and a modulo m. Using these terms, we can obtain a sequence of pseudo-random numbers x_n , using the form of LCG:

$$x_n = (ax_{n-1} + c) \quad \text{mod } m, 0 \leq x_n \leq m. \tag{11.1}$$

For large values of m, the sequence $\{x_n\}$ generated by the LCG behaves like a sample from the uniform distribution $U(0, m)$. Furthermore, the sequence $\{x_n/m\}$ resembles a random sample from the standard uniform distribution $U(0, 1)$. We can see this from the simple program below.

```
> m <- 2^20; a <- 123.89; c <- 39.75
> x <- c()
> x[1] <- 4567
> for(i in 2:10001) x[i] <- (a*x[i-1]+c) %% m
> jpeg("LCG_Hist.jpeg")
> par(mfrow=c(2,1))
> hist(x,xlab="x values", ylab="Frequency")
> hist(x/m,xlab="normalised x values", ylab="Frequency")
> dev.off()
null device
1
```

A large value of m is initiated with `m <- 2^20`, a multiplier a in `a <- 123.89`, and a constant c with `c <- 39.75`. The choice of a and c has been simply arbitrary. An initial value for the series is specified with `x[1] <- 4567`. The next values in the sequence of x_n's as required by Equation 11.1 is computed in the `for(i in 2:10001)` with `x[i] <- (a*x[i-1]+c) %% m`. The resulting histogram is seen in Figure 11.1, and shows that we have a near *uniform* set of values ranging from 0 to m. For more details about the LCG, refer to and read pages 11–27, Chapter 1 of Gentle (2003). Now, some of the interesting problems in probability will be dealt with by a simulation approach.

11.2.2 Probability Through Simulation

In this section we will solve some probability problems using a simulation approach, and we start with the birthday problem.

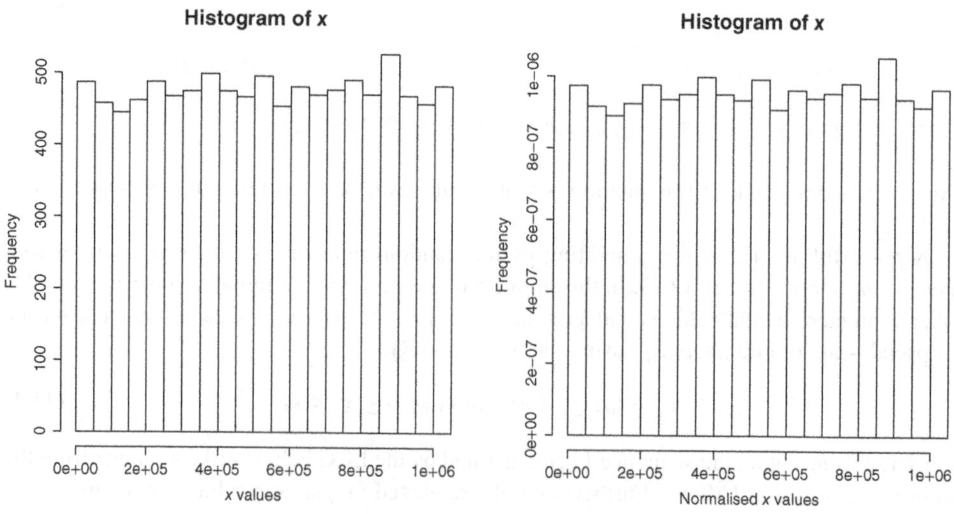

Figure 11.1 Linear Congruential Generator

Let S be our discrete sample space and A be the event of interest. The main steps in the simulation approach are as follows:

- Simulate an event $E_i, i = 1, 2, \ldots, B$, where B is a large positive integer.
- Check if E_i implies the occurrence of event A, and note I_i to be 1 if the implication is true, and I_i if 0 is otherwise.
- $\frac{\sum_{i=1}^{B} I_i}{B}$ gives us the simulated probability of the event A.

Example 11.2.1. The Birthday Problem. Here the number of cells is $n = 365$. Alternatively imagine them as 365 balls of different colors in an urn. For a fixed k, draw a ball at random and note its color before replacing it in the urn. The urn is shaken well to ensure that the balls are again in random order. This exercise is repeated k times, and then record if two balls of the same color are repeated. If yes, note 1, if no, note 0. The exercise up to this point is repeated a large number of times, say B. The average of B can then be taken as the probability of having at least two of the same birthdays in a group of k people. This approach will give us the simulated birthday probabilities.

The probabilities for the birthday probability problem can be summarized as follows:

- For a fixed k and a large B, draw B samples with replacement from an urn consisting 365 color balls, each of size k.
- For each simulated sample, note the number of occasions on which the number of different color balls is less than k.
- Sum the number of 1's in the previous step and divide it by B to obtain the simulated birthday probabilities.

An R program has been written to obtain the birthday probabilities, which can be compared with Table 5.2.

```
> # This R program for Simulated Birthday Probabilities
> diy <- 1:365
> B <- 1000
> bins <- c(2,5,10,20,30,40,50)
> simprob <- 1:length(bins)*0
> for(j in 1:length(bins)) {
+  y <- 1:B*0
+  for(i in 1:B)  {
+   x <- sample(diy,bins[j],replace=TRUE)
+   if(dim(table(x))<bins[j]) y[i] <- 1
+    }
+  simprob[j] <- mean(y)
+     }
> simprob
[1] 0.002 0.032 0.126 0.399 0.728 0.902 0.970
```

Using the `sample` function, a draw of k, R variable `bins`, balls is carried out from `diy`, days in year, with replacement (option `replace=TRUE`). To check if any birthday is selected more than once, we check if `dim(table(x))<bins[j]` holds true. If the condition is satisfied, then `y[i]` is assigned a value of 1, which is otherwise zero. The simulated birthday

Table 11.1 Theoretical and Simulated Birthday Match Probabilities

Size k	Theoretical Probability	Simulated Birthday Probability
2	0.0027	0.003
5	0.0271	0.029
10	0.1169	0.094
20	0.4114	0.417
30	0.7063	0.699
40	0.8912	0.885
50	0.9704	0.954

probability is obtained with `simprob[j] <- mean(y)`. The simulated birthday probability and theoretical probability are compared in Table 11.1. The values are close enough to each other. The reader may perform a `t-test` on them! □

Example 11.2.2. The Match Box Problem. The simulation thought process is the following. Begin with 50 sticks in each of the match boxes. Each match box is randomly selected and used, and this is continued until the point of finding one empty match box. At this time, we will note the number of remaining sticks in the non-empty match box. This process is repeated a large number of times and we then note the frequencies of the number of sticks remaining. This algorithm, which computes the simulated probabilities, for the match box problem is summarized below.

- Set the number of sticks in the match box as $N = 50$, and $B = 10000$.
- Simulate $2 \times N$ Bernoulli pseudo random observations.
- Calculate the first time either the number of heads or the number of tails exceeds 50, and note 50 minus the sum of the other events.
- Note the frequencies of 0 to 50 in the B bootstrap samples.
- Divide the values in the above step by B and we are left with the simulated probabilities.

The simulated probabilities for the other box containing exactly k matches is given by this R program segment:

```
> # Banach Match Box Problem
> match_prob <- function(x) choose(2*N-x,N)*2^{-(2*N-x)}
> # Verifing Fellers Match Box Probabilities on Page 166
> N <- 50; B <- 10000
> simfreq <- rep(0,51)
> for(i in 1:B)  {
+   maxht = minht <- 0
+   hcount = tcount <- 0
+   while(maxht<51){
+     tt <- rbinom(1,1,0.5)
+     if(tt==1) {
+       hcount <- hcount + 1
+       hremain <- 50-1
+     }
```

```
+      else {
+        tcount <- tcount + 1
+        #tremain <- 50 - tcount
+      }
+      maxht <- max(hcount,tcount)
+      minht <- min(hcount,tcount)
+      tremain <- 50-minht
+      #return(c(maxht,minht))
+    }
+    simfreq[tremain+1] <- simfreq[tremain+1]+1
+ }
> simfreq
 [1] 808 772 767 738   0   0   0
[41]   0   0   0   0   0   0   0
> simfreq <- simfreq/B
> plot(0:50,cumsum(sapply(0:50,match_prob)),ylim=c(0,1),
+ xlab="Number of Sticks Remaining", +ylab="Cumulative Probability",
+ type="o",col="green")
> title("B: The Match Box Problem")
> lines(0:50,cumsum(simfreq),"o",col="red")
> legend(x=c(35,52),y=c(-0.1,0.3),c("Theoretical","Simulated"),
+ col=c("green","red"),pch="o")
```

The `pcount` function counts the number of heads and tails in a matrix of two columns. Using the `rbinom` function, see Section 11.3 for simulation from discrete distributions, the numbers 0 or 1 for the match boxes are simulated. Now, using the `pcount` function, the number of 0's and 1's are counted. Depending on which of the match boxes becomes empty, the `if` loops `if(Nmax1>50)` or `if(Nmax0>50)`, the number of sticks in the other match box is determined and entered in the `simfreq` object. This module is repeated a large number of times B, here `B<-10000`. The theoretical and simulated probabilities match well. □

Example 11.2.3. The Coupon Collectors Problem. As with the two earlier problems, we repeat the experiment a large number of times. The algorithm for the simulated probabilities of the coupon collectors problem is given below:

- Set the number of coupons to be collected as the vector $n = 1, 2, \ldots, 100$.
- Set $B = 1000$.
- For each simulated sample, simulate the coupons drawn from an urn (with replacement) until the number of different coupons drawn equals n labels, and note down the number of trials required.
- For each n, the expected number of coupons to be collected is the average of the B numbers obtained in the previous step.

The next R program compares the theoretical expectations with the expectations based on simulated probabilities.

```
> TEn <- function(n) n*log(n) # The Theoretical Expectations
> coupons_matrix <- matrix(nrow=100,ncol=3)
> colnames(coupons_matrix) <- c("Number_of_Coupons","TEn","SPEn")
```

```
> coupons_matrix[,1] <- 1:100
> coupons_matrix[,2] <- sapply(1:100,TEn)
> coupons_matrix # Output suppressed
> coupons <- function(n){
+ cells <- 1:n
+ target <- 0
+ counts <- 0
+ collect <- NULL
+ while(length(collect)<length(cells)){
+ temp <- sample(cells,1)
+ counts <- counts+1
+ if(counts==1) collect <- temp
+ if(temp %in% setdiff(cells,collect)){
+ target <- target+1
+ collect <- c(collect,temp)
+ }
+ }
+ return(counts)
+ }
> B <- 1000
> SEn <- function(n){
+ x <- 1:B*0
+ for(i in 1:B) {
+ x[i] <- coupons(n)
+ }
+ return(mean(x))
+ }
> coupons_matrix[,3] <- sapply(1:100,SEn)
> coupons_matrix
       Number_of_Coupons          TEn     SEn
  [1,]                 1     0.000000   1.000
  [2,]                 2     1.386294   2.974

 [99,]                99   454.916865 521.858
[100,]               100   460.517019 529.590
```

This program, though a lengthier one, is fairly simple to follow. The simulated expected number of coupons and the theoretical ones are given in Table 11.2. □

Figure 11.2 gives a plot of the simulated and theoretical probabilities/expectations of the birthday, match box, and coupon collectors problems. It may be seen from the figure that the simulated and theoretical probabilities match well.

Example 11.2.4. The Buffon's Needle Problem. Georges-Louis Leclerc, Comte de Buffon posed a problem in the 18th century, in what is now popularly referred to as *Buffon's needle problem.* Consider equally spaced strips of parallel lines and drop a needle onto the surface. The lines are at a distance D apart from each other. Shonkwiler and Mendivil (2010) have explained the Buffon's needle problem as the first experiment where simulation has been used to estimate the π value. Assume that the length of the needle L is less than D. Let X denote

Table 11.2 Theoretical and Simulated Expected Number of Coupons

Number of Coupons	TEn	SEn	Number of Coupons	TEn	SEn
1	1.08	1	51	230.46	230.19
2	3.04	3	52	235.98	230.73
3	5.53	5.53	53	241.52	240.62
4	8.35	8.34	54	247.07	246.24
...	...	...	...	...	...
47	208.59	208.9	97	500.24	499.69
48	214.02	212.66	98	506.39	504.48
49	219.48	220.06	99	512.56	511.59
50	224.96	224.28	100	518.74	517.54

the distance from the center of the line to the next nearest line. Let θ be the acute angle that the needle makes with respect to the parallel lines. Then $0 \leq X \leq D/2$ and $0 \leq \theta \leq \pi/2$. The probability of the needle crossing a line, see page 2 of Shonkwiler and Mendivil (2010), is given by

$$P(\text{needle crossing a line}) = \frac{2L}{\pi D}.$$

In the next simulation study we will examine the number of times the needle crosses a line and use the *empirical probability* for the estimation of π in the above expression. The required R program now follows.

```
> # L: Needle Length; d: Distance between two lines;
> # Hn: of hits in n throws
> # Simulating if needle crosses the line
> # We needed simulated values of sin(theta).
> # Simulate values in the interval 0-1 and use it as sin(theta)
> L <- 10; d <- 25
> n <- 1e5
> theta <- runif(n,0,22/14)
> sinTheta <- sin(theta)
> x <- runif(n,0,d/2)
> SimHits <- ifelse((x<=(L/2)*sinTheta),1,0)
> # We can now estimate the value of pi
> piEstimate <- 2*L/(mean(SimHits)*d)
> piEstimate;pi
[1] 3.144407
[1] 3.141593
```

The `runif` function will be discussed in more detail in the next section. It suffices to assume at the moment that we obtain n random (and uniform) observations in the interval $(0, 22/14)$. The `ifelse` condition helps to obtain the empirical probability. The estimated value of π given by `piEstimate` in the simulation study at `3.145025` is closer to the actual value up to the first two digits. □

We next move to simulation from standard discrete distributions.

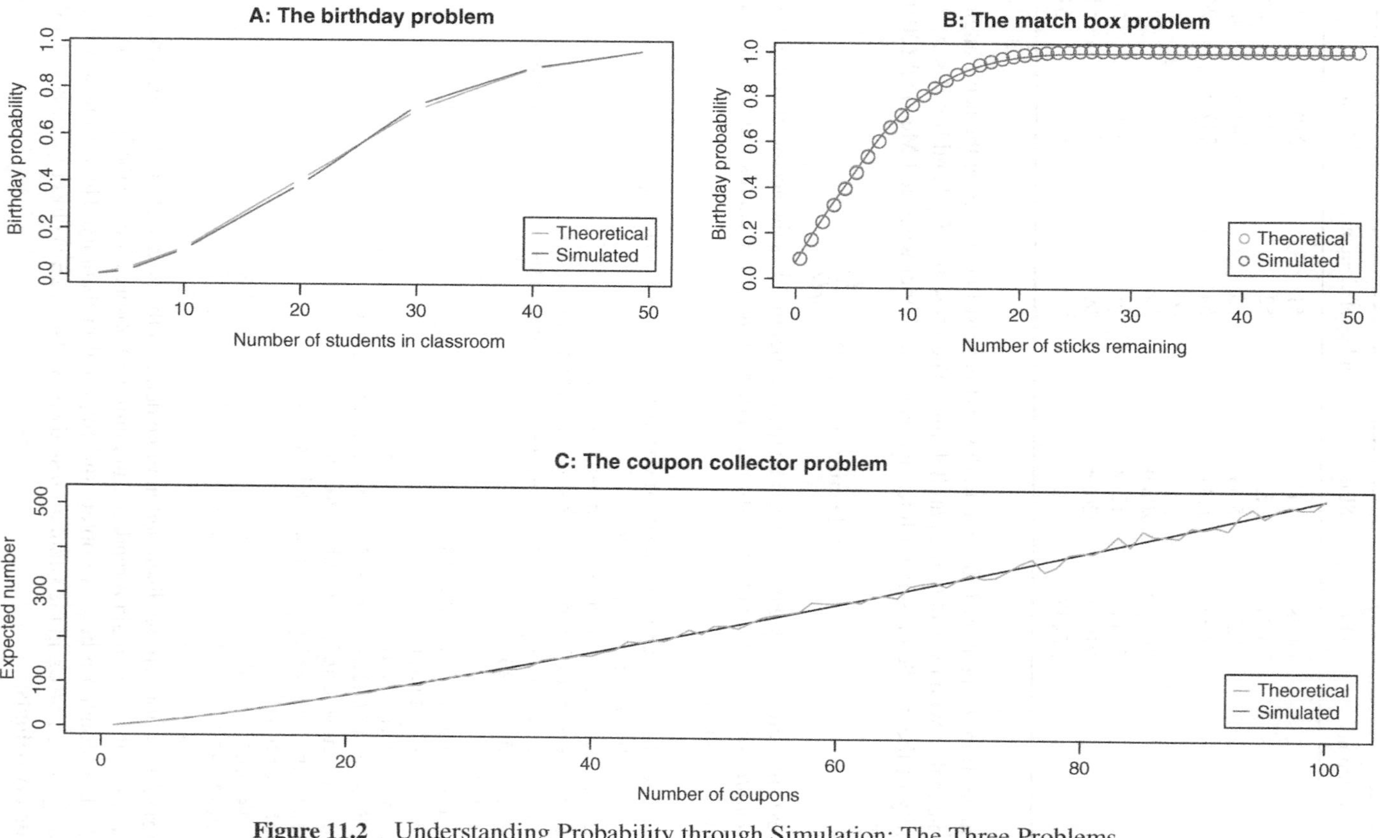

Figure 11.2 Understanding Probability through Simulation: The Three Problems

11.3 Simulation from Probability Distributions and Some Limit Theorems

Generation of random observations for some of the probability models discussed in Sections 6.2 and 6.3 will be considered now.

11.3.1 Simulation from Discrete Distributions

As mentioned earlier in Chapter 6, the wait for the fourth of the quartet (`p`, `d`, `q`, `r`) for a probability distribution ends here. The letter `r` prefixed with the abbreviation of a probability distribution enlisted in R helps us in the generation of pseudo-random observations from the target distribution. However, we will also consider the *raw* way of obtaining the pseudo numbers in a direct approach.

Discrete Uniform Distribution

If a random variable X can take one of the N possible distinct outcomes with equal probability, we say that X has a *discrete uniform distribution*, recollect the distribution discussed in detail in Section 6.2. A simple example of such a variate is if we randomly select a key from a bunch, then the probability of getting the right key to unlock the door follows a discrete uniform distribution, which is the *professors key problem*. Mathematically,

$$P(X = x_i) = \frac{1}{N}, i = 1, 2, \ldots, N.$$

Example 11.3.1. A Simple Illustration. Suppose we want to generate 100 numbers randomly from the sequence 1, 2, ..., 10. Then, the random numbers are generated by using the `sample` function.

```
> dud <- sample(c(1:10),100,replace=TRUE)
> table(dud)
dud
1 2 3 4 5 6 7 8 9 10
8 8 12 12 14 5 11 8 9 13
```

The R object name `dud` stands for *discrete uniform distribution*, of course. The `sample` function helps to generate random numbers from a given array and such an array need not be a numeric vector, as it may be a character vector as well. □

Discrete Arbitrary Distribution

The method of generating random numbers from an arbitrary discrete distribution needs the use of *the inverse transform method*. Now let the probability mass function of an arbitrary discrete RV X, which can take the values $x_1, x_2, \ldots$, be represented by $P(X = x_j) = p_j, j = 1, \ldots$. Here,

$\sum_{j=1} p_j = 1$. To generate a random number with pmf p_j, first simulate a number from $U(0, 1)$, the LCG discussed earlier may be used here, and denote it by U. The inverse transform method then generates x_j as a pseudo random number if $\sum_{i=1}^{j-1} p_j \leq U < \sum_{i=1}^{j} p_j$. That is, the value x_1 is accepted if $U < p_1$, the value x_2 if $p_1 \leq U < p_1 + p_2$, and so on. If N random numbers are required, the task is repeated N times.

Example 11.3.2. An Arbitrary Discrete Distribution. Suppose we want to generate 100 numbers randomly from the sequence 1, 2, ..., 10, where $P(X = i) = p_i$ are arbitrary. Assume that the probability vector for the 10 numbers is given by 0.05, 0.17, 0.02, 0.14, 0.11, 0.06, 0.05, 0.04, 0.17, 0.19.

To obtain the random numbers, the program is built as follows. The x and $p(x)$ are first defined in x and p_x. The cumulative distribution function of the discrete RV is obtained in F_x using the cumulative sum cumsum function. For the required number of observations N, the for loop checks which x_j value is obtained for the simulated value from $U(0, 1)$.

```
> x <- 1:10
> p_x <- c( 0.05, 0.17, 0.02, 0.14, 0.11, 0.06, 0.05,
+ 0.04, 0.17, 0.19)
> F_x <- cumsum(p_x)
> N <- 2000
> disc_sim <- numeric(length=N)
> for(i in 1:N) {
+ temp <- runif(1)
+ disc_sim[i] <- x[min(which(F_x>temp))]
+ }
> table(disc_sim)
disc_sim
  1   2   3   4   5   6   7   8   9  10
109 327  47 274 189 108 104  82 337 423
```

The reader may check if table(disc_sim) proportions are similar to p_x. □

Though the above technique is really useful, it is meaningful to check if improvements can be made to simulate the random numbers. A slight modification of investigating where x_j value should correspond to the simulated uniform random number offers better performance in terms of the computation time. Precisely, if the vector p_x is arranged in decreasing values of the probabilities, a significant improvment is achieved in terms of the computational time. However, it should be noted, in light of the repeated guidelines in Robert and Casella (2010), that if there is already a method of simulation using R available functions, it is more often preferable to use them. For instance, the sample function can be used to simulate from an arbitrary discrete distribution and as such it also uses lower computational time. These aspects are detailed as a continuation of the previous example.

Example 11.3.3. An Arbitrary Discrete Distribution. Contd. Ordered and Unordered Speed Times. Two functions ST_Unordered and ST_Ordered are defined, which simulate values from an arbitrary discrete distribution using unordered and ordered probabilities.

The `sample` function too is used and the computational times are also given. The programs explanation is not given here and is left to the reader.

```
> ST_Unordered <- function() {
+   N <- 1e7
+   x <- 1:10
+   p_x <- c(0.05,0.17,0.02,0.14,0.11,0.06,0.05,0.04,0.17,0.19)
+   F_x <- cumsum(p_x)
+   disc_sim <- numeric(length=N)
+   for(i in 1:N) {
+    temp <- runif(1)
+    disc_sim[i] <- x[min(which(F_x>temp))]
+     }
+      }
> ST_Ordered <- function() {
+   N <- 1e7
+   x <- 1:10
+   p_x <- c(0.05,0.17,0.02,0.14,0.11,0.06,0.05,0.04,0.17,0.19)
+   x <- x[order(p_x,decreasing=TRUE)]
+   F_x <- cumsum(sort(p_x,decreasing=TRUE))
+   disc_sim <- numeric(length=N)
+   for(i in 1:N) {
+    temp <- runif(1)
+    disc_sim[i] <- x[min(which(F_x>temp))]
+     }
+     }
> system.time(ST_Unordered());system.time(ST_Ordered())
   user  system elapsed
  55.38    0.03   55.66
   user  system elapsed
  54.93    0.04   55.19
> system.time(sample(1:10,size=1e7,replace=TRUE,prob=p_x))
   user  system elapsed
   0.36    0.03    0.39
```

Unsurprisingly, the use of the `sample` function is the minimum time to simulate the required number of random observations. However, it is also instructive to follow the algorithms. The reader may also note that the time depends on the computer configuration. □

The more generic form of the functions `ST_Unordered` and `ST_Ordered` are available in the ACSWR package.

Finally, we consider the problem of simulating a random permutation of n items.

Example 11.3.4. Simulating a Random Permutation. In the previous problems, the task of simulating random observations from a finite set was addressed. In those examples, if $N > x$, some elements would be selected more than once. Now consider the problem of simulating a random permutation where $N = x$ and any item can be selected once only. For the sake of simplicity, assume a random permutation of the integers $1{:}n$. The `sample` function can again be used to obtain a random permutation with `sample(1:n,n,replace=FALSE)`, which will obviously be more optimal than the `Random_Permutation` function, which will be developed here. The algorithm for simulating a random permutation is the following:

1. Initialize $k = n$.
2. Simulate a random number from $U(0, 1)$, say U, and obtain `I = round(k*U)+1`.
3. Interchange the values of `I` and `k`.
4. Set $k = k - 1$ and if $k > 1$, go to Step 1.
5. If $k = 1$, the current arrangement of the integers is a random permutation.

The function `Random_Permutation` constructed in the forthcoming R program gives us a random permutation, which implements the above algorithm.

```
> Random_Permutation <- function(n){
+ k = n; permute = 1:n
+ while(k>1){
+ t = runif(1)
+ I = round(k*t) + 1
+ a = permute[I]; b = permute[k]
+ permute[I] = b; permute[k] = a
+ k=k-1
+ print(c(k+1,I,permute))
+ }
+ return(permute)
+ }
> Random_Permutation(10)
 [1] 10 10  1  2  3  4  5  6  7  8  9 10
 [1]  9  9  1  2  3  4  5  6  7  8  9 10
 [1]  8  7  1  2  3  4  5  6  8  7  9 10
 [1]  7  7  1  2  3  4  5  6  8  7  9 10
 [1]  6  1  6  2  3  4  5  1  8  7  9 10
 [1]  5  4  6  2  3  5  4  1  8  7  9 10
 [1]  4  2  6  5  3  2  4  1  8  7  9 10
 [1]  3  4  6  5  2  3  4  1  8  7  9 10
 [1]  2  1  5  6  2  3  4  1  8  7  9 10
 [1]  5  6  2  3  4  1  8  7  9 10
> sample(1:10,10,replace=FALSE)
 [1]  2  4  5  8  1  3 10  9  7  6
```

The reader should verify that the `Random_Permutation` function indeed implements the described algorithm! □

In the rest of this subsection, simulations from popular discrete distributions are considered.

Binomial Distribution

Suppose X denotes a binomial RV with parameters (n, p). We can then generate random observations from it using the function `rbinom`. However, it is pertinent to consider the simulation technique from first principles and a useful algorithm. Can the two functions `ST_Unordered` and `ST_Ordered` be used for simulation from binomial distribution? The answer is an obvious "Yes". For example, suppose 100 observations are required from $b(12, 0.7)$. Using the options `N`, `x`, and `p_x` in conjunction with the `dbinom` function, it is a simpler task to obtain random observations from binomial distribution, as seen next.

```
> table(ST_Unordered(N=100,x=0:12,p_x=dbinom(x=0:12,size=12,
+ prob=0.7)))
 5  6  7  8  9 10 11 12
 2  7 13 26 25 19  6  2
> table(ST_Unordered(N=100,x=0:12,p_x=dbinom(x=0:12,size=12,
+ prob=0.7)))
 5  6  7  8  9 10 11 12
 4  4 15 25 19 23  8  2
> table(ST_Unordered(N=100,x=0:12,p_x=dbinom(x=0:12,size=12,
+ prob=0.7)))
 6  7  8  9 10 11 12
 7 16 25 21 20  9  2
> table(ST_Ordered(N=100,x=0:12,p_x=dbinom(x=0:12,size=12,prob=0.7)))
 5  6  7  8  9 10 11 12
 7  2 13 22 29 16  9  2
> table(ST_Ordered(N=100,x=0:12,p_x=dbinom(x=0:12,size=12,prob=0.7)))
 3  4  5  6  7  8  9 10 11 12
 1  1  2 12 15 22 26 13  5  3
> table(ST_Ordered(N=100,x=0:12,p_x=dbinom(x=0:12,size=12,prob=0.7)))
 5  6  7  8  9 10 11 12
 4 10 14 24 26 18  3  1
```

In fact, these two functions may be used for any discrete RV with a finite possible integer range, or the technically known simple RV. It is to be noted that simulation from *first principles* for the binomial distribution is inbuilt here too. The more efficient `rbinom` function too may be used for simulation from the binomial distribution.

```
> rbinom(10,1,.5)
[1] 0 1 0 1 1 1 1 0 1 0
```

Example 11.3.5. Estimating a Binomial Probability. Suppose that $X \sim B(20, 0.3)$, and we want to estimate $P(X > 13)$ based on 100 simulated observations. The desired probability is computed in the following:

```
> set.seed(123)
> sum(rbinom(100,20,.3)>13)/100
[1] 0
> 1-pbinom(13,20,0.3)
[1] 0.000261047
```

The reader should increase the number of random simulations and check the difference with `sum(dbinom(x=14:20,size=20,prob=0.3))`. □

The recurrence relationship of binomial distribution can be exploited to simulate random numbers for binomial distribution. The recurrence relationship is

$$P(X = i + 1) = \frac{n - i}{i + 1} \frac{p}{1 - p} P(X = i).$$

Using the recurrence relationship and the *inverse transform* algorithm, simulation from the binomial distribution can be carried out and the brief steps of this technique is now given.

1. Simulate a random number U from U(0,1).
2. Set $i = 0$ and compute $c = p/(1 - p)$, $prob = (1 - p)^n$, and $F = prob$.
3. If $U < F$, set $X = 0$ and stop.
4. If $U \geq F$, compute $prob = c(n - i)prob/(i + 1)$, $F = F + prob$, and $i = i + 1$ and return to Step 3.

The R function is given which follows the above algorithm:

```
Binom_Sim <- function(size,p,N) {
 q <- 1-p
 x <- numeric(N)
 for(i in 1:N) {
  temp <- runif(1)
  j <- 0; cc <- p/(1-p); prob <- (1-p)^size; F <- prob
  while(temp >= F) {
   prob <- cc*(size-j)*prob/(j+1); F <- F+prob; j <- j+1
       }
  x[i] <- j
      }
 return(x)
         }
Binom_Sim(size=10,p=0.5,N=100)
```

The next natural question is how to simulate observations for an elementary RV, that is, an RV with a countable range.

Geometric Distribution

The range of a geometric RV is the set of non-negative integers $\mathbb{Z}^+$. A question that then arises is how do we carry out simulations for the examples of an elementary RV? Consider a variant of the geometric distribution than the one specified in Equation 6.14 as

$$P(X = x) = p(1 - p)^{x-1}, x = 1, 2, \ldots .$$

To generate a random number from a geometric RV, note the following relation:

$$\sum_{x=1}^{j-1} P(X = x) = 1 - (1 - p)^{j-1},$$

and hence using an observation U from $U(0, 1)$, select that value of $X = j$ which satisfies

$$1 - (1 - p)^{j-1} \leq U < 1 - (1 - p)^j.$$

Thus, if we need n observations from a geometric RV, the Geom_Sim function as constructed next can be used for simulation:

```
Geom_Sim <- function(p,n) {
 q <- 1-p
 x <- numeric(n)
 for(i in 1:n) {
  temp <- runif(1)
  temp <- 1-temp
  j <- 0
  while(((temp>q^j) & (temp <= q^{j-1}))==FALSE) j <- j+1
  x[i] <- j
     }
 return(x)
       }
```

Example 11.3.6. Geometric Random Variables. Using the function Geom_Sim, the mean of a geometric RV across simulated samples of various sizes are computed. It may be seen that as the number of simulations increase, the accuracy increases.

```
> 0.99/0.01 # Geometric Mean
[1] 99
> mean(Geom_Sim(0.01,10))
[1] 120.7
> mean(Geom_Sim(0.01,10))
[1] 107.2
> mean(Geom_Sim(0.01,100))
[1] 106.07
> mean(Geom_Sim(0.01,1000))
[1] 104.449
> mean(Geom_Sim(0.01,10000))
[1] 101.3128
> mean(Geom_Sim(0.01,10000))
[1] 102.1636
> mean(Geom_Sim(0.01,50000))
[1] 99.76944
```

Thus, increasing the number of simulated observations leads to an increase in the accuracy. □

The reader can now use the pgeom inbuilt R function for simulation of observations from the geometric distribution. This section will close with the simulation problem of generating observations from the Poisson distribution.

Poisson Distribution

The recurrence relation for the Poisson distribution, as in the binomial distribution, will guide the simulation problem here:

$$P(X = x + 1) = \frac{\lambda}{x+1} P(X = x).$$

The algorithm for simulating observations from the Poisson distribution is the following:

1. Simulate an observation U from $U(0, 1)$.
2. Set $x = 0$, $prob = e^{-\lambda}$, and $F = prob$.
3. If $U < F$, select $X = x$ and terminate.
4. If $U \geq F$, obtain $x = x + 1$, $prob = \frac{\lambda}{x+1} prob$, $F = F + prob$, and return to the previous step.

The R function `Poisson_Sim` simulates random observations using this algorithm:

```
Poisson_Sim <- function(lambda,n) {
 x <- numeric(n)
 for(i in 1:n) {
  j <- 0; p <- exp(-lambda); F <- p
  temp <- runif(1)
  while((F>temp)==FALSE) {
   p <- lambda*p/(j+1); F <- F+p; j <- j+1
       }
  x[i] <- j
     }
 return(x)
          }
```

The reader should test the function `Poisson_Sim` for various n and λ values. We now use the command `rpois` for simulation of observations from a Poisson random variable with mean rate λ and use it to estimate a probability too.

Example 11.3.7. Estimating a Poisson Probability. Suppose $X \sim P(10)$, and $Y \sim P(20)$. We can then estimate $P(X > Y)$ based on 1000 observations as follows:

```
> x <- rpois(1000,10); y <- rpois(1000,20)
> sum(x>y)/1000
[1] 0.036
```

Thus, probabilities of interest may be computed using the random observations. □

11.3.2 *Simulation from Continuous Distributions*

We begin with simulation from the uniform distribution, which also forms the basis for generating samples from all continuous distributions.

Uniform Distribution

The probability density function of a uniform random variable over the interval (a, b) is

$$f(x) = \frac{1}{b-a}, a \leq x \leq b.$$

Simulation from this distribution was detailed in Section 11.2. However, look at the syntax of the function `runif`:

$$runif(n, min = 0, max = 1)$$

By default, for generating n observations from the unit interval, use `runif(n, min=0, max=1)`. The `runif` has already been used in the earlier sections.

We saw in Section 11.2 that the LCG returns us a sample from the uniform distribution. It is left as an exercise for the reader to figure out the exact algorithm used in `runif`. Remember, R is an open source software and you can see every line of code in it.

As an illustration, we give a simple program.

```
> runif(10,1/20,1/10)
 [1] 0.0927 0.0760 0.0767 0.0706 0.0818 0.0957 0.0756 0.0886
+ 0.0692 0.0854
> mean(runif(1e4)); var(runif(1e4))
[1] 0.493
[1] 0.0834
```

Exponential Distribution

Simulation of samples from continuous distributions easily follows from the simulated values from the standard uniform distribution, thanks to the following result.

Theorem 11.3.1 The Inverse Cumulative Distribution Function (CDF) Method. *If X is a random variable with continuous CDF F_X and $U =: F_X(x)$, then*

$$U \sim U(0, 1).$$

Consequently, if we need samples from the distribution F_X , we can use the inverse relation

$$X = F_X^{-1}(U).$$

for generating the samples from the required distribution.

Example 11.3.8. Exponential Distribution. A random variable X follows exponential distribution with mean θ if its probability density is

$$f(x; \theta) = \frac{1}{\theta} e^{-\frac{x}{\theta}}, x \geq 0, \theta > 0.$$

The CDF of exponential distribution is then

$$F(x, \theta) = 1 - e^{-\frac{x}{\theta}}, x \geq 0.$$

If U is an observation from $U(0, 1)$, we have by the discussion following the previous lemma that $F_X^{-1}(U)$ is a observation from $F_X(x, \theta)$. That is, a pseudo-observation from $F_X(x)$ may be

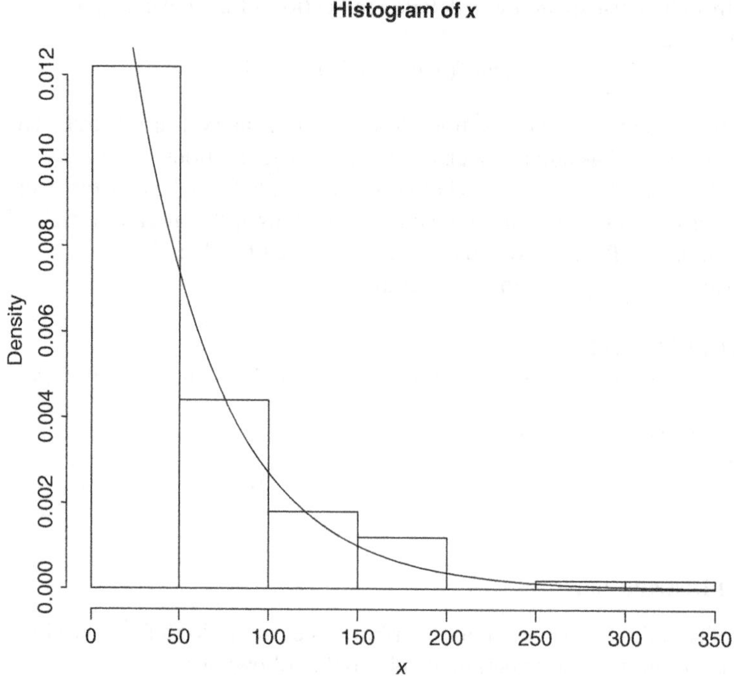

Figure 11.3 Simulation for the Exponential Distribution

generated using the relationship $x = -\theta \ln\,(1 - U)$. We can examine the correctness of the above steps in the following program:

```
> n <- 100; theta <- 50
> pseu_unif <- runif(n)
> x <- -theta*log(1-pseu_unif)
> hist(x,freq=FALSE,ylim=c(0,.012))
> curve(dexp(x,rate=1/theta),add=T)
> (rexp(10,1/theta)) # Using "rexp"
[1] 37.58 115.12 17.93 52.63 116.99 2.39 48.44 28.71
[9] 11.54 126.63
```

Thus, using the `runif` function and the transformation, observations can be simulated for the exponential distribution. The histogram, see Figure 11.3, obtained by the `hist` function gives the shape of the simulated observations and that it is a good technique is confirmed by the `curve` imposed on the histogram. □

Alternatively, using the `rexp` function, we can easily generate observations from the exponential distribution in R.

In Section 10.4 we saw the use of the Metropolis-Hastings algorithm to generate random observations from a gamma distribution. Simulation for continuous distributions, beta, and normal will be taken up again in Section 11.5. In the rest of this section we will see application and use of random observations in understanding certain limit theorems and the central limit theorem.

11.3.3 Understanding Limit Theorems through Simulation

Sections 5.10–5.12 of Chapter 5 dealt with various modes and forms of limit theorems. Wherever it was possible in the discussions therein, R programs were constructed to understand the meaning of limit theorems. The central idea in Chapter 5 made use of either the associated CDF F or expectation and variance of the random sample $X_1, X_2, \ldots$. In this section we will revisit some of the limit theorems. A simulation approach will be taken in this section to generate the data, that is, instead of looking at the quantities related with the random sample, we will use the pseudo random observations $x_1, x_2, \ldots$ and estimated sample means and variance, or the empirical CDF $\hat{F}$.

Example 11.3.9. Convergence of Uniform Minima. Let $X_1, X_2, \ldots, X_n$ be a random sample from a uniform distribution $U(0, \theta)$. Suppose the interest is in the asymptotic behavior of $nX_{(1)}$, where $X_{(1)} = \min(X_1, X_2, \ldots, X_n)$ is a function of n. Theoretically, the survival function (complement of the cumulative distribution function) is given by

$$P(nX_{(1)} > x) = P(X_{(1)} > x/n) = \prod_{i=1}^{n} P\left(X_i > \frac{x}{n\theta}\right)$$
$$= \left(1 - \frac{x/\theta}{n}\right)^n.$$

Taking limits on both sides, the asymptotic distribution of the survival function of $nX_{(1)}$ is thus the following:

$$\lim_{n\to\infty} P(nX_{(1)} > x) = \lim_{n\to\infty} \left(1 - \frac{x/\theta}{n}\right)^n = \exp\left(\frac{-x}{\theta}\right).$$

The expression on the last term is the survival function of exponential distribution with mean θ. We conduct a simulation study to understand the same using the following algorithm:

1. Consider sample sizes $n = 100, 200, \ldots, 800$.
2. For a given sample size, generate n observations from $U(0, \theta)$ and note the minimum of this sample and calculate nX_1.
3. Repeat Step 2 a large number of times, say 20.
4. Plot the empirical cumulative distribution function for each sample of size n, and also plot the CDF of an exponential random variable with mean θ.

The R program for studying the convergence of uniform minima may be easily set up using vector arrays for `ss` (sample size), `xpoints`, etc., along with the `min` and `ecdf` functions.

```
> Convergence_Uniform_Minima <- function (theta,nsimul){
+ ss <- c(10,20,50,100,200,400,600,800)
+ xpoints <- seq(0,100,5)
```

```
+ par(mfrow=c(2,4))
+ for(i in 1:length(ss)){
+ y <- c()
+ for(j in 1:nsimul){
+ y[j] <- ss[i]*min(runif(ss[i],0,theta))
+ }
+ plot(ecdf(y),verticals=TRUE,do.points=FALSE,xlim=c(0,150))
+ y <- y[order(y)]
+ z <- seq(0,150,5)
+ lines(z,pexp(z,1/theta),type="l",col="red")
+ }
+ }
> Convergence_Uniform_Minima(theta=30,nsimul=20)
```

The function `Convergence_Uniform_Minima` has two arguments, `theta` and `nsimul`. The former argument is for any parameter of the user's choice, while the latter is for the number in Step 3 explained earlier. The code `ss[i]*min(runif(ss[i],0,theta))` obtains n times the minimum in a sample of size n, and the `ecdf` function obtains the empirical distribution of $nX_{(1)}$. The exponential curve (through the `lines` function) is then imposed on the `plot` of `ecdf(y)`.

The graphs generated give us a clear understanding of the asymptotic distribution. It may be seen from Figure 11.4 that as the sample size n increases, the convergence of the minima of uniform distribution is closer to the exponential distribution. □

Example 11.3.10. Understanding the Weak Law of Large Numbers (WLLN). To understand the WLLN through simulation, consider three distributions, viz., normal, exponential, and gamma, for which the variance is theoretically known to be finite. Then generate 10 000 values from each of these distributions with means respectively at 5, 6.5, and 8. The next program along with the graph gives a clear understanding of how true the WLLN holds in reality.

```
> n <- 10000
> xnorm <- rnorm(n,5,1); xexp <- rexp(n,1/6.5)
> xgamma <- rgamma(n,4,1/2)
> plot(1:n,cumsum(xnorm[1:n])/1:n, type="l",xlab="n",
+ ylab=expression(hat(mu)),
+ main=expression(paste("A: Convergence of sample mean to ", mu)),
+ col = "red",ylim=c(4,9))
> lines(1:n,cumsum(xexp[1:n])/1:n,type="l",col="blue")
> lines(1:n,cumsum(xgamma[1:n])/1:n,type="l",col="green")
> abline(h=c(5,6.5,8),lty=2)
```

Random numbers from the normal, exponential, and gamma distribution are generated using `rnorm`, `rexp`, and `rgamma`. The remaining program is easier to follow. See Part A of Figure 11.5. □

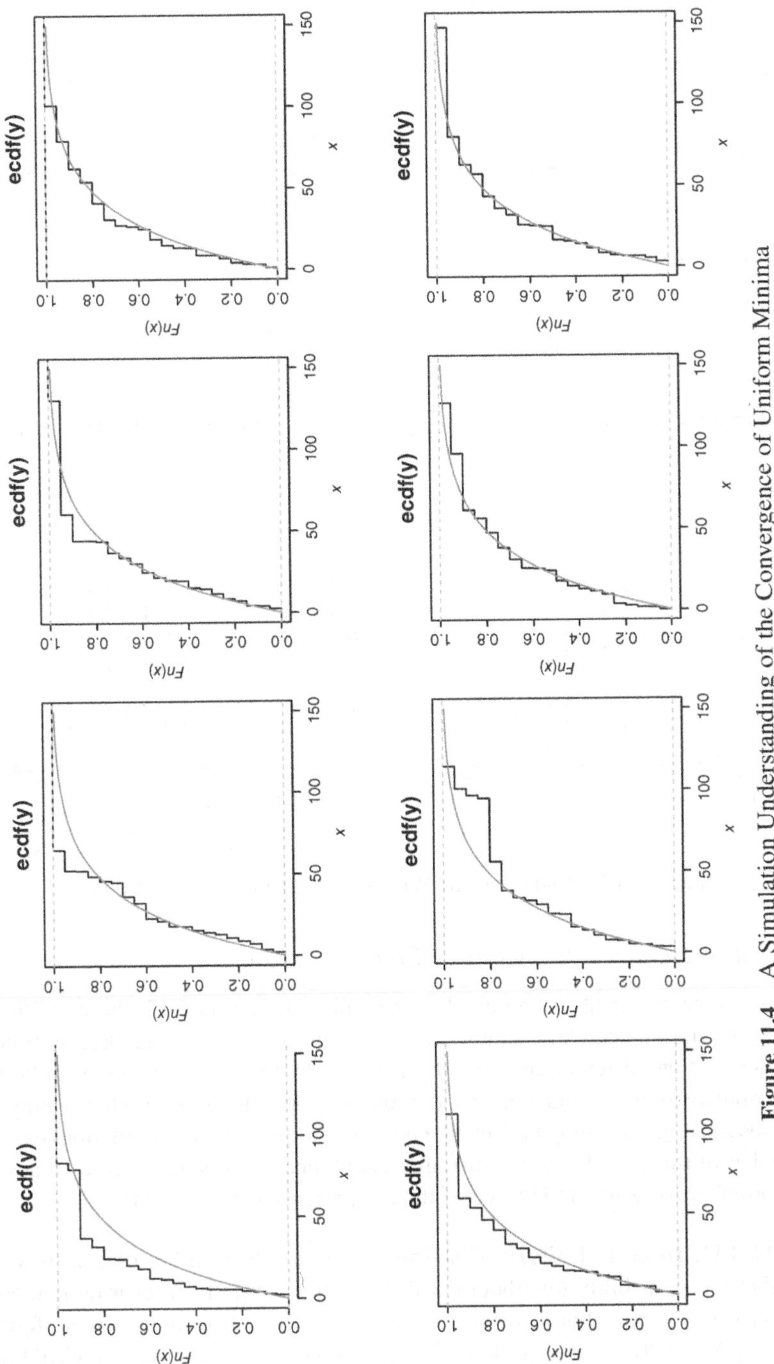

Figure 11.4 A Simulation Understanding of the Convergence of Uniform Minima

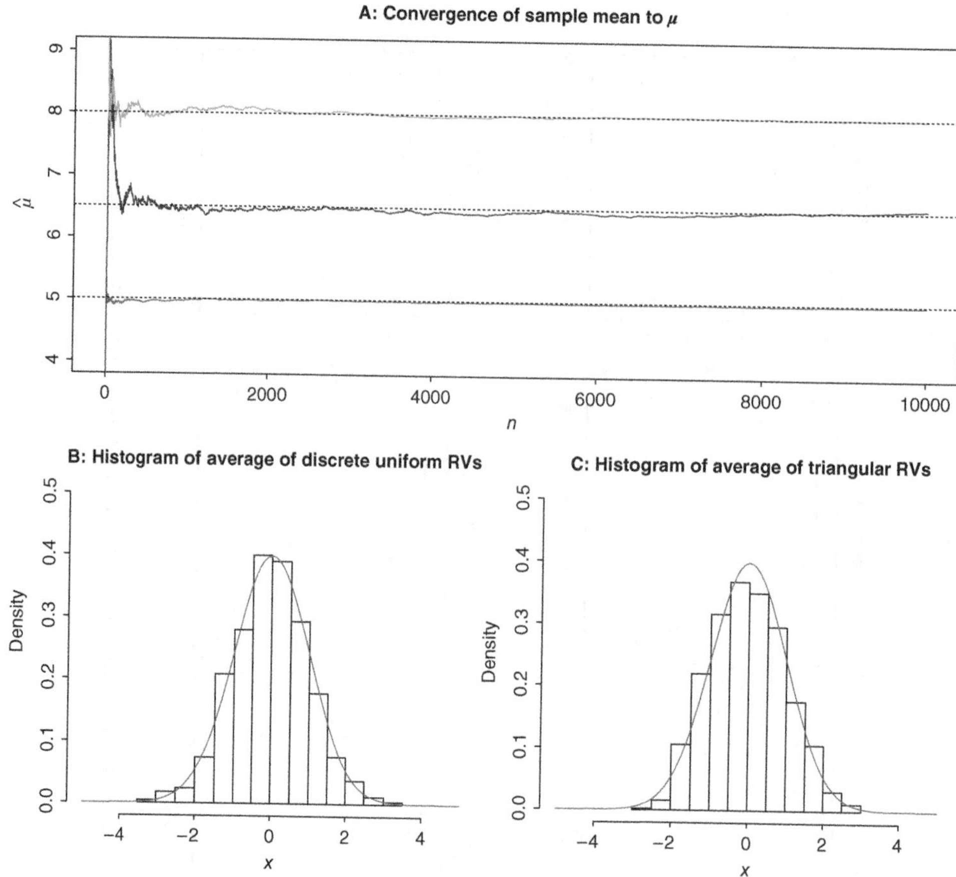

Figure 11.5 Understanding WLLN and CLT through Simulation

11.3.4 Understanding The Central Limit Theorem

The CLT is a very powerful technique. Theoretically, in Section 5.12, the conditions were stated when iid and independent sample averages converged to the standard normal distribution. In this section, different distributions are considered which are significantly different from the normal distribution, and then observations are simulated from it. Then averages of the simulated observations are computed and the module is repeated, the (simulation) experiment, a large number of times, and finally a histogram is plotted of the standardized values and the standard normal curve is fitted to inspect if the convergence is true or not!

Example 11.3.11. Discrete Uniform Distribution. If we throw a fair dice with N sides, it is known that the probability distribution will be a discrete uniform distribution. Here, we have a flat probability mass function. That is, we assume X_i is from a discrete uniform distribution $(1, \ldots, N), i = 1, 2, \ldots, n$. Define $\bar{X} = \sum_{i=1}^{n} X_i/n$. As n increases, the CLT for the iid case tells us that the asymptotic distribution of $\bar{X} - E(\bar{X})/sd(\bar{X})$ is $N(0, 1)$. Fix $N = 100$ and consider simulating a batch of 20 observations first and note the average. This step will then be repeated a large number of times, $B = 1000$. The 1000 averages will then be standardized and a histogram will be obtained to examine the appropriateness of the CLT. The program is given next.

```
> xmean <- NULL
> B <- 1000
> for(i in 1:B){
+ xmean[i]=mean(sample.int(100,size=200,replace=TRUE))
+ }
> xstan <- (xmean-mean(xmean))/sd(xmean)
> hist(xstan,prob=TRUE,main="B: Histogram of Average of Discrete
+ Uniform RVs",xlab="x",xlim=c(-5,5),ylim=c(0,0.5))
> curve(dnorm(x,mean=0,sd=1),add=TRUE,col="red")
```

Since the program is routine by now, it is self-explanatory to the reader. Part B of Figure 11.5 clearly shows that the CLT holds good for the average of random sample from a discrete uniform RV. □

Example 11.3.12. Triangular Distribution. Recollect from Example 5.12.2 of Section 5.12, the definition of a triangular distribution:

$$f(x,a,b,c) = \begin{cases} 0, & x < a, \\ \frac{2(x-a)}{(b-a)(c-a)}, & a \le x < c, \\ \frac{2}{b-a}, & x = c, \\ \frac{2(b-x)}{(b-a)(b-c)}, & c < x \le b, \\ 0, & x > b. \end{cases}$$

We do not have a standard function R to simulate an observation from the triangular distribution. However, a simple algorithm which returns simulated observations from it is given next.

- Simulate an observation from $U(0, 1)$.
- If $u \le (c - a)/(b - a)$, then take $x = a + \sqrt{(b - a)(c - a)u}$. Or else, go to the next step.
- Set $x = b - \sqrt{(b - a)(b - c)(1 - u)}$.

Thus, we will first define this simulation step using the function `rtrian` and the rest of the details will be the usual flow.

```
> a <- 10; b <- 30; c <- 14
> rtrian <- function(a,b,c){
+ u <- runif(1)
+ ifelse(u <= (c-a)/(b-a), a+sqrt((b-a)*(c-a)*u),
+ b-sqrt((b-a)*(b-c)*(1-u)))
+ }
> ntrian <- function(n,a,b,c){
+ y=NULL
```

```
+ for(i in 1:n) y[i]=rtrian(a,b,c)
+ return(y)
+ }
> x <- NULL
> B <- 1000
> for(i in 1:B) x[i] <- mean(ntrian(5,a,b,c))
> xstan <- (x-mean(x))/sd(x)
> hist(xstan,prob=TRUE,main="C: Histogram of Average of
+ Triangular RVs",xlab="x",xlim=c(-5,5),ylim=c(0,0.5))
> curve(dnorm(x,mean=0,sd=1),add=TRUE,col="red")
```

Note that we started with a highly asymmetric distribution. However, the reader can (and should) experiment with various values for a, b, and c and verify that the CLT does hold true. Part C of Figure 11.5 indicates that the CLT indeed holds for a particular choice of a, b, and c.

□

The R package `ConvergenceConcepts` is useful for understanding the concept of almost sure convergence. The important concept of *Monte Carlo simulation* will be considered and developed in the next section.

11.4 Monte Carlo Integration

Random numbers have been used since early days for evaluation of integrals. In a certain way, the Buffon's needle problem is such an example. Its simplicity also helps lay the foundation for complex algorithms. Let us begin with the algorithm and some interesting applications.

Consider the integral:

$$\theta = \int_0^1 g(x)dx.$$

If this equation is rewritten as $\theta = \int_0^1 g(x)f_U(x)dx$, where $f_U(x)$ is the probability density function of the uniform distribution on the unit interval (0, 1), it is easy to see that θ is simply the expectation

$$\theta = E[g(U)].$$

Thus, if $U_1, \ldots, U_k$ is a random sample of size k from $U(0, 1)$, we have $g(U_1), \ldots, g(U_k)$ as an iid sample with expectation θ, and it follows by the SLLN that

$$\sum_{j=1}^{k} \frac{g(U_i)}{k} \rightarrow E[g(U)] = \theta, \text{ as } k \rightarrow \infty.$$

Approximation of integrals in this fashion is referred as the *Monte Carlo* integration.

Example 11.4.1. Illustration of the Monte Carlo for Computation of some Integrals. Suppose that we want to evaluate the integrals $I_1 = \int_0^1 \exp\{e^x\}dx$ and $I_2 = \int_0^1 (1-x^2)^{3/2}dx$. The integrals can be conveniently obtained using the Monte Carlo approach:

```
> u <- runif(1000) #random sample from the U(0,1)
> int1 <- mean(exp(exp(u)))
```

```
> int1; integrate(function(x) exp(exp(x)),0,1)
[1] 6.271236
6.316564 with absolute error < 7e-14
> int2 <- mean((1-u^2)^(3/2))
> int2; integrate(function(x) {(1-x^2)^(3/2)},0,1)
[1] 0.5945052
0.5890486 with absolute error < 1.3e-05
```

Here, the function `runif` is used for simulation of observations from the standard uniform distribution. The Monte Carlo integration is easily obtained with the averaging part of the often used `mean` function. The `integrate` function has been used to verify the approximation provided by the Monte Carlo approach. □

Example 11.4.2. Can I always use this approach? Is it not obvious that if we need to evaluate, say, $I_3 = \int_{-2}^{2} e^{x+x^2} dx$, we simply simulate a sample from $U(-2, 2)$, and approximate I_3 as the mean of $g(U_i)$ with $U_i \sim U(-2, 2)$. Let us write an R program for the same.

```
> u2 <- runif(1000,-2,2)
> int3 <- mean(exp(u2+u2^2))
> int3; integrate(function(x) exp(x+x^2),-2,2)
[1] 22.63478
93.16275 with absolute error < 0.00062
```

Is this correct? □

Suppose that integrals of the type $\theta = \int_a^b g(x)dx$ are of interest. By making use of the transformation $y = (x - a)/(b - a)$, with the aid of the differential increment $dy = dx/(b - a)$, we obtain

$$\theta = \int_0^1 g(a + [b - a]y)(b - a)dy = \int_0^1 h(y)dy,$$

where $h(y) = (b - a)g(a + [b - a]y)$. Using this modified approach, the general integrals need to resolved.

Example 11.4.3. Some Examples of Monte Carlo Integration. Let us reconsider the integral $I_3 = \int_{-2}^{2} e^{x+x^2} dx$. Clearly, we need to use the substitution $y = (x + 2)/4$. After the obvious calculus steps, we need to evaluate the integral $I_3 = \frac{1}{4} \int_0^1 e^{16y^2-12y+2} dy$. As earlier, the Monte Carlo solution is now the following:

```
> int3 <- 4* mean(exp(16*u^2-12*u+2))
> int3; integrate(function(x) exp(x+x^2),-2,2)
[1] 90.75416
93.16275 with absolute error < 0.00062
> u <- runif(10^5) # Increasing the sample points
> int3 <- 4* mean(exp(16*u^2-12*u+2))
> int3
[1] 92.87321
```

Thus, increasing the number of simulation points, increases the accuracy of the integral. □

The next set of questions would be the use of the Monte Carlo approach to evaluate integrals of the type $\int_0^\infty f(x)dx$, $\int_{-\infty}^\infty f(x)dx$, and multiple integrals $\int \cdots \int f(x_1. \ldots, x_n)\, dx_1 \ldots, dx_n$ too. For example, the transformation $y = 1/(x+1)$ will transform the range of the variable from $[0, \infty)$ to the unit interval $[0, 1]$. For evaluation of a multiple integral with m variables, we repeat k generations of a set of m pseudo uniform observations to be used in Monte Carlo computation.

In Section 11.3 we simulated only from two continuous distributions. The technique in the next section will help in simulating observations from other important continuous distributions.

11.5 The Accept-Reject Technique

Direct simulation from probability distribution F will turn out to be an inefficient technique in many cases, and in a handful of cases it is simply not possible to do so. This forces us to simulate observations from a different distribution and then find a technique to *transfer* those observations to the distribution of interest through an appropriate way. First, simulation from discrete distributions will be considered.

Suppose that X is an RV of interest with pmf $\{p_j, j \geq 0\}$, and as such simulation from $\{p_j\}$ is a difficult task. Assume that an efficient technique is available to simulate observations of an RV Y with pmf $\{q_j, j \geq 0\}$. It is important that X and Y have the same range. The *accept-reject* technique then accepts the simulated values of Y for X with a probability proportional to p_X/q_Y. That is, the simulated values of Y are accepted with certain probabilities. Let c be a constant such that

$$\frac{p_j}{q_j} \leq c, \forall j \text{ with } p_j > 0. \tag{11.2}$$

The accept-reject algorithm for discrete RVs is then given in the following steps:

1. Simulate an observation Y with pmf $\{q_j, j \geq 0\}$.
2. Generate an observation from $U(0, 1)$, say U.
3. Set $X = Y$ if $U < p_Y/cq_Y$, otherwise return to the first step:

Note that Y in the algorithm corresponds to one of the potential index numbers in the range of the RV Y with pmf $\{q_j\}$. The RV X is called the *target RV* and Y the *proposal RV*.

Example 11.5.1. Simulation from an Arbitrary Distribution using Accept-Reject Algorithm. Suppose that X is a discrete RV which assumes values 1 to 10 with respective probabilities 0.05, 0.17, 0.02, 0.14, 0.11, 0.06, 0.05, 0.04, 0.17, and 0.19. Naturally, simulation from a discrete uniform distribution with $N = 10$ can serve here as the proposal density. It is immediately clear in this problem that $c = 0.19/0.1 = 1.9$. Thus, an accept-reject sampling technique here first requires us to generate a random number between 1 and 10, say i. Next, a number in the unit interval is generated and if this number is less than $p_i/(0.1 \times 1.2)$, i will be selected as a random observation for X. A *small* program is given next, which implements the accept-reject technique for the problem in hand.

```
> p_prob <- c(0.05,0.17,0.02,0.14,0.11,0.06,0.05,0.04,0.17,0.19)
> q_prob <- rep(0.1,10)
```

```
> AR_Demo <- function(p_prob,q_prob,n) {
+  X <- numeric(n)
+  m <- length(q_prob)
+  Cmax <- max(p_prob/q_prob)
+  ar_demo <- function(p_prob,q_prob) {
+  Condition <- FALSE
+  while(Condition==FALSE) {
+  temp1 <- runif(1); temp2 <- runif(1)
+  Y <- floor(m*temp1)+1
+  if(temp2<p_prob[Y]/(Cmax*q_prob[Y])) Condition <- TRUE
+  }
+  return(Y)
+  }
+  X <- replicate(n,ar_demo(p_prob,q_prob))
+  return(X)
+  }
> AR_Demo(p_prob,q_prob,100)
  [1] 10  9  3   10 10  6  5
 [27]  1  5  4    9  9 10  2
 [53]  4  9 10    9  8  9  4
 [79] 10 10 10    5  7  2  1
> round(table(AR_Demo(p_prob,q_prob,10000))/10000,2)

   1    2    3    4    5    6    7    8    9   10
0.05 0.18 0.02 0.14 0.11 0.06 0.05 0.04 0.16 0.19
> barplot(rbind(p_prob,q_prob),horiz=TRUE,col=1:2,beside=TRUE,
+ main="A: Accept-Reject Algorithm (Discrete)")
```

The function AR_Demo has been named for the program of the accept-reject technique. The steps of the technique can be easily seen as integrated in the AR_Demo function. Note that the proportions of the simulated observations for X are closer to the required probability, see Part A of Figure 11.6. □

The accept-reject technique is now extended to the case of continuous RVs. As with the discrete case, let Y be the proposal RV with pdf $g(x)$ and X denote the target RV with pdf $f(x)$. Assume that the following condition holds true:

$$\frac{f(y)}{g(y)} \leq c, \forall y.$$

The accept-reject algorithm for continuous RVs is then given in the following steps:

1. Simulate an observation Y with pdf g.
2. Generate an observation from $U(0, 1)$, say U.
3. Set $X = Y$ if $U < f(x)/cg(y)$, otherwise return to the first step.

The next example illustrates the use of the algorithm for the continuous case. The example is adapted from Example 5d of Ross (2006).

Example 11.5.2. Simulation for Beta Distribution. Let $X \sim \text{beta}(2,4)$, that is, $f(x) = 20x(1-x)^3$ be the target density and the proposal density be the standard uniform density function. Now, by using `curve(dbeta(x,2,4),xlab="x",ylab="f(x)",col="red")` and `curve(dunif(x,0,1),col="green",add=TRUE)`, it can be easily seen that the maximum value of $f(x)/g(x)$ occurs at $x = 0.25 = 1/4$. Thus, $c = \max\{f(x)/g(x)\} = 20(1/4)(1-1/4)^3 = 135/64$. Now, it is easier to use the accept-reject technique. The next program implements the accept-reject algorithm for simulation from the beta distribution using the uniform density as the proposal density.

```
> curve(dbeta(x,2,4),xlab="x",ylab="f(x)",col="red",main="B:
+ Accept-Reject Algorithm (Continuous)")
> curve(dunif(x,0,1),col="green",add=TRUE)
> Rejection_Demo1 <- function(n){
+ rd1 <- function(){
+ condition <- FALSE
+ while(condition==FALSE){
+ t1 <- runif(1); t2 <- runif(1)
+ Y <- 256*t1*(1-t1)^3/27
+ if(t2 <= Y) condition <- TRUE
+ }
+ return(t1)
+ }
+ X <- replicate(n,rd1())
+ return(X)
+ }
> Rejection_Demo1(10)
 [1] 0.30468184 0.10752535          0.07933414 0.32041217 0.42372032
> hist(Rejection_Demo1(1000),freq=FALSE,add=TRUE)
```

The explanation of the R program is left as an exercise for the reader. The result of the program is shown in Part B of Figure 11.6. □

Example 11.5.3. Simulation from Normal Distribution. Suppose random numbers are required from a normal distribution and that a virus has affected the `rnorm` function! Random observations from a standard normal distribution can be easily transformed to any other normal distribution. Using the symmetric property of normal distribution, the focus is shifted to the positive side of the normal density. The proposal density is the standard exponential distribution g and the target here is the (positive) normal density f. Now,

$$\frac{f(x)}{g(x)} = \sqrt{\frac{2}{\pi}} \exp\left\{-\frac{x^2}{2} + x\right\}.$$

Now, plot the function $\frac{f(x)}{g(x)}$ to determine the value of c required for the accept-reject technique. The plot, see the graphical output in the following R program which is not given in the text, shows that maximum value occurs at `1` and that it translates into the `fbyg(1)` value of `1.315489`, which theoretically corresponds to the value of $\sqrt{2e/\pi}$. The accept-reject criteria

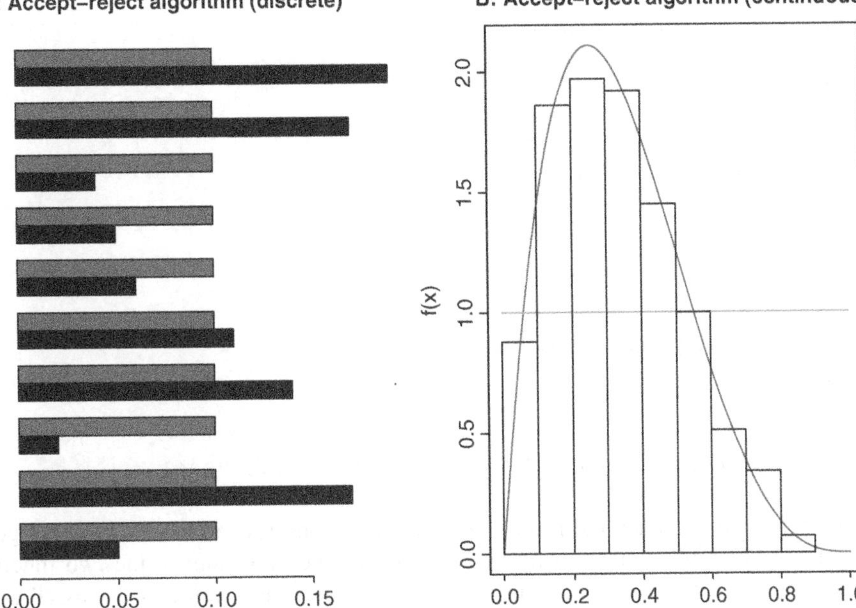

Figure 11.6 Accept-Reject Algorithm

will when turn out to be

$$\frac{f(x)}{cg(x)} = \exp\left\{-\frac{(x-1)^2}{2}\right\}.$$

Hence, the accept-reject algorithm is the following:

1. Simulate an observation Y from a standard exponential distribution, and another observation U from a standard uniform distribution.
2. If $U \leq \exp\left\{-\frac{(x-1)^2}{2}\right\}$, set $X = Y$. Otherwise go to step 1 until an X is generated.
3. Randomly assign a positive or negative sign to X.
4. Repeat the three steps a large number of times.

The next R program implements the accept-reject algorithm for the normal distribution.

```
> fbyg <- function(x) sqrt(2/pi)*exp(-x^2/2 + x)
> curve(fbyg,from=0,to=10,xlab="x",ylab="y")
> text(8,1,expression(frac(f(x),g(x))))
> seq(0,2,0.1)[which(fbyg(seq(0,2,0.1))==max(fbyg(seq(0,2,0.1))))]
[1] 1
> constant <- fbyg(seq(0,2,0.1)[which(fbyg(seq(0,2,0.1))
+ ==max(fbyg(seq(0,2,0.1))))])
> constant
```

```
[1] 1.315489
> AR_Normal <- function(n){
+ getNormal <- function(){
+ condition=FALSE
+ while(condition==FALSE){
+ y <- rexp(1); u <- runif(1)
+ if(u <= exp(-(y-1)^2/2)){
+ condition<-TRUE
+ return(y*sample(c(-1,1),1))
+ }
+ }
+ }
+ X <- replicate(n,getNormal())
+ return(X)
+ }
> AR_Normal(10)
 [1] -1.11689738 -1.38885617   0.05999845 -0.78275043
```

The `fbyg` function handles the ratio of the two functions $f(x)$ and $g(x)$. The plot generated by the `curve` function is easily seen to indicate the maximum of the two functions. Next, the `seq()[which(.==max(.)]` returns the maximum value as discussed above. The `AR_Normal` function contains a sub-function `getNormal`, which actually simulates an observation from the standard normal distribution. The sub-function is easily seen to integrate the accept-reject technique. □

The Metropolis-Hastings acceptance probability, as seen in the previous chapter, also incorporates the accept-reject technique in some sense. In fact, the accept-reject method along with the Metropolis-Hastings algorithm and the Gibbs sampler are very useful in the context of Bayesian inference, and this chapter will close with a few applications of these methods in the latter context.

11.6 Application to Bayesian Inference

Bayesian inference has been greatly enhanced during the previous two to three decades, and especially the use of Monte Carlo techniques has boosted its use and applications. In the previous section we saw that the target pdf f need not be completely specified, and it is this aspect which becomes very useful for Bayesian inference.

The *histogram prior* offers a brute-force solution for the present circumstance. For the sake of simplicity, assume that the unknown parameter is a scalar and the probability model and prior are respectively denoted by $p(\mathbf{x}|\theta)$ and $\pi(\theta)$. The general algorithm which helps implement the histogram prior approach is then given by:

- Consider a grid of legitimate points for θ from the posterior distribution.
- For the data $\mathbf{x}$ compute the likelihood $L(\theta|\mathbf{x})$.
- Obtain the product $L(\theta|\mathbf{x})\pi(\theta)$ for all the points specified in the first step.
- A random sample of $L(\theta|\mathbf{x})\pi(\theta)$ from the previous step will be a good approximation of the posterior distribution.

In the case of a binomial distribution, the parameter $\theta = p$. The use of the histogram prior is better explained by Albert's example.

Example 11.6.1. A Histogram Prior for the Proportion of Heavy Sleepers. The problem has already been discussed in Example 9.4.1. The prior probability `prior_weights` is extended over a prior grid as required in this approach. A very elementary function `getc` helps in this task along with the `sapply` function. The likelihood function is computed in the usual way. The `posterior_grid` as given in the program accomplishes the third step of the approach, while the `sample` function in the final step is obtained.

```
> p <- seq(0,1,length=100)
> x <- 11; n <- 27
> lower_limit <- seq(0,0.9,0.1); upper_limit <- seq(0.1,1,0.1)
> prior_intervals <- cbind(lower_limit,upper_limit)
> prior_weights <- c(1, 5.2, 8, 7.2, 4.6, 2.1, 0.7, 0.1, 0, 0)
> names(prior_weights) <- paste(prior_intervals[,1],"-",
+ prior_intervals[,2],sep="")
> prior_interval_weights <- prior_weights/sum(prior_weights)
> getc <- function(a,b,c) c[a>= b[,1] & a<=b[,2]]
> p_prior <- unlist(sapply(p,getc,b=prior_intervals,
+ c=prior_interval_weights))
> likelihood <- p^x*(1-p)^(n-x)
> posterior_grid <- p_prior*likelihood
> posterior_grid <- posterior_grid/sum(posterior_grid)
> posterior_sample <- sample(p,size=500,replace=TRUE,
+ prob=posterior_grid)
> par(mfrow=c(1,2))
> barplot(prior_weights,main="Histogram Prior",xlab="p")
> hist(posterior_sample,main="Posterior Distribution",xlab="p")
```

The histogram prior and the approximate posterior distribution are plotted in Figure 11.7. □

Example 11.6.2. Binomial Proportion Inference with a Non-conjugate Prior. Suppose $X_i, i = 1, \ldots, n$, is a Bernoulli trial with p being the probability of success which is unknown. The classicial estimator is then the sample average. Assume that the prior on p is given by

$$\pi(p) = 2\cos^2(4\pi p), 0 \le p \le 1.$$

The posterior distribution is then given by

$$\pi(p \mid \mathbf{x}) \propto 2p^{\sum_{i=1}^n x_i}(1-p)^{n-\sum_{i=1}^n x_i}\cos^2(4\pi p).$$

It is indeed clear from $\pi(p \mid \mathbf{x})$ that the inference is quite complex here. Now, using the Metropolis-Hastings algorithm with a normal distribution $N(p', \sigma^2)$ as the proposal distribution, the Metropolis-Hastings acceptance probability is given by

$$\alpha = \min\left\{\frac{\pi(p' \mid \sum_{i=1}^n x_i)q(p \mid p')}{\pi(p \mid \sum_{i=1}^n x_i)q(p' \mid p)}, 1\right\} = \min\left\{\frac{p'^{\sum_{i=1}^n x_i}(1-p')^{n-\sum_{i=1}^n x_i}\cos^2(4\pi p')}{p^{\sum_{i=1}^n x_i}(1-p)^{n-\sum_{i=1}^n x_i}\cos^2(4\pi p)}, 1\right\}.$$

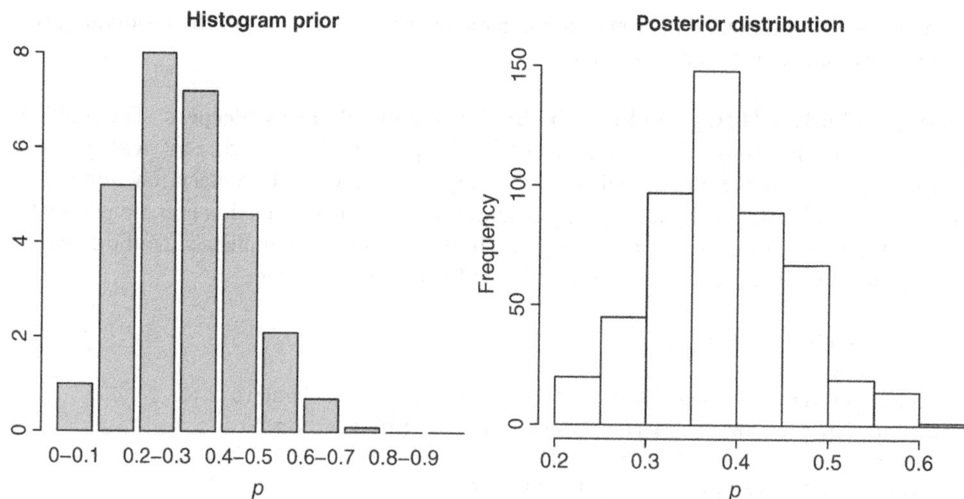

Figure 11.7 Histogram Prior in Action

The R program for the algorithm is given below.

```
> p <- seq(0,1,1e-2)
> plot(p,2*cos(4*pi*p)^2, ylab=expression(pi(p)))
> n <- 10; x <- rbinom(n=n,size=1,prob=0.65)
> Y <- sum(x)
> posterior <- choose(n,Y)*2*p^Y*(1-p)^(n-Y)*cos(4*pi*p)^2
> points(p,posterior,"l",col="red")
> Trials <- 1e4
> initialPt <- mean(x)
> # Proposal Distribution Parameters
> pprime <- 0.5
> psigma <- 0.1
> pMH <- pprime
> for(i in 2:Trials){
+ z <- rnorm(1,mean=pprime,sd=psigma)
+ alpha <- min(1,(pprime^Y*(1-pprime)^(n-Y)*cos(4*pi*pprime)^2)/
+ (z^Y*(1-z)^(n-Y)*cos(4*pi*z)^2))
+ wp <- runif(1)
+ ifelse(wp<alpha,pMH[i] <- z,pMH[i] <- pMH[i-1])
+ }
> hist(pMH,main="A Posterior Distribution Approximation")
+ #output suppressed
```

The histogram or summary of pMH may be used to carry out the inference from the posterior distribution. □

Example 11.6.3. Monte Carlo Methods for Inference from Normal Distribution. Recollect from Section 9.4.5 that the Bayesian inference from parameters from normal distributions, when both the parameters are unknown, had been deferred. The R function `normchi2post` from the `LearnBayes` package can be then used to infer. □

The interested reader may refer to the recent texts of Albert (2009), Robert and Casella (2010), and Hoff (2010).

11.7 Further Reading

Devroye (1986), Ripley (1987), Thompson (2000), and Ross (2006) are some of the authorative books on simulation. For the Monte Carlo approach, see Hammersley and Handscomb (1964), Sobol (1994), Dagpunar (2007), Dimov (2008), Liu (2001), Shonkwiler and Mendivil (2009), and, of course, Robert and Casella (2004). Robert and Casella (2010) is an R follow-up for Robert and Casella (2004). Suess and Trumbo (2010) is also a friendly guide to MCMC with R.

11.8 Complements, Problems, and Programs

Problem 11.1 Using the `p.as.plot` function from `ConvergenceConcepts`, study the convergence in probability and almost sure convergence limit theorems.

Problem 11.2 Elaborate on the details of the R program in Example 11.6.1.

Problem 11.3 Simulate 1000 observations from the standard normal distribution using `AR_Normal` function and then obtain the histogram with the option `freq=FALSE` (why?). Add the normal curve, try `curve` with `add=TRUE` option, and check if the simulated observations are satisfactory?

Problem 11.4 Using the accept-reject algorithm, generate observations from the binomial distribution as target distribution and the uniform distribution as proposal distribution. Reverse the roles and carry out the simulation and note the differences, if any.

Part IV
Linear Models

12

Linear Regression Models

Package(s): `faraway, MASS, car`
Dataset(s): `Euphorbiaceae, anscombe, tc, usc, shelf_stocking, abrasion_index, Frog_survival, flight, viscos, prostate,`

12.1 Introduction

Faraway (2002) is probably the first detailed account of the use of R for linear models. Interestingly, this book is allowed to be freely circulated and we may also print it and sell it at a cost covering the cost of print. This book makes an elegant read for the current R versions, although it was written when the R version was in the early 1.x versions. Faraway (2006) is an extended version which considers the generalized linear models, which we deal with in Chapter 17. Fox (2002) deals with regression problems in both R and S-plus. Sheather (2009) is also a very recent account of the use of R for analysis of linear models, and SAS users will also find it easier to use this book as it also gives parallel programs. Ritz and Streibig (2008) is dedicated to the applications of nonlinear regression models using R.

The covariates are also sometimes called explanatory variables, or regressors, or predictors. In general the covariate is an independent variable. The output Y is called a regressand.

A rather long route is adapted in this chapter. The reasons are two-fold. First, understanding of the statistical concepts using the simple linear regression model is of prime importance, even today. It is important to go via this route and be familiarized with the nuances of the linear regression model, whose extension to the multiple-regression model is rather straightforward. The second point of view is that using the `lm` function right away may hide some of the conceptual developments of the subject. This is not the same as saying that the developers of the function should not have given the user those many options. Thus, we take the rather lengthier route of explaining the nitty-gritty of regression using lengthier R codes than necessary. This discussion forms the matter of Section 12.2. Linear regression models, similar to most statistical techniques, need to be developed with a lot of care. It is not uncommon for any technology to be abused and it is to guard against such follies that the reader is cautioned to an extent in Section 12.3. In most of the scenarios which use the linear regression model, we

A Course in Statistics with R, First Edition. Prabhanjan Narayanachar Tattar, Suresh Ramaiah and B. G. Manjunath.

Companion Website: www.wiley.com/go/tattar/statistics

will be dealing with more than a single covariate. Thus, Section 12.4 extends the simple linear regression model to a multiple linear regression model whenever we have to deal with two or more covariates. The use of residuals for the multiple linear regression model is detailed in Section 12.5. The dependencies among the covariates have a dire impact on the estimated values of the regression coefficients and it is important to identify such relationships. Multicollinearity addresses this problem and the R techniques are put into action in Section 12.6. Sometimes, the covariates and/or the regressand may reflect that the assumptions for the linear regression model are not appropriate. In specific situations, certain transformations on the variables ensure that the use of the linear regression model continues to yield good results, see Section 12.7. With a multiple linear regression model, we need to arrive at a more reasonable model, in the sense that we have less variables than the one in the model, with all variables covering as much variability in the regressands as possible. There are multiple ways of achieving it and we will go though these techniques in Section 12.8.

12.2 Simple Linear Regression Model

In Section 4.4.3 we described the general linear regression model in equation 4.11 and used the *resistant line* to obtain the unknown slope and intercept terms. The form of the *simple linear regression model*, which will be of interest in this section, is given by

$$Y = \beta_0 + \beta_1 X + \epsilon. \tag{12.1}$$

In comparison with equation 4.11, we have $\beta_0 = a$ and $\beta_1 = b$, although the error term has not been stated there. The interpretation of β_1 is similar to b, in that it reflects the change in the regressand Y for a unit change in X. We refer to β_0 as the intercept term. However, we have an additional term in ϵ, which is the unobservable *error term*. Similar to the case of the resistant line model, we need to carry out the inference for β_0 and β_1 based on n pairs of observations: $(X_1, Y_1), (X_2, Y_2), \ldots, (X_n, Y_n)$. We state the important assumptions of the simple linear regression models:

1. The regressand and regressor have a linear relationship.
2. The observations are $(X_1, Y_1), (X_2, Y_2), \ldots, (X_n, Y_n)$ are independent observations.
3. The errors $e_1, e_2, \ldots, e_n$ are iid normal RVs with mean 0 and variance σ^2.

Using the data, and the above stated assumptions, the goal is the estimation of the parameters β_0, β_1, and σ^2. The purpose of estimating the parameters is again to understand the model 12.1. We will next consider an example and first visualize the data to ascertain whether a linear model is appropriate.

Example 12.2.1. The Height of Euphorbiaceae Tree. Botanists are interested in estimating the volume of a tree, which is often a daunting task. Under the assumption that the tree has a conical shape, the measurements of tree height and radius of the base is sufficient to estimate the volume. Since the height measurement is also cumbersome, being as much as 60 meters, the relationship between height and girth (at about 1 meter) is useful to measure the overall volume. The girth is measured in centimetres. The `Euphorbiaceae` dataset from the `gpk` package

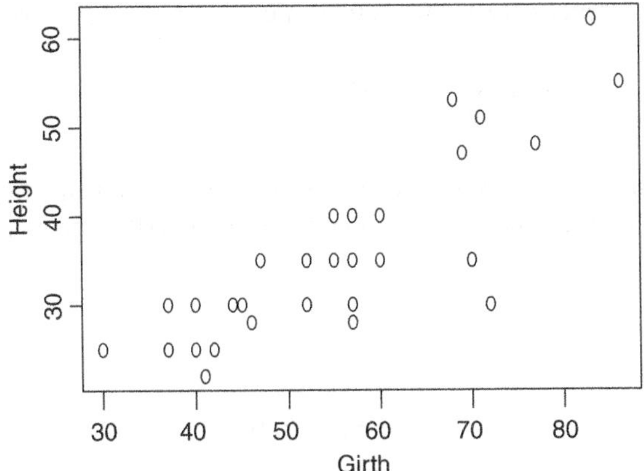

Figure 12.1 Scatter Plot for Height vs Girth of Euphorbiaceae Trees

will be used to illustrate this concept. The dataset has six different species and the ideas will be illustrated for the `Haevea brazeliensis` species. The simple linear regression model under consideration is the following:

Height of Tree = Baseline + (Effect of Girth at breast height) * (Girth at breast height) + Error.

Data is first loaded from the gpk package and a scatter plot is produced to inspect if a linear relationship exists between the height of the tree and its girth measurement of 1 meter.

```
> library(gpk)
> data(Euphorbiaceae)
> Hb <- subset(Euphorbiaceae,  Species_Name=="Haevea brazeliensis")
> plot(Hb$GBH,Hb$Height,xlab="Girth",ylab="Height")
```

It is apparent from the scatter plot, see Figure 12.1, that as the girth increases, the height of the tree increases too. Furthermore, the plot depicts a linear relationship too. □

12.2.1 *Fitting a Linear Model*

The main problem with a simple linear regression model is the estimation of unknown vector of regression coefficients $\boldsymbol{\beta} = (\beta_0, \beta_1)$ and the variance of the error term σ^2 . If we have estimates of the parameters, we can use the regression model for prediction purposes. For an intuitive discussion about the choice of the regression coefficients, the reader may refer to Chapter 6 of Tattar (2013).

For many statistical reasons, the parameters are estimated using the *least squares method.* The least-squares criterion is to find those values of β_0 and β_1 which will ensure that the sum of the squares for the difference between the actual values y_i and $\beta_0 + \beta_1 x$ over all the observations is minimized:

$$S(\beta_0, \beta_1) = \sum_{i=1}^{n} (y_i - \beta_0 - \beta_1 x_i)^2. \tag{12.2}$$

Differentiating the above equation with respect to $\boldsymbol{\beta} = (\beta_0, \beta_1)$ and equating them to zero gives us the *least-squares normal equations*, and solving them further gives us the estimators for $\boldsymbol{\beta} = (\beta_0, \beta_1)$:

$$\hat{\beta}_1 = \frac{S_{xy}}{S_{xx}}, \tag{12.3}$$

$$\hat{\beta}_0 = \overline{y} - \hat{\beta}_1 \overline{x}, \tag{12.4}$$

where

$$S_{xx} = \sum_{i=1}^{n} (x_i - \overline{x})^2, \tag{12.5}$$

$$S_{xy} = \sum_{i=1}^{n} y_i (x_i - \overline{x}). \tag{12.6}$$

Of course, the term S_{xx} is known as the *sum-of-squares* term and S_{xy} as *sum-of-cross-products* term. Towards finding an estimate of the variance σ^2, we proceed along the following lines. We first define the *model fitted values* as the regressand value predicted by the fitted model $\hat{y}_i = \hat{\beta}_0 + \hat{\beta}_1 x_1$. Next, we define *residuals* as the difference between the observed value y_i and the corresponding model fitted value $\hat{y}_i$, that is, for $i = 1, 2, \ldots, n$:

$$e_i = y_i - \hat{y}_i = y_i - \hat{\beta}_0 - \hat{\beta}_1 x_i. \tag{12.7}$$

Define the *residual* or *error sum of squares*, denoted by SS_{Res}, by:

$$SS_{Res} = \sum_{i=1}^{n} e_i^2 = \sum_{i=1}^{n} (y_i - \hat{y}_i)^2. \tag{12.8}$$

Since the residuals are based on n observations, and the parameters β_0 and β_1 are estimated from it, the degrees of freedom associated with SS_{Res} is $n - 2$. An unbiased estimator of σ^2 is given by

$$\hat{\sigma}^2 = \frac{SS_{Res}}{n-2} = MS_{Res}. \tag{12.9}$$

It is thus meaningful that an estimator of the variance is the residual mean square. Using the estimator of variance, we can carry out statistical tests for the parameters of the regression line. Mathematically, the expressions for the variance of $\hat{\beta}_0$ and $\hat{\beta}_1$ are respectively:

$$Var(\hat{\beta}_0) = \sigma^2 \left(\frac{1}{n} + \frac{\overline{x}^2}{S_{xx}} \right),$$

$$Var(\hat{\beta}_1) = \frac{\sigma^2}{S_{xx}}.$$

Using the above expressions and the estimator of the variance of the error term, we estimate the standard error of $\hat{\beta}_0$ and $\hat{\beta}_1$ using:

$$\text{se}(\hat{\beta}_0) = \sqrt{MS_{Res}\left(\frac{1}{n} + \frac{\bar{x}^2}{S_{xx}}\right)}, \tag{12.10}$$

$$\text{se}(\hat{\beta}_1) = \sqrt{\frac{MS_{Res}}{S_{xx}}}. \tag{12.11}$$

Thus, if we are interested in investigating that the covariate has an effect of magnitude, say β_{10}, we need to test the hypothesis $H^1 : \beta_1 = \beta_{10}$ against the hypothesis that it does not have an impact of magnitude $K^1 : \beta_1 \neq \beta_{10}$, a useful test statistic is

$$t_1 = \frac{\hat{\beta}_1 - \beta_{10}}{\sqrt{\frac{MS_{Res}}{S_{xx}}}}, \tag{12.12}$$

which is distributed as a t-distribution with $n - 2$ degrees of freedom. Here we have used the notation H^1 to indicate that the hypothesis testing problem is related to the regression coefficient β_1. In general, when we wish to test the hypothesis that the covariate has no effect on the regressand, the hypothesis testing problem becomes $H^1 : \beta_1 = 0$ against the hypothesis $K^1 : \beta_1 \neq 0$. Thus, an α-level test would be to reject the hypothesis H^1 if

$$|t_1| > t_{\alpha/2,n-2},$$

where $t_{\alpha/2,n-2}$ is the upper $\alpha/2$ percentile point of the t_{n-2} distribution.

Similarly, for the test statistic for the regression coefficient β_0, or the intercept term, the hypotheses problem is $H^0 : \beta_0 = \beta_{00}$ against the hypothesis $K^0 : \beta_0 \neq \beta_{00}$ is

$$t_0 = \frac{\hat{\beta}_0 - \beta_{00}}{\sqrt{MS_{Res}\left(\frac{1}{n} + \frac{\bar{x}^2}{S_{xx}}\right)}}, \tag{12.13}$$

which is again distributed as an RV with a t-distribution with $n - 2$ degrees of freedom, and the test procedure parallels the testing of β_1.

12.2.2 Confidence Intervals

Using the null distributions of $\hat{\beta}_0$ and $\hat{\beta}_1$, equivalently $\beta_{01} = 0$ and $\beta_{00} = 0$, the $100(1 - \alpha)\%$ confidence intervals of the slope and intercept are given by

$$\hat{\beta}_1 - t_{\alpha/2,n-2}se(\hat{\beta}_1) \leq \beta_1 \leq \hat{\beta}_1 + t_{\alpha/2,n-2}se(\hat{\beta}_1), \tag{12.14}$$

and

$$\hat{\beta}_0 - t_{\alpha/2,n-2}se(\hat{\beta}_0) \leq \beta_0 \leq \hat{\beta}_0 + t_{\alpha/2,n-2}se(\hat{\beta}_0). \tag{12.15}$$

Finally, we state that a $100(1-\alpha)$ percent confidence interval for σ^2 is

$$\frac{(n-2)MS_{Res}}{\chi^2_{\alpha/2,n-2}} \leq \sigma^2 \leq \frac{(n-2)MS_{Res}}{\chi^2_{1-\alpha/2,n-2}}. \tag{12.16}$$

We will illustrate all the above concepts for the `Euphorbiaceae` data.

Example 12.2.2. The Height of Euphorbiaceae Tree. Contd. The translation from formulas to programs is a vital step. We will illustrate the computations for the related formulas from Equations 12.3 to 12.16 in the following R program. The purpose is again to ensure that the formulas are well understood in terms of a program. We will begin with codes for obtaining S_{xx}, S_{xy} in R. The variables in the `data.frame Hb` will be first attached for the sake of simplicity, although we warn the reader that it is not good practice to attach variables of a data frame object.

```
> attach(Hb)
> sxx <- sum((GBH-mean(GBH))^2)
> sxx
[1] 6094.118
> sxy <- sum(Height*(GBH-mean(GBH)))
> sxy
[1] 3600.647
> beta1 <- sxy/sxx
> beta1
[1] 0.5908398
> beta0 <- mean(Height)-beta1*mean(GBH)
> beta0
[1] 2.848716
> n <- length(Height)
> sst <- sum(Height^2)-n*(mean(Height)^2)
> sst
[1] 3011.559
> ssres <- sst-beta1*sxy
> ssres
[1] 884.1533
> (sigma2 <- ssres/(n-2))
[1] 27.62979
> msres <- ssres/(n-2)
> (sebeta1 <- sqrt(msres/sxx))
[1] 0.06733384
> sebeta0 <- sqrt(msres*(1/n + (mean(GBH)^2)/sxx))
> sebeta0
[1] 3.796107
> (testbeta1 <- beta1/sebeta1)
[1] 8.774782
> (abs(qt(0.025,32)))
[1] 2.036933
> # returns the value of t-dist with 32 d.f at alpha=.05
```

The program reveals the results that for a centimeter increase in value of the girth GBH, the Height of tree will increase by beta1=0.5908398 meters. The intercept term beta0=2.848716 corresponds to the minimum tree height of the species. Similarly, the R objects sebeta1 and sebeta0 return the standard error for the slope and intercept quantities. The R code here mimics the formulas on an as-is basis and it will provide a guide towards an understanding of the theory of the linear models.

Since the absolute value of the test statistics for the slope term 8.774782 is larger than the value specified for the t-distribution 2.036933, we reject the hypothesis $H^1 : \beta_1 = 0$ that the covariate is insignificant and conclude that there is a linear relationship between the height of the tree and girth. The computations related to the confidence intervals, Equations 12.14–12.16, are as follows:

```
> (lclbeta1 <- (beta1 - abs(qt(.025,32))*sebeta1))
[1] 0.4536852
> #gives lower confidence limit for beta1
> (uclbeta1 <- (beta1 + abs(qt(.025,32))*sebeta1))
[1] 0.7279943
> #gives upper confidence limit for beta1
> (lclbeta0 <- (beta0 - abs(qt(.025,32))*sebeta0))
[1] -4.883701
> #gives lower confidence limit for beta0
> (uclbeta0 <- (beta0 + abs(qt(.025,32))*sebeta0))
[1] 10.58113
> #gives upper confidence limit for beta0
> (lclsigma2 <- (n-2)*msres/qchisq(1-.025,32))
[1] 17.86875
> #gives lower confidence limit for sigma2
> (uclsigma2 <- (n-2)*msres/qchisq(1-.975,32))
[1] 48.33878
> #gives upper confidence limit for sigma2
```

Yes, we know that the reader is asking us to put the above calculations in a more formal way. So here we report them. The 95% confidence intervals for the parameters are as follows:

$$0.4536852 \le \beta_1 \le 0.7279943$$

$$-4.883701 \le \beta_0 \le 10.58113$$

$$17.86875 \le \sigma^2 \le 48.33878$$

Since the 95% confidence interval for β_1 does not include 0, we conclude that the variable GBH has significant influence on Height. □

12.2.3 *The Analysis of Variance (ANOVA)*

In the previous sub-section, we investigated whether the covariate has an explanatory power for the regressand. However, we would like to query whether the simple linear regression model 12.1 overall explains the variation in the actual data. An answer to this question is provided by the statistical technique *Analysis of Variance*, ANOVA. This tool is nearly a century old and Gelman (2005) provides a comprehensive review of the same and explains why it is still relevant and a very useful tool today. Here, ANOVA is used to test the significance of the regression model.

We will first define two quantities, *total sum of squares*, denoted by SS_T, and *regression sum of squares*, SS_R, similar to the residual sum of squares 12.8, next:

$$SS_T = \sum_{i=1}^{n} (y_i - \bar{y})^2, \tag{12.17}$$

$$SS_R = \sum_{i=1}^{n} (\hat{y}_i - \bar{y})^2. \tag{12.18}$$

A straightforward algebraic manipulation step will give us the result that the total sum of squares SS_T is equal to the sum of regression sum of squares SS_R and residual sum of squares SS_{Res}:

$$SS_T = SS_R + SS_{Res},$$

that is,

$$\sum_{i=1}^{n} (y_i - \bar{y})^2 = \sum_{i=1}^{n} (\hat{y}_i - \bar{y})^2 + \sum_{i=1}^{n} (y_i - \hat{y})^2. \tag{12.19}$$

The *degrees of freedom* (df) for the three quantities are related as

$$df_T = df_R + df_{Res}.$$

The explicit values of df are obtained as

$$df_T = df_R + df_{Res},$$
$$n - 1 = 1 + (n - 2),$$

that is, $df_T = n - 1, df_R = 1, df_{Res} = n - 2$.
Under the hypothesis $H^1 : \beta_1 = 0$, SS_R has a χ_1^2 distribution. Since the distributions of SS_{Res} is a χ_{n-2}^2 distribution, and SS_R is independent of SS_{Res}, we can use the F-test for testing significance of the covariate. That is

$$F_0 = \frac{SS_R/df_R}{SS_{Res}/df_{Res}} = \frac{SS_R/1}{SS_{Res}/(n-2)} = \frac{MS_R}{MS_{Res}}, \tag{12.20}$$

is distributed as an F-distribution with 1 and $n - 2$ degrees of freedom. The test procedure is to reject the hypothesis H^1 if $F_0 > F_{\alpha,1,n-2}$, where $F_{\alpha,1,n-2}$ is the α percentile of an F-distribution with 1 and $n - 2$ degrees of freedom. We summarize the ANOVA procedure in the form of an ANOVA Table 12.1.

The computations and illustration of ANOVA will continue with the euphorbiaceae example.

Example 12.2.3. The Height of Euphorbiaceae Tree. (contd.) The ANOVA table calculations for the problem, which should be straightforward by now, are given below:

```
> (srs <- beta1*sxy)
[1] 2127.405
> ssres
```

```
[1] 884.1533
> sst
[1] 3011.559
> (msrs <- srs/1)
[1] 2127.405
> msres
[1] 27.62979
> (f0 <- msrs/msres)
[1] 76.9968
```

The above values can be put in the form of Table 12.2. □

12.2.4 The Coefficient of Determination

We have thus seen two methods of investigating the significance of the covariate in the regression model. An important question, in the case of the covariate being significant, is how useful the covariate is towards explaining the variation of the regressand. Recall that the total sum of squares is given by SS_T and that the regression sum of squares is given in SS_R. Thus, the ratio SS_R/SS_T gives an explanation of the total variation explained by the fitted regression model. This important measure is called the *coefficient of determination*, or the R^2, and is defined as

$$R^2 = \frac{SS_R}{SS_T} = 1 - \frac{SS_{Res}}{SS_T}. \tag{12.21}$$

A natural extension of the R^2 is quickly seen by choosing MS_R and MS_T in place of SS_R and SS_T, and this measure is more popularly known as *Adjusted-*R^2:

$$AdjR^2 = \frac{SS_R/df_R}{SS_T/df_T} = \frac{MS_R}{MS_T}. \tag{12.22}$$

Table 12.1 ANOVA Table for Simple Linear Regression Model

Source of Variation	Sum of Squares	Degrees of Freedom	Mean Square	F-Statistic
Regression	SS_R	1	MS_R	MS_R/MS_{Res}
Residual	SS_{Res}	$n-2$	MS_{Res}	
Total	SS_T	$n-1$		

Table 12.2 ANOVA Table for Euphorbiaceae Height

Source of Variation	Sum of Squares	Degrees of Freedom	Mean Square	F-Statistic
Regression	2127.405	1	2127.41	76.997
Residual	884.15	32	27.63	
Total	3011.559	33		

There are some disadvantages of the measure R^2, and this will be seen later in Section 12.4. We will first obtain these two measures for the euphorbiaceae tree.

Example 12.2.4. The Height of Euphorbiaceae Tree. (contd.) The coefficient of determination value for this dataset is `0.7064`. This is to say that approximately 71% of the variation in the tree's height is explained by the girth. Thus, it seems the linear model is a very good fit for the data. Furthermore, the adjusted R^2 value is `0.6972`. □

12.2.5 The "lm" Function from R

The linear regression model discussed thus far has been put through a lot of rudimentary codes. The `lm` function helps to create the linear regression model in R through the powerful object of class `formula`. The *tilde operator* ~ in the `formula` object helps to set up a linear regression model by allowing the user to specify the regressand on the left-hand side of the tilde ~ and the covariates on its right-hand side. This operator has also been used earlier for various graphical methods, statistical methods, etc. In conjunction with the `lm` function, we will now set up many useful linear regression models.

The main idea of working with the rudimentary codes exercise is to give a programming guide through R, and also in parallel an understanding of the underlying theory with computations. We now see how the `lm` command can be used for regression analysis.

Example 12.2.5. The Height of Euphorbiaceae Tree. (contd.) The `lm` function is now used for fitting a linear regression model for the uphborbiaceae tree data. After fitting a linear model and assigning the result to a new object, the class of the new object becomes `lm`, and a lot of useful summaries are stored in this `lm` object. We will explore the `lm` object in some detail now. The goal is to build a simple linear regression model for `Height` as a function of the covariate GBH. Hence, the formula for the `lm` function through the tilde operator becomes `Height ~ GBH`. The small program in the following builds the linear model.

```
> gbhlm <- lm(Height ~ GBH)
> class(gbhlm)
[1] "lm"
> summary(gbhlm)
Call:
lm(formula = Height ~ GBH)
Residuals:
     Min        1Q    Median       3Q       Max
-15.3892  -2.0273   0.4269   3.4509   10.1116
Coefficients:
            Estimate Std. Error t value Pr(>|t|)
(Intercept)  2.84872    3.79611   0.750    0.458
GBH          0.59084    0.06733   8.775 5.01e-10 ***
---
Signif. codes:  0 '***' 0.001 '**' 0.01 '*' 0.05 '.' 0.1 ' ' 1
Residual standard error: 5.256 on 32 degrees of freedom
Multiple R-squared:  0.7064, Adjusted R-squared:  0.6972
F-statistic:    77 on 1 and 32 DF,  p-value: 5.013e-10
```

The fitted linear model using the `lm` function is stored in the R object `gbhlm` and the `class` shows that we have indeed an `lm` object only. Next, the `summary` function reveals the details of the fitted linear regression model `gbhlm`. The regression coefficients, the values of the t-statistics, etc., may be compared with earlier results and verify that the computations earlier were correct, and as such there is no surprise here. Note that the values of multiple and adjusted R^2 given here are synchronous with earlier reported values.

The part of the output following the p-values needs an explanation. For this fitted regression model, the intercept term and the covariate GBH both have three stars, that is `***`. These symbols are called `Signif. codes` and it is a quick way to draw attention to some of the highly significant covariates in the model. In order of their importance, this idea will become clearer in Section 12.4, a `***` will be more significant than a `**` variable, and so forth. To change and customize the `Signif. codes`, see Exercise 12.4.

Next, the ANOVA table is obtained using the `anova` function in R.

```
> gbhaov <- anova(gbhlm)
> gbhaov
Analysis of Variance Table
Response: Height
          Df  Sum Sq Mean Sq F value    Pr(>F)
GBH        1 2127.41 2127.41  76.997 5.013e-10 ***
Residuals 32  884.15   27.63
---
Signif. codes:  0 '***' 0.001 '**' 0.01 '*' 0.05 '.' 0.1 ' ' 1
> summary(gbhlm$residuals)
     Min.   1st Qu.    Median      Mean   3rd Qu.      Max.
-15.3900   -2.0270    0.4269    0.0000    3.4510   10.1100
> summary(gbhlm$fitted.values)
   Min. 1st Qu.  Median    Mean 3rd Qu.    Max.
  20.57   29.44   35.34   35.21   38.30   53.66
```

Here, we used the `anova` function and created the `rpaov` object. This output must be compared with the values reported in Table 12.2. We had defined residuals earlier, and by requirement, the model fitted values of the output. These values are also summarized in the `lm` object and here we extracted them through `$residuals` and `$fitted.values`.

Some details of the `lm` object are considered later in this chapter. In fact, there are many more advantages to using the `lm` function, besides obtaining the summary of the linear fit model and the ANOVA table. The $100(1-\alpha)\%$ confidence intervals may be obtained using the `confint` function:

```
> confint(gbhlm,parm="(Intercept)",level=.99)
                0.5 %   99.5 %
(Intercept) -7.546853 13.24429
> confint(gbhlm,parm="GBH",level=.90)
           5 %       95 %
GBH 0.4767837 0.7048958
```

By default, `confint` returns 95% confidence intervals. □

12.2.6 Residuals for Validation of the Model Assumptions

We have earlier defined residuals, which is the difference between the original values and the model fitted values. In the beginning of the section, we considered the model $Y = \beta_0 + \beta_1 x + \epsilon$, and we also defined the residual for the fitted model as $e_i = y_i - \hat{\beta}_0 - \hat{\beta}_1 x_i$. We will have a preliminary look at some properties of the residuals.

Properties of the Residuals. The *mean* of the residuals is 0, that is,

$$\bar{e} = \frac{\sum_{i=1}^{n} e_i}{n} = 0.$$

The variance of the n residuals is the mean residual sum of squares MS_{Res}, or as seen earlier:

$$s_e^2 = \frac{\sum_{i=1}^{n} (e_i - \bar{e})^2}{n-2} = \frac{\sum_{i=1}^{n} (e_i)^2}{n-2} = MS_{Res}.$$

It can be proved that MS_{Res} is an unbiased estimator for the variance of the linear regression model σ^2. Finally, we need to record that the residuals are not independent. These are some of the important properties of the residuals.

Semi-Studentized Residuals. We know that the residuals are zero-mean, non-independent random variables. It has been noted by researchers and practitioners that non-independence is not a major problem and we can continue to treat them as independent variables. Thus, the Studentization method is known here as the semi-Studentization method. The semi-Studentized residuals are then defined as

$$e_i^* = \frac{e_i - \bar{e}}{\sqrt{MS_{Res}}} = \frac{e_i}{\sqrt{MS_{Res}}}. \tag{12.23}$$

The residuals, including the semi-Studentized residuals, can be used to study departures in the simple linear regression models, adapted from Kutner, et al. (2005), on the following lines:

1. The regression function $E(Y|\mathbf{x}, \boldsymbol{\beta})$ is not linear.
2. The error terms do not have constant variance, that is, $Var(\epsilon_i) \neq \sigma^2$ for some $i, i = 1, \ldots, n$.
3. The error terms are not independent.
4. The model fits all but one or a few outlier observations.
5. The error terms are not normally distributed, $\epsilon_i \nsim N(0, \sigma^2)$.
6. One or several important predictor variables have been omitted from the model.

As further stated in Kutner, et al. (2005), the diagnostics for the above problems may be visualized in the plots of residuals (or semi-Studentized residuals):

1. *Plot of residuals against predictor variable.* If the linear regression model is appropriate, the residuals are expected to fall in a horizontal band around 0. The plot should be fairly random in the positive and negative residual range across the predictor variable X.
2. *Plot of absolute or squared residuals against predictor variable.* If the residuals vary in a systematic manner in the positive and negative residual values, such curvilinear behavior will be captured in the absolute or squared residuals plot against the predictor variable.
3. *Plot of residuals against fitted values.* The purpose of residuals against fitted values is similar to the previous two plots. These plots also help to determine whether the model error has constant variance against the range of predictor variables.

4. *Plot of residuals against time*. The plot of residuals against time, observation numbers in most cases, is useful to check for randomness of the errors. That is, this plot should resemble a *random walk* and not exhibit any kind of systematic pattern.
5. *Plots of residuals against omitted predictor variables*. This plot will be more appropriate for the multiple linear regression model, Section 12.4.
6. *Box plot of residuals*. In the presence of outliers, the box plot of residuals will reflect such observations beyond the whiskers.
7. *Normal probability plot of residuals*. The assumption of normality for the errors is appropriately validated with the normal probability plot of the residuals.

From the graphical methods developed earlier in this book, we are equipped to handle the first six plots mentioned here. For the example of labor hours required for the lot size of a Toluca Company, we will illustrate these six plots.

Example 12.2.6. The Toluca Company Labour Hours against Lot Size. The Toluca Company manufactures equipment related to refrigerators. The company, in respect of a particular component of a refrigerator, has data on the labor hours required for the component in various lot sizes. Using this data, the officials wanted to find the optimum lot size for producing this part. This dataset has been downloaded from https://netfiles.umn.edu/users/nacht001/www/nachtsheim/5th/KutnerData/Chapter%20%201%20Data%20Sets/CH01TA01.txt. Of course, we are using this well-illustrated example from Kutner, et al. (2005).

A simple understanding of the predictor variable `Lot_Size` is necessary to begin the analyses.

```
> tc <- read.table("toluca_company.dat",sep="\t",header=TRUE)
> tclm <- lm(Labour_Hours~Lot_Size,data=tc)
> tclm$coefficients
(Intercept)     Lot_Size
  62.365859     3.570202
> par(mfrow=c(2,2))
> dotchart(tc$Lot_Size,main="Dot Chart for the Lot Size")
> plot.ts(tc$Lot_Size,main="Sequence Plot for the Lot Size",type="b")
> boxplot(tc$Lot_Size,horizontal=TRUE, main="A Box Plot for the
+ Lot Size")
> hist(tc$Lot_Size,main="Histogram of the Lot Size")
```

The diagram arising as a result of the above R codes is suppressed. The reader can generate them and interpret them as an exercise. The residual plots, which give us an insight into the overall fit of the simple linear regression model, are now generated in the following R program. The focus is on diagnostic plots using the residuals only, and we leave it to the reader to replicate the details with semi-Studentized residuals.

```
> tc_resid <- resid(tclm) # Note the use of the new function "resid"
> par(mfrow=c(2,3))
> plot(tc$Lot_Size,tc_resid, main="A: Plot of Residuals Vs Predictor
+ Variable", + xlab="Predictor Variable",ylab="Residuals")
> abline(h=0)
```

```
> plot(tc$Lot_Size,abs(tc_resid),main="B: Plot of Absolute Residual
+ Values Vs \n Predictor Variable", xlab="Predictor Variable",
+ ylab="Absolute Residuals")
> # Equivalently
> plot(tc$Lot_Size,tc_resid ^2,main="C: Plot of Squared Residual
+ Values Vs \n Predictor Variable", xlab="Predictor Variable",
+ ylab="Squared Residuals")
> plot(tclm$fitted.values,tc_resid, main="D: Plot of Residuals Vs
+ Fitted Values", xlab="Fitted Values",ylab="Residuals")
> abline(h=0)
> plot.ts(tc_resid, main="E: Sequence Plot of the Residuals")
> boxplot(tc_resid,main="F: Box Plot of the Residuals")
```

The `resid` function is used to extract residuals from the `tclm` linear model object. The graphics window is invoked with the code `par(mfrow=c(2,3))`. The residual plot for residuals against predictor variable is drawn with `plot(tc$Lot_Size,tc_resid,...)` and then shows that the linear regression model is appropriate since the residuals vary considerably across the horizontal band about 0 (`abline(h=0)`) and along the range of predictor variable `Lot_Size`, see Part A of Figure 12.2. The plots `plot (tc$Lot_Size,abs(tc_resid),...)` and `plot(tc$Lot_Size,tc_resid^2, ...)`, Parts B and C of Figure 12.2, reflect that there is no systematic behavior of residuals and hence the absence of curvilinear patterns for the regression model. The validity of the model assumption of variance of the error being constant across the predictor variable is visualized through the two earlier plots, and the plot of residuals against the fitted values in Part D of the same figure.

The time sequence plot of residuals, `plot.ts(tc_resid,...)`, in Part E of the figure, shows a random walk plot and hence we conclude that there is no systematic error in the dataset. Finally, Part F displays the box plot for the residuals and since all the observations (actually residuals) lie within the whiskers, it is apt to conclude that the outliers are absent. □

The Normal Probability Plot. We need to explain the normal probability plot of residuals. In the normal probability plot, the *ranked* residual values are plotted against their expected value under the normality assumption. The normal probability plot is obtained in the following steps:

- Find the rank of each residual.
- The expected value of the kth smallest residual is given by

$$E(e_{k:n}) = \sqrt{MS_{Res}}\left[\Phi^{-1}\left(\frac{k-0.375}{n+0.25}\right)\right], \tag{12.24}$$

  where Φ denotes the cumulative distribution of a standard normal variate. The subscript $k:n$ is a standard notation in the subject of *Order Statistics* and denotes the kth smallest observation of n.
- Plot the residuals $e_{k:n}$ against $E(e_{k:n})$.

If the plot of ranked residuals against the expected rank residuals is a straight line, the theoretical assumption of normal distribution for the error term is a valid assumption. In the event

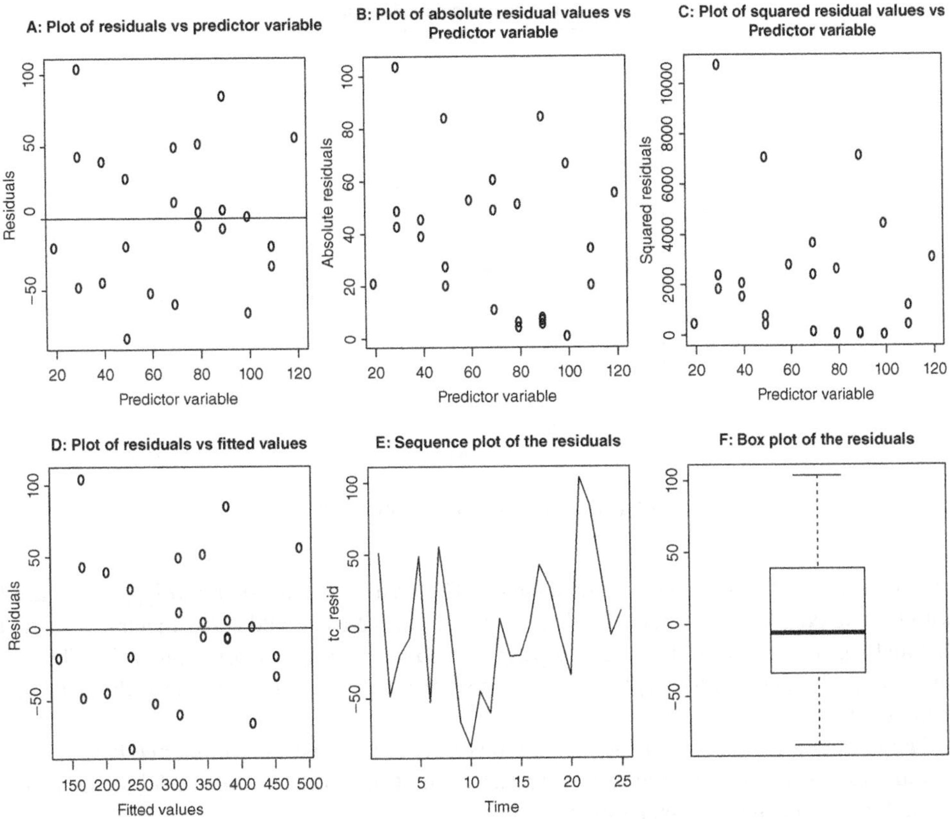

Figure 12.2 Residual Plot for a Regression Model

of this plot not reflecting a straight line, we conclude that the normality assumption is not a tenable assumption. The normal probability plot will be illustrated for the Toluca company dataset.

Example 12.2.7. The Toluca Company Labour Hours against Lot Size. Contd. The required R program is set up and executed at the R console.

```
> tcanova <- anova(tclm)
> tc_resid_rank <- rank(tc_resid)
> tc_mse <- tcanova$Mean[2]
> tc_resid_expected <- sqrt(tc_mse)*qnorm((tc_resid_rank-0.375)
+ /(length(tc$Labour_Hours)+0.25))
> plot(tc_resid_expected,tc_resid,xlab="Expected",
+ ylab="Residuals",main="The Normal Probability Plot")
> abline(0,1) # to check if the points are along a straight line
```

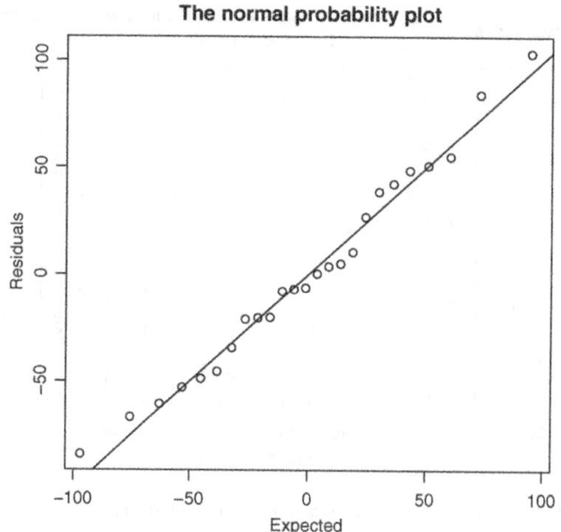

Figure 12.3 Normal Probability Plot

The first line is straightforward to understand. The mean residual square MS_{Res} is extracted with `tcanova$Mean[2]` and stored in `tc_mse`. The reader should verify that the exprected residual rank computed for `tc_resid_expected` indeed follows Equation 12.24. The plot command `plot(tc_resid,tc_resid_expected,...)` is a simple technique seen many times over.

The normal probability plot Figure 12.3 reveals that there is little difference between the residual values and the expected values. Thus, the simple linear regression model seems appropriate for the data under consideration. □

12.2.7 Prediction for the Simple Regression Model

Most often the purpose of fitting regression models is *prediction*. That is, given some values of the predictor variables, we need to predict the output values. This problem is known as *the prediction problem*.

Suppose that x_0 is the value of the predictor variable of interest. A natural estimator of the true response y_0 using the least-squares fitted model is

$$\hat{y}_0 = \hat{\beta}_0 + \hat{\beta}_1 x_0.$$

To develop a *prediction interval for the observation* y_0, we define

$$\psi = y_0 - \hat{y}_0.$$

Using the linearity property of expectations and distribution theory, we can easily see that the random variable ψ is normally distributed with mean 0 and variance

$$Var(\psi) = Var(y_0 - \hat{y}_0) = \sigma^2 \left[1 + \frac{1}{n} + \frac{(x_0 - \bar{x})^2}{S_{xx}}\right].$$

To develop the prediction confidence interval, we will again use MS_{Res} as an estimator of the variance σ^2. Thus, the $100(1-\alpha)\%$ prediction interval is given by

$$\hat{y}_0 - t_{\alpha/2,n-2}\sqrt{MS_{Res}\left(1+\frac{1}{n}+\frac{(x_0-\overline{x})^2}{S_{xx}}\right)} \leq y_0 \leq$$

$$\hat{y}_0 + t_{\alpha/2,n-2}\sqrt{MS_{Res}\left(1+\frac{1}{n}+\frac{(x_0-\overline{x})^2}{S_{xx}}\right)}. \tag{12.25}$$

Fine, we will simply use the `predict` inbuilt function of R for computations related to the prediction interval. For example, if we want to predict the number of labor hours required based on a lot size 85, we need to use the `predict` function which returns the fitted values and the 95% prediction interval:

```
> predict(tclm,newdata=data.frame(Lot_Size=85),interval
+ ="prediction")
      fit      lwr      upr
1 365.833 262.2730 469.3931
```

12.2.8 Regression through the Origin

Practical considerations may require that the regression line passes through the origin, that is, we may have information that the intercept term is $\beta_0 = 0$. In such cases, the regression model is

$$y = \beta_1 x + \epsilon. \tag{12.26}$$

In this case, the least-squares criteria becomes $S(\beta_1) = \sum_{i=1}^{n}(y_i - \beta_1 x_i)^2$ and the normal equation leads to the estimator:

$$\hat{\beta}_1 = \frac{\sum_{i=1}^{n} y_i x_i}{\sum_{i=1}^{n} x_i^2}, \tag{12.27}$$

which in return gives us the fitted model $\hat{y} = \hat{\beta}_1 x$. An unbiased estimator of the variance σ^2 would be the following:

$$\hat{\sigma}^2 = MS_{Res} = \frac{\sum_{i=1}^{n}(y_i - \hat{y}_i)^2}{n-1}. \tag{12.28}$$

It is left as an exercise for the reader to obtain the necessary expressions related to the confidence interval, prediction interval, etc. In the next example, we will illustrate this concept through a dataset.

Example 12.2.8. The Shelf-Stocking Data. A merchandiser stocks soft drinks on a shelf as a multiple number of the number of cases. The time required to put the cases on the shelves is recorded as a response. Clearly, if there are no cases to be stocked, it is natural that the time to put them on the shelf will be 0. Thus, the regression line through the origin makes sense here. A no-intercept model can be easily developed in R.

```
> shelf_stock <- read.table("shelf_stocking.dat",header=TRUE)
> names(shelf_stock)
```

```
[1] "Time"             "Cases_Stocked"
> sslm <- lm(Time ~ Cases_Stocked -1, data=shelf_stock)
> summary(sslm); anova(sslm)
Call:
lm(formula = Time ~ Cases_Stocked - 1)
Residuals:
    Min      1Q  Median      3Q     Max
-0.5252 -0.2198 -0.1202  0.1070  0.5443
Coefficients:
              Estimate Std. Error t value Pr(>|t|)
Cases_Stocked 0.402619   0.004418   91.13   <2e-16 ***
---
Signif. codes:  0 '***' 0.001 '**' 0.01 '*' 0.05 '.' 0.1 ' ' 1
Residual standard error: 0.2988 on 14 degrees of freedom
Multiple R-squared: 0.9983, Adjusted R-squared: 0.9982
F-statistic:  8305 on 1 and 14 DF,  p-value: < 2.2e-16
Analysis of Variance Table
Response: Time
              Df Sum Sq Mean Sq F value    Pr(>F)
Cases_Stocked  1 741.62  741.62  8305.2 < 2.2e-16 ***
Residuals     14   1.25    0.09
---
Signif. codes:  0 '***' 0.001 '**' 0.01 '*' 0.05 '.' 0.1 ' ' 1
> confint(sslm)
                  2.5 %    97.5 %
Cases_Stocked 0.3931431 0.4120941
> predict(sslm,data.frame(Cases_Stocked=10),interval="prediction")
       fit      lwr      upr
1 4.026186 3.378308 4.674063
```

To build an intercept-free model, the necessary modification is specified in `lm(Time ~ Cases_Stocked -1, data=shelf_stock)`. Including `-1` removes the intercept term, which otherwise is included in the default `lm` settings. The p-value for the F-statistic is highly significant at `2.2e-16`, and hence shows that the fitted linear regression model is indeed a significant model. The values of R^2 and $Adj - R^2$ at respectively `0.9983` and `0.9982` show that the regression model is a good fit. The covariate `Cases_Stocked` is found to be significant under both the t- and F- statistics. Finally, the confidence and prediction intervals are obtained in continuation of the earlier example details. □

The residual plots play a central role in validating the assumptions of the linear regression model. We have explored the relevant R functions for obtaining them.

?plot, ?qt, ?lm, ?anova, ?residuals, ?fitted, ?predict.lm

12.3 The Anscombe Warnings and Regression Abuse

Applied statistics regress in most cases towards the linear regression model. Anscombe (1973) presented four datasets which have the same values in the mean, variance, correlation, regression line, R^2 value, p-values, etc. This dataset is available in R as anscombe, and the data may be inspected following the next R session with View(anscombe).

We reproduce here select summaries:

```
> summary(anscombe)
x1 x2 x3 x4 y1 y2 y3 y4
Median : 9.0 9.0 9.0 8 7.580 8.140 7.11 7.040
Mean : 9.0 9.0 9.0 9 7.501 7.501 7.50 7.501
```

Furthermore, the ANOVA table shows that the four datasets are identical:

```
> anova(lm(y1~x1,data=anscombe))
Analysis of Variance Table
Response: y1
Df Sum Sq Mean Sq F value    Pr(>F)
x1          1 27.510 27.5100    17.99 0.002170 **
Residuals  9 13.763   1.5292
---
Signif. codes:  0 '***' 0.001 '**' 0.01 '*' 0.05 '.' 0.1 ' ' 1
> anova(lm(y2~x2,data=anscombe))
Analysis of Variance Table
Response: y2
Df Sum Sq Mean Sq F value    Pr(>F)
x2          1 27.500 27.5000  17.966 0.002179 **
Residuals  9 13.776   1.5307
---
Signif. codes:  0 '***' 0.001 '**' 0.01 '*' 0.05 '.' 0.1 ' ' 1
> anova(lm(y3~x3,data=anscombe))
Analysis of Variance Table
Response: y3
Df Sum Sq Mean Sq F value    Pr(>F)
x3          1 27.470 27.4700  17.972 0.002176 **
Residuals  9 13.756   1.5285
---
Signif. codes:  0 '***' 0.001 '**' 0.01 '*' 0.05 '.' 0.1 ' ' 1
> anova(lm(y4~x4,data=anscombe))
Analysis of Variance Table
Response: y4
Df Sum Sq Mean Sq F value    Pr(>F)
x4          1 27.490 27.4900  18.003 0.002165 **
Residuals  9 13.742   1.5269
---
Signif. codes:  0 '***' 0.001 '**' 0.01 '*' 0.05 '.' 0.1 ' ' 1
```

In the data summary, we observe that there is a lot of similarity among the median and mean of the predictor variable and the output. If we proceed with fitting regression lines, there is striking similarity between the estimated regression coefficients, MSS, p-values, etc. These summaries and the fitted regression lines leave us with the impression that the four different datasets are almost alike. However, the scatter plot in Figure 12.4 reveals an entirely different story. For

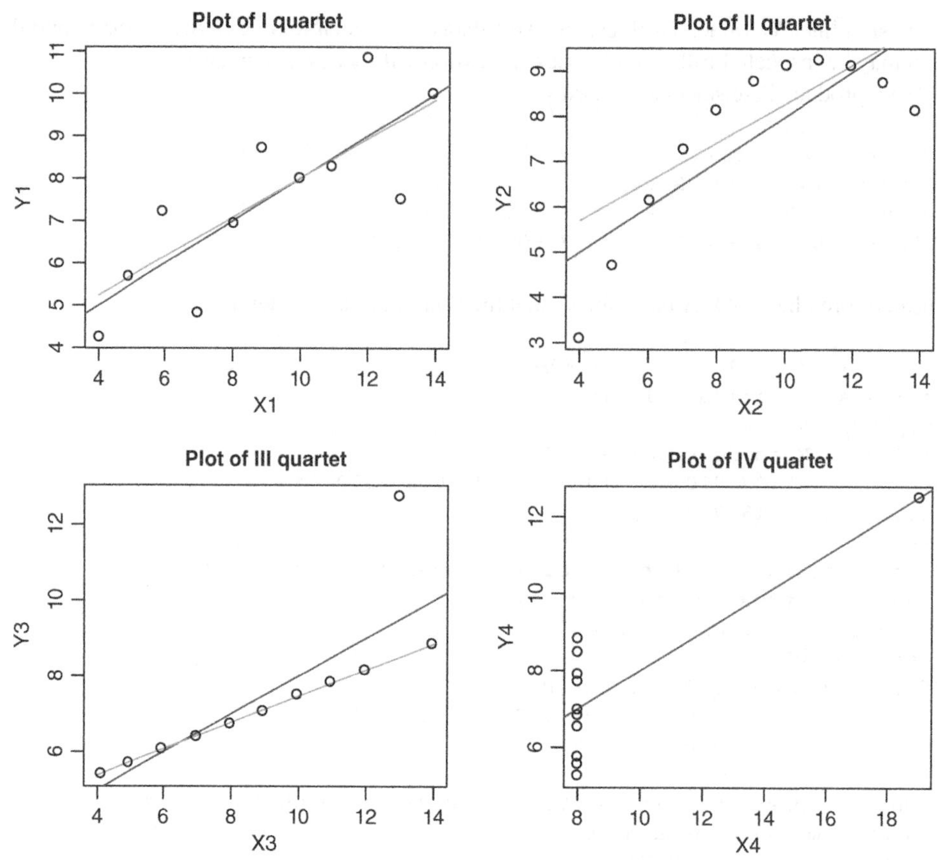

Figure 12.4 Regression and Resistant Lines for the Anscombe Quartet

the first quartet, a linear regression model seems appropriate. A non-linear association seems appropriate for the second quartet, and there appears an outlier in the third quartet. On the other hand, there does not appear to be a correlation for the fourth and final quartet. Thus, we need to exhibit real caution when carrying out data analysis.

We now fit and plot the resistant lines for the four quartets of this dataset. The regression lines are given in red and the resistant lines in green.

```
> attach(anscombe)
> rl1 <- resistant_line(x1,y1,iter=4); rl2 <- resistant_line(x2,y2,
+ iter=4)
> rl3 <- resistant_line(x3,y3,iter=4); rl4 <- resistant_line(x4,y4,
+ iter=4)
> par(mfrow=c(2,2))
> plot(x1,y1,main="Plot of I Quartet")
> abline(lm(y1~x1,data=anscombe),col="red")
> curve(rl1$coeffs[1]+rl1$coeffs[2]*(x-rl1$xCenter),add=TRUE,
+ col="green")
> plot(x2,y2,main="Plot of II Quartet")
> abline(lm(y2~x2,data=anscombe),col="red")
```

```
> curve(rl2$coeffs[1]+rl2$coeffs[2]*(x-rl2$xCenter),add=TRUE,
+ col="green")
> plot(x3,y3,main="Plot of III Quartet")
> abline(lm(y3~x3,data=anscombe),col="red")
> curve(rl3$coeffs[1]+rl3$coeffs[2]*(x-rl3$xCenter),add=TRUE,
+ col="green")
> plot(x4,y4,main="Plot of IV Quartet")
> abline(lm(y4~x4,data=anscombe),col="red")
> curve(rl4$coeffs[1]+rl4$coeffs[2]*(x-rl4$xCenter),add=TRUE,
+ col="green")
> rl1$coeffs
[1] 7.5447098 0.4617412
> rl2$coeffs
[1] 7.8525641 0.4315385
> rl3$coeffs
[1] 7.1143590 0.3461538
> rl4$coeffs
[1] NA NA
```

A very interesting thing happens in the fourth quartet. The slope has been computed as NA and the intercept is not available as a consequence of this. The reason is that 10 out of the 11 observations for the x values are the same, and due to all the thirds of the x's being the same, the slope is given as NA. Figure 12.4 shows that resistant lines fit for each quartet of the Anscombe data. Also note that the slope and intercept values are estimated differently for each data set.

For more critical abuses of the linear regression model, especially in the context of multiple covariates, the reader should consult Box (1964).

?anscombe

12.4 Multiple Linear Regression Model

In Section 12.2 we considered the case of one predictor variable. If there is more than one predictor variable, say k, we extend the simple regression model to the *multiple linear regression model*. Suppose that Y is the variable of interest and that it is dependent on some covariates $\mathbf{X} = (X_1, \dots, X_k)$. The general linear regression model is given by

$$Y = \beta_0 + \beta_1 X_1 + \dots + \beta_k X_k + \epsilon. \tag{12.29}$$

That is, the regressors are assumed to have a linear effect on the regressand. The vector $\beta = (\beta_0, \beta_1, \dots, \beta_k)$ is the vector of regression coefficients. The values of the β_j, $j = 0, 1, \dots, k$, are completely unspecified and take values on the real line. In a simple regression model, the regression coefficients have this interpretation: If the regressor $X_j, j = 1, \dots, k$, is changed by one unit while holding all other regressors at the same value, the change in the regressand Y will be β_j.

For the ith individual in the study, the model is given by

$$Y_i = \beta_0 + \beta_1 X_{i1} + \dots + \beta_k X_{ik} + \epsilon_i.$$

The errors ϵ_i are assumed to be independent and identically distributed as the normal distribution $N(0, \sigma^2)$ with unknown variance σ^2. We assume that we have a sample of size n. We will begin with the example of US crime data.

Example 12.4.1. US Crime Data. Data is available on the crime rates across 47 states in the USA, and we have additional information on 13 more explanatory variables. This dataset has been used and illustrated in Der and Everitt (2002) on the use of SAS software. The data is given in the file `US_Crime.csv`. We explain the variables, as detailed in Der and Everitt, as below.

- `R`: Crime rate – the number of offenses known to the police per 1 000 000 population.
- `Age`: Age distribution – the number of males aged 14 to 24 years per 1000 of total state population.
- `S`: Binary variable distinguishing southern states (S = 1) from the rest.
- `Ed`: Educational level – mean number of years of schooling × 10 of the population 25 years old and over.
- `Ex0`: Police expenditure – per capita expenditure on police protection by state and local governments in 1960.
- `Ex1`: Police expenditure – as Ex0, but for 1959
- `LF` Labor force participation rate per 1000 civilian urban males in the age group 14 to 24 years.
- `M`: Number of males per 1000 females.
- `N`: State population size in hundred thousands.
- `NW`: Number of non-whites per 1000.
- `U1`: Unemployment rate of urban males per 1000 in the age group 14 to 24 years.
- `U2`: Unemployment rate of urban males per 1000 in the age group 35 to 39 years.
- `W`: Wealth, as measured by the median value of transferable goods and assets or family income (unit 10 dollars).
- `X`: Income inequality: the number of families per 1000 earning below one half of the median income.

The main problem here is to build a multiple linear regression model for the crime rate `R` as a function of the rest of the demographic covariates.

In Section 12.3 we saw the effectiveness of scatter plots for the Anscombe's quartet data. If we have more than one pair of relationships to understand, we require a matrix of scatter plots. This technique is explored in the forthcoming subsection. □

12.4.1 *Scatter Plots: A First Look*

For the multiple regression data, let us use the R graphics method called `pairs`. The reader is recommended to try out the strength of this graphical utility with `example(pairs)`. In a matrix of the scatter plot, a scatter plot is provided for each variable against the other variables. Thus, the output will be a symmetric matrix of scatter plots.

Example 12.4.2. US Crime Data. Contd. For the US crime data, obtain the matrix of the scatter plot with the `pairs` function. The matrix of the scatter plot will be complemented with the correlation matrix, which is obtained using the `cor` function.

```
> data(usc)
> pairs(usc)
> round(cor(usc),2)
        R   Age         W     X
R    1.00 -0.09      0.44 -0.18
Age -0.09  1.00     -0.67  0.64
S   -0.09  0.58     -0.64  0.74
Ed   0.32 -0.53      0.74 -0.77
Ex0  0.69 -0.51      0.79 -0.63
Ex1  0.67 -0.51      0.79 -0.65
LF   0.19 -0.16      0.29 -0.27
M    0.21 -0.03      0.18 -0.17
N    0.34 -0.28      0.31 -0.13
NW   0.03  0.59     -0.59  0.68
U1  -0.05 -0.22      0.04 -0.06
U2   0.18 -0.24      0.09  0.02
W    0.44 -0.67      1.00 -0.88
X   -0.18  0.64     -0.88  1.00
```

From the first row of the matrix of scatter plots in Figure 12.5, we see that the crime rate `R` is weakly related to most of the explanatory variables. A careful examination of the first row also shows that if there is an increase in values of the variables `Ex0`, `Ex1`, and `W`, the crime rate `R` also increases. The scatter plot among the explanatory variables reveals a strong relationship between the variables `Ex0` and `Ex1`, indicating multicollinearity which is discussed in detail in Section 12.6, and a negative relationship between the variables `W` and `X`, that shows a high correlationship. □

12.4.2 *Other Useful Graphical Methods*

The matrix of a scatter plot is a two-dimensional plot. However, we can also visualize scatter plots in three dimensions. Particularly, if we have two covariates and a regressand, the three-dimensional scatter plot comes in very handy for visualization purposes. The R package `scatterplot3d` may be used to visualize three-dimensional plots. We will consider the three-dimensional visualization of scatter plots in the next example. The discussion here is slightly varied in the sense that we do not consider a real dataset for obtaining the three-dimensional plots.

Example 12.4.3. Visualization of Some Regression Models. Three-dimensional scatter plots of linear regression functions will be constructed now for the following models:

$$E(y) = 83 + 9x_1 + 6x_2, \tag{12.30}$$

$$E(y) = 83 + 9x_1 + 6x_2 + 3x_1x_2, \tag{12.31}$$

$$E(y) = 83 + 9x_1 + 6x_2 + 2x_1^4 + 3x_2^3 + 3x_1x_2, \tag{12.32}$$

$$E(y) = 83 + 9x_1 + 6x_2 - 2x_1^4 - 3x_2^3 + 3x_1x_2. \tag{12.33}$$

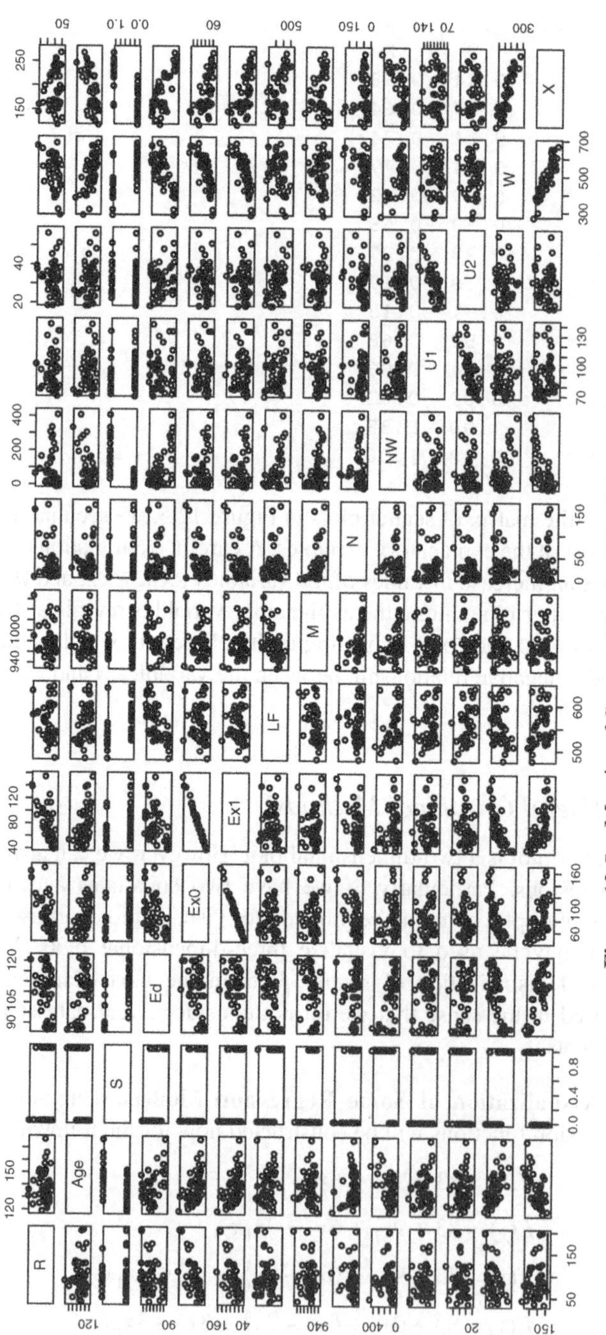

Figure 12.5 Matrix of Scatter Plot for US Crime Data

The following R codes generate the required three-dimensional plots.

```
> x1 <- rep(seq(0,10,0.5),100)
> x2 <- rep(seq(0,10,0.5),each=100)
> par(mfrow=c(2,2))
> Ey1 <- 83 + 9*x1 + 6*x2
> scatterplot3d(x1,x2,Ey1,highlight.3d=TRUE,xlim=c(0,10),
+ ylim=c(0,10),zlim=c(0,240),
+ xlab=expression(x[1]),ylab=expression(x[2]),zlab="E(y)",main =
+ expression(paste("A 3-d plot for ", E(Y*"|"*x,beta) == 83 + 9*x[1]
+ + 6*x[2])),z.ticklabs="")
> Ey2 <- 83 + 9*x1 + 6*x2 + 3*x1*x2
> scatterplot3d(x1,x2,Ey2,highlight.3d=TRUE,xlim=c(0,10),
+ ylim=c(0,10),zlim=c(0,600),
+ xlab=expression(x[1]),ylab=expression(x[2]),zlab="E(y)",main =
+ expression(paste("A 3-d plot for ",E(Y*"|"*x,beta)== 83 + 9*x[1]
+ + 6*x[2] + 3*x[1]*x[2])),z.ticklabs="")
> Ey3 <- 83 + 9*x1 + 6*x2 + 2*x1^4 + 3*x2^3 + 3*x1*x2
> scatterplot3d(x1,x2,Ey3,highlight.3d=TRUE,xlim=c(0,10),
+ ylim=c(0,10),zlim=c(0,25000),
+ xlab=expression(x[1]),ylab=expression(x[2]),zlab="E(y)",main =
+ expression(paste("A 3-d plot for ",E(Y*"|"*x,beta)== 83 + 9*x[1]
+ + 6*x[2] + 2*x[1]^4 + 3*x[2]^3 + 3*x[1]*x[2])),z.ticklabs="")
> Ey4 <- 83 + 9*x1 + 6*x2 - 2*x1^4 - 3*x2^3 + 3*x1*x2
> scatterplot3d(x1,x2,Ey4,highlight.3d=TRUE,xlim=c(0,10),
+ ylim=c(0,10),zlim=c(-23000,100),
+ xlab=expression(x[1]),ylab=expression(x[2]),zlab="E(y)",main =
+ expression(paste("A 3-d plot for ",E(Y*"|"*x,beta)==83 + 9*x[1]
+ + 6*x[2] - 2*x[1]^4 - 3*x[2]^3 + 3*x[1]*x[2])),z.ticklabs="")
```

Two vector variables `x1` and `x2` are created using the `rep` function, but with a slight difference. The expected value for the three linear models are then computed with `Ey` on three occasions. Using the `scatterplot3d` function from the same named package, we obtain the three-dimensional plots. In an easier extension of the `plot` function, we use three arguments for the `scatterplot3d` function. The `main` title for the three-dimensional plot is specified with great focus on generating the exact equation and it needs to be emphasized here that this is a non-trivial code and the reader should pay a considerable amount of attention to the R code.

In the first two three-dimensional plots of Figure 12.6, the linearity of $E(Y)$ in terms of x_1 and x_2 is apparent. Thus, a linear regression model seems appropriate. It is to be cautioned that with real datasets, some disturbance from the linearity is expected due to the error term. In the third three-dimensional plot, it appears that there may be quadratic terms for the linear regression models. □

Contour plots are again useful techniques for understanding multivariate data through slices of the dataset. In continuation of the previous regression equations, from Example 13.4.3, let us view them in terms of a contour plot.

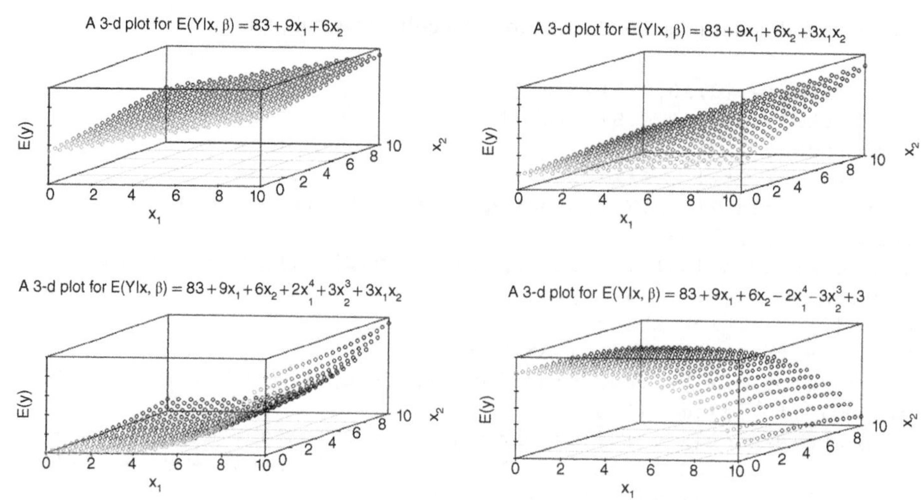

Figure 12.6 Three-Dimensional Plots

Example 12.4.4. Continuation of Example 13.4.3. To obtain the contour plot, we need to specify the output value y for each possible combination of x_1 and x_2 values. That is, if we allow 10 different values for the predictor variables x_1 and x_2, the y values must be obtained for the 100 combinations of them. This task is easily carried out using the `outer` function. This is demonstrated in the next R program.

```
> par(mfrow=c(2,2))
> x1=x2=seq(from=0,to=10,by=0.2)
> ey1 <- function(a,b) 83 + 9*a + 6*b
> Ey1 <- outer(x1,x2,ey1)
> contour(x1,x2,Ey1,main = expression(paste("Cantour plot for ",
+ E(Y*"|"*x,beta) ==83 + 9*x[1]+ 6*x[2])))
> ey2 <- function(a,b) 83 + 9*a + 6*b + 3*a*b
> Ey2 <- outer(x1,x2,ey2)
> contour(x1,x2,Ey2,main = expression(paste("Cantour plot for ",
+ E(Y*"|"*x,beta)==83 + 9*x[1]+ 6*x[2] + 3*x[1]*x[2])))
> ey3 <- function(a,b) 83 + 9*a + 6*b + 2*a^4 + 3*b^3 + 3*a*b
> Ey3 <- outer(x1,x2,ey3)
> contour(x1,x2,Ey3,main = expression(paste("Cantour plot for ",
+ E(Y*"|"*x,beta)==83 + 9*x[1] + 6*x[2] + 2*x[1]^4 + 3*x[2]^3 +
+ 3*x[1]*x[2])))
> ey4 <- function(a,b) 83 + 9*a + 6*b - 2*a^4 - 3*b^3 + 3*a*b
> Ey4 <- outer(x1,x2,ey4)
> contour(x1,x2,Ey4,main = expression(paste("Cantour plot for ",
+ E(Y*"|"*x,beta)==83 + 9*x[1] + 6*x[2] - 2*x[1]^4 - 3*x[2]^3 +
+ 3*x[1]*x[2])))
```

Here the vector variables `x1` and `x2` are created as in the previous example. However, for each combination of these variables, we need to compute the associated $E(Y|x_1, x_2)$. Thus, the

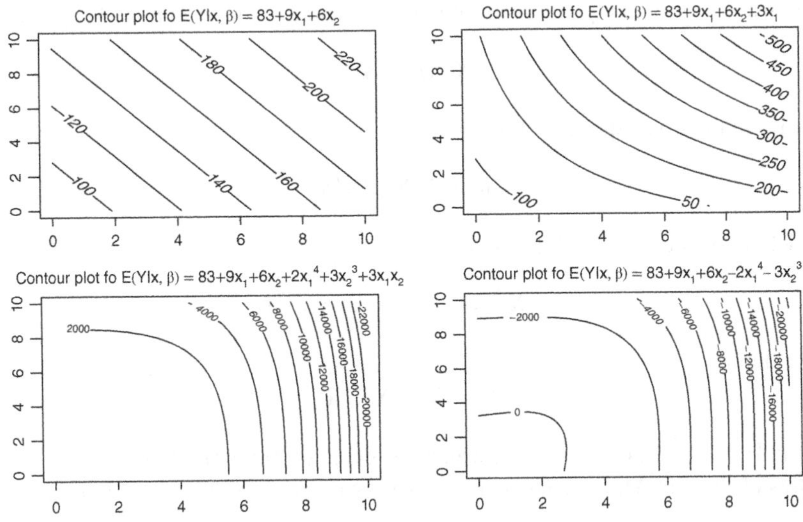

Figure 12.7 The Contour Plots for Three Models

`outer` function finds all such combinations using the function `ey`. Note that the R object `Ey` is a matrix and not a vector, and its dimension is the number of elements of `x1` and `x2`. This is a major difference from the `scatterplot3d` function. The `contour` plot function is then invoked with the R objects `x1`, `x2`, and `Ey`. The contour plots are generated for the three regression models.

As with the three-dimensional plot, the linearity is apparent for the first two contour plots of Figure 12.7, and the quadratic terms for the third example. □

Remark. *In simpler examples too, the three-dimensional plots and contour plots need good expertise to generate useful plots. Figures 12.6 and 12.7 may actually be enhanced and the reader will be asked to do the same in Exercise 7.*

12.4.3 Fitting a Multiple Linear Regression Model

Given n observations, the multiple linear regression model can be written in a matrix form as

$$\mathbf{Y} = \mathbf{X}\boldsymbol{\beta} + \boldsymbol{\epsilon}, \tag{12.34}$$

where $\mathbf{Y}' = (Y_1, Y_2, \ldots, Y_n)$, $\boldsymbol{\beta}' = (\beta_0, \beta_1, \ldots, \beta_k)$, and $\boldsymbol{\epsilon}' = (\epsilon_1, \epsilon_2, \ldots, \epsilon_n)$, and the *covariate matrix* $\mathbf{X}$[1] is

$$\mathbf{X} = \begin{bmatrix} 1 & x_{11} & x_{12} & \ldots & x_{1k} \\ 1 & x_{21} & x_{22} & \ldots & x_{2k} \\ \vdots & \vdots & \vdots & \ldots & \vdots \\ 1 & x_{n1} & x_{n2} & \ldots & x_{nk} \end{bmatrix}.$$

[1] The matrix **X** is referred as the covariate matrix. In Chapter 13, a useful variant will be introduced as *Design Matrix*.

The least-squares normal equations for the multiple linear regression model is given by

$$\mathbf{X}'\mathbf{X}\beta = \mathbf{X}'\mathbf{Y},$$

which leads to the least-squares estimator

$$\hat{\beta} = (\mathbf{X}'\mathbf{X})^{-1}\mathbf{X}'\mathbf{Y}. \tag{12.35}$$

The model fitted values $\hat{\mathbf{y}}$ are obtained as

$$\hat{\mathbf{y}} = \mathbf{X}\hat{\beta} = \mathbf{X}(\mathbf{X}'\mathbf{X})^{-1}\mathbf{X}'\mathbf{y} = \boldsymbol{H}\mathbf{y}, \tag{12.36}$$

where we define

$$\mathbf{H} = \mathbf{X}(\mathbf{X}'\mathbf{X})^{-1}\mathbf{X}'. \tag{12.37}$$

The matrix $\mathbf{H}$ is called the *hat matrix*, which has many useful properties.
Properties of the Hat Matrix. The hat matrix is symmetric and idempotent, that is,

1. $\mathbf{H} = \mathbf{H}'$, *symmetric property.*
2. $\mathbf{HH} = \mathbf{H}$, *idempotent property.*
3. Furthermore, $\mathbf{I} - \mathbf{H}$ is also symmetric and idempotent.

The hat matrix plays a vital role in determining the residual values, which in turn is very useful in model adequacy, as will be seen in the Section 12.5. Chatterjee and Hadi (1988) refer to the hat matrix as the *prediction matrix*. The importance of the hat matrix is that it serves as a bridge between the observed values and the fitted values. By definition

$$\mathbf{e} = \mathbf{y} - \hat{\mathbf{y}} = \mathbf{y} - \mathbf{X}\hat{\beta} = \mathbf{y} - \mathbf{Hy} = (\mathbf{I} - \mathbf{H})\mathbf{y}. \tag{12.38}$$

We had seen earlier, in Section 12.2, the role of the residuals in estimation of the variance σ^2. The results further extend here in the following manner:

$$\begin{aligned} SS_{Res} &= \sum_{i=1}^{n} e_i^2 = \mathbf{e}'\mathbf{e} = (\mathbf{y} - \mathbf{X}\hat{\beta})'(\mathbf{y} - \mathbf{X}\hat{\beta}) \\ &= \mathbf{y}'\mathbf{y} - \hat{\beta}'\mathbf{X}'\mathbf{y}. \end{aligned} \tag{12.39}$$

Thus, the *residual mean square* is

$$MS_{Res} = \hat{\sigma}^2 = \frac{SS_{Res}}{n-k}. \tag{12.40}$$

As in Section 12.2, MS_{Res} is an unbiased estimator of σ^2, that is,

$$E\left(\hat{\sigma}^2\right) = \sigma^2. \tag{12.41}$$

12.4.4 *Testing Hypotheses and Confidence Intervals*

12.4.4.1 Testing for Significance of the Regression Model

We need to first assert if the linear relationship between the regressand and the predictor variables is significant or not. In the terms of this hypothesis, this translates into testing for $H : \beta_1 = \beta_2 = \ldots = \beta_k = 0$ against the hypothesis $K : \beta_j \neq 0$ for at least one j. Towards the problem of testing the hypotheses H against K, we define the following:

$$\text{total sum of squares} : SS_T = \mathbf{y}'\mathbf{y} - \frac{(\mathbf{y}1)^2}{n}, \tag{12.42}$$

$$\text{residual sum of squares} : SS_{Res} = \mathbf{y}'\mathbf{y} - \hat{\beta}'\mathbf{X}'\mathbf{y}, \tag{12.43}$$

$$\text{regression sum of squares} : SS_R = \hat{\beta}'\mathbf{X}'\mathbf{y} - \frac{(\mathbf{y}1)^2}{n}. \tag{12.44}$$

In Equation 12.42, we have $\mathbf{y}1 = \sum_{i=1}^{n} y_i$. Computationally, we recognize that the regression sum of squares is obtained by exploiting the constraint $SS_T = SS_R + SS_{Res}$, that is by $SS_R = SS_T - SS_{Res}$. Under the hypothesis H, SS_R/σ^2 follows a χ_k^2 distribution, and SS_{Res}/σ^2 follows a χ_{n-k-1}^2 distribution. Furthermore, it is noted that SS_R and SS_{Res} are independent. Thus, the test statistic for the hypothesis H is the ratio of the mean of regression sum of squares to the mean of residual sum of squares, which is an F-statistic. In summary, the test statistic is

$$F_0 = \frac{SS_R/k}{SS_{Res}/(n-k-1)} = \frac{MS_R}{MS_{Res}}, \tag{12.45}$$

which is an $F_{k,n-k-1}$ distribution. Now, to test H, compute the test statistic F_0 and reject it if

$$F_0 > F_{\alpha,k,n-k-1}.$$

The ANOVA table is hence consolidated in Table 12.3.

12.4.4.2 The Role of C Matrix for Testing the Regression Coefficients

The hypothesis H tested above is a global test of model adequacy. If we reject the previous hypothesis, we may be interested in the specific predictors which are significant. Thus, there is a need to find such predictors.

Table 12.3 ANOVA Table for Multiple Linear Regression Model

Source of Variation	Sum of Squares	Degrees of Freedom	Mean Square	F-Statistic
Regression	SS_R	k	MS_R	MS_R/MS_{Res}
Residual	SS_{Res}	$n-k-1$	MS_{Res}	
Total	SS_T	$n-1$		

The least-squares estimator $\hat{\boldsymbol{\beta}}$ is an unbiased estimator of $\boldsymbol{\beta}$, and further

$$Cov(\hat{\boldsymbol{\beta}}) = \sigma^2(\mathbf{X}'\mathbf{X})^{-1}. \tag{12.46}$$

Define $\mathbf{C} = (\mathbf{X}'\mathbf{X})^{-1}$. Then the variance of the estimator of the jth regression coefficient $\hat{\beta}_j$ is $\sigma^2 C_{jj}$, where C_{jj} is the jth diagonal element of the matrix $\mathbf{C}$, and the covariance between $\hat{\beta}_j$ and $\hat{\beta}_{j'}$ is $\sigma^2 C_{jj'}$.

We are now specifically interested in testing the hypothesis $H^{(j)} : \beta_j = 0$ against the hypothesis $K^{(j)} : \beta_j \neq 0, j = 0, 1, \ldots, k$. The test statistic for the hypothesis $H^{(j)}$ is

$$t_0^{(j)} = \frac{\hat{\beta}_j}{\sqrt{\hat{\sigma}^2 C_{jj}}} = \frac{\hat{\beta}_j}{se(\hat{\beta}_j)}, j = 0, 1, \ldots, k. \tag{12.47}$$

Under the hypothesis $H^{(j)}$, the test statistic $t_0^{(j)}$ follows a t-distribution with $n - k - 1$ degrees of freedom. Thus the test procedure is to reject the hypothesis $H^{(j)}$ if $|t_0^{(j)}| > t_{\alpha/2,n-k-1}$.

Confidence Intervals

An important result, see Montgomery, et al. (2003), is the following:

$$\frac{(\hat{\boldsymbol{\beta}} - \boldsymbol{\beta})'\mathbf{X}'\mathbf{X}(\hat{\boldsymbol{\beta}} - \boldsymbol{\beta})}{kMS_{Res}} \sim F_{k,n-k}. \tag{12.48}$$

This property allows us to construct the *joint confidence region* for the vector of regression coefficients $\boldsymbol{\beta}$ as follows:

The $100(1 - \alpha)\%$ confidence intervals, region actually, for the regression coefficients is given by

$$P\left\{\frac{(\hat{\boldsymbol{\beta}} - \boldsymbol{\beta})'\mathbf{X}'\mathbf{X}(\hat{\boldsymbol{\beta}} - \boldsymbol{\beta})}{kMS_{Res}} \leq F_{\alpha,k,n-k}\right\} = 1 - \alpha.$$

In the k-dimensional space, the above inequality is a region of elliptical shape. As the next natural step, if we are interested in some specific predictor variable, the $100(1 - \alpha)\%$ confidence interval for its regression coefficient β_j is given by

$$\hat{\beta}_j - t_{\alpha/2,n-k}\sqrt{\hat{\sigma^2} C_{jj}} \leq \beta_j \leq \hat{\beta}_j + t_{\alpha/2,n-k}\sqrt{\hat{\sigma^2} C_{jj}}. \tag{12.49}$$

Finally, consider a new observation point $\mathbf{x}_0'$. A natural estimate of the future observation y_0 is $\hat{y}_0 = \mathbf{x}_0'\hat{\boldsymbol{\beta}}$. A $100(1 - \alpha)\%$ *prediction interval* is given as

$$\hat{y}_0 - t_{\alpha/2,n-k}\sqrt{\hat{\sigma}^2(1 + \mathbf{x}_0'(\mathbf{X}'X)^{-1}\mathbf{x}_0)} \leq y_0 \leq \hat{y}_0 + t_{\alpha/2,n-k}\sqrt{\hat{\sigma}^2(1 + \mathbf{x}_0'(\mathbf{X}'\mathbf{X})^{-1}\mathbf{x}_0)}. \tag{12.50}$$

The theoretical developments for multiple linear regression model will now be taken to an R session.

Example 12.4.5. US Crime Data. Continuation of Example 13.4.1. The `lm` function is deployed to fit a multiple linear regression model for the US Crime Data. The problem is to fit a linear regression model for the crime rate R as a function of the covariates, from Age to X. The covariates which give significant explanation of the crime rate are identified by the p-values. Using the lm function we build the multiple linear regression model, and then use the functions summary, confint, and anova to gather details of the fitted model.

```
> crime_rate_lm <- lm(R~Age+S+Ed+Ex0+Ex1+LF+M+N+NW+U1+U2+W+X,
+ data=usc)
> # Equivalently, crime_rate_lm <- lm(R~.,data=usc)
> summary(crime_rate_lm)
Call:
lm(formula = R ~ Age + S + Ed + Ex0 + Ex1 + LF + M + N + NW +
    U1 + U2 + W + X, data = usc)
Residuals:
    Min      1Q  Median      3Q     Max
-34.884 -11.923  -1.135  13.495  50.560
Coefficients:
             Estimate Std. Error t value Pr(>|t|)
(Intercept) -6.918e+02  1.559e+02  -4.438 9.56e-05 ***
Age          1.040e+00  4.227e-01   2.460  0.01931 *
S           -8.308e+00  1.491e+01  -0.557  0.58117
Ed           1.802e+00  6.496e-01   2.773  0.00906 **
Ex0          1.608e+00  1.059e+00   1.519  0.13836

U1          -6.017e-01  4.372e-01  -1.376  0.17798
U2           1.792e+00  8.561e-01   2.093  0.04407 *
W            1.374e-01  1.058e-01   1.298  0.20332
X            7.929e-01  2.351e-01   3.373  0.00191 **
---
Signif. codes:  0 '***' 0.001 '**' 0.01 '*' 0.05 '.' 0.1 ' ' 1
Residual standard error: 21.94 on 33 degrees of freedom
Multiple R-squared:  0.7692,    Adjusted R-squared:  0.6783
F-statistic: 8.462 on 13 and 33 DF,  p-value: 3.686e-07
> confint(crime_rate_lm)
                    2.5 %        97.5 %
(Intercept) -1.008994e+03 -374.6812339
Age          1.798032e-01    1.8998161
S           -3.864617e+01   22.0295401
Ed           4.798774e-01    3.1233247
Ex0         -5.460558e-01    3.7616925

U1          -1.491073e+00    0.2877222
U2           5.049109e-02    3.5340347
W           -7.795484e-02    0.3526718
X            3.146483e-01    1.2712173
> anova(crime_rate_lm)
Analysis of Variance Table
Response: R
          Df  Sum Sq Mean Sq F value    Pr(>F)
Age        1   550.8   550.8  1.1448 0.2924072
S          1   153.7   153.7  0.3194 0.5757727
```

```
Ed          1  9056.7   9056.7 18.8221 0.0001275 ***
Ex0         1 30760.3 30760.3 63.9278 3.182e-09 ***
Ex1         1  1530.2   1530.2  3.1802 0.0837349 .
LF          1   611.3    611.3  1.2705 0.2677989

U1          1     70.7     70.7  0.1468 0.7040339
U2          1  2696.6   2696.6  5.6043 0.0239336 *
W           1   347.5    347.5  0.7221 0.4015652
X           1  5474.2   5474.2 11.3768 0.0019126 **
Residuals 33 15878.7    481.2
---
Signif. codes:  0 '***' 0.001 '**' 0.01 '*' 0.05 '.' 0.1 ' ' 1
```

It can be seen from the output that the intercept terms, `Age`, `ED`, `U2`, and `X` are significant variables to explain the crime rate. The 95% confidence intervals also confirm it. The model is also significant, as may be seen from `p-value: 3.686e-07`, and the adjusted R^2 value is also satisfactory. The interpretation of `anova` is left to the reader. Please note that the information of some of the insignificant variables has been left out.

It becomes a bit tedious to write the variable names for a large dataset. If the model needs to consider all the variables from the `data.frame`, a simple trick is to use `lm(y~., data=data)` to include all those covariates.

A multiple linear regression model is not a trivial extension of the simple linear regression model. For instance, the R^2 and *Adj*-R^2 for this dataset are respectively `0.7692` and `0.6783`, and the difference is seen to be nearly 10%. In the case of the simple linear regression model for the fitted models `gbhlm` and `tclm`, it was not more than 2%. Let us undertake a simple task. We will add the covariates one after another and see how the R^2 and *Adj*-R^2 behave.

```
> R2Various <- AdjR2Various <- 1:13
> for(i in 2:14){
+ R2Various[i-1] <- summary(lm(usc$R~as.matrix(usc[,2:i])))$r.
+ squared
+ AdjR2Various[i-1]<- summary(lm(usc$R~as.matrix(usc[,2:i])))$adj.r.
+ squared
+ }
> round(R2Various,2)
 [1] 0.01 0.01 0.14 0.59 0.61 0.62 0.64 0.64 0.64 0.65 0.68 0.69 0.77
> round(AdjR2Various,2)
 [1] -0.01 -0.03  0.08  0.55  0.56  0.56  0.57  0.57  0.56  0.55
+   0.59  0.58  0.68
> round(R2Various-AdjR2Various,2)
 [1] 0.02 0.04 0.06 0.04 0.05 0.06 0.07 0.08 0.09 0.10 0.10 0.11 0.09
```

Note that R^2 keeps on increasing as we add more variables to the model, and that the *Adj*-R^2 can be negative too. These and other related issues will be addressed in Section 12.8. □

The model validation task for the multiple linear regression model will be undertaken next.

?pairs, ?scatterplot3d, ?contour, ?outer, ?lm

12.5 Model Diagnostics for the Multiple Regression Model

In Sub-section 13.2.6 we saw the role of residuals for model validation. We have those and a few more options for obtaining residuals in the context of multiple regression. Cook and Weisberg (1982) is a detailed account of the role of residuals for the regression models.

Residuals may be developed in one of four ways:

1. Standardized residuals
2. Semi-Studentized residuals
3. Predicted Residuals, known by its famous abbreviation as *PRESS*
4. R-Student Residuals.

12.5.1 Residuals

Standardized Residuals. Scaling the residuals by dividing them by their estimated standard deviation, which is the square root of the mean residual sum of squares, we obtain the standardized residuals as

$$d_i = \frac{e_i}{\sqrt{MS_{Res}}}, i = 1, 2, \ldots, n. \tag{12.51}$$

Note that the mean of the residuals is zero and in that sense it is present in the above expression. The standardized residuals d_i are approximately standard normal variates, and any of their absolute values greater than 3 is an indicator of the presence of an outlier.

Semi-Studentized Residuals. Recollect the definition of the hat matrix from Sub-section 13.4.3 and its usage to define the residuals as

$$\mathbf{e} = (\mathbf{I} - \mathbf{H})\mathbf{y}. \tag{12.52}$$

Substituting $\mathbf{y} = \mathbf{X}\beta + \epsilon$, and on further evaluation, we arrive at

$$\mathbf{e} = (\mathbf{I} - \mathbf{H})\epsilon. \tag{12.53}$$

Thus, the covariance matrix of the residuals is

$$\begin{aligned} \texttt{Var}(\mathbf{e}) &= \texttt{Var}((\mathbf{I} - \mathbf{H})\epsilon) \\ &= (\mathbf{I} - \mathbf{H})\texttt{Var}(\epsilon)(\mathbf{I} - \mathbf{H})' \\ &= \sigma^2(\mathbf{I} - \mathbf{H}). \end{aligned} \tag{12.54}$$

The last step follows, since $(\mathbf{I} - \mathbf{H})$ is an idempotent matrix. As the matrix $(\mathbf{I} - \mathbf{H})$ is not necessarily a diagonal matrix, the residuals have different variances and are also correlated. Particularly, it can be shown that the variance of the residual e_i is

$$\texttt{Var}(e_i) = \sigma^2(1 - h_{ii}), \tag{12.55}$$

where h_{ii} is the ith diagonal element of the hat matrix $\mathbf{H}$. Furthermore, the covariance between the residuals e_i and e_j is

$$\texttt{Cov}(e_i, e_j) = -\sigma^2 h_{ij}, \tag{12.56}$$

where h_{ij} is the $(i,j)^{th}$ diagonal element of the hat matrix. The *semi-Studentized* residuals are then defined as

$$r_i = \frac{e_i}{\sqrt{MS_{Res}(1 - h_{ii})}}, i = 1, 2, \ldots, n. \tag{12.57}$$

PRESS Residuals. The PRESS residual, also called the *predicted residual*, denoted by $e_{(i)}$, is based on a fit to data which does not include the ith observation. Define $\hat{\beta}_{(i)}$ as the least-squares estimate of the regression coefficients obtained by excluding the ith observation from the dataset. Then, the ith predicted residual $e_{(i)}$ is defined by

$$e_{(i)} = y_i - \mathbf{x}_i\hat{\beta}_{(i)}, i = 1, 2, \ldots, n.$$

The picture looks a bit scary so that we may need to fit n models to obtain the n predicted residuals. Even if we were willing to do this, for large n values, it may not be feasible to run the computer for so many hours, particularly if we can avoid it. There is an interesting relationship between the predicted residuals and the residuals, which circumvents the troublesome route of fitting n models. Equation 2.2.23 of Cook and Weisberg (1982) shows that the predicted residuals and the residuals are related by

$$e_{(i)} = \frac{e_i}{1 - h_{ii}}. \tag{12.58}$$

The variance of the ith predicted residual is

$$\texttt{Var}(e_{(i)}) = \texttt{Var}\left[\frac{e_i}{1 - h_{ii}}\right] = \frac{1}{(1 - h_{ii})^2}\left[\sigma^2(1 - h_{ii})\right] = \frac{\sigma^2}{1 - h_{ii}}. \tag{12.59}$$

The standardized prediction residual, denoted by $e^z_{(i)}$, is obtained by

$$e^z_{(i)} = \frac{e_{(i)}}{\sqrt{\texttt{Var}(e_{(i)})}} = \frac{e_i/(1 - h_{ii})}{\sqrt{\sigma^2/(1 - h_{ii})}} = \frac{e_i}{\sqrt{\sigma^2/(1 - h_{ii})}}. \tag{12.60}$$

R-Student Residuals. Montgomery, et al. (2003) mention that the Studentized residuals are useful for outlier diagnostics and that the MS_{Res} estimate of σ^2 is an *internal scaling* of the residual, since it is an internally generated estimate of σ^2. Similar to the approach of prediction residual, we can construct an estimator of σ^2 by removing the ith observation from the dataset. The estimator of σ^2 by removing the ith observation, denoted by $S^2_{(i)}$, is computed by

$$S^2_{(i)} = \frac{(n - p)MS_{Res} - e_i^2/(1 - h_{ii})}{n - p - 1}.$$

Using $S^2_{(i)}$ for scaling purposes, the *R-Student residual* is defined by

$$t_i = \frac{e_i}{S^2_{(i)}(1 - h_{ii})}, i = 1, 2, \ldots, n. \quad (12.61)$$

The utility of these residuals is studied through the next example.

Example 12.5.1. A Regression Model of the Abrasion Index for the Tire Tread. To understand the relationship between the abrasion index for the tire tread, the output y, as a linear function of the hydrated silica level x_1, silane coupling agent level x_2, and the sulfur level x_3, Derringer and Suich (1980) collected data on 14 observation points.

The appropriateness of a linear regression model through graphics for the current dataset is left as an exercise for the reader. A linear regression model for this dataset is considered and then an attempt is made to understand the four types of residuals discussed so far.

```
> abrasion_index <- read.table("abrasion_index.dat",header=TRUE)
> ailm <- lm(y~x1+x2+x3,data=abrasion_index)
> pairs(abrasion_index) # graphical output suppressed
> aianova <- anova(ailm)
> ai_fitted <- ailm$fitted.values
> ailm_mse <- aianova$Mean[length(aianova$Mean)]
> stan_resid_ai <- resid(ailm)/sqrt(ailm_mse)
> # Standardizing the residuals
> studentized_resid_ai <- resid(ailm)/(sqrt(ailm_mse*
+ (1-hatvalues(ailm))))
> #Studentizing the residuals
> # Do not wonder about writing complex codes for
+ Prediction Residuals or R Student Residuals
> # R helps! It has good function for this purpose
> pred_resid_ai <- rstandard(ailm)
> # returns the prediction residuals in a standardized form
> pred_student_resid_ai <- rstudent(ailm)
> # returns the R-Student Predicttion Residuals
> par(mfrow=c(2,2))
> plot(ai_fitted,stan_resid_ai,xlab="Fitted",ylab="Standardized
+ Residuals",
+ main="A: Plotting Standardized Residuals against Fitted Values")
> plot(ai_fitted,studentized_resid_ai,xlab="Fitted",ylab="Studentized
+ Residuals",
+ main="B: Plotting Studentized Residuals against Fitted Values")
> plot(ai_fitted,pred_resid_ai,xlab="Fitted",ylab="Prediction
+ Residuals",
+ main="C: Plotting PRESS against Fitted Values")
> plot(ai_fitted,pred_student_resid_ai,xlab="Fitted",ylab="R-Student
+ Residuals",
+ main="D: Plotting R-Student Residuals against Fitted Values")
> range(stan_resid_ai)
[1] -1.645103  1.267604
> range(studentized_resid_ai)
```

```
[1] -2.025635  1.821972
> range(pred_resid_ai)
[1] -2.025635  1.821972
> range(pred_student_resid_ai)
[1] -2.502501  2.114761
> sum(studentized_resid_ai==pred_resid_ai)
[1] 5
> length(studentized_resid_ai)
[1] 14
```

The multiple linear regression model is fitted for the abrasion index using the standard `lm` function. The `anova` is again used to facilitate the computation of mean squared error. The model fit values are stored in the `ai_fitted` vector object. The standardized residuals given in Equation 12.51 are calculated with the R code `stan_resid_ai <- resid(ailm)/sqrt(ailm_mse)`. The formula for the semi-Studentized residuals given by Equation 12.57 is implemented in the right-hand side of the assignment operator for `studentized_resid_ai`. Note that the elements h_{ii} are extracted from the fitted object `ailm` using the R function `hatvalues`. The PRESS residuals and R-Student residuals are obtained using R functions `rstandard` and `rstudent` respectively, and in our program they are stored in R objects `pred_resid_ai` and `pred_student_resid_ai`. Using the now familiar `par` and `plot` functions, we plot these four sets of residuals against the fitted values.

At the outset, the four plots A to D in Figure 12.8 look identical and hence the `range` function has been used for a small inspection that shows that we are indeed dealing with different arrays. The residual plot gives a clear answer to the presence of an outlier. The residual plot, sans the outlier, shows that the linear model is appropriate. It is to be noted that in a case such as this one, we need to first remove the outlier and then redo the entire analysis. □

12.5.2 *Influence and Leverage Diagnostics*

In the previous subsection, we saw the power of leave-one-out residuals. The residual plots help in understanding the model adequacy. We will now take measures to explain the effect of each covariate on the model fit and also of each output value on the same.

A large value of residual may arise on account of either a large value of the covariate or a large value of the output. If some observations are disparagingly distinct from the overall dataset and if the reason for this is the covariate value, then such points are called the *leverage points*. The leverage points do not affect the estimates of the regression coefficients, although they are known to drastically change the R^2 values. For the fourth quartet of the Anscombe dataset, refer to the scatter plot in Figure 12.8, any value of the regressand should correspond to the covariate value of 8. Hence, we may say that the eighth observation is a levarage point.

Another source of disparaging observations, for reasonable levels of the covariate values, may be from the output values. Such data points are called *influence points*. The influence points have a significant affect on the estimated values of the regression coefficients, and in particular tilt the model relationship towards them. For the third quarter of the Anscombe dataset, refer to the scatter plot in Figure 12.8, the outliers are clearly influential.

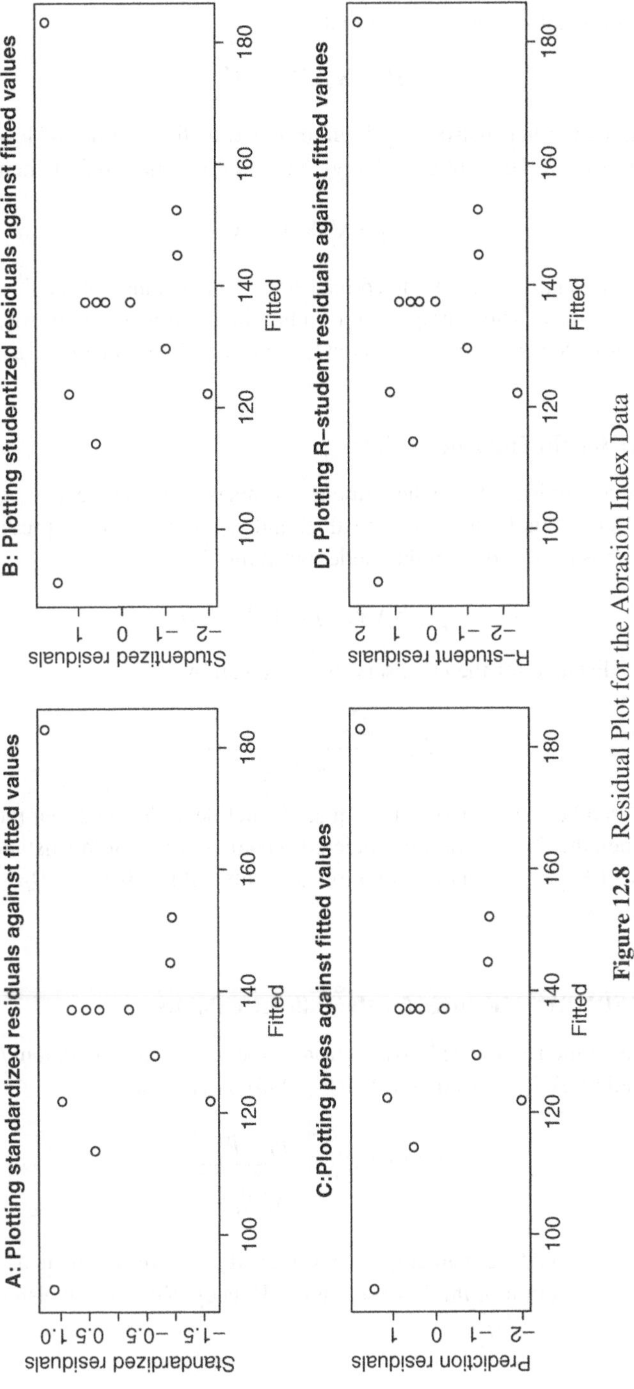

Figure 12.8 Residual Plot for the Abrasion Index Data

Leverage Points

We will recollect the definition of the hat matrix:

$$\mathbf{H} = \mathbf{X}(\mathbf{X}'\mathbf{X})^{-1}\mathbf{X}'.$$

The elements h_{ij} of the hat matrix may be interpreted as the amount of leverage exerted by the ith observation y_i on the ith fitted value $\hat{y}_i$. Note that the diagonal elements may be easily obtained as

$$h_{ii} = \mathbf{x}_i'(\mathbf{X}'\mathbf{X})^{-1}\mathbf{x}_i. \tag{12.62}$$

This hat matrix diagonal is a standardized measure of the distance of the ith observation from the center of the x-space. The average size of a hat diagonal is $\hat{h} = k/n$. Any observation for which the h_{ii} value exceeds twice the expected leverage of k/n is considered as a leverage point.

Cook's Distance for the Influence Points

The Cook's distance for identifying the influence points is based on the leave-one-out approach as seen earlier. Let $\hat{y}_i$ denote the ith fitted value, and $\hat{y}_{j,(i)}$ denote the jth predicted value when the ith observation is removed from the model building, that is,

$$y_{j,(i)} = \mathbf{x}_i\hat{\boldsymbol{\beta}}_{(i)}, j = 1, 2, \ldots, n. \tag{12.63}$$

Then the Cook's distance for the ith observation is given by

$$D_i = \frac{\sum_{j=1}^{n}(\hat{y}_j - y_{j,(i)})^2}{kMS_{Res}}. \tag{12.64}$$

The distance D_i can be interpreted as the squared Euclidean distance that the vector of fitted values moves when the ith observation is deleted. The magnitude of the distance D_i is assessed by comparing with $F_{\alpha,k,n-k}$. As a rule of thumb, any value of the distance $D_i > 1$ may be called an *influential observation*.

DFFITS and DFBETAS Measures for the Influence Points

To understand the influence of the ith observation on the regression coefficient β_j, the *DFBETAS* measure proposed by Belsley, Kuh and Welsh (1980) is given as

$$DFBETAS_{j,i} = \frac{\hat{\beta}_j - \hat{\beta}_{j,(i)}}{\sqrt{S_{(i)}^2 C_{jj}}}, \tag{12.65}$$

where C_{jj} is the jth diagonal element of the $\mathbf{C}$ matrix, and $\hat{\beta}_{j,(i)}$ is the estimate of the jth regression coefficient with the deletion of the ith observation. Belsley, Kuh, and Welsh suggest a cut-off value as $|DFBETAS_{j,i}| > 2/\sqrt{n}$.

Similarly, a measure for understanding the affect of an observation on the fitted value is given by *DFFITS*. This measure is defined as

$$DFFITS_i = \frac{\hat{y}_i - \hat{y}_{(i)}}{\sqrt{S^2_{(i)} h_{ii}}}. \tag{12.66}$$

The relevant rule of thumb is a cut-off value of $|DFFITS_i| > 2/\sqrt{k/n}$.

Example 12.5.2. A Regression Model of the Abrasion Index for the Tire Tread. Contd. Useful functions such as `hatvalues`, `cookd`, `dffits`, `dfbetas`, and `covratio` make it easy to compute all related values discussed so far. It is such an easy thing to do them in R, that it takes just one line of code to put them together.

```
> round(cbind(hatvalues(ailm),cookd(ailm),dffits(ailm),dfbetas(ailm),
+ covratio(ailm)),4)
                                 (Intercept)      x1      x2      x3
1  0.3404 0.5294 -1.7978     -0.7207  0.4247  0.9392 -0.9392 0.2794
2  0.5160 0.3231 -1.1504     -0.5619 -0.7064  0.7322  0.3603 1.8778
3  0.5957 0.0679  0.4989      0.1008 -0.3385  0.3096 -0.3096 3.5001
4  0.5160 0.8846  2.1834      1.0665  1.3406  0.6838  1.3897 0.6271
5  0.4309 0.3290  1.1974      0.3556 -0.6034 -0.4633 -0.7811 1.2474
6  0.3404 0.1397  0.7510      0.3011 -0.1774 -0.3923  0.3923 1.4611
7  0.4309 0.3589 -1.2627     -0.3750  0.6363 -0.8236 -0.4886 1.1549
8  0.3830 0.2895 -1.1319     -0.5704 -0.4538 -0.5044  0.5044 1.0815
9  0.0745 0.0022 -0.0904     -0.0904 -0.0183  0.0048 -0.0048 1.5745
10 0.0745 0.0022 -0.0904     -0.0904 -0.0183  0.0048 -0.0048 1.5745
11 0.0745 0.0015  0.0729      0.0729  0.0147 -0.0039  0.0039 1.5993
12 0.0745 0.0039  0.1202      0.1202  0.0243 -0.0064  0.0064 1.5216
13 0.0745 0.0099  0.1935      0.1935  0.0391 -0.0103  0.0103 1.3460
14 0.0745 0.0039  0.1202      0.1202  0.0243 -0.0064  0.0064 1.5216
```

Some rules of thumb were stated earlier. Also, the `plot.lm` function gives a ready plot of Cook's distances versus row labels, residuals against leverages, and Cook's distances against leverage/(1-leverage). Finally, we give a plot of the `dffits` and `dfbetas` to find the influence points, see Figure 12.9.

```
> pdf("Cooks_Distance_ailm.pdf")
> par(mfrow=c(1,3));plot(ailm,which=c(4:6))
> dev.off()
X11cairo
       1
> which(abs(as.vector(dfbetas(ailm)[,1]))>2/sqrt(14))
[1] 1 2 4 8
> which(abs(as.vector(dfbetas(ailm)[,2]))>2/sqrt(14))
[1] 2 4 5 7
```

```
> which(abs(as.vector(dfbetas(ailm)[,3]))>2/sqrt(14))
[1] 1 2 4 7
> which(abs(as.vector(dfbetas(ailm)[,4]))>2/sqrt(14))
[1] 1 4 5
> which(abs(as.vector(dffits(ailm)))>2/sqrt(14))
[1] 1 2 4 5 6 7 8
```

Since, by rule of thumb, none of the observations have Cook's distance greater than 1, there is no influential observation in the dataset. The above program gives a platform to interpret the utility of `dffits` and `dfbetas` and is left as an exercise. □

For a detailed list of R functions in the context of regression analysis, refer to the pdf file at http://cran.r-project.org/doc/contrib/Ricci-refcard-regression.pdf. The leverage points answer the problem of an outlier with respect to the covariate value. There may be at times linear dependencies among the covariates themselves, which lead to unstable estimates of the regression coefficients and this problem is known as the *multicollinearity* problem, which will be dealt with in the next section.

?influence.measures, ?resid, ?rstandard, ?rstudent, ?dffits, ?dfbetas, ?hatvalues, ?cookd, ?covratio

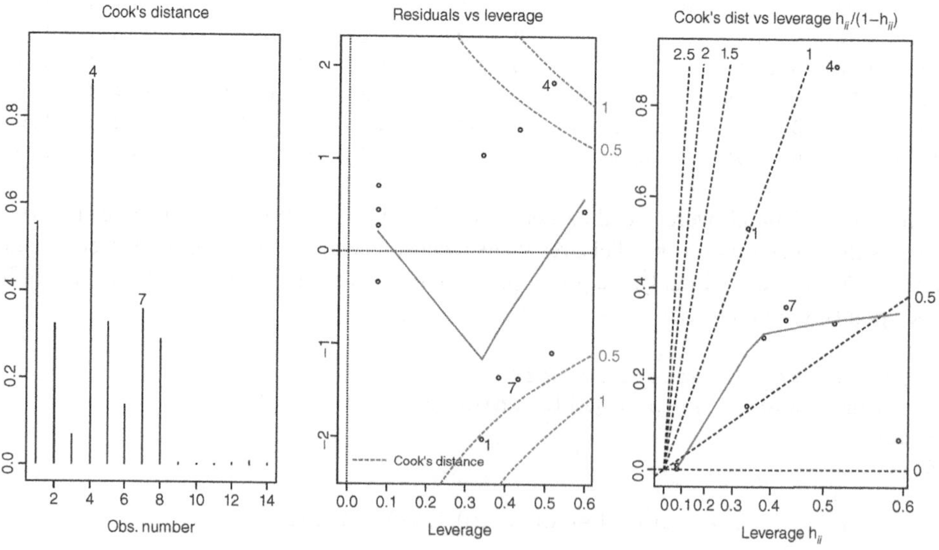

Figure 12.9 Cook's Distance for the Abrasion Index Data

12.6 Multicollinearity

Multicollinearity is best understood by splitting its spelling as "multi-col-linearity", implying a linear relationship among the multiple columns of the covariate matrix. In another sense, the columns of the covariate matrix are linearly dependent, and further it implies that the covariate matrix may not be of full rank. This linear dependence means that the covariates are strongly correlated. Highly correlated explanatory variables can cause several problems when applying the multiple regression model.

Example 12.6.1. Understanding the Problem of Multicollinearity. We fitted a multiple linear regression model for this dataset in earlier sections. The variables `Ex0` and `Ex1` are strongly correlated, as can be seen by the following:

```
> cor(usc$Ex0,usc$Ex1)
[1] 0.9935865
> cor(usc) # output suppressed
```

Let us have another look at the problem. For the rocket propellant data, Section 12.2, add small noise to the regressor GBH using the `jitter` function and rebuild the model with these two near identical regressors.

```
> data(Euphorbiaceae)
> gbhlmjit <- lm(Height ~ GBH+jitter(GBH),data=Euphorbiaceae)
> summary(gbhlmjit)
Call:
lm(formula = Height ~ GBH + jitter(GBH), data = Euphorbiaceae)
Residuals:
    Min      1Q  Median      3Q     Max
-29.242  -5.575  -1.455   5.732  27.959
Coefficients:
            Estimate Std. Error t value Pr(>|t|)
(Intercept)    8.742      2.166   4.036 0.000105 ***
GBH           -1.761      8.210  -0.214 0.830596
jitter(GBH)    2.065      8.213   0.251 0.802011
---
Signif. codes:  0 '***' 0.001 '**' 0.01 '*' 0.05 '.' 0.1 ' ' 1
Residual standard error: 9.46 on 103 degrees of freedom
Multiple R-squared:  0.404, Adjusted R-squared:  0.3925
F-statistic: 34.91 on 2 and 103 DF,  p-value: 2.654e-12
```

Now, though the linear model is significant since the p-value is `2.654e-12`, the regressor GBH is now an insignificant regressor, and its impact through the regression coefficient on `Height` changes from a positive value of `0.59084` in `gbhlm` to a negative `-1.761` in `gbhlmjit`. Thus, the multicollinearity problem needs to be identified in the multiple linear regression model. □

In general, we see that multicollinearity leads to the following problems:

1. Imprecise estimates of β, that is, which also mislead the signs of the regression coefficients
2. The t-tests may fail to reveal significant factors
3. Missing importance of predictors.

Spotting multicollinearity amongst a set of explanatory variables is a daunting task. The obvious course of action is to simply examine the correlations between these variables, and while this is often helpful, it is by no means foolproof, and more subtle forms of multicollinearity may be missed. An alternative and generally far more useful approach is to examine what are known as the *variance inflation factors* of the explanatory variables.

12.6.1 Variance Inflation Factor

The variance inflation factor $\texttt{VIF}_j$ for the jth variable is given by

$$\texttt{VIF}_j = \frac{1}{1 - R_j^2}, \tag{12.67}$$

where R_j^2 is the square of the multiple correlation coefficient from the regression of the jth explanatory variable on the remaining explanatory variables. The variance inflation factor of an explanatory variable indicates the strength of the linear relationship between the variable and the remaining explanatory variables. A rough rule of thumb is that variance inflation factors greater than ten give cause for concern.

Example 12.6.2. US Crime Data. Contd. In the previous sub-section, we fitted a full model for the US crime data. We now compute Variance Inflation Factors (VIF) of the 13 explanatory variables using the codes below. We require the R function `vif` for this purpose, which is in the library `faraway`, hence we include it in the present R session by the following codes. Also, in the spirit of understanding the concepts, we will show how the VIF for the `Age` is computed without using the `vif` function.

```
> library(faraway)
> uscrimewor <- usc[,-1] # without response variable
> vif(uscrimewor)
   Age       S        W      X
 2.698  4.877   9.969  8.409
> 1/(1-summary(lm(Age~.,data=uscrimewor))$r.square)
[1] 2.698
```

Concentrating for now on the variance inflation factors in the above output, we see that those for `Ex0` and `Ex1` are well above the value 10. As a consequence, we simply drop the variable with highest VIF in `Ex1` from consideration and now regress crime rates on the remaining 12 explanatory variables using the following code:

```
> crime_rate_lm2 <- lm(R~Age+S+Ed+Ex0-Ex1+LF+M+N+NW+U1+U2+W+X,usc)
> # Note how the variable Ex1 is removed from the model1#
```

```
> summary(crime_rate_lm2)
Call:
lm(formula = R ~ Age + S + Ed + Ex0 - Ex1 + LF + M + N + NW +
    U1 + U2 + W + X, data = usc)
Residuals:
   Min      1Q Median      3Q     Max
-38.76 -13.59   1.09   13.25   48.93
Coefficients:
              Estimate Std. Error t value Pr(>|t|)
(Intercept) -7.04e+02   1.53e+02    -4.60  5.6e-05 ***
Age           1.06e+00   4.16e-01     2.56  0.01523 *
S            -7.87e+00   1.47e+01    -0.53  0.59682
Ed            1.72e+00   6.29e-01     2.74  0.00975 **
Ex0           1.01e+00   2.44e-01     4.15  0.00021 ***
LF           -1.72e-02   1.46e-01    -0.12  0.90730
M             1.63e-01   2.08e-01     0.78  0.43842
N            -3.89e-02   1.28e-01    -0.30  0.76360
NW           -1.30e-04   6.20e-02     0.00  0.99834
U1           -5.85e-01   4.32e-01    -1.35  0.18467
U2            1.82e+00   8.46e-01     2.15  0.03883 *
W             1.35e-01   1.05e-01     1.29  0.20571
X             8.04e-01   2.32e-01     3.47  0.00145 **
---
Signif. codes:  0 '***' 0.001 '**' 0.01 '*' 0.05 '.' 0.1 ' ' 1
Residual standard error: 21.7 on 34 degrees of freedom
Multiple R-squared:  0.767,     Adjusted R-squared:  0.685
F-statistic: 9.32 on 12 and 34 DF,  p-value: 1.35e-07
> vif(uscrimewor[,-5])
  Age     S       W      X
2.671 4.865   9.956 8.354
```

The square of the multiple correlation coefficient for `crime_rate_lm2` is `0.767`, indicating that the 12 explanatory variables account for 75% of the variability in the crime rates of the 47 states. Also, recollect that `crime_rate_lm` did not have `Ex0` as a significant variable, whereas `crime_rate_lm2` shows the same variable as significant. Thus, the multicollinearity problem, if not addressed, has the potential to hide some significant variables too. The last step `vif(uscrimewor[,-5])` shows that the VIF are now all less than ten, and hence we stop further investigation of the multicollinearity problem. □

The *eigen system analysis* provides another approach to identify the presence of multicollinearity and will be considered in the next subsection.

12.6.2 Eigen System Analysis

Eigenvalues were introduced in Section 2.4. The eigenvalues of the matrix $\mathbf{X'X}$ help to identify the multicollinearity effect in the data. Here, we need to standardize the matrix $\mathbf{X}$ in the sense that each column has a mean zero and standard deviation at 1. Suppose $\lambda_1, \dots, \lambda_k$ are eigenvalues of the matrix $\mathbf{X'X}$. Let $\lambda_{\max} = \max_j\{\lambda_j\}$ and $\lambda_{\min} = \min_j\{\lambda_j\}$. Define the *condition number* and *condition indices* of $\mathbf{X}'\mathbf{X}$ respectively by

$$\kappa = \frac{\lambda_{\max}}{\lambda_{\min}}, \text{ and} \tag{12.68}$$

$$\kappa_j = \frac{\lambda_{\max}}{\lambda_j}, j = 1, \ldots, k. \tag{12.69}$$

The multicollinearity problem is not an issue for the condition number less than 100, and moderate multicollinearity exists for the values of condition numbers in the range of 100 to 1000. If the condition number exceeds the large number of 1000, the problem of linear dependence among the covariates severely exists. Similarly, any condition index κ_j in excess of 1000 is an indicator of the almost linear-dependence of the covariates, and in general if the $k' < k$ condition indices are greater than 1000, we have k' number of linear dependencies.

The decomposition of the matrix $\mathbf{X}'\mathbf{X}$ through the eigenvalues gives us the *eigen system analysis* in the sense that the matrix is decomposed with

$$\mathbf{X}'\mathbf{X} = \mathbf{T}\boldsymbol{\Lambda}\mathbf{T}', \tag{12.70}$$

where $\boldsymbol{\Lambda}$ is a $p \times p$ diagonal matrix with diagonal elements consisting of the eigenvalues of $\mathbf{X}'\mathbf{X}$ and $\mathbf{T}$ is a $p \times p$ orthogonal matrix whose columns consists of the eigenvectors of $\mathbf{X}'\mathbf{X}$. If any of the eigenvalues is closer to zero, the corresponding eigenvector gives away the associated linear dependency. We will now continue to use these techniques on the US crime dataset.

Example 12.6.3. US Crime Data. Contd. The data.frame `uscrimewor` is first converted into a matrix, and then is standardized using the `scale` function, and $\mathbf{X}'\mathbf{X}$ is obtained with `t(usc_stan)%*%usc_stan`. Using the `eigen` function, the eigenvalues and matrix of eigenvectors are first obtained. The condition number is obtained with `max(usc_eigen)/min(usc_eigen)` and the condition indices with `max(usc_eigen)/usc_eigen`.

```
> uscrimewor <- as.matrix(uscrimewor)
> usc_stan <- scale(uscrimewor)
> x1x_stan <- t(usc_stan)%*%usc_stan
> usc_eigen <- eigen(x1x_stan)
> max(usc_eigen$values)/min(usc_eigen$values) # Condition number
[1] 1081
> max(usc_eigen$values)/usc_eigen$values # Condition indices
 [1]     1.000     2.243           42.387    80.262    91.630 1080.942
> which(max(usc_eigen$values)/usc_eigen$values>1000)
[1] 13
> usc_eigen$values
 [1] 259.9811 115.9304          2.8373    0.2405
 > usc_eigen$vectors
            [,1]       [,2]          [,12]       [,13]
 [1,] -0.31718  0.124021       -0.01952 -0.010618
 [2,] -0.34001 -0.179417        0.24040 -0.005195
 [3,]  0.35610  0.214396       -0.04259  0.032819
 [4,]  0.31698 -0.299853        0.07939  0.698089
```

```
[5,]   0.31952 -0.297130      0.07611 -0.713642
[6,]   0.18310  0.400916      0.14887 -0.033483
[7,]   0.12649  0.358458      0.05198 -0.003217
[8,]   0.10731 -0.453749      0.09264 -0.008582
[9,]  -0.30357 -0.222782     -0.13307  0.022698
[10,]  0.04431 -0.118836     -0.04364 -0.004347
[11,]  0.01665 -0.400497      0.10366 -0.013567
[12,]  0.39207 -0.094476     -0.70169 -0.003024
[13,] -0.38113 -0.008553     -0.60971 -0.015409
```

The condition number κ is very high and clearly points out the presence of the multicollinearity problem. The condition indices greater than 1000 are found with `which(max (usc_eigen)/usc_eigen>1000)`, and show a linear dependency based on the condition index 13. Thus, using the 13th eigenvector, in terms of the covariates, the dependency can be written as

$$-0.0106x_{\texttt{Age}} - 0.0052x_{\texttt{S}} + 0.0328x_{\texttt{ED}} + 0.6981x_{\texttt{Ex0}} - 0.7136x_{\texttt{Ex1}} - 0.0335x_{\texttt{LF}} - 0.0032x_{\texttt{M}}$$
$$- 0.0086x_{\texttt{N}} + 0.0227x_{\texttt{NW}} - 0.0043x_{\texttt{U1}} - 0.0136x_{\texttt{U2}} - 0.0030x_{\texttt{W}} - 0.0154x_{\texttt{X}} = 0.$$

Thus, the eigensystem analysis for identifying multicollinearity is clearly illustrated here. □

?vif

12.7 Data Transformations

In Chapter 4 we came across our first transformation technique through the concept of the rootogram. In regression analysis we need transformations for a host of reasons. A partial list of reasons is as follows:

1. The linearity assumption is violated, that is, $E(y|\mathbf{x}) = \boldsymbol{\beta}\mathbf{x}$ may not be linear.
2. For the variation in the $\mathbf{x}$'s, the error variance may not be constant. This means that the variance of the y's may be a function of the mean. In fact, the assumption of constant variance is also known as the assumption of *homoscedasticity*.
3. Model errors do not follow a normal distribution.
4. In some experiments, we may have information about the need of transformations. For the model $y = \beta_0 + \beta_1 \sin x + \epsilon$, the transformation $x_1 = \sin x$ provides us with a linear model. Such information may not be available a priori, and is reflected by residual plots only.

12.7.1 Linearization

As seen in the introduction, linearity is one of our basic assumptions. In many cases, it is possible to achieve linearity by an application of transformation. Many models which have non-linear terms may be transformed to a linear model by a suitable choice of transformation. See Table 6.1 of Chatterjee and Hadi (2006), or Table 5.1 of Montgomery, et al. (2003). For example, if we have the model $Y = \alpha X^{\beta}$, by using a log transformation, we obtain

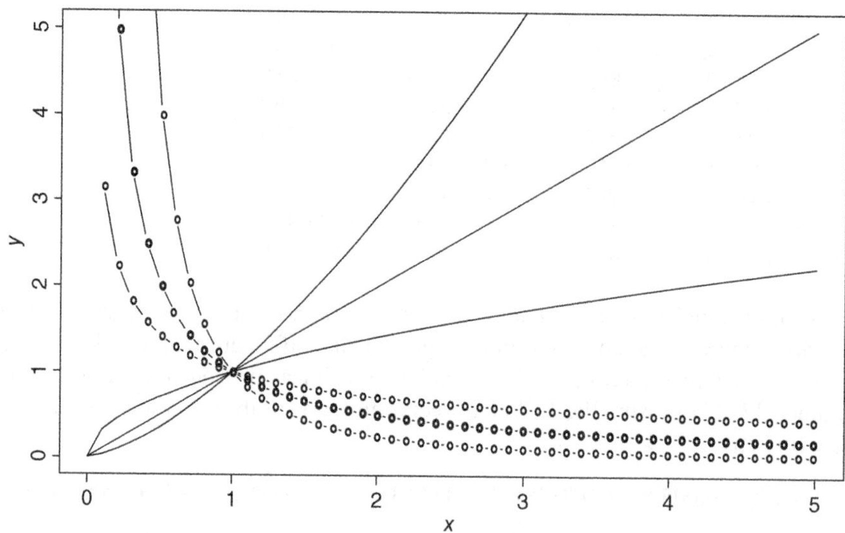

Figure 12.10 Illustration of Linear Transformation

$\log Y = \log \alpha + \beta \log x$. The transformed model is linear in terms of its parameters. Figure 12.10 displays the behavior of y for various choices of α and β (before the transformation).

```
> x <- seq(0,5,0.1)
> alpha <- 1
> par(mfrow=c(1,2))
> plot(x,y=alpha*x^{beta=1},xlab="x",ylab="y","l",lwd=1)
> points(x,y=alpha*x^{beta=0.5},"l",lwd=2)
> points(x,y=alpha*x^{beta=1.5},"l",lwd=3)
> points(x,y=alpha*x^{beta= -0.5},"b",lwd=2)
> points(x,y=alpha*x^{beta= -1},"b",lwd=3)
> points(x,y=alpha*x^{beta= -2},"b",lwd=2)
```

We will next consider an example where a transformation achieves linearization.

Example 12.7.1. Frog Survival as a Function of Age. A well-known natural phenomenon is that the number of survivors decreases with age. In the `Frog_survival` dataset from the `gpk` package, we have the number of survivors at the age of 1, 2, …, 8 years. Now, a straightforward use of the simple linear regression model gives a poor fit. Fitting a linear model for the number of `Individuals` as a function the `Age` gives an Adjusted R^2 of `0.2264`, which is quite poor. Moreover, the variable `Age` is also an insignificant variable.

Thus, there is a need to carry out a transformation to improve the model, and we attempt to model the logarithm of `Individuals` as a function of `Age`. Mathematically speaking, we are building the model $\ln(Y) = \beta_0 + \beta_1 x + \epsilon$.

```
> data(Frog_survival)
> plot(Frog_survival$Individuals,Frog_survival$Age)
+ # Output suppressed
> summary(FS1 <- lm(Individuals~Age,data=Frog_survival))
Call:
lm(formula = Individuals ~ Age, data = Frog_survival)
Residuals:
    Min      1Q  Median      3Q     Max
-3017.5 -1693.4  -381.3   943.6  5280.2
Coefficients:
            Estimate Std. Error t value Pr(>|t|)
(Intercept)   4573.2     2199.2   2.079   0.0828 .
Age           -760.3      435.5  -1.746   0.1314
---
Signif. codes:  0 '***' 0.001 '**' 0.01 '*' 0.05 '.' 0.1 ' ' 1
Residual standard error: 2822 on 6 degrees of freedom
Multiple R-squared:  0.3369, Adjusted R-squared:  0.2264
F-statistic: 3.048 on 1 and 6 DF,  p-value: 0.1314
> summary(FS2 <- lm(log(Individuals)~Age,data=Frog_survival))
Call:
lm(formula = log(Individuals) ~ Age, data = Frog_survival)
Residuals:
    Min      1Q  Median      3Q     Max
-1.9159 -0.5906 -0.1267  0.4820  2.7690
Coefficients:
            Estimate Std. Error t value Pr(>|t|)
(Intercept)   7.2212     1.1708   6.168 0.000834 ***
Age          -0.8750     0.2318  -3.774 0.009247 **
---
Signif. codes:  0 '***' 0.001 '**' 0.01 '*' 0.05 '.' 0.1 ' ' 1
Residual standard error: 1.503 on 6 degrees of freedom
Multiple R-squared:  0.7036, Adjusted R-squared:  0.6542
F-statistic: 14.24 on 1 and 6 DF,  p-value: 0.009247
```

The transformation leads to an increase in the adjusted R^2 to `0.6542` and the variable `Age` is also seen to be significant. Thus, the logarithmic transformation helped in achieving linearity for this dataset. □

12.7.2 Variance Stabilization

In general, the transformation stabilizes the variance of the error term. If the error variance is not constant for different x values, we say that the error is *heteroscedastic*. The problem of heteroscedasticity is usually detected by the residual plots.

Example 12.7.2. Injuries in Airflights. Injuries in airflights, road accidents, etc., are instances of rare occurrences, which are appropriately modeled by a Poisson distribution.

This data is adapted from Table 6.6 of Chatterjee and Hadi. Two models, before and after transformation, are fitted and checked if the transformation led to a reduction in the variance.

```
> data(flight)
> attach(flight)
> names(flight)
[1] "Injury_Incidents" "Total_Flights"
> injurylm <- lm(Injury_Incidents~Total_Flights)
> injurysqrtlm <- lm(sqrt(Injury_Incidents)~Total_Flights)
> summary(injurylm)
Call:
lm(formula = Injury_Incidents ~ Total_Flights)
Residuals:
    Min      1Q  Median      3Q     Max
-5.3351 -2.1281  0.1605  2.2670  5.6382
Coefficients:
              Estimate Std. Error t value Pr(>|t|)
(Intercept)    -0.1402     3.1412  -0.045   0.9657
Total_Flights  64.9755    25.1959   2.579   0.0365 *
---
Signif. codes:  0 '***' 0.001 '**' 0.01 '*' 0.05 '.' 0.1 ' ' 1
Residual standard error: 4.201 on 7 degrees of freedom
Multiple R-squared: 0.4872, Adjusted R-squared: 0.4139
F-statistic:  6.65 on 1 and 7 DF,  p-value: 0.03654
> summary(injurysqrtlm)
Call:
lm(formula = sqrt(Injury_Incidents) ~ Total_Flights)
Residuals:
    Min      1Q  Median      3Q     Max
-0.9690 -0.7655  0.1906  0.5874  1.0211
Coefficients:
              Estimate Std. Error t value Pr(>|t|)
(Intercept)     1.1692     0.5783   2.022   0.0829 .
Total_Flights  11.8564     4.6382   2.556   0.0378 *
---
Signif. codes:  0 '***' 0.001 '**' 0.01 '*' 0.05 '.' 0.1 ' ' 1
Residual standard error: 0.7733 on 7 degrees of freedom
Multiple R-squared: 0.4828, Adjusted R-squared: 0.4089
F-statistic: 6.535 on 1 and 7 DF,  p-value: 0.03776
> par(mfrow=c(1,2))
> plot(flight$Total_Flights, residuals(injurylm),
+ xlab="Total Flights",ylab="Residuals")
> plot(flight$Total_Flights, residuals(injurysqrtlm),
+ xlab="Total Flights",ylab="Residuals
+ Under Square Root Transformation")
```

It may be seen from the ANOVA tables that we had estimated a variance of `4.201` for the original data, that is, the simple linear regression model. The square-root transformation reduced the variance to `0.7733`, which is significant. Note that the R^2 value remains almost the same. The residual plots are not produced here. The residual plot `injurylm` shows that the variance of residuals increases with an increase in the x-value. However, the same residual plot for the `injurysqrlm` model shows that the variability of the error term remains constant across the x-values. □

Technically, we had built the model $Y^{1/2} = \beta_0 + \beta_1 x + \epsilon$. The choice of transformation is not obvious. Moreover, it is difficult to say whether the power of $1/2$ is appropriate or some other positive number. Also, it is not always easy to choose between the power transformation and logarithmic transformation. A more generic approach will be considered in the next subsection.

12.7.3 Power Transformation

In the previous two subsections, we were helped by the logarithmic and square-root transformations. Box and Cox (1962) proposed a general transformation, called the *power transformation*. This method is useful when we do not have theoretical or empirical guidelines for an appropriate transformation. The Box-Cox transformation is given by

$$Y^{\lambda} = \begin{cases} \frac{Y^{\lambda}-1}{\lambda \dot{Y}^{\lambda-1}}, & \lambda \neq 0, \\ Y \log Y, & \lambda = 0. \end{cases} \tag{12.71}$$

where $\dot{Y} = \log^{-1}\left[1/n \sum_{i=1}^{n} \log Y_i\right]$. For details, refer to Section 5.4.1 of Montgomery, et al. (2003). The linear regression model that will be built is the following:

$$Y^{\lambda} = \beta_0 + \beta_1 x + \epsilon. \tag{12.72}$$

For the choice of λ away from 0, we achieve variance stabilization, whereas for a value closer to 0, we obtain an approximate logarithmic transformation. The exact inference procedure for the choice of λ cannot be taken up here, and we simply note that the MLE technique is used for this purpose.

Example 12.7.3. The Box-Cox Transformation for Viscosity Dataset. The goal of this study is to find the impact of temperature on the viscosity of toluence-tetralin blends. This dataset is available in Problem 1, Chapter 5, of Montgomery, et al. (2003). First, the viscocity is modeled using simple linear regression. By using the `boxcox` function from the `MASS` package, we can find the MLE of λ and then use it to obtain y^{λ}, `ybc` in the R program. Using the estimated y^{λ}, a new linear model is built for `ybc` and `Temperature`.

```
> library(MASS)
> data(viscos)
> names(viscos)
[1] "Temperature" "Viscosity"
> viscoslm <- lm(Viscosity~Temperature,data=viscos)
> par(mfrow=c(1,3))
```

```
> plot(viscoslm$fitted.values,viscoslm$residuals,
+ xlab="Fitted Values",ylab="Residuals",col="red")
> bclist <- boxcox(viscoslm)
> mlelambda <- bclist$x[which(bclist$y==max(bclist$y))]
> mlelambda
[1] -0.7474747
> ygeom <- prod(viscos$Viscosity)^{1/length(viscos$Viscosity)}
> ybc <- (viscos$Viscosity^{mlelambda}-1)/(mlelambda*ygeom^
+ {mlelambda-1})
> viscosbclm <- lm(ybc~viscos$Temperature)
> plot(viscosbclm$fitted.values,viscosbclm$residuals,
+ xlab="Fitted Values", ylab="Residuals",col="red")
> summary(viscoslm)
Call:
lm(formula = Viscosity ~ Temperature, data = viscos)
Residuals:
      Min        1Q    Median        3Q       Max
-0.043955 -0.035863 -0.009305  0.019900  0.069559
Coefficients:
              Estimate Std. Error t value Pr(>|t|)
(Intercept)  1.2815107  0.0468683   27.34 1.58e-07 ***
Temperature -0.0087578  0.0007284  -12.02 2.01e-05 ***
---
Signif. codes:  0 '***' 0.001 '**' 0.01 '*' 0.05 '.' 0.1 ' ' 1
Residual standard error: 0.04743 on 6 degrees of freedom
Multiple R-squared:  0.9602, Adjusted R-squared:  0.9535
F-statistic: 144.6 on 1 and 6 DF,  p-value: 2.007e-05
> summary(viscosbclm)
Call:
lm(formula = ybc ~ viscos$Temperature)
Residuals:
      Min        1Q    Median        3Q       Max
-0.011929 -0.001858  0.000970  0.001953  0.010282
Coefficients:
                     Estimate Std. Error t value Pr(>|t|)
(Intercept)         0.2781401  0.0067156   41.42 1.33e-08 ***
viscos$Temperature -0.0083670  0.0001044  -80.17 2.54e-10 ***
---
Signif. codes:  0 '***' 0.001 '**' 0.01 '*' 0.05 '.' 0.1 ' ' 1
Residual standard error: 0.006797 on 6 degrees of freedom
Multiple R-squared:  0.9991, Adjusted R-squared:  0.9989
F-statistic:  6428 on 1 and 6 DF,  p-value: 2.536e-10
```

The `boxcox` function from the `MASS` package helps to obtain the value of λ as required in the analysis of the Box-Cox transformation. Since the value of estimated λ is `mlelambda=-0.7474747`, we have a reciprocal transformation. The `which` function is used to determine the optimum value of λ, and since the value is not closer to zero, we use the power transformation $\frac{Y^{\lambda}-1}{\lambda Y^{\lambda-1}}$ through the R objects `ygeom` and `ybc` to finally set up the linear regression model `viscosbclm`. Note the reduction in variance and also the distribution of the residuals against the fitted values in Figure 12.11. □

?log, ?sqrt, ?boxcox

12.8 Model Selection

Consider a linear regression model with ten covariates. The total number of possible models is then $\sum_{j=1}^{10}\binom{10}{j} = 1023$. The number of possible models is too enormous to investigate each one in depth. We also have further complications. Reconsider Example 12.4.5. It is seen from the output of the code `summary(crime_rate_lm)`, that the variables `S`, `Ex0`, `Ex1`, `LF`, `M`, `N`, `NW`, `U1`, and `W` are all insignificant variables by their corresponding *p*-value, as given in column `Pr(>|t|)`. What do we do with such variables? If we have to discard them, what should be the procedure? For instance, it may be recalled from Example 12.6.1 that if the variable `jitter(GBH)` is dropped, the variable `GBH` will be significant. Hence, there is a possibility that if we drop one of the variables from `crime_rate_lm`, some other variable may turn out to be significant.

The need of *model selection* is thus more of a necessity than a fancy. Any text on regression models will invariably discuss this important technique. We will see the rationale behind it with an example.

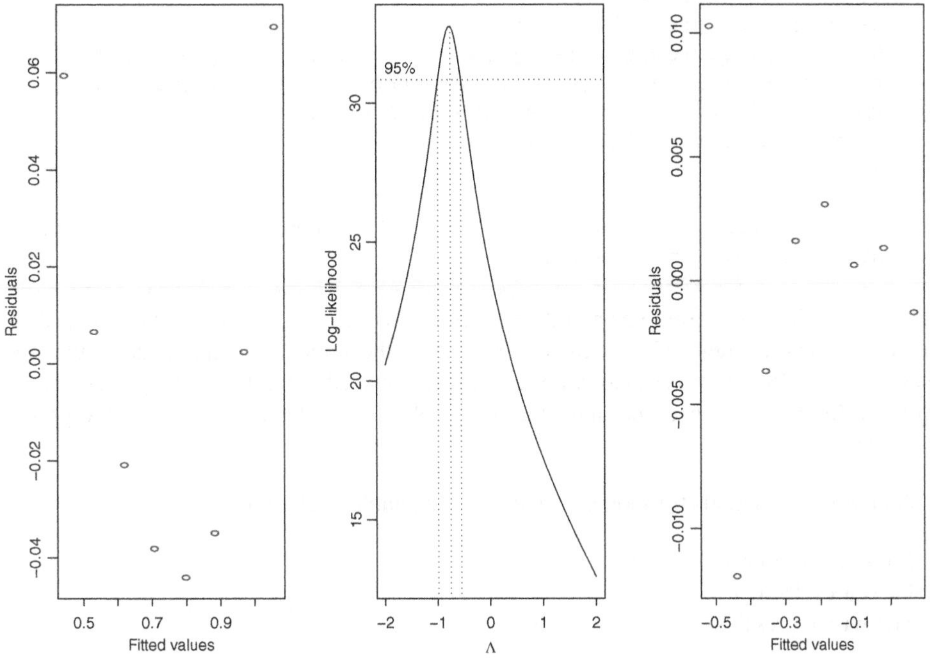

Figure 12.11 Box-Cox Transformation for the Viscosity Data

Example 12.8.1. The Prostate Cancer Example. In the prostate cancer study, we are interested in understanding the relationship between the logarithm of prostate specific antigen and the predictors including logarithms of cancer volume, prostate weight, benign prostatic hyperplasia amount, capsular penetration, and also the age, seminal vesicle invasion, Gleason score, and percentage Gleason scores 4 or 5. In this dataset, we have $n = 97$ observations and $p = 8$ number of covariates. Clearly, the total number of possible regression models is $\sum_{j=1}^{p} \binom{p}{j} = 255$. We will now obtain a plot of the residual sum of squares for each of these models. This plot is actually a beautiful programming exercise and the reader should look at Figure 12.12 first, and follow it up with a serious attempt towards obtaining it on his own. The codes have been provided here in the hope that the reader will only use it as a last resort.

```
> # The Need of Model Selection
> library(faraway)
> data(prostate)
> lspa <- prostate[,9]
> covariates <- prostate[,-9]
> covnames <- names(covariates)
> p <- length(covnames); n <- length(lspa)
> RSSmatrix <- matrix(nrow=sum(choose(8,8:1)), ncol=11)
> currrow <- 0
> for(i in 1:p) {
+  temp <- choose(p,i)
+  tempmat <- t(combn(1:8,i))
+  for(j in 1:temp) {
+   currrow <- currrow+1
+   RSSmatrix[currrow,1] <- currrow
+   RSSmatrix[currrow,tempmat[j,]+1] <- covnames[tempmat[j,]]
+   templm <- lm(lspa~.,subset(covariates,select = tempmat[j,]))
+   RSSmatrix[currrow,10] <- sum(templm$residuals^2)
+   RSSmatrix[currrow,11] <- i
+   }
+   }
> plot(RSSmatrix[,11],RSSmatrix[,10],xlab="Number of Predictors",
+ ylab="Residual Sum of Squares")
```

We confirm that the R program should be referred to as a last resort only, and hence its details are not given here. Figure 12.12 clearly shows that as the number of components of the model increases, the RSS decreases. However, the reader can verify that the model, which has least variance for a fixed p, need not have the $p - 1$ subset variables of them, as in the previous $p - 1$ case. □

A number of methods for model selection are available, including:

- Backward elimination
- Forward selection
- Stepwise regression.

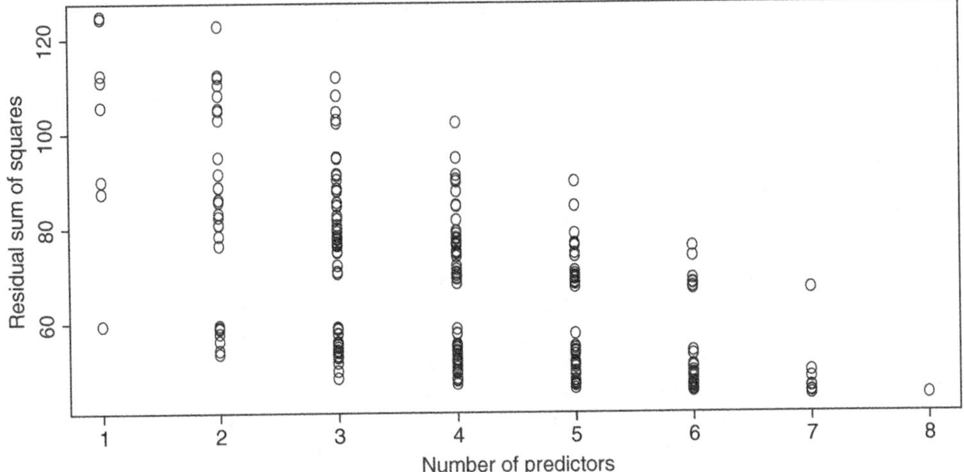

Figure 12.12 An RSS Plot for all Possible Regression Models

12.8.1 *Backward Elimination*

The backward elimination method is the simplest of all variable selection procedures and can be easily implemented without a special function/package. In situations where there is a complex hierarchy, backward elimination can be run manually while taking account of what variables are eligible for removal. This method starts with a model containing all the explanatory variables and eliminates the variables one at a time, at each stage choosing the variable for exclusion as the one leading to the smallest decrease in the regression sum of squares. An F-type statistic is used to judge when further exclusions would represent a significant deterioration in the model. The algorithm of backward selection is as follows:

1. Start with all the predictors in the model.
2. Remove the predictor with highest p-value greater than α critical.
3. Refit the model and go to 2.
4. Stop when all p-values are less than alpha critical.

The alpha critical is sometimes called the p-to-remove and does not have to be 5%. If prediction performance is the goal, then a 15 to 20% cut-off may work best, although methods designed more directly for optimal prediction should be preferred.

Example 12.8.2. The US Crime Data. Example 12.6.2. Contd. The backward elimination method is illustrated for the fitted model `crime_rate_lm2`. Here at each stage we remove the predictor with the largest p-value greater than 0.05. Since the p-value of regressor NM in the summary output of `summary(crime_rate_lm2)` is largest, we shall eliminate it first. The R function `update` will be used to re-fit a model with suitable modification.

```
> crime_rate_lm3 <- update(crime_rate_lm2,.~.-NW)
> summary(crime_rate_lm3)
Call:
lm(formula = R ~ Age + S + Ed + Ex0 + LF + M + N + U1 + U2 +
    W + X, data = usc)
Residuals:
    Min      1Q  Median      3Q     Max
-38.755 -13.587   1.089  13.242  48.921
Coefficients:
             Estimate Std. Error t value Pr(>|t|)
(Intercept) -704.12001  149.69012  -4.704 3.91e-05 ***
Age            1.06420    0.38919   2.734  0.00974 **
S             -7.88954   12.76942  -0.618  0.54068
Ed             1.72173    0.61413   2.804  0.00819 **
Ex0            1.00952    0.21793   4.632 4.85e-05 ***
LF            -0.01727    0.13814  -0.125  0.90123
M              0.16308    0.19819   0.823  0.41615
N             -0.03886    0.12634  -0.308  0.76021
U1            -0.58496    0.42003  -1.393  0.17251
U2             1.81921    0.83415   2.181  0.03600 *
W              0.13516    0.10070   1.342  0.18819
X              0.80399    0.22856   3.518  0.00123 **
---
Signif. codes:  0 '***' 0.001 '**' 0.01 '*' 0.05 '.' 0.1 ' ' 1
Residual standard error: 21.41 on 35 degrees of freedom
Multiple R-squared:  0.7669, Adjusted R-squared:  0.6936
F-statistic: 10.47 on 11 and 35 DF,  p-value: 4.008e-08
```

Since we have to remove the NM variable from the `crime_rate_lm2` fitted model, the option of `.~.-NW` achieves the required modification in the `update` function. Now the *p*-value of `LF` is the highest in the current model and hence is eliminated using the `update` function once again.

```
> crime_rate_lm4 <- update(crime_rate_lm3,.~.-LF)
> summary(crime_rate_lm4)
Call:
lm(formula = R ~ Age + S + Ed + Ex0 + M + N + U1 + U2 + W + X,
    data = usc)
Residuals:
    Min      1Q  Median      3Q     Max
-38.595 -13.628   0.876  12.927  48.991
Coefficients:
             Estimate Std. Error t value Pr(>|t|)
(Intercept) -700.19857  144.35146  -4.851 2.37e-05 ***
Age            1.06640    0.38344   2.781 0.008565 **
S             -7.18568   11.30331  -0.636 0.528984
Ed             1.70184    0.58499   2.909 0.006176 **
Ex0            1.01444    0.21139   4.799 2.77e-05 ***
```

```
M              0.15059    0.16878    0.892 0.378199
N             -0.04146    0.12290   -0.337 0.737825
U1            -0.56349    0.37804   -1.491 0.144793
U2             1.81277    0.82110    2.208 0.033720 *
W              0.13417    0.09901    1.355 0.183821
X              0.79674    0.21804    3.654 0.000816 ***
---
Signif. codes:  0 '***' 0.001 '**' 0.01 '*' 0.05 '.' 0.1 ' ' 1
Residual standard error: 21.11 on 36 degrees of freedom
Multiple R-squared:  0.7668, Adjusted R-squared:  0.702
F-statistic: 11.84 on 10 and 36 DF,  p-value: 1.125e-08
```

Now, the variables which will leave the model one after the other are N, S, S, M, U1, and W. The output for all summaries are not provided, except the final one.

```
> crime_rate_lm5 <- update(crime_rate_lm4,.~.-N)
> summary(crime_rate_lm5)
> crime_rate_lm6 <- update(crime_rate_lm5,.~.-S)
> summary(crime_rate_lm6)
> crime_rate_lm7 <- update(crime_rate_lm6,.~.-M)
> summary(crime_rate_lm7)
> crime_rate_lm8 <- update(crime_rate_lm7,.~.-U1)
> summary(crime_rate_lm8)
> crime_rate_lm9 <- update(crime_rate_lm8,.~.-W)
> summary(crime_rate_lm9)
Call:
lm(formula = R ~ Age + Ed + Ex0 + U2 + X, data = usc)
Residuals:
    Min      1Q  Median      3Q     Max
-45.344  -9.859  -1.807  10.603  62.964
Coefficients:
             Estimate Std. Error t value Pr(>|t|)
(Intercept) -524.3743    95.1156  -5.513 2.13e-06 ***
Age            1.0198     0.3532   2.887 0.006175 **
Ed             2.0308     0.4742   4.283 0.000109 ***
Ex0            1.2331     0.1416   8.706 7.26e-11 ***
U2             0.9136     0.4341   2.105 0.041496 *
X              0.6349     0.1468   4.324 9.56e-05 ***
---
Signif. codes:  0 '***' 0.001 '**' 0.01 '*' 0.05 '.' 0.1 ' ' 1
Residual standard error: 21.3 on 41 degrees of freedom
Multiple R-squared:  0.7296, Adjusted R-squared:  0.6967
F-statistic: 22.13 on 5 and 41 DF,  p-value: 1.105e-10
```

Since none of the p-values associated with the covariates in crime_rate_lm9 are greater than 0.05, we now stop the backward selection process. Notice that the R^2 for the full model of 0.7692 is reduced only slightly to 0.7296 in the final model. Thus, the removal of eight predictors causes only a minor reduction in fit. □

The above example is really taxing and there is a need to refine this before obtaining the final result. A customized R function which will achieve the same result is given next.

```
# The Backward Selection Methodology
pvalueslm <- function(lm) {summary(lm)$coefficients[,4]}
backwardlm <- function(lm,criticalalpha) {
 lm2 <- lm
 while(max(pvalueslm(lm2))>criticalalpha) {
 lm2 <- update(lm2,paste(".~.-",attr(lm2$terms,"term.labels")
+ [(which(pvalueslm(lm2)
                ==max(pvalueslm(lm2))))-1],sep=""))
 }
 return(lm2)
 }
```

12.8.2 Forward and Stepwise Selection

The forward selection method reverses the backward method. This method starts with a model containing none of the explanatory variables and then considers variables one by one for inclusion. At each step, the variable added is the one that results in the biggest increase in the regression sum of squares. An F-type statistic is used to judge when further additions would not represent a significant improvement in the model.

1. Start with no variables in the model.
2. For all predictors not in the model, check their p-value if they are added to the model. Choose the one with lowest p-value less than alpha critical.
3. Continue until no new predictors can be added.

For a function similar to `backwardlm`, refer to Chapter 6 of Tattar (2013) for an implementation of the forward selection algorithm. Stepwise regression is a combination of forward selection and backward elimination. This addresses the situation where variables are added or removed early in the process and we want to change our mind about them later. Starting with no variables in the model, variables are added as with the forward selection method. Here, however, with each addition of a variable, a backward elimination process is considered to assess whether variables entered earlier might now be removed, because they no longer contribute significantly to the model.

We will now look at another criteria for model selection: *Akaike Information Criteria*, abbreviated as AIC. Let the log-likelihood function for a fitted regression model with p covariates be denoted by $\log\left(L(\hat{\beta}_0, \hat{\beta}_1, \ldots, \hat{\beta}_p, \hat{\sigma}^2|\mathbf{y})\right)$. The total number of estimated parameters is denoted by K. The AIC for the regression model is then given by

$$\text{AIC} = 2\left[-\log\left(L(\hat{\beta}_0, \hat{\beta}_1, \ldots, \hat{\beta}_p, \hat{\sigma}^2|\mathbf{y})\right) + K\right], \tag{12.73}$$

where $K = p + 2$. The term K is referred to as the *penalty term*. The model which has the least AIC value is considered the best model. For more details, refer to Sheather (2009). The use of AIC for forward and stepwise selection will be illustrated in the following.

Example 12.8.3. The US Crime Data. Let us continue the use of the US crime dataset. The reader is assured that the steps, or R program, is actually very simple.

```
> step(crime_rate_lm,direction="both")
Start:  AIC=301.66
R ~ Age + S + Ed + Ex0 + Ex1 + LF + M + N + NW + U1 + U2 + W +
    X
        Df Sum of Sq   RSS    AIC
- NW     1       6.1 15885 299.68
- LF     1      34.4 15913 299.76
- N      1      48.9 15928 299.81
- S      1     149.4 16028 300.10
- Ex1    1     162.3 16041 300.14
- M      1     296.5 16175 300.53
<none>               15879 301.66
- W      1     810.6 16689 302.00
- U1     1     911.5 16790 302.29
- Ex0    1    1109.8 16988 302.84
- U2     1    2108.8 17988 305.52
- Age    1    2911.6 18790 307.57
- Ed     1    3700.5 19579 309.51
- X      1    5474.2 21353 313.58
Step:  AIC=299.68

Step:  AIC=291.83
R ~ Age + Ed + Ex0 + U2 + W + X
        Df Sum of Sq   RSS    AIC
<none>               17351 291.83
+ U1     1     408.6 16942 292.71
- W      1    1252.6 18604 293.11
+ Ex1    1     251.2 17100 293.14
+ LF     1     230.7 17120 293.20
+ N      1     189.6 17162 293.31
+ M      1     177.8 17173 293.35
+ S      1      71.0 17280 293.64
+ NW     1      59.2 17292 293.67
- U2     1    1628.7 18980 294.05
- Age    1    4461.0 21812 300.58
- Ed     1    6214.7 23566 304.22
- X      1    8932.3 26283 309.35
- Ex0    1   15596.5 32948 319.97
Call:
lm(formula = R ~ Age + Ed + Ex0 + U2 + W + X, data = usc)
Coefficients:
(Intercept)          Age          W X
  -618.5028       1.1252    0.1596  0.8236
```

The `step` function is a very generic function such as `summary`, `plot`, `predict`, etc., and it may be applied to many fitted regression models. This shows that the model selected by the stepwise regression includes the variables `Age`, `Ed`, `Ex0`, `U2`, `W`, and `X` in the best model. □

?choose, ?combn, ?update, ?attr, ?step

12.9 Further Reading

In this section we consider some of the regression books which have been loosely classified into different sections.

12.9.1 Early Classics

Draper and Smith (1966–98) is a treatise on applied regression analysis. Chatterjee and Hadi (1977–2006) and Chatterjee and Hadi (1988) are two excellent companions for regression analysis. Bapat (2000) builds linear models using linear algebra and the book gives the reader an indepth knowledge of the necessary theory. Christensen (2011) develops a *projective approach* for linear models. For firm foundations in linear models, the reader may also use Rao, et al. (2008). Searle (1971) is a classic book, which is still preferred by some readers.

12.9.2 Industrial Applications

Montgomery, et al. (2003) and Kutner, et al. (2005) provide comprehensive coverages of linear models with dedicated emphasis on industrial applications.

12.9.3 Regression Details

Belsley, Kuh and Welsh (1980), Fox (1991), Cook (1998), Cook and Weisberg (1982), Cook and Weisberg (1994), and Cook and Weisberg (1999) are the monographs which have details about regression diagnostics. For a robust regression model, the reader will find a very useful source in Rousseeuw and Leroy (1987).

12.9.4 Modern Regression Texts

Andersen and Skovgaard (2010) consider many variants of regression models which have linear predictors. Gelman and Hill (2007) develop hierarchical regression models. Freedman (2009) is an instant classic which lays more emphasis on matrix algebra. Sengupta and Rao (2003), Clarke (2008), Seber and Lee (2003), and Rencher and Schaalje (2008) are also useful accounts of the linear models.

12.9.5 R for Regression

Fox (2002) is an early text on the use of R software for regression analysis. Faraway (2002) is an open source book which has detailed R programs for linear models.

12.10 Complements, Problems, and Programs

Problem 12.1 Fit a simple linear regression model for the Galton dataset as seen in Example 4.5.1. Compare the values of the regression coefficients of the linear regression model for this dataset with the previously obtained resistant line coefficients.

Problem 12.2 Verify that Equation 12.19 is satisfied for Example 13.2.3. Fit the resistant lines model for this dataset, and verify whether the ANOVA decomposition holds for the fitted values obtained using the resistant line model.

Problem 12.3 Extend the concept of R^2 and $AdjR^2$ for the resistant line model. Create an R function which will extract these two measures for a fitter resistant line model and obtain these values for the Galton dataset, `rp`, and `tc`.

Problem 12.4 The `Signif. codes` as obtained by `summary(lm)` may be easily customized in R to use your own cut-off points, and symbols too. There are two elements to this, first the cut-off points for the p-values and the default settings are `cutpoints = c(0, 0.001, 0.01, 0.05, 0.1, 1)`, and the second part has the symbols in `symbols = c("***", "**", "*", ".", " ")`. Change these default settings to, say, `symbols = c("$$$", "$$", "$", ".", " ")` by first running `fix(printCoefmat)`. Edit the `printCoefmat` and save it. The changes in this object are then applied in an R session by running the code `assignInNamespace("printCoefmat", printCoefmat, "stats")` at the console. Customize your `Signif. codes` and complete the program!

Problem 12.5 The model validation in Example 13.2.6 for the Toluca Company dataset has been carried out using the residuals. The semi-Studentized residuals also play a critical role in determining departures from the assumptions of the linear regression model. Obtain the six plots as in that example with the semi-Studentized residuals.

Problem 12.6 The model validation aspects need to be checked for the Rocket propellant problem, Example 13.2.1. Complete the program for the fitted simple linear regression model and draw the appropriate conclusions.

Problem 12.7 In Example 13.4.3, change the range of the variables `x1` and `x2` to `x1 <- rep(seq(-10,10,0.5),100)` and `x2 <- rep(seq(-10,10, 0.5),each=100)` and redo the three-dimensional plot, especially for the third linear regression model. Similarly, for the contour plot of the same model, change the variable ranges to `x1=x2=seq(from=-5,to=5, by=0.2)` and redraw the contour plot. What are your typical observations?

Problem 12.8 For the fitted linear model `crime_rate_lm`, using the `usc` dataset, obtain the plot of residuals against the fitted values.

Problem 12.9 Verify the properties of the hat matrix **H** given in Equation 12.37 for the fitted object `crime_rate_lm`, or any other fitted multiple linear regression model of your choice.

Problem 12.10 Using self-defined functions for *DFFITS* and *DFBETAS*, as given in Equations 12.66 and 12.65, say `my_dffits` and `my_dfbetas`, compute the values for an `ailm` fitted object and compare the results with the R functions `dffits` and `dfbetas`.

Problem 12.11 The VIF given in Equation 12.67 for a covariate requires computation of R^2, as obtained in the regression model when the covariate is an output and other covariates are input variables for it. Thus, using `1/(1-summary(lm(xi~x1+...+xi-1+xi+1+...+xp))$r.squared)`, the VIF of the covariate x_i may be obtained. Verify the VIFs obtained in Example 13.6.2.

Problem 12.12 Identify if the multicollinearity problems exist for the fitted `ailm` object using (i) VIF method, and (ii) eigen system analysis.

Problem 12.13 Carry out the Box-Cox transformation method for the `bacteria_study` and compare it with the result in Example 13.7.1 of the log transformation technique, `bacterialoglm`.

Problem 12.14 For the prostate cancer problem discussed in Example 13.8.1, find the best possible linear regression model using (i) step-wise, (ii) forward, and (iii) backward selection technique.

13

Experimental Designs

Package(s): BHH2, AlgDesign, granova, multcomp, car, agricolae, phia
Dataset(s): olson, tensile, girder, Hardness, reaction, rocket, rocket_Graeco, battery, bottling, SP, intensity

13.1 Introduction

Experimental Designs, also known as Design of Experiments (DOE), is one of the most important pillars of statistics.

Section 13.2 will introduce the important principles of experimental design, beginning with an interesting real experiment. The first model of the experimental design will be deliberated in Section 13.3, and its extensions to the *block design* will be detailed in Section 13.4. An effective extension and important class of models of *factorial design* will be taken up in Section 13.5.

13.2 Principles of Experimental Design

Salsburg (2001) has written a very interesting and historical account in his book titled "The Lady Tasting Tea". The first chapter, with the same title as the book, has this amazing story of a lady who declared in a cafeteria that she can clearly distinguish between two variants of tea: (i) tea poured into milk, and (ii) milk poured into tea. As Salsburg puts it "A thin, short man, with thick glasses and a Vandyke beard beginning to turn gray, pounced on the problem", and a live experiment rolled on. The lady was then sent a sequence of different patterns of tea poured into milk cups and milk poured into tea cups. For each cup, the lady would have one sip following which she would declare the process she felt was the underlying preparation, and the results would be noted down. The lady would not be told whether her observation was correct or not at the end of each experiment. This experiment performed by the Vandyke bearded scientist became very famous and laid the foundations of DOE. The reader may be curious to know the answer to two points: (i) Who is this Vandyke bearded scientist? and (ii) What was the result of the experiment? Of course, it was Sir Ronald Fisher who had this Vandyke-styled beard and

A Course in Statistics with R, First Edition. Prabhanjan Narayanachar Tattar, Suresh Ramaiah and B. G. Manjunath.

Companion Website: www.wiley.com/go/tattar/statistics

he put the importance of *randomization* in action for the tea tasting expert lady. It is important to note here that the goal of the experiment was to test if that lady's claim was correct or not! The randomization prevents the effect of false guesses on the results. If the results of the "The Lady Tasting Tea" experiment were declared, then it was a possibility that people would have failed the concept of "randomization" and not distinguished the fact that this experiment was about the claim of the lady. The lady was correct with all her ten guesses and this was thanks to the fact that she was indeed an expert in making the distinction between the two methods of tea preparation. Salsburg (2001) has built this story in a more fascinating writing and the reader should read the same for more details.

The three important concepts of DOE are (i) Randomization, (ii) Replication, and (iii) Blocking.

Randomization. An experimenter may or may not have biases while conducting an experiment. This influence needs to be done away with before we run the experiment. For example, if Fisher had sent first five times tea poured with milk, and then next five times milk poured with tea to the lady, we are actually having just two observations and not ten observations. Similarly, sending the two types of tea alternatively also sets in predictability. Thus, it is necessary to *mix things up* and what can be better than sending the tea in a random order for removing the experimenter's bias.

Replication. In "The Lady Tasting Tea" example, randomization alone does not help us if we were sending just two cups of tea to the lady. We need to ensure that the number of cups of "tea poured into milk" and "milk poured into tea" is large enough to support our randomization technique mentioned earlier.

Blocking. Consider an artificial example where we have to decide if the students learn better in classrooms with or without air conditioning (AC). For students from Classes I to IV, we have been careful enough to allocate enough numbers of students to the classrooms with and without AC. Despite our caution, suppose that we have accidentally put all the boys in the classrooms with AC and all the girls in the classrooms without AC. Assume that the result shows that boys perform better than girls. Is the result acceptable? Or assume that the results show that AC students get higher marks than non-AC students. Are the results still acceptable? As we know that the results are not acceptable, we must understand that there are some natural obstacles/restrictions in the nature of the experimental units. This variation in the experimental units cannot be allowed to ruin the results of the experiments. Thus, we need to form *blocks* which remove this kind of bias/error from the experiment.

We will now consider the simple experimental design, where the importance of randomization will play the central role, in the next section.

13.3 Completely Randomized Designs

Completely Randomized Designs (CRD) is one of the first steps in DOE, and it is a simple setup which involves replication and randomization. If the source of variation in the output is only due to the treatments, CRD is appropriate to deduce the more effective treatments.

13.3.1 The CRD Model

Let Y_{ij} denote the jth experimental unit for the ith treatment, with $j = 1, 2, \cdots, r$, and $i = 1, 2, \cdots, v$. We assume that the number of observations for each treatment is the same as for any other treatment. Suppose that the experimenter believes that the average yield due to treatment i is μ_i. The CRD model is then expressed by

$$Y_{ij} = \mu_i + \epsilon_{ij}, j = 1, 2, \cdots, r, i = 1, 2, \cdots, v, \tag{13.1}$$

where $\epsilon_{ij} \sim N(0, \sigma^2), \forall i, j$. This model 13.1 is known as the *means model*. The more general and useful mathematical model for the CRD is

$$Y_{ij} = \mu + \tau_i + \epsilon_{ij}, j = 1, 2, \cdots, r, i = 1, 2, \cdots, v. \tag{13.2}$$

The CRD model 13.2 in this form is known as the *effects model*. The effects model is more feasible from a practical point of view. In this form the mean μ is thought of as some guaranteed yield in the absence of any kind of treatment. This parameter is also known as the *baseline* or *control treatment*. The parameter values τ_i are a reflection of the effect due to the treatment i. We will consider the second format of the model throughout the rest of this section. The error component, or the noise factor, ϵ_{ij} are noise factors associated with the (i,j) experimental unit. We will assume that the errors are iid as $N(0, \sigma^2)$, where the variance of the normal distribution is not known. Thus, the CRD model says that the probability distribution of the experimental units Y_{ij} is $N(\mu + \tau_i, \sigma^2)$. The means and effects model are also related in the sense of defining $\mu_i = \mu + \tau_i, i = 1, 2, \cdots, v$.

In both models 13.1 and 13.2, each treatment receives an equal number of experimental units, that is, each treatment i receives r number of units. These kinds of models are called *balanced designs*. In practical setups, it may not be feasible to allocate equal numbers of units, and we allow the i-th treatment of $r_i, i = 1, 2, \cdots, v$, number of units. In this case, the model is called the *unbalanced design*. The inferential aspects of balanced or unbalanced models do not vary drastically from each other, at least for the CRD model, and the coverage for the balanced model is provided in the rest of this section.

The movement to *Design Matrix* from *Covariate Matrix*. The covariates **x**'s are missing in the effects model 13.2! In fact, the **x**'s will not appear in the rest of this chapter either. Recollect that the median polish model 4.14 also did not have the covariates **x**'s. However, the covariates are very much present in these models and they have a well-defined format. Indeed, the covariates are *designed* to appear in a specific way and this is the reason why we call the covariate matrix the *Design Matrix*. The models in this broad area completely determine the exact structure of the covariate matrix. In R, the function `model.matrix` will generate the exact design matrix, and we will come to this function later.

Consider the effects in model 13.2. Suppose we have $v = 3$ treatments and $r = 4$ observations for each of the treatments. Let the treatment effect be denoted by $\tau_i, i = 1, 2, 3$, and let X_i take the value of 1 if treatment i is assigned to the observation, and 0 otherwise, $i = 1, 2, 3$. The design matrix $\mathbf{X}$ is then defined as in Table 13.1. Note that it is important to drop one of the X_1, X_2, X_3!

The next small sub-section will help in random allocation of the treatments to the experimental units.

13.3.2 Randomization in CRD

Suppose that we have v number of treatments and that the ith treatment, $i = 1, 2, \cdots, v$, is allocated r number of experimental units. Let $N = v \times r$ be the total number of available experimental units.

Table 13.1 Design Matrix of a CRD with $v = 3$ Treatments and $r = 4$ Observations

Observation	Intercept	X_1	X_2
1	1	1	0
2	1	1	0
3	1	1	0
4	1	1	0
5	1	0	1
6	1	0	1
7	1	0	1
8	1	0	1
9	1	0	0
10	1	0	0
11	1	0	0
12	1	0	0

Example 13.3.1. Allocation of Experimental Units to Treatments. Randomization for CRD is really simple in R. Here, we have $v = 3$ and $r = 4$ and thus $N = 12$ units. Let the 12 units be labeled from 1 to 12. Now, these 12 units need to be randomly assigned to one of the three treatments, `LETTERS[1:3]`. We use the `sample` function to randomly assign the units to treatments.

```
> treatments <- LETTERS[1:3] # 3 treatments in action
> replicates <- c(4,4,4) # number of replicates
> total_units <- 1:sum(replicates)
> unsort_tr <- rep(treatments,replicates)
> unsort_numbers <- sample(total_units,length(total_units))
> cbind(unsort_tr,unsort_numbers)
      unsort_tr unsort_numbers
 [1,] "A"       "9"
 [2,] "A"       "6"
 [3,] "A"       "11"
 [4,] "A"       "8"
 [5,] "B"       "4"
 [6,] "B"       "10"
 [7,] "B"       "2"
 [8,] "B"       "12"
 [9,] "C"       "3"
[10,] "C"       "7"
[11,] "C"       "5"
[12,] "C"       "1"
```

The above allocation is to be interpreted as follows. Treatment `A` is assigned the experimental units 9, 6, 11, and 8, treatment `B` is assigned 4, 10, 2, and 12, whereas treatment `C` is allocated with units 3, 7, 5, and 1. Note that this allocation is done before conducting the experiment. The reader may get a different allocation based on running the code at the R terminal. □

The statistical inference for the CRD model will now be discussed.

13.3.3 Inference for the CRD Models

A few standard notations are in order. The ith treatment sample sum (mean), denoted by $y_{i.}$ ($\bar{y}_{i.}$) and total sample sum (mean), $y_{..}$ ($\bar{y}_{..}$), are defined by

$$y_{i.} = \sum_{j=1}^{r} y_{ij} \quad \text{and } \bar{y}_{i.} = \tfrac{y_{i.}}{v}, \tag{13.3}$$

$$y_{..} = \sum_{i=1}^{a} y_{i.} \quad \text{and } \bar{y}_{..} = \tfrac{y_{..}}{N}. \tag{13.4}$$

Define the *total (corrected) sum of squares*, denoted by SS_T, as

$$SS_T = \sum_{i=1}^{v} \sum_{j=1}^{r} (y_{ij} - \bar{y}_{..})^2. \tag{13.5}$$

The ANOVA technique partitions the SS_T as the sum of two components: (i) the sum of squares due to treatments SS_{Tr}, and (ii) the sum of squares due to error SS_E. Here, SS_{Tr} and SS_E are defined by

$$SS_{Tr} = r \sum_{i=1}^{v} (\bar{y}_{i.} - \bar{y}_{..})^2, \tag{13.6}$$

$$SS_E = \sum_{i=1}^{v} \sum_{j=1}^{r} (y_{ij} - \bar{y}_{i.})^2. \tag{13.7}$$

Note that SS_{Tr} accounts for the *between treatments* effect, and SS_E accounts for the *within treatments* difference. Here, SS_T has $N - 1$ degrees of freedom, whereas SS_{Tr} and SS_E have respectively $v - 1$ and $r - 1$ degrees of freedom. It is easy to verify that

$$SS_T = SS_{Tr} + SS_E.$$

Define

$$S_i^2 = \frac{\sum_{j=1}^{r} (y_{ij} - \bar{y}_{i.})^2}{r - 1}, i = 1, \cdots, v.$$

That is, S_i^2 is the sampling variance of the i-th treatment. We can pool these v sampling variances and obtain the following:

$$\frac{(r-1)S_1^2 + \cdots + (r-1)S_v^2}{(r-1) + \cdots + (r-1)} = \frac{\sum_{i=1}^{v} \sum_{j=1}^{r} (y_{ij} - \bar{y}_{i.})^2}{\sum_{i=1}^{v}(r-1)} = \frac{SS_E}{N - v} = MS_E,$$

where MS_E denotes the *mean error sum of squares*. Note that S_i^2 is an estimator of the variance σ^2 for the i-th treatment, and it may be seen that $SS_E/(N - v)$ is an estimator of the common variance within each of the treatments. Similarly, we can also use the variation of the treatment averages from the grand average, under the assumption that there is no difference among the treatment means, for estimation of σ^2. That is, the *mean treatment sum of squares* is given by

$$\frac{SS_{Tr}}{v-1} = \frac{r \sum_{i=1}^{r} (\bar{y}_{i.} - \bar{y}_{..})}{v - 1} = MS_{Tr}$$

Table 13.2 ANOVA for the CRD Model

Source of Variation	Sum of Squares	Degrees of Freedom	Mean Square	F-Statistic
Between Treatments	SS_{Tr}	$v-1$	MS_{Tr}	MS_{Tr}/MS_E
Error within Treatments	SS_E	$N-v$	MS_E	
Total	SS_T	$N-1$		

An interesting hypothesis testing problem is about the equality of effect of the treatment means: $H : \tau_1 = \cdots = \tau_v = \tau$, say, against the alternative $K : \tau_i \neq \tau_j$, for some $i \neq j$. The details can then be presented in the ANOVA Table 13.2.

In light of Theorem 6.6.2, the sampling distribution of MS_E and MS_{Tr} may be seen as an χ^2-distribution with $N-v$ and $v-1$ degrees of freedom respectively. Finally, the sampling distribution of MS_{Tr}/MS_E is seen to be an F-distribution, see Theorem 6.3.4, with $(N-v, v-1)$ degrees of freedom.

Before a formal illustration of the CRD model, let us take an EDA route for understanding ANOVA. The package `granova` has a very interesting graphical tool `granova.1w`, where `1w` stands for "one-way layout". The illustration through `example(granova.1w)` is first considered. The `granova` may be useful for outlier identification, skewness, etc.

Example 13.3.2. `granova` Tool for Weight Gain Problem. The weight change for 72 young female *anorexia* patients is available in the `MASS` package. Understand more about the dataset with `?anorexia`. The patients were randomly allocated to three different treatments: `CBT`, `Cont`, and `FT`. The aim is to find if the weight gain is the same across the three treatments. First, the weight gain is defined by `anorexia[,3]-anorexia[,2]` and stored in `w.gain`. The ANOVA technique with `aov` clearly shows that the weight gain across the three treatments is significantly: `aov(w.gain ~ anorexia[,1])`.

```
> library(MASS)
> data(anorexia)
> w.gain <- anorexia[,3]-anorexia[,2]
> summary(aov(w.gain ~ anorexia[,1]))
               Df Sum Sq Mean Sq F value   Pr(>F)
anorexia[, 1]   2  614.6 307.322  5.4223 0.006499 **
Residuals      69 3910.7  56.677
---
Signif. codes:  0 '***' 0.001 '**' 0.01 '*' 0.05 '.' 0.1 ' ' 1
> pdf("Anorexia_granova.pdf")
> granova.1w(w.gain,group=anorexia[,1])
$grandsum
     Grandmean          df.bet        df.with          MS.bet         MS.with
          2.76            2.00          69.00          307.32           56.68
        F.stat          F.prob SS.bet/SS.tot
          5.42            0.01           0.14
$stats
      Size Contrast Coef Wt'd Mean  Mean Trim'd Mean  Var. St. Dev.
Cont    26           -3.21     -0.49 -0.45        -1.16 63.82     7.99
```

```
CBT     29          0.24     3.63  3.01       1.80 53.41     7.31
FT      17          4.50     5.15  7.26       7.91 51.23     7.16
> dev.off()
null device
          1
```

At the center of the plot in Figure 13.1, we see the total sample mean of the observations as given in Equation 13.3. The blue box represents within sum of squares given in Equation 13.6, and the red box between sum of squares in Equation 13.6. Since we reject the hypothesis that the weight gain by different treatments are equal, it may be seen from Figure 13.1 that the weight gain is at a maximum for `FT` treatment at `7.2647`. □

In the next example, we will find out how R handles the covariates for the CRD model!

Example 13.3.3. The Tensile Strength Experiment. Page 70 of Montgomery (2005). An engineer wants to find out if the cotton weight percentage in a synthetic fiber effects the tensile strength. Towards this, the cotton weight percentage is fixed at 5 different levels of 15, 20, 25, 30, and 35. Each level of the percentage is assigned five experimental units and the tensile strength is measured for each of them. The randomization is specified in the `Run_Number` column. The goal of the engineer is to investigate if $H : \tau_{15} = \tau_{20} = \cdots = \tau_{35}$, where the

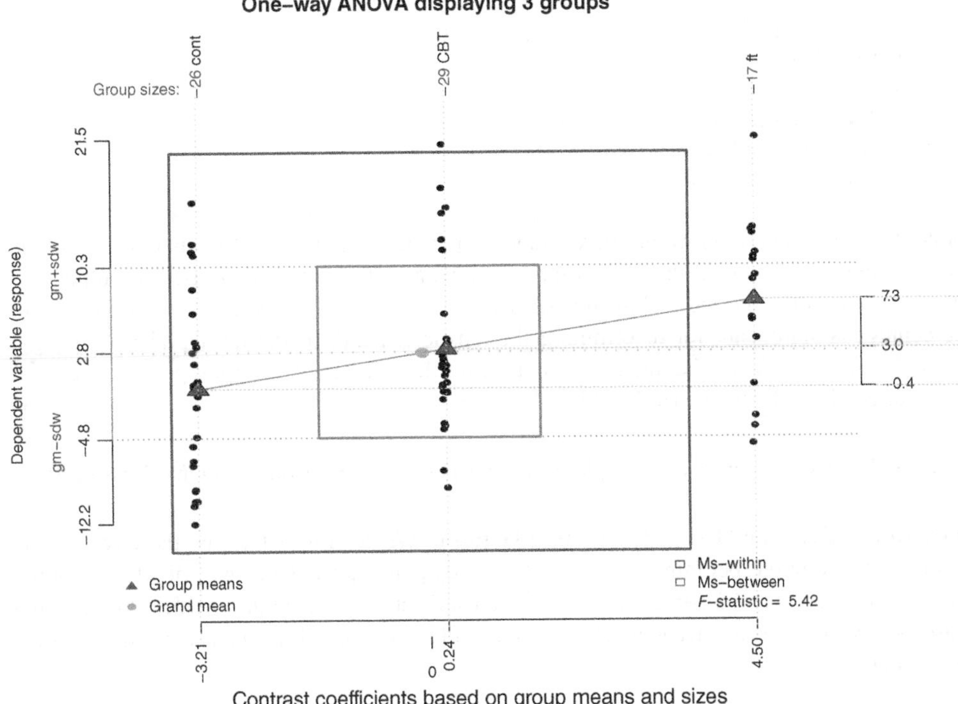

Figure 13.1 "Granova" Plot for the Anorexia Dataset

subscript denotes the percentage level. Towards this goal, a CRD model is fitted and the ANOVA table is obtained following the next program.

```
> data(tensile)
> tensile$CWP <- as.factor(tensile$CWP)
> tensile_aov <- aov(Tensile_Strength~CWP, data=tensile)
> summary(tensile_aov)
            Df Sum Sq Mean Sq F value   Pr(>F)
CWP          4  475.8  118.94   14.76 9.13e-06 ***
Residuals   20  161.2    8.06
---
Signif. codes:  0 '***' 0.001 '**' 0.01 '*' 0.05 '.' 0.1 ' ' 1
> model.matrix(tensile_aov)
   (Intercept) CWP20 CWP25 CWP30 CWP35
1            1     1     0     0     0
2            1     0     0     1     0
3            1     1     0     0     0
4            1     0     0     0     1

12           1     0     0     0     0
13           1     0     1     0     0
14           1     1     0     0     0

24           1     0     0     1     0
25           1     0     0     0     0
attr(,"assign")
[1] 0 1 1 1 1
attr(,"contrasts")
attr(,"contrasts")$CWP
[1] "contr.treatment"
```

Note that since the cotton weight percentage is specified in numeric, R reads it as a numeric vector. However, it is vital that the variable be read as a `factor`, otherwise the output will be drastically different and technically wrong. The p-value clearly specifies that the weight percentage is significant for determining the tensile strength of the fabric. The R function `model.matrix` shows that the design matrix for the CRD model is appropriately prepared as required along the lines in Table 13.1. □

We will consider one more example for the CRD model 13.2 from Dean and Voss (1999).

Example 13.3.4. The Olson Heart Lung Dataset. We need to determine the effect of the number of revolutions per minute (`rpm`) of the rotary pump head of an Olson heart–lung pump on the fluid flow rate `Liters_minute`. The rpm's are replicated at 50, 75, 100, 125, and 150 levels with respective frequencies 5, 3, 5, 2, and 5. The fluid flow rate is measured in liters per minute.

```
> data(olson)
> par(mfrow=c(2,2))
```

```
> plot(olson$rpm,olson$Liters_minute,xlim=c(25,175),xlab="RPM",
+ ylab="Flow Rate",main="Scatter Plot")
> boxplot(Liters_minute~rpm,data=olson,main="Box Plots")
> aggregate(olson$Liters_minute,by=list(olson$rpm),mean)
  Group.1      x
1      50 1.1352
2      75 1.7220
3     100 2.3268
4     125 2.9250
5     150 3.5292
> olson_crd <- aov(Liters_minute ~ as.factor(rpm), data=olson)
> olson_crd
Call:
   aov(formula = Liters_minute ~ as.factor(rpm), data = olson)
Terms:
                as.factor(rpm) Residuals
Sum of Squares        16.12551   0.02084
Deg. of Freedom              4        15
Residual standard error: 0.03727412
Estimated effects may be unbalanced
> summary(olson_crd)
               Df Sum Sq Mean Sq F value Pr(>F)
as.factor(rpm)  4 16.126   4.031    2902 <2e-16 ***
Residuals      15  0.021   0.001
---
Signif. codes:  0 '***' 0.001 '**' 0.01 '*' 0.05 '.' 0.1 ' ' 1
> confint(olson_crd)
                      2.5 %    97.5 %
(Intercept)       1.0996698 1.1707302
as.factor(rpm)75  0.5287795 0.6448205
as.factor(rpm)100 1.1413527 1.2418473
as.factor(rpm)125 1.7233291 1.8562709
as.factor(rpm)150 2.3437527 2.4442473
> anovaPlot(olson_crd,main="Box-Hunter-Hunter ANOVA Plot")
> granova.1w(olson$Liters_minute,group=olson$rpm,
+ main="Graphical ANOVA")
$grandsum
    Grandmean        df.bet        df.with          MS.bet          MS.with
     F.stat       F.prob SS.bet/SS.tot
        2.30         4.00          15.00            4.03             0.00
        2901.61         0.00            1.00
$stats
    Size Contrast Coef Wt'd Mean Mean Trim'd Mean Var. St. Dev.
50     5         -1.16      1.42 1.14        1.13 0.00       0.01
75     3         -0.58      1.29 1.72        1.72 0.00       0.03
100    5          0.03      2.91 2.33        2.33 0.00       0.02
125    2          0.63      1.46 2.92        2.92 0.01       0.08
150    5          1.23      4.41 3.53        3.52 0.00       0.05
```

The scatter plot clearly indicates, Figure 13.2, that as the RPM is increasing, there is an increase in the flow rate too. This is further confirmed by the box plot which shows that the average, actually median, levels are different, and since there is no overlap of the quantiles, the difference is also significant. The ANOVA table may be visualized as displayed by the output of `granova.1w`, and the Box-Hunter-Hunter ANOVA plot is left to the reader for interpretation.

Since the p-value, in `Pr(>F)`, is significantly zero, we reject the hypothesis that the treatment effects are equal. The 95% confidence intervals for the four treatments do not contain 0 and hence we can conclude that each of the treatments has a non-zero `rpm` because of it. □

Validation of the model assumptions is considered next.

13.3.4 Validation of Model Assumptions

The CRD model is a linear regression model, as in 12.1. The assumptions for the model are the same as detailed in Section 12.2, that is, linearity, independent, and normality assumptions. For the model under consideration, the plots, as in Section 12.2.6, give us all that is required. The demonstration is carried out for Example 13.3.3.

Example 13.3.5. The Tensile Strength Experiment. Contd. The following plots are obtained for testing the model adequacy of the CRD model for the tensile strength experiment:

- Plot of Residuals vs Predictor Variable
- Plot of Absolute Residual Values vs Predictor Variable
- Normal Q-Q Plot
- Plot of Residuals vs Fitted Values
- Sequence Plot of the Residuals
- Box Plot of the Residuals

The next program gives the required plots.

```
> tensile_resid <- residuals(tensile_aov)
> pdf("Tensile_Model_Assumptions.pdf")
> par(mfrow=c(2,3))
> plot(tensile$CWP,tensile_resid,main="Plot of
+ Residuals Vs Predictor Variable",ylab="Residuals",
+ xlab="Predictor Variable")
> plot(tensile$CWP,abs(tensile_resid),main="Plot of
+ Absolute Residual Values \n Vs Predictor Variable",
+ ylab="Absolute Residuals", xlab="Predictor Variable")
> qqnorm(residuals(tensile_aov))
> qqline(residuals(tensile_aov))
> plot(tensile_aov$fitted.values,tensile_resid, main="Plot of
+ Residuals Vs Fitted Values",ylab="Residuals", xlab="Fitted
+ Values")
> plot.ts(tensile_resid, main="Sequence Plot of the Residuals")
> boxplot(tensile_resid,main="Box Plot of the Residuals")
> dev.off()
null device
          1
```

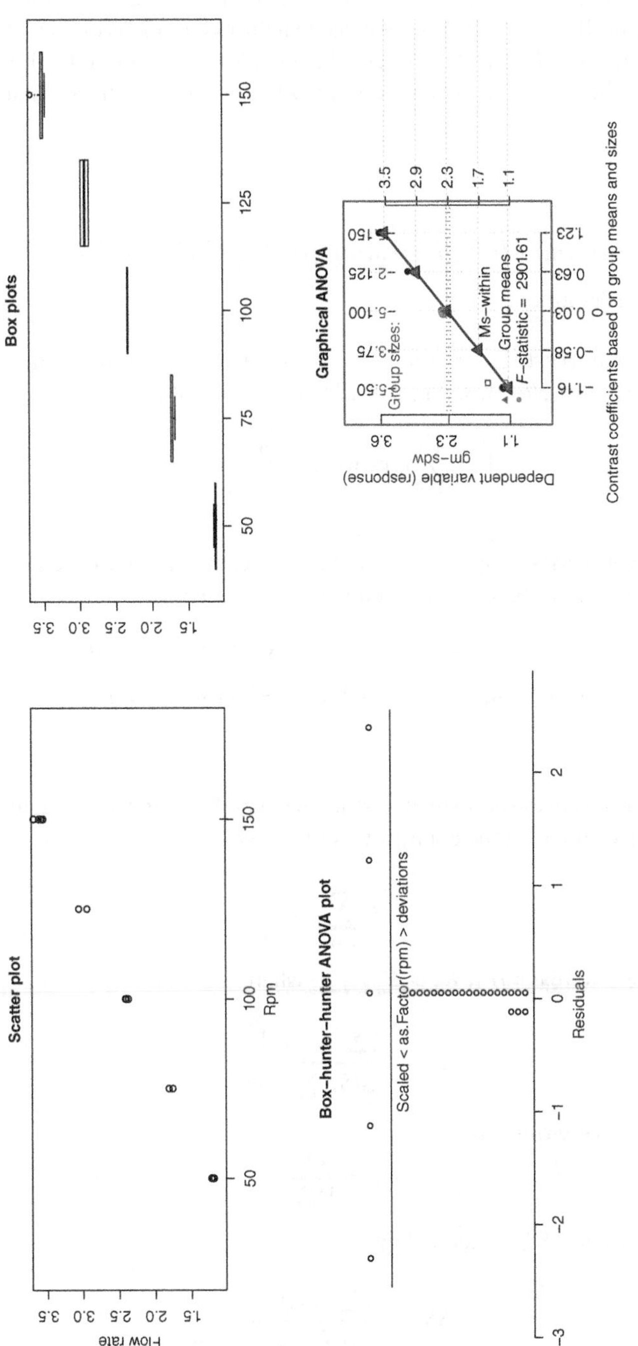

Figure 13.2 Box Plots for the Olson Data

The randomness in the plots, see Figure 13.3, "Plot of Residuals vs Predictor Variable", "Plot of Absolute Residual Values vs Predictor Variable", "Plot of Residuals vs Fitted Values", and "Sequence Plot of the Residuals" clearly indicate that the assumptions of linearity and independence are appropriate for the tensile dataset. The box plot "Box Plot of the Residuals" shows that there are no outliers, and finally the "Normal Q-Q Plot" justifies the normality assumption for the error term.

□

13.3.5 Contrasts and Multiple Testing for the CRD Model

Let us begin with a definition.

Definition 13.3.1 Contrast. *Let $\tau_i, i = 1, \cdots, v$, denote the effects of v treatments. A linear combination of treatment effects, say Γ, is said to be a* contrast *if*

$$\Gamma = \sum_{i=1}^{v} c_i \tau_i, \text{ where } \sum_{i=1}^{v} c_i = 0. \tag{13.8}$$

Example 13.3.6. Contrasts. Suppose that we have v treatments whose effects are denoted by $\tau_i, i = 1, \cdots, v$. The following are then examples of contrasts:

$$\tau_1 - \tau_2, c_1 = 1, c_2 = -1, c_3 = \cdots = c_v = 0,$$
$$\text{In general, } \tau_i - \tau_j, c_i = 1, c_j = -1, c_k = 0, k \neq i, j.$$

□

The statistical interest is in the problem of testing the hypothesis $H : \Gamma = 0$ against the alternative $K : \Gamma \neq 0$. An estimate of the contrast Γ is given by

$$\hat{\Gamma} = \sum_{i=1}^{v} c_i y_{i.}.$$

The test procedure is to reject H if $F_0 > F_{\alpha,1,N-v}$, where

$$F_0 = \frac{\left(\sum_{i=1}^{v} c_i y_{i.}\right)^2}{vMS_E \sum_{i=1}^{v} c_i^2}.$$

The test statistic F_0 is rewritten as

$$F_0 = \frac{MS_C}{MS_E},$$

where $MS_C = SS_C/1$ and SS_C is defined by

$$SS_C = \frac{\left(\sum_{i=1}^{r} c_i y_{i.}\right)^2}{v \sum_{i=1}^{r} c_i^2}.$$

Some contrasts are considered in the next example.

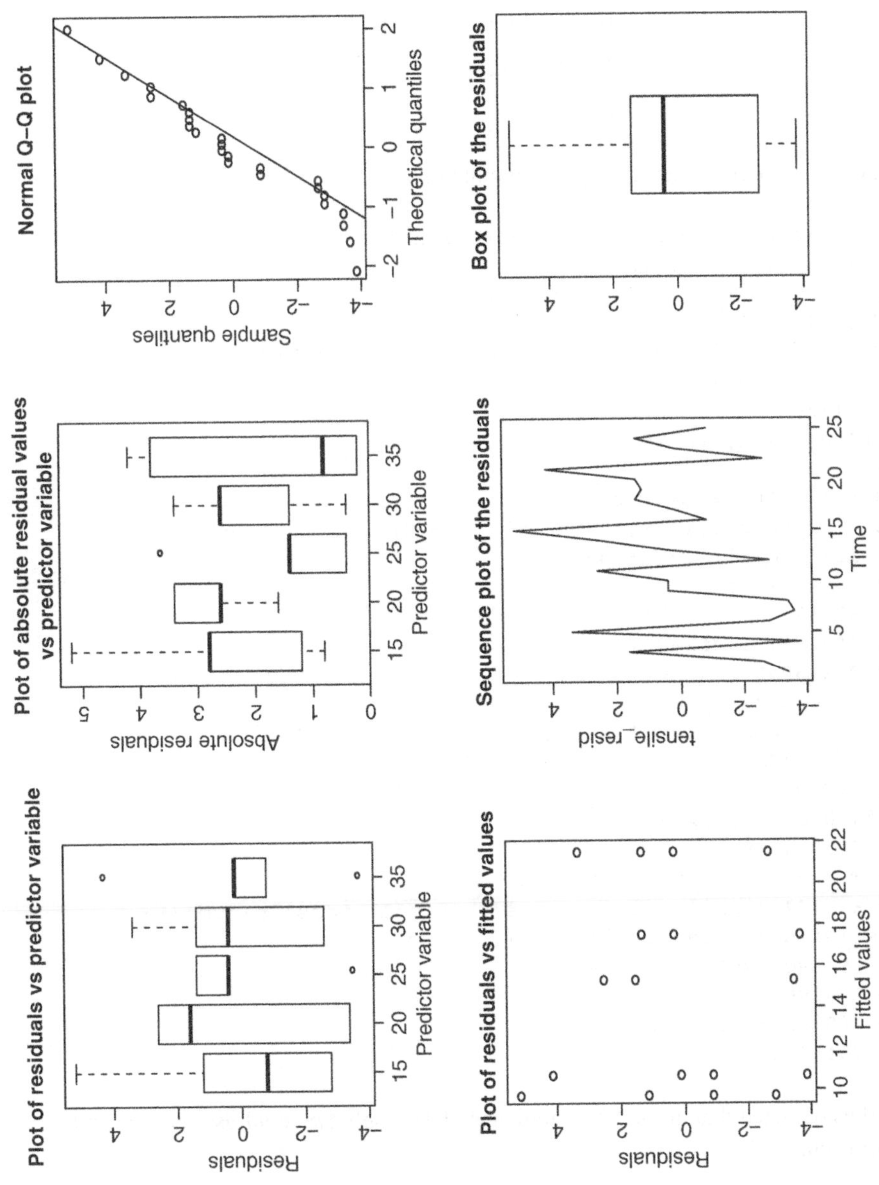

Figure 13.3 Model Adequacy Plots for the Tensile Strength Experiment

Example 13.3.7. Contrast for the Tensile Strength Experiment. The four contrasts considered are given in the following:

$$H^{(1)} : \tau_4 = \tau_5$$
$$H^{(2)} : \tau_1 + \tau_3 = \tau_4 + \tau_5$$
$$H^{(3)} : \tau_1 = \tau_3$$
$$H^{(4)} : 4\tau_2 = \tau_1 + \tau_3 + \tau_4 + \tau_5$$

The next program gives the necessary computations.

```
> tensileisum <- aggregate(tensile$Tensile_Strength,by=
+ list(tensile$CWP),FUN=sum)$x
> mse <- summary(tensile_aov)[[1]][2,3]
> # H : t4 = t5
> ssc <- ((tensileisum[4]-tensileisum[5])^2)/(5*2)
> (f0 <- ssc/mse)
[1] 36.17866
> 1-pf(f0,df1=1,df2=20)
[1] 7.011202e-06
> # H : t1 + t3 = t4 + t5
> ssc <- ((tensileisum[1]+tensileisum[3]-tensileisum[4]-
+ tensileisum[5])^2)/(5*4)
> (f0 <- ssc/mse)
[1] 3.877171
> 1-pf(f0,df1=1,df2=20)
[1] 0.06295952
> # H : t1 = t3
> ssc <- ((tensileisum[1]-tensileisum[3])^2)/(5*2)
> (f0 <- ssc/mse)
[1] 18.87097
> 1-pf(f0,df1=1,df2=20)
[1] 0.0003147387
> # H : 4t2 = t1 + t3 + t4 + t5
> ssc <- ((4*tensileisum[2]-tensileisum[1]-tensileisum[3]-
+ tensileisum[4]-tensileisum[5])^2)/(5*20)
> (f0 <- ssc/mse)
[1] 0.1004963
> 1-pf(f0,df1=1,df2=20)
[1] 0.7545203
```

It may thus be noted that at the 5% significance level, only two contrasts $\tau_4 - \tau_5$ and $\tau_1 - \tau_3$ are significant. □

The problem of multiple testing was dealt with in Section 7.15. Here, the results are specialized to the CRD model.

If the hypothesis H is rejected, we know that at least two treatment levels have significantly different effects. This calls for techniques which will help the reader to identify which treatments are significantly different. The details of the multiple comparison problem may be found in Miller (1981), Hsu (1996), and Bretz, et al. (2011).

For the multiple testing problem we are familiar with the Bonferroni's method and the Holm's method. Tukey's *honest significant differences*, HSD, and Dunnett's procedures are detailed next.

In a CRD model with r treatment levels, the interest is in comparison of the equality for each possible combination of the levels, that is, there are $\binom{r}{2}$ possible hypotheses. Tukey's procedure uses the distribution of the *Studentized range statistic*:

$$q = \frac{\bar{y}_{\max} - \bar{y}_{\min}}{\sqrt{MS_E/v}}, \tag{13.9}$$

where $\bar{y}_{\max}$ and $\bar{y}_{\min}$ are the largest and smallest sample means out of the v possible means. Tukey's HSD procedure declares two means to be significantly different if the absolute value of their differences exceeds

$$T_\alpha = q_\alpha(v,f)\sqrt{MS_E/n},$$

where $q_\alpha(v,f)$ is the upper α percentage point of q and f is the number of degrees of freedom associated with the MS_E. Thus, a $100(1-\alpha)$ % confidence interval for all possible pairs of means is given by

$$\bar{y}_{i.} - \bar{y}_{j.} - q_\alpha(v,f)\sqrt{MS_E/r} \le \tau_i - \tau_j \le \bar{y}_{i.} - \bar{y}_{j.} + q_\alpha(v,f)\sqrt{MS_E/r}, i \ne j.$$

Suppose that one of the v treatment levels is a *control* level and comparisons are required with respect to this control level. The Dunnett's procedure offers a solution in this case. The hypotheses are then $H_i : \tau_i = \tau_v, i = 1, \cdots, v-1$, which then need to be tested against the set of hypotheses $K_i : \tau_i \ne \tau_v, i = 1, \cdots, v-1$. The Dunnett's procedure begins with computation of the differences:

$$|\bar{y}_{i.} - \bar{y}_{a.}|, i = 1, \cdots, v-1.$$

The test procedure is to reject the hypothesis H_i at size α if

$$|\bar{y}_{i.} - \bar{y}_{a.}| > d_\alpha(v-1,f)\sqrt{MS_E/r},$$

where $d_\alpha(v-1,f)$ corresponds to Dunnett's distribution.

The four methods of multiple testing are next illustrated for the tensile strength experiment.

Example 13.3.8. Multiple Testing for the Tensile Strength Experiment. The R package `multcomp` is useful for multiple testing. For more details about the package, refer to Bretz, et al. (2011). R codes are in action now.

```
> library(multcomp)
> tensile.mc <- glht(tensile_aov, linfct = mcp(CWP="Dunnett"),
+ alternative="two.sided")
> summary(tensile.mc)
  Simultaneous Tests for General Linear Hypotheses
Multiple Comparisons of Means: Dunnett Contrasts
Fit: aov(formula = Tensile_Strength ~ CWP, data = tensile)
```

```
Linear Hypotheses:
             Estimate Std. Error t value Pr(>|t|)
20 - 15 == 0    5.600      1.796   3.119  0.01867 *
25 - 15 == 0    7.800      1.796   4.344  0.00115 **
30 - 15 == 0   11.800      1.796   6.572  < 0.001 ***
35 - 15 == 0    1.000      1.796   0.557  0.94693
---
Signif. codes:  0 '***' 0.001 '**' 0.01 '*' 0.05 '.' 0.1 ' ' 1
(Adjusted p values reported -- single-step method)
> summary(tensile.mc,test=adjusted(type="bonferroni"))
  Simultaneous Tests for General Linear Hypotheses
Multiple Comparisons of Means: Dunnett Contrasts
Fit: aov(formula = Tensile_Strength ~ CWP, data = tensile)
Linear Hypotheses:
             Estimate Std. Error t value Pr(>|t|)
20 - 15 == 0    5.600      1.796   3.119  0.02164 *
25 - 15 == 0    7.800      1.796   4.344  0.00126 **
30 - 15 == 0   11.800      1.796   6.572 8.43e-06 ***
35 - 15 == 0    1.000      1.796   0.557  1.00000
---
Signif. codes:  0 '***' 0.001 '**' 0.01 '*' 0.05 '.' 0.1 ' ' 1
(Adjusted p values reported -- bonferroni method)
> summary(tensile.mc,test=adjusted(type="holm"))
  Simultaneous Tests for General Linear Hypotheses
Multiple Comparisons of Means: Dunnett Contrasts
Fit: aov(formula = Tensile_Strength ~ CWP, data = tensile)
Linear Hypotheses:
             Estimate Std. Error t value Pr(>|t|)
20 - 15 == 0    5.600      1.796   3.119 0.010818 *
25 - 15 == 0    7.800      1.796   4.344 0.000944 ***
30 - 15 == 0   11.800      1.796   6.572 8.43e-06 ***
35 - 15 == 0    1.000      1.796   0.557 0.583753
---
Signif. codes:  0 '***' 0.001 '**' 0.01 '*' 0.05 '.' 0.1 ' ' 1
(Adjusted p values reported -- holm method)
> TukeyHSD(tensile_aov)
  Tukey multiple comparisons of means
    95% family-wise confidence level
Fit: aov(formula = Tensile_Strength ~ CWP, data = tensile)
$Cotton_Weight_Percentage
       diff         lwr        upr     p adj
20-15   5.6   0.2270417 10.9729583 0.0385024
25-15   7.8   2.4270417 13.1729583 0.0025948
30-15  11.8   6.4270417 17.1729583 0.0000190
35-15   1.0  -4.3729583  6.3729583 0.9797709
25-20   2.2  -3.1729583  7.5729583 0.7372438
30-20   6.2   0.8270417 11.5729583 0.0188936
35-20  -4.6  -9.9729583  0.7729583 0.1162970
30-25   4.0  -1.3729583  9.3729583 0.2101089
35-25  -6.8 -12.1729583 -1.4270417 0.0090646
35-30 -10.8 -16.1729583 -5.4270417 0.0000624
```

The `glht` function represents the *General Linear Hypotheses* according to the description in the `multcomp` package. In Dunnett, Bonferroni, and Holm's multiple testing procedures, the treatment level `15` is taken as a base for the purposes of comparison. The difference between treatment levels is shown through the *p*-values. The interpretation of the results is along similar lines as earlier and obvious too. □

The tensile strength experiment is an example of a balanced design. Fortunately, there is a slight change of r_i, instead of the r, but all the results continue to hold. In R there are no changes in the structure of the commands and functionality. Thus, the user can easily solve the multiple testing problem for the Olson dataset, which is an example of an unbalanced design.

Example 13.3.9. The Olson Heart Lung Dataset. Contd. For the sake of brevity, only the R codes are given here.

```
olson.mc <- glht(olson_crd, linfct = mcp(rpmf="Dunnett"),
alternative="two.sided")
summary(olson.mc)
summary(olson.mc,test=adjusted(type="bonferroni"))
summary(olson.mc,test=adjusted(type="holm"))
TukeyHSD(olson_crd)
```

The reader should complete the exercise of running the program and analyze the results. □

?sample, ?aov, ?granova.1w, ?aggregate, ?residuals, ?qqnorm, ?qqline, ?glht

13.4 Block Designs

In the CRD model, the source of variation arises due to the different treatment levels. It is also assumed that the nuisance factor is completely unknown and uncontrollable. In the case of the nuisance factor being known and controllable, the experiment can be designed to account for such a source of error through *blocking*.

13.4.1 *Randomization and Analysis of Balanced Block Designs*

In a block model, a comparison needs to be carried out for the different treatment levels and blocks. In a balanced block design, each block will have one observation per treatment level. It is to be noted that randomization is only carried out on the treatments within a block. The *effects model* for a balanced block design model is specified by

$$Y_{ij} = \mu + \tau_i + \beta_j + \epsilon_{ij}, i = 1, \cdots, v, j = 1, \cdots, b, \tag{13.10}$$

where μ is the overall mean, τ_i is the effect of the i-th treatment, and β_j is the effect of the j-th block. Also, define $N = v \times b$. As previously we assume that the error term ϵ_{ij} follows a Gaussian distribution $N(0, \sigma^2)$.

The randomization for the above design 13.10 is illustrated next.

Example 13.4.1. Randomization for a Balanced Block Design. Suppose that we have $b = 4$ blocks and $v = 5$ treatment levels. Thus, we need $b \times v = 20$ experimental units. The problem is that of allocating the units in such a way that meets the requirements of the model. The next R program achieves the randomization.

```
> b <- 4; v <- 5
> eunits <- 1:b*v
> b_alloc <- rep(1:b,each=v)
> tlevel_alloc <- NULL
> for(i in 1:b) tlevel_alloc[((i-1)*v+1):(i*v)] <-
+ sample(1:v,rep=FALSE)
> cbind(sample(1:(b*v),rep=FALSE),b_alloc,tlevel_alloc)
         b_alloc tlevel_alloc
 [1,] 13       1            2
 [2,] 18       1            4
 [3,]  9       1            3
 [4,]  5       1            1
 [5,] 15       1            5
 [6,]  3       2            2

[19,]  7       4            4
[20,] 12       4            2
```

Note the slight programming difference in randomization for block designs with that in a CRD model.

□

Towards inference for the randomized block design, define the following quantities:

$$y_{i.} = \sum_{j=1}^{b} y_{ij}, \quad \bar{y}_{i.} = \frac{y_{i.}}{b}, i = 1, \cdots, v,$$

$$y_{.j} = \sum_{i=1}^{v} y_{ij}, \quad \bar{y}_{.j} = \frac{y_{.j}}{v}, j = 1, \cdots, b,$$

$$y_{..} = \sum_{i=1}^{v}\sum_{j=1}^{b} y_{ij}, \quad \bar{y}_{..} = \frac{y_{..}}{bv}.$$

The decomposition of the total sum of squares SS_T is given below:

$$SS_T = SS_{Tr} + SS_{blocks} + SS_E, \tag{13.11}$$

where

$$SS_T = \sum_{i=1}^{v}\sum_{j=1}^{b} (y_{ij} - \bar{y}_{..})^2,$$

$$SS_{Tr} = b\sum_{i=1}^{v} (\bar{y}_{i.} - \bar{y}_{..})^2,$$

Table 13.3 ANOVA for the Randomized Balanced Block Model

Source of Variation	Sum of Squares	Degrees of Freedom	Mean Square	F-Statistic
Between Treatments	SS_{Tr}	$v-1$	MS_{Tr}	MS_{Tr}/MS_E
Between Blocks	SS_{blocks}	$b-1$	MS_{blocks}	MS_{blocks}/MS_E
Error	SS_E	$(v-1)(b-1)$	MS_E	
Total	SS_T	$N-1$		

$$SS_{blocks} = v\sum_{j=1}^{b}(\bar{y}_{.j}-\bar{y}_{..})^2,$$

$$SS_E = \sum_{i=1}^{v}\sum_{j=1}^{b}(y_{ij}-\bar{y}_{i.}-\bar{y}_{.j}+\bar{y}_{..})^2.$$

Observe that SS_T has $N-1$ degrees of freedom, SS_{Tr} has $v-1$ df, SS_{blocks} has $b-1$ df, and finally, SS_E has $(v-1)(b-1)$ df. Thus, the ANOVA table is then set up as given in Table 13.3. The balanced block design will be illustrated now.

Example 13.4.2. Strength Dataset of a Girder Experiment. Consider the girder experiment, which has 9 blocks and 4 treatments. The aim of the experiment is to find if the shear strength depends on the blocks, varying from `S1.1` to `S4.2`, or on the method of preparation: `Aarau`, `Karisruhe`, `Lehigh`, and `Cardiff`. A bit of data preparation is needed from the csv file, and post the preparation, the ANOVA table is obtained using the `aov` function in R. Recollect the analysis of this dataset in Example 4.5.3 of Section 4.5 through the median polish algorithm. The data arrangement is slightly different in the block design model.

```
> data(girder)
> names(girder)[2:5] <- c("Aar","Kar","Leh","Car")
> gf <- as.character(rep(girder$Girder,each=4))
> mf <- as.character(rep(colnames(girder)[2:5],9))
> ss <- NULL # Shear Strength
> for(i in 1:nrow(girder)) ss <- c(ss, as.numeric(girder[i,2:5]))
> girdernew <- data.frame(mf, gf, ss)
> ssaov <- aov(ss~gf + mf, data=girdernew)
> summary(ssaov)
            Df Sum Sq Mean Sq F value  Pr(>F)
gf           8 0.0895  0.0112   1.619   0.172
mf           3 1.5138  0.5046  73.027 3.3e-12 ***
Residuals   24 0.1658  0.0069
---
Signif. codes:  0 '***' 0.001 '**' 0.01 '*' 0.05 '.' 0.1 ' ' 1
> model.matrix(ssaov)
   (Intercept) gfS1.2  mfCar mfKar mfLeh
1            1      0      0     0     0
2            1      0      0     1     0
```

```
3        1    0    0    0    1
4        1    0    1    0    0
5        1    0    0    0    0
6        1    0    0    1    0
7        1    0    0    0    1
8        1    0    1    0    0

33       1    0    0    0    0
34       1    0    0    1    0
35       1    0    0    0    1
36       1    0    1    0    0
```

After reading the data, the names of the variables have been curtailed to ensure the output of `model.matrix` displays all the variables in a single line. The codes `rep(girder$Girder,each=4)` and `rep(colnames(girder)[2:5],9)` with `as.character` ensures that the block design is clearly told that these two inputs are factors. The vector `ss` now contains the shear strength for each combination of the method of preparation and the girder. Finally, `aov(ss gf + mf, data=girdernew)` sets up the required block design in R. The interpretation is as follows. The large p-value of `0.172` with `girderf` suggests that the blocks have insignificant effect on the output. However, the method of preparation is found to have significant effects on the strength of the material.

□

As seen in Models 13.2, 13.10, etc., these linear models need to be investigated for model assumptions and other regression diagnostics too. *Can it be said without loss of generality that leverages are not a concern in DOE since all the covariate values are fixed*? Now, we consider an example from Montgomery (2005), wherein we will investigate issues related to model adequacy.

Example 13.4.3. Hardness Example. Four types of tip are used which form the blocks in this experiment. The variable of interest is the hardness which further depends on the type of metal coupon. For each type of tip, the hardness is observed for four different types of metal coupon. In the next R segment, an ANOVA is first obtained to check if the tip type and coupon type effect the hardness of the coupon. The assumption of normality for the model error is validated through the "Q-Q" plot. Diagnostic measures, leverage points, etc., are obtained using the functions as seen earlier for the linear regression model and the CRD model, Sections 12.5 and 13.3.

```
> data(hardness)
> hardness$Tip_Type <- as.factor(hardness$Tip_Type)
> hardness$Test_Coupon <- as.factor(hardness$Test_Coupon)
> hardness_aov <- aov(Hardness~Tip_Type+Test_Coupon,data=hardness)
> summary(hardness_aov)
            Df Sum Sq Mean Sq F value   Pr(>F)
Tip_Type     3  0.385 0.12833   14.44 0.000871 ***
Test_Coupon  3  0.825 0.27500   30.94 4.52e-05 ***
Residuals    9  0.080 0.00889
---
```

```
Signif. codes:  0 '***' 0.001 '**' 0.01 '*' 0.05 '.' 0.1 ' ' 1
> p <- 7
> diagnostics_matrix <- matrix(nrow=nrow(hardness),ncol=8)
> colnames(diagnostics_matrix) <- c("Obs No.","y","Pred y",
+ "Residual","Leverage","S.Residual","Cooks.Dist","Outlier")
> diagnostics_matrix[,1] <- 1:nrow(hardness)
> diagnostics_matrix[,2] <- hardness$Hardness
> diagnostics_matrix[,3] <- hardness_aov$fitted.values
> diagnostics_matrix[,4] <- round(hardness_aov$residuals,3)
> diagnostics_matrix[,5] <- influence(hardness_aov)$hat
> diagnostics_matrix[,6] <- round(rstandard(hardness_aov),3)
> diagnostics_matrix[,7] <- round(cooks.distance(hardness_aov),3)
> diagnostics_matrix[,8] <- diagnostics_matrix[,6]*sqrt((16-p-1)/
+ (16-p-diagnostics_matrix[,6]^2))
> diagnostics_matrix
      Obs No.    y  Cooks.Dist  Outlier
 [1,]       1  9.3       0.056   -0.686
 [2,]       2  9.4       0.014    0.336
 [3,]       3  9.6       0.125   -1.069
 [4,]       4 10.0       0.222    1.512

[15,]      15 10.0       0.014    0.336
[16,]      16 10.2       0.000    0.000
> par(mfrow=c(2,3)); plot(hardness_aov,which=1:6)
+ # Output suppressed
```

The R `lm` complementary functions `influence`, `rstandard`, and `cooks.distance` have again been used for the diagnostics of the fitted `hardness_aov` object. The "Q-Q" plot, see Figure 13.4, shows that the normality assumption is appropriate for the current dataset. Since the Cooks distance does not exceed 1 for any of the observations, we do not have any influential observation. □

13.4.2 Incomplete Block Designs

The constraints of the real world may not allow each block to have an experimental unit for every treatment level. The restriction may force allocation of only $k < v$ units within each block. Such models are called *incomplete block designs*. If in an incomplete block design, any two treatments pair appearing together, across the blocks, occurring an equal number of times, the designs are then called *balanced incomplete block designs*, abbreviated as BIBD. It may be seen that a BIBD may be constructed in $\binom{v}{k}$ different ways.

The setup is now recollected again. We have v treatments, b distinct blocks, k is the number of units appearing in a block, and $N = k \times b = r \times v$ is the total number of observations, where r is the number of times a treatment appears in the design. Then, the number of times each pair of treatments appears in the same block is given by

$$\lambda = \frac{r(k-1)}{v-1}. \tag{13.12}$$

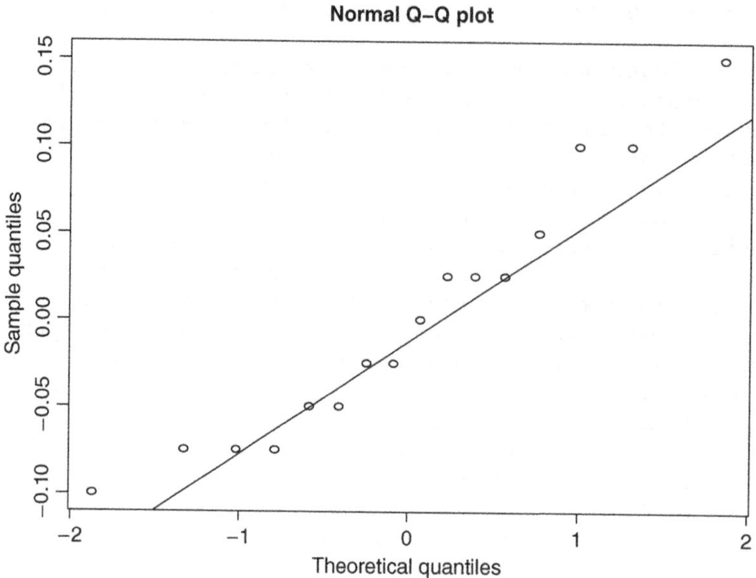

Figure 13.4 A qq-Plot for the Hardness Data

The statistical model for BIBD is given by

$$Y_{ij} = \mu + \tau_i + \beta_j + \epsilon_{ij}, i = 1, 2, \cdots, v, j = 1, 2, \cdots, b, \tag{13.13}$$

where Y_{ij} is the ith observation in the jth block, μ is the overall mean, τ_i is the effect of the ith treatment, and β_j is the effect of the jth block. The error term ϵ_{ij} is assumed to follow $N(0, \sigma^2)$. The total variability needs to be handled in a slightly different manner. Define

$$Q_i = y_{i.} - \frac{1}{k}\sum_{j=1}^{b} n_{ij} y_{.j}, i = 1, \cdots, v, \tag{13.14}$$

where

$$n_{ij} = \begin{cases} 1, & \text{if treatment } i \text{ appears in block } j, \\ 0, & \text{otherwise.} \end{cases}$$

Using the Q_i's, the *adjusted treatment sum of squares* is defined by

$$SS_{(adj)Tr} = \frac{k\sum_{i=1}^{v} Q_i^2}{\lambda v}.$$

Thus, the total variability is partitioned by

$$SS_T = SS_{(adj)Tr} + SS_{blocks} + SS_E, \tag{13.15}$$

where

$$SS_{blocks} = \frac{1}{k}\sum_{j=1}^{b} y_{.j}^2 - \frac{y_{..}^2}{N},$$

Table 13.4 ANOVA for the BIBD Model

Source of Variation	Sum of Squares	Degrees of Freedom	Mean Square	F-Statistic
Between Treatments	$SS_{(adj)Tr}$	$v-1$	MS_{Tr}	$\frac{MS_{Tr}}{MS_E}$
Between Blocks	SS_{blocks}	$b-1$	MS_{blocks}	$\frac{MS_{blocks}}{MS_E}$
Error	SS_E	$N-v-b+1$	MS_E	
Total	SS_T	$N-1$		

$$SS_T = \sum_{j=1}^{b}\sum_{i=1}^{n_{ij}} y_{ij}^2 - \frac{y_{..}^2}{N},$$

$$SS_E = SS_T - SS_{(adj)Tr} - SS_{blocks}.$$

The ANOVA table for BIBD model is given in Table 13.4.

The function `BIB.test` from the `agricolae` package is useful to fit a BIBD model.

Example 13.4.4. Chemical Reaction Experiment. For a chemical reaction experiment, the blocks arise due to the `Batch` number, `Catalyst` of different types from the treatments, and the reaction time is the output. Due to a restriction, all the catalysts cannot be analysed within each batch and hence we need to look at the BIBD model. Using the `BIB.test` function from the `agricolae` package, a summary of the ANOVA model related to the BIBD model is obtained.

```
> library(agricolae)
> data(reaction)
> attach(reaction)
> BIB.test(block=Batch,trt=Catalyst,y=Reaction)
ANALYSIS BIB:  Reaction
Class level information
Block:  1 2 3 4
Trt  :  1 2 3 4
Number of observations:  16
Analysis of Variance Table
Response: Reaction
            Df Sum Sq Mean Sq F value   Pr(>F)
block.unadj  3  55.00 18.3333  28.205 0.001468 **
trt.adj      3  22.75  7.5833  11.667 0.010739 *
Residuals    5   3.25  0.6500
---
Signif. codes:  0 '***' 0.001 '**' 0.01 '*' 0.05 '.' 0.1 ' ' 1
coefficient of variation: 1.1 %
Reaction Means: 72.5
```

The computed ANOVA table shows that both the catalyst and the batch have a significant effect on the reaction of the units. □

Two very important variations of the BIBD will be considered in the rest of the section.

13.4.3 Latin Square Design

In each of the Examples 13.4.1 to 13.4.4, and the blocking models 13.2 and 13.10, we had a single source of known and controllable source of variation and we use the *blocking principle* to overcome this. Suppose now that there are two ways or sources of the variation which may be controlled through blocking! Consider the following example from Montgomery (2001), page 144.

Example 13.4.5. Rocket Propellant Example. Five different formulations of a rocket propellant x_1 may be used in an aircrew escape system at the observed burning rate Y. Here, each of the formulations is prepared by mixing from a batch of raw materials x_2, which can support only five formulations required for the purpose of testing. However, each of the formulations is prepared by different operators x_3, who in turn may have substantial differences in their skills and experience. Thus, the source of variation for this experiment arises from the type of raw material and skill and experience of the operators. Model 13.10 thus needs to be extended so that the burning rate can be modeled for the different formulations at each level of raw material and operator. □

In the above example, we need to ensure that each type of formulation occurs exactly once for the type of raw material and also that each formulation is prepared exactly once by each of the five operators. This type of problem is handled by the *Latin Square Design*, abbreviated as *LSD*, and we use the Latin letters to represent the type of formulations. A simple technique is to set up an LSD for say p formulations, set up in the first row of the design as 1, 2, …, p, the second row as 2, 3, …, k,1, the third row as 3, 4, …, p, 2, 1, and so forth until the last row as p, $p-1$, …, 3, 2, 1. There are many other techniques available for creating an LSD, such as Wichmann-Hill, Marsaglia-Multicarry, Mersenne-Twister, Super-Duper, etc. A couple of illustrations are given next using the `design.lsd` function from the `agricolae` package.

Example 13.4.6. Setting up LSDs. A simple 3-treatment LSD is first set up, and then a 5-treatment LSD is produced. First, we show how the entire LSD setup looks for two examples, and then follow it up with the simple rectangular displays of LSD.

```
> design.lsd(letters[1:3],kinds="super-duper")
  plots row col letters[1:3]
1     1   1   1            a
2     2   1   2            b
3     3   1   3            c
4     4   2   1            c
5     5   2   2            a
6     6   2   3            b
7     7   3   1            b
8     8   3   2            c
9     9   3   3            a
> design.lsd(letters[1:3],kinds="super-duper")
  plots row col letters[1:3]
1     1   1   1            a
2     2   1   2            b
3     3   1   3            c
```

```
4       4   2   1           b
5       5   2   2           c
6       6   2   3           a
7       7   3   1           c
8       8   3   2           a
9       9   3   3           b
> matrix(design.lsd(LETTERS[1:3])[,4],nrow=3)
     [,1] [,2] [,3]
[1,] "A"  "C"  "B"
[2,] "B"  "A"  "C"
[3,] "C"  "B"  "A"
> Formulations <- paste("F",1:5,sep="")
> matrix(design.lsd(Formulations,kinds="Marsaglia-Multicarry")
+ [,4],nrow=5)
     [,1] [,2] [,3] [,4] [,5]
[1,] "F1" "F5" "F2" "F3" "F4"
[2,] "F2" "F1" "F3" "F4" "F5"
[3,] "F3" "F2" "F4" "F5" "F1"
[4,] "F4" "F3" "F5" "F1" "F2"
[5,] "F5" "F4" "F1" "F2" "F3"
```

Thus, we have used the `design.lsd` function to set up LSDs. □

The LSD model and its statistical analyses is now detailed. The LSD statistical model is specified by

$$Y_{ijk} = \mu + \tau_i + \beta_j + \gamma_k + \epsilon_{ijk}, i, j, k = 1, \cdots, p. \tag{13.16}$$

Here, τ_i will continue to represent the effect of the i-th treatment (or formulation), β_j for the row (block) effect (raw material), and γ_k for the column (block) effect (operator). The errors are assumed to follow normal distribution $N(0, \sigma^2$. The ANOVA decomposition of the *sum of squares* for the LSD model 13.16 will be as follows:

$$SS_T = SS_{Row} + SS_{Column} + SS_{Tr} + SS_E, \tag{13.17}$$

where

$$SS_T = \sum_{i=1}^{p}\sum_{j=1}^{p}\sum_{k=1}^{p} y_{ijk}^2 - \frac{y_{...}^2}{p^2},$$

$$SS_{Row} = \frac{1}{p}\sum_{j=1}^{p} y_{.j.}^2 - \frac{y_{...}^2}{p^2},$$

$$SS_{Column} = \frac{1}{p}\sum_{k=1}^{p} y_{..k}^2 - \frac{y_{...}^2}{p^2},$$

$$SS_{Tr} = \frac{1}{p}\sum_{i=1}^{p} y_{i..}^2 - \frac{y_{...}^2}{p^2}, \text{ and}$$

$$SS_E = SS_T - SS_{Treatment} - SS_{Row} - SS_{Column}.$$

Table 13.5 ANOVA for the LSD Model

Source of Variation	Sum of Squares	Degrees of Freedom	Mean Square	F-Statistic
Between Treatments	SS_{Tr}	$p-1$	MS_{Tr}	$\frac{MS_{Tr}}{MS_E}$
Between Rows	SS_{Row}	$p-1$	MS_{Row}	$\frac{MS_{Row}}{MS_E}$
Between Columns	SS_{Column}	$p-1$	MS_{Column}	$\frac{MS_{Column}}{MS_E}$
Error	SS_E	$(p-1)(p-2)$	MS_E	
Total	SS_T	p^2-1		

The ANOVA table for the LSD is given in Table 13.5. For Example 13.4.5, the R method is illustrated next.

Example 13.4.7. Rocket Propellant Example. The data from Table 4.9 of Montgomery (2002) is available on the `rocket`. After reading the data in R, we check for the LSD arrangement with `matrix(rocket$treat,nrow=5)`. Since each of the formulations, raw materials, and operators is supposed to be a factor variable, the plot of the burning rate (`y` in the data frame) against these variables will give us a box plot. The graphical output (the figure is suppressed here) clearly indicates that the burning rate `y` depends on each of the three factors. The `aov` function is again used for analyzing the model here.

```
> data(rocket)
> matrix(rocket$treat,nrow=5)
     [,1] [,2] [,3] [,4] [,5]
[1,] "A"  "B"  "C"  "D"  "E"
[2,] "B"  "C"  "D"  "E"  "A"
[3,] "C"  "D"  "E"  "A"  "B"
[4,] "D"  "E"  "A"  "B"  "C"
[5,] "E"  "A"  "B"  "C"  "D"
> par(mfrow=c(1,3)) # Graphical output suppressed again
> plot(y~op+batch+treat,rocket)
> rocket.lm <- lm(y~factor(op)+factor(batch)+treat,rocket)
> anova(rocket.lm)
Analysis of Variance Table
Response: y
              Df Sum Sq Mean Sq F value   Pr(>F)
factor(op)     4    150  37.500  3.5156 0.040373 *
factor(batch)  4     68  17.000  1.5937 0.239059
treat          4    330  82.500  7.7344 0.002537 **
Residuals     12    128  10.667
---
Signif. codes:  0 '***' 0.001 '**' 0.01 '*' 0.05 '.' 0.1 ' ' 1
```

The analysis output clearly shows that the formulation level (`treat`) and the type of operator (`op`) clearly influence the burning rate (`y`). □

Table 13.6 The GLSD Model

LSD			GSD			GLSD		
A	B	C	α	β	γ	Aα	Bβ	Cγ
B	C	A	β	γ	α	Bβ	Cγ	Aα
C	A	B	γ	α	β	Cγ	Aα	Bβ

There are many other useful variants of LSD and the reader may refer to Chapter 10 of Hinkelmann and Kempthorne (2008) for the same. An extension of the LSD is considered in the next topic.

13.4.4 Graeco Latin Square Design

Suppose that there is an extra source of randomness for the Rocket Propellant problem in Example 13.4.5 in *test assemblies*, which forms an additional type of treatment. Now, it is obvious that this is a second treatment which may be again addressed by another LSD. Let us denote the second treatment by Greek letters, say $\alpha, \beta, \gamma, \delta$, and ϵ. There is symbolic confusion in the sense that the Greek letters of β, γ, and ϵ may be confused with the notations used in Model 13.16. However, we will use the notations as elements of the LSD matrix. It should be clear from the context whether the notations are as in the Greek letters required or in the statistical model. Now, the LSD matrices for the two treatments are superimposed on each other to obtain the *Graeco-Latin Square Design* model. Table 13.6 shows how superimposing is done for two simple LSDs to obtain the GLSD.

In more formal terms, the Graeco-Latin square design model, abbreviated as *GLSD*, is specified by

$$Y_{ijk} = \mu + \tau_i + \psi_l + \beta_j + \gamma_k + \epsilon_{iljk}, i, l, j, k = 1, \cdots, p, \tag{13.18}$$

where ψ_l now denotes the effect of the additional treatment. A couple of GLSDs will be first set up.

Example 13.4.8. Setting up the GLSDs. The function `design.graeco` from the `agricolae` package helps in setting up a GLSD. In general, LSDs and GLSDs are also nice to visualize and this example will visualize the latter through the R program. Essentially, we would like to produce a GLSD of any order, which can be displayed as in the form of Table 13.6. If we were to *skip* the Greek letters and obtain the GLSD as two LSDs superimposed on each other, the task is fairly simple. First, we create two LSDs using `design.lsd` and use the `paste` function to get the desired result. However, the Greek letters can be displayed in a plot and hence the GLSD can be visualized.

```
> LSD1 <- matrix(design.lsd(LETTERS[1:3])[,4],nrow=3)
> LSD2 <- matrix(design.lsd(LETTERS[4:6])[,4],nrow=3)
> GLSD <- matrix(paste(LSD1,LSD2,sep=""),nrow=3)
> LSD1; LSD2; GLSD
```

```
     [,1] [,2] [,3]
[1,] "A"  "C"  "B"
[2,] "B"  "A"  "C"
[3,] "C"  "B"  "A"
     [,1] [,2] [,3]
[1,] "D"  "F"  "E"
[2,] "E"  "D"  "F"
[3,] "F"  "E"  "D"
     [,1] [,2] [,3]
[1,] "AD" "CF" "BE"
[2,] "BE" "AD" "CF"
[3,] "CF" "BE" "AD"
> GLSD_Length <- function(n){
+ Greek <- c("alpha","beta","gamma","delta","epsilon","zeta","eta",
+ "theta","iota","kappa","lambda","mu","nu","xi","omicron","pi",
+ "rho","sigma","tau","upsilon","phi","chi","psi","ometa")
+ Latin <- LETTERS[1:n]
+ greek <- 1:n; latin <- 1:n
+ My_Graeco <- design.graeco(latin,greek)
+ My_Graeco
+ Latin_Matrix <- matrix(as.numeric(My_Graeco[,4]),nrow=n) # Latin
+ Greek_Matrix <- matrix(as.numeric(My_Graeco[,5]),nrow=n) # Greek
+ plotSquareMatrix <- function(X,Y){
+ n <- nrow(X)
+ reverseIndex <- n:1
+ plot(0:(n+1),0:(n+1),type="n",axes=FALSE,xlab="",ylab="")
+ title("A Graeco-Latin Square Design")
+ for(i in 1:n){
+ for(j in 1:n){
+ text(j,reverseIndex[i], as.expression(substitute(A (B),
+  list(A = as.name(Latin[X[i,j]]),B = as.name(Greek[Y[i,j]])))))
+ }
+ }
+ }
+ plotSquareMatrix(Latin_Matrix,Greek_Matrix)
+ }
> GLSD_Length(10)
```

The first three lines of the above program simply superimpose two LSDs and give a GLSD as an output. Next, we define the function `GLSD_Length`, which will help generate a GLSD of order n. The `design.graeco` function can create a GLSD of order 14, although we have considered more Greek letters. Thus, the objects `Greek` and `Latin` store the Greek and Latin letters. A GLSD is obtained using the `design.graeco` function. The matrices `Latin_Matrix` and `Greek_Matrix` constitutes two LSDs, which need to be superimposed upon each other. The function `plotSquareMatrix` is defined within the `GLSD_Length` function, which helps to visualize a square matrix, as seen at the console

A Graeco–Latin Square Design

H(ι)	B(θ)	I(γ)	G(η)	F(ζ)	A(β)	C(α)	D(δ)	J(ϵ)	E(κ)
E(α)	D(ϵ)	B(ι)	I(θ)	A(η)	F(δ)	H(β)	J(γ)	C(κ)	G(ζ)
D(β)	G(α)	J(κ)	B(ϵ)	I(ι)	H(η)	F(γ)	C(θ)	E(ζ)	A(δ)
F(θ)	J(β)	A(α)	C(ζ)	B(κ)	I(ϵ)	D(η)	E(ι)	G(δ)	H(γ)
J(η)	F(ι)	C(β)	H(α)	E(δ)	B(ζ)	I(κ)	G(ϵ)	A(γ)	D(θ)
I(ζ)	C(η)	F(ϵ)	E(β)	D(α)	G(γ)	B(δ)	A(κ)	H(θ)	J(ι)
B(γ)	I(δ)	E(η)	F(κ)	G(β)	J(α)	A(θ)	H(ζ)	D(ι)	C(ϵ)
C(δ)	E(γ)	G(θ)	A(ι)	H(ϵ)	D(κ)	J(ζ)	F(α)	B(η)	I(β)
A(ϵ)	H(κ)	D(ζ)	J(δ)	C(γ)	E(θ)	G(ι)	B(β)	I(α)	F(η)
G(κ)	A(ζ)	H(δ)	D(γ)	J(θ)	C(ι)	E(ϵ)	I(η)	F(β)	B(α)

Figure 13.5 Graeco-Latin Square Design

on a graphical device. The R code in the loop `for(j in 1:n)` is motivated from http://stackoverflow.com/questions/13169318/r-creating-vectors-of-latin-greek-expression-for-plot-titles-axis-labels-or-l. The resulting display is given in Figure 13.5. □

The ANOVA decomposition of the *sum of squares* for the GLSD model 13.18 will be as follows:

$$SS_T = SS_{Row} + SS_{Column} + SS_{Latin} + SS_{Greek} + SS_E, \tag{13.19}$$

where

$$SS_{Row} = \frac{1}{p}\sum_{j=1}^{p} y_{..j.}^2 - \frac{y_{....}^2}{p^2}, \qquad SS_{Column} = \frac{1}{p}\sum_{k=1}^{p} y_{...k}^2 - \frac{y_{....}^2}{p^2},$$

$$SS_{Latin} = \frac{1}{p}\sum_{i=1}^{p} y_{i...}^2 - \frac{y_{....}^2}{p^2}, \qquad SS_{Greek} = \frac{1}{p}\sum_{l=1}^{p} y_{.i..}^2 - \frac{y_{....}^2}{p^2}$$

$$SS_T = \sum_{i=1}^{p}\sum_{j=1}^{p}\sum_{k=1}^{p} y_{iljk}^2 - \frac{y_{....}^2}{p^2}, \quad SS_E = SS_T - SS_{Latin} - SS_{Greek} - SS_{Row} - SS_{Column}.$$

The ANOVA table for the GLSD is given in Table 13.7. For Example 13.4.5, the R method is illustrated next.

Example 13.4.9. Extending the Rocket Example. In continuation of Example 13.4.7 of the Rocket Propellant data, we now have the added blocking factor in test assemblies. This dataset is available in the `rocket_Graeco` data frame from the companion package. Using

Table 13.7 ANOVA for the GLSD Model

Source of Variation	Sum of Squares	Degrees of Freedom	Mean Square	F-Statistic
Between Latin Treatments	SS_{Latin}	$p-1$	MS_{Latin}	$\frac{MS_{Latin}}{MS_E}$
Between Greek Treatments	SS_{Greek}	$p-1$	MS_{Greek}	$\frac{MS_{Greek}}{MS_E}$
Between Rows	SS_{Row}	$p-1$	MS_{Row}	$\frac{MS_{Row}}{MS_E}$
Between Columns	SS_{Column}	$p-1$	MS_{Column}	$\frac{MS_{Column}}{MS_E}$
Error	SS_E	$(p-1)(p-3)$	MS_E	
Total	SS_T	p^2-1		

`assembly` as the additional blocking variable, we continue to use the `lm` function and then the `anova` function to obtain the results.

```
> data(rocket_Graeco)
> par(mfrow=c(2,2))
> plot(y~op+batch+treat+assembly,rocket_Graeco) # output suppressed
> rocket.glsd.lm <- lm(y~factor(op)+factor(batch)+treat+assembly,
+ rocket_Graeco)
> anova(rocket.glsd.lm)
Analysis of Variance Table
Response: y
               Df Sum Sq Mean Sq F value   Pr(>F)
factor(op)      4    150   37.50  4.5455 0.032930 *
factor(batch)   4     68   17.00  2.0606 0.178311
treat           4    330   82.50 10.0000 0.003344 **
assembly        4     62   15.50  1.8788 0.207641
Residuals       8     66    8.25
---
Signif. codes:  0 '***' 0.001 '**' 0.01 '*' 0.05 '.' 0.1 ' ' 1
```

The result, in comparison with the ANOVA table in Example 13.4.7, shows that using the `assembly` as an additional variable reduces the experimental errors from `128` to `66`, although we now have reduced degrees of freedom. □

We now move to more important and complex experimental designs.

13.5 Factorial Designs

Factorial designs[1] are useful in experiments involving two or more factor variables. Suppose that there are two factor variables, with variable 1 having a levels and variable 2 having b levels. A factorial design investigates all possible combinations of the levels of the factors.

[1] The term *factorial* here refers as in *factors* and not the mathematical formula as $n! = n \times (n-1) \times \cdots \times 2 \times 1$.

In simple words, if factor A is at a levels, factor B at b levels, and factor C at c levels, a factorial design will investigate all possible levels $a \times b \times c$. It is then common practice to say that factors are *crossed*, implying that each factor variable level also has a corresponding observation among the levels of other factors. In factorial designs, the interest is more often to determine if there is an *interaction* between some combination of the factor levels. What does interaction really mean? In general, the *main effects* of a factor are observed to be the changes in the regressand due to the changes of the factor levels. However, if the changes in such expected values of the regressand also depend on the levels of other factor variables, we believe that there is an interaction effect between the factor variables. In the previously discussed designs in Sections 13.3 and 13.4, the factors were implicitly assumed to not have any kind of interaction among their different levels. Recollect from the three-dimensional scatter plot in Figure 12.6 and the cantor plot in Figure 12.7, the model 12.31 consisted of straight lines or planes only. However, for the models 12.31 and Figure 13.6, the three-dimensional plots and cantor plots had curvi-linear shapes in them, which is then an indication of the presence of interaction among the variables.

Sir R.A. Fisher advocated the use of a complex design like factorial designs with "No aphorism is more frequently repeated in connection with field trials, than that we must ask Nature a few questions, or, ideally, one question, at a time. The writer is convinced that this view is wholly mistaken." To understand this advantage, consider two factorial variables at two levels each. Suppose that two factor variables, A and B, are both available at levels high H and low L. Then the four possible combinations of the two treatments are $A^H B^H, A^H B^L, A^L B^H$, and $A^L B^L$. If low refers to the absence of factor levels, it is also a common practice to denote these respective combination levels with *ab*, *a*, *b*, and (1). Suppose we are interested in finding the effect of changing the factors A and B. A rule of thumb is to take two observations at each combination level of the factors in the presence of the experimental error. Now, the effect of treatment factor A is found by the difference in the combination level of $A^H B^L - A^L B^L$, while that of B is with $A^L B^H - A^L B^L$. Thus, we require data on the three combination levels $A^H B^L$, $A^L B^L$, and $A^L B^H$, or equivalently six observations only. In a full factorial experiment, we would also have two more data points at the combination level $A^H B^H$. Now, we can obtain two main effects for A with $A^H B^H - A^L B^H$ and $A^H B^L - A^L B^L$, and two main effects for B too with $A^H B^H - A^L B^H$ and $A^H B^L - A^L B^L$.

In the remainder of this section, we will consider some useful factorial designs. The focus will be only on *fixed effects models*.

13.5.1 Two Factorial Experiment

Consider the case of two factor variables. Suppose that factor A is at a levels, and B at b levels. The *two factorial* design model is given by

$$Y_{ijk} = \mu + \tau_i + \beta_j + (\tau\beta)_{ij} + \epsilon_{ijk}, i = 1, \cdots, a, j = 1, \cdots, b, k = 1, \cdots, n. \tag{13.20}$$

Here, μ is the overall mean effect, τ_i is the effect of the i-th factor level of A, β_j is the j-th effect of the factor B, and $(\tau\beta)_{ij}$ is the interaction effect between the variables. The ANOVA decomposition of the *sum of squares* for the two factorial experiments is given by

$$SS_T = SS_A + SS_B + SS_{AB} + SS_E, \tag{13.21}$$

where

$$SS_T = \sum_{i=1}^{a} \sum_{j=1}^{b} \sum_{k=1}^{n} (y_{ijk} - \bar{y}_{...})^2,$$

$$SS_A = bn \sum_{i=1}^{a} (\bar{y}_{i..} - \bar{y}_{...})^2,$$

$$SS_B = an \sum_{j=1}^{b} (\bar{y}_{.j.} - \bar{y}_{...})^2,$$

$$SS_{AB} = n \sum_{i=1}^{a} \sum_{j=1}^{b} (\bar{y}_{ij.} - \bar{y}_{i..} - \bar{y}_{.j.} + \bar{y}_{...})^2,$$

$$SS_E = \sum_{i=1}^{a} \sum_{j=1}^{b} \sum_{k=1}^{n} (y_{ijk} - \bar{y}_{ij.})^2.$$

The computation of SS_{AB} involves two stages. Since such issues do not exist when we use R, we skip this detail. The ANOVA table for the two-factorial model is given in Table 13.8. The hypotheses problems of interest here are the following:

1. Testing for Factor A:

$$H^A : \tau_1 = \cdots = \tau_a = 0 \text{ against } K^A : \tau_i \neq 0, \text{ for some } i.$$

2. Testing for Factor B:

$$H^B : \beta_1 = \cdots = \beta_b = 0 \text{ against } K^B : \beta_j \neq 0, \text{ for some } j.$$

3. Testing for the Interaction of factors:

$$H^{AB} : (\tau\beta)_{ij} = 0, \forall i,j, \text{ against } K^{AB} : (\tau\beta)_{ij} \neq 0, \text{ for some } i,j.$$

The two-factorial experiment is now illustrated with an example from Montgomery (2005).

Table 13.8 ANOVA for the Two Factorial Model

Source of Variation	Sum of Squares	Degrees of Freedom	Mean Square	F-Statistic
Treatment A	SS_A	$a-1$	MS_A	$\frac{MS_A}{MS_E}$
Treatment B	SS_B	$b-1$	MS_B	$\frac{MS_B}{MS_E}$
Interaction	SS_{AB}	$(a-1)(b-1)$	MS_{AB}	$\frac{MS_{AB}}{MS_E}$
Error	SS_E	$ab(n-1)$	MS_E	
Total	SS_T	$abn-1$		

Example 13.5.1. Two Factorial Experiment for Battery Data. An engineer designs a battery to be used in a device, which will be subject to extreme variations in temperature, and as a blocking variable he has some control on the type of plate material among three different choices. The engineer has no control on the temperature variations once the device leaves the factory. Thus, the task of the engineer is to investigate two major problems: (i) The effect of material type and temperature on the life of the device, and (ii) Finding the type of material which has least variation among the varying temperature levels. The temperature in the study is at three levels of 15, 70, and 125^0 Fahrenheit, while there are three different types of material. For each combination of the temperature and material, four replications of the life of the battery are tested. This dataset is available in the `battery.txt` file. Thus, the *two-factorial experiment* for this problem is given by

$$Y_{\text{Life},ijk} = \mu + \tau_{\text{Temperature},i} + \beta_{\text{Material},j} + (\tau\beta)_{ij} + \epsilon_{ijk}, i,j = 1,2,3, k = 1,2,3,4.$$

The reader may refer to Example 5.3.1 of Montgomery (2005) for more details of this experiment.

```
> data(battery)
> names(battery) <- c("L","M","T")
> battery$M <- as.factor(battery$M)
> battery$T <- as.factor(battery$T)
> battery.aov <- aov(L~M*T,data=battery)
> model.matrix(battery.aov)
   (Intercept) M2 M3 T70 T125 M2:T70 M3:T70 M2:T125 M3:T125
1            1  0  0   0    0      0      0       0       0
2            1  0  0   0    0      0      0       0       0
3            1  0  0   0    0      0      0       0       0
4            1  0  0   0    0      0      0       0       0
5            1  1  0   0    0      0      0       0       0

32           1  1  0   0    1      0      0       1       0
33           1  0  1   0    1      0      0       0       1
34           1  0  1   0    1      0      0       0       1
35           1  0  1   0    1      0      0       0       1
36           1  0  1   0    1      0      0       0       1
attr(,"assign")
[1] 0 1 1 2 2 3 3 3 3
attr(,"contrasts")
attr(,"contrasts")$M
[1] "contr.treatment"
attr(,"contrasts")$T
[1] "contr.treatment"
> summary(battery.aov)
            Df Sum Sq Mean Sq F value   Pr(>F)
M            2  10684    5342   7.911  0.00198 **
T            2  39119   19559  28.968 1.91e-07 ***
M:T          4   9614    2403   3.560  0.01861 *
Residuals   27  18231     675
---
Signif. codes:  0 '***' 0.001 '**' 0.01 '*' 0.05 '.' 0.1 ' ' 1
```

The reader is advised to interpret the working design matrix as given by `model.matrix (battery.aov)`. The factor variables have been renamed for simplicity's sake only. Using the `aov` function, the linear model for this factorial experiment is set up. The code `summary(battery.aov)` shows that both material and temperature and their interaction are significant variables for explaining the life of the device. Now that it is known that the interaction effect is significant, a question that arises is what does it look like? Using the two functions `plot.design` and `interaction.plot`, the average life at the different factor levels are visualized. The multiple comparisons are obtained using the `glht` function from the `multcomp` package.

```
> par(mfrow=c(1,2))
> plot.design(L~M+T,data=battery)
> interaction.plot(battery$T,battery$M,battery$L,type="b",pch=19,
+ fixed=TRUE,xlab="Temperature",ylab="Average life")
> glht(battery.aov,linfct=mcp(M="Dunnett"),alternative="two.sided",
+ interaction=TRUE)
         General Linear Hypotheses
Multiple Comparisons of Means: Dunnett Contrasts
Linear Hypotheses:
           Estimate
2 - 1 == 0    21.00
3 - 1 == 0     9.25
Warning message:
In mcp2matrix(model, linfct = linfct) :
  covariate interactions found -- default contrast might be
+ inappropriate
> glht(battery.aov,linfct=mcp(M="Tukey"),alternative="two.sided",
+ interaction=TRUE)
         General Linear Hypotheses
Multiple Comparisons of Means: Tukey Contrasts
Linear Hypotheses:
           Estimate
2 - 1 == 0    21.00
3 - 1 == 0     9.25
3 - 2 == 0   -11.75
Warning message:
In mcp2matrix(model, linfct = linfct) :
  covariate interactions found -- default contrast might be
+ inappropriate
> glht(battery.aov,linfct=mcp(T="Tukey"),alternative="two.sided",
+ interaction=TRUE)
         General Linear Hypotheses
Multiple Comparisons of Means: Tukey Contrasts
Linear Hypotheses:
               Estimate
70 - 15 == 0     -77.50
125 - 15 == 0    -77.25
125 - 70 == 0      0.25
```

```
Warning message:
In mcp2matrix(model, linfct = linfct) :
  covariate interactions found -- default contrast might be
+ inappropriate
```

The use of the "simpler" `plot.design` function in Part A of Figure 13.6 shows that the average life increases across the material type (from 1 to 3), whereas it decreases as the temperature of the region increases. However, the interaction plot, as given in Part B of Figure 13.6, clearly shows that at Temperature `T` 70^0 Fahrenheit, the average life for Material `M` 2 is longer than that for `M` at 3, a clear interaction effect between the temperature and material type. To verify whether this interaction is statistically significant, we may use `testInteractions` from the package `phia`.

```
> testInteractions(battery.aov,fixed="T",across="M")
F Test:
P-value adjustment method: holm
               M1     M2 Df Sum of Sq       F    Pr(>F)
 15         -9.25  11.75  2     886.2  0.6562 0.5268904
 70        -88.50 -26.00  2   16552.7 12.2574 0.0004892 ***
125        -28.00 -36.00  2    2858.7  2.1169 0.2799107
Residuals                27   18230.8
---
Signif. codes:  0 '***' 0.001 '**' 0.01 '*' 0.05 '.' 0.1 ' ' 1
```

The interaction effect at `Temperature=70` is clearly seen to be significant in the above output. With the main and interaction effects as understood by us, it is not important to focus on the *model assumptions*. Since the two-factorial experiment is again an example of a linear regression model, the techniques of model assumption from Chapter 12 carry over and are used for the `battery.aov lm` object.

```
> p <- 9
> diagnostics_matrix <- matrix(nrow=nrow(battery),ncol=8)
> colnames(diagnostics_matrix) <- c("Obs No.","y","Pred
+ y","Residual","Levarage","S.Residual","Cooks.Dist","Outlier")
> diagnostics_matrix[,1] <- 1:nrow(battery)
> diagnostics_matrix[,2] <- battery$L
> diagnostics_matrix[,3] <- battery.aov$fitted.values
> diagnostics_matrix[,4] <- round(battery.aov$residuals,3)
> diagnostics_matrix[,5] <- influence(battery.aov)$hat
> diagnostics_matrix[,6] <- round(rstudent(battery.aov),3)
> diagnostics_matrix[,7] <- round(cooks.distance(battery.aov),3)
> diagnostics_matrix[,8] <- diagnostics_matrix[,6]*sqrt((16-p-1)/
+ (16-p-diagnostics_matrix[,6]^2))
Warning message:
In sqrt((16 - p - 1)/(16 - p - diagnostics_matrix[, 6]^{ :
+ NaNs produced
> round(diagnostics_matrix,3)
```

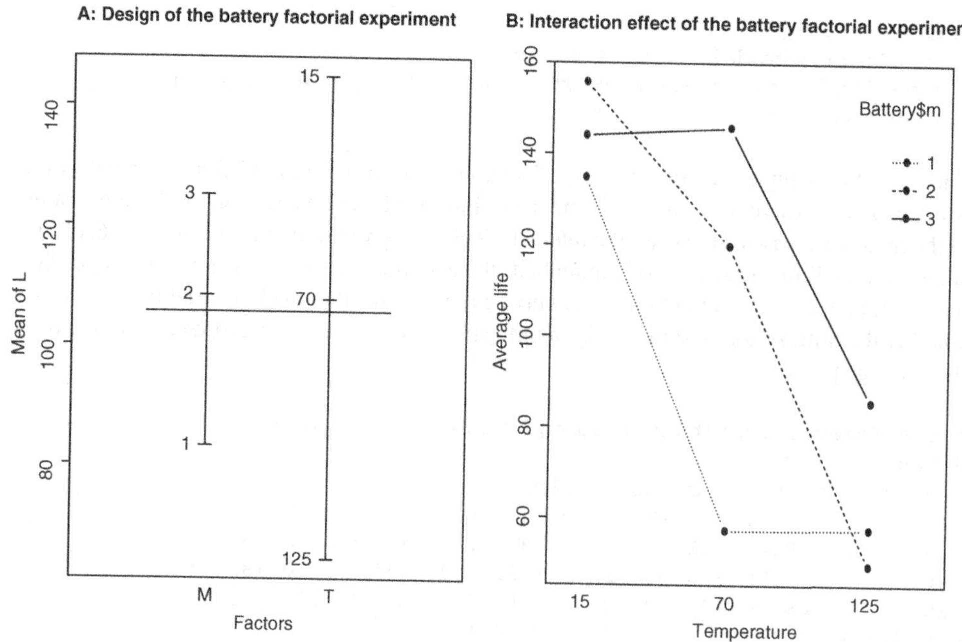

Figure 13.6 Design and Interaction Plots for 2-Factorial Design

```
      Obs No.   y Pred y Residual Levarage S.Residual Cooks.Dist
[1,]        1 130 134.75    -4.75     0.25     -0.207      0.002
[2,]        2  74 134.75   -60.75     0.25     -3.100      0.270
[3,]        3 155 134.75    20.25     0.25      0.897      0.030
[4,]        4 180 134.75    45.25     0.25      2.140      0.150
[5,]        5 150 155.75    -5.75     0.25     -0.251      0.002

[32,]      32  45  49.50    -4.50     0.25     -0.196      0.001
[33,]      33  96  85.50    10.50     0.25      0.460      0.008
[34,]      34  82  85.50    -3.50     0.25     -0.153      0.001
[35,]      35 104  85.50    18.50     0.25      0.817      0.025
[36,]      36  60  85.50   -25.50     0.25     -1.139      0.048
```

The interpretation and the R program is left as an exercise for the reader. □

The extension of the two-factorial experiment is discussed in the next subsection.

13.5.2 Three-Factorial Experiment

A natural extension of the two-factorial experiment will be the *three-factorial experiment*. Let the three factors be denoted by A, B, and C, each respectively at a, b, and c factor levels. Consequently, there are now three more interaction terms to be modeled for in $(\tau\gamma)$, $(\beta\gamma)$, and $(\tau\beta\gamma)$. Towards a complete crossed model, we need each replicate (of index l) to cover all possible factor combinations. Thus, the three-way factorial model is then modeled by

$$Y_{ijkl} = \mu + \tau_i + \beta_j + \gamma_k + (\tau\beta)_{ij} + (\tau\gamma)_{ik} + (\beta\gamma)_{jk} + (\tau\beta\gamma)_{ijk} + \epsilon_{ijkl},$$
$$i = 1, \cdots, a, j = 1, \cdots, b, k = 1, \cdots, c, l = 1, \cdots, n. \quad (13.22)$$

The total sum of squares decomposition equation is then

$$SS_T = SS_A + SS_B + SS_C + SS_{AB} + SS_{AC} + SS_{BC} + SS_{ABC} + SS_E, \quad (13.23)$$

where

$$SS_T = \sum_{i=1}^{a}\sum_{j=1}^{b}\sum_{k=1}^{c}\sum_{l=1}^{n} y_{ijkl}^2 - \frac{y_{....}^2}{abcn},$$

$$SS_A = \frac{1}{bcn}\sum_{i=1}^{a} y_{i...}^2 - \frac{y_{....}^2}{abcn},$$

$$SS_B = \frac{1}{acn}\sum_{j=1}^{b} y_{.j..}^2 - \frac{y_{....}^2}{abcn},$$

$$SS_C = \frac{1}{abn}\sum_{j=1}^{c} y_{..k.}^2 - \frac{y_{....}^2}{abcn},$$

$$SS_{AB} = \frac{1}{cn}\sum_{i=1}^{a}\sum_{j=1}^{b} y_{ij..}^2 - \frac{y_{....}^2}{abcn} - SS_A - SS_B,$$

$$SS_{AC} = \frac{1}{bn}\sum_{i=1}^{a}\sum_{k=1}^{c} y_{i.k.}^2 - \frac{y_{....}^2}{abcn} - SS_A - SS_C,$$

$$SS_{BC} = \frac{1}{an}\sum_{j=1}^{a}\sum_{k=1}^{b} y_{.jk.}^2 - \frac{y_{....}^2}{abcn} - SS_B - SS_C,$$

$$SS_{ABC} = \frac{1}{n}\sum_{i=1}^{a}\sum_{j=1}^{b}\sum_{k=1}^{c} y_{ijk.}^2 - \frac{y_{....}^2}{abcn} - SS_A - SS_B - SS_C - SS_{AB} - SS_{AC} - SS_{BC},$$

$$SS_E = SS_T - SS_A - SS_B - SS_C - SS_{AB} - SS_{AC} - SS_{BC} - SS_{ABC}.$$

The ANOVA table for the three-factorial design model is given in Table 13.9.

Since the details of the two-factorial experiment extend in a fairly straightforward manner to the current model, the model will be illustrated with two examples from Montgomery (2005).

Example 13.5.2. A Three-Factorial Experiment for Bottling Data. The Example 5.3 from Montgomery (2005) is discussed here through the R program, and the current example also benefits from Lalanne (2006), the R companion of Montgomery's book. The height of the filling of a soft drinks bottle is required to be as consistent as possible and is controlled through three factors: (i) the percent carbonation of the drink, (ii) the operating pressure in the filler, and

Table 13.9 ANOVA for the Three-Factorial Model

Source of Variation	Sum of Squares	Degrees of Freedom	Mean Square	F-Statistic
Treatment A	SS_A	$a-1$	MS_A	$\frac{MS_A}{MS_E}$
Treatment B	SS_B	$b-1$	MS_B	$\frac{MS_B}{MS_E}$
Treatment C	SS_C	$c-1$	MS_c	$\frac{MS_C}{MS_E}$
Interaction (AB)	SS_{AB}	$(a-1)(b-1)$	MS_{AB}	$\frac{MS_{AB}}{MS_E}$
Interaction (AC)	SS_{AC}	$(a-1)(c-1)$	MS_{AC}	$\frac{MS_{AC}}{MS_E}$
Interaction (BC)	SS_{BC}	$(b-1)(c-1)$	MS_{BC}	$\frac{MS_{BC}}{MS_E}$
Interaction (ABC)	SS_{ABC}	$(a-1)(b-1)(c-1)$	MS_{ABC}	$\frac{MS_{ABC}}{MS_E}$
Error	SS_E	$abc(n-1)$	MS_E	
Total	SS_T	$abcn-1$		

(iii) the line speed which is the number of bottles filled per minute. The first factor variable of the percent of carbonation is available at three levels of 10, 12, and 14, the operating pressure is at 25 and 30 psi units, while the line speeds are at 200 and 250 bottles per minute. Two complete replicates are available for each combination of the three factor levels, that is, 24 total number of observations. In this experiment, the deviation from the required height level is measured.

The R formula for a three-factorial experiment may be set up using `aov(y~a+b+c+(a*b)+(a*c)+(b*c)+(a*b*c),data)`, or simply with `aov(y~.^3,data)`. It is nice to know both the options! In the case of the two-factorial experiment, the investigation requires us only to find out whether there is an interaction effect between two factor variables in the model, and the `interaction.plot` function has been useful for that purpose. However, in the three-factorial experiment, there are overall four interaction variables. A simple extension of the `interaction.plot` function is to obtain such plots while holding the other factorial variable at a specified level. Thus, an extension of the `interaction.plot` function is first defined and then the various plots are obtained.

```
> data(bottling)
> # # Preliminary investigation for interaction effect
> windows(height=15,width=20)
> par(mfrow=c(2,2))
> plot.design(Deviation~.^3,data=bottling)
> IP_subset <- function(ab,colIndex,ss_char)}
+ abcd <- ab[,colIndex]
+ abcd <- abcd[abcd[,3]==ss_char,]
+ vnames <- names(abcd)
+ interaction.plot(x.factor=abcd[,1],trace.factor=abcd[,2],
+ response=abcd[,4],
+ type="b",xlab=vnames[1],ylab=vnames[4],trace.label=vnames[2]){
> IP_subset(bottling,c(3,4,2,1),"10")
```

```
> IP_subset(bottling,c(3,4,2,1),"12")
> IP_subset(bottling,c(3,4,2,1),"14")
> title("Understanding Height of Bottling -
+ Interaction Plots",outer=TRUE,line=-1)
> par(mfrow=c(1,2))
> IP_subset(bottling,c(2,3,4,1),"200")
> IP_subset(bottling,c(2,3,4,1),"250")
> par(mfrow=c(1,2))
> IP_subset(bottling,c(2,4,3,1),"25")
> IP_subset(bottling,c(2,4,3,1),"30")
```

The newly-defined function `IP_subset` needs an explanation. There are three arguments for this function. Recollect that the plot function `interaction.plot` is essentially a "Two-way Interaction Plot". Thus, there is a need of a function which checks for the interaction between two factor variables when the third variable is held constant. Thus, given the `data.frame`, the newly-defined function `IP_subset` finds the required `data.frame`, the `colIndex`, which has four integers required for the first two entries, which have the two-factor variable to be investigated for the interaction effect when the third-factor variable is held at a constant `ss_char`. The fourth entry of `colIndex` contains the output values. Note that the data frame is generic and any control over the two-factor variables, the variables to be held constant, and the output needs to be clearly specified in `colIndex`. The `plot.design`, as in the north-east block of Figure 13.7, clearly indicates linearity across each of the input (factor) variables. The investigation of the interaction effect between `Pressure` and `Speed` is ruled out in the remaining three plots of Figure 13.7. The interpretation for the remaining two combinations of the factor variables program, as included in the above R module, is left to the reader. Now that the interaction effect is understood, it is time to analyze the data.

```
> summary(bottling.aov <- aov(Deviation~.^3,bottling))
                            Df Sum Sq Mean Sq F value   Pr(>F)
Carbonation                  2 252.75  126.38 178.412 1.19e-09 ***
Pressure                     1  45.37   45.37  64.059 3.74e-06 ***
Speed                        1  22.04   22.04  31.118  0.00012 ***
Carbonation:Pressure         2   5.25    2.63   3.706  0.05581 .
Carbonation:Speed            2   0.58    0.29   0.412  0.67149
Pressure:Speed               1   1.04    1.04   1.471  0.24859
Carbonation:Pressure:Speed   2   1.08    0.54   0.765  0.48687
Residuals                   12   8.50    0.71
---
Signif. codes:  0 '***' 0.001 '**' 0.01 '*' 0.05 '.' 0.1 ' ' 1
> summary(aov(Deviation~ Carbonation + Pressure + Speed+
+ (Carbonation*Pressure)
+ +(Carbonation*Speed)+(Pressure*Speed)+
+ (Carbonation*Speed*Pressure),data=bottling))
+ # Equivalent way and hence output is not provided
```

The use of `aov` and `summary` above gives us the desired output. Cleary, the ANOVA Table 13.9 for the height of the bottling variable shows that while the main effects are

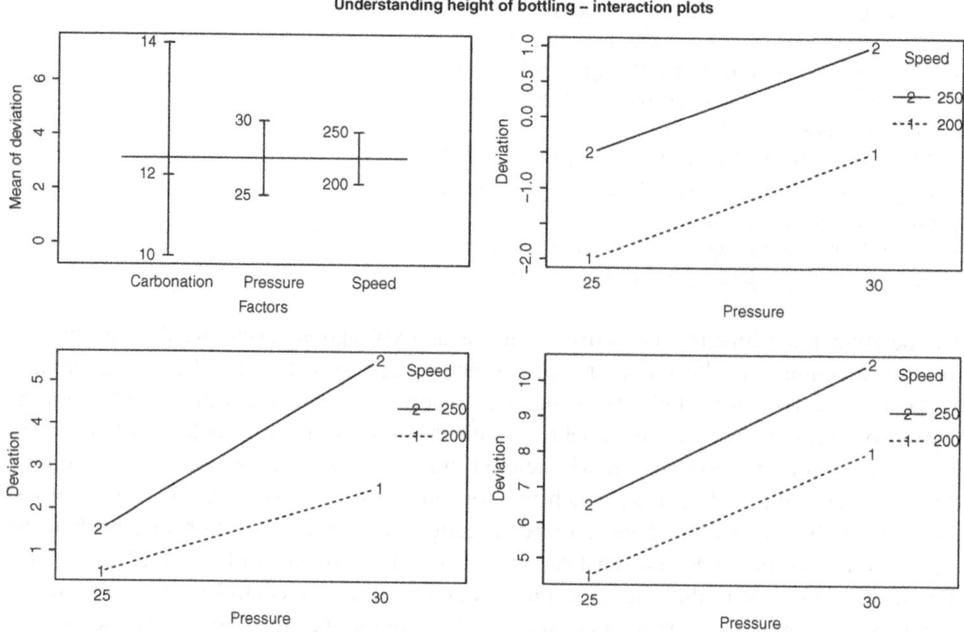

Figure 13.7 Understanding Interactions for the Bottling Experiment

significant, p-values for the interaction effects are all large enough and hence, it is appropriate to conclude that the interaction effects are insignificant. □

Example 13.5.3. Understanding Strength of Paper with a Three-Factorial Experiment. The strength of a paper depends on three variables: (i) the percentage of hardwood concentration in the raw pulp, (ii) the vat pressure, and (iii) the cooking time of the pulp. The hardwood concentration is tested at three levels of 2, 4, and 8 percentage, the vat pressure at 400, 500, and 650, while the cooking time is at 3 and 4 hours. For each combination of the these three factor variables, 2 observations are available, and thus a total of $3 \times 3 \times 2 \times 2 = 36$ observations. The goal of the study is investigation of the impact of the three factor variables on the strength of the paper, and the presence of the interaction effect, if any. The dataset is available in the `Strength_Paper.csv` file and the source is Problem 5.16 of Montgomery (2005).

```
> data(SP)
> plot.design(Strength~.^3,data=SP)
> windows(width=10,height=5)
> par(mfrow=c(1,3))
> IP_subset(SP,c(2,3,1,4),"2")
> IP_subset(SP,c(2,3,1,4),"4")
> IP_subset(SP,c(2,3,1,4),"8")
> par(mfrow=c(1,2))
```

```
> IP_subset(SP,c(1,2,3,4),"3")
> IP_subset(SP,c(1,2,3,4),"4")
> par(mfrow=c(1,3))
> IP_subset(SP,c(1,3,2,4),"400")
> IP_subset(SP,c(1,3,2,4),"500")
> IP_subset(SP,c(1,3,2,4),"650")
> summary(SP.aov <- aov(Strength~.^3,SP))
                              Df Sum Sq Mean Sq F value   Pr(>F)
Hardwood                       2  3.764   1.882   2.458 0.113792
Pressure                       2 24.041  12.020  15.701 0.000113 ***
Cooking_Time                   1 14.694  14.694  19.194 0.000360 ***
Hardwood:Pressure              4 14.224   3.556   4.645 0.009422 **
Hardwood:Cooking_Time          2  0.304   0.152   0.198 0.821750
Pressure:Cooking_Time          2  4.951   2.475   3.233 0.063137 .
Hardwood:Pressure:Cooking_Time 4  1.751   0.438   0.572 0.686497
Residuals                     18 13.780   0.766
---
Signif. codes:  0 '***' 0.001 '**' 0.01 '*' 0.05 '.' 0.1 ' ' 1
```

The presence of the interaction effects is clearly brought out by the `IP_subset` plots. The validation of the same is obtained from the `summary` of the fitted `aov` object. The question now is whether the interaction effects are statistically significant? The answer is again provided by the `testInteractions` function from the `phia` package.

```
> testInteractions(SP.aov,fixed="Hardwood",across="Pressure")
F Test:
P-value adjustment method: holm
          Pressure1 Pressure2 Df Sum of Sq       F    Pr(>F)
2            -3.775     -1.75  2   28.5517 18.6477 0.0001231 ***
4            -0.825     -1.25  2    3.2317  2.1107 0.1501486
8            -0.925     -1.80  2    6.4817  4.2333 0.0622582 .
Residuals                     18   13.7800
---
Signif. codes:  0 '***' 0.001 '**' 0.01 '*' 0.05 '.' 0.1 ' ' 1
> testInteractions(SP.aov,fixed="Cooking_Time",across="Pressure")
F Test:
P-value adjustment method: holm
          Pressure1 Pressure2 Df Sum of Sq       F   Pr(>F)
3           -1.3833     -2.05  2    13.121  8.5697 0.002428 **
4           -2.3000     -1.15  2    15.870 10.3650 0.002023 **
Residuals                     18    13.780
---
Signif. codes:  0 '***' 0.001 '**' 0.01 '*' 0.05 '.' 0.1 ' ' 1
```

Thus, the significance of the interaction effects has also been established here. □

The principle of *blocking* in the context of factorial experiments is taken up in the next subsection.

13.5.3 Blocking in Factorial Experiments

The two- and three-factorial experiments discussed above are extensions of the basic CRD model. In Section 13.4, we saw that replication does not alone eliminate the source of error and that the principle of blocking helps improve the efficiency of the experiment. Similarly, in the case of factorial experiments, practical considerations sometimes dictate that the replication principle cannot be implemented uniformly and that the factorial experiments may be improved through the introduction of a blocking route. The blocking model for a two-factorial experiment is stated next:

$$Y_{ijk} = \mu + \tau_i + \beta_j + (\tau\beta)_{ij} + \delta_k + \epsilon_{ijk}, i = 1, \cdots, a, j = 1, \cdots, b, k = 1, \cdots, n. \tag{13.24}$$

The total sum of squares decomposition equation for the model 13.24 is then

$$SS_T = SS_{Blocks} + SS_A + SS_B + SS_{AB} + SS_E, \tag{13.25}$$

where

$$SS_T = \sum_{i=1}^{a}\sum_{j=1}^{b}\sum_{k=1}^{n} y_{ijk}^2 - \frac{y_{...}^2}{abn},$$

$$SS_{Blocks} = \frac{1}{ab}\sum_{k=1}^{n} y_{..k}^2 - \frac{y_{...}^2}{abn},$$

$$SS_A = \frac{1}{bn}\sum_{i=1}^{a} y_{i..}^2 - \frac{y_{...}^2}{abn},$$

$$SS_B = \frac{1}{an}\sum_{j=1}^{b} y_{.j.}^2 - \frac{y_{...}^2}{abn},$$

$$SS_{AB} = \frac{1}{n}\sum_{i=1}^{a}\sum_{j=1}^{b} y_{ij.}^2 - \frac{y_{...}^2}{abn} - SS_A - SS_B,$$

$$SS_E = SS_T - SS_A - SS_B - SS_C - SS_{AB} - SS_{AC} - SS_{BC} - SS_{ABC}.$$

The corresponding ANOVA table for the blocking factorial experiment 13.24 is given in Table 13.10.

Example 13.5.4. Blocking for Intensity Dataset. The intent of this experiment is to help the engineer to improve the ability of detecting targets on a radar system. The two variables chosen, which are believed to have the most impact on detecting the abilities of the radar system, are marked as the amount of background noise and type of filter on the screen. The background noise `Ground` is classified into one of three levels: `low`, `medium`, and `high`. The two types of filter are available. However, there are different operators who use the radar system and this information forms the blocks. The dataset is available in the `intensity.txt` file. The `formula` for the `aov` object needs to be specialized for the factorial experiment with blocking. The R program next delivers the required computation.

Table 13.10 ANOVA for Factorial Models with Blocking

Source of Variation	Sum of Squares	Degrees of Freedom	Mean Square	F-Statistic
Blocks	SS_{Blocks}	$n-1$	MS_{Blocks}	$\frac{MS_{Blocks}}{MS_E}$
Treatment A	SS_A	$a-1$	MS_A	$\frac{MS_A}{MS_E}$
Treatment B	SS_B	$b-1$	MS_B	$\frac{MS_B}{MS_E}$
Interaction (AB)	SS_{AB}	$(a-1)(b-1)$	MS_{AB}	$\frac{MS_{AB}}{MS_E}$
Error	SS_E	$(ab-1)(n-1)$	MS_E	
Total	SS_T	$abn-1$		

```
> data(intensity)
> intensity.aov <- aov(Intensity~
+ Ground*Filter+Error(Operator),intensity)
> summary(intensity.aov)
Error: Operator
          Df Sum Sq Mean Sq F value Pr(>F)
Residuals  3 402.17  134.06
Error: Within
               Df  Sum Sq Mean Sq F value    Pr(>F)
Ground          2  335.58  167.79 15.1315 0.0002527 ***
Filter          1 1066.67 1066.67 96.1924 6.447e-08 ***
Ground:Filter   2   77.08   38.54  3.4757 0.0575066 .
Residuals      15  166.33   11.09
---
Signif. codes:  0 '***' 0.001 '**' 0.01 '*' 0.05 '.' 0.1 ' ' 1
> intensity.aov
Call:
aov(formula = Intensity ~ Ground * Filter + Error(Operator),
    data = intensity)
Grand Mean: 94.91667
Stratum 1: Operator
Terms:
                Residuals
Sum of Squares   402.1667
Deg. of Freedom         3
Residual standard error: 11.57824
Stratum 2: Within
Terms:
                   Ground    Filter Ground:Filter Residuals
Sum of Squares   335.5833 1066.6667       77.0833  166.3333
Deg. of Freedom         2         1             2        15

Residual standard error: 3.329998
Estimated effects may be unbalanced
```

The reader is asked to compare the results with Montgomery (2005) and Lalanne (2006); for more details post an attempt of interpretation of results here. □

The theory and applications of *Experimental Designs* extend far beyond the models discussed here and thankfully the purpose of the current chapter has been to consider some of the important models among them.

13.6 Further Reading

Kempthorne (1952), Cochran and Cox (1958), Box, Hunter, and Hunter (2005), Federer (1955), and of course, Fisher (1971) are some of the earliest treatises in this area.

Montgomery (2005), Wu and Hamada (2000–9), and Dean and Voss (1999) are some of the modern accounts in DOE. Casella (2008) is a very useful source with emphasis on computations using R. The web link http://cran.r-project.org/web/views/ExperimentalDesign.html is very useful for the reader interested in almost exhaustive options for DOE analysis using R.

13.7 Complements, Problems, and Programs

Problem 13.1 Identify which of the design models studied in this chapter are appropriate for the datasets available in the `BHH2` package. The list of datasets available in the package may be found with `try(data(package="BHH2"))`. The exercise may also be repeated for design-related packages such as `agricolae`, `AlgDesign`, and `granova`.

Problem 13.2 Carry out the diagnostic tests for the `olson_crd` fitted model in Example 13.3.4. Repeat a similar exercise for the ANOVA model fitted in Example 13.3.2.

Problem 13.3 Multiple comparison tests of Dunnett, Tukey, Holm, and Bonferroni have been explored in Example 13.3.8. The confidence intervals are reported only for `TukeyHSD`. The reader should obtain the confidence intervals for the rest of the multiple comparison tests contrasts.

Problem 13.4 Explore the use of the functions `design.crd` and `design.rcbd` from the `agricolae` package for setting up CRD and block designs.

Problem 13.5 The function `granova.2w` may be applied on the `girdernew` dataset with a slight modification. Create a new data frame `girdernew2 <- girdernew[,c(3,1,2)]`. Note that an additional R package `rgl` will be required though. Test the code `granova.2w( girdernew2, ss gf + mf)` and make an attempt to interpret the output.

Problem 13.6 In the fitted models `ssaov`, `hardness_aov`, `rocket_aov`, `rocket.aov`, and `rocket.glsd.aov` discussed in Section 13.4, investigate the presence of an interaction effect through the use of the `interaction.plot` graphical function.

Problem 13.7 Perform the diagnostic tests on the BIBD model in Example 13.4.4.

Problem 13.8 Investigate the presence of outliers and influential measures for the fitted models `rocket.lm` and `rocket.glsd.lm` in the respective Examples 13.4.7 and 13.4.9.

Problem 13.9 Obtain the confidence intervals for the contrasts of the fitted model `battery.aov` in Example 13.5.1.

Problem 13.10 Carry out the diagnostic tests for the fitted models `bottling.aov`, `SP.aov`, and `intensity.aov`.

14

Multivariate Statistical Analysis - I

Package(s): `ICSNP`, `scatterplot3d`, `aplpack`, `mvtnorm`, `foreign`
Dataset(s): `cardata`, `stiff`, `iris`, `hw`, `calcium`, `mfp`, `rootstock`, `waterquality`, `pw`, `sheishu`

14.1 Introduction

In many real-world problems, data is seldom univariate. We have more than one variable, which needs a good understanding of the underlying uncertain phenomenons. Thus, we need a set of tools to handle this type of data, and this is provided by *Multivariate Statistical Analysis* (MSA), a branch of the subject. We saw in the previous chapters on regression, that multiple regressors explain the regressand. Sometimes experiments may need a deeper study of the covariates themselve. In particular, we are now concerned with a random vector, the characteristics of which form the crux of this and the next chapter.

In Section 14.2 we look at graphical plots, which give a deeper insight into the structure of the dataset. The core concepts of MSA are introduced in Section 14.3. Sections 14.4 and 14.5 deal with the inference problem related to the mean vectors of multivariate data, whereas inference related with the variance-covariance matrix are performed in Sections 14.7 and 14.8. Multivariate Analysis of Variance, abbreviated as MANOVA, tools are introduced and illustrated in Section 14.6 and some tests for independence of sub-vectors are addressed in Section 14.9. Advanced topics of multivariate statistical analysis are carried over to the next chapter.

14.2 Graphical Plots for Multivariate Data

In Chapter 12 we saw the use of scatter plots and pairs (matrix of scatter plots). A slight modification of the matrix of a scatter plot is considered here, which gives more insight into the multivariate aspect of the dataset. Multi-dimensional data can be still visualized in two dimensions and a particularly effective technique provided by Chernoff faces is detailed. We will begin with a multivariate dataset.

A Course in Statistics with R, First Edition. Prabhanjan Narayanachar Tattar, Suresh Ramaiah and B. G. Manjunath.

Companion Website: www.wiley.com/go/tattar/statistics

Example 14.2.1. Car Data. We consider the car dataset consisting of 13 variables and 74 car variables. This example is drawn from Hárdle and Simar (2007), Appendix B.3, which has been earlier analyzed by Chambers, et al. (1983). The variable description, variables names as in the dataset in verbatim font, and the notation of random variable in italics, are given in the following:

- Price: `P`, X_1
- Mileage (in miles per gallon): `M`, X_2
- Repair record 1978 (rated on a 5-point scale; 5 best, 1 worst): `R78`, X_3
- Repair record 1977 (scale as before): `R77`, X_4
- Headroom (in inches): `H`, X_5
- Rear seat clearance (distance from front seat back to rear seat, in inches): `R`, X_6
- Trunk space (in cubic feet): `Tr`, X_7
- Weight (in pound): `W`, X_8
- Length (in inches): `L`, X_9
- Turning diameter (clearance required to make a U-turn, in feet): `T`, X_{10}
- Displacement (in cubic inches): `D`, X_{11}
- Gear ratio for high gear: `G`, X_{12}
- Company headquarter (1 for U.S., 2 for Japan, 3 for Europe): `C`, X_{13}

Let us now plot the matrix of scatter plots and examine the correlation among the 13 variables. The matrix of scatter plots can be customized to extract a lot of information. For instance, we use the functions `panel.hist` and `panel.cor`, which have been defined in the R example of `pairs` function, seen by running `example(pairs)` at the R terminal. The dataset is first imported into R and then the `pairs` function is applied to it with the options of `panel.hist` and `panel.cor`.

```
> panel.hist <- function(x, ...)
+  {
+       usr <- par("usr"); on.exit(par(usr))
+       par(usr = c(usr[1:2], 0, 1.5) )
+       h <- hist(x, plot = FALSE)
+       breaks <- h$breaks; nB <- length(breaks)
+       y <- h$counts; y <- y/max(y)
+       rect(breaks[-nB], 0, breaks[-1], y, col="cyan", ...)
+  }
> panel.cor <- function(x, y, digits=2, prefix="", cex.cor, ...) {
+       usr <- par("usr"); on.exit(par(usr))
+       par(usr = c(0, 1, 0, 1))
+       r <- abs(cor(x, y))
+       txt <- format(c(r, 0.123456789), digits=digits)[1]
+       txt <- paste(prefix, txt, sep="")
+       if(missing(cex.cor)) cex.cor <- 0.8/strwidth(txt)
+       text(0.5, 0.5, txt, cex = cex.cor * r)
+  }
> data(cardata)
> pairs(cardata[,2:14],diag.panel=panel.hist,
+ lower.panel=panel.smooth,
```

```
+ upper.panel=panel.cor)
+ # as some data is missing, we remove them and replot below
> pairs(na.omit(cardata[,2:14]),diag.panel=panel.hist,
+ lower.panel=panel.smooth, upper.panel=panel.cor)
```

Figure 14.1 is the output of the previous R program. The price `P` appears to be weakly correlated with the other components of the random vector. Strong associations appear among the variables `M`, `W`, `L`, `T`, `D`, and `G`. In this figure, as we look at the upper panel for the correlation coefficients, the lower panel also needs to be checked for the scatter plot. Of course, the diagonal elements indicate the spread of the variables themselves. Thus, using the options in `diag.panel`, `lower.panel`, and `upper.panel`, the `pairs` becomes a very effective tool for visualization of multivariate data. □

Chernoff (1973) gave a very innovative technique to visualize multivariate data, which considers each variate as some dimension of the human face, say nose, ears, smile, cheeks, etc. Interpretation of three-dimensional plots itself is difficult, even if we were to deploy features such as rotation of the plots. Certainly, visualization in more than three dimensions is not possible. Thus, the Chernoff technique of visualizing the multivariate data through faces is very helpful and such a plot is of course well known as the *Chernoff faces*. We deploy this method here using the graphical function `faces` from the R package `aplpack`.

Example 14.2.2. Car Data. Contd. The first 25 data points are considered here for purposes of brevity.

```
> library(aplpack)
> faces(cardata[1:25,2:14])
[1] "Warning: NA elements have been exchanged by mean values!!"
effect of variables:
 modified item       Var
 "height of face   " "P"
 "width of face    " "M"

 "height of ear    "  "M"
```

Note that the missing values have been replaced by the average values of that variate. The diagram is given in Figure 14.2.

A car freak reader will not be surprised by the Chernoff faces, as the cars labeled 14 to 16 are Cadillac luxury car models Deville, Eldorado, and Seville, whereas the ones labeled 2, 3, 21, and 25 (yes, the ones with grim faces), are low-end hatchback cars, respectively AMC-Pacer, AMC-Spirit, Chevrolet Monza, and Datsun-510. □

Chernoff faces gives one facet of data visualization of multivariate data. There are many other similar techniques, though we will not dwell more on them. In the next Section 14.3 we consider more basic aspects of the multivariate and define the multivariate normal distribution in more detail.

?pairs, ?faces

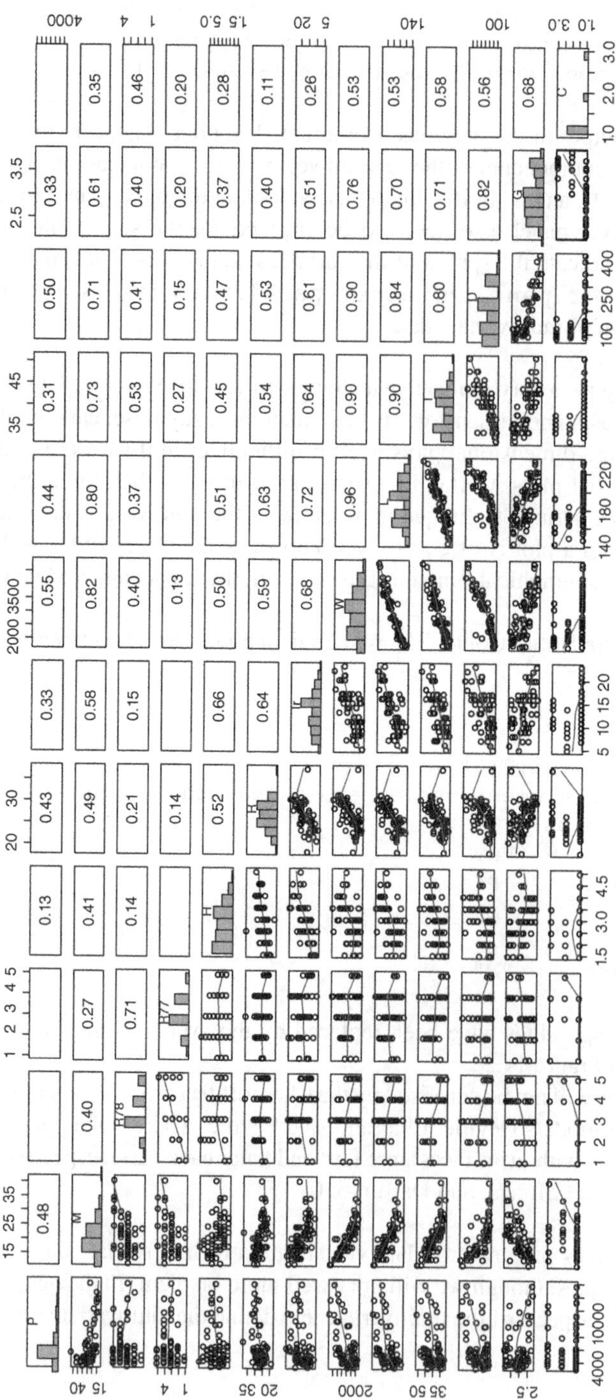

Figure 14.1 A Correlation Matrix Scatter Plot for the Car Data

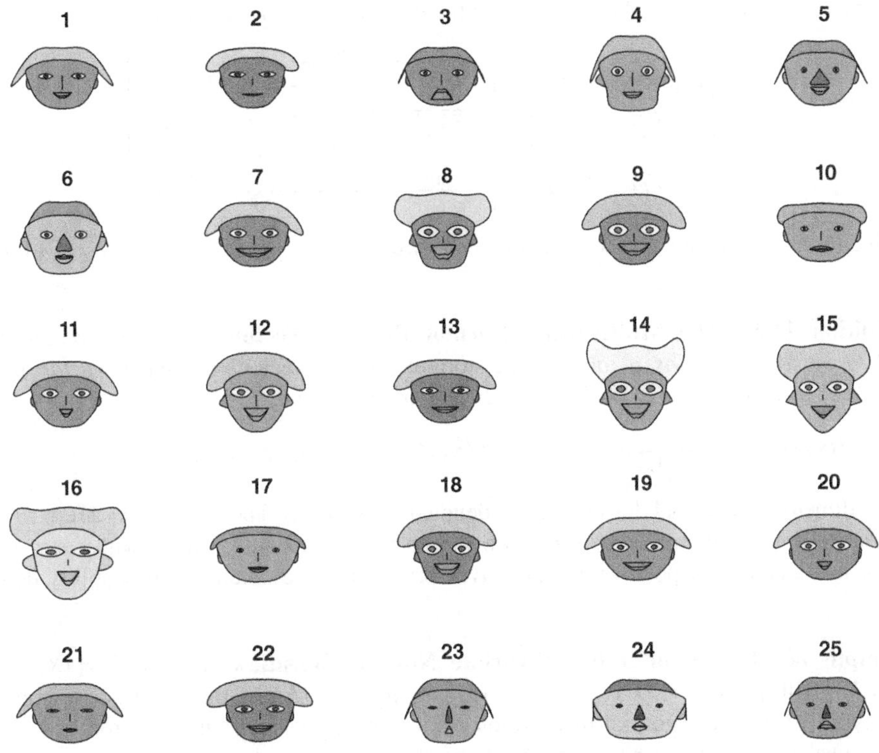

Figure 14.2 Chernoff Faces for a Sample of 25 Data Points of Car Data

14.3 Definitions, Notations, and Summary Statistics for Multivariate Data

14.3.1 Definitions and Data Visualization

We will denote a p-random vector by $\mathbf{X} = (X_1, X_2, \ldots, X_p)$, and its n replicates by $\mathbf{X_1}, \mathbf{X_2}, \ldots, \mathbf{X_n}$. The random vector of the ith replicate is denoted as $\mathbf{X_i} = (X_{i1}, X_{i2}, \ldots, X_{ip})$, $i = 1, 2, \ldots, n$. The mean vector and variance-covariance matrix of $\mathbf{X}$ are respectively denoted as

$$E(\mathbf{X}) = \boldsymbol{\mu} = (E(X_1), E(X_2), \ldots, E(X_p)), \tag{14.1}$$

$$Var(\mathbf{X}) = \boldsymbol{\Sigma} = E(\mathbf{X} - \boldsymbol{\mu})'(\mathbf{X} - \boldsymbol{\mu}) \tag{14.2}$$

$$= \begin{bmatrix} \sigma_{11} & \sigma_{12} & \cdots & \sigma_{1p} \\ \sigma_{21} & \sigma_{22} & \cdots & \sigma_{2p} \\ \vdots & \vdots & \cdots & \vdots \\ \sigma_{p1} & \sigma_{p2} & \cdots & \sigma_{pp} \end{bmatrix}. \tag{14.3}$$

Note that the matrix $Var(\mathbf{X}) = \boldsymbol{\Sigma}$ is a symmetric matrix, that is, $\sigma_{ij} = \sigma_{ji}, i, j = 1, 2, \ldots, p$.

Sometimes, we may also be interested in the *correlation matrix* defined by

$$\rho = \begin{bmatrix} \rho_{11} & \rho_{12} & \cdots & \rho_{1p} \\ \rho_{21} & \rho_{22} & \cdots & \rho_{2p} \\ \vdots & \vdots & \cdots & \vdots \\ \rho_{p1} & \rho_{p2} & \cdots & \rho_{pp} \end{bmatrix} = \begin{bmatrix} \frac{\sigma_{11}}{\sqrt{\sigma_{11}}\sqrt{\sigma_{11}}} & \frac{\sigma_{12}}{\sqrt{\sigma_{11}}\sqrt{\sigma_{22}}} & \cdots & \frac{\sigma_{1p}}{\sqrt{\sigma_{11}}\sqrt{\sigma_{pp}}} \\ \frac{\sigma_{12}}{\sqrt{\sigma_{11}}\sqrt{\sigma_{22}}} & \frac{\sigma_{22}}{\sqrt{\sigma_{22}}\sqrt{\sigma_{22}}} & \cdots & \frac{\sigma_{2p}}{\sqrt{\sigma_{22}}\sqrt{\sigma_{pp}}} \\ \vdots & \vdots & \cdots & \vdots \\ \frac{\sigma_{1p}}{\sqrt{\sigma_{11}}\sqrt{\sigma_{pp}}} & \frac{\sigma_{2p}}{\sqrt{\sigma_{22}}\sqrt{\sigma_{pp}}} & \cdots & \frac{\sigma_{pp}}{\sqrt{\sigma_{pp}}\sqrt{\sigma_{pp}}} \end{bmatrix}.$$

Each correlation coefficient will be a number between –1 and +1, that is, $-1 \leq \rho_{ij} \leq +1, i,j = 1, \cdots, p$.

Definition 14.3.1 The Multivariate Normal Random Vector. *A random vector* $\mathbf{X}$ *is said to be distributed as a* multivariate normal random vector *with mean vector* $\boldsymbol{\mu}$ *and variance-covariance matrix* $\boldsymbol{\Sigma}$*, if its density function is given by*

$$f(\mathbf{x}) = \frac{1}{(2\pi)^{p/2}|\boldsymbol{\Sigma}|^{1/2}} e^{-(x-\mu)'\Sigma^{-1}(x-\mu)/2}, \ if - \infty < x_i < \infty, i = 1, 2, \cdots, p. \tag{14.4}$$

The p-dimensional normal density will be denoted by $N_p(\boldsymbol{\mu}, \boldsymbol{\Sigma})$. The case of $p = 2$ refers to the bivariate normal random distribution. For bivariate normal random variables with a zero-mean vector and a couple of positive and negative correlations, we obtain the probability density plots.

Example 14.3.1. Plot of a few Bivariate Normal Densities. Assume $\mathbf{X} = (X_1, X_2) \sim N_2(\boldsymbol{\mu}, \boldsymbol{\Sigma})$, with $\mu_1 = \mu_2 = 0$, $\rho_{11} = \rho_{22} = 1$, $\rho_{12} = \rho_{21} = \pm 0.5$ or ± 0.9. That is, we consider four types of bivariate normal distribution. Using the `dmvnorm` function from the `mvt-norm` package and `scatterplot3d` from the same named package, we generate the three-dimensional plots of bivariate normal densities.

```
> x <- rep(seq(-4,4,.2),each=41)
> y <- rep(seq(-4,4,.2),41)
> sigma5 <- matrix(c(1,.5,.5,1),nrow=2)
> sigma_5 <- matrix(c(1,-.5,-.5,1),nrow=2)
> sigma9 <- matrix(c(1,.9,.9,1),nrow=2)
> sigma_9 <- matrix(c(1,-.9,-.9,1),nrow=2)
> dxy5 <- dmvnorm(cbind(x,y),sigma=sigma5)
> dxy_5 <- dmvnorm(cbind(x,y),sigma=sigma_5)
> dxy9 <- dmvnorm(cbind(x,y),sigma=sigma9)
> dxy_9 <- dmvnorm(cbind(x,y),sigma=sigma_9)
> scatterplot3d(x, y, dxy5, highlight.3d=TRUE,type="l",xlab="x",
+ ylab="y",zlab="Bivariate Density Function",main="Bivariate Normal
+ Density with Correlation 0.5")
> scatterplot3d(x, y, dxy_5, highlight.3d=TRUE,type="l",xlab="x",
+ ylab="y",zlab="Bivariate Density Function",main="Bivariate Normal
+ Density with Correlation -0.5")
> scatterplot3d(x, y, dxy9, highlight.3d=TRUE,type="l",xlab="x",
+ ylab="y",zlab="Bivariate Density Function",main="Bivariate Normal
+ Density with Correlation 0.9")
> scatterplot3d(x, y, dxy_9, highlight.3d=TRUE,type="l",xlab="x",
+ ylab="y",zlab="Bivariate Density Function",main="Bivariate Normal
+ Density with Correlation -0.9")
```

The resulting three-dimensional plots for the bivariate normal densities are displayed in Figure 14.3. The user must experiment with different values in the mean vector and the variance-covariance matrix to get a firm grip over the bivariate normal densities. □

Example 14.3.2. Normally Distributed and Uncorrelated Random Variables do not imply that the Random Variables are Independent. Melnick and Tenenbein (1982) have demystified the popular notion that normally distributed and uncorrelated random variable are independent random variables. To see this, consider the following counter example. Let X be a standard normal variable, and define

$$Y = \begin{cases} -X \text{ if } |x| < c, \\ X \text{ if } |x| > c. \end{cases}$$

For small values of c, the correlation between X and Y is nearly equal to 1, and for large c values, it is −1. Thus it tells us that there must be some intermediate value of c, which should make the correlation value close to 0, and this value is in the vicinity of 1.54. However, as the X values completely determine the corresponding Y value, they are certainly not independent. In the following R program and Figure 14.4, we see the above-mentioned theory.

```
> x <- rnorm(300)
> constant <- c(.005,1.54,5)
> y1 <- ifelse(abs(x)>constant[1],x,-x)
> y2 <- ifelse(abs(x)>constant[2],x,-x)
> y3 <- ifelse(abs(x)>constant[3],x,-x)
> layout(matrix(c(1,2,3,3),2,byrow=TRUE))
> plot(x,y1,col="blue",ylab="y-values",xlab="x-values","p",
+ main="c = 0.005")
> plot(x,y3,col="green",pch=21,ylab="y-values",xlab="x-values",
+ "p",main="c = 5")
> plot(x,y2,col="red",ylab="y-values",xlab="x-values","p",
+ main="c = 1.54")
```

First, standard normal deviates are obtained using the `rnorm` simulator and stored in the object `x`. Three constant values are stored with `c(0.005,1.54,5)` and the associated `y1-y3` objects are generated with the `ifelse` control loop. We have not considered the `layout` options earlier. The `layout` function divides the device into rows and columns as specified by the matrix. It is a very effective method of obtaining multiple plots in a single frame. The resulting Figure 14.4 confirms the earlier discussion. □

We now describe some standard methods of estimation of the mean vector and the variance-covariance matrix. Define

$$\hat{\mu} = \overline{\mathbf{X}} = \frac{\sum_{i=1}^{n} \mathbf{X_i}}{n}, \tag{14.5}$$

$$\hat{\Sigma} = \frac{1}{n}\sum_{i=1}^{n}(\mathbf{X_i} - \overline{\mathbf{X}})(\mathbf{X_i} - \overline{\mathbf{X}})' = \frac{n-1}{n}\mathbf{S}. \tag{14.6}$$

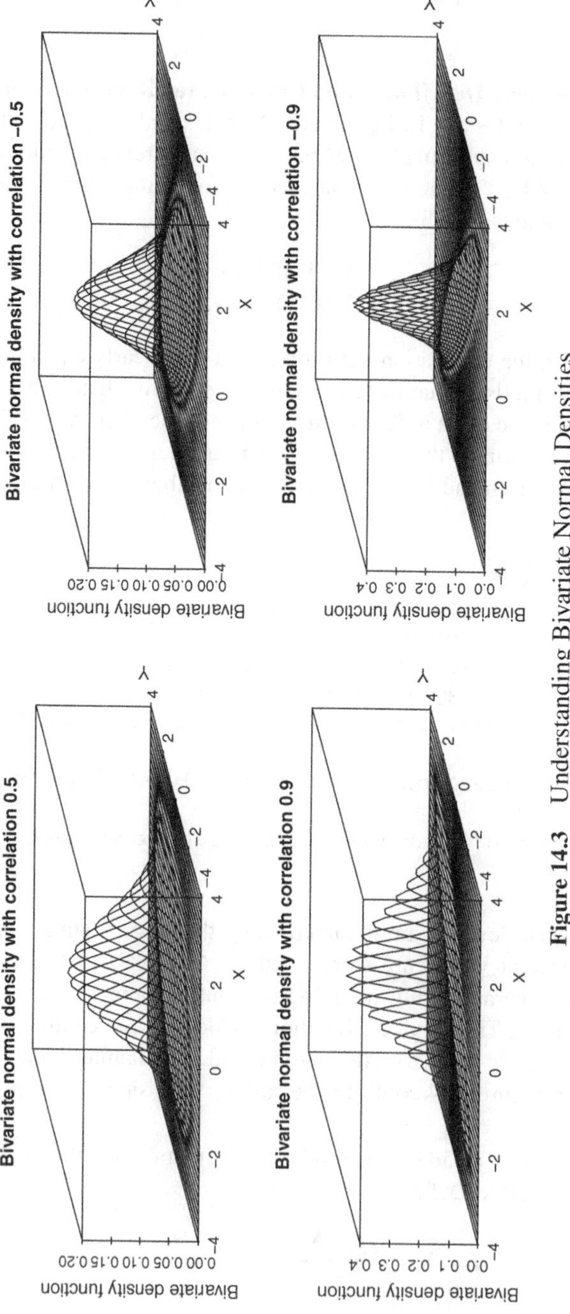

Figure 14.3 Understanding Bivariate Normal Densities

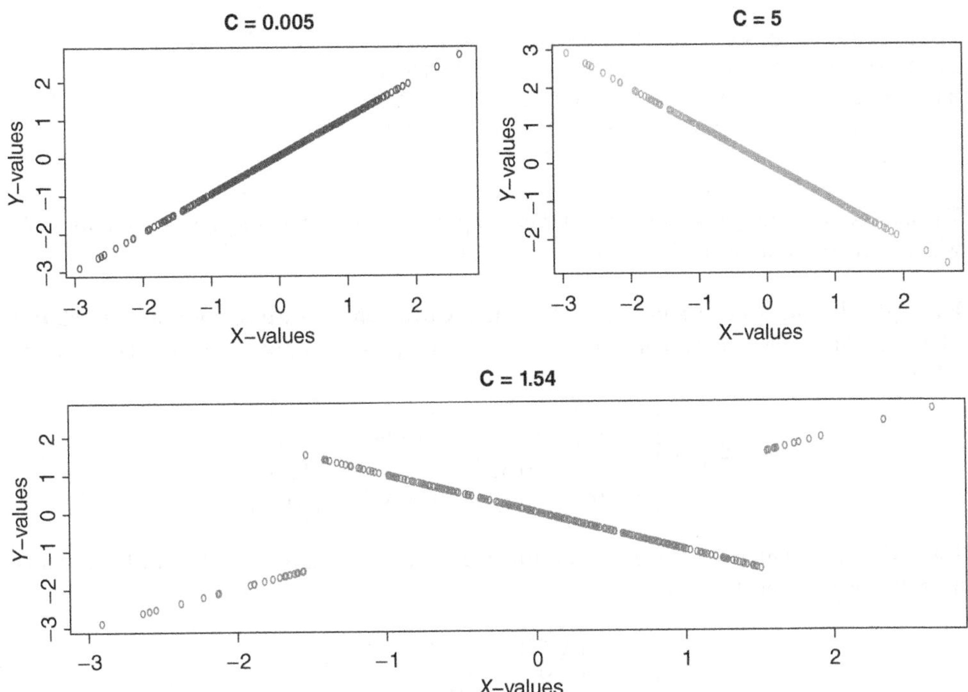

Figure 14.4 A Counter Example of the Myth that Uncorrelated and Normal Distribution imply Independence

Result 4.11 of Johnson and Wichern (2006) shows that the estimators $\hat{\boldsymbol{\mu}}$ and $\hat{\boldsymbol{\Sigma}}$ are respectively MLE's of their parameters.

Example 14.3.3. The Board Stiffness Dataset. Four measures of stiffness of 30 boards are available. The first measure of stiffness is obtained by sending a shock wave down the board, the second measure is obtained by vibrating the board, and the remaining are obtained from static tests. We see that the mean, variance-covariance matrix, as well as the correlation matrix are very easy to compute.

```
> data(stiff)
> mean(stiff)
      x1       x2       x3       x4
1906.100 1749.533 1509.133 1724.967
> var(stiff)
          x1        x2       x3        x4
x1 105616.30  94613.53 87289.71  94230.73
x2  94613.53 101510.12 76137.10  81064.36
x3  87289.71  76137.10 91917.09  90352.38
x4  94230.73  81064.36 90352.38 104227.96
> cor(stiff)
```

```
          x1        x2        x3        x4
x1 1.0000000 0.9137620 0.8859301 0.8981212
x2 0.9137620 1.0000000 0.7882129 0.7881034
x3 0.8859301 0.7882129 1.0000000 0.9231013
x4 0.8981212 0.7881034 0.9231013 1.0000000
> pairs(stiff)
```

The matrix of scatter plots indicate that there might be an *outlier* among the observations. We will say more about this in the coming subsection. □

Example 14.3.4. Conversion of a Variance-Covariance Matrix into a Correlation Matrix. The variance-covariance matrix for the four parameters of the `iris` dataset is the following:

$$\hat{\mathbf{\Sigma}}_{iris} = \begin{bmatrix} 0.6857 & -0.0424 & 1.2743 & 0.5163 \\ -0.0424 & 0.1900 & -0.3297 & -0.1216 \\ 1.2743 & -0.3297 & 3.1163 & 1.2956 \\ 0.5163 & -0.1216 & 1.2956 & 0.5810 \end{bmatrix}.$$

The task is to obtain $\hat{\rho}$ from the given estimated variance-covariance matrix $\hat{\mathbf{\Sigma}}$. First, define the following diagonal matrix:

$$\mathbf{V}^{1/2} = \begin{bmatrix} \sqrt{\sigma_{11}} & 0 & \cdots & 0 \\ 0 & \sqrt{\sigma_{22}} & \cdots & 0 \\ 0 & 0 & \cdots & \sqrt{\sigma_{pp}} \end{bmatrix}.$$

It can then be shown that $\mathbf{V}^{1/2}\rho\mathbf{V}^{1/2} = \mathbf{\Sigma}$. Thus, the sample correlation matrix can be obtained by the relation

$$\hat{\rho} = (\mathbf{V}^{1/2})^{-1}\hat{\mathbf{\Sigma}}(\mathbf{V}^{1/2})^{-1}.$$

The variance-covariance matrix $\hat{\mathbf{\Sigma}}$ is now converted into a correlation matrix in R. An R function `cov2cor` is also available for the same purpose, which will be used to confirm our understanding.

```
> covmat <- round(var(iris[,1:4]),4)
> v1_2 <- covmat*0; diag(v1_2)=sqrt(diag(covmat))
> cormat <- solve(v1_2)%*%covmat%*%solve(v1_2)
> cormat
             Sepal.Length Sepal.Width Petal.Length Petal.Width
Sepal.Length    1.0000000  -0.1174687    0.8717360   0.8179881
Sepal.Width    -0.1174687   1.0000000   -0.4284721  -0.3659896
Petal.Length    0.8717360  -0.4284721    1.0000000   0.9628602
Petal.Width     0.8179881  -0.3659896    0.9628602   1.0000000
> cov2cor(cormat)
             Sepal.Length Sepal.Width Petal.Length Petal.Width
Sepal.Length    1.0000000  -0.1174687    0.8717360   0.8179881
Sepal.Width    -0.1174687   1.0000000   -0.4284721  -0.3659896
Petal.Length    0.8717360  -0.4284721    1.0000000   0.9628602
Petal.Width     0.8179881  -0.3659896    0.9628602   1.0000000
```

Note that any arbitrary square matrix cannot be a variance-covariance matrix. For such inappropriate matrices, you will find that the correlation matrix, if converted, will contain elements which will be less than –1 or greater than 1. □

14.3.2 Early Outlier Detection

An important concept for analysis of multivariate data is given by the *Mahalanobis distance.*

Definition 14.3.2 *The* **Mahalanobis distance** *of a vector* **x** *from a group of vectors with mean* $\boldsymbol{\mu}$ *and covariance matrix* $\mathbb{S}$ *is given by*

$$D^2 = (\mathbf{x} - \boldsymbol{\mu})\mathbb{S}^{-1}(\mathbf{x} - \boldsymbol{\mu}). \tag{14.7}$$

Thus, for each vector $i, i = 1, \ldots, n$, the Mahalanobis distance D^2 may be computed and any unusually large value may then be marked as an outlier. The Mahalanobis distance is also called the *generalized squared distance.*

It is a familiar story that outliers, as in univariate cases, need to be addressed as early as possible. Graphical methods become a bit difficult if the number of variables is more than three. Johnson and Wichern (2006) suggest we should obtain the standardized values of the observations with respect to each variable, and they also recommend looking at the matrix of scatter plots. The four steps listed by them are:

- Obtain the dot plot for each variable.
- Obtain the matrix of scatter plots.
- Obtain the standardized scores for each variable, $z_{ik} = (x_{ik} - \overline{x_k})/\sqrt{s_{kk}}$, for $i = 1, 2, \cdots, n$, and $k = 1, 2, \cdots, p$. Check for large and small values of these scores.
- Obtain the generalized squared distances $(\mathbf{x_i} - \overline{\mathbf{x}})'\mathbf{S}^{-1}(\mathbf{x_i} - \overline{\mathbf{x}})$. Check for large distances.

A dot plot is also known as a *Cleveland dot plot* and it is set up using the `dotchart` function, which in turn is a substitute to the bar plot. In this plot, a dot is used to represent the magnitude of the observation along the x-axis with the observation number on the y-axis.

Example 14.3.5. The Board Stiffness Dataset. Contd. The matrix of scatter plots from Figure 14.5 already indicates the presence of an outlier. Next, look at the dot plots of each of the variables.

```
> par(mfrow=c(4,1),cex=.5)
> dotchart(stiff[,1],main="Dotchart of X1")
> dotchart(stiff[,2],main="Dotchart of X2")
> dotchart(stiff[,3],main="Dotchart of X3")
> dotchart(stiff[,4],main="Dotchart of X4")
```

The dot chart in Figure 14.6 clearly shows that, for each variable, there is one observation at the right-hand side of the diagram whose value is very large compared with the rest of the observations. This is a clean case of the presence of an outlier. If all the four points on the dot chart belong to one observation, we have one outlier, else there may be more outliers. The standardized values are obtained using the `scale` function.

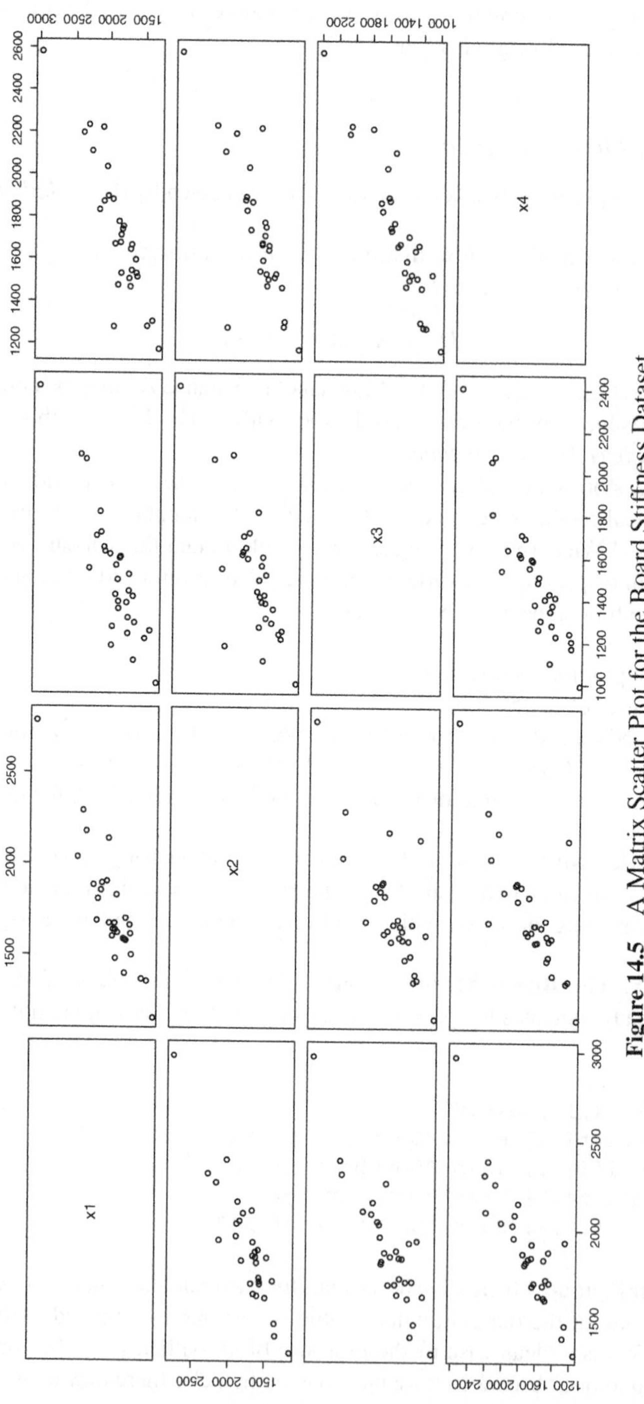

Figure 14.5 A Matrix Scatter Plot for the Board Stiffness Dataset

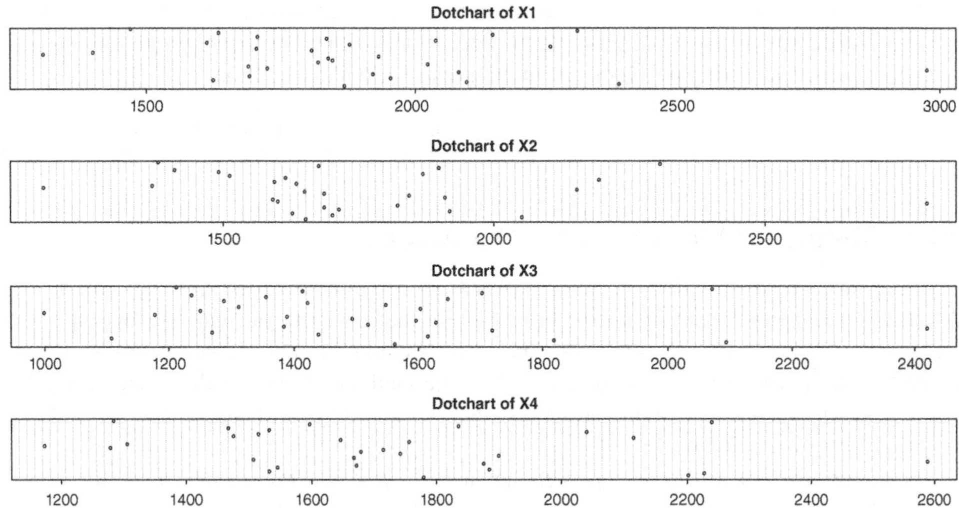

Figure 14.6 Early Outlier Detection through Dot Charts

```
> cbind(stiff,round(scale(stiff),1))
     x1   x2   x3   x4   x1   x2   x3   x4
1  1889 1651 1561 1778 -0.1 -0.3  0.2  0.2
2  2403 2048 2087 2197  1.5  0.9  1.9  1.5
3  2119 1700 1815 2222  0.7 -0.2  1.0  1.5
4  1645 1627 1110 1533 -0.8 -0.4 -1.3 -0.6
5  1976 1916 1614 1883  0.2  0.5  0.3  0.5

9  2983 2794 2412 2581  3.3  3.3  3.0  2.7

30 1490 1382 1214 1284 -1.3 -1.2 -1.0 -1.4
```

Note that the last four columns are standardized values. From our knowledge of the univariate normal cases, we guess that the observation labeled 9 must be an outlier, since three of the four components are in excess of the 3 sigma distance of the mean 0. Multivariate data have a lot of surprises as we see from the outliers given by the generalized squared distances. We now calculate the generalized squared distances for each of the observations.

```
> mahalanobis(stiff,colMeans(stiff),cov(stiff))
 [1]  0.6000129  5.4770196  7.6166439  5.2076098  1.3980776

[29]  6.2837628  2.5838186
```

As we mentioned earlier, we have a surprise outlier in the observation labeled 16 in addition to that labeled 9. Though each of its components is within the control level sense of the univariate data, the generalized squared distance for observation 16 is unusually high. □

We have seen some interesting graphical plots for the multivariate data. The multivariate normal distribution has also been introduced here, along with a few of its properties. We will next consider some testing problems for multivariate normal distribution.

?dmvnorm, ?scatterplot3d, ?solve, ?cov2cor

14.4 Testing for Mean Vectors : One Sample

Suppose that we have random vector samples from a multivariate normal distribution, say $N_p(\boldsymbol{\mu}, \boldsymbol{\Sigma})$. In Chapter 7, we saw testing problems for the univariate normal distribution. If the variance-covariance matrix $\boldsymbol{\Sigma}$ is known to be a diagonal matrix, that is components are uncorrelated random variables, we can revert back to the methods discussed there. However, this is not generally the case for multivariate distributions and they need specialized methods for testing hypothesis problems.

For the problem of testing $H : \boldsymbol{\mu} = \boldsymbol{\mu}_0$ against $K : \boldsymbol{\mu} \neq \boldsymbol{\mu}_0$, we consider two cases here: (i) $\boldsymbol{\Sigma}$ is known, and (ii) $\boldsymbol{\Sigma}$ is unknown. Suppose that we have n samples of random vectors from $N_p(\boldsymbol{\mu}, \boldsymbol{\Sigma})$, which we will denote as $\{\mathbf{X}_1, \mathbf{X}_2, \cdots, \mathbf{X}_n\}$. The sample of random vectors is the same as saying that we have iid random vectors.

14.4.1 Testing for Mean Vector with Known Variance-Covariance Matrix

If the variance-covariance matrix is known, the test statistic is a multivariate extension of the Z-statistic, and is given by

$$Z^2 = n(\overline{\mathbf{x}} - \boldsymbol{\mu}_0)'\boldsymbol{\Sigma}^{-1}(\overline{\mathbf{x}} - \boldsymbol{\mu}_0). \tag{14.8}$$

Under the hypothesis $H : \boldsymbol{\mu} = \boldsymbol{\mu}_0$, the test statistic Z^2 is distributed as a chi-square variate with p degrees of freedom, and a χ_p^2 random variable. The computations are fairly easy and we do that in the next example.

Example 14.4.1. The Importance of Handling the Covariances. Rencher (2002). Consider the height and weight of 20 college-age males. This dataset is available in the csv file `Height_Weight.csv`. Assume that the variance-covariance matrix is known as $\boldsymbol{\Sigma} = [20, 100; 100, 1000]$, and that the hypothesis of interest is $H : \boldsymbol{\mu} = \boldsymbol{\mu}_0 = [70, 170]$, where the height is measured in inches and the weight in pounds.

```
> data(hw)
> mu0 <- c(70,170)
> n <- nrow(hw)
> sigma <- matrix(c(20, 100, 100,1000),nrow=2)
> meanx <- mean(hw)
> z2 <- n*t(meanx-mu0)%*%solve(sigma)%*%(meanx-mu0)
> z2 # the test statistic value
[1] 8.4026
> qchisq(1-.05,2) # 95% confidence level and 2 d.f.
[1] 5.991465
```

Since the calculated χ^2 value is greater than the tabulated value, we reject the hypothesis that the average height and weight are at 70 and 170 units respectively. If we were to ignore the correlation between the height and weight, we have the following conclusions:

```
> htest <- (meanx[1]-70)/(sqrt(sigma[1,1]/n)) # testing for height
> wtest <- (meanx[2]-170)/(sqrt(sigma[2,2]/n)) # testing for weight
> as.numeric(htest);as.numeric(wtest)
[1] 1.45
[1] -0.7495332
```

The absolute value of each of these tests is less than 1.96, and hence we would have failed to reject the hypothesis H, which is not the case when the correlations are adjusted for. Thus, we learn an important story that whenever the correlations are known, it is always better to adjust the statistical procedure for them. □

Example 14.4.2. The Board Stiffness Data. Contd. Suppose that the variance-covariance matrix for this data is known as

$$\Sigma_0 = 10^4 \times \begin{bmatrix} 11 & 9 & 9 & 9 \\ 9 & 10 & 8 & 8 \\ 9 & 8 & 9 & 9 \\ 9 & 8 & 9 & 10 \end{bmatrix}$$

The hypothesis testing problem is $H : \mu = 10^3 \times [2 \quad 1.5 \quad 1.5 \quad 2]$ against the hypothesis $K : \mu \neq 10^3 \times [2 \quad 1.5 \quad 1.5 \quad 2]$. Repeating the above program with small changes, we get the value of the test statistics, and also the critical value.

```
> n <- nrow(stiff)
> sigma <- matrix(10^4*c(11,9,9,9,9,10,8,8,9,8,9,9,9,8,9,10),nrow=4)
> mu0 <- 10^3*c(2,1.5,1.5,2)
> meanx <- mean(stiff)
> z2 <- n*t(meanx-mu0)%*%solve(sigma)%*%(meanx-mu0)
> z2 # the test statistic value
         [,1]
[1,] 365.9636
> qchisq(1-.05,4) #95% confidence level and 4 d.f.
[1] 9.487729
```

The test procedure thus rejects the hypothesis H, since the value of the test statistic is larger than the critical value. □

14.4.2 Testing for Mean Vectors with Unknown Variance-Covariance Matrix

It turns out that in many practical settings, the variance-covariance matrix is unknown. Therefore, we need to extend the test procedure for this important case. The Hotelling's T^2-statistic is given by

$$T^2 = n(\bar{\mathbf{x}} - \boldsymbol{\mu}_0)'\mathbf{S}^{-1}(\bar{\mathbf{x}} - \boldsymbol{\mu}_0), \tag{14.9}$$

where **S** is the sampling covariance matrix. Under the hypothesis H, the test statistic T^2 is distributed as Hotellings' T^2 distribution with p and $\upsilon = n - 1$ degrees of freedom.

Example 14.4.3. The Calcium in Soil and Turnip Greens Data of Rencher (2002). Kramer and Jensen (1969) collected data on three variables at ten different locations. The variables of interest are (i) x_1: available calcium in the soil, (ii) x_2: exchangeable soil calcium, and (iii) x_3: turnip green calcium. Suppose the hypothesis of interest is $H : \boldsymbol{\mu} = [15.0\ 6.0\ 2.85]$.

```
> data(calcium)
> n <- nrow(calcium)
> meanx <- mean(calcium[,-1])
> varx <- var(calcium[,-1])
> mu0 <- c(15,6,2.85)
> t2 <- n*t(meanx-mu0)%*%solve(varx)%*%(meanx-mu0)
> t2
[1] 24.55891
```

If we compare the test statistic value with a Hotelling's distribution with three degrees of freedom and non-centrality parameter 9 at 95% significance level, the critical value is 16.766, and thus we will have to reject the null-hypothesis. □

The Hotellings' T^2 can be converted to an F-statistics using the transformation:

$$\frac{\upsilon - p + 1}{\upsilon p} T^2_{p,\upsilon} = F_{p,\upsilon-p+1}. \tag{14.10}$$

An R function for calculating the test statistic is available in the `ICSNP` package. The test function `HotellingsT2` implements the F-test by comparing if the mean of a normal vector equals some specified null vector. We can easily carry out the F-test for the above example.

Example 14.4.4. The Calcium in Soil and Turnip Greens Data of Rencher (2002). Contd. First call up the `ICSNP` library and then use the function `HotellingsT2` for the calcium problem.

```
> library(ICSNP)
> HotellingsT2(calcium[,-1],mu=mu0,test="f")

        Hotelling's one sample T2-test

data:  calcium[, -1]
T.2 = 6.3671, df1 = 3, df2 = 7, p-value = 0.02068
alternative hypothesis: true location is not equal to c(15,6,2.85)
```

The conclusion on using any of the methods does not vary and we are led to reject the hypothesis H. □

It is known that the likelihood-ratio tests are very generic methods for testing hypothesis problems. The likelihood-ratio test of $H : \boldsymbol{\mu} = \boldsymbol{\mu}_0$ against $K : \boldsymbol{\mu} \neq \boldsymbol{\mu}_0$ is given by

$$\Lambda = \left(\frac{|\hat{\boldsymbol{\Sigma}}|}{|\hat{\boldsymbol{\Sigma}}_0|} \right)^{n/2} = \left(\frac{|\sum_{i=1}^{n}(\mathbf{x}_i - \overline{\mathbf{x}})(\mathbf{x}_i - \overline{\mathbf{x}})'|}{|\sum_{i=1}^{n}(\mathbf{x}_i - \boldsymbol{\mu}_0)(\mathbf{x}_i - \boldsymbol{\mu}_0)'|} \right)^{n/2}. \tag{14.11}$$

It is further known from the general theory of the likelihood ratios that the above-mentioned test statistics follow a chi-square random variate. Yes, the computations are not trivial for the χ^2-test based on the likelihood-ratio test, and hence the `ICSNP` package will be used to bail us out of this scenario. The illustration is continued with the previous data-set.

Example 14.4.5. The Calcium in Soil and Turnip Greens Data of Rencher (2002). Contd. The option of `test="f"` needs to be replaced with `test="chi"` in the previous R line to carry out the χ^2-test for testing the hypothesis H.

```
> HotellingsT2(calcium[,-1],mu=mu0,test="chi")
        Hotelling's one sample T2-test
data:  calcium[, -1]
T.2 = 24.5589, df = 3, p-value = 1.909e-05
alternative hypothesis: true location is not equal to c(15,6,2.85)
```

The conclusion does not change and, as earlier, the hypotheses H is rejected in confirmation with earlier methods. □

The problem of testing $H : \boldsymbol{\mu} = \boldsymbol{\mu}_0$ against $K : \boldsymbol{\mu} \neq \boldsymbol{\mu}_0$ will be considered for the two-sample problem in Section 14.5.

?qchisq, ?var, ?solve, ?HotellingsT2

14.5 Testing for Mean Vectors : Two-Samples

Consider the case of random vector samples from two plausible populations, $N(\boldsymbol{\mu}_1, \boldsymbol{\Sigma}_1)$ and $N(\boldsymbol{\mu}_2, \boldsymbol{\Sigma}_2)$. Such scenarios are very likely if new machinery and a population labeled 1 refers to samples obtained under the new machinery and that labeled 2 refers to the samples under older machinery. As the comparison of the mean vectors become sensible only if the covariance matrices are equal, we assume that the covariance matrices are equal, but not known. That is, $\boldsymbol{\Sigma}_1 = \boldsymbol{\Sigma}_2 = \boldsymbol{\Sigma}$, with $\boldsymbol{\Sigma}$ unknown.

Suppose that we have samples from the two populations as $\mathbf{X}_{11}, \mathbf{X}_{12}, \cdots, \mathbf{X}_{1n_1}$, $\mathbf{X}_{1i} \sim N_p(\boldsymbol{\mu}_1, \boldsymbol{\Sigma})$, and $\mathbf{X}_{21}, \mathbf{X}_{22}, \cdots, \mathbf{X}_{2n_2}$, $\mathbf{X}_{2i} \sim N_p(\boldsymbol{\mu}_2, \boldsymbol{\Sigma})$. The hypothesis of interest is to test $H : \boldsymbol{\mu}_1 = \boldsymbol{\mu}_2$ against $K : \boldsymbol{\mu}_1 \neq \boldsymbol{\mu}_2$. The estimates of the mean vectors from each of the populations is given by $\overline{\mathbf{x}}_j = \sum_{i=1}^{n_j} \mathbf{x}_{ji}/n_j, j = 1, 2$.

We will first define the matrices of *sum squares* and *cross-products* as below:

$$\mathbf{W}_1 = \sum_{i=1}^{n_1}(\mathbf{x}_{1i} - \overline{\mathbf{x}}_1)(\mathbf{x}_{1i} - \overline{\mathbf{x}}_1)' = (n_1 - 1)\mathbf{S}_1, \tag{14.12}$$

$$\mathbf{W}_2 = \sum_{i=1}^{n_2}(\mathbf{x}_{2i} - \overline{\mathbf{x}}_2)(\mathbf{x}_{2i} - \overline{\mathbf{x}}_2)' = (n_2 - 1)\mathbf{S}_2. \tag{14.13}$$

Further define the *pooled covariance matrix*:

$$\mathbf{S}_{pl} = \frac{1}{n_1 + n_2 - 2}\left[(n_1 - 1)\mathbf{S}_1 + (n_2 - 1)\mathbf{S}_2\right] = \frac{1}{n_1 + n_2 - 2}\left[\mathbf{W}_1 + \mathbf{W}_2\right]. \tag{14.14}$$

The Hotelling's T^2 test statistic is then given by

$$T^2 = \frac{n_1 n_2}{n_1 + n_2}(\overline{\mathbf{x}}_1 - \overline{\mathbf{x}}_2)'\mathbf{S}_{pl}^{-1}(\overline{\mathbf{x}}_1 - \overline{\mathbf{x}}_2). \tag{14.15}$$

The test statistic T^2, under the hypothesis H, is distributed as Hotelling's T^2 distribution with parameters p and $n_1 + n_2 - 2$. We list below some important properties of the Hotelling's T^2 statistic:

1. Hotelling's T^2 distribution is skewed.
2. For a two-sided alternative hypothesis, the critical-region is one-tailed.
3. A necessary condition for the inverse of the pooled covariance matrix to exist is that the $n_1 + n_2 - 2 > p$.
4. A straightforward, not necessarily simple, transformation of the Hotelling's statistic gives us an F-statistic.

As in the previous section, we may also use the likelihood-ratio tests, which lead to an appropriate χ^2-test, for large n of course, see Rencher (2002) or Johnson and Wichern (2006). In the next illustrative example, we obtain the Hotelling's test statistics, the associated F-statistic, and the likelihood-ratio test.

Example 14.5.1. Psychological Tests for Males and Females. A psychological study consisting of four tests was conducted on male and female groups and the results were noted. Since the four tests are correlated and each one is noted for all the individuals, we are interested in knowing if the mean vector of the test scores is the same across the gender group. The four tests here are as follows:

- x_1: pictorial inconsistencies
- x_2: paper form board
- x_3: tool recognition
- x_4: vocabulary.

Assume that the covariance matrix is the same for both the groups, and that it is unknown. We will write a small program for calculating the Hotelling's T^2 statistic, and use the function from the `ICSNP` package for the F- test and the chi-square tests.

```
> data(mfp)
> males <- mfp[,1:4]; females <- mfp[,5:8]
> nm <- nrow(males); nf <- nrow(females)
> meanm <- colMeans(males); meanf <- colMeans(females)
> sigmam <- var(males); sigmaf <- var(females)
> sigmapl <- (1/(nm+nf-2))*((nm-1)*sigmam+(nf-1)*sigmaf)
> t2 <- ((nm*nf)/(nm+nf))*(t(meanm-meanf)%*%solve(sigmapl)%*%
+ (meanm-meanf))
> nm;nf;meanm;meanf;sigmapl;t2
[1] 32
[1] 32
    M_y1     M_y2     M_y3     M_y4
15.96875 15.90625 27.18750 22.75000
    F_y1     F_y2     F_y3     F_y4
12.34375 13.90625 16.65625 21.93750
         M_y1      M_y2      M_y3      M_y4
M_y1 7.164315  6.047379  5.693044  4.700605
M_y2 6.047379 15.894153  8.492440  5.855847
M_y3 5.693044  8.492440 29.356351 13.980847
M_y4 4.700605  5.855847 13.980847 22.320565
        [,1]
[1,] 97.6015
> HotellingsT2(males,females,test="f")
        Hotelling's two sample T2-test
data:  males and females
T.2 = 23.2197, df1 = 4, df2 = 59, p-value = 1.464e-11
alternative hypothesis: true location difference is not
+ equal to c(0,0,0,0)
> HotellingsT2(males,females,test="chi")
        Hotelling's two sample T2-test
data:  males and females
T.2 = 97.6015, df = 4, p-value < 2.2e-16
alternative hypothesis: true location difference is not
+ equal to c(0,0,0,0)
```

After importing the dataset, the first few lines of the code obtain the quantities n_1, n_2, $\overline{\mathbf{x}}_1$, $\overline{\mathbf{x}}_2$, $\mathbf{S}_1$, and $\upsilon\mathbf{S}_2$. The pooled variance as specified in Equation 14.14 is computed by the R code line beginning with `t2`. The computations are illustrated to clarify the formulas. The R function `HotellingsT2` is then used to obtain the results in the routine way.

Comparing the value of the test statistic T^2 with critical value $T^2_{0.01,4,62} = 15.373$, we are led to reject the hypothesis of equal mean vectors for the gender groups. □

?HotellingsT2

14.6 Multivariate Analysis of Variance

The ANOVA deals with testing of k-means being equal in the univariate case. A host of ANOVA techniques was seen in Chapter 13. For the multivariate case, we have the generalization *multivariate analysis of variance*, more commonly simply known as MANOVA. The data structure can be easily displayed in tabular form, and we adapt the notation from Rencher (2002).

Suppose we want to test for equality of mean of k-vector samples. Let $\mathbf{y}_{ij}$ denote observation j from population i, $i = 1, 2, \cdots, k, j = 1, 2, \cdots, n$. We assume that $\mathbf{y}_{ij} \sim N(\boldsymbol{\mu}_i, \boldsymbol{\Sigma})$. The observation model is specified by

$$\begin{aligned} \mathbf{y}_{ij} &= \boldsymbol{\mu} + \boldsymbol{\alpha}_i + \boldsymbol{\epsilon}_{ij} \\ &= \boldsymbol{\mu}_i + \boldsymbol{\epsilon}_{ij}, i = 1, 2, \cdots, k, j = 1, 2, \cdots, n. \end{aligned} \tag{14.16}$$

Here $\boldsymbol{\epsilon} \sim N(\boldsymbol{\mu}, \boldsymbol{\Sigma})$, and $\boldsymbol{\alpha}_i$ is the *mean effect* in the ith population. The hypothesis of interest is given by $H : \boldsymbol{\mu}_1 = \boldsymbol{\mu}_2 = \cdots = \boldsymbol{\mu}_k$. To test the hypothesis H, we need to define, as usual, the "between" and "within" sum of squares matrices, denoted by $\mathbf{H}$ and $\mathbf{E}$ respectively:

$$\begin{aligned} \mathbf{H} &= n \sum_{i=1}^{k} (\overline{\mathbf{y}}_{i.} - \overline{\mathbf{y}}_{..})(\overline{\mathbf{y}}_{i.} - \overline{\mathbf{y}}_{..})^T \\ &= \frac{1}{n} \sum_{i=1}^{k} \mathbf{y}_{i.}\mathbf{y}_{i.}^T - \frac{1}{kn}\mathbf{y}_{..}\mathbf{y}_{..}^T, \end{aligned} \tag{14.17}$$

$$\begin{aligned} \mathbf{E} &= \sum_{i=1}^{k} \sum_{j=1}^{n} (\mathbf{y}_{ij} - \overline{\mathbf{y}}_{i.})(\mathbf{y}_{ij} - \overline{\mathbf{y}}_{i.})^T \\ &= \sum_{ij} \mathbf{y}_{ij}\mathbf{y}_{ij}^T - \frac{1}{n} \sum_{i} \mathbf{y}_{i.}\mathbf{y}_{i.}^T. \end{aligned} \tag{14.18}$$

Let v_H and v_E respectively denote the rank of $\mathbf{H}$ and $\mathbf{E}$. There are four different statistics to test for H and they are now explained in some detail.

14.6.1 Wilks Test Statistic

The *Wilks test statistic* for H is given by

$$\Lambda = \frac{|\mathbf{E}|}{|\mathbf{E} + \mathbf{H}|}. \tag{14.19}$$

In the above expression, $|.|$ denotes the determinant of the matrix. The multivariate literature refers to Λ as Wilks' Λ. The test statistic can be equivalently expressed in terms of the eigenvalues $\lambda_i, i = 1, \cdots, s$ of $\mathbf{E}^{-1}\mathbf{H}$, where s is the rank of $\mathbf{E}^{-1}\mathbf{H}$, and is given by

$$\Lambda = \prod_{i=1}^{s} \frac{1}{1 + \lambda_i}. \tag{14.20}$$

The Wilks' Λ takes values in the interval $[0,1]$. Thus, the test procedure is to reject H if $\Lambda \leq \Lambda_{\alpha,p,\upsilon_E,\upsilon_H}$. These ideas and concepts are next illustrated using the well-known root-stack dataset.

Example 14.6.1. Apple of Different Rootstock. The variables description is listed:

- y_1 = trunk girth at 4 years ($mm \times 100$)
- y_2 = extension growth at 4 years (m)
- y_3 = trunk girth at 15 years ($mm \times 100$)
- y_4 = weight of tree above ground at 15 years ($lb \times 1000$)

The goal is to test if the mean vector of the four variables is the same across six stratas of the experiment, that is, $H : \boldsymbol{\mu}_1 = \boldsymbol{\mu}_2 = \cdots = \boldsymbol{\mu}_6$. We will first use a laborious approach to obtain the Wilks' Λ and test the hypothesis. The R function will follow these tedious codes later.

```
> # rootstock.dta is available at
> # http://www.stata-press.com/data/r10/rootstock.dta
> library(foreign)
> rootstock <- read.dta("rootstock.dta")
> rootstock1 <- rootstock[rootstock[,1]==1,2:5]
> rootstock2 <- rootstock[rootstock[,1]==2,2:5]
> rootstock3 <- rootstock[rootstock[,1]==3,2:5]
> rootstock4 <- rootstock[rootstock[,1]==4,2:5]
> rootstock5 <- rootstock[rootstock[,1]==5,2:5]
> rootstock6 <- rootstock[rootstock[,1]==6,2:5]
> n <- 8; p <- 4; vh <- 5; ve <- 6*(8-1); k <- 6
> ymm<- colSums(rootstock[,2:5])
> y1m <- colSums(rootstock1)
> y2m <- colSums(rootstock2)
> y3m <- colSums(rootstock3)
> y4m <- colSums(rootstock4)
> y5m <- colSums(rootstock5)
> y6m <- colSums(rootstock6)
> H <- ((y1m%*%t(y1m))/n) + ((y2m%*%t(y2m))/n)+((y3m%*%t(y3m))/n)
+ +((y4m%*%t(y4m))/n) + ((y5m%*%t(y5m))/n)+((y6m%*%t(y6m))/n)
+ - (ymm%*%t(ymm))/(k*n)
> E <- matrix(0,nrow=4, ncol=4);
> for(i in 1:nrow(rootstock)) {
+ a <- as.numeric(rootstock[i,2:5])
+ E <- E + a%*%t(a)
+ }
> E <- E - (((y1m%*%t(y1m))/n) + ((y2m%*%t(y2m))/n)
+ +((y3m%*%t(y3m))/n)+((y4m%*%t(y4m))/n) + ((y5m%*%t(y5m))/n)
+ +((y6m%*%t(y6m))/n))
> E_H <- E+H
> wlambda <- det(E)/(det(E_H))
> options(digits=3)
> E;H;E_H;wlambda
        y1    y2    y3    y4
[1,] 0.320  1.70 0.554 0.217
[2,] 1.697 12.14 4.364 2.110
```

```
[3,] 0.554  4.36 4.291 2.482
[4,] 0.217  2.11 2.482 1.723
         y1    y2    y3    y4
[1,] 0.0736 0.537 0.332 0.208
[2,] 0.5374 4.200 2.355 1.637
[3,] 0.3323 2.355 6.114 3.781
[4,] 0.2085 1.637 3.781 2.493
        y1    y2     y3    y4
[1,] 0.394  2.23  0.886 0.426
[2,] 2.234 16.34  6.719 3.747
[3,] 0.886  6.72 10.405 6.263
[4,] 0.426  3.75  6.263 4.216
[1] 0.154
```

From the data object `rootstock`, the data for each stratum is extracted with the code `rootstock1 <- rootstock[rootstock[,1]==1,2:5]`. We have exactly eight observations from each stratum and hence `n <- 8`, and similarly the other scalar numbers are created. The R function `colSums` is essentially used to capture terms such as $\mathbf{y}_{i.}$ and $\mathbf{y}_{..}$. To obtain the matrix **H**, the R code `((y1m%*%t(y1m))/n)+ ... +((y6m%*%t(y6m))/n) - (ymm%*%t(ymm))/(k*n)` imitates Formula 14.17. To obtain the matrix **E**, the R program takes it into two steps. In the first step, it simply captures the first part of Formula 14.18, that is the $\sum_{ij}\mathbf{y}_{ij}\mathbf{y}_{ij}^T$ part with the `for` loop `for(i in 1:nrow(rootstock))`. The rest of Equation 14.18 is computed with `E <- E - (((y1m%*%t(y1m))/n) + ... + ((y6m%*%t(y6m))/n))`. The rest of the R program is trivial to follow.

The calculated values of Wilks lambda `0.154` is less than the theoretical value of 0.455 (corresponding to $p = 4$, $\upsilon_H = 5$, $\upsilon_E = 42$). Thus, we reject the hypothesis that the mean vector is the same for the six strata. The R function `manova` shows the same result:

```
> attach(rootstock)
> rs <- rootstock[,1]
> rs <- factor(rs,ordered=is.ordered(rs)) # Too important a step
> root.manova <- manova(cbind(y1,y2,y3,y4)~rs)
> summary(root.manova, test = "Wilks")
          Df Wilks approx F num Df den Df  Pr(>F)
rs         5 0.154     4.94     20    130 7.7e-09 ***
Residuals 42
---
Signif. codes:  0 '***' 0.001 '**' 0.01 '*' 0.05 '.' 0.1 ' ' 1
```

Complex computational statistics, at least from a vector and matrix point of view, is completely followed through a rudimentary approach and then verified through the R function `manova`. □

14.6.2 Roy's Test

It is beyond the scope of the current work to clearly underpin the statistical motivation of *Roy's test*. An elegant description of the Roy's test can be found in Section 6.1.4 of Rencher (2002).

We now give a watered-down version of Roy's test. Let λ_1 denote the largest eigenvalue of the matrix $\boldsymbol{E}^{-1}\boldsymbol{H}$. The *Roy's largest root test* is given by

$$\theta = \frac{\lambda_1}{1+\lambda_1}. \tag{14.21}$$

The test procedure is then to reject the hypothesis H if $\theta \geq \theta_{\alpha,s,m,N}$, where $s = \min\{\upsilon_H, p\}, m = \frac{1}{2}(|\upsilon_H - p| - 1), N = \frac{1}{2}(\upsilon_E - p - 1)$.

For the rootstock dataset, the one-line R code below gives the result based on the Roy's test.

```
> summary(root.manova, test = "Roy")
          Df  Roy approx F num Df den Df Pr(>F)
rs         5 1.88     15.8      5     42  1e-08 ***
Residuals 42
---
Signif. codes:  0 '***' 0.001 '**' 0.01 '*' 0.05 '.' 0.1 ' ' 1
```

The Roy's test also rejects the hypothesis H that the mean vector for the six strata are equal.

14.6.3 Pillai's Test Statistic

Let $\lambda_1, \cdots, \lambda_s$ denote the s eigenvalues of the matrix $\mathbf{E}^{-1}\mathbf{H}$. The *Pillai test statistic* is then given by

$$V^{(s)} = \text{tr}[(\boldsymbol{E}+\boldsymbol{H}^{-1})\boldsymbol{H}] = \sum_{i=1}^{s} \frac{\lambda_i}{1+\lambda_i}. \tag{14.22}$$

The test procedure is to reject H if $V^{(s)} \geq V_\alpha^{(s)}$. In R, we carry out the Pillai's method as below.

```
> summary(root.manova, test = "Pillai")
          Df Pillai approx F num Df den Df Pr(>F)
rs         5   1.30     4.07     20    168  2e-07 ***
Residuals 42
---
Signif. codes:  0 '***' 0.001 '**' 0.01 '*' 0.05 '.' 0.1 ' ' 1
```

The Pillai's test statistic confirms the findings of the Wilks's and Roy's test that the mean vector for the six strata are significantly different. Finally, we look at the fourth test for testing the hypothesis H, that the strata mean vectors are equal to the Lawley-Hotelling test statistic.

14.6.4 The Lawley-Hotelling Test Statistic

The *Lawley-Hotelling statistic* is defined by:

$$U^{(s)} = \text{tr}(\boldsymbol{E}^{-1}\boldsymbol{H}). \tag{14.23}$$

The test procedure is to reject the hypothesis H for large values of $U^{(s)}$. This is illustrated in R.

```
> summary(root.manova, test = "Hotelling")
          Df Hotelling-Lawley approx F num Df den Df   Pr(>F)
rs         5             2.92     5.48     20    150 2.6e-10 ***
Residuals 42
---
Signif. codes:  0 '***' 0.001 '**' 0.01 '*' 0.05 '.' 0.1 ' ' 1
```

Thus, it is concluded that all the four statistical tests lead to the same conclusion, that the mean vector for the six strata are different. From a theoretical point of view, there is no reason to prefer one of the four methods over the others. A general advice is to use all the four methods. Consider one more example before closing the MANOVA section.

Example 14.6.2. Testing for Physico-chemical Properties of Water in Four Cities. Water samples from four cities are collected and their physico-chemical properties for ten variables, such as `pH`, `Conductivity`, `Total_Dissolved_Solid`, etc., are measured. We would then like to test if the properties are the same across the four cities and in which case a same water treatment approach can be adopted for all cities. The MANOVA test is used for statistical analysis of the problem. This example is drawn from Gore, et al. (2006). This dataset is also available in the R package `gpk` and the dataset name is `Waterquality`.

```
> data(Waterquality)
> attach(Waterquality)
> City <- factor(City,ordered=is.ordered(City))
> WQ.manova <- manova(cbind(pH,Conductivity,Total_Dissolved_Solid,
+ Alkalinity,Hardness,
+ Calcium_Hardness,Magnesium_Hardness,Chlorides,Sulphates)~City)
> summary(WQ.manova, test = "Wilks")
          Df    Wilks approx F num Df den Df    Pr(>F)
City       3 0.030522   12.758     27 149.59 < 2.2e-16 ***
Residuals 59
---
Signif. codes:  0 '***' 0.001 '**' 0.01 '*' 0.05 '.' 0.1 ' ' 1
> summary(WQ.manova, test = "Roy")
          Df    Roy approx F num Df den Df    Pr(>F)
City       3 6.3098   37.158      9     53 < 2.2e-16 ***
Residuals 59
---
Signif. codes:  0 '***' 0.001 '**' 0.01 '*' 0.05 '.' 0.1 ' ' 1
> summary(WQ.manova, test = "Pillai")
          Df Pillai approx F num Df den Df    Pr(>F)
City       3  1.909   10.305     27    159 < 2.2e-16 ***
Residuals 59
---
Signif. codes:  0 '***' 0.001 '**' 0.01 '*' 0.05 '.' 0.1 ' ' 1
> summary(WQ.manova, test = "Hotelling")
          Df Hotelling-Lawley approx F num Df den Df    Pr(>F)
City       3           8.5864   15.795     27    149 < 2.2e-16 ***
Residuals 59
---
Signif. codes:  0 '***' 0.001 '**' 0.01 '*' 0.05 '.' 0.1 ' ' 1
```

Since each of the four statistical tests indicates that the mean vector of the ten variates across the four cities are significantly different from each other, the water treatment program across the cities has to be different. □

?det, ?manova, ?summary.manova

We will next look at testing hypotheses problems related to the variance-covariance matrices.

14.7 Testing for Variance-Covariance Matrix: One Sample

In MSA, the covariance matrix plays the role of the scale parameter. We thus naturally encounter the problem of testing $H : \boldsymbol{\Sigma} = \boldsymbol{\Sigma}_0$. Let us begin with the testing problems of covariance matrix in the one sample case.

Let $\mathbf{S}$ denote the sample covariance matrix of $\boldsymbol{\Sigma}$. Define $\upsilon = n - 1$. The *likelihood ratio test statistic* for the hypothesis $H : \boldsymbol{\Sigma} = \boldsymbol{\Sigma}_0$ is given by

$$u = \upsilon[\ln |\boldsymbol{\Sigma}_0| - \ln |\mathbf{S}| + tr(\mathbf{S}\boldsymbol{\Sigma}_0^{-1}) - p], \tag{14.24}$$

where υ is the degrees of freedom of $\mathbf{S}$, ln is the natural logarithm (base e), and tr is the trace, sum of diagonal matrix, of a matrix. For large υ values, u is approximately distributed as a χ^2-random variable with $p(p+1)/2$ degrees of freedom. For moderate-sized samples, Rencher (2002) recommends the use of the following modification:

$$u' = u\left[1 - \frac{1}{6\upsilon - 1}\left(2p + 1 - \frac{2}{p+1}\right)\right]. \tag{14.25}$$

The test procedure is to reject the hypothesis H if the values of u or u' are greater than $\chi^2_{[\alpha,p(p+1)/2]}$. Both the test statistics u and u' are computed in the next example.

Example 14.7.1. Understanding the Height-Weight Relationship. This is a continuation of Example 14.4.1, where we have the height and weight of 20 college-age males. Here, test if the covariance matrix is indeed $\boldsymbol{\Sigma}_0 = [20, 100; 100, 1000]$.

```
> data(hw)
> sigma0 <- matrix(c(20, 100, 100, 1000),nrow=2)
> sigma <- var(hw)
> v <- nrow(hw)-1
> p <- ncol(hw)
> u <- v*(log(det(sigma0))-log(det(sigma)) + sum(diag(sigma%*%solve
+ (sigma0)))-p)
> u1 <- (1- (1/(6*v-1))*(2*p+1 - 2/(p+1)))*u
> u;u1;qchisq(1-0.05,p*(p+1)/2)
[1] 11.09374
[1] 10.66832
[1] 7.814728
```

The R code `u <- v*(log(det(sigma0))...` does the computation as required in Equation 14.24, while `u1 <- (1- (1/(6*v-1))...` does the computation for Equation 14.25. Comparing with the critical values of $\chi^2_{[\alpha,p(p+1)/2]}$, with `p <- ncol(hw)`, since the values of u and u' are greater than the critical value, we reject the hypothesis $H : \mathbf{\Sigma} = \mathbf{\Sigma}_0$ and conclude that $\mathbf{\Sigma} \neq \mathbf{\Sigma}_0$. □

14.7.1 *Testing for Sphericity*

The problem of testing if the components of a random vector are independent is equivalent to the problem of testing $H : \mathbf{\Sigma} = \sigma^2\mathbf{I}$, where $\mathbf{I}$ is the identity matrix. We would like to caution the reader to always keep in mind the counter-example of Section 14.3. The hypothesis is that we are testing equivalent tests if all the correlations among the component are equal to zero, that is, it examines if the components are independent.

Note that if the hypothesis H holds true, the ellipsoid $(\mathbf{x} - \boldsymbol{\mu})'\mathbf{\Sigma}^{-1}(\mathbf{x} - \boldsymbol{\mu}) = c^2$ becomes $(\mathbf{x} - \boldsymbol{\mu})'(\mathbf{x} - \boldsymbol{\mu}) = \sigma^2 c^2$, which is the equation of a sphere. Here, c is some non-negative constant, that is, $c > 0$. Hence, the problem of a test for independence of the components is also known as *tests of sphericity*.

The log-likelihood ratio test for $H : \mathbf{\Sigma} = \sigma^2\mathbf{I}$ is given by

$$LR = \left[\frac{|\mathbf{S}|}{(tr\,(\mathbf{S})\,/p)^p}\right]^{n/2},$$

which on further evaluation leads to

$$-2\ln(LR) = -n(\ln(|\mathbf{S}|) - p\ \ln(tr(\mathbf{S})/p)) = -n\ln(u),$$

where $u = (LR)^{2/n}$. The test statistic u can be restated in terms of the eigenvalues as

$$u = \frac{p^p \prod_{i=1}^{p} \lambda_i}{(\sum_{i=1}^{p} \lambda_i)^p}, \tag{14.26}$$

where $\lambda_1, \lambda_2, \cdots, \lambda_p$ are the eigenvalues of the sample covariance matrix $\mathbf{S}$. An improvement of u by u' is further given by

$$u' = -\left(\upsilon - \frac{2p^2 + p + 2}{6p}\right)\ln(u), \tag{14.27}$$

where υ is the degrees of freedom of $\mathbf{S}$. The statistic u', under the hypothesis H, has a χ^2 distribution with $p(p+1)/2 - 1$ degrees of freedom. The test procedure is to reject the hypothesis H if $u' > \chi^2_{[\alpha,p(p+1)/2-1]}$.

Example 14.7.2. The Linguistic Probe Word Analysis. Probe words are used to test the recall ability of words in various linguistic contexts. In this experiment the response time to 5 different probe words are recorded for 11 individuals. The interest in the experiment is to examine if the response times to the different words are independent or not. The failure to reject the hypothesis of sphericity implies that the response times can be compared using ANOVA.

```
> data(pw)
> sigma <- var(pw[2:6])
> p <- ncol(pw)-1; v <- nrow(pw)-1
> u <- p^p*(det(sigma))/(sum(diag(sigma))^p)
> u1 <- -(v-(2*p^2+p+2)/(6*p))*log(u)
> u;u1
[1] 0.03948874
[1] 26.17709
```

Note here that the R program code `u <- p^p*(det(sigma))/(sum(diag (sigma))^p)` does not imitate the expression given in Equation 14.26, though the code for `u1` follows Equation 14.27. However, we will leave it to the reader to obtain the relationship between determinants and eigenvalues, which will assure that the program is correct.

Since the calculated χ^2 value is greater than the critical value of 23.68479, we reject the sphericity hypothesis. □

?qchisq

14.8 Testing for Variance-Covariance Matrix: *k*-Samples

Consider the case when we have samples from k-populations, that is, $\mathbf{X}_j \sim N(\boldsymbol{\mu}_j, \boldsymbol{\Sigma}_j)$, for $j = 1, 2, \cdots, k$. For the jth sample, we have a sample of size n_j. The hypothesis of interest here is $H : \boldsymbol{\Sigma}_1 = \boldsymbol{\Sigma}_2 = \cdots = \boldsymbol{\Sigma}_k$. Also, define the following:

- $\mathbf{S}_j$: the sample covariance matrix of the jth population;
- $\upsilon_j = n_j - 1$: the degrees of freedom associated with the estimated covariance matrix $\mathbf{S}_j$.

Technically, we need to have $\upsilon_i > p, j = 1, 2, \cdots, k$ for ensuring that the estimated covariance matrices are non-singular. Define the pooled sample covariance matrix by

$$\mathbf{S}_{pl} = \frac{\sum_{j=1}^{k} \upsilon_j \mathbf{S}_j}{\sum_{j=1}^{k} \upsilon_j}.$$

The test statistic for the hypothesis $H : \boldsymbol{\Sigma}_1 = \boldsymbol{\Sigma}_2 = \cdots = \boldsymbol{\Sigma}_k$ is then given by the following:

$$M = \frac{|\mathbf{S}_1|^{\upsilon_1/2}|\mathbf{S}_2|^{\upsilon_2/2}\cdots|\mathbf{S}_k|^{\upsilon_k/2}}{|\mathbf{S}_{pl}|^{\sum_{j=1}^{k}\upsilon_j/2}}. \tag{14.28}$$

The range of values for M is between 0 and 1, with values closer to 1 favoring the hypothesis H, and values closer to 0 leading to its rejection. This can be easily seen by rewriting the expression of M as

$$M = \left(\frac{|\mathbf{S}_1|}{|\mathbf{S}_{pl}|}\right)^{\upsilon_1/2}\left(\frac{|\mathbf{S}_2|}{|\mathbf{S}_{pl}|}\right)^{\upsilon_2/2}\cdots\left(\frac{|\mathbf{S}_k|}{|\mathbf{S}_{pl}|}\right)^{\upsilon_k/2}. \tag{14.29}$$

An expression for $\ln(M)$ is given by

$$\ln(M) = \frac{1}{2}\sum_{j=1}^{k}\upsilon_i \ln(|\mathbf{S}_j|) - \frac{1}{2}\left(\sum_{j=1}^{k}\upsilon_j\right)\ln(|\mathbf{S}_{pl}|). \tag{14.30}$$

The hypothesis $H : \mathbf{\Sigma}_1 = \mathbf{\Sigma}_2 = \cdots = \mathbf{\Sigma}_k$ may be tested using the *exact M-test* with $-2 \ln M$, see page 258 of Rencher (2002).

To test the hypothesis $H : \mathbf{\Sigma}_1 = \mathbf{\Sigma}_2 = \cdots = \mathbf{\Sigma}_k$, we may also use the Box's χ^2 and F-approximations for the probability distribution of M. Towards this, we will first define c_1 as follows:

$$c_1 = \left[\sum_{j=1}^{k} \frac{1}{v_j} - \frac{1}{\sum_{j=1}^{k} v_j}\right] \left[\frac{2p^2 + 3p - 1}{6(p+1)(k-1)}\right]. \tag{14.31}$$

It can then be proved that

$$u = -2(1 - c_1)\ln(M), \tag{14.32}$$

is distributed as a χ^2 random variable with $(k-1)p(p+1)/2$ degrees of freedom.

The steps for obtaining the F-approximation may appear cumbersome, but its benefits are also equally rewarding. As with the χ^2 approximation, we will first define the required quantities. Define c_2 as a function of c_1 by

$$c_2 = \frac{(p-1)(p+2)}{6(k-1)} \left[\sum_{j=1}^{k} \frac{1}{v_j^2} - \frac{1}{(\sum_{j=1}^{k} v_j)^2}\right], \tag{14.33}$$

and also define the quantities a_1, a_2, b_1, b_2 in the following:

$$a_1 = \frac{1}{2}(k-1)p(p+1), \quad a_2 = \frac{a_1 + 2}{|c_2 - c_1^2|},$$

$$b_1 = \frac{1 - c_1 - a_1/a_2}{a_1}, \quad b_2 = \frac{1 - c_1 + 2/a_2}{a_2}.$$

We have two scenarios here: (i) $c_2 > c_1^2$, and (ii) $c_2 < c_1^2$. In case (i), the appropriate F-statistic is

$$F = -2b_1 \ln(M), \tag{14.34}$$

and in case (ii), it is

$$F = -\frac{2a_2b_2 \ln(M)}{a_1(1 + 2b_2 \ln(M))}. \tag{14.35}$$

In both cases, the approximation follows the F_{a_1,a_2} distribution, and the test procedure is to reject the hypothesis H if $F > F_\alpha$.

Example 14.8.1. Psychological Tests for Males and Females. Contd. We have considered the problem of testing hypothesis of equality of mean vectors in Section 14.5. We will now test if the covariance matrices for the male and female groups are equal or not, that is, $H : \mathbf{\Sigma}_M = \mathbf{\Sigma}_F$. We first compute the exact M test statistic value, and then calculate the Box's χ^2 and F test statistic values.

```
> # Testing for Equality of Covariance Matrices
> data(mfp)
> males <- mfp[,1:4]; females <- mfp[,5:8]
> nm <- nrow(males);nf <- nrow(females)
> p <- 4; k <- 2
> vm <- nm-1; vf <- nf-1
> meanm <- mean(males); meanf <- mean(females)
> sigmam <- var(males); sigmaf <- var(females)
> sigmapl <- (1/(nm+nf-2))*((nm-1)*sigmam+(nf-1)*sigmaf)
> ln_M <- .5*(vm*log(det(sigmam))+vf*log(det(sigmaf)))
+ -.5*(vm+vf)*log(det(sigmapl))
> exact_test <- -2*ln_M # the Exact Test
> exact_test
[1] 14.5606
> # The Box's chi-square approximation
> c1 <- (sum(c(1/vm,1/vf))- (1/sum(c(vm,vf))))*((2*p^2+3*p-1)
+ /(6*(p+1)*(k-1)))
> u <- -2*(1-c1)*ln_M
> qchisq(1-0.05,(k-1)*p*(p+1)/2)
[1] 18.30704
> u; qchisq(1-0.05,(k-1)*p*(p+1)/2)
[1] 13.55075
[1] 18.30704
> c2 <- ((p-1)*(p+2)/(6*(k-1)))*(sum(c(1/vm,1/vf)^2)-
+ (1/(sum(c(vm,vf))^2)))
> a1 <- (k-1)*p*(p+1)/2; a2 <- (a1+2)/(abs(c2-c1^2))
> b1 <- (1-c1-a1/a2)/a1; b2 <- (1-c1+2/a2)/a2
> if(c2>c1^2) {Ftest = -2*b1*ln_M} else {Ftest = (2*a2*b2*ln_M)/
+ (a1*(1+2*b2*ln_M))}
> Ftest; qf(1-.05,10,Inf)
[1] 1.354283
[1] 1.830704
```

The R code `ln_M <- .5*(vm*log(det(sigmam))...` delivers the computation for Equation 14.30 and `exact_test <- -2*ln_M` obtains the required exact M test statistic of `14.5606`. Compared with the critical value, Appendix Table A.14 of Rencher (2002), of 19.74, we will be rejecting the hypothesis that the covariance matrices for males and females are equal.

To obtain the Box's χ^2, and F-statistics, we need to obtain the c_1 and c_2 values. The R codes `c1 <- ...` and `c2 <- ...` clearly implement the required formulas, as given in Equations 14.31 and 14.33 . The program for Box's χ^2 statistic in Equation 14.32 is carried out with `u <- -2*(1-c1)*ln_M` and the resultant value is `13.55075`, and a comparison with the critical value for `qchisq(1-0.05,(k-1)*p*(p1)/2)+` in `18.30704` again leads to rejecting the hypothesis.

For our problem, we have that $c_2 > c_1^2$, although the R program takes care of both scenarios. The details of obtaining a_1, a_2, b_1, and b_2 is left to the reader. The computation of the F-statistic is handled by the `if-else` control loop for both the cases, as given in Equations 14.34 and 14.35. All the three procedures lead to rejection of the hypothesis. □

14.9 Testing for Independence of Sub-vectors

The test of sphericity addresses the problem of testing if all the covariates are independent or not. A very likely practical problem could be that we may know beforehand that certainly not all the components are independent. However, we may also have knowledge that though the first three components and the next four components are related, it may be the case that the set of the first three components are independent of the set of the next four components. We would thus like to have some statistical tests to help us prove if our hypothesis is true or not. In fact, we need methods to help us test any combination of vectors as independent or not, and the methods in this section exactly help us to accomplish this.

Consider the p-dimensional random vector $\mathbf{x} = (x_1, x_2, \cdots, x_p)$. Suppose that we are interested to find if the sub-vectors $\mathbf{x_1}, \mathbf{x_2}, \cdots, \mathbf{x_k}$ are a k mutually independent sets of sub-vectors. The notation needs a bit of explanation. If $k = p$, we are testing if all the components are independent. We denote p_j for the number of elements in the jth sub-vector $\mathbf{x}_j$, and we require that $\sum_{j=1}^{k} p_j = p$. Note that $(\mathbf{x}_1, \mathbf{x}_2, \cdots, \mathbf{x}_k)$ denotes a partitioning of $\mathbf{x}$ and not a random sample of size k of $\mathbf{x}$.

Let $\mathbf{\Sigma}_{jj'}$ denote the covariance matrix between the sub-vectors $\mathbf{x_j}$ and $\mathbf{x_{j'}}, j \neq j'$. The hypothesis for independence of the sub-vectors can then be stated symbolically as $H : \mathbf{\Sigma}_{jj'} = \mathbf{0}, j \neq j'$, and in matrix notation as below:

$$H : \mathbf{\Sigma} = \begin{pmatrix} \mathbf{\Sigma}_{11} & \mathbf{0} & \cdots & \mathbf{0} \\ \mathbf{0} & \mathbf{\Sigma}_{22} & \cdots & \mathbf{0} \\ \vdots & \vdots & & \vdots \\ \mathbf{0} & \mathbf{0} & \cdots & \mathbf{\Sigma}_{kk} \end{pmatrix}. \tag{14.36}$$

Let us denote the partition of estimated covariance matrix by the following:

$$\mathbf{S} = \begin{pmatrix} \mathbf{S}_{11} & \mathbf{S}_{12} & \cdots & \mathbf{S}_{1k} \\ \mathbf{S}_{12} & \mathbf{S}_{22} & \cdots & \mathbf{S}_{2k} \\ \vdots & \vdots & & \vdots \\ \mathbf{S}_{1k} & \mathbf{S}_{2k} & \cdots & \mathbf{S}_{kk} \end{pmatrix}. \tag{14.37}$$

The likelihood ratio test statistic for the hypothesis H is given by

$$u = \frac{|\mathbf{S}|}{|\mathbf{S}_{11}||\mathbf{S}_{22}| \cdots |\mathbf{S}_{kk}|}. \tag{14.38}$$

A χ^2 approximation of the distribution of u is given by

$$u' = -\upsilon\, c\, \ln(u), \tag{14.39}$$

where υ and c are determined by the following:

$$c = 1 - \frac{1}{12f\upsilon}(2a_3 + 3a_2), \quad f = \frac{a_2}{2},$$

$$a_2 = p^2 - \sum_{j=1}^{k} p_j^2, \quad a_3 = p^3 - \sum_{j=1}^{k} p_j^3, \quad \upsilon = n - 1. \tag{14.40}$$

We reject the hypothesis H if $u' > \chi^2_{\alpha, f}$.

Example 14.9.1. The Seishu Wine Study. The odor and taste of wines are recorded in a study. It is believed that the variables such as the *pH* concentration, alcohol content, total sugar, etc., explain the odor and taste of the wine. The variables are enumerated below.

1. y_1 : Taste
2. y_2 : Odor
3. x_1 : pH
4. x_2 : Acidity 1
5. x_3 : Acidity 2
6. x_4 : Sake meter
7. x_5 : Direct reducing sugar
8. x_6 : Total sugar
9. x_7 : Alcohol
10. x_8 : Formyl nitrogen

Note that the variables y_1 and y_2 are in some sense outputs, or regressands, and appear to be a function of the other regressors. The (input) variables x_1, x_2, x_3 are the acidic content, whereas x_4, x_5, x_6 are the sugar content of the wine, and the remaining variables describe the alcohol and nitrogen content. It is thus natural to believe that we have here four types of sub-vectors, which may be mutually exclusive. Mathematically speaking, we are interested in testing if the sub-vectors $(y_1, y_2), (x_1, x_2, x_3), (x_4, x_5, x_6), (x_7, x_8)$ are a mutually exclusive subsets of vector. The following R program deals with the related computations.

```
> data(sheishu)
> noc <- c(2,3,3,2)
> nov <- 10
> v <- nrow(sheishu)-1
> varsheishu <- var(sheishu)
> s11 <- varsheishu[1:2,1:2]
> s22 <- varsheishu[3:5,3:5]
> s33 <- varsheishu[6:8,6:8]
> s44 <- varsheishu[9:10,9:10]
> u <- det(varsheishu)/(det(s11)*det(s22)*det(s33)*det(s44))
> a2 <- nov^2 - sum(noc^2)
> a3 <- nov^3 - sum(noc^3)
> f <- a2/2
> cc <- 1 - (2*a3 + 3*a2)/(12*f*v)
> u1 <- -v*cc*log(u)
> u; a2; a3; f; cc; u1
[1] 0.01627025
[1] 74
[1] 930
[1] 37
[1] 0.8383038
[1] 100.1221
> qchisq(1-0.001,37)
[1] 69.34645
```

Using the `var` function, we first obtain **S** as required in Equation 14.37, and the partitions with `s11`, `s22`, `s33`, and `s44`. The test statistic u as required by Equation 14.38 is computed by `u <- det(varsheishu)/(det(s11)*...*det(s44))`. The constants required in Equation 14.40 are easily obtained in the variables `a2`, `a3`, `f`, `v`, and `cc`, which further help to obtain u' given by Equation 14.39, calculated with `u1 <- -v*cc*log(u)`. Since the

$u1$ value exceeds `qchisq(1-0.001,37)` equal to `69.34645`, we reject the hypothesis of independence of sub-vectors. □

?chisq, ?det

In the next chapter on MSA, we will consider some of the more advanced topics, which are more useful in an applied context.

14.10 Further Reading

Anderson (1953, 1984, and 2003) is the first comprehensive and benchmark book in this area of statistics. Rencher (2002), Johnson and Wichern (2007), Hair, et al. (2010), Hardle and Simar (2007), and Izenman (2008) are some of the modern accounts of multivariate statistical analysis. Everitt (2005) has handled the associated computations through R and S-Plus. However, as Everitt (2005) and Everitt and Hothorn (2011) are dwelling more in advanced methods of MSA, we believe that the reader can benefit from the coverage given in this and the next chapter.

14.11 Complements, Problems, and Programs

Problem 14.1 The `iris` data has been introduced in AD2. Obtain the matrix of scatter plots for (i) the overall dataset (removing the `Species`), and (ii) three subsets according to the `Species`. Obtain the average of the four characteristics by the `Species` group and using the `faces` function from the `aplpack` package, plot the Chernoff faces. Do the Chernoff faces offer enough insight to identify the group?

Problem 14.2 For the board stiffness data discussed in Example 14.3.3, obtain the covariance matrix and then using the `cov2cor` function, obtain the correlation matrix.

Problem 14.3 The *Mahalanobis distance* D^2 given in Equation 14.7 is easily obtained in R using the `mahalanobis` function. Using this function, obtain the distance of the observations from the entire dataset for the board stiffness dataset and investigate for presence of outliers. Repeat the exercise for the presence of outliers in the `iris` dataset too.

Problem 14.4 Using the `HotellingsT2` function from the `ICSNP` package, test whether average sepal and petal length and width for `setosa` species equals [5.936 2.770 4.260 1.326] in the `iris` dataset.

Problem 14.5 Using the `HotellingsT2` function from the `ICSNP` package, test whether average sepal and petal length and width for `setosa` species equals that of `versicolor` in the `iris` dataset.

Problem 14.6 Run the example code of the function `HotellingsT2`, that is run `example(HotellingsT2)`, and explore the options available with this function.

Problem 14.7 Carry out the MANOVA analysis for the `iris` datasets, where the hypothesis problem is that the mean of the multivariate vector of the four variables are equal across the three types of species.

Problem 14.8 Using base matrix tools of R, create a function which returns the value of Roy's test statistic given in Equation 14.21.

Problem 14.9 Repeat the above exercise for the Pillai and Lawley-Hotelling tests respectively given in Equations 14.22 and 14.23.

Problem 14.10 For the `iris` dataset, test the hypothesis $\mathbf{\Sigma}_{setosa} = \mathbf{\Sigma}_{versicolor} = \mathbf{\Sigma}_{virginica}$. Repeat the exercise for the stack loss problem too.

Problem 14.11 Test whether the `Sepal` and `Petal` characteristics are independent of each other in the `iris` dataset.

15

Multivariate Statistical Analysis - II

Package(s): `DAAG`, `HSAUR2`, `qcc`
Dataset(s): `iris`, `socsupport`, `chemicaldata`, `USairpollution`, `hearing`, `cork`, `adjectives`, `life`

15.1 Introduction

In the previous chapter we built on some of the essential multivariate techniques. The results there helped set up a platform to stage more practical applications. The classification and discriminant analysis techniques work well for classifying observations into distinct groups. This topic forms the content of Section 15.2. Canonical correlations help to identify if there are groups of variables present in a multivariate vector, which will be dealt with in Section 15.3. Principal Component Analysis (PCA) helps in obtaining a new set of fewer variables, which have the overall variation of the original set of variables. This multivariate technique will be developed in Section 15.4, whereas specific areas of application of the technique will be dealt in Section 15.5. Multivariate data may also be used to find a new set of variables using *Factor Analysis*, check Section 15.6.

15.2 Classification and Discriminant Analysis

The application of MSA is to classify the data into distinct groups. This task is achieved through two steps: (i) Discriminant Analysis, and (ii) Classification. In the first step we identify linear functions, which describe the similarities and differences among the groups. This is achieved through the relative contribution of variables towards the separation of groups and finds an optimal plane which separates the groups. The second task is allocation of the observations to the groups identified in the first step. This is broadly called *Classification*. We will begin with the first task in the forthcoming subsection.

A Course in Statistics with R, First Edition. Prabhanjan Narayanachar Tattar, Suresh Ramaiah and B. G. Manjunath.

Companion Website: www.wiley.com/go/tattar/statistics

15.2.1 Discrimination Analysis

Suppose that there are two groups characterized by two multivariate normal distributions: $N_p(\mu_1, \Sigma)$ and $N_p(\mu_2, \Sigma)$. It is assumed that the variance-covariance matrix Σ is the same for both the groups. Assume that we have n_1 observations $\mathbf{X}_{11}, \mathbf{X}_{12}, \dots, \mathbf{X}_{1n_1}$ from $N_p(\boldsymbol{\mu}_1, \Sigma)$ and n_2 observations $\mathbf{X}_{21}, \mathbf{X}_{22}, \dots, \mathbf{X}_{2n_2}$ from $N_p(\boldsymbol{\mu}_2, \Sigma)$. The *discriminant function* is a linear combination of the p variables, which will maximize the distance between the two group's mean vectors. Thus, we are seeking a vector $\mathbf{a}$, which achieves the required objective.

As a first step, the $n_1 + n_2$ vectors are transformed to $n_1 + n_2$ scalars through $\mathbf{a}$ as below:

$$\begin{aligned} z_{1i} &= \mathbf{a}'\mathbf{X}_{1i}, \quad i = 1, \dots, n_1, \\ z_{2i} &= \mathbf{a}'\mathbf{X}_{2i}, \quad i = 1, \dots, n_2. \end{aligned} \tag{15.1}$$

Define the means of the transformed scalars and the pooled variance as below:

$$\begin{aligned} \bar{z}_1 &\equiv \frac{\sum_{i=1}^{n_1} \mathbf{a}'\mathbf{x}_{1i}}{n_1} = \mathbf{a}'\bar{\mathbf{x}}_1, \\ \bar{z}_2 &\equiv \frac{\sum_{i=1}^{n_2} \mathbf{a}'\mathbf{x}_{2i}}{n_2} = \mathbf{a}'\bar{\mathbf{x}}_2, \\ \mathbf{S}_{pl} &= \frac{(n_1 - 1)\mathbf{S}_1 + (n_2 - 1)\mathbf{S}_2}{n_1 + n_2 - 2}, \text{ exists iff } n_1 + n_2 - 2 > p. \end{aligned} \tag{15.2}$$

Since the goal is to find that $\mathbf{a}$ which maximizes the distance between the group means, the problem is to maximize the squared distance:

$$\frac{\{\mathbf{a}'(\bar{\mathbf{x}}_1 - \bar{\mathbf{x}}_2)\}^2}{\mathbf{a}'\mathbf{S}_{pl}\mathbf{a}}. \tag{15.3}$$

The maximum of the squared distance occurs at $\mathbf{a}$ given by

$$\mathbf{a} = \mathbf{S}_{pl}^{-1}(\bar{\mathbf{x}}_1 - \bar{\mathbf{x}}_2). \tag{15.4}$$

An illustration of the discriminant analysis steps is done through the next example.

Example 15.2.1. Discriminant Function for the "setosa" species in Iris Data. Suppose that based on the four variables of sepal length and width, and petal length and width, we need to find $\mathbf{a}$ which will maximize the distance between the two groups: "setosa" and "not a setosa" species. The formulas are clearly illustrated in the following R program.

```
> data(iris)
> x1bar <- colMeans(iris[iris$Species=="setosa",1:4])
> x2bar <- colMeans(iris[iris$Species!="setosa",1:4])
> table(iris$Species)
    setosa versicolor  virginica
        50         50         50
> S_pl <- ((49*var(iris[iris$Species=="setosa",1:4])+
+              99*var(iris[iris$Species!="setosa",1:4]))/148)
```

```
> x1bar;x2bar; S_pl
Sepal.Length  Sepal.Width Petal.Length  Petal.Width
       5.006        3.428        1.462        0.246
Sepal.Length  Sepal.Width Petal.Length  Petal.Width
       6.262        2.872        4.906        1.676
             Sepal.Length Sepal.Width Petal.Length Petal.Width
Sepal.Length    0.3350257  0.11456216   0.30867703  0.11523649
Sepal.Width     0.1145622  0.12163784   0.09939189  0.05661081
Petal.Length    0.3086770  0.09939189   0.46590676  0.19514730
Petal.Width     0.1152365  0.05661081   0.19514730  0.12436892
> solve(S_pl)
                   [,1]
Sepal.Length   3.186486
Sepal.Width   11.719430
Petal.Length -10.841575
Petal.Width   -2.773537
```

Thus, the discriminant function is given by $z = -3.186486x_1 + 11.719430x_2 - 10.841575x_3 - 2.773537x_4$. □

The use of the discriminant function for classification is considered next.

15.2.2 Classification

Let $\mathbf{x}_{new}$ be a new vector of observation. The goal is to classify it into one of the groups by using the discriminant function. The simple, and fairly obvious, technique is to first obtain the discriminant score by

$$z_{new} = \mathbf{a}'\mathbf{x}_{new} = (\bar{\mathbf{x}}_1 - \bar{\mathbf{x}}_2)'\mathbf{S}_{pl}^{-1}\mathbf{x}_{new}.$$

Next, classify $\mathbf{x}_{new}$ to group 1 or 2 accordingly, as z_{new} is closer to $\bar{z}_1$ or $\bar{z}_2$. A simple illustration is done next.

Example 15.2.2. Classification for Iris Data. The above description is captured in the next R program. We simply verify if the original observations are correctly identified by the discriminant function or not.

```
> a <- solve(S_pl)%*%(x1bar-x2bar)
> z1bar <- t(a)%*%x1bar
> z2bar <- t(a)%*% x2bar
> pred_gr <- NULL
> for(i in 1:150) {
+  mynew <- t(a)%*%t(as.matrix(iris[i,1:4]))
+  pred_gr[i] <- ifelse(abs(mynew-z1bar)>abs(mynew-z2bar),
+ "not setosa","setosa")
+   }
> pred_gr
```

```
  [1] "setosa"     "setosa"     "setosa"     "setosa"

 [43] "setosa"     "setosa"     "setosa"     "setosa"
 [49] "setosa"     "not setosa" "not setosa" "not setosa"
 [55] "not setosa" "not setosa" "not setosa" "not setosa"

[145] "not setosa" "not setosa" "not setosa" "not setosa"
```

For the original observations, the discriminant function has properly identified their groups. □

The function `lda` from the `MASS` package handles the *Linear Discriminant Analysis* very well. The particular reason for not using the function here is that our focus has been elucidation of the formulas in the scheme of flow of the theory. The results arising as a consequence of using the `lda` function by the command `lda(GROUP~X1+X2, data=rencher)` is a bit different and the reader is asked to figure out the same. It goes without an explicit mention that the reader has a host of other options using the `lda` function.

?colMeans, ?solve, ?lda

15.3 Canonical Correlations

In multivariate data, we may have the case that there are two distinct subsets of vectors, with each subset characterizing certain traits of the unit of measurement. As an example, the marks obtained by a student in the examination for different subjects is one subset of measurements, whereas the performance in different sports may form another subset of measurements. Canonical correlations help us to understand the relationship between such sets of vector data.

Let $\mathbf{y}' = (y_1, y_2, \cdots, y_p)$ and $\mathbf{x}' = (x_1, x_2, \cdots, x_q)$ be two set of vectors measured on the same experimental unit. The goal of a canonical correlation study is to obtain vectors $\mathbf{a}$ and $\mathbf{b}$ such that correlation between $\mathbf{y}$ and $\mathbf{x}$ is a maximum, that is, $\texttt{Cor}(\mathbf{a}'\mathbf{y}, \mathbf{b}'\mathbf{x})$ is a maximum.

The sample covariance matrix for the vector $(y_1, \cdots, y_p, x_1, \cdots, x_q)$ is

$$\mathbf{S} = \begin{pmatrix} \mathbf{S}_{yy} & \mathbf{S}_{yx} \\ \mathbf{S}_{xy} & \mathbf{S}_{xx} \end{pmatrix}, \tag{15.5}$$

where $\mathbf{S}_{yy}$ is the sample covariance matrix of $\mathbf{Y}$, $\mathbf{S}_{xy}$ is the sample covariance matrix between $\mathbf{X}$ and $\mathbf{Y}$, and $\mathbf{S}_{xx}$ of $\mathbf{X}$. A *measure of association* between the $\mathbf{y}'$s and the $\mathbf{x}'$s is given by

$$R_M^2 = |\mathbf{S}_{yy}^{-1}\mathbf{S}_{yx}\mathbf{S}_{xx}^{-1}\mathbf{S}_{xy}| = \prod_{i=1}^{s} r_i^2, \tag{15.6}$$

where $s = \min(p, q)$, and $r_1^2, r_2^2, \cdots, r_s^2$ are the eigenvalues of $\mathbf{S}_{yy}^{-1}\mathbf{S}_{yx}\mathbf{S}_{xx}^{-1}\mathbf{S}_{xy}$. Note that the association measure R_M^2 will be a poor measure, since each of the r_i^2 values is between 0 and 1, and hence the product of such numbers approach 0 faster. However, the eigenvalues provide a useful measure of association between the vectors. Particularly, the square root of the eigenvalues leads to useful interpretations of the measures of the association. The collection of the square root of the eigenvalues $\{r_1, r_2, \ldots, r_s\}$ has been named the *canonical correlations* in the multivariate literature. Without loss of generality we assume that $r_1^2 \geq r_2^2 \geq \ldots \geq r_s^2$.

As mentioned in Rencher (2002), the best overall measure of association between the $\mathbf{x}'$s and $\mathbf{y}'$s is the largest squared canonical correlation r_1^2. However, the other eigenvalues $\{r_2, \ldots, r_s\}$ leading to the squared canonical correlations $\{r_2^2, \ldots, r_s^2\}$ also provide measures of supplemental dimensions of linear relationships between the $\mathbf{x}'$s and $\mathbf{y}'$s.

The two important properties of canonical correlations as listed by Rencher are the following:

- Canonical correlations are scale invariant, scales of the $\mathbf{x}'$s as well as the $\mathbf{y}'$s.
- The first canonical correlation r_1 is the maximum correlation among all linear combinations between the $\mathbf{x}'$s and the $\mathbf{y}'$s.

See Chapter 11 of Rencher for a comprehensive coverage of canonical correlations. We can test the independence of the $\mathbf{x}'$s and the $\mathbf{y}'$s using any of the four tests discussed in Section 14.6. The concepts are illustrated for the Chemical Dataset of Box and Youle (1955) and are illustrated in Rencher.

Example 15.3.1. Chemical Reaction Experiment. In this experiment temperature (x_1), concentration (x_2), and time (x_3) have influence on three yield variables, namely outputs, the percentage of unchanged starting material (y_1), the percentage converted to the desired product (y_2), and the percentage of unwanted by-product (y_3). The cross-products and squares of the input variables are also believed to influence the three outputs, and hence we need to take this information into account when we construct the canonical correlations between these two sets of variables. That is, we now have nine input variables and three output variables. An R program, using the inbuilt `cancor` function, is put into action for canonical correlation analysis.

```
> data(chemicaldata)
> names(chemicaldata)
[1] "y1" "y2" "y3" "x1" "x2" "x3"
> chemicaldata$x12 <- chemicaldata$x1*chemicaldata$x2;
> chemicaldata$x13 <- chemicaldata$x1*chemicaldata$x3;
> chemicaldata$x23 <- chemicaldata$x2*chemicaldata$x3
> chemicaldata$x1sq <- chemicaldata$x1^{2}
> chemicaldata$x2sq <- chemicaldata$x2^{2}
> chemicaldata$x3sq <- chemicaldata$x3^{2}
> S_Total <- cov(chemicaldata)
> cancor_xy <- sqrt(eigen(solve(S_Total[1:3,1:3])%*%S_Total
+ [1:3,4:12]
+ %*%solve(S_Total[4:12,4:12])%*%S_Total[4:12,1:3])$values)
> cancor_xy
[1] 0.9899 0.9528 0.4625
> cancor(chemicaldata[,1:3],chemicaldata[,4:12])
$cor
[1] 0.9899 0.9528 0.4625
$xcoef
        [,1]    [,2]    [,3]
y1 0.03633 0.1057 0.1371
y2 0.01054 0.1414 0.1113
y3 0.01638 0.1097 0.1802
$ycoef
```

```
           [,1]       [,2]          [,9]
x1    -0.189983  1.451850  -0.9081431
x2    -0.325733  0.986862   0.0363422

x3sq -0.006645 -0.010175   0.0972184
$xcenter
   y1    y2    y3
20.18 56.34 20.78
$ycenter
      x1      x3      x12      x13      x23     x1sq     x2sq     x3sq
  167.32    6.50  4536.82  1087.34   177.86 28031.21   755.99    44.78
```

In this case, we have $s = \min\{3, 9\} = 3$, that is, we can have three canonical correlations between $\mathbf{y}'$s and $\mathbf{x}'$s. The cross-product and squares term are integrated into the original data frame `chemicaldata`, itself with the first three columns for $\mathbf{y}'$s and the rest for $\mathbf{x}'$s. Before using the R canonical correlation function `cancor`, we attempt to obtain them using formulas 15.5 and 15.6. Thus, the covariance matrix `S_Total` is first obtained. Next, the code `solve(S_Total[1:3,1:3])%*% ... %*%S_Total[4:12,1:3])` does the computation for $\mathbf{S}_{yy}^{-1}\mathbf{S}_{yx}\mathbf{S}_{xx}^{-1}\mathbf{S}_{xy}$. Using `eigen(matrix)$values` for the eigenvalues and followed by `sqrt`, we get the three canonical correlations, as specified in Equation 15.6, between the $\mathbf{y}'$s and $\mathbf{x}'$s as `0.9899 0.9528 0.4625`.

By using the `cancor` function on the data frame `chemicaldata`, the previous result is confirmed in the `$cor` values.

Finally, we would like to test the hypothesis $H : \boldsymbol{\Sigma}_{xy} = \mathbf{0}$. The four tests seen in Section 14.6 may be used to confirm if $\mathbf{y}$ is independent of $\mathbf{x}$ or not.

```
> y <- as.matrix(chemicaldata[,1:3])
> x <- as.matrix(chemicaldata[,4:12])
> chemical_manova <- manova(y~x)
> summary(chemical_manova,test="Wilks")
          Df   Wilks approx F num Df den Df  Pr(>F)
x          9 0.00145     6.54     27   21.1 2.1e-05 ***
Residuals  9
---
Signif. codes:  0 '***' 0.001 '**' 0.01 '*' 0.05 '.' 0.1 ' ' 1
> summary(chemical_manova,test="Roy")
          Df  Roy approx F num Df den Df  Pr(>F)
x          9 48.9     48.9      9      9 1.4e-06 ***
Residuals  9
---
Signif. codes:  0 '***' 0.001 '**' 0.01 '*' 0.05 '.' 0.1 ' ' 1
> summary(chemical_manova,test="Pillai")
          Df Pillai approx F num Df den Df Pr(>F)
x          9    2.1     2.34     27     27  0.016 *
Residuals  9
---
Signif. codes:  0 '***' 0.001 '**' 0.01 '*' 0.05 '.' 0.1 ' ' 1
> summary(chemical_manova,test="Hotelling")
          Df Hotelling-Lawley approx F num Df den Df  Pr(>F)
```

```
x           9                 59      12.4      27      17 9.5e-07 ***
Residuals   9
---
Signif. codes:  0 '***' 0.001 '**' 0.01 '*' 0.05 '.' 0.1 ' ' 1
```

All the four type tests reject the hypothesis H that the two sets of vectors are independent, and hence the canonical correlations among them may be accepted. □

The next section is a very important concept in multivariate analysis.

?cancor, ?summary.manova

15.4 Principal Component Analysis – Theory and Illustration

Principal Component Analysis (PCA) is a powerful data reduction tool. In the earlier multivariate studies we had p components for a random vector. PCA considers the problem of identifying a new set of variables which explain more variance in the dataset. Jolliffe (2002) explains the importance of PCA as "The central idea of principal component analysis (PCA) is to reduce the dimensionality of a dataset consisting of a large number of interrelated variables, while retaining as much as possible of the variation present in the dataset." In general, most of the ideas in multivariate statistics are extensions of the concepts from univariate statistics. PCA is an exception!

Jolliffe (2002) considers the PCA theory and applications in a monumental way. Jackson (1991) is a very elegant exposition of PCA applications. For useful applications of PCA in chemometrics, refer to Varmuza and Filzmoser (2009). The development of this section is owed in a large extent to Jolliffe (2002) and Rencher (2002).

PCA may be useful in the following two cases: (i) too many explanatory variables relative to the number of observations; and (ii) the explanatory variables are highly correlated. Let us begin with a brief discussion of the math behind PCA.

15.4.1 The Theory

We begin with a discussion of *population principal components*. Consider a p-variate normal random vector $\mathbf{x} = (x_1, \dots, x_p)$ with mean $\boldsymbol{\mu}$ and variance-covariance matrix $\boldsymbol{\Sigma}$. We assume that we have a random sample of n observations. The goal of PCA is to return a new set of variables $\mathbf{y} = (y_1, \dots, y_p)$, where each $y_i, i = 1, 2, \dots, p$ is some linear combination of the x_is. Furthermore, and importantly, the y_i's are in decreasing order of importance in the sense that y_i has more information about $\mathbf{x}$'s than y_j, whenever $i < j$. The y_i's are constructed in such a way that they are uncorrelated. Information here is used to convey the fact that the $Var(y_i) \geq Var(y_j)$ whenever $i < j$.

From its definition, the PCAs are linear combinations of the $\mathbf{x}$'s. The ith principal component is defined by

$$y_i = a_{i1}x_1 + a_{i2}x_2 + \cdots + a_{ip}x_p, i = 1, 2, \dots, p. \tag{15.7}$$

We know from the linearity of variance that we can specify the $\mathbf{a}_i = (a_{i1}, a_{i2}, \dots, a_{ip})$ in such a way that variance of y_i can be infinite. Thus we may end up with components such that variance is infinite for each of them, which is of course meaningless. We will thus impose a restriction:

$$\mathbf{a}_i^T\mathbf{a}_i = 1, i = 1, 2, \ldots, p.$$

We need to find $\mathbf{a}_1$ such that $\texttt{Var}(y_1)$ is a maximum. Next, we need to obtain $\mathbf{a}_2$ such that

$$\mathbf{a}_2^T\mathbf{a}_1 = 0,$$

and in general

$$\mathbf{a}_i^T\mathbf{a}_j = 0, i \neq j.$$

For the first component, mathematically, we need to solve the maximization problem

$$\max \mathbf{a}_1^T\mathbf{\Sigma}\mathbf{a}_1 - \lambda(\mathbf{a}_1^T\mathbf{a}_1 - 1), \tag{15.8}$$

where λ is a Lagrangian multiplier. As with an optimization problem, we will differentiate the above expression and equate the result to 0 for obtaining the optimal value of $\mathbf{a}$:

$$\mathbf{\Sigma}\mathbf{a}_1 - \lambda\mathbf{a}_1 = 0,$$

$$(\mathbf{\Sigma} - \lambda\mathbf{I})\mathbf{a}_1 = 0.$$

Thus, we see that λ is an eigenvalue of $\mathbf{\Sigma}$ and $\mathbf{a}_1$ is the corresponding eigenvector. Since we need to maximize $\mathbf{a}_1^T\mathbf{\Sigma}\mathbf{a}_1 = \mathbf{a}_1^T\lambda\mathbf{a}_1 = \lambda\mathbf{a}_1^T\mathbf{a}_1 = \lambda$, we select the maximum of the eigenvalue and its corresponding eigenvector for $\mathbf{a}_1$.

Let $\lambda_1, \ldots, \lambda_p$ denote the p eigenvalues of $\mathbf{\Sigma}$. We assume that the eigenvalues are distinct. Without loss of generality, we further assume that $\lambda_1 > \lambda_2 \ldots > \lambda_p$. For the first PC we select the eigenvector corresponding to λ_1, that is, $\mathbf{a}_1$ is the eigenvector related to λ_1.

The second PC $\mathbf{a}_1$ needs to maximize $\mathbf{a}_2^T\mathbf{\Sigma}\mathbf{a}_2$ and with the restriction that $\texttt{Cov}(\mathbf{a}_1^T\mathbf{x}, \mathbf{a}_2^T\mathbf{x}) = 0$. Note that, post a few matrix computational steps,

$$\texttt{Cov}\left(\mathbf{a}_1^T\mathbf{x}, \mathbf{a}_2^T\mathbf{x}\right) = \mathbf{a}_1^T\mathbf{\Sigma}\mathbf{a}_2 = \lambda\mathbf{a}_1^T\mathbf{a}_2.$$

Thus, the constraint that the first two PCs are uncorrelated may be specified by $\mathbf{a}_1^T\mathbf{a}_2 = 0$. The maximization problem for the second PC is specified in the equation below:

$$\max \mathbf{a}_2^T\mathbf{\Sigma}\mathbf{a}_2 - \lambda(\mathbf{a}_2^T\mathbf{a}_2 - 1) - \phi\mathbf{a}_1^T\mathbf{a}_2. \tag{15.9}$$

where λ, ϕ are the Lagrangian multipliers. We need to optimize the above equation and obtain the second PC. As we generally do with optimization problems, we will differentiate the maximization statement with respect to $\mathbf{a}_2$ and obtain:

$$\mathbf{\Sigma}\mathbf{a}_2 - \lambda\mathbf{a}_2 - \phi\mathbf{a}_1 = 0,$$

which by multiplication of the left-hand side by $\mathbf{a}_1^T$ gives us

$$\mathbf{a}_1^T\mathbf{\Sigma}\mathbf{a}_2 - \lambda\mathbf{a}_1^T\mathbf{a}_2 - \phi\mathbf{a}_1^T\mathbf{a}_1 = 0. \tag{15.10}$$

Since $\mathbf{a}_1^T\mathbf{a}_2 = 0$, the first two terms of the above equation equal zero and since $\mathbf{a}_1^T\mathbf{a}_1 = 1$, we get $\phi = 0$. Substituting this into the two displayed expressions above, we get $\mathbf{\Sigma}\mathbf{a}_2 - \lambda\mathbf{a}_2 = 0$. On readjustment, we get $(\mathbf{\Sigma} - \lambda\mathbf{I})\mathbf{a}_2 = 0$, and we again see λ as the eigenvalue of $\mathbf{\Sigma}$. Under the assumption of distinct eigenvalues for $\mathbf{\Sigma}$, we choose the second largest eigenvalue and its corresponding eigenvector for $\mathbf{a}_2$. We proceed in a similar way for the rest of the $(p-1)$ PCs. As with the first PC, $\mathbf{a}_j$ is chosen as the eigenvector corresponding to λ_j for $j = 2, \dots, p$.

The variance of the jth principal component y_j is

$$\texttt{Var}\{y_j\} = \lambda_j, j = 1, 2, \dots, p. \tag{15.11}$$

The amount of variation explained by the jth PC is

$$P_j = \frac{\lambda j}{\sum_{j=1}^{m} \lambda_j}.$$

Since the PCs are uncorrelated, the variation explained by the first m PCs is

$$P^{(m)} = \frac{\sum_{j=1}^{m} \lambda_j}{\sum_{j=1}^{p} \lambda_j}, m \leq p. \tag{15.12}$$

The variance explained by the PCs are best understood through a *screeplot*. A screeplot looks like the profile of a mountain where after a steep slope a flatter region appears that is built by fallen and deposited stones (called scree). Therefore, this plot is often named as the SCREE PLOT. It is investigated from the top until the debris is reached. This explanation is from Varmura and Filzmoser (2009).

The development thus far focuses on population principal components, which involve unknown parameters $\boldsymbol{\mu}$ and $\mathbf{\Sigma}$. Since these parameters are seldom known, the *sample principal components* are obtained by replacing the unknown parameters with their respective MLEs. If the observations are on different scales of measurements, a practical rule is to use the sample correlation matrix instead of the covariance matrix.

The covariance between observation i and PC j is given by

$$\text{Cov}(x_i, y_j) = \lambda_j a_{ji}, i = 1, 2, \dots, n, j = 1, 2, \dots, p,$$

and the correlation is

$$\begin{aligned} r_{x_i, y_j} &= \frac{\lambda_j a_{ji}}{\sqrt{\text{Var}(x_i)\text{Var}(y_j)}} \\ &= \frac{a_{ji}\sqrt{\lambda_j}}{s_i}. \end{aligned}$$

However, if the PCs are extracted from the correlation matrix, then

$$\rho_{x_i, y_j} = a_{ji}\sqrt{\lambda_j}.$$

The concepts will be demonstrated in the next subsection.

15.4.2 *Illustration Through a Dataset*

We will use two datasets for the usage of PCA.

Example 15.4.1. US Air Pollution Data. The dataset `Usairpollution` from the `HSAUR2` package will be used to demonstrate PCA. A brief description of the variables in this dataset is given below:

- `SO2`: Sulphur dioxide content of air in micrograms per cubic meter.
- `Temp`: Average annual temperature in OF.
- `Manu`: Number of manufacturing enterprises employing 20 or more workers.
- `Pop`: Population size (1970 census) in thousands.
- `Wind`: Average annual wind speed in miles per hour.
- `Precip`: Average annual precipitation in inches.
- `Days`: Average number of days with precipitation per year.

The problem of interest here is to understand the dependency of `SO2` on the other variables. Since the units of measurements are not the same across the variables, we will need to form the PCs based on the correlation matrix. The pairs function is used to understand the relationship among the variables here. Recollect the definition of `panel.cor` and `panel.hist` from Chapter 14 and use them to visualize `USairpollution`. The graphical output is suppressed and the reader should make preliminary investigations into the dataset.

The PCs are obtained in R with the `princomp` function and the correlation matrix requirement is made explicit with the option `cor=TRUE`. The `summary.princomp` returns the eigenvalues, proportion of the variance P_j, and the cumulative variance percentages. The `pairs` function is applied over the principal component variables $\mathbf{y}$'s to check if the orthogonality condition of `Cor`($\mathbf{y}_i, \mathbf{y}_j, i \neq j$, is satisfied or not. The R function `screeplot` helps to determine the number of principal components to be chosen. Finally, the part of an `princomp` object in `$loadings` gives the relationship between the variables and PCs.

```
> library(HSAUR2)
> data(USairpollution)
> pairs(USairpollution[,-1],upper.panel=panel.cor)
> usair.pc <- princomp(USairpollution[,-1],cor=TRUE)
> summary(usair.pc)
Importance of components:
                       Comp.1 Comp.2 Comp.3 Comp.4 Comp.5   Comp.6
Standard deviation      1.482  1.225 1.1810 0.8719 0.3385 0.185600
Proportion of Variance  0.366  0.250 0.2324 0.1267 0.0191 0.005741
Cumulative Proportion   0.366  0.616 0.8485 0.9752 0.9943 1.000000
> pairs(usair.pc$scores)
> screeplot(usair.pc)
> usair.pc$loadings
Loadings:
        Comp.1 Comp.2 Comp.3 Comp.4 Comp.5 Comp.6
temp     0.330 -0.128  0.672 -0.306 -0.558 -0.136
manu    -0.612 -0.168  0.273  0.137  0.102 -0.703
popul   -0.578 -0.222  0.350                0.695
wind    -0.354  0.131 -0.297 -0.869 -0.113
precip          0.623  0.505 -0.171  0.568
predays -0.238  0.708         0.311 -0.580
```

```
                 Comp.1 Comp.2 Comp.3 Comp.4 Comp.5 Comp.6
SS loadings       1.000  1.000  1.000  1.000  1.000  1.000
Proportion Var   0.167  0.167  0.167  0.167  0.167  0.167
Cumulative Var   0.167  0.333  0.500  0.667  0.833  1.000
```

The `summary` shows that if we need 80% of the variation is to be explained by the PCs, we can choose the first three PCs, and if 90% coverage is required, the first four PCs will provide us with the coverage. The output of `pairs(usair.pc$scores)` in Figure 15.1 shows that the orthogonality requirement of PCs is satisfied here. The debris in the screeplot of `usair.pc`, Part A of Figure 15.2, clearly shows that the first four PCs are required to explain the variation of the original dataset. The covariance between the variables and the PCs may be investigated by the reader. □

Example 15.4.2. The Hearing Loss Data. Jackson (1991) describes in detail the "Hearing Loss" data. A study was carried out by the Eastman Kodak Company, which involved the measurement of hearing loss. Such studies are called *audiometric* studies. This dataset contains 100 males, each aged 39, who had no history of noise exposure or hearing disorders. A method of measuring the hearing capabilities is the use of an instrument called an *audiometer*. Here, the individual is exposed to a signal of a given frequency with an increasing intensity until the signal is perceived. Observations are obtained for intensities: 500 Hz, 1000 Hz, 2000 Hz, and 4000 Hz. This signal perception is carried out for both ears.

We will first read the data, and look at the covariance and correlation matrix.

```
> data(hearing)
> round(cor(hearing[,-1]),2)
      L500 L1000 L2000 L4000 R500 R1000 R2000 R4000
L500  1.00  0.78  0.40  0.26 0.70  0.64  0.24  0.20
L1000 0.78  1.00  0.54  0.27 0.55  0.71  0.36  0.22

R4000 0.20  0.22  0.33  0.71 0.13  0.22  0.37  1.00
> round(cov(hearing[,-1]),2)
       L500 L1000  L2000  L4000  R500 R1000 R2000  R4000
L500  41.07 37.73  28.13  32.10 31.79 26.30 14.12  25.28
L1000 37.73 57.32  44.44  40.83 29.75 34.24 25.30  31.74

R4000 25.28 31.74  68.99 269.12 18.19 27.22 67.26 373.66
```

The above results can be matched with Tables 5.2 and 5.3 of Jackson (1991). All the variables have the same unit of measurement and hence the covariance matrix can be used here to obtain the PCs. We look at the screeplot and decide on the number of PCs.

```
> hearing.pc <- princomp(hearing[,-1])
> screeplot(hearing.pc)
```

The screeplot in Part B of Figure 15.2 suggests that four PCs suffice for explaining the variation contained among the eight variables. □

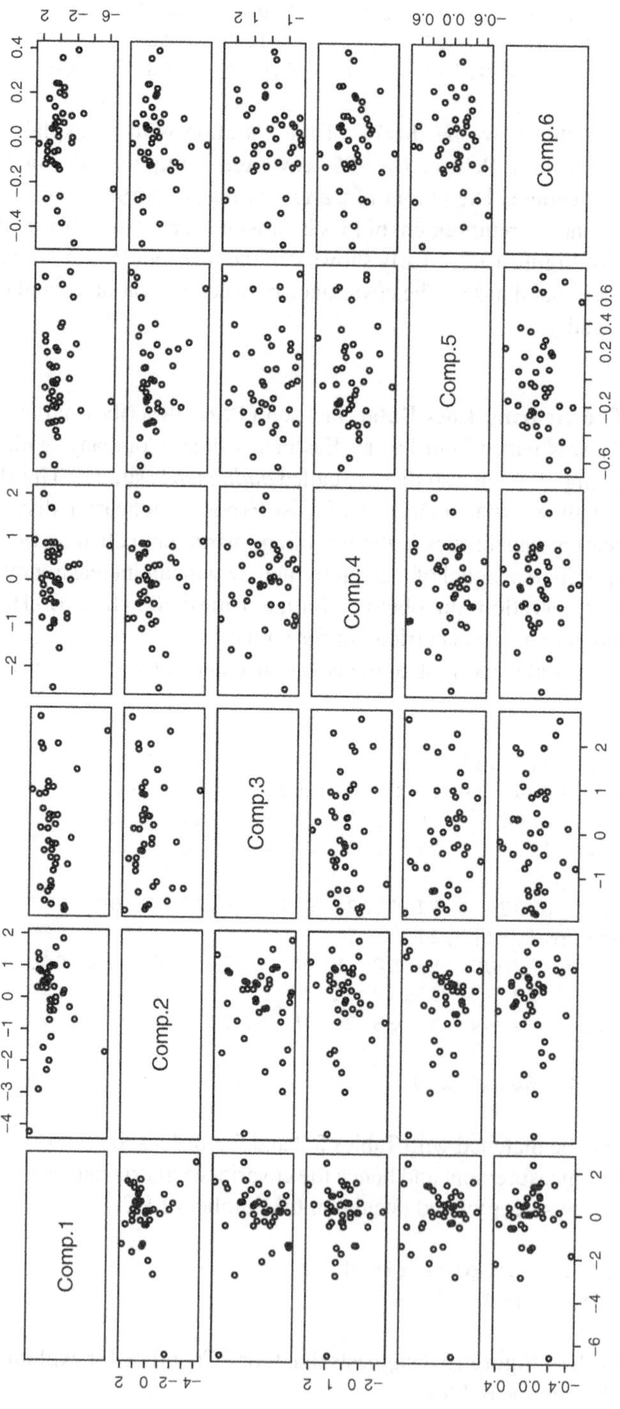

Figure 15.1 Uncorrelatedness of Principal Components

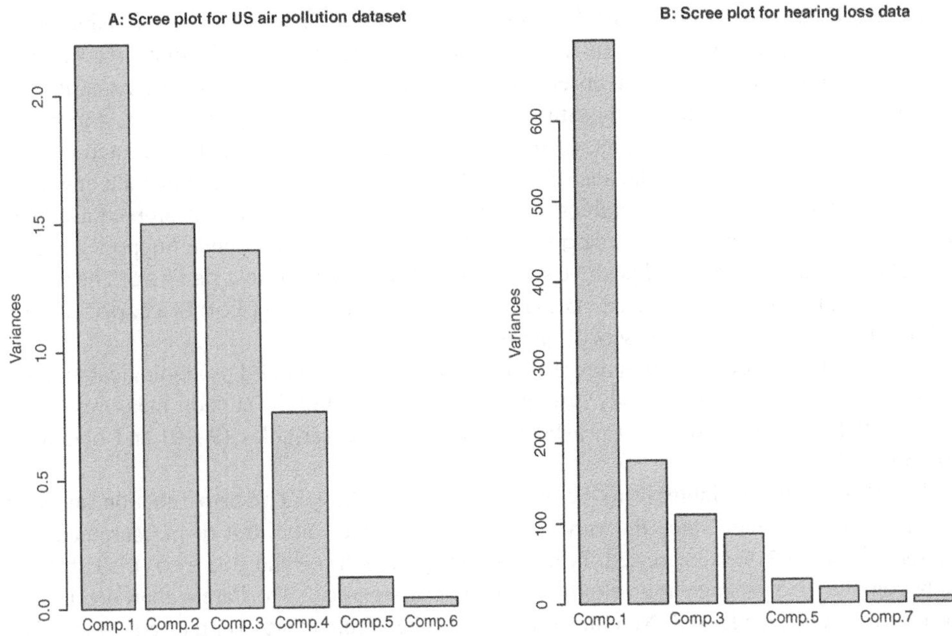

Figure 15.2 Scree Plots for Identifying the Number of Important Principal Components

In the next subsection, we focus on the applications of PCA.

?pairs, ?princomp, ?prcomp, ?summary.princomp, ?screeplot

15.5 Applications of Principal Component Analysis

Jolliffe (2002) and Jackson (1991) are two detailed treatises which discuss variants of PCA and their applications. PCA can be applied and/or augmented by statistical techniques such as ANOVA, linear regression, Multidimensional scaling, factor analysis, microarray modeling, time series, etc.

15.5.1 PCA for Linear Regression

Section 12.6 indicated the problem of multicollinearity in linear models. If the covariates are replaced with the PCs, the problem of multicollinearity will cease, since the PCs are uncorrelated with each other. It is thus the right time to fuse the multicollinearity problems of linear models with PCA. We are familiar with all the relevant concepts and hence will take the example of Maindonald and Braun (2009) for throwing light on this technique. Maindonald and Braun (2009) have made the required dataset available in their package `DAAG`. See Streiner and Norman (2003) for more details of this study.

Example 15.5.1. The socsupport Dataset. The dataset socsupport is available in the DAAG package. This dataset contains 19 predictor variables as follows. The first eight variables describe the characteristics of the observation such as age, gender, country, marital status in \verbmarital, live with status in variable livewith, employment, firstyr, and enrollment. Variable pairs, (9,10), (11,12), (13,14), and (15,16) are nested pairs of information in the sense that the answer of the first component may determine the answer of the second component. Here, variables 9, 11, 13, and 15 are respective indicators of availability of emotional satisfaction, tangible support existence, affectionate support existence in affect, and availability of positive social interaction in the variable psisat. The respective other half of these pairs (emotionalsat, tangiblesat, affectsat, psisat) of information are based on some sets of questions.

The output, Beck depression index (BDI), is a score of the standard psychological measure of depression. The aim of the study is to understand the effect of the support measures (9–19) on the BDI. We will first perform a PCA analysis on the variables (9–19) and obtain the important PCs.

The PCs for the variables 9 to 19 are created using the princomp function and then ss.pr1 is generated. Since the variables do not have the same unit of measurement, the option of cor=TRUE is exercised. In this example, we will use the pareto.chart function from the qcc package as an alternative to the screeplot. The Pareto chart details may be referred to in Chapter 4.3. Note the advantage of the Pareto chart over the screeplots. If we decide to use the PCs, which offer us 90% of the variation in the original data, the first six PCs provide the necessary coverage, see summary(ss.pa1) and the Pareto chart output in Figure 15.3.

```
> library(DAAG)
> data(socsupport)
> names(socsupport)
 [1] "gender"   "age"          "country"      "marital"      "livewith"

[16] "psisat"   "esupport"    "psupport"     "supsources"    "BDI"
> sum(is.na(socsupport[,9:19]))
[1] 10
> # Since observations are missing, we will remove them to
+ obtain the PCs
> ss.pr1 <- princomp(as.matrix(na.omit(socsupport[,9:19])),cor=TRUE)
> # screeplot(ss.pr1)
> library(qcc)
> pareto.chart(summary(ss.pr1)[[1]])
> summary(ss.pr1)
Importance of components:
                          Comp.1    Comp.2      Comp.4      Comp.5
Standard deviation     2.4967051 1.1620727  0.79328034  0.71977169
Proportion of Variance 0.5666851 0.1227648  0.05720852  0.04709739
Cumulative Proportion  0.5666851 0.6894500  0.85223245  0.89932984
                           Comp.6     Comp.7      Comp.9     Comp.10
Standard deviation     0.66590642 0.47892850  0.33771822  0.28154276
Proportion of Variance 0.04031194 0.02085205  0.01036851  0.00720603
```

```
Cumulative Proportion  0.93964178 0.96049383  0.98830796  0.99551399
                           Comp.11
Standard deviation     0.222139794
Proportion of Variance 0.004486008
Cumulative Proportion  1.000000000
```

Next, obtain the pairs diagram for the first six PC scores. The pairs diagram in Figure 15.3 indicates the presence of an outlier, which needs to be removed from further analyses. The outlier can be identified from the console using the simple `sort` function.

```
> pcscores <- ss.pr1$scores[,1:6]
> pairs(pcscores)
> sort(ss.pr1$scores[,1],decreasing=TRUE)[1:10]
      36       30             81       73
9.898667 5.614594     3.902259 3.703742
       2       75
3.497409 3.297526
```

As in Maindonald and Braun, we will use the first six PC scores to build a regression model for the BDI. Furthermore, we remove missing observations using `complete.cases` and the outlier through a simple trick, which may be easily figured out by the reader. Following this, we obtain the PCs for the refined predictors and then build a linear model for this setup. The next block of R codes is aimed at these steps.

```
> pcscores <- ss.pr1$scores[,1:6]
> soccases <- complete.cases(socsupport[,9:19])
> soccases[36] <- FALSE
> ss.pr <- princomp(as.matrix(socsupport[soccases,9:19]),cor=TRUE)
> ss.lm <- lm(socsupport$BDI[soccases]~ss.pr$scores[,1:6])
> summary(ss.lm)
Call:
lm(formula = socsupport$BDI[soccases] ~ ss.pr$scores[, 1:6])
Residuals:
     Min       1Q   Median        3Q      Max
-13.8017  -4.9450  -0.2718    3.1257  36.1143
Coefficients:
                             Estimate Std. Error t value Pr(>|t|)
(Intercept)                   10.4607     0.8934  11.709  < 2e-16 ***
ss.pr$scores[, 1:6]Comp.1      1.3113     0.3732   3.513 0.000723 ***
ss.pr$scores[, 1:6]Comp.2     -0.3959     0.7329  -0.540 0.590526
ss.pr$scores[, 1:6]Comp.3      0.6036     0.7860   0.768 0.444744
ss.pr$scores[, 1:6]Comp.4      1.4248     1.0576   1.347 0.181610
ss.pr$scores[, 1:6]Comp.5      2.1459     1.1841   1.812 0.073622 .
ss.pr$scores[, 1:6]Comp.6      1.2882     1.2848   1.003 0.318967
---
Signif. codes:  0 '***' 0.001 '**' 0.01 '*' 0.05 '.' 0.1 ' ' 1
```

```
Residual standard error: 8.428 on 82 degrees of freedom
Multiple R-squared: 0.1908, Adjusted R-squared: 0.1315
F-statistic: 3.222 on 6 and 82 DF,  p-value: 0.006837
```

Note that except for the first PC, the remaining PCs do not have a significant power in the explanation of BDI. For interesting further details, see Section 13.1 of Maindonald and Braun (2009). □

It is thus seen how the PCA helps to reduce the number of variables in the linear regression model. Note that even if we replace the original variables with equivalent PCs, the problem of multicollinearity is fixed.

15.5.2 Biplots

Gower and Hand (1996) have written a monograph on the use of biplots for multivariate data. Gower, et al. (2011) is a recent book on biplots complemented with the R package `UBbipl`, and is also an extension of Gower and Hand (1996). Greenacre (2010) has implemented all the biplot techniques in his book. This book has R codes for doing all the data analysis, and he has also been very generous to gift it to the world at http://www.multivariatestatistics.org/biplots.html. For theoretical aspects of biplots, the reader may also refer to Rencher (2002), Johnson and Wichern (2007), and Jolliffe (2002) among others. For a simpler and effective understanding of the biplots, see the Appendix of Desmukh and Purohit (2007).

The biplot is a visualization technique of the data matrix **X** through two coordinate systems representing the observations (row) and variables (columns) of the dataset. In this method, the variance-covariance between the variable and the distance between the observations, are plotted in a single figure, and to reflect this facet the prefix "bi" is used here. In this plot, the distance between the points, which are observations, represents the Mahalanobis distance between them. The length of a vector, displayed on the plot, from the origin to the coordinates, represents the variance of the variable with the angle between the variables (represented by the vectors) denoting the correlation. If the angle between the vectors is small, it will indicate that the vectors are strongly correlated.

For the sake of simplicity, we will assume that the data matrix **X**, consisting of n observations of a p-dimensional vector, is a centered matrix in the sense that each column has a zero mean. By the *singular value decomposition, SVD,* result, we can write the matrix **X** as

$$\mathbf{X} = \mathbf{U}\mathbf{\Lambda}\mathbf{V}', \tag{15.13}$$

where $\mathbf{U}$ is an $n \times r$ matrix, $\mathbf{\Lambda}$ is an diagonal $r \times r$ matrix, and $\mathbf{V}$ is an $p \times r$ matrix. By the properties of SVD, we have $\mathbf{U}'\mathbf{U} = \mathbf{I}_r$ and $\mathbf{V}'\mathbf{V} = \mathbf{I}_r$. Furthermore, $\mathbf{\Lambda}$ has diagonal elements in $\lambda_1 \geq \lambda_2 \geq \ldots \geq \lambda_r > 0$. We will consider a simple illustration of the SVD for the famous "Cork" dataset of Rao (1973).

Example 15.5.2. Understanding SVD for the Cork Dataset. Thickness of cork borings in four directions of North, South, East, and West are measured for 28 trees. The problem here is to examine if the bark deposit is the same in all directions.

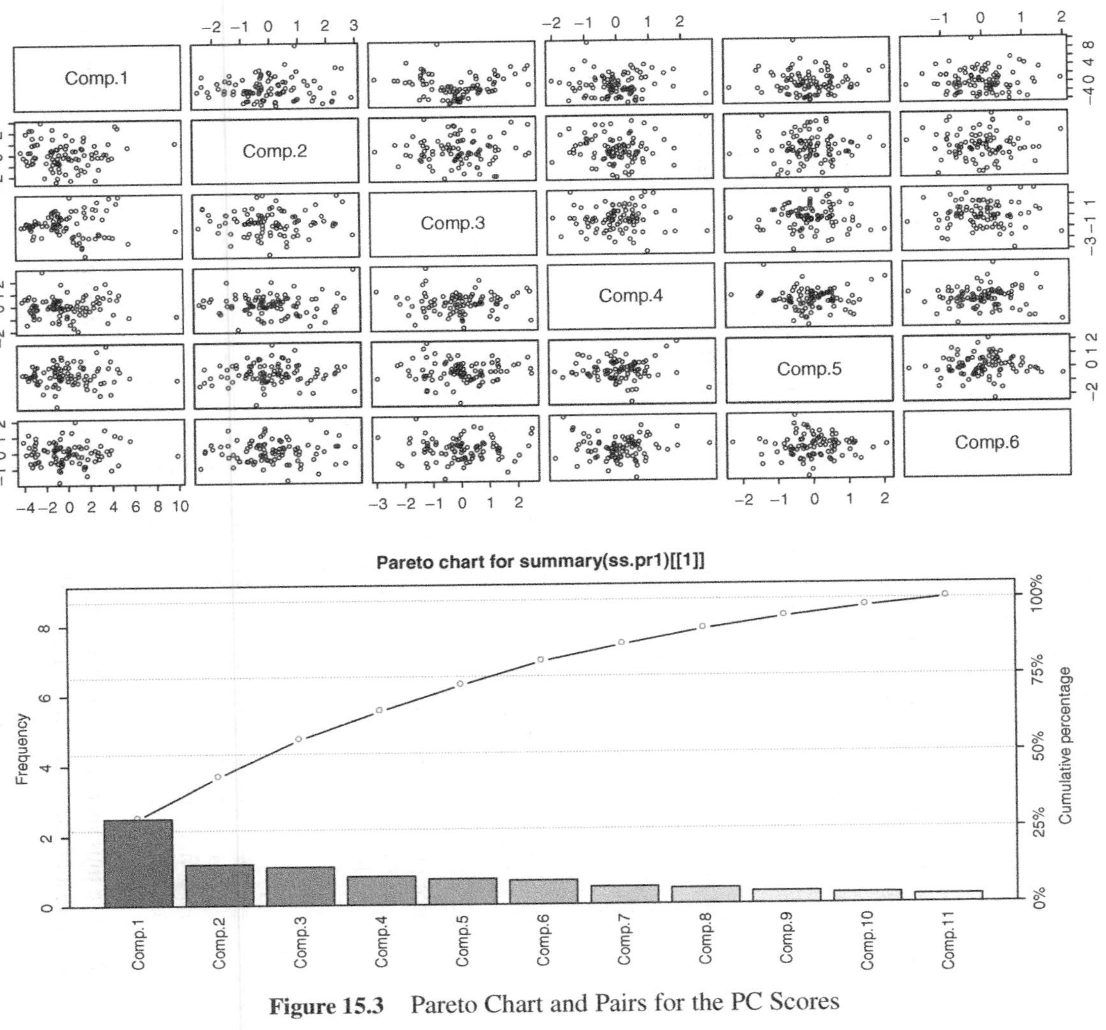

Figure 15.3 Pareto Chart and Pairs for the PC Scores

```
> data(cork)
> corkcent <- cork*0
> corkcent[,1] <- cork[,1]-mean(cork[,1])
> corkcent[,2] <- cork[,2]-mean(cork[,2])
> corkcent[,3] <- cork[,3]-mean(cork[,3])
> corkcent[,4] <- cork[,4]-mean(cork[,4])
> corkcentsvd <- svd(corkcent)
> t(corkcentsvd$u)%*%corkcentsvd$u
             [,1]          [,2]          [,3]          [,4]
[1,] 1.000000e+00  1.778092e-17  4.857226e-17  6.711211e-17
[2,] 1.778092e-17  1.000000e+00 -1.387779e-16 -8.023096e-17
[3,] 4.857226e-17 -1.387779e-16  1.000000e+00 -1.309716e-16
[4,] 6.711211e-17 -8.023096e-17 -1.309716e-16  1.000000e+00
> t(corkcentsvd$v)%*%corkcentsvd$v
              [,1]          [,2]          [,3]          [,4]
[1,]  1.000000e+00  1.110223e-16 -8.326673e-17 -1.110223e-16
[2,]  1.110223e-16  1.000000e+00 -1.665335e-16  1.665335e-16
[3,] -8.326673e-17 -1.665335e-16  1.000000e+00  3.330669e-16
[4,] -1.110223e-16  1.665335e-16  3.330669e-16  1.000000e+00
> round(corkcentsvd$u %*% diag(corkcentsvd$d) %*% t(corkcentsvd$v),2)
       [,1]   [,2]   [,3]   [,4]
 [1,] 21.46  19.82  26.32  31.82
 [2,]  9.46   6.82  16.32  17.82
 [3,]  5.46  10.82  14.32  12.82

[26,]  -0.54 -12.18 -12.68  -5.18
[27,]  -7.54  -9.18 -10.68   4.82
[28,]  -2.54   7.82   7.32  -2.18
> round(corkcent,2)
   North   East  South   West
1  21.46  19.82  26.32  31.82
2   9.46   6.82  16.32  17.82
3   5.46  10.82  14.32  12.82

26 -0.54 -12.18 -12.68  -5.18
27 -7.54  -9.18 -10.68   4.82
28 -2.54   7.82   7.32  -2.18
> corkcentsvd$d
[1] 163.03355  40.17752  25.40940  22.16929
```

We have thus seen the use of SVD for the cork dataset. This example will be carried forward to the rest of the discussion in this section. □

Notice the decline of the singular values, λ values, for the cork dataset. In the spirit of PCA, we tend to believe that if such a decline is steep, we can probably have a good understanding of the dataset if we resort to some plots which use two variables. In fact, such a result is validated by a theorem of Eckart and Young (1936). We need to connect the SVD result with the well-known *quadratic decomposition, QR,* result, which is now stated. The QR decomposition says that any $n \times p$ matrix can be expressed as

$$\mathbf{X} = \mathbf{G}\mathbf{H}', \tag{15.14}$$

where $\mathbf{G}$ is an $n \times r$ matrix and $\mathbf{H}$ is an $p \times r$ matrix, and r is the rank of matrix $\mathbf{X}$. In a certain sense, the goal is to understand the variance among the n observations through the matrix $\mathbf{G}$ and the variance among the p variables through $\mathbf{H}$. The matrices $\mathbf{G}$ and $\mathbf{H}$ may be obtained as a combination of the SVD elements as $\mathbf{G} = \mathbf{U}\Lambda^{\alpha}$ and $\mathbf{H} = \Lambda^{1-\alpha}\mathbf{V}$. For different choices of α, we have different representations for $\mathbf{X}$. The three most common choices of α are 0, 1/2, and 1, see Gabriel (1971). We mention some consequences of these choices, see Khatree and Naik (1999).

- $\alpha = 1/2$. In the this case, the QR matrices may be expressed in terms of the SVD matrices as

$$\mathbf{g}_i' = (\sqrt{\lambda_1}u_{1i}, \sqrt{\lambda_2}u_{2i}, \dots, \sqrt{\lambda_p}u_{pi}), i = 1, 2, \dots, n,$$

$$\mathbf{h}_j' = (\sqrt{\lambda_1}v_{1j}, \sqrt{\lambda_2}v_{2j}, \dots, \sqrt{\lambda_p}v_{pj}), j = 1, 2, \dots, p. \tag{15.15}$$

  For the choice $\alpha = 1/2$, we place an equal emphasis on the variables and the observations.
- $\alpha = 0$. Here

$$\mathbf{g}_i' = (u_{1i}, u_{2i}, \dots, u_{pi}), i = 1, 2, \dots, n,$$

$$\mathbf{h}_j' = (\lambda_1 v_{1j}, \lambda_2 v_{2j}, \dots, \lambda_p v_{pj}), j = 1, 2, \dots, p. \tag{15.16}$$

  The distance between the vectors $\mathbf{g}_i$ approximates the squared Mahalanobis distance between the observation vectors. Furthermore, the inner product between the vectors $\mathbf{h}_j$ approximates the covariances between them and length of a vector $\mathbf{h}_j$ gives its variance.
- $\alpha = 1$. Here,

$$\mathbf{g}_i' = (\lambda_1 u_{1i}, \lambda_2 u_{2i}, \dots, \lambda_p u_{pi}), i = 1, 2, \dots, n,$$

$$\mathbf{h}_j' = (v_{1j}, v_{2j}, \dots, v_{pj}), j = 1, 2, \dots, p. \tag{15.17}$$

  For this case, the distance between $\mathbf{g}_i$'s is the usual Euclidean distance between them and the values of $\mathbf{g}_i$ equals the principal component score for the observations, whereas the values of $\mathbf{h}_j$ refer to the principal component loadings.

  For the cork dataset, we will obtain the biplot for the choice $\alpha = 1/2$.

Example 15.5.3. Understanding SVD for the Cork Dataset. Contd. The `biplot` function R can be readily used for the analysis.

```
> corkcentpca <- princomp(corkcent,cor=TRUE)
> summary(corkcentpca)
Importance of components:
                          Comp.1     Comp.2     Comp.3     Comp.4
Standard deviation     1.8965419 0.50362240 0.28303246 0.26341193
Proportion of Variance 0.8992178 0.06340888 0.02002684 0.01734646
Cumulative Proportion  0.8992178 0.96262670 0.98265354 1.00000000
> biplot(corkcentpca,scale=1/2)
```

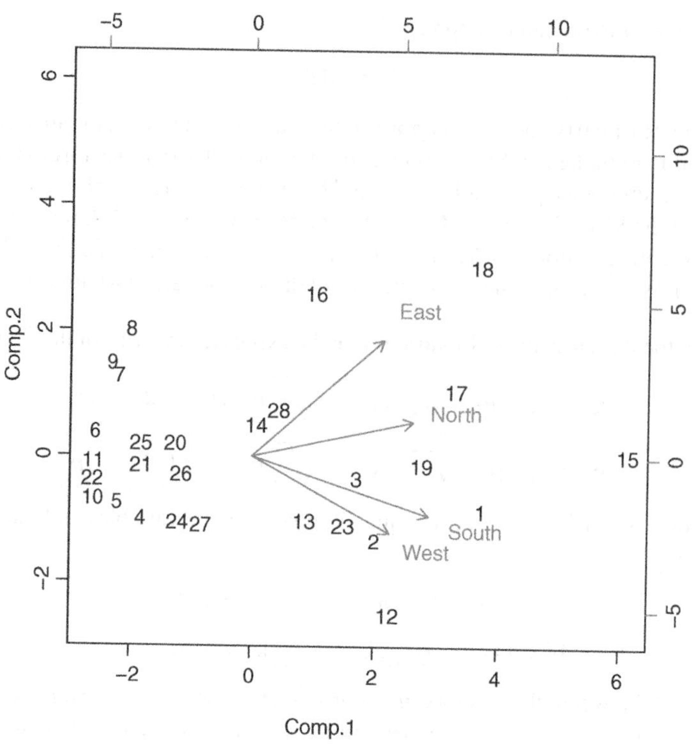

Figure 15.4 Biplot of the Cork Dataset

The first two PCs explain `96.26%` of the variation in the four variables. The principal component can be interpreted as the weighted average of the original variables. The original variables are all positively correlated with respect to the first component. It can be seen from Figure 15.4 that `North` and `East` are positively correlated with the second component and `South` and `West` are negatively correlated. Hence, we have a contrast in `North + East - South - West`. Furthermore, observations numbered 12 and 18 have maximum difference with respect to PC 1, while 6, 10, and 11 observations have maximum difference with observation 15 with respect to PC 2.

?pareto.chart, ?complete.cases, ?svd, ?biplot

15.6 Factor Analysis

We will have a look at another important facet of multivariate statistical analysis: *Factor Analysis*. The data observations $\mathbf{x}_i, i = 1, \ldots, n$, are assumed to arise from an $N(\boldsymbol{\mu}, \boldsymbol{\Sigma})$ distribution. Consider a hypothetical example where the correlation matrix is given by

$$\text{Cor}(\mathbf{X}) = \begin{pmatrix} 1 & 0.89 & 0.01 & 0.04 & 0.023 \\ & 1 & 0.02 & 0.042 & -0.03 \\ & & 1 & 0.93 & 0.98 \\ & & & 1 & 0.94 \\ & & & & 1 \end{pmatrix}$$

Here, we can see that the first two components are strongly correlated with each other and also appear to be independent of the rest of the components. Similarly, the last three components are strongly correlated among themselves and independent of the first two components. A natural intuition is to think of the first two components arising due to one *factor* and the remaining three due to a second *factor*. The factors are also sometimes called *latent variables*.

The development in the rest of the section is only related to *orthogonal factor model* and it is the same whenever we talk about the factor analysis model. For other variants, refer to Basilevsky (1994), Reyment and J'oreskog (1996), and Brown (2006).

15.6.1 The Orthogonal Factor Analysis Model

Let $\mathbf{x} = (x_1, x_2, \dots, x_p)$ be a p-vector. To begin with, we will assume that there are m factors with $m < p$ and that each of the x_i's is a function of the m factors. The *factor analysis model* is given by

$$\begin{aligned}
x_1 - \mu_1 &= \lambda_{11}f_1 + \lambda_{12}f_2 + \dots + \lambda_{1m}f_m + u_1, \\
x_2 - \mu_2 &= \lambda_{21}f_1 + \lambda_{22}f_2 + \dots + \lambda_{2m}f_k + u_2, \\
&\vdots \\
x_p - \mu_p &= \lambda_{p1}f_1 + \lambda_{p2}f_2 + \dots + \lambda_{pm}f_k + u_p,
\end{aligned} \tag{15.18}$$

where $u_i, i = 1, \dots, p$, are normally distributed errors associated with the variable $x_i, i = 1, \dots, p$. In the factor analysis model, the $\lambda_{ij}, i = 1, \dots, p, j = 1, \dots, k$, are the regression coefficients between the observed variables and the factors. Two points need to be observed. In the factor analysis literature, the regression coefficients are called *loadings*, which indicate how the weights of the x's depend on the factors f's. The loadings are denoted by λ's, which we thus far used for eigenvalues and eigenvectors. However, the notation of λ's for the loadings is standard in the factor analysis literature and in the rest of this section they will denote the loadings and not quantities related to eigenvalues.

We will now use the matrix notation and then state the essential assumptions. The (orthogonal) factor model may be stated in matrix form as

$$\mathbf{x} - \boldsymbol{\mu} = \boldsymbol{\Lambda}\mathbf{f} + \mathbf{u}, \tag{15.19}$$

where

$$\begin{aligned}
\mathbf{x} &= (x_1, \dots, x_p)^T, \\
\boldsymbol{\mu} &= (\mu_1, \dots, \mu_p)^T, \\
\mathbf{f} &= (f_1, \dots, f_m)^T, \\
\mathbf{u} &= (u_1, \dots, u_p)^T, \\
\boldsymbol{\Lambda} &= \begin{pmatrix} \lambda_{11} & \lambda_{12} & \cdots & \lambda_{1m} \\ \lambda_{11} & \lambda_{12} & \cdots & \lambda_{1m} \\ \vdots & \vdots & & \vdots \\ \lambda_{l1} & \lambda_{p2} & \cdots & \lambda_{pm} \end{pmatrix}.
\end{aligned}$$

The essential assumptions related to the factors are as follows:

$$E(\mathbf{f}) = 0, \tag{15.20}$$

$$\text{cov}(\mathbf{f}) = \mathbf{I}, \tag{15.21}$$

$$E(\mathbf{u}) = \mathbf{0}, \tag{15.22}$$

$$\text{cov}(\mathbf{u}) = \boldsymbol{\Psi} = \text{diag}(\psi_1, \psi_2, \ldots, \psi_p), \text{ and} \tag{15.23}$$

$$\text{cov}(\mathbf{f}, \mathbf{u}) = \mathbf{0}. \tag{15.24}$$

Under the above assumptions, we can see that the variance of component x_i can be expressed in terms of the loadings as

$$\text{var}(x_i) = \underbrace{\lambda_{i1}^2 + \lambda_{i2}^2 + \cdots + \lambda_{im}^2}_{\text{communality}} + \underbrace{\psi_i}_{\text{specific variance}}. \tag{15.25}$$

Define $h_i^2 = \lambda_{i1}^2 + \lambda_{i2}^2 + \cdots + \lambda_{im}^2, i = 1, \ldots, p$. Thus, the variance of a component can be written as the sum of a common variance component and a specific variance component. It is common practice in the factor analysis literature to refer to h_i^2 as the *common variance* and the specific variance ψ_i as *specificity, unique variance*, or *residual variance*.

The covariance matrix $\boldsymbol{\Sigma}$ can be written in terms of $\boldsymbol{\Lambda}$ and $\boldsymbol{\Psi}$ as

$$\boldsymbol{\Sigma} = \boldsymbol{\Lambda}^T\boldsymbol{\Lambda} + \boldsymbol{\Psi}. \tag{15.26}$$

Using the above relationship, we can arrive at the next expression:

$$\text{cov}(\mathbf{x}, \mathbf{f}) = \boldsymbol{\Lambda}.$$

We will consider three methods for estimation of the loadings and communalities: (i) The Principal Component Method, (ii) The Principal Factor Method, and (iii) Maximum Likelihood Function. We omit a fourth important technique of estimation of factors in "Iterated Principal Factor Method".

15.6.2 Estimation of Loadings and Communalities

We will first consider the principal component method. Let $\mathbf{S}$ denote the sample covariance matrix. The problem is then to find an estimator $\hat{\boldsymbol{\Lambda}}$, which will approximate $\mathbf{S}$ such that

$$\mathbf{S} \cong \hat{\boldsymbol{\Lambda}}\hat{\boldsymbol{\Lambda}}^T + \hat{\boldsymbol{\Psi}}. \tag{15.27}$$

In this approach, the last component $\hat{\boldsymbol{\Psi}}$ is ignored and we approximate the sampling covariance matrix by a *spectral decomposition*:

$$\mathbf{S} = \mathbf{CDC}^T, \tag{15.28}$$

where $\mathbf{C}$ is an orthogonal matrix constructed with normalized eigenvectors, $\mathbf{c_i}\mathbf{c_i}^T = \mathbf{1}$, of $\mathbf{S}$ and $\mathbf{D}$ is a diagonal matrix with eigenvalues of $\mathbf{S}$. That is, if $\theta_1, \ldots, \theta_p$ are the eigenvalues of $\mathbf{S}$, then $\mathbf{D} = \text{diag}\{\theta_1, \ldots, \theta_p\}$. Since the eigenvalues θ_i of the positive semi-definite matrix $\mathbf{S}$ are all positive or zero, we can factor $\mathbf{D}$ as

$$\mathbf{D} = \mathbf{D}^{1/2}\mathbf{D}^{1/2},$$

and substituting this in (15.28), we get

$$\begin{aligned}\mathbf{S} &= \mathbf{C}\mathbf{D}^{1/2}\mathbf{D}^{1/2}\mathbf{C}^T \\ &= (\mathbf{C}\mathbf{D}^{1/2})(\mathbf{C}\mathbf{D}^{1/2})^T.\end{aligned} \tag{15.29}$$

This suggests that we can use $\hat{\mathbf{\Lambda}} = \mathbf{C}\mathbf{D}^{1/2}$. However, we seek a $\hat{\mathbf{\Lambda}}$ whose order is less than p, and hence we consider the first m largest θ eigenvalues and take $\mathbf{D} = \text{diag}(\theta_1, \ldots, \theta_m)$ and $\mathbf{C}$ with their corresponding eigenvectors. Thus, an useful estimator of $\mathbf{\Lambda}$ is given by

$$\hat{\mathbf{\Lambda}} = \left(\sqrt{\theta_1}\mathbf{c}_1, \sqrt{\theta_2}\mathbf{c}_2, \ldots, \sqrt{\theta_m}\mathbf{c}_m\right). \tag{15.30}$$

Note that the ith diagonal element of $\hat{\mathbf{\Lambda}}\hat{\mathbf{\Lambda}}^T$ is the sum of squares of $\hat{\mathbf{\Lambda}}$. We can then use this to estimate the diagonal elements of $\hat{\mathbf{\Psi}}$ by

$$\hat{\psi}_i = s_{ii} - \sum_{j=1}^{m} \hat{\lambda}_{ij}^2, \tag{15.31}$$

and using this relationship approximate $\mathbf{S}$ by

$$\mathbf{S} \cong \hat{\mathbf{\Lambda}}\hat{\mathbf{\Lambda}}^T + \hat{\mathbf{\Psi}}. \tag{15.32}$$

Since, here, the sums of squares of the rows and columns of $\hat{\mathbf{\Lambda}}$ equal the communalities and eigenvalues respectively, an estimate of the ith communality is given by

$$\hat{h}_i^2 = \sum_{j=1}^{m} \hat{\lambda}_{ij}^2. \tag{15.33}$$

Similarly, we have

$$\sum_{i=1}^{p} \hat{\lambda}_{ij}^2 = \sum_{i=1}^{p} (\sqrt{\theta_j} c_{ij})^2 = \theta_j \sum_{i=1}^{p} (c_{ij})^2 = \theta_j, \tag{15.34}$$

where the last equality follows from the fact that $\mathbf{c}_i\mathbf{c}_i^T = 1$. Using the estimates of $\hat{\psi}_i$ and $\hat{h}_i^2$ in (15.29), we obtain a partition of the variance of the ith variable as

$$s_{ii} = \hat{\lambda}_{i1}^2 + \ldots + \hat{\lambda}_{im}^2 + \hat{\psi}_i. \tag{15.35}$$

The contribution of the jth factor to the total sample variance is therefore

$$\hat{\lambda}_{1j}^2 + \ldots + \hat{\lambda}_{pj}^2. \tag{15.36}$$

We will now illustrate the concepts with a solved example from Rencher (2002).

Example 15.6.1. Renchers Example 13.3.2. A girl rates seven of her acquaintances on a grade of 1 to 9 based on the five adjectives kind, intelligent, happy, likable, and just.

```
> data(adjectives)
> adjectivescor <- cor(adjectives[,-1])
> round(adjectivescor,3)
             Kind Intelligent  Happy Likeable  Just
Kind        1.000       0.296  0.881    0.995 0.545
Intelligent 0.296       1.000 -0.022    0.326 0.837
Happy       0.881      -0.022  1.000    0.867 0.130
Likeable    0.995       0.326  0.867    1.000 0.544
Just        0.545       0.837  0.130    0.544 1.000
> adj_eig <- eigen(adjectivescor)
> cumsum(adj_eig$values)/sum(adj_eig$values)
[1] 0.6526490 0.9603115 0.9938815 1.0000000 1.0000000
> adj_eig$vectors[,1:2]
           [,1]       [,2]
[1,] -0.5366646 -0.1863665
[2,] -0.2875272  0.6506116
[3,] -0.4342879 -0.4734720
[4,] -0.5374480 -0.1692745
[5,] -0.3896959  0.5377197
> loadings1 <- adj_eig$vectors[,1]*sqrt(adj_eig$values[1])
> loadings2 <- adj_eig$vectors[,2]*sqrt(adj_eig$values[2])
> cbind(loadings1,loadings2)
      loadings1  loadings2
[1,] -0.9694553 -0.2311480
[2,] -0.5194021  0.8069453
[3,] -0.7845174 -0.5872412
[4,] -0.9708704 -0.2099491
[5,] -0.7039644  0.6669269
> communalities <- (adj_eig$vectors[,1]*sqrt(adj_eig$values[1]))^2
+ + (adj_eig$vectors[,2]*sqrt(adj_eig$values[2]))^2
> round(communalities,3)
[1] 0.993 0.921 0.960 0.987 0.940
> specific_variances <- 1-communalities
> round(specific_variances,3)
[1] 0.007 0.079 0.040 0.013 0.060
> var_acc_factors <- adj_eig$values
> round(var_acc_factors,3)
[1] 3.263 1.538 0.168 0.031 0.000
> prop_var <- adj_eig$values/sum(adj_eig$values)
> round(prop_var,3)
[1] 0.653 0.308 0.034 0.006 0.000
> cum_prop <- cumsum(adj_eig$values)/sum(adj_eig$values)
> round(cum_prop,3)
[1] 0.653 0.960 0.994 1.000 1.000
```

Note that for this example, we may need further adjustments if we wish to use the `factanal` function of R.

□

We will next consider the *principal factor method*. In the previous method we have omitted $\mathbf{\Psi}$. In the principal factor method we use an initial estimate of $\mathbf{\Psi}$, say $\hat{\mathbf{\Psi}}$, and factor for $\mathbf{R} - \hat{\mathbf{\Psi}}$, or $\mathbf{S} - \hat{\mathbf{\Psi}}$, whichever is appropriate:

$$\mathbf{R} - \hat{\mathbf{\Psi}} \cong \hat{\mathbf{\Lambda}}\hat{\mathbf{\Lambda}}^T, \tag{15.37}$$

$$\mathbf{S} - \hat{\mathbf{\Psi}} \cong \hat{\mathbf{\Lambda}}\hat{\mathbf{\Lambda}}^T, \tag{15.38}$$

where $\hat{\mathbf{\Lambda}}$ is as specified in (15.30) with the eigenvalues and eigenvectors of $\mathbf{S} - \hat{\Psi}$ or $\mathbf{R} - \hat{\Psi}$. Since the ith diagonal element of $\mathbf{S} - \hat{\mathbf{\Psi}}$ is the ith communality, we have $\hat{h}_i^2 = s_{ii} - \hat{\psi}_i$. In the case of $\mathbf{S} - \hat{\Psi}$, we have $\hat{h}_i^2 = 1 - \hat{\psi}_i$. For more details, refer to Section 13.2 of Rencher (2002). We will illustrate these computations as a continuation of the previous example.

Example 15.6.2. Example 15.6.1. Contd. To the best of our knowledge, the Principal Factor Method of estimation of factors does not have a ready-to-use function in R. We have developed an ad-hoc function for the same.

```
> RPsi <- adjectivescor
> for(i in 1:nrow(RPsi)){
+     RPsi[i,i] <- max(abs(RPsi[i,-i]))
+ }
> RPsi_eig <- eigen(RPsi)
> cumsum(RPsi_eig$values)/sum(RPsi_eig$values)
[1] 0.7043136 1.0110721 1.0175840 1.0175356 1.0000000
> RPsi_eig$vectors[,1:2]
           [,1]       [,2]
[1,] -0.5479823 -0.1775575
[2,] -0.2721324  0.6556565
[3,] -0.4310945 -0.4604984
[4,] -0.5486491 -0.1587823
[5,] -0.3725601  0.5489237
> loadings1 <- RPsi_eig$vectors[,1]*sqrt(RPsi_eig$values[1])
> loadings2 <- RPsi_eig$vectors[,2]*sqrt(RPsi_eig$values[2])
> communalities <- (RPsi_eig$vectors[,1]*sqrt(RPsi_eig$values[1]))^2
+ + (RPsi_eig$vectors[,2]*sqrt(RPsi_eig$values[2]))^2
> specific_variances <- 1-communalities
> var_acc_factors <- RPsi_eig$values
> prop_var <- RPsi_eig$values/sum(RPsi_eig$values)
> round(prop_var,3)
[1]  0.704  0.307  0.007  0.000 -0.018
> cum_prop <- cumsum(RPsi_eig$values)/sum(RPsi_eig$values)
> round(cum_prop,3)
[1] 0.704 1.011 1.018 1.018 1.000
> lambda <- cbind(loadings1,loadings2)
> lambda
          [,1]       [,2]       [,3]      [,4]      [,5]
[1,] 1.0000000 0.31512040 0.87039495 1.0019415 0.5177525
```

```
[2,] 0.3151204  1.00000000 -0.04542739 0.3328682 0.8265158
[3,] 0.8703950 -0.04542739  1.00000000 0.8592584 0.1617328
[4,] 1.0019415  0.33286820  0.85925837 1.0000000 0.5329202
[5,] 0.5177525  0.82651577  0.16173275 0.5329202 1.0000000
```

The computations may be cross-checked with page 423 of Rencher. The proportion of variance for the first principal factor is .704.

□

Finally, we conclude this section with a discussion of the Maximum Likelihood Estimation method. Under the assumption that the observations $\mathbf{x}_1, \ldots, \mathbf{x}_n$ are a random sample from $N(\boldsymbol{\mu}, \boldsymbol{\Sigma})$, it may be shown that the estimates $\hat{\boldsymbol{\Lambda}}$ and $\hat{\boldsymbol{\Psi}}$ satisfy the following set of equations:

$$\mathbf{S}\hat{\boldsymbol{\Psi}}\hat{\boldsymbol{\Lambda}} = \hat{\boldsymbol{\Lambda}}\left(\mathbf{I} + \hat{\boldsymbol{\Lambda}}^T\hat{\boldsymbol{\Psi}}^{-1}\hat{\boldsymbol{\Lambda}}\right), \tag{15.39}$$

$$\hat{\boldsymbol{\Psi}} = \text{diag}\left(\mathbf{S} - \hat{\boldsymbol{\Lambda}}\hat{\boldsymbol{\Lambda}}^T\right), \tag{15.40}$$

$$\hat{\boldsymbol{\Lambda}}^T\hat{\boldsymbol{\Psi}}^{-1}\hat{\boldsymbol{\Lambda}} \quad \text{is diagonal.} \tag{15.41}$$

The equations need to be solved iteratively, and happily for us R does that. The MLE technique is illustrated in the next example. We need to address a few important questions before then.

The important question is regarding the choice of the number of factors to be determined. Some rules given in Rencher are stated in the following.

- Select m as equal to the number of factors necessary, which account for a pre-specified percentage of the variance accounted by the factors, say 80%.
- Select m as the number of eigenvalues that are greater than the average eigenvalue.
- Use a screeplot to determine m.
- Test the hypothesis that m is the correct number of factors, that is, $H : \boldsymbol{\Sigma} = \boldsymbol{\Lambda}\boldsymbol{\Lambda}^T + \boldsymbol{\Psi}$.

We leave it to the reader to find out more about the concept of *Rotation* and give a summary of them, adapted from Hair, et al. (2010).

- **Varimax Rotation** is the most popular orthogonal factor rotation method, which focuses on simplifying the columns of a factor matrix. It is generally superior to other orthogonal factor rotation methods. Here, we seek to rotate the loadings, which maximize the variance of the squared loadings in each column of $\hat{\boldsymbol{\Lambda}}^*$.
- **Quartimax Rotation** is a less powerful technique than varimax rotation, which focuses on simplifying the columns of the factor matrix.
- **Oblique Rotation** obtains the factors such that the extracted factors are correlated, and hence it identifies the extent to which the factors are correlated.

Example 15.6.3. Life Expectancies. We have read about this dataset in Example 3.2.8. This example is borrowed from Section 5.9 of Everitt and Hothorn (2011). We need to determine the factor model at which the number of factors are such that the statistic U is insignificant. For this dataset, the number of factors k is three and hence a three-factor is adequate.

```
> data(life)
> factanal(life,factors=1)$PVAL
   objective
1.879555e-24
```

```
> factanal(life,factors=2)$PVAL
   objective
1.911514e-05
> factanal(life,factors=3)
Call:
factanal(x = life, factors = 3)
Uniquenesses:
   m0   m25   m50   m75    w0   w25   w50   w75
0.005 0.362 0.066 0.288 0.005 0.011 0.020 0.146
Loadings:
    Factor1 Factor2 Factor3
m0  0.964   0.122   0.226
m25 0.646   0.169   0.438
m50 0.430   0.354   0.790
m75         0.525   0.656
w0  0.970   0.217
w25 0.764   0.556   0.310
w50 0.536   0.729   0.401
w75 0.156   0.867   0.280
               Factor1 Factor2 Factor3
SS loadings      3.375   2.082   1.640
Proportion Var   0.422   0.260   0.205
Cumulative Var   0.422   0.682   0.887
Test of the hypothesis that 3 factors are sufficient.
The chi square statistic is 6.73 on 7 degrees of freedom.
The p-value is 0.458
> factanal(life,factors=4)$PVAL
Error in factanal(life, factors = 4) :
  unable to optimize from this starting value
> round(factanal(life,factors=3,scores="reg")$scores,3)
                         Factor1 Factor2 Factor3
Algeria                   -0.258   1.901   1.916
Cameroon                  -2.782  -0.723  -1.848
Madagascar                -2.806  -0.812  -0.012

Colombia                  -0.241  -0.295   0.429
Ecuador                   -0.723   0.442   1.592
```

The loadings for Factor 1 are strongly associated with the variables `m0` and `w0`, which represent the life force at birth. Similarly, Factor 2 is associated with older women, and Factor 3 is associated with older men. □

We have thus learnt about fairly complex and powerful techniques in multivariate statistics. The techniques vary from classifying observations to specific class, identifying group of independent (sub) vectors, reducing the number of variables, and determining hidden variables which possibly explain the observed variables. More details can be found in the references concluding this chapter.

?eigen, ?cumsum, ?factanal

15.7 Further Reading

We will begin with a disclaimer that the classification of the texts in different sections is not perfect.

15.7.1 The Classics and Applied Perspectives

Anderson (1958, 1984, and 2003) are the first primers on MSA. Currently, Anderson's book is in its third edition and it is worth noting that the second and third editions are probably the only ones which discuss the *Stein effect* in depth. Chapter 8 of Rao (1973) provides the necessary theoretical background for multivariate analysis and also contains some of Rao's remarkable research in multivariate statistics. In a certain way, one chapter may have more results than we can possibly cover in a complete book. A vector space approach for multivariate statistics is to be found in Eaton (1983, 2007). Mardia, Kent, and Bibby (1979) is an excellent treatise on multivariate analysis and considers many geometrical aspects. The geometrical approach is also considered in Gnanadesikan (1977, 1997), and further robustness aspects are also developed within it. Muirhead (1982), Giri (2004), Bilodeau and Brenner (1999), Rencher (2002), and Rencher (1998) are among some of the important texts on multivariate analysis. We note here that our coverage is mainly based on Rencher (2002).

Jolliffe (2002) is a detailed monograph on Principal Component Analysis. Jackson (1991) is a remarkable account on the applications on PCA. It is needless to say that if you read through these two books, you may become an authority on PCA.

Missing data, EM algorithms, and multivariate analysis have been aptly handled in Schafer (1997) and in fact many useful programs have been provided in S, which can be easily adapted in R. In this sense, this is a stand-alone reference book which deals with missing data. Of course, McLachlan and Krishnan (2008) may also be used!

Johnson and Wichern (2007) is a popular course, which does apt justice between theory and applications. Hair, et al. (2010) may be commonly found on a practitioner's desk. Izenman (2008) is a modern flavor of multivariate statistics with converage of the fashionable area of *machine learning*. Sharma (1996) and Timm (2002) also provide a firm footing in multivariate statistics.

Gower, et al. (2011) discuss many variants of biplots, which is an extension of Gower and Hand (1996). Greenacre (2010) is an open source book with in-depth coverage of biplots.

15.7.2 Multivariate Analysis and Software

The two companion volumes of Khatree and Naik (1999) and Khatree and Naik (2000) provide excellent coverage of multivariate analysis and computations through SAS software. It may be noted, one more time, that the programs and logical thinking are of paramount importance rather than a particular software. It is worth recording here that these two companions provide a fine balance between the theoretical aspects and computations. H'ardle and Simar (2007) have used "XploRe" software for computations. Last, and not least, the most recent book of Everitt and Hothorn (2011) is a good source for multivariate analysis through R. Varmuza and Filzmoser (2009) have used R software with a special emphasis on the applications to Chemometrics. Husson, et al. (2011) is also a recent arrival, which integrates R with multivariate analysis. Desmukh and Purohit (2007) also present PCA, biplot, and other multivariate aspects in R, though their emphasis is more on microarray data.

15.8 Complements, Problems, and Programs

Problem 15.1 Explore the R examples for linear discriminant analysis and canonical correlation with `example(lda)` and `example(cancor)`.

Problem 15.2 In the "Seishu Wine Study" of Example 16.9.1, the tests for independence of four sub-vectors lead to rejection of the hypothesis of their independence. Combine the subvectors `s11` with `s22` and `s33` with `s44`. Find the canonical correlations between these combined subvectors. Furthermore, find the canonical correlations for each subvector while pooling the others together.

Problem 15.3 Principal components offer effective reduction in data dimensionality. In Examples 15.4.1 and 15.4.2, it is observed that the first few PCs explain most of the variation in the original data. Do you expect further reduction if you perform PCA on these PCs? Validate your answer by running `princomp` on the PCs.

Problem 15.4 Find the PCs for the stack loss dataset, which explain 85% of the variation in the original dataset.

Problem 15.5 Perform the PCA on the `iris` dataset along the two lines: (i) the entire dataset, (ii) three subsets according to the three species. Check whether the PC scores are significantly different across the three species using an appropriate multivariate testing problem.

Problem 15.6 For the US crime data of Example 13.4.2, carry out the PCA for the covariates and then perform the regression analysis on the PC scores. Investigate if the multicollinearity problem persists in the fitted regression model based on the PC scores.

Problem 15.7 How do outliers effect PC scores? Perform PCA on the board stiffness dataset of Example 16.3.5 with and without the detected outliers therein.

Problem 15.8 Check out for the example of the `factanal` function. Are factors present in the `iris` dataset? Develop the complete analysis for the problem.

16

Categorical Data Analysis

Package(s): `gdata`
Dataset(s): `UCBAdmissions`, `Titanic`, `HairEyeColor`, `VADeaths`, `faithful`, `atombomb`, `Filariasistype`

16.1 Introduction

Discrete data may be classified into two forms: (i) nominal data, and (ii) ordinal data. Nominal data consists of variables which have labels. For example, the variable gender consists of two labels, male and female. As such, though we may denote males by 0 and females by 1, it is not the case here that 1 is greater than 0, and thus the name for the variable is a nominal variable. On the other hand, if we consider the rank of a student on the basis of marks, the first rank signifies more value than the second rank. Such variables are called ordinal variables. Categorical data analysis is concerned about analysis of these kind of variables.

Categorical Data Analysis, abbreviated as CDA, requires data to be entered in a specific format, viz., the contingency tables. In particular, in R, the data has to be read in a table format. Some of the standard datasets, for CDA, shipped along with R software include `UCBAdmissions`, `Titanic`, `HairEyeColor`, and `VADeaths`. Note that earlier datasets, such as `iris`, are of the class `data.frame`. The above-mentioned datasets are of the class `table` or `matrix`, as can be verified in the next (small) program.

```
> class(UCBAdmissions);class(Titanic);class(HairEyeColor)
> class(VADeaths)
[1] "table"
[1] "table"
[1] "table"
[1] "matrix"
```

We will begin with graphical methods for the categorical data in Section 16.2. In Section 16.3, we will discuss the all-important odds ratio. Simpson's paradox poses genuine problems in the

A Course in Statistics with R, First Edition. Prabhanjan Narayanachar Tattar, Suresh Ramaiah and B. G. Manjunath.

Companion Website: www.wiley.com/go/tattar/statistics

analysis of categorical data. An illustration of the paradox will be seen in Section 16.4. The role of binomial, multinomial, and Poisson distributions as statistical models for categorical data will be dealt with in Section 16.5. A brief discussion of the problem of *overdispersion* is the matter of Section 16.6. Statistical tests for independence of attributes will be taken up in Section 16.7. The final section will contain measures of agreement for ordinal data. Regression methods for categorical data will be considered in the final chapter of the book.

16.2 Graphical Methods for CDA

The use of graphics for data analysis has perhaps been most elegantly explained by Friendly (2000):

VISUALIZATION = GRAPHING + FITTING + GRAPHING + ...

Friendly adds in clarification that the visualization approach for data analysis is encompassed in this way: (i) expose information and structure of the data, (ii) complement the graphs with numerical summaries, and (iii) explore more suitable models. In this section we will focus more on the graphical method, and follow up the *friendly* approach in later sections.

The important graphical techniques for understanding the structure of categorical data is enlisted as follows:

- Bar and Stacked Bar Charts
- Spine and Stacked Spine Charts
- Pie Chart
- Four Fold Plots
- Mosaic Plots

16.2.1 Bar and Stacked Bar Plots

In a bar plot the values (or frequencies) of the categories are plotted against the names of the categories. The plotted values are drawn proportional to values of the variables. Bar diagrams are essentially one-dimensional diagrams in the sense that the scale on one axis is sufficient to reveal the complete information. An important advantage of bar diagrams is that they can give insight into nominal variables too. More complexity in the data can be handled using what is known as the stacked bar plot. Bar plots are introduced first and their variations of stacked bar are handled later.

Example 16.2.1. The Virginia Deaths Dataset. For the year 1940, data related to death rates per 1000 persons has been recorded in Virginia City. The age groups have been partitioned into five groups: `50-54`, `55-59`, `60-64`, `65-69`, `70-74`. Furthermore, we have information about the urban/rural status along with gender information. The death rates for the rural male across the different age groups is visualized through a bar plot with the R function `barplot`, see Figure 16.1.

The bar plots are displayed in decreasing order of the death rates `sort(VADeaths[,1], dec=TRUE)`. The range on the y-axis is set the same for both genders, to ensure that comparison of the bar plots becomes reasonable. Colors with `col`, title with `main`, and `legend` give more character to the bar plots. Note that the bar plots may be simply generated with

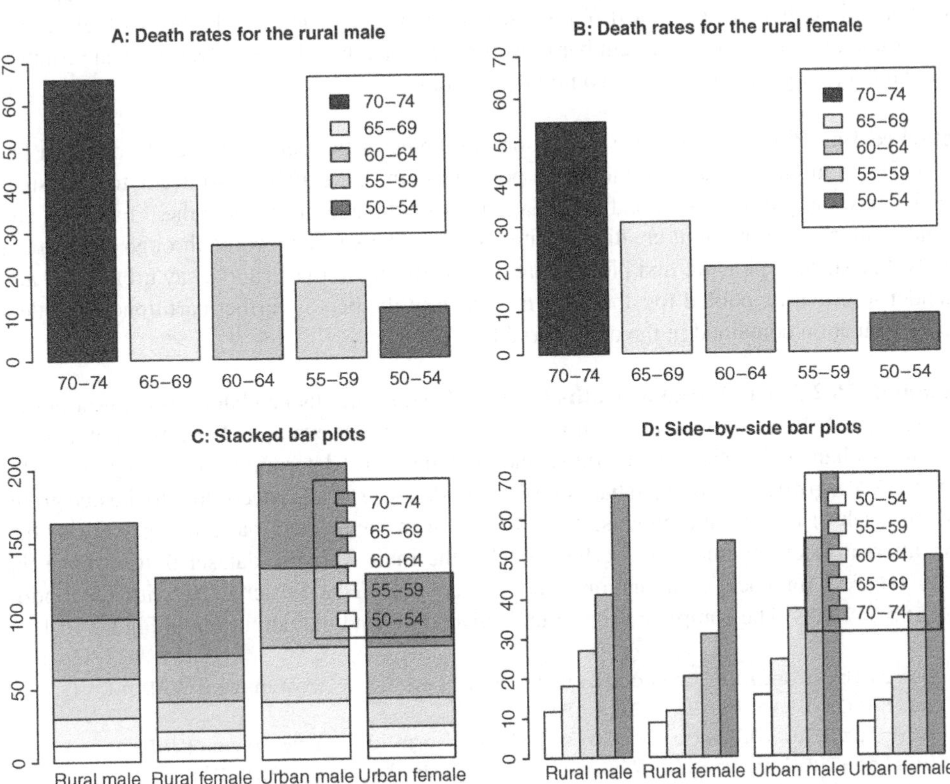

Figure 16.1 Death Rates among the Rural Population

`barplot(VADeaths[,1])` and `bar plot(VADeaths[,2])`. However, it does not just suffice to generate the plots, it is also important to provide the details.

```
> VADeaths[,1]
50-54 55-59 60-64 65-69 70-74
 11.7  18.1  26.9  41.0  66.0
> VADeaths[,2]
50-54 55-59 60-64 65-69 70-74
  8.7  11.7  20.3  30.9  54.3
> barplot(sort(VADeaths[,1],dec=TRUE),ylim=c(0,70),
+ main="A: Death Rates for the Rural Male",
+ col=c("blue","beige","grey","yellow", "brown"),
+ legend=names(sort(VADeaths[,1],dec=TRUE)))
> barplot(sort(VADeaths[,2],dec=TRUE),ylim=c(0,70),
+ main="B: Death Rates for the Rural Female",
+ col=c("blue","beige","grey","yellow", "brown"),
+ legend=names(sort(VADeaths[,2],dec=TRUE)))
```

The distribution of death rates across the age groups for rural males and females appears similar, although there are some differences, as seen in parts A and B of Figure 16.1. However, we would not like to have different bar plots for the urban data. Especially, if we can visualize the data in a single diagram, this would be preferred. □

Stacked Bar Plots. Suppose we have more variables in the data and need to obtain a bar plot. For example, the data on the urban population in `VADeaths` also needs to be visualized. Thus, the plot should reveal information across the age groups and the urban/rural and gender information without creating additional plots. This is achievable through stacked bar plots. In a stacked plot, we first plot the bar plot according to one criteria, say urban/rural and gender information pooled together, and then each of the bars is further partitioned to reflect the information contained in the other variable.

Example 16.2.2. The Virginia Deaths Dataset. Contd. The stacked bar plots are now generated for the `VADeaths` data in a continuation of the previous example. For four combinations of rural-urban and male-female traits, and first bars are determined according to `colSums(VADeaths)`. Now each bar is further divided (or stacked) according to the age group within each of these combinations. This will result in the stacked bar plot for `VADeaths`. An alternative arrangement of the bar plot for the multi-variable dataset is to arrange the bars (stacks) for each combination near one another. This is achieved with the option `beside=TRUE`. The complete R program is given now and the output file in Figure 16.1.

```
> barplot(VADeaths,col=colors()[1:5],legend = row.names(VADeaths),
+ main="C: Stacked Bar Plots")
> barplot(VADeaths,col=colors()[1:5],legend = row.names(VADeaths),
+ beside=TRUE,ylim=c(0,75),main="D: Side-by-side Bar Plots")
> title("Barplots Arrangement for VADeaths",outer=TRUE,line=-1)
```

Figure 16.1, Parts C and D, shows that the death rate is highest in the age group `70-74` and decreases along the age group. It may also be seen that the death rate is highest among the urban males. Even though the death rate appears very high among males, there is no significant difference between the death rates of females among urban or rural populations. □

Example 16.2.3. The Old Faithful Geyser Data. Volcanic eruptions at the Yellowstone National Park, Wyoming, USA, are so frequent that data collection of eruptions and time between consecutive eruptions collection is very easy to obtain. Data is collected on two variables, the time length of an eruption, and the time between two eruptions. The `summary` statistics shows that the time between any two eruptions is for a minimum of `1.6` minutes and maximum of `5.1`. Similarly, the `waiting` time between two eruptions ranges from `41-96` minutes. The `eruptions` are divided into 9 intervals and `waiting` time into 13 intervals. A bar plot will be used to gain more insight into the `faithful` variables.

```
> summary(faithful)
   eruptions        waiting
 Min.   :1.600   Min.   :43.0
 1st Qu.:2.163   1st Qu.:58.0
 Median :4.000   Median :76.0
```

```
 Mean    :3.488   Mean    :70.9
 3rd Qu.:4.454   3rd Qu.:82.0
 Max.    :5.100   Max.    :96.0
> eruptions_int <- cut(faithful$eruptions,seq(1.5,5.5,0.5))
> waiting_int <- cut(faithful$waiting,seq(40,100,5))
> layout(matrix(c(1,2,3,3),2,byrow=TRUE))
> barplot(table(eruptions_int),main="A Bar Diagram for Eruption
+ Frequencies",col=colors()[88:96])
> barplot(table(waiting_int), main="A Bar Diagram for Waiting Times
+ \n Between Two Eruptions",col=colors()[181:193])
> barplot(table(eruptions_int,waiting_int),main="A Stacked Bar
+ Diagram Explaining Frequency Distribution \n of Eruptions for the
+ Waiting Times",col=colors()[88:96])
```

Note how low eruption times are more likely to occur if the time between the two eruptions is shorter. Similarly, it can be deduced that if the time between two eruptions is larger, that the duration of the eruption will also likely be larger. Can you try to deduce/refute the claims from Figure 16.2. □

16.2.2 *Spine Plots*

In the bar plot we obtain a plot of the variable frequencies against the variable label. Notice that the bar's height varies and the width is constant. A *spine plot* does the task the other way round and varies the width of the bar and keeps the height at a constant. That is, the height of the variable labels is kept the same and the width of the spine cord will be used to display the frequencies of the variable labels. At the outset it may appear that there might not be a great advantage in interchanging the fixed width with fixed height. The examples will clarify whether we can extract additional information or not. We will illustrate this concept using the Virginia Death rates data.

Example 16.2.4. Spine Plots for Virginia Death Rates. We will first obtain the spine chart for the rural area and then for the complete dataset. The size of graphics is invoked to be of width 20 inches `width=20` with a height of 10 inches `height=10`. The `par` function with the option of `mfrow=c(1,2)` divides the graphic device into 1 row and 2 columns. The options of `cex.lab=0.8` and `cex.axis=0.8` are specified to ensure that the font size scale of labels and axis is reduced by a factor of `0.8`, which in turn is useful to print out all the labels and axis on the graphical device. The program will be followed by more explanation.

```
> windows(width=20, height=10)
> par(mfrow=c(1,2),cex.lab=0.8,cex.axis=0.8)
> spineplot(VADeaths[,1:2],main="A: Death Rates for Rural Area",
+ col=c("lawngreen","lightgreen"))
> abline(h=0.5,lwd=2,col="red")
> abline(v=c(0.2,0.4,0.6,0.8),lwd=2,col="red")
> spineplot(VADeaths,main="B: Death Rates for Complete Data",
+ col=c("lawngreen","lightgreen"))
> abline(h=c(0.25,0.5,0.75),lwd=2,col="red")
> abline(v=c(0.2,0.4,0.6,0.8),lwd=2,col="red4")
```

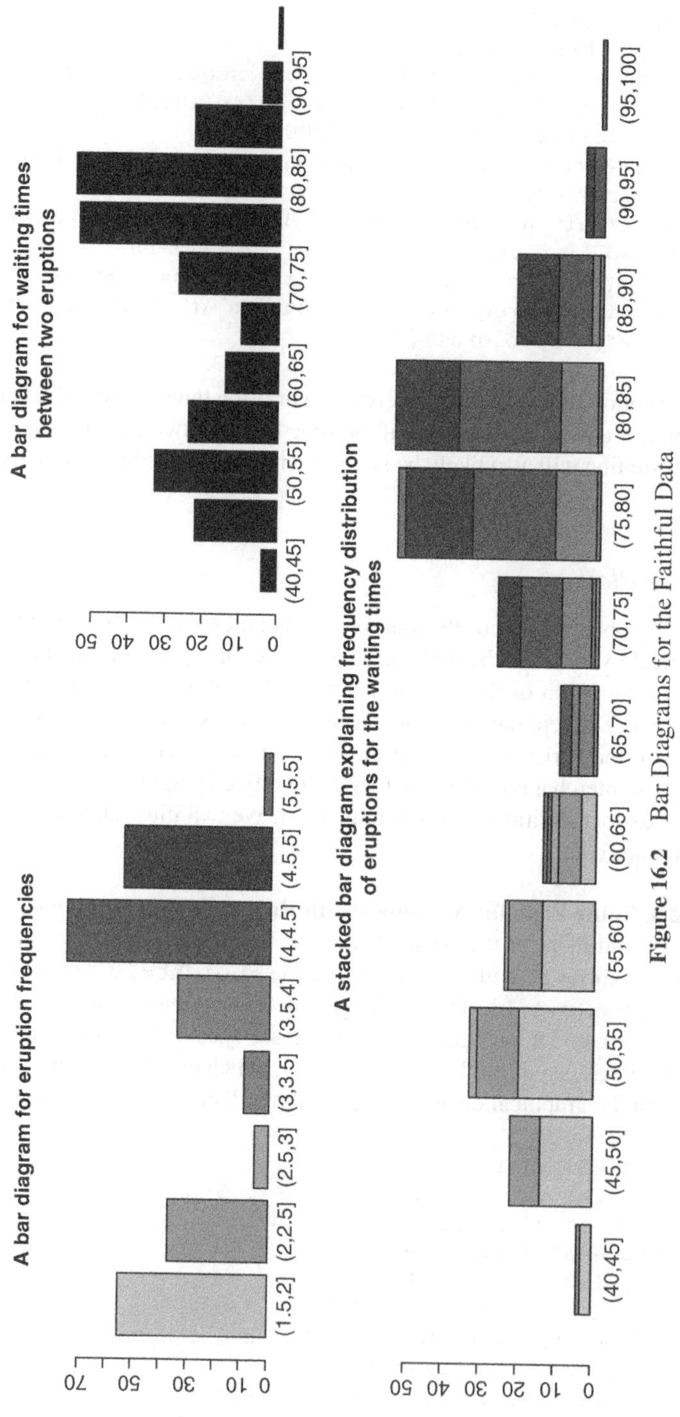

Figure 16.2 Bar Diagrams for the Faithful Data

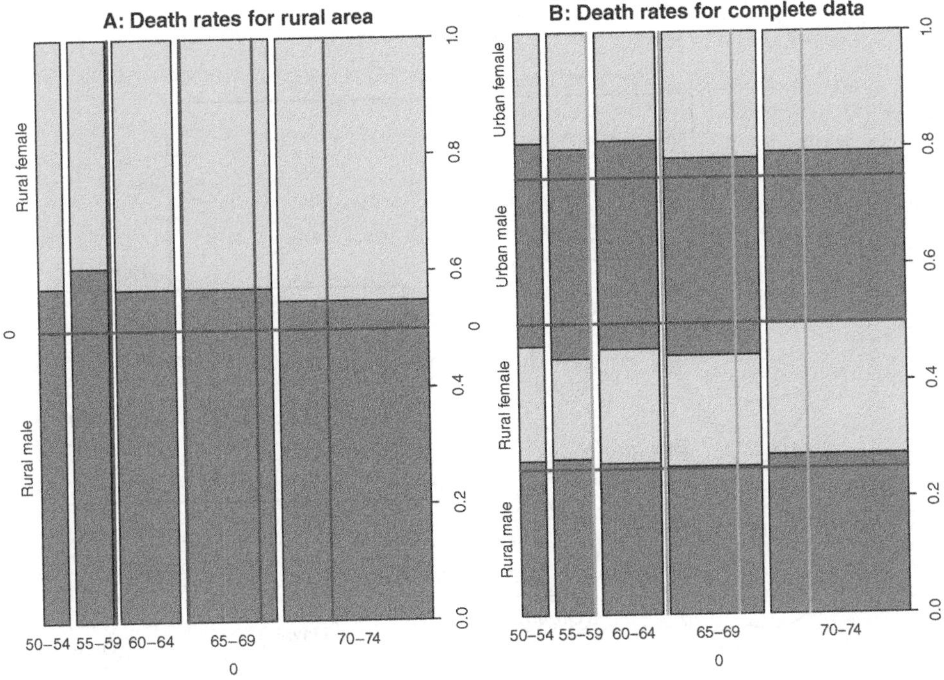

Figure 16.3 Spine Plots for the Virginia Death Rates

The data for rural areas is selected with `VADeaths[,1:2]`. The function `spineplot` on the selected data, with the options of `main` and `col`, gives Part A of Figure 16.3. In general, we would be interested to test the hypothesis that the death rates are equal for males and females across the age group. In visualization terms, the hypothesis means that if we divide the graph into the number of groups as the required gender and age group, we should have near equal regions for each pair of the age-gender combination. Hence, we add horizontal (`h`) and vertical (`v`) lines using the `abline` at the appropriate points of `0.5` and `c(0.2,0.4,0.6,0.8)` respectively. Clearly, in Part A, the figure hardly reflects equal regions. Thus, we are inclined to believe that the death rates indeed depend on the gender and age group. A similar conclusion also holds for the complete dataset `VADeaths`. □

Spine plots are very effective for *two-way* variables. However, it cannot be extended for additional variables. This shortcoming is removed in the next graphical method that we discuss.

16.2.3 Mosaic Plots

Multivariate categorical data can be visualized using mosaic plots. In a mosaic display, the frequencies of the contingency table are represented by a collection of rectangles (or tiles) whose area is proportional to the cell frequency. The working of a mosaic plot is best illustrated using an example, and we use the `HairEyeColor` data available in the `datasets` package.

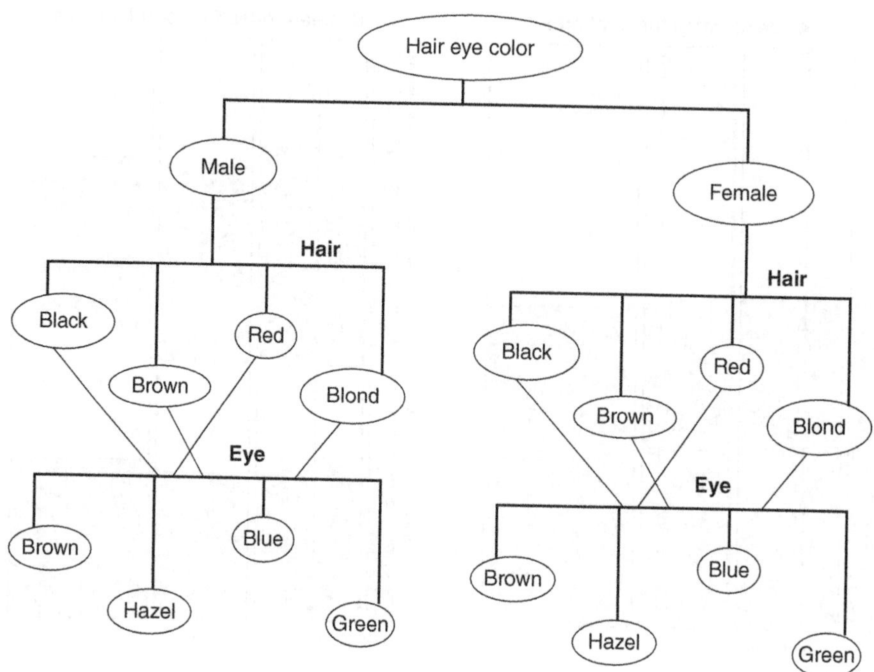

Figure 16.4 A Diagrammatic Representation of the Hair Eye Color Data

Example 16.2.5. Understanding the Mosaic Plots using the Hair Eye Color Dataset. In this dataset, it is observed that students have different combinations of hair and eye colors. Eyes are colored brown, blue, hazel and green, whereas the hair colors are black, brown, red, and blond. The gender of the student can further be male or female. Figure 16.4 describes the data flow.

Visualizing contingency table frequencies becomes more complex. However, mosaic plots take one variable at a time and help to create a meaningful and catchy display. For this dataset, the basic summaries are as below:

```
> HairEyeColor # Data in an array format
, , Sex = Male
       Eye
Hair    Brown Blue Hazel Green
  Black    32   11    10     3
  Brown    53   50    25    15
  Red      10   10     7     7
  Blond     3   30     5     8

, , Sex = Female
       Eye
Hair    Brown Blue Hazel Green
  Black    36    9     5     2
```

```
Brown    66   34    29    14
Red      16    7     7     7
Blond     4   64     5     8
```

```
> rowSums(HairEyeColor[,,1])+rowSums(HairEyeColor[,,2])
> # Frequencies by Hair Color
Black Brown Red Blond
108 286 71 127
> colSums(HairEyeColor[,,1])+colSums(HairEyeColor[,,2])
> # Frequencies by Eye Color
Brown Blue Hazel Green
220 215 93 64
> sum(HairEyeColor[,,1]);sum(HairEyeColor[,,2])
> # Frequencies by Gender
[1] 279
[1] 313
> (rowSums(HairEyeColor[,,1])+rowSums(HairEyeColor[,,2]))/
+ sum(HairEyeColor)
Black Brown Red Blond
0.1824324 0.4831081 0.1199324 0.2145270
```

Suppose we decide to obtain a plot which will reveal a pattern according to the following order: (i) `Hair` Color distribution, (ii) `Eye` Color distribution, and finally (iii) Gender (`Sex`) distribution. To obtain the mosaic plot here, let us first look at the `Hair` color distribution. Note that the normalized frequencies by the hair color are `0.1824324`, `0.4831081`, `0.1199324`, and `0.2145270`. Thus, the proportion of width of the bars for the hair color representation is approximately 0.2, 0.5, 0.1, and 0.2 respectively for the colors `Black` to `Blond`. Having fixed the approximate areas for the hair criteria, we now undertake the criteria for further classification by the `Eye` color criteria. We will first obtain the frequency by eye criteria across the genders, while retaining the split by the hair color criteria. After obtaining this matrix, we will divide each row by its cumulative sum, which will give us the distribution of the eye color across the hair color criteria. This is computed below as:

```
> eyecol <- HairEyeColor[,,1]+HairEyeColor[,,2]
> eyecol/rowSums(eyecol)
       Eye
Hair      Brown   Blue   Hazel  Green
  Black 0.62963 0.1852 0.13889 0.0463
  Brown 0.41608 0.2937 0.18881 0.1014
  Red   0.36620 0.2394 0.19718 0.1972
  Blond 0.05512 0.7402 0.07874 0.1260
```

Now, each bar will be appropriately divided according to the normalized frequencies in the above output. That is, the `Black` will be divided into regions proportional to `0.62963`, `0.1852`, `0.13889`, and `0.0463` respectively for the `Eye` colors `Brown`, `Blue`, `Hazel`, and `Green`. Now, we will have achieved 16 regions. Finally, we will require the distribution of the gender for the above matrix, which displays the frequency for the eye and hair color criteria. Though things look too complex, it is not very difficult to manage the computations.

Note that we need to have 32 summaries to completely handle the mosaic plot for this dataset. After understanding this fact, it is easy to know what should come in the next R codes:

```
> HairEyeColor[,,1]/eyecol
       Eye
Hair        Brown      Blue     Hazel     Green
  Black 0.4705882 0.5500000 0.6666667 0.6000000
  Brown 0.4453782 0.5952381 0.4629630 0.5172414
  Red   0.3846154 0.5882353 0.5000000 0.5000000
  Blond 0.4285714 0.3191489 0.5000000 0.5000000
> HairEyeColor[,,2]/eyecol
       Eye
Hair        Brown      Blue     Hazel     Green
  Black 0.5294118 0.4500000 0.3333333 0.4000000
  Brown 0.5546218 0.4047619 0.5370370 0.4827586
  Red   0.6153846 0.4117647 0.5000000 0.5000000
  Blond 0.5714286 0.6808511 0.5000000 0.5000000
> mosaicplot(HairEyeColor)
```

In light of all the above codes, we finally obtain the mosaic plot using the `mosaicplot` function, which is now a lot easier to interpret, see Figure 16.5. Particularly, what can you conclude about the distribution pattern in the `HairEyeColor` dataset? □

?barplot, ?spineplot, ?pie, ?fourfoldplot, ?mosaicplot

16.2.4 Pie Charts and Dot Charts

A pie chart is a circular plot with sectors whose areas are proportional to the frequency of the classes. It is a very popular technique among many people who tend to visualize data and is commonly seen in newspapers, television channels, etc. For the Old Faithful geyser, the pie charts for the eruption time frequencies, and the time between two eruptions are shown below. The dot chart was already introduced in Chapter 14.

Example 16.2.6. The Old Faithful Geyser Data. Pie Charts. Contd. The bar plot has been used earlier for the variables `eruptions_int` and `waiting_int`. Pie charts are obtained in R using the `pie` function. The optional arguments used here have been used and explained for earlier plots and will not be detailed here, though there are some semantic differences.

```
> par(mfrow=c(1,2),cex=0.8)
> pie(table(eruptions_int),main="Pie Chart for the Eruption Time
+ Frequencies",radius=2,init.angle=180,clockwise=TRUE)
> pie(table(waiting_int),main="Pie Chart for the Waiting Time
+ Between Two Eruptions",radius=2,init.angle=180,clockwise=TRUE)
```

The additional options here include `radius`, `init.angle`, and `clockwise`. The reader may simply run `pie(table(eruptions_int))` and `pie(table(waiting_int))` and reason out the requirement of these options coded here. Parts A and B of Figure 16.6 give the pie chart for both the variables of interest. □

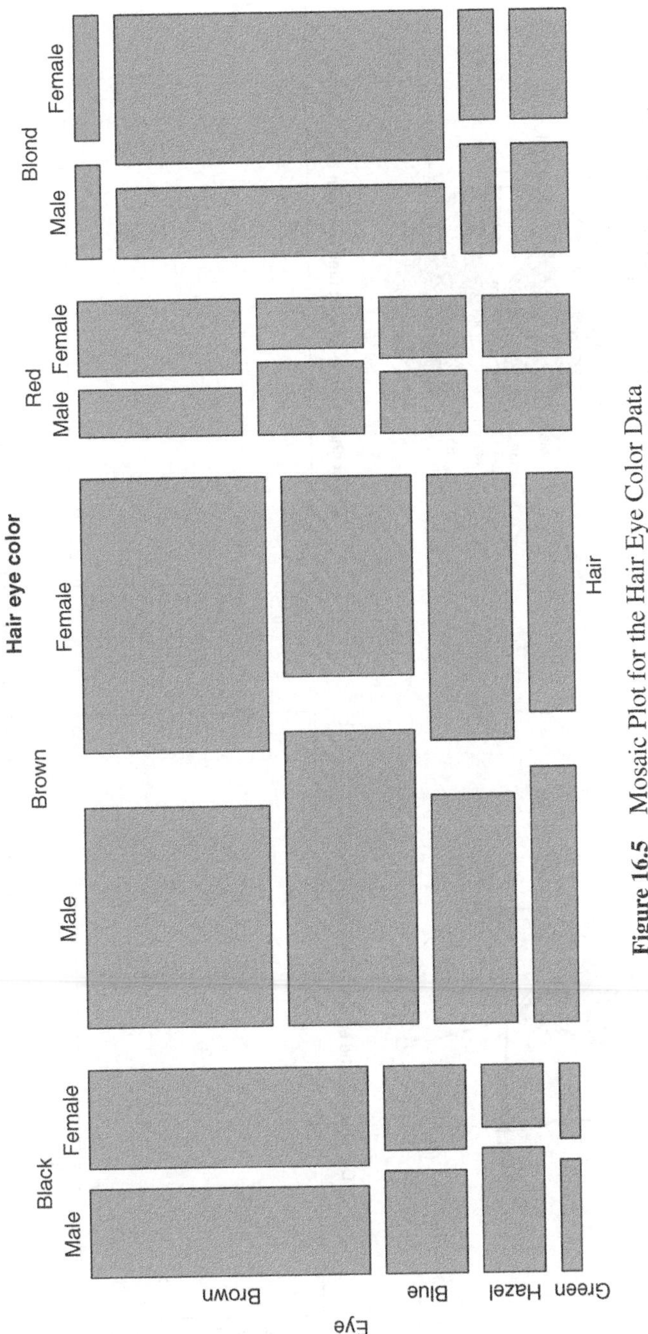

Figure 16.5 Mosaic Plot for the Hair Eye Color Data

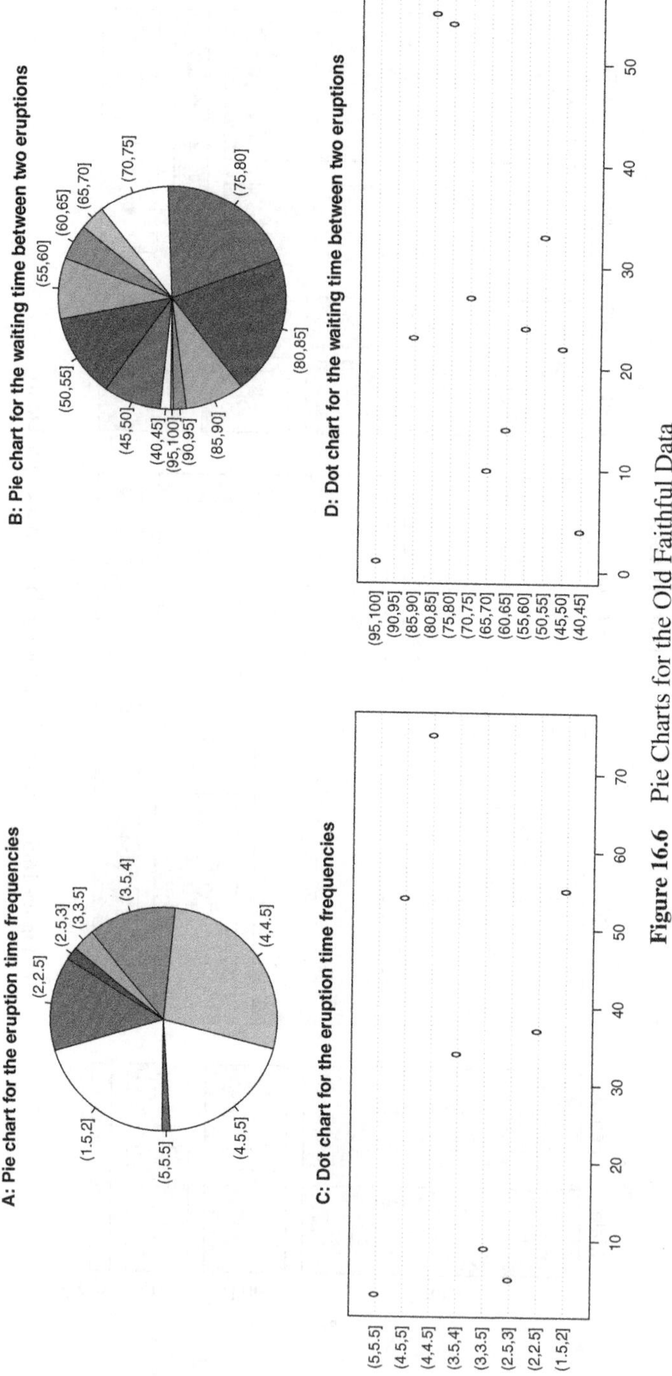

Figure 16.6 Pie Charts for the Old Faithful Data

R has a very important warning about pie charts and this warning must always be remembered. Following Cleveland and McGill's investigation, R displays the following warning for pie charts: *Pie charts are a very bad way of displaying information. The eye is good at judging linear measures and bad at judging relative areas. A bar chart or dot chart is a preferable way of displaying this type of data. Cleveland (1985), page 264: "Data that can be shown by pie charts always can be shown by a dot chart. This means that judgements of position along a common scale can be made instead of the less accurate angle judgements."* Hence, we will also obtain dot charts for the two variables here.

Example 16.2.7. The Old Faithful Geyser Data. Dot Chart. Contd. The dot chart was used earlier in Section 14.2. A slight improvement over the plotting techniques will be considered for the variables `eruptions_int` and `waiting_int`.

```
> ei_freq <- as.numeric(table(eruptions_int))
> ei_names <- names(table(eruptions_int))
> dotchart(ei_freq,labels=ei_names,main="C: Dot Chart for the
+ Eruption Time Frequencies")
> wi_freq <- as.numeric(table(waiting_int))
> wi_names <- names(table(waiting_int))
> dotchart(wi_freq,labels=wi_names,main="D: Dot Chart for the
+ Waiting Time Between Two Eruptions")
```

Is the advantage of the dot chart, Parts C and D, over the pie chart apparent to you? □

16.2.5 Four-Fold Plots

The four-fold plot is a specialized way of visualizing cell frequency of 2×2 tables. In this plot, the cell frequency n_{ij} in each cell of a four-fold table is shown by a quarter circle whose radius is proportional to $\sqrt{(n_{ij})}$. The area is thus proportional to the cell count. Note that in a pie chart, the angles of the segments are varied and the radius is kept the same, whereas in a four-fold plot, the angles of the segments are kept constant and the radius is varied. These aspects are clarified in the next popular example of University of California, Berkeley admissions data.

Example 16.2.8. Understanding the Four-Fold Plot using UCB Admissions Data. The `UCBAdmissions` dataset available in the `datasets` package is one of the popular datasets for the analysis of categorical data analysis. In the year 1975, it was observed that for six departments, 1198 male applicants were admitted to the courses and 1493 male applications were rejected. For females, the accepted and rejected numbers were 557 and 1278 respectively. A further split of this information across six departments is also available and this information will be taken up later as required. For this dataset, the forthcoming R program gives us the four-fold plot and the pie chart. The plot function `fourfoldplot` will be useful to obtain the four-fold plots.

```
> UCBoverall <- aperm(UCBAdmissions, c(2, 1, 3))
> par(mfrow=c(1,2))
> fourfoldplot(margin.table(UCBoverall, c(1, 2)),std="ind.max",
```

```
+ main="Four Fold Plot for UCB Admissions")
> pie(margin.table(UCBoverall, c(1, 2)),
+ labels=c("Male Admitted","Female Admitted",
+ "Male Rejected","Female Rejected"),radius=2,
+ main="Pie Chart for UCB Admissions")
```

The `aperm(UCBAdmissions, c(2, 1, 3))` code aggregates the frequencies for the `Gender-Admit` across the six departments. Marginal tables can be obtained using the `margin.table` function, while the `radius` option is used here to produce aesthetic graphs. The ratio of male to female acceptance is `(1198/1493)/(557/1278) = 1.84108`, which apparently favors the males. If the ratio is nearly equal to 1, see Section 16.3, we expect a near circle. □

In general, the four-fold plot can be used to visualize $2 \times 2 \times k$ contingency tables too. As an example, it is known from the above that the `UCBAdmissions` data is available across six departments. Thus, we would like to see how the patterns are revealed for the six departments.

Example 16.2.9. Understanding the Four-Fold Plot using UCB Admissions Data. Contd. The R code `fourfoldplot(UCBAdmissions,...)` gives us the required four-fold plot for the UCBAdmissions data.

```
> fourfoldplot(UCBAdmissions,mfrow=c(2,3),space=0.4,
+ col=c("lightgreen","lawngreen"),
+ main="Four Fold Plots for the 6 Departments of UCB")
```

The output of the preceding program is provided in Figure 16.7. The interpretation and more details of the four-fold plot, see Figure 16.8, will be taken up in Section 16.3. The `space` option must be experimented on by the reader for different values. □

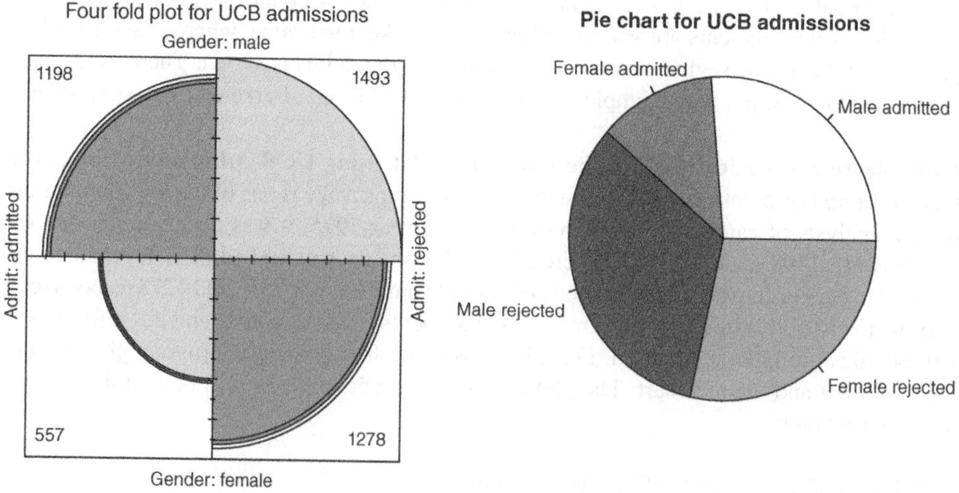

Figure 16.7 Four-Fold Plot for the Admissions Data

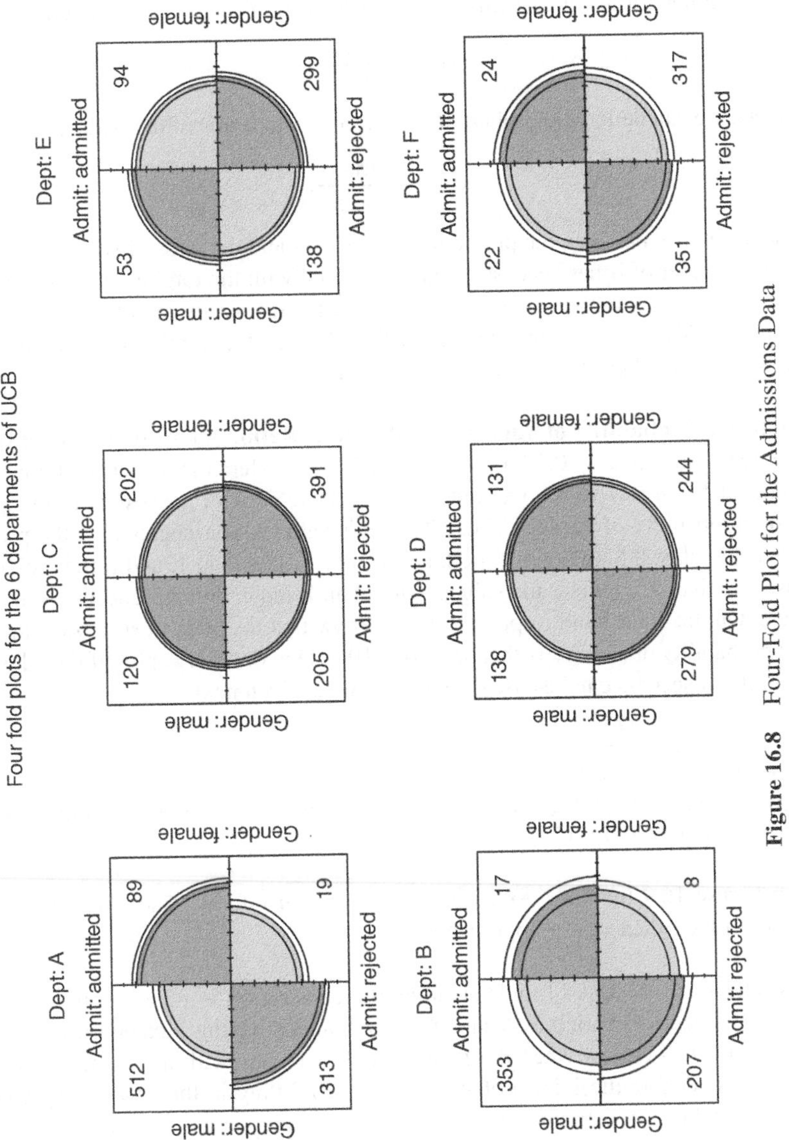

Figure 16.8 Four-Fold Plot for the Admissions Data

16.3 The Odds Ratio

The odds ratio is a very important measure of association in a 2×2 contingency table. Suppose that an experiment results in a binary outcome, where we denote 1 for success and 0 for failure. Let the probability of success be defined by π. Though earlier we have used the symbol π for the irrational number, it is not a confusion here. The *odds of success* is then defined by

$$\texttt{odds} = \frac{\pi}{1-\pi}. \tag{16.1}$$

Alternatively, we can define the probability of success π in terms of the odds as

$$\pi = \frac{\texttt{odds}}{1+\texttt{odds}}. \tag{16.2}$$

The subtle difference between the probability of success and the odds of success is that probability is the number of times success occurs compared with the total number of trials, while odds of success is the number of times success occurs against the number of failures. This means that the odds value can also be greater than 1 when the number of times success can occur exceeds the number of times failure can occur.

Example 16.3.1. Probability of Success and the Odds Ratio. If the probability of success is $\pi = 0.2 = 1/5$, then $\texttt{odds} = 0.2/(1-0.2) = 0.25 = 1/4$. Here the odds is better understood as 1/4 rather 0.25. In this sense, we understand that the odds of success is in the ratio 1:4, whereas the probability of success is 1/5. The odds value is non-negative. If the probability of success is less than 0.5, the odds ratio takes a value of less than 1, and if the probability of success is more than 0.5, it takes the value greater than 1, indicating that success is more likely than failure. On the other hand, suppose that we know that the odds of success is in the ratio 10:1. The probability of success is then $\pi = 10/(10+1) = 0.9091$. A plot of the odds against the probability of success can be easily obtained, and is given next.

```
> pi <- seq(0,1,0.05)
> odds <- pi / (1- pi)
> plot(pi,odds,xlab="Probability of Success", ylab="The Odds Ratio",
+ main="Understanding the Odds Ratio","l")
```

Note from Figure 16.9 that as $\pi \to 1$, the odds approach infinity, since the quantity in the denominator of the $\texttt{odds} = \frac{\pi}{1-\pi}$ approaches 0. □

We now undertake the task of understanding the odds ratio for a 2×2 contingency table. Consider two categorical variables X and Y, with X and Y having 2 categories each. Let n_{ij} denote the number of counts when the i category of X occurs with the j category of Y, and $i,j = 1,2$. Let π_{ij} denote the joint probability of (X, Y) falling in the i-row and j column of the rectangular table. An estimate of π_{ij} is then given by $\hat{\pi}_{ij} = p_{ij} = n_{ij}/n, i,j = 1,2$, where $n = n_{11} + n_{12} + n_{21} + n_{22}$. The odds ratio for a 2×2 contingency table is then defined by

$$\texttt{odds} = \theta = \frac{\pi_{11}/\pi_{12}}{\pi_{21}/\pi_{22}} = \frac{\pi_{11}\pi_{22}}{\pi_{12}\pi_{21}}. \tag{16.3}$$

Note that the odds ratio does not change for the transpose of the 2×2 contingency table. Hence, the odds ratio is sometimes called the *cross-product ratio*. For more details, see Chapter 2 of Agresti (2007).

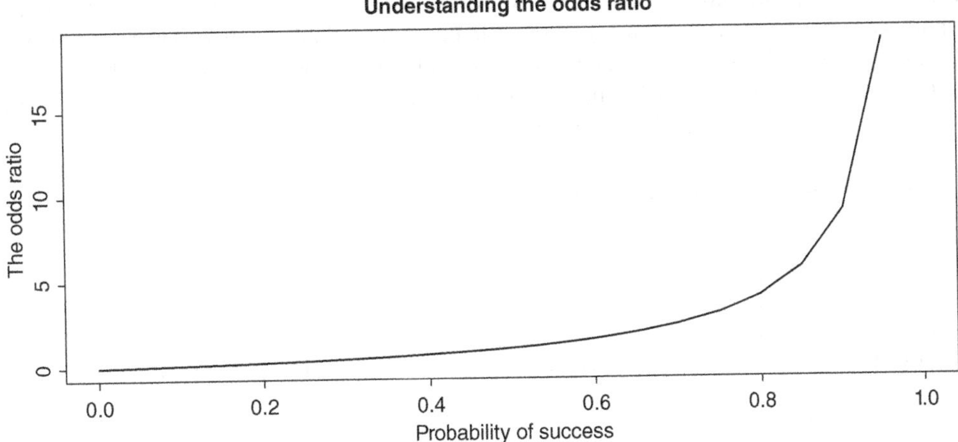

Figure 16.9 Understanding the Odds Ratio

Example 16.3.2. The Odds Ratio for Afterlife Believers. A survey was conducted to see if the afterlife believers depend on the gender of the person, see page 22 or Agresti (2007). The survey had a total of $n = 1127$ respondents, with 625 females, the rest being males. The number of believers in the afterlife for the two genders are respectively 509 and 398. The odds ratio of believers in the afterlife for males against females is then

```
> Afterlife <- matrix(c(509,116,398,104),byrow=TRUE,dimnames=list(c(
+ "Females","Males"),c("Yes","No")),nrow=2)
> Afterlife
        Yes  No
Females 509 116
Males   398 104
> pi1 <- Afterlife[1,1]/(Afterlife[1,1]+Afterlife[1,2])
> pi2 <- Afterlife[2,1]/(Afterlife[2,1]+Afterlife[2,2])
> (pi1/(1-pi1))/(pi2/(1-pi2))
[1] 1.146595
```

which means that there are more believers of afterlife among `Females` than `Males`. □

Example 16.3.3. The UCBAdmissions. This example will be repeated more often in this chapter. The accept-reject data of candidates by gender, and across departments, is available in the `UCBAdmissions` dataset. The n_{ij} values for the problem is obtained as

```
> margin.table(UCBAdmissions, c(1, 2))
          Gender
Admit      Male Female
  Admitted 1198    557
  Rejected 1493   1278
```

The function `margin.table` returns the overall count across the `A-F` departments. The odds ratio for a male admittance to a female admittance is then `(1198 * 1278)/(557 * 1493)`, with the answer being `1.84108`. □

Example 16.3.4. Did more Children Survive in the Titanic? The Titanic, and movies based on it, is a very popular as well as tragic story and data is available on its survivors. It remains for us to analyze if efforts were made to save the children. Let us have a quick look here. The data for the survivors is available in the datasets as `Titanic`. A small change and we will obtain the `fourfoldplot` for the child survivors.

```
> childTitanic <- apply(Titanic, c(3, 4), sum)
> childTitanic
       Survived
Age       No Yes
  Child   52  57
  Adult 1438 654
> fourfoldplot(childTitanic,std="ind.max") # output suppressed
> (57/52)/(654/1438)
[1] 2.410198
```

The odds ratio for the child survivors against adult survivors is `(57/52)/(654/1438)` is `2.410198`, which shows that children were given more priority in the rescue operations. Note that a naive approach may have suggested that more adults were saved than the children. □

?margin.table, ?prop.table

16.4 The Simpson's Paradox

The Simpson's paradox presents an intriguing fact about independence of the attributes. We consider the hypothetical example of Simonoff (2003). The marketing head of a company carries out a survey in two cities for two weeks to investigate the recall rates of a certain product. The observation is that the recall rate has improved in both of the cities at the end of two weeks, as reflected in the Table 16.1.

The first four rows of the table show that there has been an increase in the percentage recall of the product in both the cities. However, the last two rows show that the recall percentages pooled together have decreased. Thus, we see that across two weeks, there has been a decrease in the recall percentage from 70% to 50%. This is the famous ***Simpson's paradox***. From a probabilistic point of view, the results are not surprising at all. The anxious reader may

Table 16.1 Simpson's Data and the Paradox

City	Week	Recall	Don't recall	Total
New York	1	60	140	60/200 (37%)
	2	320	480	320/800 (40%)
Los Angeles	1	640	160	640/800 (80%)
	2	180	20	180/200 (90%)
Combined	1	700	300	700/1000 (70%)
	2	500	500	500/1000 (50%)

refer to Chapter 3 of Leonard (2000) for detailed coverage of the paradox. To put the paradox in probabilistic terms, consider two events A and B with $P(A|B) > P(A|B^c)$. It is then possible to find another event C such that $P(A|B, C) < P(A|B^c, C)$. A famous example of the Simpson's paradox is about the gender bias in admission to six departments to graduate schools at Berkeley, check with `?UCBAdmissions`.

16.5 The Binomial, Multinomial, and Poisson Models

Under the assumption that categorical data are generated by certain probability models, we will now consider the inference part of this.

16.5.1 *The Binomial Model*

Suppose that in a survey we ask people if they agree with the issues raised by the "United Against Corruption" civil society. In such a survey, the respondents are requested to answer the "Yes" or "No" options. If n responses are obtained, the number of "Yes" answers may be modeled by a binomial distribution. A checklist for analysis of such data is provided by Simonoff (2003), page 55:

- The number of trials n is fixed.
- Each trial results in a binary outcome.
- The probability of obtaining a success p remains the same in each trial.
- The trials are independent.

Let X denote the number of success in the n trials. Then, the pmf of X is given by

$$p(x, n, p) = \binom{n}{x} p^x(1-p)^x, x = 0, 1, \cdots, n, 0 \leq p \leq 1.$$

The binomial model has already been introduced in Section 6.2. We have seen in Chapter 7 that a natural estimator of p is the $\hat{p} = x/n$. A $100(1-\alpha)\%$ confidence interval, also called the *Wald interval*, given by

$$\hat{p} \pm z_{\alpha/2}\sqrt{\frac{\hat{p}(1-\hat{p})}{n}}, \tag{16.4}$$

whereas the *Wilson confidence interval*, actually the *score interval*, is given by

$$\hat{p}\frac{n}{n+z_{\alpha/2}^2} + \frac{1}{2}\frac{z_{\alpha/2}^2}{n+z_{\alpha/2}^2} \pm \sqrt{\frac{\hat{p}(1-\hat{p})}{n}\frac{n^2z_{\alpha/2}^2}{(n+z_{\alpha/2}^2)^2} + \frac{1}{4}\frac{z_{\alpha/2}^4}{(n+z_{\alpha/2}^2)^2}}. \tag{16.5}$$

For details of the Wilson score interval, refer to page 57 of Simonoff (2003). The Wald and Wilson confidence intervals will be illustrated now. The option of `method="wilson"` in the `binconf` function from the `Hmisc` package gives a ready implementation of obtaining the Wilson's confidence interval. However, we will use the function `WilsonCI` from the `ACSWR` package.

Example 16.5.1. United Against Corruption Society. Suppose that 10 658 out of 15 000 respondents support the issues raised by the "United Against Corruption" civil society. We would like to construct the Wald and Wilson confidence intervals for p. Here $n = 15000$ and $\hat{p} = 0.7105333$.

Note that the Wald confidence interval is fairly easy to compute. The reader can check the implementation of the `WilsonCI` function with the Formula 16.5.

```
> x <- 10658; n <- 15000
> phat <- x/n
> # Wald Confidence Interval
> c(phat-1.96*sqrt(phat*(1-phat)/n),phat+1.96*sqrt(phat*(1-phat)/n))
[1] 0.7032756 0.7177911
> WilsonCI(x,n,alpha=0.05)
[1] 0.7031598 0.7176736
> prop.test(x=10658,n=15000)$conf.int
[1] 0.7031890 0.7177694
attr(,"conf.level")
[1] 0.95
> prop.test(x=10658,n=15000,correct=FALSE)$conf.int
[1] 0.7032225 0.7177363
attr(,"conf.level")
[1] 0.95
```

Thus, any appropriate hypothesis testing problem of $H : p = p_0$ can be carried out through the confidence intervals or the `prop.test` function and the Wilson confidence interval can be obtained with the use of the `WilsonCI` function from `ACSWR` package. □

16.5.2 *The Multinomial Model*

If the respondents have more than two response options, we need to extend the binomial distribution to the multinomial distribution, as seen earlier in Section 6.4. Particularly, if there are k possible response options, the probability mass function of the multinomial distribution is given by

$$p(\mathbf{x}, n, \mathbf{p}) = \begin{cases} \dfrac{n!}{\prod_i n_i!} \prod_{i=1}^{k} p_i^{x_i}, & x_i = 0, 1, \cdots, n, i = 1, \cdots, k, p_i \geq 0, \\ 0, & \text{otherwise,} \end{cases}$$

where, $\mathbf{x} = (x_1, \cdots, x_k)$, and $x_i, i = 1, \cdots, k$ is the number of favorable responses for the ith option, and $\mathbf{p} = (p_1, \cdots, p_k)$. Quesenberry and Hurst (1964) have obtained the *simultaneous confidence intervals* for $\mathbf{p}$, where the $100(1 - \alpha)\%$ for p_i is given by:

$$\frac{1}{2(n + \chi^2_{k-1,1-\alpha})}\left[\chi^2_{k-1,1-\alpha} + 2x_i \pm \sqrt{\chi^2_{k-1,1-\alpha}\left\{\chi^2_{k-1,1-\alpha} + \frac{4x_i(n - x_i)}{n}\right\}}\right], \tag{16.6}$$

where $\chi^2_{k-1,1-\alpha}$ refers to the $(1-\alpha)$ quantile of a χ^2 distribution with $K-1$ degrees of freedom. To obtain the set of simultaneous confidence intervals to ensure that the overall confidence level is at level α, substitute α with α/k in Equation 16.6.

Example 16.5.2. The Louisiana Lottery. Simonoff (2003) discusses this example where the winning four-digit for a game is chosen using four machines. Basically, one of the balls numbered 0 to 9 is to be selected at random. The digits appearing in the winning spin frequencies are tabled. We need to test if the game is fair or not. Thus, we need to test the hypothesis $H : p_i = 0.1, i = 1, \cdots, 10$. The following R program constructs the Quesenberry-Hurst $100(1-\alpha)\%$ simultaneous confidence intervals, and the binomial confidence interval too from Equation 16.4 , for **p**.

```
> x <- c(206,200,206,223,176,215,202,223,213,204)
> binom_CI <- matrix(nrow=10,ncol=2,
+ dimnames=list(NULL,c("binomLCL","binomUCL")))
> for(i in 1:10) binom_CI[i,] <- as.numeric(prop.test(x[i],2068,
+ p=0.1,correct=FALSE,conf.level=1-alpha/k)$conf.int)
> data.frame(x,x/sum(x),binom_CI,QH_CI(x,alpha=0.05))
     x   x.sum.x.   binomLCL  binomUCL     QH_lcl    QH_ucl
1  206 0.09961315 0.08261944 0.1196464 0.07200503 0.1362526
2  200 0.09671180 0.07996878 0.1165164 0.06954368 0.1329766
3  206 0.09961315 0.08261944 0.1196464 0.07200503 0.1362526
4  223 0.10783366 0.09015493 0.1284895 0.07902125 0.1454919
5  176 0.08510638 0.06941775 0.1039446 0.05978476 0.1197865
6  215 0.10396518 0.08660431 0.1243325 0.07571193 0.1411516
7  202 0.09767892 0.08085179 0.1175602 0.07036322 0.1340695
8  223 0.10783366 0.09015493 0.1284895 0.07902125 0.1454919
9  213 0.10299807 0.08571789 0.1232921 0.07488667 0.1400644
10 204 0.09864603 0.08173535 0.1186036 0.07118368 0.1351615
```

The Quesenbery-Hurst simultaneous confidence intervals are set up using the `QH_CI` function. The program is a simple implementation of the formulas and does not require additional explanation. Since 0.1 lies within each of the ten confidence intervals, Quesenberry and Hurst, as well as the binomial, we do not have evidence to reject the hypothesis H. The results, `binomLCL` and `binomUCL`, may be compared with the table on page 67 of Simonoff (2003). □

16.5.3 The Poisson Model

The Poisson model is also useful in CDA. Let X denote a Poisson random variable with parameter λ. The Poisson model is given by

$$P(X=x) = \begin{cases} \dfrac{e^{\lambda}\lambda^x}{x!}, & x = 0, 1, 2, \cdots, \lambda > 0, \\ 0, & \text{otherwise.} \end{cases}$$

Then $100(1-\alpha)\%$ large sample confidence interval for λ, based on a random sample of size n, is given by

$$\bar{X} \pm z_{\alpha/2}\sqrt{\frac{\bar{X}}{n}}, \tag{16.7}$$

where $\bar{X} = \sum_{i=1}^{n} X_i/n$. A $100(1-\alpha)\%$ *score interval*, based on the score function, is given by

$$\bar{X} + \frac{z_{\alpha/2}^2}{2n} \pm \frac{z_{\alpha/2}}{\sqrt{n}}\sqrt{\bar{X} + \frac{z_{\alpha/2}^2}{4n}}. \tag{16.8}$$

Example 16.5.3. Goal Scoring Example of Simonoff (2003). We will illustrate the results on page 72 of Simonoff (2003). The goal scoring data of the hockey team "New Jersey Devils" and the goals scored against the team are first stated and then we will construct the large-sample and score confidence intervals for them.

```
> # The Poisson Models
> goals <- 0:9
> NJDGS <- c(3,9,24,18,14,7,3,2,1,1)
> NJDGA <- c(6,21,17,16,12,9,1)
> alpha <- 0.05
> NJDGSmean <- sum(goals*NJDGS)/sum(NJDGS)
> NJDGAmean <- sum(0:6*NJDGA)/sum(NJDGA)
> # Large Sample Confidence Interval
> c(NJDGSmean-qnorm(1-alpha/2)*sqrt(NJDGSmean/sum(NJDGS)),
+ NJDGSmean+qnorm(1-alpha/2)*sqrt(NJDGSmean/sum(NJDGS)))
[1] 2.682297 3.439655
> c(NJDGAmean-qnorm(1-alpha/2)*sqrt(NJDGAmean/sum(NJDGA)),
+ NJDGAmean+qnorm(1-alpha/2)*sqrt(NJDGAmean/sum(NJDGA)))
[1] 2.123703 2.803126
> # Score Intervals
> c(NJDGSmean+(qnorm(1-alpha/2)^2/(2*sum(NJDGS)))-(qnorm(1-
+ alpha/2)/sqrt(sum(NJDGS)))*sqrt(NJDGSmean+
+ (qnorm(1-alpha/2)^2)/(4*sum(NJDGS))),
+ NJDGSmean+(qnorm(1-alpha/2)^2/(2*sum(NJDGS)))+(qnorm(1-
+ alpha/2)/sqrt(sum(NJDGS)))*sqrt(NJDGSmean+
+ (qnorm(1-alpha/2)^2)/(4*sum(NJDGS))))
[1] 2.704996 3.463802
> c(NJDGAmean+(qnorm(1-alpha/2)^2/(2*sum(NJDGA)))-(qnorm(1-
+ alpha/2)/sqrt(sum(NJDGA)))*sqrt(NJDGAmean+
+ (qnorm(1-alpha/2)^2)/(4*sum(NJDGA))),
+ NJDGAmean+(qnorm(1-alpha/2)^2/(2*sum(NJDGA)))+(qnorm(1-
+ alpha/2)/sqrt(sum(NJDGA)))*sqrt(NJDGAmean+
+ (qnorm(1-alpha/2)^2)/(4*sum(NJDGA))))
[1] 2.146320 2.827356
```

The program unfolds as follows. The second term of the large sample confidence interval in Equation 16.7 of $z_{\alpha/2}\sqrt{\bar{X}/n}$ is calculated with `qnorm(1-alpha/2)*sqrt(NJDGSmean/`

`sum(NJDGS))`. The first two terms for the score intervals given by Equation 16.8 are easy to obtain and are implemented in the R computation with `(qnorm(1-alpha/2)/sqrt(sum(NJDGS)))*sqrt(NJDGSmean+(qnorm(1-alpha/2)^2)/(4*sum(NJDGS)))`. The rest of the code is simpler to understand.

The confidence intervals, large samples, for the goals scored and those against them are respectively `(2.682297, 3.439655)` and `(2.123703, 2.803126)`. The respective score intervals are `(2.704996, 3.463802)` and `(2.146320, 2.827356)`. □

?prop.test, ?qchisq, ?qnorm

16.6 The Problem of Overdispersion

Overdispersion and underdispersion are common problems in the application of binomial and Poisson models. A main reason for this is the fact that these models are completely determined by a single parameter. Especially, when the data is heterogeneous, these models are not able to account the variability in the data.

Example 16.6.1. The Zero-Inflated Poisson Model. Suppose that we have a dataset where there are a large number of 0's. A simulated data illustrates the overdispersion phenomenon.

```
> sampleset <- c(rpois(n=100,lambda=2), rep(0,30))
> est_lambda <- mean(sampleset)
> est_lambda; var(sampleset)
[1] 1.6
[1] 2.52
```

Thus, we see the shortcomings of the Poisson model in this example. We refer the reader to Section 4.5 of Simonoff (2003). □

The overdispersion problem may be overcome with the use of the EM algorithm.

16.7 The χ^2- Tests of Independence

Chapter 4 of Faraway (2006) has an in-depth survey of the χ^2-tests of independence. Here, we will consider the core χ^2- tests of independence of attributes. We consider the hypothesis H that the cell probabilities equal certain fixed values π_{ij}. The expected frequencies are then given by $\mu_{ij} = n\pi_{ij}$. The *Pearson χ^2-statistic* for H is

$$\chi^2 = \sum_{i=1}^{I}\sum_{j=1}^{K}\frac{(n_{ij} - \mu_{ij})^2}{\mu_{ij}}$$

If there is departure in the hypothesis H, it is expected that some values of $(n_{ij} - \mu_{ij})^2$ will be large, and thereby the value of χ^2, and thus the associated p-value will be very close to 0. We next examine the independence of the attributes for the Japanese atomic bomb survivors.

Example 16.7.1. Cancer Death Rates for the Japanese Atomic Bomb Survivors. In the second section, we successfully read the relevant data in a contingency table format. It is time for action, and we will use the chi-square test for independence of the attributes.

```
> chisq.test(atombombxtabs)
 Chi-squared test for given probabilities
data:  atombombxtabs
X-squared = 12337.16, df = 83, p-value < 2.2e-16
> summary(atombombxtabs)
Call: xtabs(formula = Frequency ~ Radians + Count.Type +
+  Count.Age.Group)
Number of cases in table: 4861
Number of factors: 3
Test for independence of all factors:
 Chisq = 992.9, df = 71, p-value = 1.557e-162
 Chi-squared approximation may be incorrect
```

The small p-value indicates that the attributes are not independent. □

Example 16.7.2. Filariasis and Different Parasites Analysis. Filariasis is a common infection which occurs in many tropical and subtropical countries. Filariasis is caused by different types of parasites. Gore, et al. (2007) reports a study in Nigeria, which was conducted to observe the prevalence of filariasis due to various parasite types. The study included 13 communities. In each of the communities, a record is made of the number of individuals examined for filariasis, the total number infected by it, the total number of infected cases due to *Onchocerca volvulus*, and other infections. The purpose is to investigate if the proportion of infected cases due to *O. volvulus* across the different communities is equal or not to the total number of individuals examined. Furthermore, it is also desired to find out if the proportion of infected cases due to *O. volvulus* across the communities is the same as that given for the number of infected cases. The R program below gives the answers.

```
> data(Filariasistype)
> prop.test(x=Filariasistype[,4],n=Filariasistype[,2])
 13-sample test for equality of proportions without continuity
 correction
data:  Filariasistype[, 4] out of Filariasistype[, 2]
X-squared = 52.76, df = 12, p-value = 4.539e-07
alternative hypothesis: two.sided
sample estimates:
 prop 1  prop 2   prop 12 prop 13
0.10277 0.15306   0.33333 0.22222
Warning message:
In prop.test(x = Filariasistype[, 4], n = Filariasistype[, 2]) :
  Chi-squared approximation may be incorrect
> prop.test(x=Filariasistype[,4],n=Filariasistype[,3])
 13-sample test for equality of proportions without continuity
 correction
data:  Filariasistype[, 4] out of Filariasistype[, 3]
```

```
X-squared = 16.88, df = 12, p-value = 0.1541
alternative hypothesis: two.sided
sample estimates:
 prop 1  prop 2   prop 12 prop 13
 0.7429  0.8333   0.8966  0.4444
Warning message:
In prop.test(x = Filariasistype[, 4], n = Filariasistype[, 3]) :
  Chi-squared approximation may be incorrect
```

The analysis clearly shows that though the number of cases due to *O. volvulus* depends upon the communities, if we consider the number of individuals examined, this count is independent of the community if the important factor of the number of infected persons is taken into consideration. □

?chisq.test

16.8 Further Reading

Refer to the same title section of the next chapter.

16.9 Complements, Problems, and Programs

Problem 16.1 Obtain stacked bar plots for `UCBAdmissions`, `HairEyeColor`, and `Titanic` datasets.

Problem 16.2 Plot the mosaic plots for the datasets in the previous problem and record your observations.

Problem 16.3 From the `Titanic` dataset, obtain the odds ratio of survivors for the following: (i) `Adult` vs `Child`, (ii) `Male` vs `Female`, (iii) for each of the `Class` as in `1st`, `2nd`, `3rd`, and `Crew`. For the `UCBAdmissions`, compute the overall odds ratio of `Admit` for `Male` vs `Female` and across each of the department `A-F`.

Problem 16.4 Find the Wilson confidence interval for the probability of admission of a female candidate in the `UCBAdmissions` data.

Problem 16.5 Perform the χ^2 tests for the datasets in the first problem here.

17

Generalized Linear Models

Package(s): `gdata`, `RSADBE`
Dataset(s): `chdage`, `lowbwt`, `sat`, `Disease`, `BS`, `caesareans`

17.1 Introduction

In Chapter 16 we discussed many useful statistical methods for analysis of categorical data, which may be nominal or ordinal data. The related regression problems were deliberately not touched upon there, the reason for omission being that the topic is more appropriate here. We will see in the next section that the linear regression methods of Chapter 12 are not appropriate for explaining the relationship between the regressors and discrete regressands. The statistical models, which are more suitable for addressing this problem, are known as the *generalized linear models*, which we abbreviate to GLM.

In this chapter, we will consider the three families of the GLM: logistic, probit, and log-linear models. The logistic regression model will be covered in more detail, and the applications of the others will be clearly brought out in the rest of this chapter.

We first begin with the problem of using the linear regression model for count/discrete data in Section 17.2. The exponential family continues to provide excellent theoretical properties for GLMs and the relationship will be brought out in Section 17.3. The important logistic regression model will be introduced in Section 17.4. The statistical inference aspects of the logistic regression model is developed and illustrated in Section 17.5. Similar to the linear regression model, we will consider the similar problem of model selection in Section 17.6. Probit and Poisson regression models are developed in Sections 17.7 and 17.8.

17.2 Regression Problems in Count/Discrete Data

By count/discrete data, we refer to the case where the regressand/output is discrete. That is, the output y takes values in the set $\{0, 1\}$, or $\{0, 1, 2, \dots\}$. As in the case of the linear regression model, we have some explanatory variables which effect the output y. We will immediately see the shortcomings of the approach of the linear regression model.

A Course in Statistics with R, First Edition. Prabhanjan Narayanachar Tattar, Suresh Ramaiah and B. G. Manjunath.

Companion Website: www.wiley.com/go/tattar/statistics

Example 17.2.1. Linear Model for Binary Outcome – Pass/Fail Indicator as Linear Function of the SAT Score. Johnson and Albert (1999) give a simple example of the drawbacks of the linear regression model approach for count data. The Scholastic Assessment Test (SAT) scores for the Mathematics subject, denoted by the variable `Sat` in the dataset `sat`, of students at the time of admission to a course is available, and it is known whether or not in a later examination the student completed the course, denoted by `Pass`. The variable `Sat` is the input variable x, while the output variable `Pass` is the regressand y. The course completion status `Pass` takes only two possible values 0 (fail) or 1 (pass). The task is to predict y based on the covariate x. The scatter plot looks as in Figure 17.1.

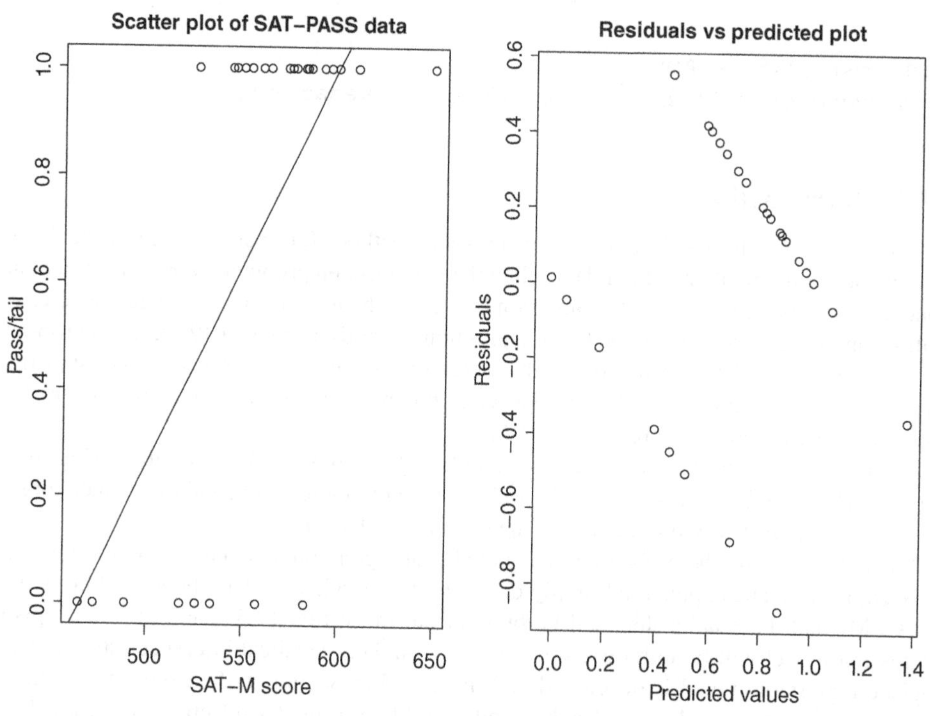

Figure 17.1 A Conditional Density Plot for the SAT Data

Though the scatter plot does not suggest that a linear model is appropriate, we will model for y, `Pass` here, in terms of the covariate x in `Sat`. Let us check how well the linear regression model of earlier chapters works here.

```
> library(RSADBE)
> data(sat)
> par(mfrow=c(1,2))
> plot(sat$Sat,sat$Pass,xlab="SAT-M Score",ylab="Pass/Fail",
+ main="Scatterplot of SAT-PASS Data")
> satlm <- lm(Pass~Sat,data=sat)
```

```
> abline(reg=satlm)
> predict(satlm)
      1        2        24        25        29        30
0.44667  0.50593  0.88370 -0.01260   0.65407  0.62444
> predict(satlm,newdata=list(Sat=c(300,750)))
     1      2
-1.220  2.113
> plot(predict(satlm),satlm$residuals,xlab="Predicted Values",ylab=
+ "Residuals",main="Residuals vs Predicted Plot")
```

First, the scatter plot is obtained using the `plot` function, and then the linear model is fitted using the `lm` function, which is the diagram on the left-hand side of Figure 17.1. The regression line is drawn on the scatter plot using the option of `reg` with the `abline` graphical function. The shortcomings of the linear regression model are seemingly apparent. For instance, the predicted values, `predict(...)`, for a few students have values in excess of 1 and also a few have less than 0. In simple words, we see that for discrete and bounded random variables, the predicted values from the simple linear regression model can overshoot the boundaries. Finally, the residuals-vs-predicted plot, the right-hand panel of Figure 17.1, indicates two parallel lines, which is very unlikely if a linear model is appropriate. Thus we need a model which overcomes such limitations. □

Example 17.2.2. Understanding the Relationship between Coronary Heart Disease and the Age of the Patient. A well-known explanation of heart disease is that as age increases, the risk of coronary heart disease also increases. The current dataset and the example may be found in Chapter 1 of Hosmer and Lemeshow (1990–2013). We will first plot the indicator value of coronary heart disease (CHD) against the age of the patient with the usual `plot` command.

It is fairly clear from the plot, Figure 17.2, that there is not a strong association between the CHD indicator and the age of the patient. However, a different way of re-plotting the same data gives a useful insight. Let us group the patients into certain age intervals, and calculate the percentage of the patients who have CHD. The patients are grouped in the interval groups 19–29, 29–34, 34–39, …, 54–59, and 59–69 using the `cut` function. The number of patients falling in these age groups are obtained with `table(agegrp,chdage$CHD)`. The code `prop.table(mytable,1)` gives row-wise percentages, and with option of 2 in place of `1`, the column-wise percentages. The second column of this proportions table gives the percentage of CHD patients in these age groups. We will then plot this percentage against the center of the intervals with the `points(...)` option.

```
> data(chdage)
> plot(chdage$AGE,chdage$CHD,xlab="AGE",ylab="CHD Indicator",
+ main="Scatter plot for CHD Data")
> agegrp <- cut(chdage$AGE,c(19,29,34,39,44,49,54,59,69),include.
+ lowest=TRUE, labels=c(25,seq(31.5,56.5,5),64.5))
> mp <- c(25,seq(31.5,56.5,5),64.5) # mid-points
> chd_percent <- prop.table(table(agegrp,chdage$CHD),1)[,2]
> points(mp,chd_percent,"l",col="red")
```

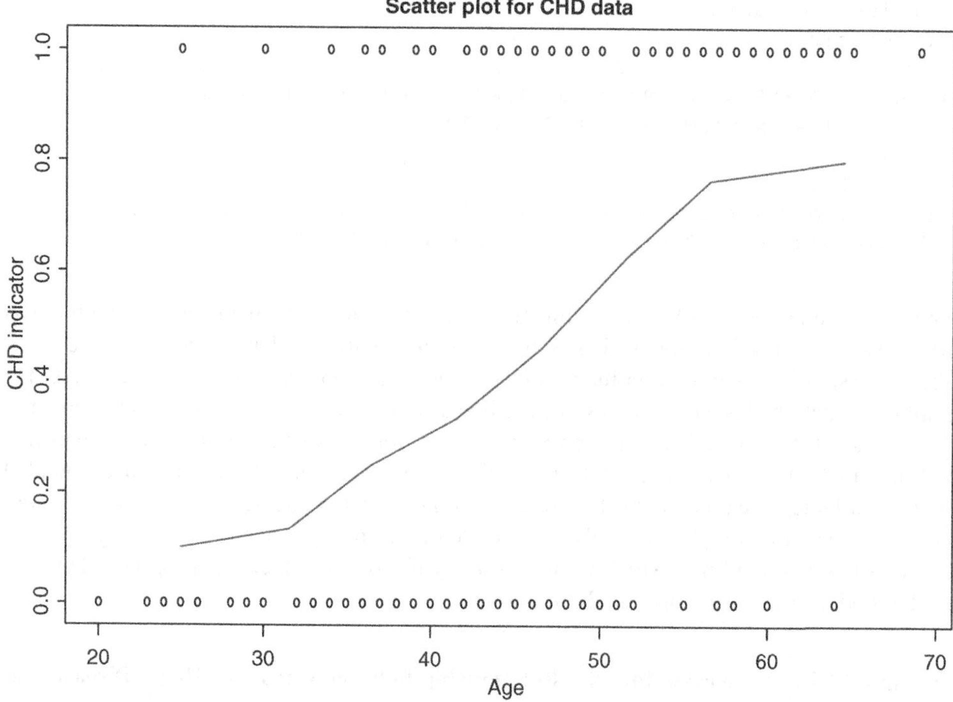

Figure 17.2 Understanding the Coronary Heart Disease Data in Terms of Percentage

The `red` curve in Figure 17.2 shows us that the percentage of people having CHD is increasing as age increases. Furthermore, the shape of the curve is "S" shaped. In particular, it looks like a *sigmoid* function. It is this fact that forms the basis of the *logistic regression model.* □

We will now digress a bit from applications and attempt to understand the general underlying theory of GLMs. A brief look at the important members of the GLM family will be discussed here.

?quantile, ?aggregate, ?cdplot, ?cut

17.3 Exponential Family and the GLM

The exponential family of distribution was introduced in Chapter 7. Chapter 3 of Dobson (2002) highlights the role of the *exponential family* for the GLM's considered in this chapter. Recall the definition of the exponential family from Chapter 7 as

$$f(y|\theta) = s(y)t(\theta)\exp[a(y)b(\theta)],$$

where a, b, s, t are some known functions. This form of exponential family may be rewritten as

$$f(y|\theta) = \exp[a(y)b(\theta) + c(\theta) + d(y)],$$

Table 17.1 GLM and the Exponential Family

Probability Model	Name of Link Function	Link Function	Mean Function
Normal	Identity	$\mathbf{X}\boldsymbol{\beta} = \mu$	$\mu = \mathbf{X}\boldsymbol{\beta}$
Exponential/Gamma	Inverse	$\mathbf{X}\boldsymbol{\beta} = \mu^{-1}$	$\mu = (\mathbf{X}\boldsymbol{\beta})^{-1}$
Inverse Gaussian	Inverse Squared	$\mathbf{X}\boldsymbol{\beta} = \mu^{-2}$	$\mu = (\mathbf{X}\boldsymbol{\beta})^{-1/2}$
Poisson	Log	$\mathbf{X}\boldsymbol{\beta} = \log(\mu)$	$\mu = \exp(\mathbf{X}\boldsymbol{\beta})$
Binomial	Logit	$\mathbf{X}\boldsymbol{\beta} = \log\left\{\frac{\mu}{1-\mu}\right\}$	$\mu = \frac{\exp\{\mathbf{X}\boldsymbol{\beta}\}}{1+\exp\{\mathbf{X}\boldsymbol{\beta}\}}$

where $c(\theta) = \exp(t(\theta))$ and $d(y) = \exp(s(y))$. If $a(y) = y$, the distribution is said to be in *canonical form* and in this case $b(\theta)$ is called the *natural parameter* of the distribution. We had seen some members of the exponential family in Section 7.2.1. The dependency of GLM on the exponential family is now discussed.

Consider an independent sample $Y_1, Y_2, \dots, Y_n$, with the following characteristics:

- Each observation $Y_i, i = 1, 2, \dots, n$, is a distribution from the exponential family.
- The distributions of Y_i are of the same form, that is, all are either normal, or all binomial, etc.
- The canonical form Y_i is specified by

$$f(y_i|\theta_i) = \exp[a(y_i)b(\theta_i) + c(\theta_i) + d(y_i)] \tag{17.1}$$

This translates into the form that the joint probability density function of the random sample $Y_1, Y_2, \dots, Y_n$, is given by

$$f(y_1, \dots, y_n|\theta_1, \dots, \theta_n) = \exp\left[\sum_{i=1}^{n} a(y_i)b(\theta_i) + \sum_{i=1}^{n} c(\theta_i) + \sum_{i=1}^{n} d(y_i)\right]. \tag{17.2}$$

In a GLM, we are interested in estimation of the n parameters θ_i. The trick is to consider some function of θ_i, say μ_i, such that $E(Y_i) = \mu_i$, and then allow the n μ_i's to vary as a function of $p, p < n$, regression coefficients. That is, we define μ_i by

$$g(\mu_i) = \mathbf{x}_i\boldsymbol{\beta}, i = 1, 2, \dots, n, \tag{17.3}$$

where $\mathbf{x}_i$ is the covariate vector associated with $y_i, i = 1, \dots, n$. The function $g(.)$ is called the *link function* of the GLM. Some essential requirements of the function g is that it should be monotonic and differentiable. Table 17.1 gives a summary of important members of the GLM. There will be more focus on *logistic regression* in this chapter.

17.4 The Logistic Regression Model

We saw in the previous section how the probability curve is a sigmoid curve. Now we will introduce the concepts in a more formal and mathematical way. We have found the paper of

Czepiel, http://czep.net/stat/mlelr.pdf, to be in the most appropriate pedagogical manner and this section is a liberal adaptation of the same. Let the binary outcomes be represented by $Y_i, i = 1, 2, \ldots, n$, and the covariates associated with them be respectively $\mathbf{x}_i, i = 1, 2, \ldots, n$. The covariate is assumed to be a vector of the k elements, that is, $\mathbf{x} = (x_1, x_2, \ldots, x_k)$. Without loss of generality, we can write the covariate vector as $\mathbf{x} = (x_0, x_1, x_2, \ldots, x_k)$, with $x_0 \equiv 1$. The probability of success is specified by $\pi_i = P(Y_i = 1)$. The *logistic regression* model is then given by

$$\pi(\mathbf{x}) = P(Y = 1) = \frac{e^{\mathbf{x}\boldsymbol{\beta}}}{1 + e^{\mathbf{x}\boldsymbol{\beta}}} = \frac{e^{\sum_{i=0}^{k} \beta_i x_i}}{1 + e^{\sum_{i=0}^{k} \beta_i x_i}}, \tag{17.4}$$

where $\boldsymbol{\beta} = (\beta_0, \beta_1, \ldots, \beta_p)$ is the vector of regression coefficients. The probability of a failure has the simple form:

$$P(Y = 0) = 1 - \pi(x) = 1 - \frac{e^{\mathbf{x}\boldsymbol{\beta}}}{1 + e^{\mathbf{x}\boldsymbol{\beta}}} = \frac{1}{1 + e^{\mathbf{x}\boldsymbol{\beta}}}.$$

An important identity in the context of logistic regression is the form of the *odds ratio*, abbreviated and denoted as *OR*:

$$OR = \frac{\pi(\mathbf{x})}{1 - \pi(\mathbf{x})} = \frac{e^{\mathbf{x}\boldsymbol{\beta}}}{1 + e^{\mathbf{x}\boldsymbol{\beta}}} \left\{ \frac{1}{1 + e^{\mathbf{x}\boldsymbol{\beta}}} \right\}^{-1} = e^{\mathbf{x}\boldsymbol{\beta}}. \tag{17.5}$$

Taking the logarithm on both sides of the above equation, we get the form of logistic regression model:

$$\ln(OR) = \ln\left(\frac{\pi(\mathbf{x})}{1 - \pi(\mathbf{x})}\right) = \mathbf{x}\boldsymbol{\beta} = \sum_{i=0}^{k} \beta_i x_i.$$

The expression $\ln(\pi(\mathbf{x})/(1 - \pi(\mathbf{x})))$ is known as the *logit function* and since it is linear in the covariates, the logistic regression model, based on the logit function, is a particular class of the well-known generalized linear models. The logistic regression model is given by

$$y = \pi(\mathbf{x}) + \epsilon, \tag{17.6}$$

where ϵ is the error term. Thus, if $y = 1$, the error is $1 - \pi(\mathbf{x})$ with probability $\pi(\mathbf{x})$. Otherwise, the error is $-\pi(\mathbf{x})$ with probability $1 - \pi(\mathbf{x})$. That is

$$\epsilon = \begin{cases} 1 - \pi(\mathbf{x}), & \text{with probability } \pi(\mathbf{x}) \text{ if } y = 1, \\ -\pi(\mathbf{x}), & \text{with probability } 1 - \pi(\mathbf{x}) \text{ if } y = 0. \end{cases} \tag{17.7}$$

Hence, the error ϵ has a binomial distribution with mean $E(\epsilon) = 0$ and variance $Var(\epsilon) = \pi(\mathbf{x})(1 - \pi(\mathbf{x}))$. The next section will deal with the inferential aspect of $\boldsymbol{\beta}$.

17.5 Inference for the Logistic Regression Model

17.5.1 Estimation of the Regression Coefficients and Related Parameters

The likelihood function based on n observations is given by

$$L(\boldsymbol{\beta}, \mathbf{y}) = \prod_{i=1}^{n} \pi(\mathbf{x}_i)^{y_i} [1 - \pi(\mathbf{x}_i)]^{1 - y_i}. \tag{17.8}$$

As in the most cases, it is easier to work with the log-likelihood function:

$$\begin{aligned}\ln[L(\boldsymbol{\beta}, \mathbf{y})] &\propto \sum_{i-1}^{n} \{y_i \ln(\pi(\mathbf{x}_i)) + (1 - y_i)\ln(1 - \pi(\mathbf{x}_i))\} \\ &= \sum_{i=1}^{n} y_i \ln\left\{\frac{\pi(\mathbf{x}_i)}{1 - \pi(\mathbf{x}_i)}\right\} + \sum_{i=1}^{n} \ln(1 - \pi(\mathbf{x}_i)) \\ &= \sum_{i=1}^{n} y_i \mathbf{x}_i \boldsymbol{\beta} - \sum_{i=1}^{n} \ln(1 + e^{\mathbf{x}_i\boldsymbol{\beta}}). \end{aligned} \tag{17.9}$$

Differentiating the above log-likelihood function with respect to $\beta_j, j = 0, 1, 2, \ldots, k$, we obtain the *score* function:

$$\begin{aligned}\frac{\partial \ln[L(\boldsymbol{\beta}, \mathbf{y})]}{\partial \beta_j} &= \sum_{i=1}^{n} y_i \mathbf{x}_i - \sum_{i=1}^{n} \left[\frac{1}{1 + e^{\mathbf{x}_i\boldsymbol{\beta}}}\right] e^{\mathbf{x}_i\boldsymbol{\beta}} \mathbf{x}_i \\ &= \sum_{i=1}^{n} y_i \mathbf{x}_i - \sum_{i=1}^{n} \pi(\mathbf{x}_i)\mathbf{x}_i \\ &= \sum_{i=1}^{n} (y_i - \pi(\mathbf{x}_i))\mathbf{x}_i. \end{aligned} \tag{17.10}$$

Let us denote the covariate matrix, as in earlier chapters, by $\mathbf{X}$, the probability of success vector by $\boldsymbol{\pi} = \{\pi_1, \pi_2, \ldots, \pi_n\}$, and the outcome vector by $\mathbf{y} = (y_1, y_2, \ldots, y_n)$. The normal equation, obtained by equating the above equation to zero, for the logistic regression model is then given by

$$\mathbf{X}'(\mathbf{y} - \boldsymbol{\pi}) = 0. \tag{17.11}$$

The above equation looks similar to the normal equation of the linear models. However, Equation 17.11 cannot be solved immediately as the vector $\boldsymbol{\pi}$ contains the vector of regression coefficients. We need the help of a different algorithm to obtain the estimates of the regression coefficients. This algorithm is generally known as the *iterated reweighted least squares*, abbreviated as IRLS, algorithm. In the context of the logistic regression model, the IRLS algorithm is given below, see Fox http://socserv.mcmaster.ca/jfox/Courses/UCLA/logistic-regression-notes.pdf.

- Initialize the vector of regression coefficients $\mathbf{b}_0 = \mathbf{0}$.
- The tth improvement of the regression coefficients is given by

$$\mathbf{b}_t = \mathbf{b}_{t-1} + (\mathbf{X}'\mathbf{V}_{t-1}\mathbf{X})^{-1}\mathbf{X}'(\mathbf{y} - \boldsymbol{\pi}_{t-1}), \tag{17.12}$$

  where $\mathbf{V}_{t-1}$ is a diagonal matrix with the ith diagonal element given by $\pi_{i,t-1}(1 - \pi_{i,t-1})$, and $\pi_{i,t-1} = 1/(1 + \exp(-\mathbf{x}_i'\mathbf{b}_{t-1}))$.
- Repeat the above step until $\mathbf{b}_t$ is close to $\mathbf{b}_{t-1}$.
- The asymptotic covariance matrix of the regression coefficients is given by $(\mathbf{X}'\mathbf{V}\mathbf{X})$, see next sub-section.

In the next example, we will develop an example which will clearly bring out the steps of the IRLS algorithm. The use of the R function `glm` directly returns us the estimates of the regression coefficients. However, the working of the IRLS algorithm does not become clear, and the first time the reader *may feel* that IRLS is some kind of black box. It is to be understood that software does not hide anything, R or any other statistical software. The onus of clear understanding of software functionality is with the reader, and sometimes the authors. For the sake of simplicity, we will focus on the simple GLM case of a single covariate only. The IRLS function is first given and discussed.

```
irls <- function(output, input) {
input <- cbind(rep(1,length(output)),input)
bt <- 1:ncol(input)*0 # Initializing the regression coefficients
probs <- as.vector(1/(1+exp(-input%*%bt)))
temp <- rep(1,nrow(input))
while(sum((bt-temp)^2)>0.0001) {
temp <- bt
bt <- bt+as.vector(solve(t(input)%*%diag(probs*(1-probs))
%*%input)%*%(t(input)%*%(output-probs)))
probs <- as.vector(1/(1+exp(-input%*%bt)))
}
return(bt)
}
```

The `irls` R function defined here should return us the estimates as required by the IRLS algorithm and in particular Equation 17.12 computations are to be handled here. Given the covariate values for the n observations from a dataset, the first step is to take care of the intercept term, and thus we first begin by inserting a column of 1's with `input <- cbind(rep(1,length(output)),input)`. The initial estimate of regression coefficients is set equal to 0, and hence the initial probabilities π_i's will be zero too, see `bt` and `probs` in the `irls` program. The regression coefficient vector for the previous iteration will be denoted by `temp` and so long as the improvement of the current iteration, vector distance, and the previous iteration is greater than `1e-4`, the iterations will be carried out in the `while` loop. The iteration as required by Equation 17.12 is provided by the R code `solve(t(input)%*%diag(probs*(1-probs))%*%input)%*%(t(input) %*%(output-probs))`. When the convergence criteria is met, the vector of regression coefficients is returned by `return(bt)` as the output. The `irls` function will be tested for the coronary heart disease problem and the results will be further verified with the R `glm` function.

Example 17.5.1. Understanding the Relationship between Coronary Heart Disease and the Age of the Patient. Contd. We will now see how the above `irls` function compares with the R modules. The R function `glm` will be useful to build GLM, and it works on similar lines as the linear model function `lm`. The formula ~ as used in `lm` continues to hold for `glm` and does not need further elaboration.

```
> data(chdage)
> chdglm <- glm(chdage$CHD~chdage$AGE,family='binomial')
> irls(chdage$CHD,chdage$AGE)
```

```
[1] -5.3094530  0.1109211
> chdglm$coefficients
(Intercept)  chdage$AGE
 -5.3094534   0.1109211
 > summary(chdglm)
Call:
glm(formula = chdage$CHD ~ chdage$AGE, family = "binomial")
Deviance Residuals:
    Min       1Q   Median      3Q      Max
-1.9718  -0.8456  -0.4576   0.8253   2.2859
Coefficients:
               Estimate Std. Error z value Pr(>|z|)
(Intercept) -5.30945    1.13365   -4.683 2.82e-06 ***
chdage$AGE   0.11092    0.02406    4.610 4.02e-06 ***
- - -
Signif. codes:  0 '***' 0.001 '**' 0.01 '*' 0.05 '.' 0.1 ' ' 1
(Dispersion parameter for binomial family taken to be 1)
    Null deviance: 136.66  on 99  degrees of freedom
Residual deviance: 107.35  on 98  degrees of freedom
AIC: 111.35
Number of Fisher Scoring iterations: 4
```

Thus, the `irls` function returns the precise answer as the R function `glm` as seen by the output for `irls(chdage$CHD,chdage$AGE)` and `chdglm$coefficients`. It is now hoped that the reader is really comfortable with the IRLS algorithm.

The `summary` function shows that AGE is a significant variable for explaining CHD. Further description will follow in the rest of this section. □

Estimates of the link function and odds ratio is straightforwardly obtained by plugging in the values of the estimated regression coefficients, that is,

$$\hat{\pi}(x) = \mathbf{x}\hat{\beta},$$

$$\hat{OR} = e^{\mathbf{x}\hat{\beta}}.$$

We will next consider an example of the *multiple logistic regression*, that is when we have more than one covariates.

Example 17.5.2. The Low Birth-Weight Problem. Low birth weight of new-born infants is a serious concern. If the weight of the new-born is less than 2500 grams, we consider that instance as a low-birth weight case. A study was carried out at Baystate Medical Center in Springfield, Massachusetts. Table 17.2 gives a description of the variables in the study.

The multiple logistic regression model will be built for the low birth weight category LOW as a function of the covariates AGE, LWT, RACE, and FTV.

```
> data(lowbwt)
> lowglm <- glm(LOW~AGE+LWT+RACE+FTV,data=lowbwt,family='binomial')
> lowglm$coefficients
(Intercept)          AGE        RACE3           FTV
 1.29536575 -0.02382297 0.43310843 -0.04930832
```

Table 17.2 The Low Birth-Weight Variables

Serial Number	Description	Abbreviation
1	Identification Code	ID
2	Low Birth Weight	LOW
3	Age of Mother	AGE
4	Weight of Mother at Last Menstrual Period	LWT
5	Race	RACE
6	Smoking Status During Pregnancy	SMOKE
7	History of Premature Labor	PTL
8	History of Hypertension	HT
9	Presence of Uterine Irritability	UI
10	Number of Physician Visits During the First Trimester	FTV
11	Birth Weight	BWT

Note that converting RACE as a factor has multiplied itself by two variables, since we have modeled it as a *factor variable* and not as a continuous variable. The reasoning is similar as in the linear models.

□

The estimated vector of regression coefficients $\hat{\boldsymbol{\beta}}$ needs to be tested for significance. The first step towards this would be to obtain an estimate of the variance-covariance matrix of $\hat{\boldsymbol{\beta}}$.

17.5.2 Estimation of the Variance-Covariance Matrix of $\hat{\beta}$

We have seen earlier in Chapter 7 that the variance of the score function gives the Fisher information. Thus, to obtain the variance-covariance matrix of $\hat{\boldsymbol{\beta}}$, we look at the second-order partial derivatives of the log-likelihood function. The technique of estimating the variance-covariance matrix of $\hat{\boldsymbol{\beta}}$ follows from the theory of the maximum likelihood estimation, see Rao (1973). Differentiating the partial differential equations of the log-likelihood function of sub-section 8.4.1, we get

$$\frac{\partial^2 \ln[L(\beta, y)]}{\partial \beta_j^2} = -\sum_{i=1}^{n} x_{ij}^2 \pi_i (1 - \pi_i),$$

$$\frac{\partial^2 \ln[L(\beta, y)]}{\partial \beta_j \partial \beta_{j'}} = -\sum_{i=1}^{n} x_{ij} x_{ij'} \pi_i (1 - \pi_i),$$

for $j, j' = 0, 1, \ldots, k$. The Fisher information for $\boldsymbol{\beta}$, denoted by $I(\boldsymbol{\beta})$, consists of elements as specified in the above two equations. Adapting the results from Chapter 7, the inverse matrix of the information matrix gives us the variance-covariance matrix of $\hat{\boldsymbol{\beta}}$, that is,

$$var(\hat{\boldsymbol{\beta}}) = I^{-1}(\hat{\boldsymbol{\beta}}) = (\mathbf{X}'\mathbf{V}\mathbf{X})^{-1}. \tag{17.13}$$

Thus, we specifically have that the variance of the estimator of regression coefficient β_j, denoted by $\mathtt{v\hat{a}r}(\hat{\beta}_j)$ as the jth diagonal element of $\mathtt{var}(\hat{\boldsymbol{\beta}})$. Similarly, the covariance between the estimators of two regression coefficients, denoted by $\mathtt{c\hat{o}v}(\hat{\beta}_j, \hat{\beta}_{j'})$, as the (j, j') element of $\mathtt{var}(\hat{\boldsymbol{\beta}})$.

In R, it is easier to obtain the variance-covariance matrix for a fitted logistic regression model. For the Low Birth-Weight example, we can obtain this using the listed object `cov.unscaled`.

```
> lowglm_summary <- summary(lowglm)
> lowglm_summary$cov.unscaled
            (Intercept)     AGE     LWT   RACE2   RACE3     FTV
(Intercept)      1.1480 -0.0220 -0.0045 -0.0373 -0.1339  0.0054
AGE             -0.0220  0.0011  0.0000  0.0031  0.0013 -0.0010
LWT             -0.0045  0.0000  0.0000 -0.0008  0.0003 -0.0001
RACE2           -0.0373  0.0031 -0.0008  0.2479  0.0571 -0.0003
RACE3           -0.1339  0.0013  0.0003  0.0571  0.1312  0.0058
FTV              0.0054 -0.0010 -0.0001 -0.0003  0.0058  0.0280
```

17.5.3 *Confidence Intervals and Hypotheses Testing for the Regression Coefficients*

The natural hypotheses testing problem is inspection for the significance of the regressors, that is, $H^{(j)} : \beta_j = 0, j = 1, 2, \dots, k$. The *Wald test statistics* for $H^{(j)}$ is given by

$$W_j = \frac{\hat{\beta}_j}{\hat{\mathrm{SE}}(\hat{\beta}_j)}, j = 0, 1, \dots, k. \tag{17.14}$$

Under the hypotheses $H^{(j)}$, the Wald statistics W_j (asymptotically) follow a standard normal distribution. Furthermore, the $100(1-\alpha)\%$ confidence interval for β_j is given by

$$\hat{\beta}_j \pm z_{\alpha/2}\hat{\mathrm{SE}}(\hat{\beta}_j), j = 0, 1, \dots, k. \tag{17.15}$$

We will illustrate these concepts for the low birth-weight study problem.

Example 17.5.3. The Low Birth-Weight Problem. Contd. The Wald statistics values and the corresponding p-values are given in the third and fourth columns of the "Coefficients" table of the `summary` function, that is:

```
> lowglm_summary$coefficients[,3:4]
            z value Pr(>|z|)
(Intercept)  1.2090   0.2267
AGE         -0.7063   0.4800
LWT         -2.1778   0.0294
RACE2        2.0164   0.0438
RACE3        1.1956   0.2318
FTV         -0.2948   0.7681
> confint(lowglm)
```

```
Waiting for profiling to be done...
                  2.5 %   97.5 %
(Intercept) -0.7603   3.4594
AGE           -0.0917   0.0413
LWT           -0.0278  -0.0020
RACE2          0.0230   1.9910
RACE3         -0.2787   1.1462
FTV           -0.3899   0.2707
```

Note that at $\alpha = 0.05$ level of significance, `LWT` and `RACE` would be two significant variables in explaining the low birth weight `LOW`. The 95% confidence intervals for the regression coefficients confirm the hypotheses test results, since `0` does not lie in the intervals for `LWT` and `RACE`. For details about *profiling*, refer to Dalgaard (2008). □

An overall model level significance test needs to be in place. Towards this test, we need to first define the notion of *deviance*, and this topic will be taken up in sub-section 17.5.5. First, we need to define the various types of residuals on the lines of linear models for the logistic regression model.

?diag, ?glm, ?family, ?coefficients, ?summary.glm, ?deviance, ?confint

17.5.4 Residuals for the Logistic Regression Model

Recollect from the definition of residuals for the linear regression model as defined in Section 12.5 that the residual is the difference between actual and predicted y values. Similarly, the residuals for the logistic regression model is defined by

$$r_i = y_i - \hat{\pi}_i(\mathbf{x}_i), i = 1, \ldots, n. \tag{17.16}$$

The residuals r_i are sometimes called the *response residual*. The different variants of the residuals which will be useful are defined next, see Chapter 7 of Tattar (2013). The hat matrix $\mathbf{H}$ played an important role in defining the residuals for the linear regression model, recall Equation 12.37. A similar matrix will be required for the logistic regression model, and we have the problem here that the observation y is not a straightforward linear in terms of the regression coefficient. A linear approximation for the fitted values $\hat{\pi}$, which gives a similar hat matrix for the logistic regression model, has been proposed by Pregibon (1981), see Section 5.3 of Hosmer and Lemeshow (1990–2013). The hat matrix for the logistic regression matrix will be denoted by $\mathbf{H}_{LR}$, the subscript LR denotes logistic regression and not linear regression, and is defined by

$$\mathbf{H}_{LR} = \mathbf{V}^{1/2}\mathbf{X}(\mathbf{X}'\mathbf{V}\mathbf{X})^{-1}\mathbf{X}'\mathbf{V}^{1/2}, \tag{17.17}$$

where $\mathbf{V}$ is a diagonal matrix with

$$v_i = \hat{\pi}(\mathbf{x}_i)(1 - \hat{\pi}(\mathbf{x}_i)), i = 1, \ldots, n.$$

The diagonal elements, hat values, h_{ii}, or simply h_i, are given by

$$h_i = \hat{\pi}(\mathbf{x}_i)(1 - \hat{\pi}(\mathbf{x}_i))\mathbf{x}_i'(\mathbf{X}'\mathbf{V}\mathbf{X})^{-1}\mathbf{x}_i = v_i b_i, i = 1, \ldots, n, \tag{17.18}$$

with $v_i \equiv \hat{\pi}(\mathbf{x}_i)(1 - \hat{\pi}(\mathbf{x}_i))$ capturing the model-based estimator of the variance of y_i and $b_i \equiv \mathbf{x}_i'(\mathbf{X}'\mathbf{V}\mathbf{X})^{-1}\mathbf{x}_i$ computing the weighted distance of $\mathbf{x}_i$ from the average of the covariate design matrix $\bar{\mathbf{x}}$. Similar to the linear regression model case, the diagonal element h_i is useful for obtaining the variance of the residual:

$$\texttt{Var}(e_i) = \hat{\pi}(\mathbf{x}_i)(1 - \hat{\pi}(\mathbf{x}_i))(1 - h_i), i = 1, \ldots, n. \tag{17.19}$$

The *Pearson residual* for the logistic regression model is then defined by

$$r_i^P = \frac{y_i - \hat{\pi}_i(\mathbf{x}_i)}{\sqrt{\hat{\pi}(\mathbf{x}_i)(1 - \hat{\pi}(\mathbf{x}_i))}}, i = 1, \ldots, n. \tag{17.20}$$

The *standardized Pearson residual* is defined by

$$r_i^{P\_Stan} = \frac{r_i^P}{\sqrt{1 - h_i}}, i = 1, \ldots, n. \tag{17.21}$$

The *deviance residual* for the logistic regression model is defined as signed square root of the contribution of the observation to the sum of the model deviance and is given by

$$r_i^{dev} = \text{sign}\,\{r_i\}\sqrt{-2[y_i \log(\hat{\pi}_i(\mathbf{x}_i)) + (1 - y_i)\log(1 - \hat{\pi}_i(\mathbf{x}_i))]}. \tag{17.22}$$

The residuals are obtained for a disease outbreak dataset, which is adapted from Kutner, et al. (2005).

Example 17.5.4. Disease Outbreak Problem. The purpose of this health study is investigation of an epidemic outbreak due to mosquitoes. A random sample, from two sectors of a city, among the individuals has been tested to determine if they had contracted the disease forming the binary outcome Y. The variables of age `x1`, socioeconomic status (of three categories lower, middle, and upper) through data variables `x2` and `x3`, and sector of the city `x4`, are used to determine if the disease has been contracted by the individual. This dataset is available in the file `Disease_Outbreak.csv` and imported into the R session as `Disease data.frame` object. First, a logistic regression model will be fitted with `glm(y ~.,data=Disease)` and the fitted model `DO_LR` will be used to obtain the residuals: response, deviance, Pearson, standardized Pearson, and the important hat values. The R functions `glm`, `residuals` with the options of `response`, `deviance`, and `pearson`, `hatvalues`, and `fitted` will help us to obtain the quantities defined in Equations 17.16–17.22.

```
> data(Disease)
> DO_LR <- glm(y~.,data=Disease,family='binomial')
> LR_Residuals <- data.frame(Y = Disease$y,Fitted = fitted(DO_LR),
+ Hatvalues = hatvalues(DO_LR),Response = residuals(DO_LR,
+ "response"), Deviance = residuals(DO_LR,"deviance"),
+ Pearson = residuals(DO_LR,"pearson"),
+ Pearson_Standardized = residuals(DO_LR,"pearson")/
+ sqrt(1-LR_Residuals$Hatvalues))
```

```
> LR_Residuals
   Y Fitted Hatvalues Response Deviance Pearson Pearson_Standardized
1  0 0.2090    0.0387  -0.2090   -0.685  -0.514               -0.524
2  0 0.2190    0.0404  -0.2190   -0.703  -0.529               -0.541
3  0 0.1058    0.0332  -0.1058   -0.473  -0.344               -0.350
4  0 0.3710    0.0895  -0.3710   -0.963  -0.768               -0.805
5  1 0.1108    0.0252   0.8892    2.098   2.833                2.869

94 0 0.1630    0.0460  -0.1630   -0.596  -0.441               -0.452
95 1 0.1589    0.0326   0.8411    1.918   2.300                2.339
96 0 0.1138    0.0254  -0.1138   -0.491  -0.358               -0.363
97 0 0.0919    0.0241  -0.0919   -0.439  -0.318               -0.322
98 0 0.1712    0.0356  -0.1712   -0.613  -0.455               -0.463
```

The plots of residuals against the fitted values of the type `plot(fitted,residuals)`, unlike the linear regression model, are not very useful. A deviation from the tested path is required to obtain meaningful residual plots and will be developed now. □

Recollect from Equation 17.7 that the mean and variance of the error term are respectively $E(\epsilon) = 0$ and $Var(\epsilon) = \pi(\mathbf{x})(1 - \pi(\mathbf{x}))$. Thus, the *LOESS* plot, refer to Section 8.4, of errors against the fitted values should reflect a line around 0 if the assumption of the logistic regression is appropriate. This perspective will be explored as a continuation of the previous example.

Example 17.5.5. Disease Outbreak Problem. Contd. The residuals against the fitted values plot are easily obtained. We need to complement the residual plots with the LOESS approximation. Thus, the `loess` function is used in the usual way `loess(y~x)`. The fitted LOESS curve will then be added to the residual plot and investigated if the line is approximately at 0.

```
> par(mfrow=c(2,2))
> plot(LR_Residuals$Fitted,LR_Residuals$Response,
+ xlab="Fitted Values",ylab="Response Residual")
> response_loess <- loess(Response~Fitted,data=LR_Residuals)
> points(response_loess$x,predict(response_loess))
> plot(LR_Residuals$Fitted,LR_Residuals$Deviance,
+ xlab="Fitted Values", ylab="Deviance Residual")
> deviance_loess <- loess(Deviance~Fitted,data=LR_Residuals)
> points(deviance_loess$x,predict(deviance_loess))
> plot(LR_Residuals$Fitted,LR_Residuals$Pearson,
+ xlab="Fitted Values", ylab="Pearson Residual")
> pearson_loess <- loess(Pearson~Fitted,data=LR_Residuals)
> points(pearson_loess$x,predict(pearson_loess))
> plot(LR_Residuals$Fitted,LR_Residuals$Pearson_Standardized,
+ xlab="Fitted Values", ylab="Standardized Pearson Residual")
> pearson_standardized_loess <- loess(Pearson~Fitted,
+ data=LR_Residuals)
```

```
> points(pearson_standardized_loess$x,predict(pearson_
+ standardized_loess))
> title(main="The Loess Approach for Residual Validation of Logistic
+ Regression Model",outer=TRUE,line=-2)
```

Figure 17.3 shows that the logistic regression model is appropriate for the disease outbreak data problem. □

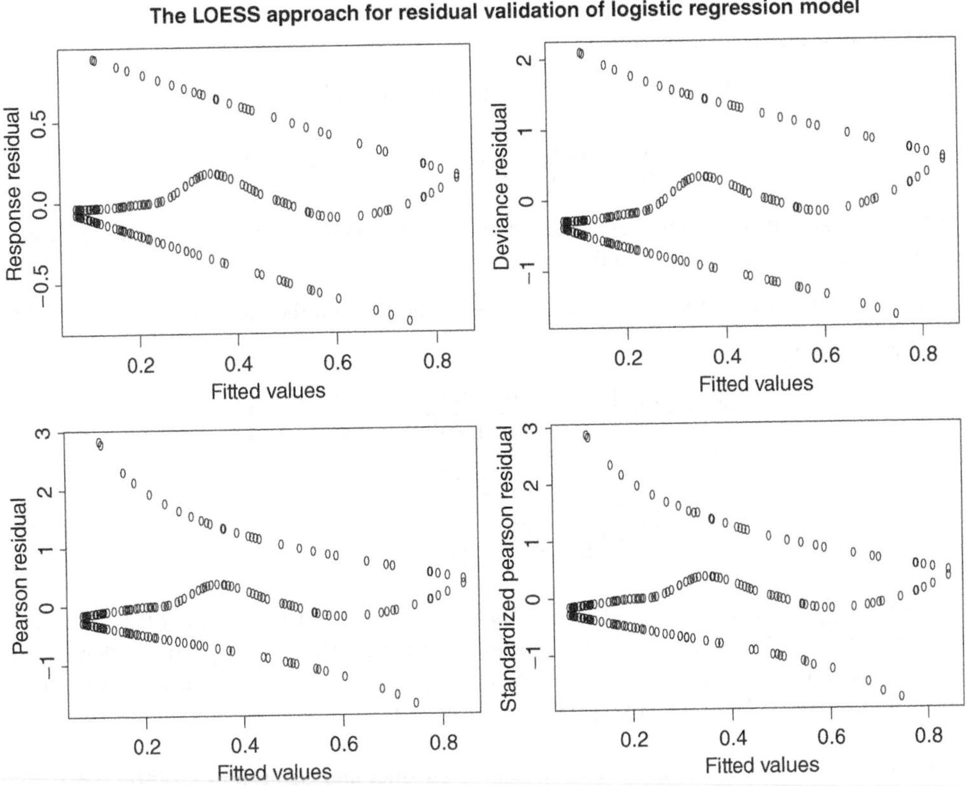

Figure 17.3 Residual Plots using LOESS

The residuals have more importance than validation of the model assumptions. The overall fit of the model will be investigated next.

17.5.5 Deviance Test and Hosmer-Lemeshow Goodness-of-Fit Test

Testing for the significance of the GLM model is carried out using *Deviance Statistic*, denoted by D, by comparing the likelihood function for the fitted model, which includes the covariates, with the likelihood of the *saturated model*. A saturated model is that model which takes into consideration all possible parameters and thus results in a perfect fit in the sense that all successful outcomes are predicted as success and failures predicted as failed. The deviance statistic D is then defined by

$$D = -2\ln\left[\frac{\text{(likelihood of the fitted model)}}{\text{(likelihood of the saturated model)}}\right].$$

Since the saturated model, by definition, leads to a perfect fit, we have $\hat{\pi}_i = y_i$, and thus

$$\text{likelihood of the saturated model} = \prod_{i=1}^{n} y_i^{y_i} \times (1-y_i)^{1-y_i} = 1.$$

Thus, the deviance statistic becomes

$$\begin{aligned} D &= -2\ln(\text{likelihood of the fitted model}) - 0 \\ &= -2\sum_{i=1}^{n}\left[y_i \ln\left(\frac{\hat{\pi}_i}{y_i}\right) + (1-y_i)\log\left(\frac{1-\hat{\pi}_i}{1-y_i}\right)\right]. \end{aligned}$$

To know the significance of the set of the independent variables, we need to compare the value of D with and without the set of independent variables/covariates. That is

$$G = \text{D(model without the variables)} - D\text{(model with the variables)}. \tag{17.23}$$

We further see that

$$\begin{aligned} G &= -2\ln\left[\frac{\text{(likelihood without the variables)}}{\text{(likelihood with the variables)}}\right] \\ &= -2\ln\left[\frac{\left(\frac{n_1}{n}\right)^{n_1}\left(\frac{n_0}{n}\right)^{n_0}}{\prod_{i=1}^{n}\hat{\pi}_i^{y_i}[1-\hat{\pi}_i]^{1-y_i}}\right] \end{aligned} \tag{17.24}$$

where $n_0 = \sum_{i=1}^{n} y_i$ and $n_1 = \sum_{i=1}^{n}(1-y_i)$. Basically, we are substituting the MLEs of π and $1-\pi$ for the model without the set of independent variables. Under the hypothesis that all the regression coefficients are not significant, the test statistic G follows a χ^2- distribution with k degrees of freedom. With the appropriate significance level, it is possible to infer the model significance using the G statistic. This G statistic may be seen as the parallel of the F statistic in the linear model case. For more details, refer to Hosmer and Lemeshow (2000).

Example 17.5.6. The Low Birth-Weight Problem. Contd. Recall that the R object `lowglm_summary` had been used to store summary values of the `glm` object in `lowglm`. To calculate the G-statistic, which is not directly given in R, we note that the summarized object gives us the `deviance` and `null.deviance` of the model. Thus,

```
> gstat_lowbwt <- lowglm_summary$null.deviance - lowglm_summary
+ $deviance
> gstat_lowbwt
[1] 12.09909
> 1-pchisq(gstat_lowbwt,5)
[1] 0.03345496
> with(lowglm, pchisq(null.deviance - deviance,df.null - df.residual,
+ lower.tail = FALSE)) # Equivalently
[1] 0.0335
```

The p-value is significant at the 0.05 level, which leads us to reject the hypothesis H and conclude that at least one or even all of k variable effects are significantly different from zero. □

17.6 Model Selection in Logistic Regression Models

We consider "Stepwise Logistic Regression" for the best variable selection in a logistic regression model. The most important variable is the one that produces maximum change in the log-likelihood relative to a model containing no variables. That is, maximum change in the value of the G-statistic is considered as the most important variable. The complete process of step-wise logistic regression is given in S number of steps.

Step 0

- Consider all plausible variables, say k.
- Fit "intercept only model", and evaluate the log-likelihood L_0.
- Fit each of the possible k univariate logistic regression models and note the log-likelihood values $L_j^{(0)}$. Furthermore, calculate the G-statistic for each of the k-models, $G_j^{(0)} = -2(L_0 - L_j^{(0)})$.
- Obtain the p-value for each model.
- The most important variable is then the one with least p-value, $p_{e_l}^{(0)} = \min(p_j^{(0)})$
- Denote the most important variable by x_{e_1}.
- Define the entry criteria p-value as p_E, which will at any time throughout this procedure decide if the variable is to be included or not. That is, the variable with the least p-value must be less than p_E to be selected in the final model.
- If none of the variables have the p-value less than p_E, we stop.

Step 1. The Forward Selection Step

- Replace L_0 of the previous step with $L_{e_1}^{(1)}$.
- Fit $k-1$ models with variables x_{e_1} and the remaining variables x_j, $j = 1, 2, \ldots, k$, and j distinct from e_1.
- For each of the $k-1$ models, calculate the log-likelihood $L_{e_1 j}^{(1)}$ and the G-statistics $G_j^{(1)} = -2(L_{e_1}^{(1)} - L_{e_1 j}^{(1)})$, and the corresponding p-values, denoted $p_j^{(1)}$.
- Define $p_{e_2}^{(1)} = \min(\overset{(1)}{\underset{j}{\mathrm{p}}})$
- If $p_{e_2}^{(1)} = p_E$, stop.

Step 2A. The Backward Elimination Step

- Adding x_{e_2} may leave x_{e_1} statistically insignificant.
- Let $L_{-e_j}^{(2)}$ denote the log-likelihood of the model with variable e_j removed.
- Calculate the likelihood-ratio test of these reduced models with respect to the full model at the beginning of this step $G_{-e_j}^{(2)} = -2(L_{e_j}^{(2)} - L_{e_1 e_2}^{(2)})$, and calculate the p-values $p_{-e_j}^{(2)}$.
- Deleted variables must result in a maximum p-value of the modified model.
- Denote x_{r_2} as the variable which is to be removed, and define $p_{r_2}^{(2)} = \max(p_{-e_1}^{(2)}, p_{-e_2}^{(2)})$.
- To remove variables, we need to have a value p_R with respect to which we compare $p_{r_2}^{(2)}$.

- We need to have $p_R > p_E$. (Why?)
- Variables are removed if $p_{r_2}^{(2)} > p_R$.

Step 2B. The Forward Selection Phase

- Continue the forward selection method with $k - 2$ remaining variables and find $p_{e_3}^{(2)}$.
- Let x_{e_3} be the variable associated with $p_{e_3}^{(2)}$.
- If the $p_{e_3}^{(2)}$ is less than p_E, proceed to Step 3, otherwise stop.

Step 3

- Fit the model including the variable selected in the previous step and perform backward elimination and then forward selection phase.
- Repeat until the last Step S.

Step S

- Stopping happens if all the variables have been selected in the model.
- It also happens if all the p-values in the model are less than p_R, and the remaining variables have p-values exceeding p_E.

The `step` function in R may be used to build a model. The criteria used there is the Akaike Information Criteria, AIC. To the best of our knowledge, there is no package/function which will implement stepwise logistic regression using the G-statistic generated p-values. The Hosmer and Lemeshow (2000) approach of model selection will be used here.

Example 17.6.1. Stepwise Regression for Low Birth-Weight Study. Let us begin by reading the dataset into R and with some essential data manipulations.

```
> data(lowbwt)
> attach(lowbwt)
> RACE_2=RACE_3=c()
> for(i in 1:nrow(lowbwt)){
+ if(lowbwt$RACE[i]==1) {RACE_2[i] <- 0;RACE_3[i] <- 0}
+ if(lowbwt$RACE[i]==2) {RACE_2[i] <- 1;RACE_3[i] <- 0}
+ if(lowbwt$RACE[i]==3) {RACE_2[i] <- 0;RACE_3[i] <- 1}
+ }
> design <- cbind(rep(1,nrow(lowbwt)),lowbwt[,3],
+ lowbwt[,4],RACE_2,RACE_3,lowbwt[,10])
> colnames(design)=c("intercept", "AGE","LWT",
+ "RACE_2","RACE_3","FTV")
> n <- nrow(design)
> n1 <- sum(lowbwt$LOW); n0 <- n-n1
> nullloglik <- n1*log(n1/n) + n0*log(n0/n)
```

We have thus obtained the null-log-likelihood value. We will first define two functions which will calculate the log-likelihood value `glmllv` and given two log-likelihood values, and will return the p-values for the fitted GLM `pvalue`.

```
> # Functions which calculate the log-likelihood
> # values and the p-value
> glmllv <- function(glm, x) {
+ glm <- glm; y <- glm$y
+ x1 <- cbind(rep(1,length(y)),x)
+ coeff <- glm$coefficients
+ logitx <- x1%*%coeff;
+ pix <- exp(logitx)/(1+exp(logitx))
+ llvalue <- sum(y*log(pix))+sum((1-y)*log(1-pix))
+ return(llvalue)
+ }
> pvalue <- function(lik1,lik0,df){
+ gstat <- -2*(lik0-lik1)
+ pval <- 1-pchisq(gstat,df)
+ return(pval)
+ }
```

We will now set the entry and exit criteria and decide which variable will first enter the model.

```
> #The p-values for entry and exit criteria
> pe <- 0.25; pr <- 0.4
> # Selecting the first variable to be included in the model
> glm_AGE <- glm(LOW~AGE,family='binomial')
> ll_AGE <- glmllv(glm_AGE,AGE)
> (pvalue_AGE <- pvalue(ll_AGE,nullloglik,1))
[1] 0.09664596
> glm_LWT <- glm(LOW~LWT,family='binomial')
> ll_LWT <- glmllv(glm_LWT,LWT)
> (pvalue_LWT <- pvalue(ll_LWT,nullloglik,1))
[1] 0.01445812
> glm_RACE_2 <- glm(LOW~RACE_2,family='binomial')
> ll_RACE_2 <- glmllv(glm_RACE_2,RACE_2)
> (pvalue_RACE_2 <- pvalue(ll_RACE_2,nullloglik,1))
[1] 0.1985105
> glm_RACE_3 <- glm(LOW~RACE_3,family='binomial')
> ll_RACE_3 <- glmllv(glm_RACE_3,RACE_3)
> (pvalue_RACE_3 <- pvalue(ll_RACE_3,nullloglik,1))
[1] 0.1829021
> glm_FTV <- glm(LOW~FTV,family='binomial')
> ll_FTV <- glmllv(glm_FTV,FTV)
> (pvalue_FTV <- pvalue(ll_FTV,nullloglik,1))
[1] 0.3792461
```

We see that the minimum p-value of `0.0145` is associated with the `LWT` variable, and is also less than p_E. We include this variable in the model now and move to Step 1.

```
> #Selecting the variables for the Step 1
> glm_LWT <- glm(LOW~LWT,family='binomial')
> ll_LWT <- glmllv(glm_LWT,LWT)
```

```
> glm_LWT_AGE <- glm(LOW~LWT+AGE,family='binomial')
> ll_LWT_AGE <- glmllv(glm_LWT_AGE,cbind(LWT,AGE))
> (pvalue_LWT_AGE <- pvalue(ll_LWT_AGE,ll_LWT,1))
[1] 0.2106024
> glm_LWT_RACE_2 <- glm(LOW~LWT+RACE_2,family='binomial')
> ll_LWT_RACE_2 <- glmllv(glm_LWT_RACE_2,cbind(LWT,RACE_2))
> (pvalue_LWT_RACE_2 <- pvalue(ll_LWT_RACE_2,ll_LWT,1))
[1] 0.05723459
> glm_LWT_RACE_3 <- glm(LOW~LWT+RACE_3,family='binomial')
> ll_LWT_RACE_3 <- glmllv(glm_LWT_RACE_3,cbind(LWT,RACE_3))
> (pvalue_LWT_RACE_3 <- pvalue(ll_LWT_RACE_3,ll_LWT,1))
[1] 0.442516
> glm_LWT_FTV <- glm(LOW~LWT+FTV,family='binomial')
> ll_LWT_FTV <- glmllv(glm_LWT_FTV,cbind(LWT,FTV))
> (pvalue_LWT_FTV <- pvalue(ll_LWT_FTV,ll_LWT,1))
[1] 0.5457832
```

Since the p-value associated with RACE_2 is the least and is less than p_E, it can be selected in our model. We will now check if some variable needs to leave the model.

```
> #Backward Elimination Method of Step 2
> # Since Race is consists of both RACE_2 and RACE_3,
> # we include both in Step 2
> glm_LWT_RACE <- glm(LOW~LWT+RACE_2+RACE_3,family='binomial')
> ll_LWT_RACE <- glmllv(glm_LWT_RACE, cbind(LWT,RACE_2,RACE_3))
> glm_RACE <- glm(LOW~RACE_2+RACE_3)
> ll_RACE <- glmllv(glm_RACE,cbind(RACE_2,RACE_3))
> pvalue(ll_LWT_RACE,ll_LWT,2)
[1] 0.06615272
> pvalue(ll_LWT_RACE,ll_RACE,1)
[1] 1.554312e-15
```

Since the maximum of these two p-values is less than p_R, we retain the variable RACE in the model. That is, the backward elimination step has not removed any variable. We need to redo Step 2 until we reach Step S described earlier.

```
> #Step 3 continues the Step 2 untill stopping criteria
> glm_LWT_RACE_AGE <- glm(LOW~LWT+RACE_2+RACE_3+AGE)
> ll_LWT_RACE_AGE <- glmllv(glm_LWT_RACE_AGE,cbind(LWT,RACE_2,
+ RACE_3,AGE))
> (pvalue_LWT_RACE_AGE <- pvalue(ll_LWT_RACE_AGE,ll_LWT_RACE,1))
[1] 1
> glm_LWT_RACE_FTV <- glm(LOW~LWT+RACE_2+RACE_3+FTV)
> ll_LWT_RACE_FTV <- glmllv(glm_LWT_RACE_FTV,cbind(LWT,RACE_2,
+ RACE_3,FTV))
> (pvalue_LWT_RACE_FTV <- pvalue(ll_LWT_RACE_FTV,ll_LWT_RACE,1))
[1] 1
```

Since none of the p-values associated variables AGE and FTV is less than p_E, we cannot enter the variables into the model. Thus, our best model includes the variables LTW and RACE. □

We will next illustrate the concept of the *backward regression* selection method using the AIC criteria.

Example 17.6.2. Backward Selection Method for Low Birth-Weight Study. We will again use the `step` function with the `backward` option for the direction to get the desired result.

```
> lowbwt <- read.xls("lowbwt.xls",sheet=1,header=TRUE)
> lowbwt <- lowbwt[,-1]
> lowglm <- glm(LOW~.,data=lowbwt,family='binomial')
> lowbackglm <- step(lowglm,direction="backward")
> step(lowglm,direction="backward")
Start:  AIC=20
LOW ~ AGE + LWT + RACE + SMOKE + PTL + HT + UI + FTV + BWT
        Df Deviance    AIC
- SMOKE  1     0.00  18.00
- AGE    1     0.00  18.00
- RACE   1     0.00  18.00
- UI     1     0.00  18.00
- PTL    1     0.00  18.00
- FTV    1     0.00  18.00
- LWT    1     0.00  18.00
- HT     1     0.00  18.00
<none>         0.00  20.00
- BWT    1   204.19 222.19
Step:  AIC=18
LOW ~ AGE + LWT + RACE + PTL + HT + UI + FTV + BWT
        Df Deviance    AIC
- AGE    1     0.00  16.00
- PTL    1     0.00  16.00
- LWT    1     0.00  16.00
- FTV    1     0.00  16.00
- HT     1     0.00  16.00
- RACE   1     0.00  16.00
- UI     1     0.00  16.00
<none>         0.00  18.00
- BWT    1   209.89 225.89

Step:  AIC=4
LOW ~ BWT
        Df Deviance    AIC
<none>         0.00   4.00
- BWT    1   234.67 236.67
Call:  glm(formula = LOW ~ BWT, family = "binomial", data = lowbwt)
Coefficients:
(Intercept)          BWT
   2976.010       -1.186
Degrees of Freedom: 188 Total (i.e. Null);  187 Residual
Null Deviance:     234.7
Residual Deviance: 4.931e-07 AIC: 4
> summary(lowbackglm)
```

```
Call:
glm(formula = LOW ~ BWT, family = "binomial", data = lowbwt)
Deviance Residuals:
       Min          1Q      Median          3Q         Max
-4.986e-04  -2.107e-08  -2.107e-08   2.107e-08   2.472e-04
Coefficients:
             Estimate Std. Error z value Pr(>|z|)
(Intercept)  2976.010 218927.077   0.014     0.99
BWT            -1.186     87.251  -0.014     0.99
(Dispersion parameter for binomial family taken to be 1)
    Null deviance: 2.3467e+02  on 188  degrees of freedom
Residual deviance: 4.9313e-07  on 187  degrees of freedom
AIC: 4
Number of Fisher Scoring iterations: 25
```

Thus, only the `BWT` variable has been selected for the best explanation of the `LOW` birth indicator.

□

An alternative to the binary regression problem, as discussed here with the logistic regression model, is given by the probit model and we will discuss this in the next section.

?step

17.7 Probit Regression

Bliss (1935) proposed the use of the *probit regression model* for problems where the response variable is a binary variable. Recall that in the logistic regression model we used the logit transformation of the link function to ensure that the predicted probabilities were always in the unit interval. Bliss suggested modeling the link function using the normal cumulative distribution.

Let Y denote the binary outcome as earlier and the covariates be represented by $\mathbf{x} = (1, x_1, \ldots, x_k)$. The probit regression model is constructed through the use of an *auxiliary RV* denoted by Y^*, see Chapter 7 of Tattar (2013). The auxiliary RV Y^* is then modeled as the multiple linear regression model:

$$Y^* = \beta_0 + \beta_1 x_1 + \ldots + \beta_k x_k + \epsilon = \mathbf{X}\boldsymbol{\beta} + \epsilon,$$

where the error ϵ follows the normal distribution $N(0, \sigma^2)$. Without loss of generality we assume $\sigma = 1$. The vectors $\mathbf{X}$ and $\boldsymbol{\beta}$ have their usual meanings. The probit regression model is then developed as a *latent variable model* through the use of the auxiliary RV:

$$Y = \begin{cases} 1, \text{ if } Y^* > 0, & \text{or } \mathbf{X}\boldsymbol{\beta} > -\epsilon, \\ 0, & \text{otherwise.} \end{cases} \tag{17.25}$$

The *probit model* is then given by

$$P(Y = 1|\mathbf{X}) = P(Y^* > 0) = P(\epsilon < \mathbf{X}\boldsymbol{\beta}) = \Phi(\mathbf{X}\boldsymbol{\beta}), \tag{17.26}$$

where Φ denotes the cumulative distribution of a standard normal variable. If we have n pairs of observations $(Y_1, \mathbf{X}_1), (Y_2, \mathbf{X}_2), \ldots, (Y_n, \mathbf{X}_n)$, the statistical inference for $\boldsymbol{\beta}$ may be carried out through the likelihood function given by

$$\ln L(\boldsymbol{\beta}|\text{data}) = \sum_{i=1}^{n} (y_i \ln \Phi(\mathbf{X}_i \boldsymbol{\beta}) + (1 - y_i) \ln(1 - \Phi(\mathbf{X}_i \boldsymbol{\beta}))).$$

It is obvious that this likelihood function will be difficult to evaluate. A probit regression model is set up in R, again using the `glm` function with the option `binomial(probit)`. Since the fitted probit model is again a member of the `glm` class, the techniques available and discussed for the logistic regression model are also available for the fitted probit model. For the sake of paucity, the mathematical details of the probit model will be skipped. First, we consider the simple probit model, followed with an example of multiple probit model.

Example 17.7.1. Probit Model for the CHD Data. We need to use `binomial(probit)` as the `family` option in the `glm` function to fit a probit model.

```
> # The Probit Regression Model
> data(chdage)
> chdprobit <- glm(CHD~AGE,data=chdage,family=binomial(probit))
> summary(chdprobit)
Call:
glm(formula = CHD ~ AGE, family = binomial(probit), data = chdage)
Deviance Residuals:
    Min         1Q    Median        3Q       Max
-1.9713   -0.8608   -0.4499    0.8359    2.3269
Coefficients:
            Estimate Std. Error z value Pr(>|z|)
(Intercept) -3.14573    0.62460  -5.036 4.74e-07 ***
AGE          0.06580    0.01335   4.930 8.20e-07 ***
---
Signif. codes:  0 '***' 0.001 '**' 0.01 '*' 0.05 '.' 0.1 ' ' 1
(Dispersion parameter for binomial family taken to be 1
    Null deviance: 136.66  on 99  degrees of freedom
Residual deviance: 107.50  on 98  degrees of freedom
AIC: 111.50
Number of Fisher Scoring iterations: 4
> summary(glm(CHD~AGE,data=chdage,family='binomial'))$coefficients
              Estimate Std. Error   z value     Pr(>|z|)
(Intercept) -5.3094534 1.13365365 -4.683488 2.820338e-06
AGE          0.1109211 0.02405982  4.610224 4.022356e-06
```

A comparison with the logistic regression model, see Example 17.5.1, shows that the coefficients are similar, though not the same. The AGE is found to be a significant variable, as in the case of the logistic regression model.

The confidence intervals and model significance may be obtained in R for this model, as seen next.

```
> confint(chdprobit)
Waiting for profiling to be done...
```

```
                   2.5 %      97.5 %
(Intercept) -4.41109357 -1.97605229
AGE          0.04070297  0.09278964
> with(chdprobit, pchisq(null.deviance - deviance,df.null
+ - df.residual,lower.tail = FALSE))
[1] 6.649872e-08
```

Since 0 does not lie in the 95% confidence intervals for either of the intercept terms or AGE, we again conclude that the variable is significant. Finally, since the overall p-value for the fitted model is very close to 0, 6.649872e-08, the fitted model is a significant model. □

A lot of similarity exists between the logistic regression and the probit regression regarding the model building in R, since both are generated using the glm function. Especially, the computational and inference methods remain almost the same. We will close this section with an illustration of the step-wise regression method for the probit regression model.

Example 17.7.2. Stepwise Regression for the Probit Regression Model with an Application to the Low Birth Weight Study. We are now familiar with this dataset. Hence, we will directly show how to perform the stepwise regression for the probit regression model.

```
> lowprobit <- glm(LOW~.,data=lowbwt,binomial(probit))
> step(lowprobit,direction="both")
Start:  AIC=20
LOW ~ AGE + LWT + RACE + SMOKE + PTL + HT + UI + FTV + BWT
         Df Deviance    AIC
- RACE    1     0.00  18.00
- UI      1     0.00  18.00
- AGE     1     0.00  18.00
- SMOKE   1     0.00  18.00
- PTL     1     0.00  18.00
- FTV     1     0.00  18.00
- LWT     1     0.00  18.00
- HT      1     0.00  18.00
<none>          0.00  20.00
- BWT     1   203.74 221.74
Step:  AIC=18
LOW ~ AGE + LWT + SMOKE + PTL + HT + UI + FTV + BWT
         Df Deviance    AIC
- PTL     1     0.00  16.00
- AGE     1     0.00  16.00
- LWT     1     0.00  16.00
- FTV     1     0.00  16.00
- SMOKE   1     0.00  16.00
- UI      1     0.00  16.00
- HT      1     0.00  16.00
<none>          0.00  18.00
+ RACE    1     0.00  20.00
- BWT     1   208.46 224.46
```

```
Step:  AIC=4
LOW ~ BWT
         Df Deviance     AIC
<none>              0.00    4.00
+ UI      1         0.00    6.00
+ LWT     1         0.00    6.00
+ AGE     1         0.00    6.00
+ PTL     1         0.00    6.00
+ RACE    1         0.00    6.00
+ HT      1         0.00    6.00
+ FTV     1         0.00    6.00
+ SMOKE   1         0.00    6.00
- BWT     1       234.67  236.67
Call:  glm(formula = LOW ~ BWT,
family = binomial(probit), data = lowbwt)
Coefficients:
(Intercept)            BWT
     928.57          -0.37
Degrees of Freedom: 188 Total (i.e. Null);  187 Residual
Null Deviance:      234.7
Residual Deviance: 8.798e-07 AIC: 4
```

Note that the probit regression model has also identified `BWT` as the single most important regressor of the low birth-weight indicator, as in the logistic regression model in the previous section. □

The next section will deal with a different type of discrete variable.

?glm, ?step

17.8 Poisson Regression Model

The logistic and probit regression models are useful when the discrete output is a binary variable. By an extension, we can incorporate multi-nominal variables too. However, these variables are class indicators, or nominal variables. In Section 16.5, the role of the Poisson RV was briefly indicated in the context of discrete data. If the discrete output is of a quantitative type and there are covariates related to it, we need to use the *Poisson regression model*.

The Poisson regression models are useful in two *slightly* different contexts: (i) the events arising as a percentage of the *exposures*, along with covariates which may be continuous or categorical, and (ii) the exposure effect is constant with the covariates being categorical variables only. In the first type of modeling, the parameter (rate λ) of the Poisson RV is specified in terms of the units of exposure. As an example, the quantitative variable may refer to the number of accidents per thousand vehicles arriving at a traffic signal, or the number of successful sales per thousand visitors on a web page. In the second case, the regressand Y may refer to the count in each cell of a contingency table. The Poisson model in this case is popularly referred to as the *log-linear model*. For a detailed treatment of this model, refer to Chapter 9 of Dobson (2002).

Let Y_i denote the number of responses from n_i events for the ith exposure, $i = 1, \ldots, n$, and let $\mathbf{x}_i$ represent the vector of explanatory variables. The *Poisson regression model* is stated as

$$E(Y_i|\mathbf{x}_i, \boldsymbol{\beta}) = \mu_i = n_i e^{\boldsymbol{\beta}^T \mathbf{x}_i}, i = 1, \ldots, n. \tag{17.27}$$

Here, the natural link function is the logarithmic function

$$\ln \mu_i = \ln n_i + \boldsymbol{\beta}^T \mathbf{x}_i.$$

The extra term ln n_i that appears in the link function is referred to as the *offset* term. It is important to clearly specify here the form of the pmf of Y:

$$f(y_i|\mathbf{x}_i, \boldsymbol{\beta}) = \frac{\mu_i^{y_i} e^{-\mu_i}}{y_i!}, i = 1, \ldots, n.$$

The likelihood function is then given by

$$L(\boldsymbol{\beta}|\text{data}) = \prod_{i=1}^{n} f(y_i|\mathbf{x}_i, \boldsymbol{\beta}) = \frac{\prod_{i=1}^{n} \mu_i^{y_i} e^{-\sum_{i=1}^{n} \mu_i}}{\prod_{i=1}^{n} y_i!}. \tag{17.28}$$

The (ML) technique of obtaining $\boldsymbol{\beta}$ is again based on the IRLS algorithm. However, this aspect will not be dealt with here. It is assumed that the ML estimate is available for $\hat{\boldsymbol{\beta}}$, as returned by say R software, and by using it we will then look at other aspects of the model. The *fitted values* from the Poisson regression model are given by

$$\hat{y}_i = \hat{\mu}_i = n_i e^{\hat{\boldsymbol{\beta}}^T \mathbf{x}_i}, i = 1, \ldots, n, \tag{17.29}$$

and hence the residuals are

$$e_i = y_i - \hat{y}_i, i = 1, \ldots, n. \tag{17.30}$$

Note that the mean and variance of the Poisson model are equal, and hence an estimate of the variance of the residual is $\sqrt{e_i}$, which leads to the *Pearson residuals*:

$$r_i = \frac{e_i}{\sqrt{\hat{y}_i}}, i = 1, \ldots, n. \tag{17.31}$$

A χ^2 goodness-of-fit test statistic is then given by

$$\chi^2 = \sum_{i=1}^{n} r_i^2 = \sum_{i=1}^{2} \frac{e_i^2}{\hat{y}_i}. \tag{17.32}$$

These concepts will be demonstrated through the next example.

Example 17.8.1. British Doctors Smoking and Coronary Heart Disease. The data for this example is taken from Table 9.1 of Dobson (2002) and available in the file `British_Smokers.csv`. The problem is to investigate the impact of smoking tobacco among British doctors, refer to Example 9.2.1 of Dobson. In the year 1951, a survey was sent out to all British doctors asking them whether or not they smoked tobacco and their age group

Age_Group. The data also collected the person-years Person_Years of the doctors in the respective age group. A follow-up after ten years reveals the number of deaths Deaths, the smoking group indicator Smoker_Cat. The data is slightly re-coded to extract variables with Age_Cat taking values 1 to 5 respectively for the age groups 35-44, 45-54, 55-64, 65-74, and 75-84. To check the presence of the non-linear impact of the variable age, the square of the Age_Cat is created in Age_Square. The variable Smoke_Age is created, which takes the Age_Cat values for the smokers' group and 0 for the non-smokers. The number of deaths is standardized to 100 000 Person_Years.

The glm model can be built using the link function family='poisson' with the offset option.

```
> data(BS)
> BS_Pois <- glm(Deaths~Age_Cat+Age_Square+Smoke_Ind+Smoke_Age,
+ offset=log(Person_Years), data=BS,family='poisson')
> logLik(BS_Pois)
'log Lik.' -28 (df=5)
> summary(BS_Pois)
Call:
glm(formula = Deaths ~ Age_Cat + Age_Square + Smoke_Ind + Smoke_Age,
    family = "poisson", data = BS, offset = log(Person_Years))
Deviance Residuals:
      1        2         9       10
 0.4382  -0.2733    -0.4106  -0.0127
Coefficients:
            Estimate Std. Error z value Pr(>|z|)
(Intercept) -10.7918     0.4501  -23.98  < 2e-16 ***
Age_Cat       2.3765     0.2079   11.43  < 2e-16 ***
Age_Square   -0.1977     0.0274   -7.22  5.1e-13 ***
Smoke_Ind     1.4410     0.3722    3.87  0.00011 ***
Smoke_Age    -0.3075     0.0970   -3.17  0.00153 **
- - -
Signif. codes:  0 '***' 0.001 '**' 0.01 '*' 0.05 '.' 0.1 ' ' 1
(Dispersion parameter for poisson family taken to be 1)
    Null deviance: 935.0673  on 9  degrees of freedom
Residual deviance:   1.6354  on 5  degrees of freedom
AIC: 66.7
Number of Fisher Scoring iterations: 4
> with(BS_Pois, pchisq(null.deviance - deviance,
+ df.null - df.residual,lower.tail = FALSE))
[1] 1e-200
> confint(BS_Pois)
Waiting for profiling to be done...
            2.5 % 97.5 %
(Intercept) -11.7   -9.9
Age_Cat       2.0    2.8
Age_Square   -0.3   -0.1
Smoke_Ind     0.7    2.2
Smoke_Age    -0.5   -0.1
```

The R output clearly shows that each of the variables included is significant for the number of deaths. However, we are not really interested in this aspect of the model! We would like to know if the death rates for smokers is higher than that for non-smokers, and if it is higher, then by how much? This will be answered through the next discussion. □

For a binary regressand, we can obtain a precise answer for the influence of the variable on the rate of the Poisson model through the concept of the *rate ratio*. The rate ratio, denoted by *RR*, gives the impact of the variable on the rate, by looking at the ratio of the expected value of Y, when the variable is present to the expected value when it is absent:

$$RR = \frac{E(Y|x=1)}{E(Y|x=0)} = e^{\beta}.$$

If the *RR* value is closer to unity, it implies that the indicator variable has no influence on Y. The confidence intervals, based on the invariance principle of MLE, is obtained with a simple exponentiation of the confidence intervals for the estimated regression coefficient β.

Example 17.8.2. British Doctors Smoking and Coronary Heart Disease. Contd. Apart from the computation of *RR*, we will quickly look at the residuals (Pearson) and the χ^2 goodness-of-fit test statistics.

```
> exp(BS_Pois$coefficients)
(Intercept)       Age_Cat  Age_Square    Smoke_Ind    Smoke_Age
       0.00         10.77        0.82         4.22         0.74
> exp(confint(BS_Pois))
Waiting for profiling to be done...
              2.5 % 97.5 %
(Intercept)   0.00   0.00
Age_Cat       7.23  16.34
Age_Square    0.78   0.87
Smoke_Ind     2.09   9.01
Smoke_Age     0.61   0.89
> residuals(BS_Pois,'pearson')
     1      2      3      4      5      6      7      8      9     10
 0.444 -0.272 -0.152  0.235 -0.057 -0.766  0.135  0.655 -0.405 -0.013
> sum(residuals(BS_Pois,'pearson')^2)
[1] 1.550
> 1-pchisq(1.55,5)
[1] 0.907229
```

The confidence intervals for *RR* do not include 1 in any of them. Furthermore, the RR value for `Smoke_Ind` is `4.22`, which indicates that the death rate for smokers is four times higher than that for the non-smokers. The Pearson residuals are all small enough, which rule out the presence of any outlier. The χ^2 goodness-of-fit test statistic indicates that the fitted model is good enough! □

Example 17.8.3. The Caesarean Cases. An increasing concern has been the number of Caesarean deliveries, especially in private hospitals. We have obtained the small dataset from http://www.oxfordjournals.org/our_journals/tropej/online/ma_chap13.pdf. Here, we know the number of births, the type of hospital (private or public), and the number of Caesareans. We would like to model the number of Caesareans as a function of the number of births and the type of hospital. A Poisson regression model is fitted for this dataset.

```
> data(caesareans)
> names(caesareans)
[1] "Births"          "Hospital_Type" "Caesareans"
> cae_pois <- glm(Caesareans~Hospital_Type+Births,data=caesareans,
+ family='poisson')
> summary(cae_pois)
Call:
glm(formula = Caesareans ~ Hospital_Type + Births,
+ family = "poisson",
    data = caesareans)
Deviance Residuals:
    Min        1Q    Median       3Q       Max
-2.3270  -0.6121  -0.0899   0.5398   1.6626
Coefficients:
               Estimate Std. Error z value Pr(>|z|)
(Intercept)    1.351e+00  2.501e-01   5.402 6.58e-08 ***
Hospital_Type 1.045e+00  2.729e-01   3.830 0.000128 ***
Births         3.261e-04  6.032e-05   5.406 6.45e-08 ***
- - -
Signif. codes:  0 '***' 0.001 '**' 0.01 '*' 0.05 '.' 0.1 ' ' 1
(Dispersion parameter for poisson family taken to be 1)
    Null deviance: 99.990  on 19  degrees of freedom
Residual deviance: 18.039  on 17  degrees of freedom
AIC: 110.80
Number of Fisher Scoring iterations: 4
```

The analysis shows that Caesarean sections are about twice as common in public hospitals as in private ones. □

?glm, ?step

17.9 Further Reading

Agresti (2007) is a very nice introduction for a first course in CDA. Simonoff (2003) has a different approach to CDA and is addressed to a more advanced audience. Johnson and Albert (1999) is a dedicated text for analysis of ordinal data from a Bayesian perspective. Congdon (2005) is a more exclusive account of Bayesian methods for CDA. Graphics of CDA are different in nature, as the scale properties are not necessarily preserved here. Specialized graphical methods have been developed in Friendly (2000). Though Friendly's book uses SAS as the sole software for statistical analysis and graphics, it is a very good account of the ideas and thought processes for CDA. Blascius and Greenacre (1998), Chen, et al. (2008), and Unwin, et al. (2005) are advanced level edited collections of research papers with dedicated emphasis on the graphical and visualization methods for data.

McCullagh and Nelder (1983–9) is among the first set of classics which deals with GLM. Kleinbaum and Klein (2002–10), Dobson (1990–2002), Christensen (1997), and Lindsey (1997) are a handful of very good introductory books in this field. Hosmer and Lemeshow (1990–2013) forms the spirit of this chapter for details on logistic regression. GLMs have evolved in more depth than we can possibly address here. Though we cannot deal with all of them, we will see here the other directional dimensions of this field. Bayesian methods are the natural alternative school for considering the inference methods in GLMs. Dey, Ghosh, and Mallick (2000) is a very good collection of peer reviewed articles for Bayesian methods in the domain of GLM. Agresti (2002, 2007) and Congdon (2005) also deal with Bayesian analysis of GLMs.

Chapter 13 of Dalgaard (2008), Chapter 7 of Everitt and Hothorn (2010), Chapter 6 of Faraway (2006), Chapter 8 of Maindonald and Braun (2006), and Chapter 13 of Crawley (2007) are some good introductions to GLM with R.

17.10 Complements, Problems, and Programs

Problem 17.1 The `irls` function given in Section 17.5 needs to be modified for incorporating more than one covariate. Extend the program which can then be used for any logistic regression model.

Problem 17.2 Obtain the 90% confidence intervals for the logistic regression model `chdglm`, as discussed in Example 17.5.1. Also, carry out the deviance test to find if the overall fitted model `chdglm` is a significant model? Validate the assumptions of the logistic regression model.

Problem 17.3 Suppose that you have a new observation $\mathbf{x}_{new}$. Find details with `?predict.glm` and use them for prediction purposes for any $\mathbf{x}_{new}$ of your choice with `chdglm`.

Problem 17.4 The likelihood function for the logistic regression model is given in Equation 17.8 . It may be tempting to write a function, say `lik_Logistic`, which is proportional to the likelihood function. However, `optimize` does not return the MLE! Write a program and check if you can obtain the MLE.

Problem 17.5 The residual plot technique extends to the probit regression and the reader should verify the same for the fitted probit regression models in Section 17.7.

Problem 17.6 Obtain the 99% confidence intervals for the `lowprobit` model in Example 17.8.2.

Appendix A

Open Source Software–An Epilogue

Shakun Gupta

Open source software is computer software that is available in source code form. The source code is provided under a software license which permits the users to use, study, change, improve, and distribute the software. An example of the source code is as seen for the `mean` function in Section 1.1.

Open source software is made available for anyone to use or modify, as its source code is made available. The software use is subject only on the stipulation that any enhancements or changes are freely available to the public. With open source software, users, scientists, engineers, and everyone else, are granted the right to both of the program's *functionality* and *methodology*. The users only have the rights to functionality of a proprietary software program.

Definition from the Open Source Initiative (OSI) Foundation
Introduction

Open source does not just mean access to the source code. The distribution terms of open source software must comply with the following criteria:

1. *Free Redistribution*. The license shall not restrict any party from selling or giving away the software as a component of an aggregate software distribution containing programs from several different sources. The license shall not require a royalty or other fee for such a sale.
2. *Source Code*. The program must include the source code, and must allow distribution in source code as well as compiled form. Where some form of a product is not distributed with the source code, there must be a well-publicized means of obtaining the source code for no more than a reasonable reproduction cost, preferably downloading via the Internet

A Course in Statistics with R, First Edition. Prabhanjan Narayanachar Tattar, Suresh Ramaiah and B. G. Manjunath.

Companion Website: www.wiley.com/go/tattar/statistics

without charge. The source code must be the preferred form in which a programmer can modify the program. A deliberately obfuscated source code is not allowed. Intermediate forms such as the output of a preprocessor or translator are not allowed.

3. *Derived Works*. The license must allow modifications and derived works, and must allow them to be distributed under the same terms as the license of the original software.
4. *Integrity of the Author's Source Code*. The license may restrict the source code from being distributed in modified form, only if the license allows the distribution of "patch files" with the source code for the purpose of modifying the program at build time. The license must explicitly permit distribution of the software built from the modified source code. The license may require derived works to carry a different name or version number from the original software.
5. *No Discrimination Against Persons or Groups*. The license must not discriminate against any person or group of persons.
6. *No Discrimination against Fields of Endeavor*. The license must not restrict anyone from making use of the program in a specific field of endeavor. For example, it may not restrict the program from being used in a business, or from being used for genetic research.
7. *Distribution of License*. The rights attached to the program must apply to all to whom the program is redistributed without the need for execution of an additional license by those parties.
8. *License must not be Specific to a Product*. The rights attached to the program must not depend on the program being part of a particular software distribution. If the program is extracted from that distribution and used or distributed within the terms of the program's license, all parties to whom the program is redistributed should have the same rights as those that are granted in conjunction with the original software distribution.
9. *License must not Restrict other Software*. The license must not place restrictions on other software that is distributed along with the licensed software. For example, the license must not insist that all other programs distributed on the same medium must be open source software.
10. *License must be Technology-Neutral*. No provision of the license may be predicated on any individual technology or style of interface.

Merits and Demerits of Open Source Software

There are a number of merits inherent in the use of open source software.

1. *Low Cost*. The source code of the open source software is freely available. Also the commercial versions and the support associated with the software is typically cheaper.
2. *Ease of Customization*. The user has full access to the source code. So, the code can be customized according to their requirements.
3. *Open Platforms*. The open source software solutions are typically developed using open tools, which reduces 'lock-in' with specific vendors or software platforms.
4. *Ease of Integration*. Typically, all the open source software packages are developed by keeping integration in mind.
5. *Community Support*. The most popular open source solutions are supported by an active community of many developers. So, it becomes easy to reach to the core of any issue.
6. *Rapid Problem Resolution*. When a bug is reported in the open source software, the solution is released as a patch in a very short period of time. Also, as the full source code is available, the problem can be resolved by the user also.

There are some demerits too.

1. *Not Enterprise-Level.* The open source software solutions can lack some of the features provided by enterprise scales solutions.
2. *Lack of Commercial Support.* Open source solutions lack commercial support, and service-level guarantees.
3. *Lack of Documentation.* Open source solutions typically provide only a small amount of documentation.
4. *Poor usability.* In general, open source solutions have remained focused primarily on the technical architecture and feature set.

Motivation for Programmers and Students

Although there is a lack of financial incentive to program software, motivation can be seen as a form of personal satisfaction for programmers.

- Sense of "intellectual gratification" as a result of writing software. This intellectual gratification is similar to the feeling of a scientific discovery.
- Personal satisfaction comes from the act of writing software as an equivalent to creative self expression.
- Rediscovery of creativity, which has been lost through the mass production of commercial software products.
- Creating a tool better suited to the programmer's or community use.
- Economic motivations like rewards, possible future career endeavors.

Examples of Usage

- *Government Agencies.* Government Agencies are utilizing open source infrastructure software, such as the Linux operating system and the Apache Web-server into software, to manage information
- *Education.* Colleges and organizations use software to educate their students. Open source technology is being adopted by many institutions, because it can save these institutions from paying companies to provide them with these administrative software systems.
- *Enterprises.* Enterprises are the biggest consumers of open source software. As open source software is commercially free, it significantly reduces the expenditure on the IT division.

Some Famous Open Source Software

We use open source software in our day-to day lives. Here are some of the famous ones:

- Linux Kernel
- GNU utilities and compilers
- Ubuntu
- Apache
- Google Android Google Chrome
- VLC, Wordpress
- Mysql
- Mozilla
- GNU Plot
- LaTeX, and of course
- R

Appendix B

The Statistical Tables

Statistical tables have played a very prominent role in the development of the subject, especially before the advent of the computer era. Through powerful software evolution, it may appear to be a very trivial matter. However, the contribution of pioneering Statisticians, such as Sir R.A. Fisher, Karl Pearson, and many eminent others cannot be undermined simply because those tasks can be easily carried out in a software with the user not even being aware of them being in action. The importance of *statistical tables* may be understood with Horgan (2008), Appendix C, giving the standard normal tables as a useful reference point to her table. In this very brief appendix, we attempt to help the reader to generate some of such tables.

Let us first undertake the task of generating Table A.2 of Snedecor and Cochran (1980) on page 464. The standard density function for z-values varying from 0 to 2.99 with a delta of 0.01 is required to generate this table. To set up this, first declare `z <- seq(0,2.9,0.1); zpart <- seq(0,0.09,0.01)`. The half-line simple R code `dnorm(outer(z,zpart,"+"))` accomplishes the task, and to obtain the four decimal accuracy, as required on their page 464, simply round off the result with `round(dnorm(outer(z,zpart,"+")),4)`.

Next, consider setting up Table A.3 from the same reference, page 465. The `z` needs to be slightly changed to `z <- seq(0,3.9,0.1)` and the next line to `round (0.5-pnorm(outer(z,zpart,"+"),lower.tail=FALSE),4)`. Obviously, the row and column names need to be changed according to the user's taste. However, the very brief section here is a modest attempt as a tribute to our eminent scientists from previous centuries who have made things very simple for us.

A Course in Statistics with R, First Edition. Prabhanjan Narayanachar Tattar, Suresh Ramaiah and B. G. Manjunath.

Companion Website: www.wiley.com/go/tattar/statistics

Bibliography

Adke, S.R. and Manjunath, S.M. (1984). *An Introduction to Markov Processes*. Wiley Eastern India.

Agresti, A. (1996–2007). *An Introduction to Categorical Data Analysis*, 2e. J. Wiley

Albert, J. (2007–9). *Bayesian Computations with R*, 2e. Springer

Albert, J. and Rizzo, M. (2012). *R by Example*. Springer.

Andersen, P.K. and Skovgaard, L.T. (2010). *Regression with Linear Predictors*. Springer.

Anderson, T.W. (1958–2003). *Introduction to Multivariate Statistical Analysis*, 3e. J. Wiley.

Anscombe, F.J. (1973). Graphs in Statistical Analysis. *American Statistician*, **27**, 17–21.

Ash, R.B. (1969). *Basic Probability Theory*. Dover.

Ash, R.B. and Doléans-Dade, C. (1972–2000). *Probability and Measure Theory*. 2e. Academic Press. Title of first edition was "Real Analysis and Probability".

Aspin, A A. (1948). An Examination and Further Development of a Formula Arising in the Problem of Comparing Two Mean Values. *Biometrika*, 88–96.

Athreya, K.B. and Lahiri, S. (2005). *Measure Theory and Probability Theory*. Springer.

Balakrishnan, N. and Nevzorov, V.B. (2003). *A Primer on Statistical Distributions*. J. Wiley.

Baclawski, K. (2008). *Introduction to Probability with R*. Chapman & Hall/CRC.

Bapat, R.B. (1993–2012). *Linear Algebra and Linear Models*, 3e. Springer.

Barnard, G.A., Jenkins, G.M., and Winsten, C.B. (1962). Likelihood Inference and Time Series. *Journal of Royal Statistical Society*, Series A, **125**, 321–372.

Basu, A.K. (1998). *Measure Theory and Probability*. Prentice Hall of India.

Berger, J.O. (1980–85). *Statistical Decision Theory*, 2e. Springer.

Berger, J.O. and Woolpert, R.L. (1988). *The Likelihood Principle*, 2e. IMS.

Bernardo, J. and Smith, A. (1994). *Bayesian Theory*. John Wiley, New York.

Belsley, D.A., Kuh, E., and Welsch, R.E. (1980). *Regression Diagnostics: Identifying Influential Data and Sources of Collinearity*, John Wiley, New York.

Bhat, B.R. (1980–2012). *Modern Probability Theory*, 4e. New Age Publisher.

Bhattacharya, R.N. and Waymire, E.C. (1990–2009). *Stochastic Processes with Applications*. J. Wiley. Also reprinted in 2009 as Volume 61 by SIAM, Philadelphia.

Bilder, C.R. and Loughin, T.M. (2015). *Analysis of Categorical Data with R*. CRC Press.

Billingsley, P. (1979–95). *Probability and Measure*, 3e. John Wiley, New York.

Bilodeau, M. and Brenner, D. (1999). *Theory of Multivariate Statistics*. Springer.

Blackwell, D. and Ramamoorthi, R.V. (1982). A Bayes but not Classically Sufficient Statistic.

Blasius, J. and Greenacre, M. (1998). *Visualization of Categorical Data*. Academic Press, New York.

A Course in Statistics with R, First Edition. Prabhanjan Narayanachar Tattar, Suresh Ramaiah and B. G. Manjunath.

Companion Website: www.wiley.com/go/tattar/statistics

Bliss, C.I. (1935). The Calculation of the Dosage-Mortality Curve. *Ann. Appl. Biol.* **22**, 134–167. *Ann. Statist.* **10**, 1025–1026.

Bolstad, W.M. (2007). *Introduction to Bayesian Statistics*, 2e. J. Wiley.

Box, G.E., Jenkins, G.M., and Reinsel, G. C. (1969–2011). *Time Series Analysis: Forecasting and Control*, 4e. J. Wiley.

Box, G.E.P. and Youle, P.V. (1955). The Exploration of Response Surfaces: An Example of the Link between the Fitted Surface and the Basic Mechanism of the System. *Biometrics*, **11**, 287–323.

Box, G.E.P. and Tiao, G. (1973). *Bayesian Inference in Statistical Analysis*. Addison-Wesley, Reading, MA.

Box, G.E.P., Hunter, J.S., and Hunter, W.G. (1978–2005). *Statistics for Experimenters Design, Innovation, and Discovery*, 2e. J. Wiley.

Box. G.E.P. and Cox, D.R. (1964). An Analysis of Transformations. *Journal of the Royal Statistical Society*. Series B. **26**, 211–224.

Breiman, L. (1968–92). *Probability*. SIAM, Philadelphia.

Bretz, F., Hothorn, T., and Westfall, P. (2011). *Multiple Comparisons Using R*. CRC Press.

Broemeling, L.D. (2009). *Bayesian Methods for Measures of Agreement*. Chapman & Hall/CRC Press.

Brown, T.A. (2006–15). *Confirmatory Factor Analysis for Applied Research*, 2e. Guilford Publications, Chicago.

Cacoullos, T. (1989). *Exercises in Probability*. Springer.

Capiński, M. and Zastawniak, T. (2001). *Probability Through Problems*. Springer.

Carlin, B. and Louis, T. (1996–2000). *Bayes and Empirical Bayes Methods for Data Analysis*, 2e. Chapman & Hall, New York.

Casella, G. (2008). *Statistical Design*. Springer.

Casella, G. and Berger, R.L. (2002). *Statistical Inference*, 2e. Duxbury.

Chambers, J.M., Cleveland, W.S., Kleiner, B., and Tukey, P.A. (1983). *Graphical Methods for Data Analysis*. Wadsworth & Brooks/Cole.

Chandra, T K. and Chatterjee, D. (2001). *A First Course in Probability*. Narosa Publishing House, India.

Chatterjee, S. and Hadi, A.S. (1977–2006). *Regression Analysis by Examples*, 4e. J. Wiley.

Chatterjee, S. and Hadi, A.S. (1988). *Sensitivity Analysis in Linear Regression*. J. Wiley.

Chaumont, I. and Yor, M. (2003). *Excercises in Probability*. Cambridge University Press.

Chen, C., Härdle, W., and Unwin, A. (2008). *Handbook of Data Visualization*. Springer.

Chernick, M.R. (1999–2008). *Bootstrap Methods: A Guide for Practitioners and Researchers*, 2e. J. Wiley.

Chernoff, H. (1973). Using Faces to Represent Points in K-Dimensional Space Graphically. *Journal of the American Statistical Association*, **68**, no. 342, 361–368.

Christensen, R. (1990–7). *Log-Linear Models and Logistic Regression*, 2e. Springer.

Christensen, R. (1987–2011). *Plane Answers to Complex Questions: The Theory of Linear Models*, 4e. Springer.

Chow, Y.S. and Teicher, H. (1978–95). *Probability Theory: Independence, Interchangeability, Martingales*, 3e. Springer-Verlag, New York.

Chung, K.L. (1968–2001). *A Course in Probability Theory*, 3e. Academic Press, New York.

Chung, K.L. and AitSahlia, F. (1979–2003). *Elementary Probability Theory*, 4e. Springer.

Clarke, B.R. (2008). *Linear Models*. J. Wiley.

Cleveland, W.S. (1985). *The Elements of Graphing Data*. Wadsworth: Monterey, CA.

Cochran, W.G. and Cox, G. (1950–8). *Experimental Design*, 2e. J. Wiley.

Congdon, P. (2005). *Bayesian Models for Categorical Data*. J. Wiley.

Conover, W.J. (1971–99). *Practical Nonparametric Statistics*, 3e. J. Wiley.

Cook, R.D. (1998). *Regression Graphics*. J. Wiley.

Cook, R.D. and Weisberg, S. (1982). *Residuals and Influence in Regression*. Chapman & Hall.

Cook, R.D. and Weisberg, S. (1994). *An Introduction to Regression Graphics*. J. Wiley.

Cook, R.D. and Weisberg, S. (1999). *Applied Regression Including Computing and Graphics*. J. Wiley.
Cox, D.R. and Hinkley, D.V. (1974). *Theoretical Statistics*. Chapman & Hall.
Cox, D. and Lewis, P. (1966). *The Statistical Analysis of Series of Events*. Chapman & Hall.
Cramér, H. (1946). *Mathematical Methods of Statistics*. Princeton Press.
Crawley, M. (2007–13). *The R Book*, 2e. J. Wiley.
Dagpunar, J.S. (2007). *Simulation and Monte Carlo*. J. Wiley.
Dalgaard, P. (2002–8). *Introductory Statistics with R*, 2e, Springer-Verlag, New York.
Das, M.N. (1989). *Statistical Methods and Concepts*. Wiley, Eastern India.
DasGupta, A. (2008). *Asymptotic Theory of Statistics and Probability*. Springer.
DasGupta, A. (2010). *Fundamentals of Probability: A First Course*. Springer.
DasGupta, A. (2011). *Probability for Statistics and Machine Learning*. Springer.
Dasu, J. and Johnson, T. (2003). *Exploratory Data Mining and Data Cleaning*. J. Wiley.
de Finetti, B. (1974–5). *Theory of Probability – A Critical Introductory Treatment*, Vols 1 and 2. J. Wiley.
DeGroot, M.H. and Schervish, M.J. (1975–2012). *Probability and Statistics*, 4e. Addison-Wesley, Reading, MA.
Dean, A. and Voss, D. (1999). *Design and Analysis of Experiments*. Springer.
Dekking, F.M., Kraaikamp, C., Lopuhaa, H.P., and Meester, L.E. (2005). *A Modern Introduction to Probability and Statistics*. Springer.
Dempster, A.P., Laird, N.M., and Rubin, D.B. (1977). Maximum Likelihood from Incomplete Data via the EM Algorithm (with discussion). *Journal of the Royal Statistical Society B*, **39**, 1–38.
Der, G. and Everitt, B.S. (2002). *A Handbook of Statistical Analysis using SAS*, 2e. CRC Press.
Derringer, G. and Suich, R. (1980). Simultaneous Optimization of Several Response Variables. *Journal of Quality Technology*, **12**, 214–219.
Deshmukh, S.R. and Purohit, S.G. (2007). *Microarray Data – Statistical Analysis Using R*. Narosa Publishing House, India.
Desu, M.M. and Raghavarao, D. (2004). *Nonparametric Statistical Methods for Complete and Censored Data*. CRC Press.
Devroye, L. (1986). *Non-Uniform Random Variate Generation*. Springer.
Dey, D.K., Ghosh, S.K., and Mallick, B.K. (2000). *Generalized Linear Models – A Bayesian Perspective*. Marcel Dekker.
Diaconis, P. and Holmes, S. (2002). A Bayesian Peek into Feller Volume I. *Sankhya*. **64**, Series A, 820–41.
Dickey, D.A. and Arnold, J.T. (1995). Teaching Statistics with Data of Historic Significance: Galileo's Gravity and Motion Experiments. *Journal of Statistics Education*, **3**(1). Dimov, I.T. (2008). *Monte Carlo Methods for Applied Scientists*. World Scientific.
Diggle, P.J., Heagerty, P., Liang, K-Y., and Zeger, S. L. (1994–2002). *Analysis of Longitudinal Data*, 2e. Oxford University Press.
Dobrow, R.P. (2013). *Probability With Applications and R*. J. Wiley.
Dobson, A.J. (1990–2002). *An Introduction to Generalized Linear Models*, 2e. Chapman & Hall/CRC Press, New York.
Doob, J.L. (1953). *Stochastic Processes*. J. Wiley.
Draper, N.R. and Smith, H. (1966–98). *Applied Regression Analysis*, 3e. J. Wiley.
Dunn and Master (1982). Obtained from http://openlearn.open.ac.uk/mod/resource/view.php?id=165509.
Durrett, R. (2009). *Elementary Probability for Applications*. Cambridge University Press.
Durrett, R. (1991–2010). *Probability: Theory and Examples*, 4e. Cambridge University Press.
Dworsky, L.D. (2008). *Probably Not: Future Prediction Using Probability and Statistical Inference*. J. Wiley.
Dynkin, E.B. (1951). Necessary and Sufficient Statistics for a Family of Probability Distributions. English translation in *Select. Transl. Math. Statist. Prob.* **I** (1961) 23–41.
Eaton, M.L. (1983–2007). *Multivariate Statistics: A Vector Space Approach*. IMS.

Eckart, C. and Young, G. (1936). The Approximation of One Matrix by Another of Lower Rank. *Psychometrika*, **1**, 211–218.

Efron, B. (1979). Bootstrap Methods: Another Look at the Jackknife. *Ann. Statist.*, **7**, 1–26.

Efron, B. and Tibshirani, R. (1993). *An Introduction to the Bootstrap*. Chapman & Hall.

Everitt, B.S. (2005). *An Rand S-PLUS® Companion to Multivariate Analysis*. Springer.

Everitt, B.S. and Hothorn, T. (2006–10). *A Handbook of Statistical Analyses Using R*, 2e. CRC Press.

Everitt, B.S. and Hothorn, T. (2011). *An Introduction to Applied Multivariate Analysis with R*. Springer.

Faraway, J.J. (2002). Practical Regression and Anova using R. Freely distributed notes.

Faraway, J.J. (2006). *Extending the Linear Model with R*. CRC Press.

Federer, W.T. (1955). *Experimental Design: Theory and Applications*. Oxford and IBH Publishing Co., Calcutta.

Feldman, R.M. and Valdez-Flores, C. (2010). *Applied Probability and Stochastic Processes*, 2e. Springer.

Feller, W. (1950–68). *An Introduction to Probability Theory and Its Applications*, Volume I, 3e. J. Wiley.

Feller, W. (1965–71). *An Introduction to Probability Theory and Its Applications*, Volume II, 2e. J. Wiley.

Fisher, R.A. (1925–71). *The Design of Experiments*, 8e. Reprinted by Hafner Publishing Company, New York. Also contained in *Statistical Methods, Experimental Design, and Scientific Inference*. Oxford University Press, London 1990.

Fox, J. (1991). *Regression Diagnostics*. Sage.

Fox, J. (2002). *An R and S-Plus Companion to Applied Regression*. Sage.

Freedman, D.A. (2009). *Statistical Models: Theory and Practice*. Cambridge University Press.

Freedman, D., Pisani, R., and Purves, R. (1978–2007). *Statistics*, 4e. Norton.

Freund, R.J. and Wilson, W.J. (2003). *Statistical Methods*, 2e. Academic Press, New York.

Frieden, B.R. and Gatenby, R.A. (2007). *Exploratory Data Analysis Using Fisher Information*. Springer.

Friendly, M. (2000). *Visualizing Categorical Data*. SAS.

Gabriel, K.R. (1971). The Biplot Graphical Display of Matrices with Application to Principal Component Analysis. *Biometrika*, **58**, 453–467.

Geisser, S. and Johnson, W. (2006). *Modes of Parametric Statistical Inference*. J. Wiley.

Gelman, A. (2005). Analysis of Variance–Why it is More Important Than Ever. *Ann. Statist.* **33**, 1–33.

Gelman, A., Carlin, J., Stern, H., and Rubin, D. (1995–2004). *Bayesian Data Analysis*, 2e. Chapman & Hall, New York.

Gelman, A. and Hill, J. (2007). *Data Analysis Using Regression and Multilevel/Hierarchical Models*. Cambridge University Press.

Gentle, J.E. (2009). *Computational Statistics*. Springer-Verlag, New York.

Gentle, J.E. (2003). *Random Number Generation and Monte Carlo Methods*, 2e. Springer-Verlag, New York.

Gentle, J.E. (2007). *Matrix Algebra, Theory, Computations, and Applications in Statistics*. Springer.

Geyer, C.J. (2001). Stat 8153 Lecture Notes.

Geyer, C.J. (2001). Stat 5101 Probability and Statistics.

Geyer, C.J. (2003). Maximum Likelihood in R. Available at www.stat.umn.edu/geyer/5931/mle/mle.pdf.

Ghosh, J.K., Delampady, M., and Samanta, T. (2006). *Introduction to Bayesian Analysis*. Springer.

Gibbons, J.D. and Chakraborti, S. (1971–2003). *Nonparametric Statistical Inference*, 4e. Marcel Dekker.

Giri, N.C. (1996–2004). *Multivariate Statistical Analysis*, 2e. Marcel Dekker.

Gnanadesikan, R. (1977–97). *Methods for Statistical Data Analysis of Multivariate Observations*, 2e. John Wiley, New York.

Gnedenko, B.V. (1978). *The Theory of Probability*. Mir Publishers.

Gnedenko, B.V. and Khinchin, A.Ya. (1964). *An Elementary Introduction to Probability Theory*, 6e, Nauka. (Also, republished by Dover).

Goon, A.M., Gupta, M.K., and Dasgupta, B. (1973). *An Outline of Statistical Theory*. World Press Private.

Gore, A.P., Paranjape, S.A., and Kulkarni, M.B. (2006). 100 Data Sets for Statistics Education. Department of Statistics, University of Pune.

Govindrajalu, Z. (2007). *Nonparametric Inference*, World Scientific.

Gower, J.C. and Hand, D.J. (1996) *Biplots*. Chapman & Hall, London.

Gower, J.C., Gardner-Lubbe, S., and le Roux, N. (2011). *Understanding Biplots*. J. Wiley.

Greenacre, M. (2010). Biplots in Practice. Available at http://www.multivariatestatistics.org.

Grimmet, G. and Stirzaker, D. (2001). *One Thousand Excercises in Probability*. Oxford University Press.

Gupta, M.R. and Chen, Y. (2011). *Theory and Use of the EM Algorithm*. Now Publishers Inc.

Gut, A. (2007). *An Intermediate Course in Probability*, 2e. Springer.

Hair, J.F., Black, W.C., Babin, B.J., and Anderson, R.E. (2009). *Multivariate Data Analysis*, 7e. Pearson Education.

Hajėk, J., Sidak, Z., and Sen, P.K. (1967–99). *Theory of Rank Tests*, 2e. Academic Press, New York.

Halmos, P.R. and Savage, L.J. (1949). Application of the Radon-Nikodym Theorem to the Theory of Sufficient Statistics. *Ann. Math. Statist.* **20**, 225–241.

Hammersley, J.M., and Handscomb, D.C. (1964). *Monte Carlo Methods*. J. Wiley.

Hampel, F.R. (1975). Beyond Location Parameters: Robust Concepts and Methods. Proceedings of the 40th Session of the ISI, **46**, 375–391.

Härdle, W. and Simar, L. (2007). *Applied Multivariate Statistical Analysis*. Springer.

Hastie, T., Tibshirani, R., and Freidman. J. (2001–10). *The Elements of Statistical Inference*, 2e. Springer

Hastings, W. (1970). Monte Carlo Sampling Methods Using Markov Chains and Their Application. *Biometrika*, **57**, 97–109.

Hedeker, D., and Gibbons, R.D. (2006). *Longitudinal Data Analysis*. J. Wiley.

Hinkelmann, K. and Kempthorne, O. (2008). *Design and Analysis of Experiments*. Volume 1: Introduction to Experimental Design. J. Wiley.

Hoaglin, D.C., Mosteller, F., and Tukey, J.W. (1985). *Exploring Data Tables, Trends, and Shapes*. J. Wiley.

Hoaglin, D.C., Mosteller, F., and Tukey, J.W. (1991). *Fundamentals of Exploratory Analysis of Variance*. J. Wiley.

Hoel, P.G., Port, S.C., and Stone, C.J. (1971). *Introduction to Probability Theory*. Houghton Mifflin.

Hoff, P.D. (2010). *A First Course in Bayesian Statistical Methods*. Springer.

Hogg, R.V. and Craig, A.T. (1978). *Introduction to Mathematical Statistics*, 4e. Macmillan.

Hogg, R.V., Tanis, E.A., and Zimmerman, D. (1977–2015). *Probability and statistical inference*, 9e. Macmillan.

Hollander, M. and Wolfe, D.A. (1973–99). *Nonparametric Statistical Methods*, 2e. J. Wiley.

Horgan, J. (2008). *Introduction to Probability With R*. J. Wiley.

Hosmer, D.W. and Lemeshow, S. (1989–2000). *Applied Logistic Regression*, 2e. J. Wiley.

Hsu, J.C. (1996). *Multiple Comparisons: Theory and methods*. Chapman & Hall.

Husson, F., Lé, S., and Pagés, J. (2011). *Exploratory Multivariate Analysis by Example Using R*. Chapman & Hall/CRC Press.

Iacus, S.M. (2009). *Simulation and Inference for Stochastic Differential Equations: With R Examples*. Springer.

Izenman, A.J. (2008). *Modern Multivariate Statistical Techniques*. Springer.

Jackson, J.E. (1991). *A User's Guide to Principal Components*. John Wiley, New York.

Jeffreys, H. (1939–61). *Theory of Probability*. Clarendon Press.

Jiang, J. (2010). *Large Sample Techniques for Statistics*. Springer.

Johnson, N.L. and Kotz, S. (1969–1972). *Distributions in Statistics*, (4 vols.). John Wiley, New York.

Johnson, N.L. and Kotz, S. (1977). *Urn Models and Their Application*. J. Wiley.

Johnson, R.A. and Wichern, D.W. (1982–2007). *Applied Multivariate Statistical Analysis*, 6e. Pearson Education.

Johnson, V.E. and Albert, J. (1999). *Ordinal Data Modeling*. Springer.

Jolliffe, I.T. (1986–2002). *Principal Component Analysis*, 2e. Springer.

Kallenberg, O. (1997–2002). *Foundations of Modern Probability*, 2e. Springer.

Karlin, S. and Taylor, H.M. (1966–75). *A First Course in Stochastic Processes*, 2e. Academic Press, New York.

Karlin, S. and Taylor, H. (1981). *A Second Course in Stochastic Processes*. Academic Press, New York.

Kay, S. and Xu, C. (2008). Cramer-Rao Lower Bound Computation Via the Characteristic Function. Available at http://www.ele.uri.edu/faculty/kay/New%20web/downloadable%20files/CRLB_via_CF.pdf

Keener, R.W. (2010). *Theoretical Statistics*. Springer.

Kempthorne, O. (1952). *Design and Analysis of Experiments*. John Wiley, New York.

Kendall, M. and Stuart, A. (1945–79). *The Advanced Theory of Statistics*, 4e. Griffin.

Kerns, G.J. (2010). *Introduction to Probability and Statistics Using R*. Open Source.

Khattree, R. and Naik, D.N. (1999). *Applied Multivariate Statistics with SAS Software*, 2e. John Wiley, New York.

Khattree, R. and Naik, D.N. (2000). *Multivariate Data Reduction and Discrimination with SAS Software*, John Wiley, New York.

Kim, S.H. and Cohen, A.S. (1998). On the Behrens-Fisher Problem: A review. *Journal of Educational and Behavioral Statistics*, **23**(4), 356–377.

Kleinbaum, D.G. and Klein, M. (1994–2010). *Logistic Regression: A Self-Learning Text*, 3e. Springer.

Knight, K. (2000). *Mathematical Statistics*. Chapman & Hall/CRC Press, New York.

Kotz, S. and Nadarajah, S. (2004). *Multivariate t Distributions and Their Applications*. Cambridge University Press.

Kolmogorov, A.N. (1933). Grundbegriffe der Wahrscheinlichkeitsrechnung. English translation: *Foundations of the Theory of Probability*. Chelsea, New York (1956).

Kramer, C.Y. and Jensen, D.R. (1969). Fundamentals of Multivariate Analysis, Part I. Inference about Means. *Journal of Quality Technology*, **1** (2), 120–133.

Kutner, M.H., Nachtsheim, C.J., Neter, J., and Li, W. (1974–2005). *Applied Linear Statistical Models*, 5e. McGraw-Hill.

Lehmann, E.L. (1975). *Nonparametrics: Statistical Methods Based on Ranks*. Holden-Day. Also republished by Prentice Hall in 1998 and Springer in 2006.

Lehmann, E.L. and Casella, G. (1983–98). *Theory of Point Estimation,* 2e. Springer.

Lehmann, E.L. and Romano, J.P. (1958–2005). *Testing Statistical Hypotheses,* 3e. Springer.

Lehmann, E.L. and Scheffé, H. (1950, 1955, 1956). Completeness, Similar Regions and Unbiased Estimation. *Sankhya*, **10**, 305–340; **15**, 219–236. (Corr: 17, 250.)

Leonard, T. (2000). *A Course in Categorical Data Analysis*. CRC Press.

Liang, K.-Y. and Zeger, S.L. (1986). Longitudinal Data Analysis Using Generalized Linear Models. *Biometrika*, **73**, 13–22.

Liese, F. and Miescke, K.J. (2008). *Statistical Decision Theory: Estimation, Testing, and Selection*. Springer.

Lindley, D.V. (1965). *Introduction to Probability and Statistics from Bayesian Viewpoint*. Parts 1 and 2. Cambridge University Press.

Linnik, J.V. (1968). *Statistical Problems with Nuisance Parameters (Scripta Technica, Trans.)*. Providence, RI: American Mathematical Society. (Original work published 1966.)

Lindsey, J.K. (1997). *Applying Generalized Linear Models*. Springer.

Little, R.J. and Rubin, D.B. (1987–2002). *Statistical Analysis with Missing Data*, 2e. J. Wiley.

Liu, J.S. (2002). *Monte Carlo Strategies in Scientific Computing*. Springer-Verlag, New York.

Loéve, M. (1955-78). *Probability Theory*, Vols. 1–2, 4e. Springer-Verlag, New York.

Mahalanobis, P.C. (1999). Why Statistics? *Resonance*.

Mahmoud, H.M. (2009). *Pólya Urn Models*. CRC Press.

Maindonald, J. and Braun, W.J. (2003–10). *Data Analysis and Graphics Using R – an Example-Based Approach*, 3e. Cambridge University Press.

Mardia, K.V., Kent, J.T., and Bibby, J.M. (1979). *Multivariate Analysis*. Academic Press, New York.

Marian, J-M. and Robert, C.P. (2007). *Bayesian Core: A Practical Approach to Computational Bayesian Statistics*. Springer.

Martinez, W.L. and Martinez, A.R. (2005). *Exploratory Data Analysis with MATLAB*. Chapman & Hall/CRC, New York.

McCullagh, P. and Nelder, J.A. (1983–89). *Generalized Linear Models*. Chapman & Hall/CRC, New York.

McCulloch, C.E. and Searle, S.R. (2001). *Generalized, Linear, and Mixed Models*. J. Wiley.

McLachlan, G. and Krishnan, T. (1998–2008). *The EM Algorithm and Extensions*. J. Wiley.

McNeil, D. (1977). *Interactive Data Analysis*. John Wiley, New York.

Medhi, J. (1992). *Stochastic Processes*, 2e. New Age Publishers.

Millar, R.B. (2011). *Maximum Likelihood Estimation and Inference*. J. Wiley.

Miller, R.G. Jr. (1966–81). *Simultaneous Statistical Inference*, 2e. Springer.

Minka, T.P. (2001). Bayesian Inference of a Uniform Distribution. Obtained from research.microsoft.com/en-us/um/people/minka/papers/uniform.html.

Monahan, J.F. (2011). *Numerical Methods of Statistics,* 2e. Cambridge University Press.

Montgomery, D.C. (1976–2012). *Design and Analysis of Experiments*, 8e. J. Wiley.

Montgomery, D.C. (1985–2012). *Introduction to Statistical Quality Control*, 7e. J. Wiley.

Montgomery, D.C., Peck, E.A., and Vining, G.G. (1983–2012). *Introduction to Linear Regression Analysis*, 5e. J. Wiley.

Mood, A.M., Graybill, F.A., and Boes, D.C. (1950–74). *Introduction to the Theory of Statistics*. McGraw, Tokyo.

Mosteller, F. (1965). *Fifty-challenging Problems in Probability with Solutions*. Dover Publications.

Mosteller, F. and Tukey, J.W. (1977). *Data Analysis and Regression*. Addison-Wesley, Reading, MA.

Muirhead, R.J. (1982). *Aspects of Multivariate Statistical Theory*. J. Wiley.

Mukhopadhyay, N. (2000). *Probability and Statistical Inference*. Marcel Dekker.

Murrell, P. (2005). *R Graphics*, Boca Raton, Florida, USA: Chapman & Hall/CRC, New York.

Myatt, G.J. (2007). *Making Sense of Data*. J. Wiley.

Nahin, P.J. (2008). *Digital Dice – Computational Solutions to Practical Probability Problems*. Princeton University Press.

Nolan, D. and Speed, T. (2000). *Stat Labs – Mathematical Statistics Through Applications*. Springer.

Ntzoufras, I. (2009). *Bayesian Modeling Using Winbugs*. J. Wiley.

Oja, H. (2010). *Multivariate Nonparametric Methods with R*. Springer.

Ott, E.R. (1967). Analysis of Means – A Graphical Procedure. *Industrial Quality Control*, **24**(2), 101–109.

Parthasarathy, K.R. (1978–2005). *Introduction to Probability and Measure*. Macmillan India Limited. Republished by Hindustan Book Agency.

Parzen, E. (1960). *Modern Probability Theory and Its Applications*. J. Wiley.

Pawitan, Y. (2001). *In All Likelihood*. Oxford Science Publications.

Press, S.J. (1988–2003). *Subjective and Objective Bayesian Statistics*, 2e. J. Wiley.

Pregibon, D. (1981). Logistic Regression Diagnostics. *The Annals of Statistics*, 705–724.

Purohit, S.G., Gore, S.D., and Deshmukh, S.R. (2008). *Statistics Using R*. Narosa Publishing House, India.

Quenouille, M.H. (1949). Approximate Tests of Correlation in Time-Series. *J. Roy. Statist. Soc. B*, **11**, 68–84.

Quesenberry, C.P. and Hurst, D.C. (1964). Large Sample Simultaneous Confidence Intervals for Multinomial Proportions. *Technometrics*, **6**(2), 191–195.

R Development Core Team (2009a), *An Introduction to R*, R Foundation for Statistical Computing, Vienna, Austria, URL http://www.R-project.org, ISBN 3-900051-12-7.

Ramasubramaniam, S. (1997). The Normal Distribution I, II. *Resonance* **2** (1997), no.6, pp. 15–24; no.7, pp. 27–37.

Ramsay, J.O., Hooker, G., and Graves, S. (2009). *Functional Data Analysis with R and MATLAB*. Springer.

Rao, C.R. (1973). *Linear Statistical Inference and Its Applications*, 2e. J. Wiley.

Rao, C.R., Toutenburg, H., Shalabh, H.C., and Schomaker, M. (1995–2008). *Linear Models and Generalizations: Least Squares and Alternatives*, 3e. Springer.

Rencher, A.C. (1998). *Multivariate Statistical Inference and Applications*. John Wiley, New York.

Rencher, A.C. (2002). *Methods of Multivariate Analysis*, 2e. J. Wiley.

Rencher, A.C. and Schaalje, G.B. (2000–8). *Linear Models in Statistics*, 2e. J. Wiley.

Reyment, R.A. and J'oreskog, K.G. (1996). *Applied Factor Analysis in the Natural Sciences*. Cambridge University Press.

Ripley, B.D. (1987). *Stochastic Simulation*. J. Wiley.

Ritz, C. and Streibig, J.C. (2008). *Nonlinear Regression with R*. Springer-Verlag, New York.

Robert, C.P. (2001). *The Bayesian Choice*. 2e. Springer-Verlag, New York.

Robert, C.P. and Casella, G. (1999–2004). *Monte Carlo Statistical Methods*, 2e. Springer.

Robert, C. and Casella, G. (2010). *Introducing Monte Carlo Methods with R*. Springer.

Robinson, G.K. (1976). Properties of Students t and of the Behrens-Fisher Solution to the Two Means Problem. *The Annals of Statistics,* **4**(5), 963–971.

Rohatgi, V.K. and Saleh, A.K.Md. (1975–2000). *An Introduction to Probability and Statistics*, 2e. J. Wiley.

Romano, J.P. and Siegel, A.F. (1986). *Counterexamples in Probability and Statistics*. CRC Press.

Rosenthall, J.S. *A First Look at Rigorous Probability Theory*, 2e. World Scientific.

Ross, S.M. (1996). *Stochastic Processes*, 2e. J. Wiley.

Ross, S.M. (2006). *Simulation*, 4e. Elsevier.

Ross, S.M. (1985–2014). *An Introduction to Probability Models*, 11e. Elsevier.

Ross, S.M. and Pek'oz, E.A. (2007). *A Second Course in Probability*. AMC. www.ProbabilityBookstore.com.

Rousseeuw, P.J. and Leroy, A.M. (1987). *Robust Regression and Outlier Detection*. J. Wiley.

Royden, H.L. (1963–87). *Real Analysis*, 3e. Prentice Hall of India.

Ryan, T.P. (2007). *Modern Experimental Design*. J. Wiley.

Salsburg, D. (2001). *The Lady Tasting Tea*. W. H. Freeman & Company.

Samaniego, F.J. (2010). *A Comparison of the Bayesian and Frequentist Approaches to Estimation*. Springer.

Sarkar, D. (2008). *Lattice: Multivariate Data Visualization with R*. Springer-Verlag, New York.

Savage, L.J. (1954–72). *The Foundations of Statistics*. Wiley, New York. Second revised edition published by Dover Publications.

Schafer, J.L. (2000). *Analysis of Incomplete Multivariate Data*. Chapman & Hall/CRC Press, New York.

Scheffe, H. (1943). On Solutions of the Behrens-Fisher Problem, Based on the t-Distribution. *The Annals of Mathematical Statistics*, **14**(1), 35–44.

Schervish, M.J. (1995). *Theory of Statistics*. Springer.

Schwarz, W. (2007). *40 Puzzles and Problems in Probability and Mathematical Statistics*. Springer.

Searle, S.R. (1971). *Linear Models*. J. Wiley.

Seber, G.A.F. (2008). *A Matrix Handbook for Statisticians*. J. Wiley.

Seber, G.A.F. and Lee, A.J. (1977–2003). *Linear Regression Analysis*, 2e. J. Wiley.

Sen, P.K., Singer, J M., and de Lima, A.C.P. (2009). *From Finite Sample to Asymptotic Methods in Statistics*. Cambridge University Press.

Sengupta, D. and Rao, S.J. (2003). *Linear Models: An Integrated Approach*. World Scientific.

Shao, J. (2003). *Mathematical Statistics*, 2e. Springer.

Shao, J., and Tu, D. (1996). *The Jackknife and Bootstrap*. Springer.

Sharma, S. (1996). *Applied Multivariate Techniques*. J. Wiley.

Sheather, S.J. (2009). *A Modern Approach to Regression with R*. Springer.

Sheshkin, D.J. (1997–2011). *Handbook of Parametric and Nonparametric Statistical Procedures*, 5e. Chapman & Hall/CRC Press, New York.

Shiryaev, A.N. (1979–95). *Probability*, 2e. Springer-Verlag, New York.

Shonkwiler, R.W. and Mendivil, F. (2010). *Explorations in Monte Carlo Methods*. Springer.

Shoukri, M.M. (2003). *Measures of Interobserver Agreement*. Chapman & Hall/CRC Press, New York.

Siegel, S. (1956). *Nonparametric Statistics for the Behavioral Sciences*. McGraw Hill.

Siegel, S. and J.W. Tukey (1960). A Nonparametric Sum of Ranks Procedure for Relative Spread in Unpaired Samples. *Journal of the American Statistical Association*, **55**, 429–445; correction, ibid., 56, 1005 (1961).

Silverman, B.W. (1985). *Density Estimation for Statistics and Data Analysis*. Chapman & Hall/CRC Press, New York.

Simonoff, J.S. (1996). *Smoothing Methods in Statistics*. Springer.

Simonoff, J.S. (2003). *Analyzing Categorical Data*. Springer.

Sivia, D.S. with J. Skilling. (2006). *Data Analysis – A Bayesian Tutorial*. Oxford.

Snedecor, G.W. and Cochran, W.G. (1980). *Statistical Methods*, 7e. Iowa State University, Ames, IA. Press.

Sobol, I.M. (1994). *A Primer for the Monte Carlo Method*. CRC Press.

Spector, P. (2008). *Data Manipulation With R*. Springer.

Sprent, P. and Smeeton, N.C. (2000). *Applied Nonparametric Statistical Methods*, 3e, Chapman & Hall, New York.

Srivastava, M.K. and Srivastava, N. (2009). *Statistical Inference – Testing of Hypothesis*. Prentice Hall of India.

Steenbergen, M.R. (2006). Maximum Likelihood Programming in R. Available at www.unc.edu/monogan/computing/r/MLE_in_R.pdf.

Stoyanov, J. (1997). *Counterexamples in Probability*, 2e. J. Wiley.

Streiner, D.L. and Norman, G.R. (2003). *Health Measurement Scales. A Practical Guide to their Development and Use*, 3e. Oxford University Press.

Suess, E.A. and Trumbo, B.E. (2010). *Introduction to Probability Simulation and Gibbs Sampling with R*. Springer.

Sveshnikov, A.A. (1968). *Problems in Probability Theory*. Saunders, Philadelphia, PA.

Tattar, P.N. (2013). *R Statistical Application Development by Example Beginner's Guide*. Packt Publishing Ltd.

Taylor, H.M. and Karlin, S. (1984–98). *An Introduction to Stochastic Modeling*, 3e. Academic Press. (4th Edition in 2011 has been co-authored by Pinsky.)

Thompson, J.R. (2000). *Simulation*. J. Wiley.

Timm, N.H. (2002). *Applied Multivariate Analysis*. Springer.

Tukey, J.W. (1962). The Future of Data Analysis. *Ann. Statist.* 1–67.

Tukey, J.W. (1977). *Exploratory Data Analysis*. Addison-Wesley, Reading, MA.

Tukey, J.W. (1980). We Need Both Exploratory and Confirmatory. *The American Statistician*, **34**(1), 23–25.

Ugarte, M.D., Militino, A.F., and Arnholt, A.T. (2008). *Probability and Statistics with R*. CRC Press.

Unwin, A., Theus, M., and Hoffman, H. (2005). *Graphics of Large Datasets Visualizing a Million*. Springer.

Varmuza, K. and Filzmoser, P. (2009). *Introduction to Multivariate Statistical Analysis in Chemometrics*. Springer.

Venables, W.N. and Ripley, B.D. (2002). *Modern Applied Statistics with S-PLUS*, 4e. Springer-Verlag, New York.

Venables, W.N., Smith, D.M., and the R Core Team. (2015). An Introduction to R. (Comes with the R Software.)

Velleman, P.F. and Hoaglin, D.C. (2004). *ABC of Exploratory Data Analysis*. Duxbury Press, Boston. Republished in 2004 by The Internet-First University Press.

Verzani, J. (2005). *Using R for Introductory Statistics*. Chapman & Hall.

Wasserman, L. (2004). *All of Statistics*. Springer.

Wasserman, L. (2006). *All of Nonparametric Statistics*. Springer-Verlag, New York.

Weisberg, H.F. (1992). Central Tendency and Variability. Sage University Papers Series.

Welch, B.L. (1938). The Significance of the Difference Between Two Means When the Population Variances are Unequal. *Biometrika*, **29**(3–4), 350–362.

Welch, B.L. (1947). The Generalization of Student's Problem When Several Different Population Variances are Involved. *Biometrika*, 28–35.

Wilcox, R.R. (2009). *Basic Statistics*. Oxford University Press.

Wilcoxon, F. (1945). Individual Comparisons by Ranking Methods. *Biometrics*, **1**, 80–83.

Wilks, S.S. (1962). *Mathematical Statistics*. J. Wiley.

Williams, D. (2001). *Weighing the Odds: A Course in Probability and Statistics*. Cambridge University Press.

Wu, C.F.J. and Hamada, M. (2000–9). *Experiments: Planning, Analysis, and Parameter Design Optimization*, 2e. J. Wiley.

Wu, X. and Kumar, V. (2009). *The Top Ten Algorithms in Data Mining*. Taylor & Francis Group.

Youden, W.J. and Beale, H.P. (1934). A Statistical Study of the Local Lesion Method for Estimating Tobacco Mosaic Virus. *Contrib. Boyce Thompson Inst*, **6**, 437–454.

Zacks, S. (1971). *The Theory of Statistical Inference*. J. Wiley.

Zuur, A.F., Ieno, E.N., and Meesters, E.H.W.G. (2009). *A Beginner's Guide to R*. Springer.

Author Index

A Course in Statistics with R, First Edition. Prabhanjan Narayanachar Tattar, Suresh Ramaiah and B. G. Manjunath.

Companion Website: www.wiley.com/go/tattar/statistics

Subject Index

A Course in Statistics with R, First Edition. Prabhanjan Narayanachar Tattar, Suresh Ramaiah and B. G. Manjunath.

Companion Website: www.wiley.com/go/tattar/statistics

R Codes

A Course in Statistics with R, First Edition. Prabhanjan Narayanachar Tattar, Suresh Ramaiah and B. G. Manjunath.

Companion Website: www.wiley.com/go/tattar/statistics

Printed and bound by CPI Group (UK) Ltd, Croydon, CR0 4YY